**Piotr Bienkowski** is Curator of Egyptian and Near Eastern Antiquities in the National Museums and Galleries on Merseyside and Honorary Research Fellow at the University of Liverpool. He was editor of the archaeological journal *Levant* from 1987 to 1992 and has directed archaeological projects in Jordan. He is the author or editor of many publications on the archaeology and culture of the ancient Near East and Egypt, including *Jericho in the Late Bronze Age, Early Edom and Moab: The Beginning of the Iron Age in Southern Jordan*, and *Treasures from an Ancient Land: The Art of Jordan*.

**Alan Millard** is Rankin Professor of Hebrew and Ancient Semitic Languages at the University of Liverpool. He has participated in archaeological projects across the Near East; among his scholarly and popular works on the subject are *The Eponyms of the Assyrian Empire, 910–612 B.C.*, *Treasures from Bible Times*, and *Discoveries from the Time of Jesus*.

# Dictionary
# of the
# Ancient Near East

# Dictionary
# of the
# Ancient Near East

*Edited by*

Piotr Bienkowski and Alan Millard

**PENN**

University of Pennsylvania Press
Philadelphia

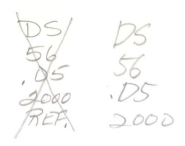
First published in the United Kingdom by British Museum Press

First published in the United States of America 2000 by
University of Pennsylvania Press
Philadelphia, Pennsylvania 19104-4011

10 9 8 7 6 5 4 3 2 1
A catalogue record for this book is available from the Library of Congress

ISBN 0-8122-3557-6

Designed and typeset in Minion by Andrew Shoolbred

Printed in Great Britain by Butler & Tanner Ltd, Frome and London

# Contents

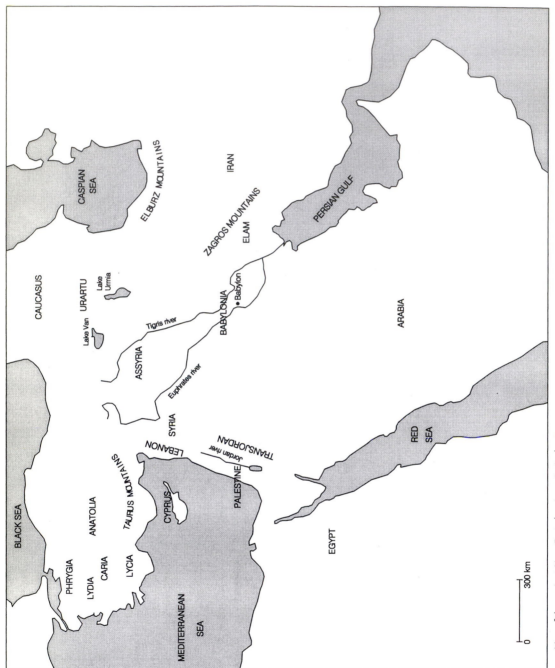

Map of the ancient Near East showing principal areas.

| YEARS bp/BC | MESOPOTAMIA | | IRAN | ANATOLIA | LEVANT |
|---|---|---|---|---|---|
| 1.5 million bp | | | | | |
| | | | Lower Palaeolithic | | |
| 150,000 bp | | | | | |
| | | | Middle Palaeolithic | | |
| 45,000 bp | | | | | |
| | | | Upper Palaeolithic | | |
| 20,000 bp | | | | | |
| | | | Epipalaeolithic | | |
| 10,500bp/9500 BC | | | | | (Natufian) |
| 9000 BC | Pre-Pottery Neolithic A/Proto-Neolithic | | Proto-Neolithic | | Pre-Pottery Neolithic A |
| 8500 BC | | | | Aceramic Neolithic | |
| 8000 BC | | | Aceramic Neolithic | | Pre-Pottery Neolithic B |
| 7500 BC | Late Aceramic Neolithic | | | | |
| 7000 BC | | | | | |
| 6500 BC | Hassuna, Samarra | | Ceramic Neolithic | Ceramic Neolithic | |
| 6000 BC | | | | | Pottery Neolithic |
| 5500 BC | *North* Halaf | *South* | | | |
| 5000 BC | Ubaid | Ubaid | | Chalcolithic | |
| 4500 BC | | | Chalcolithic | | Chalcolithic |
| 4000 BC | | | | | |
| 3500 BC | Uruk | | | | |
| 3000 BC | Late Uruk/Jemdet Nasr | | Proto-Elamite | | |
| | | | | | Early Bronze Age |
| 2500 BC | Early Dynastic | | Old Elamite | Early Bronze Age | |
| | Akkadian | | | | |
| 2000 BC | Ur III | | Shimashki | | |
| | Old Assyrian | Isin/Larsa Old Babylonian | Sukkalmah | Hittite Old Kingdom | Middle Bronze Age |
| 1500 BC | Middle Assyrian | Kassite | Middle Elamite | Hittite New Kingdom | Late Bronze Age |
| 1000 BC | Neo-Assyrian | | Neo-Elamite | Neo-Hittite Urartu Phrygian kingdom Lydian kingdom | Iron Age |
| 500 BC | Neo-Babylonian | | | | |
| | | | Achaemenid Persian | | |

VII

# List of contributors

**Editors**
Piotr Bienkowski, *Curator of Egyptian and Near Eastern Antiquities, National Museums and Galleries on Merseyside, and Honorary Research Fellow, University of Liverpool*

Alan Millard, *Rankin Professor of Hebrew and Ancient Semitic Languages, University of Liverpool*

**Additional contributors**
Douglas Baird, *Lecturer in Near Eastern Archaeology, University of Liverpool*

Jeremy Black, *University Lecturer in Akkadian, Oriental Institute, University of Oxford*

Paul T. Collins, *freelance lecturer in the ancient Near East, London*

Stephanie Dalley, *Shillito Fellow in Assyriology, Oriental Institute, University of Oxford*

Anthony Green, *Lecturer in Near Eastern Archaeology, Free University of Berlin*

Gwendolyn Leick, *Lecturer in Anthropology, Richmond College, the American International University, London*

Michael Macdonald, *Research Fellow, Oriental Institute, University of Oxford*

Roger Matthews, *Director, British Institute of Archaeology at Ankara*

Gerald L. Mattingly, *Lecturer, Johnson Bible College, Knoxville, Tennessee*

Graham Philip, *Lecturer in Archaeology, University of Durham*

Geoffrey D. Summers, *Lecturer in Archaeology, Middle East Technical University, Ankara*

# Preface

The principal purpose of this dictionary is to provide a handy one-volume reference work accessible to anyone with an interest in the ancient Near East, as well as students and specialists in different areas who require a wider view. The definition of the ancient Near East used in this book follows that used in the British Museum: Mesopotamia, Iran, Anatolia, the Caucasus, the Levant and Arabia. Deciding what to include and exclude was not easy, and a major constraint was the maximum word limit allocated for the book. The biggest difficulty was with the ever increasing number of archaeological sites; we have included individual entries on all significant ones while trying to strike a balance between areas and periods.

The chronological range covered by the entries stretches from the earliest periods (Lower Palaeolithic, c.1.5 million years ago) to the fall of Babylon to the Persian Cyrus the Great in 539 BC. This date marks the incorporation of the lands of the ancient Near East into a larger empire and the point after which many of the main sources for the history and culture come from outside the Near East, from the writings of ancient Greek historians. In many ways, too, the culture of the Persian period is quite different in character from what preceded it, with the ancient Near East becoming increasingly connected with the classical world, so 539 BC seemed as good an end-date as any for the dictionary's main coverage. Nevertheless, several entries briefly cover later peoples and dynasties, since these are unavoidably mentioned in entries on sites where settlement continued into and beyond the Persian period.

The chronological table and the entries follow the so-called 'Middle Chronology' (see the Chronology entry). Readers may notice that dates for early prehistoric periods often differ significantly from those available in even recently published general works. This is because until the last few years it has not been possible to calibrate reliably the radiocarbon dates for early sites in order to calculate an absolute date BC (see the Radiocarbon dating entry for explanation), and many prehistoric dates in other publications are uncalibrated. Calibrated dates (i.e. dates in 'real' years BC) for Neolithic sites are about a thousand years earlier than uncalibrated dates. Prehistorians are now more confident about the reliability of their calibrations, and throughout this book the dates for prehistoric periods from the Neolithic onwards are given in calibrated, 'real' dates BC.

The entries are supplemented by an appendix listing the kings of the main dynasties of the ancient Near East and their dates (Middle Chronology) up to the end of the Neo-Babylonian period. The overall map of the ancient Near East at the front of the book shows the position of the main areas, and may be used to locate the more detailed maps provided with individual entries.

Spelling of ancient Near Eastern personal and place names is a continual source of difficulty, and while we have been consistent with the spelling of individual names, readers should be aware that other spellings are used elsewhere, so, for example, Aššur/Ashur/Asshur/Assur are the same name (denoting a town, a land and a god).

The ancient Near East was not a homogeneous area but a diverse collection of changing cultures. Many entries attempt to give an overview of particular topics across the whole geographical area and chronological range. Inevitably within the space of a few hundred words the rich written materials from Mesopotamia often predominate, but we have been careful to avoid homogenization and have attempted to cover other distinct traditions.

Accompanying nearly all entries are short bibliographies in alphabetical order. Where possible these include the primary publications on sites or topics, through which we hope to guide the reader to reliable and full treatments of the subjects.

Topics may be located under individual entries and by consulting the index. Throughout the text, an asterisk before a word indicates that there is a main entry on that topic (e.g. *Cyrus); an asterisk is added only on the first occurrence of a particular word in any one entry. We have endeavoured to make the index as comprehensive as possible so that readers can search for sites and topics not covered by specific headings in the text. Several common topics covered by individual entries (e.g. Mesopotamia, Assyria) have been deliberately indexed only to the main entry, since they occur too frequently throughout the book to make their full indexing helpful.

## Acknowledgements

The editors thank all the contributors of entries for their support and for their help in deciding what to include and to exclude. The curatorial staff of the Department of Western Asiatic Antiquities at the British Museum kindly read a draft of the manuscript and provided helpful comments. Many other colleagues all over the world, too numerous to name individually, gave valuable advice and support, and to all of them we owe a debt of gratitude. We acknowledge the support we received from our respective institutions, the National Museums and Galleries on Merseyside and the University of Liverpool.

Nina Shandloff, Joanna Champness, Jemima Scott-Holland, Antonia Brook, Nicola Denny and Emma Way of British Museum Press gave excellent help and advice concerning the production of the book.

We would like to thank the copy-editor, John Banks, and designer, Andrew Shoolbred, whose helpful suggestions have greatly enhanced the clarity of the book.

Credits for photographs are listed at the end of each caption. Unless otherwise stated the line drawings are by John-Gordon Swogger, and maps and plans by Simon Griffin and Piotr Bienkowski. For photographs from the collections of the British Museum, we are grateful to the staff of the British Museum Photographic Service. Abbreviations used for British Museum object registration numbers in the captions are:

WA:     Department of Western Asiatic Antiquities
Or. Dr.: Original drawing by Austen Henry Layard, in the Department of Western Asiatic Antiquities
OA:     Department of Oriental Antiquities
PRB:    Department of Prehistoric and Romano-British Antiquities
BMC:    British Museum Catalogue reference to a coin in the Department of Coins and Medals

*Piotr Bienkowski*
*Alan Millard*

# A

**Achaemenids**   The Achaemenids were a *dynasty from *Iran whose empire, originating in the sixth century BC and lasting for more than two hundred years, stretched from *Egypt in the west to north-west *India in the east, and as far as the Black Sea to the north.

The legendary founder of the dynasty, Achaemenes (the *Greek form of the *Persian *Hakhamanish*), ruled one of the Persian tribes of the Iranian plateau; if he really existed, which is uncertain, it was probably around the late eighth century BC. Later, Darius I (see below) claimed that he was the ninth *king of a dynasty which had started with Achaemenes.

*Cyrus II (Cyrus the Great) of the Achaemenid dynasty became king of *Anshan in 559 BC, and within twenty years had conquered all his neighbours, entered *Babylon and automatically acquired all of the Neo-Babylonian empire's possessions: *Syria, *Palestine, *Phoenicia and North *Arabia. Cyrus' son, Cambyses II (530–522 BC), conquered Egypt in 525 BC but died while returning home to deal with an uprising. His successor Darius I (522–486 BC), perhaps a usurper, quelled the rebellions and then re-organized the empire into provinces called satrapies, ruled by Persian governors. The capital was moved from *Pasargadae to *Persepolis, with the winter residence at *Susa.

During the reigns of Cyrus II and Darius I, Zoroastrianism became the state *religion of Persia. The prophet Zoroaster (or Zarathustra), who may have lived about 600 BC or earlier in Bactria, east of Iran, taught that there was only one *god, Ahura Mazda, the 'Wise Lord', although other local gods continued to be worshipped.

One of a pair of gold armlets with terminals in the form of winged monsters, originally inlaid with coloured stones, from the Oxus Treasure. 11.5 cm wide. Achaemenid, fifth to fourth century BC. WA 124017.

Ahura Mazda was believed to have created good, which was opposed by evil (Ahriman).

Under Darius the Achaemenid empire reached its greatest extent, with the annexation of the Indus Valley in India. He attempted to conquer the mainland Greek states, but with his defeat at the battle of Marathon in 490 BC and that of Xerxes (486–465 BC) at Salamis in 480 BC, the period of Achaemenid expansion ended. Their successors were weak and faced by intrigues, scandals and rebellions in the satrapies. The last true Achaemenid ruler, Darius III (336–330 BC), was defeated by Alexander the Great at the battle of Gaugemela in northern Iraq in 331 BC. Darius escaped, but was murdered by one of his own satraps, Bessos of Bactria, while Alexander took over his empire. Bessos proclaimed himself King Artaxerxes IV but was defeated and put to death in 329 BC.

The Achaemenids had a wealth of resources available within the frontiers of their empire – *building materials, *gold, *silver, lapis lazuli, *ivory, *artists and *craftsmen – which they used to create a distinct imperial style of art and architecture. Achaemenid art, based upon *Elamite, *Median or *Assyrian motifs and models, was designed to impress and to present a picture of power and stability. Their *sculpture is on a monumental scale, but produces its effect from being static and repetitive, rather than realistically depicting events. The most frequent depiction on *seals and relief sculpture is of a hero mastering beasts, a traditional Near Eastern motif, here presenting a message of power, order and harmony.          PB

J.M. COOK, *The Persian Empire* (London 1983).

M.A. DANDAMAEV, *A Political History of the Achaemenid Empire* (Leiden 1989).

R.N. FRYE, *The Heritage of Persia*, 2nd ed. (London 1976).

M.C. ROOT, 'Art and Archaeology of the Achaemenid Empire', *Civilizations of the Ancient Near East*, ed. J.M. Sasson (New York 1995) 2615–37.

H. SANCISI-WEERDENBURG *et al.* (eds), *Achaemenid History* 1–8 (Leiden 1987–94).

F. WIESEHÖFER, *Ancient Persia* (London 1996).

**Adad (Hadad)**   The *god who embodied the power of storms was known to the *Sumerians as Ishkur. The *Akkadian equivalent of this deity was Adad (also called Hadad, Haddu, Addu or Adda). More at home in the West *Semitic area was a related deity called Wer or Mer. Most ancient Near Eastern peoples worshipped a storm-god (see Weather-gods), and Adad was sometimes equated with the *Hurrian god Teshup or the *Kassite god Buriash (whose name may be distantly connected with the *Greek god of the north wind, Boreas).

Ishkur/Adad was usually regarded as the son of *An/Anu. According to an older tradition, he was the son of *Enlil. His wife was the goddess Shala, possibly of

Design on a haematite cylinder seal of the Old Babylonian period, perhaps cut in Yamhad (Aleppo), showing the storm-god (probably Adad) with horned helmet and clubs, facing a goddess, and at right angles two bull men holding the tendrils of a stylized tree beneath a winged sun disk. Height 2.8 cm. WA 129580.

Hurrian origin, also treated as the wife of *Dagan. The minor deities Shullat and Hanish served as his ministers.

The worship of Ishkur probably goes back as far as the Early Dynastic period at least: the sign for his name (the same as the sign for 'wind') appears in the earliest list of gods. Karkara, a town in *Babylonia whose name was also written with the sign 'wind', was a cult centre of Adad. Later Anu and Adad shared a double temple, with twin ziggurats, at the *Assyrian capital *Ashur.

While Ishkur, associated with the Sumerian south, tended to be connected with thunderstorms, hail and flood, Adad also had a beneficial aspect as a god of fruitful rain and mountain streams, possibly in areas where rain was more important for *agriculture.

A representation of lightning symbolized such storm-gods. The beast of Ishkur is thought to have been the lion-dragon; that of Adad was the lion-dragon or the bull.

Storm clouds were called Adad's 'bull-calves'.

In the west, Aleppo was a major centre of the cult of Adad from an early time, a text from *Mari reporting an oracle he gave there. The tablets from *Ugarit often call him *Baal and preserve myths about him, but as Adad or Hadad he occurs in many texts and personal names from the Late Bronze Age *Levant. In the *Iron Age, Adad was the god of *Aram-Damascus and its *dynasty (he was known there as Ramman, 'the thunderer'), and was revered throughout the *Aramaean states. He is shown in Neo-*Hittite *sculpture holding a thunderbolt and sometimes standing on an ox.                    JAB

D.O. EDZARD, 'Mesopotamien: Die Mythologie der Sumerer und Akkader', *Götter und Mythen im Vorderen Orient*, Vol. 1 of *Wörterbuch der Mythologie*, ed. H.W. Haussig (Stuttgart 1965) 135.

J.C. GREENFIELD, 'Hadad', *Dictionary of Deities and Demons in the Bible*, eds K. van der Toorn, B. Becking and P.W. van der Horst (Leiden/New York 1995) 716–26.

W.P. RÖMER, 'Ein Eršemma-Lied für Iškur (CT 15, 15–16)', *Zikir šumim: Assyriological Studies Presented to F.R. Kraus on the Occasion of his Seventieth Birthday*, eds G. van Driel *et al.* (Leiden 1982) 298–317.

A. VANEL, *L'iconographie du dieu de l'orage dans le Proche-Orient ancien jusqu'au VII siècle avant J.-C.* (Paris 1965).

N. WYATT, 'The Relationship of the Deities Dagan and Hadad', *Ugarit-Forschungen* 12 (1980) 375–9.

**Adad-nirari**  Adad-nirari, 'the god *Adad is my helper', was the name of three *Assyrian *kings.

Adad-nirari I (c.1307–1275 BC) expanded Assyria's frontiers in all directions, following the assertion of independence by Ashur-uballit I (c.1365–1330 BC). While he defeated local tribes and princes in the north-east to secure his borders, he put most effort into fighting the *Hurrian state of *Mitanni-Hanigalbat to the west. Its king was captured, sworn to loyalty and reinstated. The

Excavations at Tell al-Rimah uncovered a stela of Adad-nirari III standing in a small shrine. The stela, 1.3 m high, records the king's campaign in the west. The lower part celebrates the power of the governor, Nergal-eresh, who erected the stela. After his downfall, that part was erased (by courtesy of Stephanie Dalley).

next king rebelled, abetted by the *Hittites, leading Adad-nirari to march west and take control of the territory up to the Euphrates. Adad-nirari corresponded with the Hittite kings who had previously been allied with *Babylonia. Early in his reign he had defeated the *Kassite king of *Babylon and advanced the Assyrian *boundary in the south-east. The numerous inscriptions record building work in *Ashur and at the captured Mitannian town of Taidu on the *Khabur, whence many *stone vases were taken to Ashur. The inscriptions include for the first time truly narrative accounts of military campaigns (see Annals and chronicles).

Adad-nirari II (911–891 BC) continued his father Ashur-dan II's reassertion of Assyrian power, subduing *Aramaean rulers as far west as the *Balikh *river, regaining areas lost 150 years earlier in eight campaigns, and marching north-east across the *Zagros and to Lake Van. In fighting Babylon he secured the frontier along the Lower Zab river. He built at Ashur, *Nineveh, Shibaniba (Tell Billa) and Apqu (Tell Abu Marya) west of Nineveh.

Adad-nirari III (810–783 BC), son of *Shamshi-Adad V and Sammu-ramat (*Semiramis), has left few monuments of his own, but the *Eponym Chronicle reports many campaigns in the east, against the *Medes and the Mannaeans, and in the south, where *Chaldaean kings became his vassals and he was received as king in Babylon. Officials governing large provinces became more powerful (see Provincial administration), erecting monuments which lauded the king while reporting victories in such a way that it is clear the governors were responsible. Nergal-eresh, controlling much of Upper *Mesopotamia, tells of tribute from *Damascus (captured by Assyria for the first time), *Samaria, *Tyre and Sidon. Shamshi-ilu, the commander-in-chief, regulated the border between Hamath (*Hama) and Arpad in his master's name. Building works of the king are known from Ashur, Nineveh and *Nimrud.          ARM

Adad-nirari I:

A.K. GRAYSON, *Assyrian Royal Inscriptions* 1 (Wiesbaden 1972) 57–79.

——, *Assyrian Rulers of the Third and Second Millennia BC (to 1115 BC)* (Toronto 1987) 128–79.

M. MUNN-RANKIN, 'Assyrian Military Power 1300–1200 B.C.', *Cambridge Ancient History* 2.2, 2nd ed. (Cambridge 1975) 274–9.

Adad-nirari II:

A.K. GRAYSON, *Assyrian Royal Inscriptions* 2 (Wiesbaden 1976) 81–97.

——, *Assyrian Rulers of the Early First Millennium BC 1 (1114–859 BC)* (Toronto 1991) 142–62.

——, 'Assyria: Ashur-dan II to Ashur-nirari V (934–745 B.C.)', *Cambridge Ancient History* 3.1, 2nd ed. (Cambridge 1982) 249–51.

Adad-nirari III:

A.K. GRAYSON, *Assyrian Rulers of the Early First Millennium BC II (858–745 BC)* (Toronto 1996) 200–38.

——, 'Assyria: Ashur-dan II to Ashur-nirari V (934–745 B.C.)', *Cambridge Ancient History* 3.1, 2nd ed. (Cambridge 1982) 271–6.

**Adapa** According to *Babylonian legend, Adapa was an ancient 'wise man' or 'sage' (*apkallu*) of *Eridu, which was reputed to be the earliest city of *Sumer. His wisdom and position had been granted to him by the *god *Ea. Having 'broken the wings' of the south wind, Adapa was summoned for punishment by the supreme god *Anu. Ea had told Adapa that he would be offered the bread and water of death. Meanwhile, though, the two gatekeepers of heaven, *Dumuzi and Gishzida (Ningishzida), had interceded with Anu on Adapa's behalf, causing a change of heart, and Anu instead offered the sage the bread and water of eternal life. But Adapa refused, thus losing the chance of immortality. The story is often regarded as an explanatory myth of the mortality of man.          JAB

J.D. BING, 'Adapa and Mortality', *Ugarit-Forschungen* 16 (1984) 53–6.

S.M. DALLEY, *Myths from Mesopotamia* (Oxford 1990) 182–8.

H.-P. MÜLLER, 'Mythos als Gattung des archaischen Erzählens und die Geschichte von Adapa', *Archiv für Orientforschung* 29 (1983/4) 75–89.

S.A. PICCHIONI, *Il poemetto di Adapa* (Budapest 1981).

**Administration** In ancient Near Eastern kingdoms, the *king was the head of state and normally commander-in-chief of the army (see Military organisation). In between him and the masses of unskilled workers were several layers of officials and bureaucrats. Most information comes from *Babylonian and *Assyrian *cuneiform texts, although administrative systems elsewhere were similar if less sophisticated and bureaucratic.

The most senior officials of state were part of the *royal court based in the *palace. Next, normally reporting directly to the king, were *provincial governors and *city mayors; then superintendents of tradesmen and labourers; then freemen (see Social classes), palace officials, tradesmen and tenant farmers; and finally *slaves. *Temples had their own administration with a separate hierarchy of officials responsible for the property of the temple and for administering staff, including *priests and priestesses, *scribes, *craftsmen, *water carriers and doorkeepers. Temple administrators in Babylonia normally held permanent appointments, while cultic officials might change every few days. Their salaries were formed from the offerings made to the temples, not only *food and drink but also *textiles and *silver items.

During the *Ur III period there appear to have been separate civilian and military administrations, but it is not clear how they were distinguished in practice. The Ur III state was probably the earliest centralized state, with rigid bureaucratic control of the *economy, recording every last detail and compiling monthly and annual reports. This contrasts strongly with the Neo-*Assyrian period which was essentially decentralized, with administrative control delegated to provincial governors to run their territories without constant central interference.

At every level of administration, scribes were assigned to officials to read and write their memos, *letters and dispatches. It was not unusual for sons to inherit their fathers' offices. High posts in the administration were often awarded to members of the royal *family, and sometimes individuals held several military and civilian posts. In the Neo-Assyrian administration, *eunuchs formed a discrete, trusted element, although originally their function had been to protect the *harem. The collective term for Neo-Assyrian royal officials was 'eunuchs and bearded ones'.

There was no distinction between officials' public and private lives, or concern for what today we regard as integrity of office. Payments ('bribes') for services or for legal decisions in one's favour were routine, accepted and not regarded as immoral or as an abuse of office.  PB

G. BECKMAN, 'Royal Ideology and State Administration in Hittite Anatolia', *Civilizations of the Ancient Near East*, ed. J.M. Sasson (New York 1995) 529–43.

R.D. BIGGS and McG. GIBSON (eds), *The Organization of Power: Aspects of Bureaucracy in the Ancient Near East* (Chicago 1987).

I.M. DIAKONOFF, *Structure of Society and State in Early Dynastic Sumer* (Malibu 1974).

M. HELTZER, *The Internal Organization of the Kingdom of Ugarit* (Wiesbaden 1982).

J.N. POSTGATE, 'Royal Ideology and State Administration in Sumer and Akkad', *Civilizations of the Ancient Near East*, ed. J.M. Sasson (New York 1995) 395–411.

J.F. ROBERTSON, 'The Social and Economic Organization of Ancient Mesopotamian Temples', *Civilizations of the Ancient Near East*, ed. J.M. Sasson (New York 1995) 443–54.

## Adonis

Adonis was the name given by the *Greeks to a *god who they thought was originally Near Eastern. The name comes from the *Semitic word *adon* ('lord'). In fact there is no precise Near Eastern equivalent to Adonis and to the detailed Greek mythology concerning him, although he has been identified with a Phoenician god in *Byblos who is referred to as DA.MU in the *Amarna Letters. Adonis is a typical 'dying god', sentenced by Zeus to four months in the *underworld, the rest of the year spent with Aphrodite, in conjunction with whom he was normally worshipped. In the *Hellenistic period a *festival for him is attested at Byblos, which involved the whole population first in mourning, then in joy. Some elements of Adonis are present in the myths concerning *Baal and *Dumuzi, who also descended into the underworld.  PB

M.H. POPE and W. RÖLLIG, 'Syrien: Die Mythologie der Ugariter und Phönizier', *Götter und Mythen im Vorderen Orient*, Vol. 1 of *Wörterbuch der Mythologie*, ed. H.W. Haussig (Stuttgart 1965) 234–5.

S. RIBICHINI, *Adonis: Aspetti 'orientali' di un mito greco* (Rome 1981).

——, 'Adonis', *Dictionary of Deities and Demons in the Bible*, eds K. van der Toorn, B. Becking and P.W. van der Horst (Leiden/New York 1995) 12–17.

B. SOYEZ, *Byblos et la fête des Adonies* (Leiden 1977).

## Adoption

Adoption is known from *Mesopotamian and *Hittite texts dating to the second and first millennia BC, particularly the Old and Middle Babylonian periods. Most of the documentation is in the form of *law codes and adoption *contracts, although the Hittite evidence comes from historical texts. The usual adoption formula in *Akkadian was to 'take for son/daughtership', although individuals could also be adopted as brothers, sisters or fathers. From *Nuzi come examples of *women adopted in order to be given away in *marriage. A written contract between the adopter and the parent or guardian of the adoptee could record the adoption, stating the nature of the adoptive relationship. The contract might also state the penalties should either party repudiate the agreement, which ranged from fines, or loss of promised assets, to *slavery.

The reasons for adoption were many: to adopt an heir, or an apprentice, to keep property in the *family, to free slaves or to legitimate illegitimate *children. Having children to support you in old age was stated as a reason. Sometimes infant children were adopted, but usually the arrangement was between adults. Hittite kings adopted their grandsons, nephews or sons-in-law, presumably to strengthen their claim as heirs. At Nuzi, a peculiar form of land sale took the form of an adoption, perhaps to circumvent a law against giving away inherited property. The buyer was adopted and given land as an inheritance in exchange for a gift of equivalent value or to clear a debt.  PB

E.-M. CASSIN, *L'adoption à Nuzi* (Paris 1938).

M. DE J. ELLIS, 'An Old Babylonian Adoption Contract from Tell Harmal', *Journal of Cuneiform Studies* 27 (1975) 130–51.

F.W. KNOBLOCH, 'Adoption', *Anchor Bible Dictionary* 1, ed. D.N. Freedman (New York 1992) 76–9.

S. PAUL, 'Adoption Formulae: A Study of Cuneiform and Biblical Legal Clauses', *Maarav* 2 (1979–80) 173–85.

## Adultery

The institution of *marriage was respected in the ancient Near East, and morals and *laws defined and protected the behaviour that was acceptable to each culture. In most places, adultery was regarded as an illicit act that a *woman could commit against her husband and against the *religious scruples of their society. In legal, economic and moral terms, a man's extramarital sexual activity was regarded as an offence against the husband, fiancé or father of another woman, not against his wife. This widespread double standard reflected the patriarchal nature of ancient society. In the *Bible, adultery is distinguished from 'fornication' and defined as voluntary *sexual intercourse by a married male or female with a person other than his or her spouse. Even in Hebrew society, the extramarital sex of a married man was not necessarily condemned by law, and the practice of polygamy and concubinage meant that adultery was understood differently than it is today.

Beginning c.2000 BC, Near Eastern laws prescribed the circumstances under which individuals were accused of committing adultery and the punishment for those who were found guilty. The so-called code of *Ur-Nammu and the Middle Assyrian laws provided for the death penalty for an adulteress caught *in flagrante delicto*, but her male counterpart was set free. This assumes that the woman enticed the man, and he did not know she was married. In

*Hammurabi's code, which includes sixty-eight sections that relate to the *family institution, both a wife and her lover caught in the act were bound and thrown into the water. In this case, her guilt or innocence was determined by the '*river ordeal'. The wife and the guilty man could be pardoned, by the husband of the adulteress and the *king, respectively. If a wife was accused of adultery, she was subjected to the river ordeal. The law makes it clear that her survival exonerated her husband, and she still had to pay a fine. It is worth noting that Numbers 5 says that *Israelite wives accused of being unfaithful were also subjected to an ordeal.

Literary evidence for the prosecution of adulterers is scant. In one case that was covered by Old Babylonian law, a married woman was accused of adultery and of making unwarranted use of her husband's property. The husband could have had her executed or enslaved, but she was shaven, had her nose pierced and was led around the *city in public humiliation. The fate of her paramour is unknown. The people of ancient *Mesopotamia worried about the social disgrace of a sexual scandal, since such marital infidelity brought dishonour upon the husband.

In the Bible, adultery was a capital offence (Leviticus 20: 10; Deuteronomy 22: 22–4). As in *Hittite law, both consenting parties to adultery were to be executed. The double standard did not exist in these instances, and equal punishment was exacted on both man and woman. In *Hebrew law, it did not make any difference if the man was unaware that the woman was married. The Hittite and Middle Assyrian law allowed the husband to kill an adulterous couple on the spot and suffer no penalty himself, but this was prohibited in ancient Israel. Adultery carried a moral stigma and was viewed as an affront to the gods in *Mesopotamia, and its religious implications were very serious in the Hebrew purview. Adultery was prohibited by the seventh commandment (Exodus 20: 14; Deuteronomy 5: 18). For the Israelites, adultery was regarded as a treacherous act that had long-term consequences (Proverbs 2, 5, 6, and 7). The term 'adultery' was used figuratively for religious idolatry. Adultery was, in fact, regarded as a sin against God (Genesis 20: 6; 39: 9), and in both *Ugaritic and *Egyptian texts it was called the 'great sin'               GLM

E.A. GOODFRIEND, 'Adultery', *The Anchor Bible Dictionary* 1, ed. D.N. Freedman (New York 1992) 82–6.

S. GREENGUS, 'A Textbook Case of Adultery in Ancient Mesopotamia', *Hebrew Union College Annual* 40–1 (1969–70) 33–44.

W.G. LAMBERT, 'Morals in Ancient Mesopotamia', *Jaarbericht van het Vooraziatisch-Egyptisch Genootschap ex Oriente Lux* 15 (1958) 184–96.

K. VAN DER TOORN, *Sin and Sanction in Israel and Mesopotamia: A Comparative Study* (Assen 1986).

R. WESTBROOK, 'Adultery in Ancient Near Eastern Law', *Revue Biblique* 97 (1990) 542–80.

——, 'The Enforcement of Morals in Mesopotamian Law', *Journal of the American Oriental Society* 104 (1984) 753–6.

**Aegean**  The Aegean Sea lies between mainland *Greece and western *Anatolia, and includes the islands of Crete,

Late Mycenaean III 'pilgrim flask' from Gezer in Palestine, a typical import from Mycenaean Greece during the Late Bronze Age. Height 16.5 cm. WA 104961.

the Cyclades and Rhodes. The latter two show less *archaeological evidence for contact with areas east of the Aegean, but links between Crete and the Near East reached a peak in the second millennium BC, probably stimulated by Aegean need for *tin and *copper to produce *bronze.

Cretan civilization of that period is referred to as 'Minoan', after the legendary King Minos. Minoan goods appear in increasing numbers in western Anatolia and the *Levant until the political and economic collapse of Minoan Crete some time during the Late *Bronze Age. *Wall paintings, similar in style to those found in Minoan palaces, have been excavated at Middle Bronze Age *Alalakh and Tel Kabri, and at Tell ed-Dab'a in Egypt, the probable *Hyksos capital of Avaris.

*Cuneiform and Egyptian texts of the second millennium BC refer to a place called 'Keftiu/Kaptaru'. Keftiu could be reached only by ship, was regarded as a major power and had particularly close contacts with Egypt. It is normally identified with Crete or the Aegean, although there is some disagreement. Inscriptions on Egyptian wall paintings describe gift-bearers from Keftiu as inhabitants of 'islands in the midst of the sea'. Keftiu is recorded as exporting mineral and *medicinal items, *wood, fine *pottery, oil, an *alcoholic beverage, grain and *metals. A variety of goods was exchanged between Keftiu/Kaptaru and *Mari, some at least through *Ugarit. In recent years, a controversial theory has proposed that as early as 2000 BC Levantine and Egyptian influence on the Aegean played a central role in the formation of Greek civilization, although it is more likely that the later Minoan rulers of Crete emulated various aspects of Near Eastern culture.

After the demise of Minoan Crete, trading activities with the Near East were taken over by Mycenaean Greece until the collapse of most of the kingdoms in c.1200 BC. Mycenaean pottery is found widely in the Near East, but the absence of other artefacts suggests that it reflects *trade and not Mycenaean settlement or colonization.

*Hittite texts mention a place called Ahhiyawa, which has been explained as the Hittite way of writing Greek *Achaiwa*, equated with the Achaean Greeks of the Homeric epics, and therefore describing Mycenaean Greece. Although the people of Ahhiyawa are mentioned as trading across the eastern Mediterranean, the identification with Mycenaean Greece is not universally accepted. Other suggestions for the location of Ahhiyawa are an Anatolian kingdom, or an island kingdom off the Anatolian coast, perhaps Rhodes.　　　　　PB

A.B. KNAPP, 'Island Cultures: Crete, Thera, Cyprus, Rhodes, and Sardinia', *Civilizations of the Ancient Near East*, ed. J.M. Sasson (New York 1995) 1433–49.

C. LAMBROU-PHILLIPSON, *Hellenorientalia: The Near Eastern Presence in the Bronze Age Aegean, ca. 3000–1000 B.C.* (Jonsered 1990).

M. MARAZZI, 'Mykener in Vorderasien', *Reallexikon der Assyriologie* 8 (Berlin/New York 1997) 528–34.

**Afterlife:** see Death and funerary beliefs and customs

**Agriculture** The Near East witnessed some of the earliest cultivation of crops and herding of *animals anywhere in the world.

Crop cultivation started independently in a few separate locations across the Near East, according to genetic and palaeobotanical evidence. The cultivation of different crops spread from different settings. The earliest, most prominent cultivated crops seem to be einkorn and emmer wheat, two-row barley, lentils and peas. There is currently a reasonable but not uncontested case for seeing cultivation in the southern *Levant during Pre-Pottery *Neolithic A between 9300 and 8500 BC. By 8500 BC cultivation seems to be more widespread in the Near East.

Whatever the date of the appearance of cultivation, most authorities now suggest that herding appeared somewhat later, and probably followed as a consequence of the adoption of sedentary life and cultivation. The period between 8000 and 7000 BC is generally seen as the time when the herding of sheep and goat commenced, although some argue for later, others for earlier in this period. There is now a claim for pig domestication as early as 9000 BC in Turkey and occasional not well substantiated claims for early animal domestication in the *Zagros. Cattle and pig appear to be domesticated by the beginning of the seventh millennium BC in most parts of the Near East. By the seventh millennium BC the classic foundations of Near Eastern agriculture were established, based on dry farming and herding using these domesticates.

Other major developments followed to produce a classic formula for Near Eastern agriculture. In some areas animal herding began to be managed separately from cultivation, allowing increases in herd size and a degree of specialization in pastoral production. This was a strong element in the life of *nomadic groups exploiting the dry steppe and desert areas throughout *prehistoric and historical periods. An important development for all pastoral communities was the exploitation of 'secondary' products like milk and its products, hair and wool.

Some time after the domestication of grain crops, probably between 6000 and 4500 BC, fruit crops were added to the range of cultivars. In particular the olive and grape became important features of cultivation in hilly areas and the date in drier areas. Their secondary products oil and *wine became particularly important within early Near Eastern lifestyles.

When agriculture penetrated the major alluvial *river systems of central and southern *Mesopotamia (probably after 7000 BC) with their low rainfall, *irrigation would have been essential for crop production. Irrigation, apart from increasing the dependability of crop production, can markedly increase yields. By the time of the first texts indicating the nature of Mesopotamian agriculture in the third millennium BC we see a highly sophisticated and well regulated agricultural regime that ensured massive crop yields.

Thus evolved an agricultural mosaic with distinctive features that characterized the Near East until the nineteenth century AD.　　　　　DB

J.N. POSTGATE, *Early Mesopotamia: Society and Economy at the Dawn of History* (London 1992) chapters 8 and 9.

C. REDMAN, *The Rise of Civilization* (San Francisco 1978).

**Ahmar, (Tell):** see Til Barsip

**Ai** Ai is a *Hebrew place-name meaning 'the ruin' which appears in the *Bible, most prominently as a site destroyed during the *Israelite conquest (see Exodus; Israel and Judah). In 1838 Edward Robinson proposed that it be identified with the 11-ha site of et-Tell, north of *Jerusalem in *Palestine. This identification is now generally accepted; suggested alternatives for ancient Ai – nearby Khirbet Khaiyan and Khirbet Khudriya – are in fact Byzantine settlements.

Ai/et-Tell has been excavated by *Garstang (1928), Judith Marquet-Krause (1933–5) and Joseph Callaway (1964–72). The site was occupied throughout the Early Bronze Age, first as an unfortified *village, later as a walled town destroyed and rebuilt three times. This town consisted of a *fortified *palace and *temple compound on the 'acropolis', *houses, a possible *market and four town *gates. Imported *Egyptian alabaster and *stone vessels and certain stone construction techniques point to links with the First and Second Dynasties in Egypt. After the last destruction, the site was abandoned until the beginning of the *Iron Age, when a small unwalled village was built on the summit of the mound. The houses were characterized by the use of pillars and arches. The new occupants dug cisterns in the rock to collect rain *water, terraced and cultivated the slopes of the hill, and later built granaries. This village was abandoned in the eleventh century BC, and the site was never resettled.

The excavations revealed no destruction level which might have been associated with the Israelite conquest, and this is often cited as evidence that the biblical references to Ai are not historical, but the Hebrew name 'the ruin' may indicate that it was only temporarily occupied at that time.                                                            PB

J.A. CALLAWAY, *The Early Bronze Age Sanctuary at Ai (et-Tell)* (London 1972).
——, *The Early Bronze Age Citadel and Lower City at Ai (et-Tell)* (Cambridge, MA 1980).
——, 'Ai', *The New Encyclopedia of Archaeological Excavations in the Holy Land*, ed. E. Stern (Jerusalem 1993) 39–45.
J. MARQUET-KRAUSE, *Les fouilles de 'Ay (et-Tell), 1933–1935* (Paris 1949).

## Ain Dara

**Ain Dara** A large *tell north-west of Aleppo, with a main mound and an extensive lower city, excavated principally by Ali Abou Assaf in 1976, 1978 and 1980–5, revealing occupation of medieval, *Hellenistic, *Persian, *Iron and Late Bronze Ages. The major discovery is a *temple in level VII, which the excavator dated 1300–740 BC, divided into three phases. The building was set in a courtyard with a well and its plan is like the Late Bronze Age area H temple at *Hazor and the Iron Age one at Tell Tayinat. The floors were paved in white limestone to contrast with the grey basalt blocks of the walls. Entry was through a porch flanked by towers and carved *stone *animals. Two footprints were chiselled in the outer threshold and one, almost a metre long, in the inner. Two rows of carvings adorned the façade. The next room was lined with basalt blocks carved in high relief with figures of *gods and geometrical patterns. Three steps rose to the sanctuary, which also had carved decoration, one block showing a god between two bull-men. In the final phase a corridor was built around the temple with more carved slabs forming a dado outside and showing *kings and gods inside. Although many are damaged, the majority of the reliefs, which number over 150 and are all in Syro-*Hittite style dating to the ninth to eighth centuries BC, apparently depicted lions and sphinxes or mountain deities, indicating a dedication to *Ishtar in the excavator's opinion. Identification with the *town of Kunulua, mentioned in *Assyrian inscriptions, is unsubstantiated.                                                    ARM

A. ABOU ASSAF, *Der Tempel von 'Ain Dara* (Mainz 1990).
——, 'Die Kleinfunden aus 'Ain Dara', *Damaszener Mitteilungen* 9 (1996) 47–111.

## Ain Ghazal

**Ain Ghazal** Ain Ghazal is located on the south-eastern edge of the modern *Jordanian capital Amman, near the edge of the hilly and wooded zone on the eastern flank of the Jordan rift valley. It is, therefore, in an area that receives enough rainfall for reliable dry farming, but is within striking distance of the more arid steppe lands to the east. The site sits by a major spring on either side of the major river, the Wadi Zerqa. *Water is abundant.

Ain Ghazal has been excavated since 1979 by Gary Rollefson. Occupied from c.8200 BC, the site is distinguished by the significant growth it underwent by the end of the aceramic *Neolithic period, reaching c.12 ha at 7000 BC. In the earlier seventh millennium BC it extended over 20 ha although it may have been less densely occupied at this period.

During the Middle Pre-Pottery Neolithic B (c.8000 BC) the site was characterized by evenly spaced 'pier' *houses arranged in rows on terraces. Each such building was characterized by a rectangular space divided into three by large piers, whose thickness suggests they supported the roof as well as serving as room divisions. Such buildings are found on either side of the Jordan Valley at this period, for example at *Jericho as well. A sunken hearth is often found in one of these chambers. The buildings are notable for their thick plaster floors, sometimes decorated with red ochre paint.

In this phase caches of half-size plaster statues have been found buried on the site. These depict human-like figures and at some point stood upright. Fragments of such statues have been found at Jericho as well so the

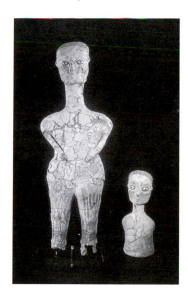

Cache of plaster statues as discovered at Ain Ghazal. Pre-Pottery Neolithic B, c.8000 BC (courtesy of Gary Rollefson).

Two of the Pre-Pottery Neolithic plaster statues from Ain Ghazal, now in Amman Archaeological Museum. Their heights are 84 cm and 32.4 cm (courtesy of Piotr Bienkowski).

practices with which they were associated may have been quite widespread. Their rarity and nature suggest they may have played a relatively public role, but whether the whole community was involved in such communal rites or extended *family groups is certainly not clear. They may have been associated with mortuary *rituals in that mortuary practices at this period included separation of skulls from bodies with, in a few cases, the skulls plastered and retained in specific contexts.

Architecture changes in the Late Pre-Pottery Neolithic B, c.7500 BC. Larger, more compartmentalized buildings with sub-floor compartments, perhaps to aid ventilation and drainage, are typical. Family sizes, storage needs, and the way buildings were used had undoubtedly changed. Distinct structures include a circular building with four sub-floor channels that led to a central feature unfortunately damaged. The channels and this central feature may have been employed in maintaining a fire or furnace. Interpretations of this building include a ritual building/*temple or an industrial installation – certainly a communal or public installation is suggested. In the part of the settlement on the opposite side of the Zerqa a rectangular building is designated as a temple principally for its three upright slabs. Alternatively this building might have been a dwelling with certain features of ritual importance for those who inhabited it.

In the earliest seventh millennium BC simple buildings without plaster floors replace the complex Late Pre-Pottery Neolithic B ones. In addition small rectangular 'corridor' buildings with basements divided into compartments also typify this phase, perhaps not dissimilar to the *Beidha buildings. Later in the seventh millennium BC, in the Pottery Neolithic, simpler rectangular structures are constructed without plastered floors and generally showing less investment. The excavators have suggested less intensive occupation in the seventh millennium BC, with part of the community perhaps taking sheep and goat herds into the steppe or desert areas. On the other hand there are substantial features to the settlement including a large 15-m long thick wall demarcating, in a massive way, one area from others, and a walled street is present. *Burial practice has changed, with bodies being buried off site or disposed of in other ways and no separated skulls present.

The evidence for subsistence activities is important. Cultivated cereal and probably leguminous crops are found from the earliest levels of the settlement. Large quantities of legumes are found in one Late Pre-Pottery Neolithic B building showing their importance alongside simple hulled wheat and barley. From 8000 BC, whilst goats show no morphological changes associated with domestication, the population structure represented at Ain Ghazal suggests human manipulation of herds. With the appearance of significant numbers of sheep after 7500 BC and even more after 7000 BC we see the increasing importance of herded as against hunted animals and perhaps increased utilization of the steppe. The need to pasture *animals may have had a profound impact on these large sedentary communities and resulted in their eventual abandonment.                                              DB

G. ROLLEFSON, A. SIMMONS and Z. KAFAFI, 'Neolithic Cultures at Ain Ghazal, Jordan', *Journal of Field Archaeology* 19/4 (1992) 443–70.

G. ROLLEFSON, 'Changes in Architecture and Social Organization at Neolithic 'Ain Ghazal', *The Prehistory of Jordan II: Perspectives from 1997*, eds H.G.K. Gebel, Z. Kafafi and G.O. Rollefson (Berlin 1997) 287–308.

**Akitu festival:** see New Year ceremonies

**Akkad** *Sargon made the town of Agade his capital about 2300 BC and it gave its name to northern *Babylonia, paired with *Sumer and *Semitized as Akkad. The location is unknown. Although it became unimportant after the end of Sargon's *dynasty, Babylonian *kings still undertook building works there in the sixth century BC.

The dynasty of Akkad created a centralized *administration, but only small *archives are available from provincial centres (e.g. Umma, Gasur (=*Nuzi)). As a Semitic dynasty, the kings of Akkad brought Semitic deities to prominence, especially *Ishtar. The Semitic *Akkadian *language was used for royal inscriptions, alone and beside *Sumerian, and widely for *letters and administrative and legal deeds, beginning its rise to dominate the whole land. Akkad's impact is most evident today in its *art. The vigour of some Early Dynastic III *seal designs reached a peak in magnificently modelled figures of men and *animals in more open arrangements, frequently with heraldic balance, and a variety of new motifs appeared, including scenes from *myth and legend (apparently *Anzû, *Etana, a supernatural battle). The long-lived 'presentation scene', showing the seal's owner being presented to a *god or the king is introduced and names of owners are more frequently engraved on seals. Vigour and realism also mark the fragments of Akkadian *sculpture, above all the stela of *Naram-Sin found at *Susa, and *copper cast figures, notably the head of a king from *Nineveh and the kneeling figure inscribed for *Naram-Sin from Bassetki.

The kings of the dynasty, *Sargon, his sons Rimush and Manishtusu, and his grandson *Naram-Sin, ruled a realm extending into *Iran and up to the *Anatolian foothills, with some control up the Euphrates into northwestern *Syria. Pressures from *Guti tribes in the northeast, revolt against heavy *taxes imposed on conquered areas and, probably, severe drought brought decline under Naram-Sin's son Shar-kali-sharri, and eventual extinction. Yet the memory of this empire and its rulers remained alive as a model until the end of Babylonian civilization.                                              ARM

P. AMIET, *L'art d'Agade* (Paris 1976).

D.R. FRAYNE, *Sargonic and Gutian Periods (2334–2113 BC)* (Toronto 1993).

C.J. GADD, 'The Dynasty of Agade and the Gutian Invasion', *Cambridge Ancient History* 1.2, 2nd ed. (Cambridge 1971) 417–63.

J. GOODNICK WESTENHOLZ, *Legends of the Kings of Akkade* (Winona Lake, IN 1997).

M. LIVERANI (ed.), *Akkad, the First World Empire* (Padua 1993).

**Akkadian** Akkadian is an overall term for all dialects of *Assyrian and *Babylonian, the eastern branch of the *Semitic *language family. Attested from the middle of the third millennium BC (Early Dynastic III, *Ebla) until the first century AD, it preserves the oldest written Semitic texts. Akkadian shares common Semitic features of consonantal word base, inflected according to regular patterns for nominal and verbal forms, with consequent phonetic shifts. Nominal forms distinguish subject, object and oblique cases in the singular (e.g. *kalbum, kalbam, kalbim*), subject and object or oblique in the plural (*kalbū, kalbē*). As in all Semitic languages, the genitive relationship is expressed by attaching the possessed in as short a form as possible to the possessor (*wardum* 'slave', *warad šarrim* 'slave of the king'). There is no definite article. Akkadian developed the verbal system in its own way, with prefixed forms for finite actions (Preterite *ipqid*, 'he delivered', Imperfective *ipaqqid*, 'he delivers, will deliver', Perfective used in a sequence of verbs, *iptaqid*, 'he has delivered, will have delivered'), a suffixed form for conditions (Stative *paqid, paqdat*, 'he is delivering, she is delivering', often passive). Four themes mark the simple sense (G or I, *ipqid*, etc.), intensive or factitive (D or II, *upaqqid*, 'he supplied, cared for'), causative (S or III, *ušapqid*, 'he made deliver'), passive or reflexive (N or IV, *ippaqid* (for *inpaqqid*), 'he was delivered'). Derived forms with infixed *t*, denoting reciprocal or passive, occasionally reflexive, action, occur in the first three themes and infixed *tan*, denoting repeated or enduring action, in all four.

Over the centuries the language changed: Old Akkadian (c.2600–2000 BC) displays many archaic forms. The two main streams can then be seen to diverge as Old Babylonian, considered the 'golden age' of Akkadian (c.2000–1600 BC) and Old Assyrian (c.2000–1700 BC) preserving certain adjacent vowels uncontracted, against Babylonian. In Middle Babylonian (c.1600–1000 BC) case endings lose distinction, final *m* is lost from nominal forms and phonetic changes occur, and Middle Assyrian (c.1500–1000 BC) shares those features and displays others. Neo-Babylonian and Neo-Assyrian both suffer Aramaic influence, c.1000–600 BC; Late Babylonian shows strong Aramaic influence, 600 BC onwards. Scribes of Middle Babylonian also maintained a literary form of the language derived from Old Babylonian which is termed Standard Babylonian or the Hymnal-Epic Dialect and is found, for example, in the standard form of the *Gilgamesh epic and Assyrian royal inscriptions.

Akkadian has a large vocabulary, with many words unique to it, even the prepositions 'to' and 'in' (*ana, ina*). Sumerian influenced it strongly, providing many nouns (e.g. Sumerian *é.gal*, Akkadian *ekallum*, 'palace') and causing the verb to stand at the end of a clause. Beside the *Aramaic influence noted, *Hurrian and West Semitic words entered in the second millennium BC and *Persian and *Greek later in the first millennium BC. ARM

J. HUEHNERGARD, *A Grammar of Akkadian* (Atlanta, GA 1997).
A. UNGNAD, L. MATOUŠ and H.A. HOFFNER, *Akkadian Grammar* (Atlanta, GA 1992).
W. VON SODEN, *Grundriss der akkadischen Grammatik* (Rome 1995).

**Al Jauf:** see Duma

**Al Mina:** see Alalakh; Greeks

**Alaca Hüyük** The mound of Alaca Hüyük is located north of Yozgat, 180 km east of Ankara in north-central *Anatolia, modern Turkey. Excavated by Hamit Koşay in the 1930s, Alaca Hüyük is best known for its spectacularly rich tombs of Early *Bronze Age date, as well as its impressive architecture of the *Hittite period.

The site was first settled in the *Chalcolithic period, late in the fourth millennium BC. During the Early Bronze Age, in the late third millennium BC, extremely rich *burials were deposited. These graves took the form of stone-lined chambers at the bottom of shafts, with *wooden roofs. Each of the thirteen excavated burials was of a single individual, male or female, accompanied by a wealth of objects, especially *metal artefacts such as solar disks, weapons, *jewellery, libation vessels, swords, daggers and animal standards, frequently of *gold or *silver. After the burial had been sealed by a wooden and clay roof, *feasts and animal *sacrifices took place, and the remains were deposited in the pit above each tomb. Parallels in the metalwork and *pottery from these

The Sphinx Gate at Alaca Hüyük (courtesy of Roger Matthews).

Finial for a pole in the form of a silver bull, inlaid with gold, on a copper peg, an example of the craftsmanship displayed in the tombs at Alaca Hüyük. Height 24 cm. c.2300 BC. WA 135851.

contemporary with the mention of Alalakh as a dependency in the *Ebla *archives. The first palace was built c.2000 BC, contemporary with the Third Dynasty of *Ur. Later, it became a vassal of *Yamhad; the level VII palace archive illustrates Alalakh's commercial relations with Syria, *Babylonia and *Cyprus. The palace had two or three storeys, with some rooms painted with *wall paintings similar to Minoan examples from Crete. Storerooms contained elephant tusks for making *ivory inlays.

Level VII was destroyed by *Hattusilis I; the city was rebuilt and became a vassal of *Mitanni. This period is described in the '*autobiographical' inscription on the statue of Idrimi (c.1500 BC), perhaps written after his death, in which he tells of his exile from Yamhad and successful return to power in Alalakh. Idrimi's son, Niqmepa, built the level IV palace which was destroyed, probably by the *Hittites, in c.1430 BC. The palace plan was an early version of the *bīt hilāni. The palace archives consisted of *diplomatic, *administrative and legal texts (see Law), which document the growing presence of *Hurrians in north Syria through personal names and loan words.

tombs, which occur in various forms across much of northern Anatolia in the Early Bronze Age, suggest connections with the metal-rich cultures of the *Caucasus well to the east, and may indicate an influx of *Indo-European speakers into Anatolia.

During the Middle and Late Bronze Ages (c.2000–1200 BC), Alaca Hüyük became a major Hittite city, located only 30 km north-east of the great Hittite capital *city of *Hattusas. Alaca was circled by a wall with towers and a monumental *gateway. A large *palace was constructed just inside the city wall, with open courtyard and suites of rooms. The main gate at Alaca in the Hittite period featured two large *stone sphinxes, with relief processional and hunting scenes, carved on adjacent stone blocks. Areas of *housing and streets lined with *shops have also been excavated. Alaca appears to have been abandoned towards the end of the second millennium BC during the general collapse of the Hittite empire.

RM

J.G. MACQUEEN, *The Hittites and Their Contemporaries in Asia Minor*, 2nd ed. (London 1996).

J. YAKAR, *The Later Prehistory of Anatolia: The Late Chalcolithic and Early Bronze Age* (Oxford 1985).

**Alalakh** Identified with modern Tell Atchana, Alalakh lies in the *Amuq plain on the modern *Syrian–Turkish border, just east of the River Orontes. *Woolley's excavations, from 1937–9 and 1946–9, uncovered seventeen levels of occupation from the Early Bronze Age to the end of the Late Bronze Age, including a sequence of *palaces and *temples, on a mound measuring 750 by 300 m. Alalakh's history is one of vassaldom to more powerful Syrian neighbours, but its prime importance is its archives of about five hundred *Akkadian *cuneiform tablets, principally from levels VII and IV, which illuminate the structure of Syrian society in the second millennium BC.

The earliest levels were below the water table, but were

The son of King Idrimi of Alalakh had this statue carved and inscribed to commemorate his father's adventurous life. Height 1.035 m. Early fourteenth century BC. WA 130738-9.

Alalakh continued under Mitannian rule until its conquest by *Suppiluliumas I in c.1366 BC. Hittite inscriptions, *seals and a stela testify to Hittite control of the city. Alalakh was destroyed c.1200 BC, probably by the *Sea Peoples, and never re-occupied.

Woolley also excavated the nearby harbour town of Al Mina, occupied primarily from the late ninth century BC until the early *Hellenistic period, where storerooms of imported Aegean and Cypriot pottery were found.     PB

D. COLLON, *The Seal Impressions from Tell Atchana/Alalakh* (Neukirchen/Vluyn 1975).

——, *The Alalakh Cylinder Seals* (Oxford 1982).

M. DIETRICH and O. LORETZ, 'Die Inschrift der Statue des Königs Idrimi von Alalah', *Ugarit-Forschungen* 13 (1981) 201–69.

M. HEINZ, *Tell Atchana/Alalakh: Die Schichten VII–XVII* (Neukirchen/Vluyn 1992).

D.L. STEIN, 'Alalakh', *The Oxford Encyclopedia of Archaeology in the Near East* 1, ed. E.M. Meyers (New York 1997) 55–9.

D.J. WISEMAN, *The Alalakh Tablets* (London 1953).

C.L. WOOLLEY, *A Forgotten Kingdom* (London 1953).

——, *Alalakh: An Account of the Excavations at Tell Atchana in the Hatay, 1937–1949* (Oxford 1955).

## Alashiya

The land of Alashiya is first mentioned in texts from *Mari dating to the eighteenth century BC. Thereafter 'Alashiya' occurs with increasing frequency, usually in connection with *copper production and *trade, in texts from *Babylon, *Alalakh, *Hatti and *Egypt and in the *Amarna Letters. With the end of the Late Bronze Age in c.1200/1150 BC, references to Alashiya cease (although the term 'Elishah' in the *Bible is probably equivalent, referring to a maritime nation in the *Aegean which supplied coloured fabrics to *Tyre). A Hittite text referring to a battle between the Hittites and Alashiyan *ships suggests that Alashiya was affected by the disruptions connected with the *Sea Peoples.

Since 1864, many scholars have argued that Alashiya was the name used during the second millennium BC for all or part of *Cyprus. Although the equation still arouses controversy, it is now generally accepted. Texts portray Alashiya as a flourishing, multi-ethnic kingdom engaged in state-organized copper production and export, with close connections to the *Levant and Hatti, a picture which fits well with the archaeological evidence from Cyprus. The copper industry was very important on Cyprus, especially in the Middle and Late Bronze Ages, contemporary with the Alashiya references. As Cypriot international relations and copper exports expanded, there was a corresponding increase in the number of textual references to Alashiya. During the Late Bronze Age, the most important site on Cyprus appears to have been Enkomi, and it has been suggested that it was the capital of the kingdom of Alashiya, or conceivably that 'Alashiya' referred specifically to Enkomi itself.     PB

A.B. KNAPP, '*Alashiya, Caphtor/Keftiu*, and Eastern Mediterranean Trade: Recent Studies in Cypriote Archaeology and History', *Journal of Field Archaeology* 12 (1985) 231–50.

—— (ed.), *Sources for the History of Cyprus II: Near Eastern and Aegean Texts from the Third to the First Millennia BC* (New York 1996).

R.S. MERRILLEES, *Alasia Revisited* (Paris 1987).

J.D. MUHLY, 'The Land of *Alashiya*: References to *Alashiya* in the Texts of the Second Millennium BC and the History of Cyprus in the Late Bronze Age', *Acts of the First International Cyprological Congress*, ed. V. Karageorghis (Nicosia 1972) 201–19.

## Albright, William Foxwell (1891–1971)

Few scholars in the history of ancient Near Eastern studies are linked with as many subdisciplines as W.F. Albright, who preferred to call himself an 'Orientalist'. Born of missionary parents in Chile, Albright's interest in ancient Near Eastern and *biblical history, languages and literature developed early and led to his Johns Hopkins University PhD in *Assyriology, in 1916. When Albright accepted a fellowship to study in *Jerusalem in 1920, his eyes opened on to an enormous range of research interests. He served as director of the American School of Oriental Research for most of the period between 1920 and 1936 and edited the *Bulletin of the American Schools of Oriental Research* from 1930 to 1968. Albright contributed much to the vitality of the institute and its parent organization (ASOR) in the USA, and this East Jerusalem research centre was renamed after him in 1970.

From 1929 until 1958, Albright taught at Johns Hopkins, where he supervised fifty-nine doctoral dissertations and extended his influence through the careers of his students (e.g. Cross, Freedman, Wright, Bright, Mendenhall). The list of Albright's publications contains over one thousand entries in many different fields of study (e.g. Egyptian and Semitic languages, *Israelite history and religion, *Mesopotamian chronology, Dead Sea Scrolls, Syro-Palestinian archaeology). Major books include *The Archaeology of Palestine and the Bible*, *The Archaeology of Palestine*, *Archaeology and the Religion of Israel*, and *Yahweh and the Gods of Canaan*. The 'Albrightian synthesis' is best reflected in his magnificent *From the Stone Age to Christianity: Monotheism and the Historical Process*, 2nd ed. (1957). This title and the book's encyclopaedic content illustrate Albright's desire to arrange minute details into orderly sequences. While many of his positions on historical, linguistic and biblical debates have been rejected by later scholarship (along with much of the 'biblical archaeology' agenda), Albright's attempt to integrate data from many disciplines into a coherent picture presents a challenge to the contemporary trend to compartmentalize. This synthetic approach was successful in many regards and stands as a clear sign of his genius.

Though trained primarily as a linguist, Albright immediately saw the value of *archaeology for biblical studies. He took a leading role in excavations at Tell el-Ful, Bethel, Beth Zur and Ader, and in South Yemen. His excavation technique was far from perfect, but his major contribution to the methodological development of Palestinian archaeology resulted from four seasons of digging (1926–32) at Tell Beit Mirsim, in southern *Palestine. Here Albright applied his typological approach to build on *Petrie's pioneering efforts and produced a firm ceramic chronology for the Palestinian Middle Bronze, Late Bronze and Iron Ages.                    GLM

'Celebrating and Examining W.F. Albright', special thematic issue of *Biblical Archaeologist* 56 (1993) 1–45.

D.N. FREEDMAN (ed.), *The Published Works of William Foxwell Albright: A Comprehensive Bibliography* (Cambridge, MA 1975).

B.O. LONG, *Planting and Reaping Albright: Politics, Ideology, and Interpreting the Bible* (College Station, PA 1997).

P. MACHINIST, 'William Foxwell Albright: The Man and His Work', *The Study of the Ancient Near East in the Twenty-first Century: The William Foxwell Albright Centennial Conference*, eds J.S. Cooper and G.M. Schwartz (Winona Lake, IN 1996) 385–403.

L.G. RUNNING and D.N. FREEDMAN, *William Foxwell Albright: A Twentieth-century Genius* (New York 1975).

G.W. VAN BEEK, *The Scholarship of William Foxwell Albright: An Appraisal* (Atlanta, GA 1989).

## Alcoholic beverages: see Beer; Wine

## Aleppo: see Yamhad

**Alikosh**   The site of Alikosh is located in the Deh Luran plain at the foot of the *Zagros mountains, east of the southern stretch of the Tigris. It is, at 145 m above sea level, relatively low-lying and is also in a relatively arid zone, the area of the site receiving just enough rainfall for dry farming today. It is a small site less than 1.5 ha in area. Two major aceramic *Neolithic phases of settlement, the Bus Mordeh and Alikosh phases, are followed by an early ceramic Neolithic phase, the Muhammed Jaffar. The Muhammed Jaffar phase belongs to the period shortly after c.7000 BC. The aceramic phases must predate this and probably are contemporary with the Pre-Pottery Neolithic B in the *Levant.

In all phases there are limited exposures of architecture as the site was excavated to reveal the changes in subsistence economy and environment associated with the adoption of farming and herding (see Agriculture). The picture revealed is still a classic of subsistence and environment reconstruction and provides the best picture of such developments on the eastern edge of the *Fertile Crescent.

In the Bus Mordeh phase the cultivation of wheat and barley is attested, but a large range of other *plants are found more commonly, especially small seeded legumes which were probably gathered. It is suggested that sheep show evidence indicating their domestication and that the presence of goat in an open steppe environment means they were introduced in herds. However, this suggestion of the appearance of herding could be disputed. Gazelle, onager, wild cattle and pig were certainly hunted. *Obsidian and sea shells attest to participation in exchanges bringing materials from considerable distances, obsidian from at least 800 km away.

In the succeeding Alikosh phase cultivated cereals are much more important although significant quantities of wild foods were still gathered. There seems more convincing evidence for the presence of herded goats. It is perhaps only with this late aceramic Neolithic phase that we see the appearance of a fully fledged mixed farming economy in the steppe lands at the foot of the southern Zagros. Apart from obsidian and sea shells, *copper and turquoise also reached the site over some distance, hinting at a broadening of contacts.

Intriguingly in the early Pottery Neolithic Muhammed Jaffar phase the seeds of wild plants substantially outnumber those from cultivated wheat and barley. The analysts suggest that this indicates the extensive presence of weeds of cultivation, some of which may have been useful in their own right. In this phase goats show incontrovertible evidence of changes in anatomy associated with domestication.                    DB

F. HOLE et al., *Prehistory and Human Ecology of the Deh Luran Plain* (Ann Arbor, MI 1969).

**Alphabet**   The first two letters of the *Greek script gave their names to the *writing system which uses a distinct sign to represent each major sound in a *language. The letters which the Greeks adopted from the *Phoenicians, probably in the ninth century BC, had their origin a thousand years earlier. The oldest specimens that are partly intelligible are the thirty or so Proto-Sinaitic inscriptions from the region of the Egyptian turquoise mines at Serabit el-Khadem in western *Sinai. Egyptian inscriptions in the same place, both formal and graffiti, show that the mines were operated over a long period, but the inscriptions in question can be dated to the middle of the second millennium BC. In 1916 Sir Alan Gardiner proposed to treat the twenty-four to thirty signs used in these texts as a form of the alphabet, identifying some on the basis of their resemblance to the meanings of the names given to the Phoenician and *Hebrew letters, borrowed but meaningless in Greek (a wavy line for Greek *mu*, Hebrew *mem*, 'water'). He surmised that the initial sound of the name alone was taken, so that each sign marked a consonant (*mem*=*m*), the principle of acrophony. On this basis he read a repeated group of signs *lb'lt*, in *Canaanite 'for the lady, mistress', a sense which agrees well with the Egyptian dedications to Hathor in a shrine at the site, she being 'the mistress'. Although little more can be read because the inscriptions are brief and damaged, this carries conviction. The inscriptions can be attributed to workmen hired in Canaan where, we assume, the script had been invented. The inventor was a *scribe unhappy with Egyptian and *Babylonian systems, which could not represent Canaanite well. He analysed his language to isolate each main phoneme, then created a sign for each by acrophony. In reality, he made a simple syllabary, each sign standing for a consonant followed by any vowel, but in effect it was an alphabet. No word began with a vowel in Canaanite, so the process did not produce signs for vowels, and *Semitic languages have been written satisfactorily in that way ever since (as Arabic and modern Hebrew are). When the Greeks adopted the alphabet, it was essential for them to mark vowels – the word for 'no' is *ou* – and so they took signs for Semitic sounds which they did not have and used them for vowels (thus *w* became *u*).

From the end of the Middle Bronze Age and through the Late Bronze Age there is a small number of inscriptions scratched on *pottery, *metal objects and *stone which display signs related to Proto-Sinaitic. At *Ugarit scribes apparently translated the alphabetic principle into *cuneiform for writing on clay in their Babylonian tradition. On some tablets they wrote the signs in order, presenting the oldest examples of the order familiar from Hebrew and Greek, with signs for some sounds that later merged in Phoenician and Hebrew (e.g. *th* and *sh*) and three added at the end for writing *Hurrian. That script was also engraved on stone and metal and occasionally written on pottery vessels before they were baked. If only those pieces survived, they would present a use of writing

similar to that represented by the alphabetic texts from Canaan. This allows the conclusion that Canaanite scribes wrote all sorts of texts on perishable papyrus or leather rolls or *wooden tablets.

During the twelfth and eleventh centuries BC the alphabet reached standard form in the *Levant, the twenty-two letters being read from right to left, under Egyptian influence. Most examples from this time are owners' names incised for unknown purposes on over forty *bronze arrowheads. The oldest intelligible sentences occur on the sarcophagus of Ahiram of *Byblos (see Coffins), dated about 1000 BC. From that time onwards the history of the alphabet can be traced in several branches. In the Levant the *Israelites and their *Transjordanian neighbours adopted it and the *Aramaeans carried it eastwards so that it replaced cuneiform and, under the *Persians, reached *India to beget the scripts used for Sanskrit, Mongolian and other tongues, as well as many local Near Eastern scripts (Palmyrene, Elymaic, Mandaic), 'square' Hebrew and, via *Nabataean, Arabic. The Phoenicians spread the alphabet around the Mediterranean, most notably to the Greeks to whom the European alphabets are owed. ARM

J.F. HEALEY, *The Early Alphabet* (London 1990).

B.S.J. ISSERLIN, 'The Earliest Alphabetic Writing', *Cambridge Ancient History* 3.1, 2nd ed. (Cambridge 1982) 794–818.

L.H. JEFFERY, 'Greek Alphabetic Writing', *Cambridge Ancient History* 3.1, 2nd ed. (Cambridge 1982) 819–33.

A.R. MILLARD, 'The Infancy of the Alphabet', *World Archaeology* 17 (1986) 390–8.

Among the earliest examples of alphabetic writing are those from Serabit el-Khadem in western Sinai. Signs on the side of this sphinx are read *lb'lt* ('for Baalat' or 'for the lady'). Length 24.7 cm. c.1600 BC. EA 41748.

(*below*) Bronze arrowhead inscribed with the owner's name in early Phoenician letters, 'Arrow of Ada' son of Ba'la'. Length 9.1 cm. c.1100 BC. WA 136753.

(*right*) Chart showing the development of four letters of the alphabet from the earliest examples through the main lines until the Persian empire when the Aramaic script became the ancestor of modern Arabic, Hebrew and many others.

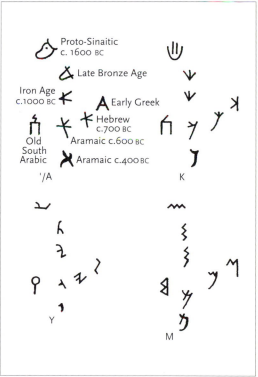

Scene on a seal from Uruk (c.3000 BC) showing a stepped structure on an animal's back, perhaps a dais for an altar, cult statue or offering table.

Altar of King Tukulti-Ninurta I of Assyria (mid thirteenth century BC) showing the king approaching, then kneeling in worship, before a similar altar supporting a god's symbol (original in Vorderasiatisches Museum, Berlin).

J. NAVEH, *Early History of the Alphabet: An Introduction to West Semitic Epigraphy and Palaeography* (Jerusalem 1987).

B. SASS, *The Genesis of the Alphabet and Its Development in the Second Millennium B.C.* (Wiesbaden 1988).

K. GALLING, *Der Altar in den Kulturen des alten Orients* (Berlin 1925).

R.D. HAAK, 'Altar', *Anchor Bible Dictionary* 1, ed. D.N. Freedman (New York 1992) 162–7.

W. ZWICKEL, *Räucherkult und Räuchergeräte* (Göttingen 1990).

**Altars**   In the ancient Near East, an altar was any surface on which offerings and *sacrifices were made or placed for a deity, actually or symbolically. Altars could be portable or stationary, plain or elaborate, located in a *temple or outside, for example even on hilltops. Unfortunately, any *stone object with a depression and without obvious function found archaeologically tends to be identified as an altar, but it is not always clear that its use was cultic.

The earliest temple altars at *Eridu in the fifth millennium BC and En Gedi in *Palestine in the *Chalcolithic period were placed opposite the *doorway, a position which became standard. In *Mesopotamia the altar was usually placed before the image of the *god, or in front of a statue of the worshipping *king. Archaeological evidence for *Israelite altars confirms the evidence of the *Old Testament that altars for burnt offerings stood in the forecourt of the temple, while *incense altars were found inside. Open altars unrelated to temples were common throughout the *Bronze Age; an impressive Early Bronze Age altar at *Megiddo, in an area surrounded by temples, is large, circular and mounted by a flight of steps. More portable altars include examples in which incense was burned in temples, common in the *Levant in the *Persian period, libation altars with depressions for liquid offerings, or bowls placed on ceramic stands.

Mesopotamian altars tended to be more elaborate, often carved in an architectural style representing a miniature temple, or showing scenes of worship or protective figures on the sides. Altars are also depicted on *kudurrus, stelae and *seals, the illustrations showing how they were actually used. Emblems of deities were placed on altars to receive worship (see Divine symbols). Sometimes a statue of a deity itself served as an altar, with the god's symbol placed on the animal's back. Seals depict stepped structures on the backs of deities' animals, which may have been daises for altars, cult statues or offering tables.                                                                PB

**Amarna Letters**   This is the name given to a collection of cuneiform tablets found in 1887 at Amarna, c.280 km south of Cairo in *Egypt, by a woman digging ancient mudbrick for use as fertilizer. Further illicit and legal digging brought the total to 382 tablets. Each tablet now has its own identity number and the prefix EA, and they are held in museums all over the world (the majority in the Vorderasiatische Museum, Berlin, the British Museum and the Egyptian Museum, Cairo).

Amarna was the site of the capital city founded by the Pharaoh Akhenaten (Amenophis IV) (c.1352–1336 BC). The tablets came originally from 'The Place of the Letters of the Pharaoh', the official records office of the capital. They span a period of between fifteen and thirty years, beginning around the thirtieth year of Amenophis III (c.1390–1352 BC), to no later than the first year of Tutankhamun's reign (c.1336–1327 BC). The majority date to the time of Akhenaten. The archive consists mostly of *letters received; eleven were written in Egypt and are either file copies or letters simply not sent.

Forty-three tablets are diplomatic correspondence in the *Akkadian language between Egypt and the great powers of western Asia – *Babylon, *Assyria, *Mitanni, *Hatti and *Alashiya – in which the 'great *kings' address each other as 'brother'. The letters refer to political matters, *trade agreements, arrangement of diplomatic *marriages and exchange of presents, with some lengthy inventories of the gifts (see Diplomacy).

Three hundred and seven tablets are correspondence with the *Canaanite city-states of *Syria and *Palestine, which were part of the Egyptian empire. These consist mostly of routine and standardized expressions of loyalty from the tributary rulers, who address the pharaoh as 'my lord'. The letters provide a fairly detailed picture of Egyptian power in Canaan, recording the intrigues of the local rulers who ask for help against each other and the threat that homeless groups such as the *Habiru posed.

Cuneiform tablet, a letter from Tushratta, king of Mitanni, to Pharaoh Amenophis III, concerning the visit of a statue of the goddess Shaushka (=Ishtar) of Nineveh to Egypt. At the end an ink-written note in Egyptian hieratic (cursive hieroglyphic) records the date that the letter was received in Egypt. Amarna Letter no. 23. WA 29793.

Most of the tablets are written in dialects of the Babylonian language, but two are in Hittite, and one each in *Hurrian and Assyrian. Thirty-two of the tablets are not letters or inventories attached to letters: they include *Akkadian *myths and epics, syllabaries, lexical texts, a god list, a Hurrian tale, and a list of equivalent Egyptian and Akkadian words which came from a *scribal *school. The Amarna *archive is unique, but presumably similar archives existed elsewhere and have not survived or been discovered. The earlier Amarna Letters from the time of Amenophis III must have been transferred from his capital, Thebes; presumably, certain letters were taken back to Thebes when Amarna was abandoned. The tablets which survived at Amarna are 'dead letters' which were left behind when the *royal court moved.  PB

B.J. KEMP, *Ancient Egypt: Anatomy of a Civilization* (London 1989) 223–7.
M. LIVERANI, *Three Amarna Essays* (Malibu 1979).
W.L. MORAN, *The Amarna Letters* (London 1992).
N. NA'AMAN, 'Amarna Letters', *Anchor Bible Dictionary* 1, ed. D.N. Freedman (New York 1992) 174–81.

**Amlash:** see Marlik

**Ammon, Ammonites** Ammon was a tiny *Iron Age kingdom, somewhat like a city-state, in *Transjordan. The Ammonites shared a border with the *Moabites to the south and the various peoples who occupied Gilead to the north. The kingdom of Ammon centred on its principal town, Rabbah or Rabbath-ammon, the modern capital city of Jordan, Amman, whose name is derived from the ancient *Semitic name. Geographical references in ancient texts and a homogeneous material culture seem to centre the Ammonite cultural sphere between the Jabbok (modern Wadi Zerqa) in the north and the region around Madaba in the south. Ammon's east and west boundaries were fixed by the *Syrian desert and the Jordan Valley respectively. The source of the Jabbok is in the valley floor below the ancient citadel of Rabbath-ammon, which was called the 'city of waters' in 2 Samuel 12: 27.

According to the *Bible, the eponymous ancestor of the Ammonites, Ben-'ammi, was the son of Lot, but evidence of human occupation in this region dates back to the *Palaeolithic. The earliest known settlement in the confines of modern Amman is *Ain Ghazal, a *village with impressive remains that reach back to the *Natufian and Pre-Pottery *Neolithic periods. *Water resources and a relatively hospitable *climate made this an attractive region for almost continuous occupation through the millennia. Towards the end of the Late Bronze Age, the inhabitants of Ammon – as in other parts of Transjordan – began to coalesce into a tribal state with a national identity. This land-tied tribalism produced a clear national or ethnic identity between the eighth and sixth centuries BC, as evident in material remains, *language and *religion.

Limestone statue of Yerah 'Azar from Amman Citadel, late eighth century BC, inscribed with his name and those of his father and grandfather (courtesy of Piotr Bienkowski).

Thanks to the Bible and the discovery of numerous, albeit brief, inscriptions, the names of eleven Ammonite *kings are known, but no precise chronology can be constructed. Most of the contacts between *Israel and Ammon were hostile, and the Hebrew prophets denounced the Ammonites. According to the *Assyrian texts, the Ammonites were among the *Levantine states that fought against *Shalmaneser III at Qarqar in 853 BC. Even though the Ammonites reached the peak of their cultural development between the eighth and sixth centuries BC, they were vassals of the Assyrians for most of this period. Ammon lost its independence when the *Babylonians conquered much of the Levant early in the sixth century BC, and the Ammonite people were incorporated into the *Persian *provincial system.

The Ammonites' material culture was very distinctive by the seventh and sixth centuries BC. They produced a high-quality style of *pottery and are well known for their numerous figurines and limestone *sculptures. The latter included images of kings and perhaps even portrayed their chief deity, Milkom. A group of anthropoid clay *coffins from Ammon dates to the *Iron Age. Ammonite script was derived from *Aramaic, and their language was a *Semitic dialect closely related to *Hebrew, Moabite and *Edomite. Ammonite names often included the theophoric element 'Il' or 'El', and 'Milkom' and '*Baal' were also used.                                   GLM

L. G. HERR, 'Ammon', *The Oxford Encyclopedia of Archaeology in the Near East* 1, ed. E.M. Meyers (New York 1997) 103–5.

—— 'What Ever Happened to the Ammonites?' *Biblical Archaeology Review* 19 (1993) 26–35, 68.

U. HÜBNER, *Die Ammoniter: Untersuchungen zur Geschichte, Kultur und Religion eines transjordanischen Volkes im I. Jahrtausend v. Chr.* (Wiesbaden 1992).

Ø.S. LABIANCA and R.W. YOUNKER, 'The Kingdoms of Ammon, Moab and Edom: The Archaeology of Society in Late Bronze/Iron Age Transjordan (ca. 1400–500 BCE)', *The Archaeology of Society in the Holy Land*, ed. T.E. Levy (New York 1995) 399–415, 590–4.

B. MACDONALD, *Ammon, Moab and Edom: Early States/Nations of Jordan in the Biblical Period* (Amman 1994).

R.W. YOUNKER, 'Ammonites', *Peoples of the Old Testament World*, eds A.J. Hoerth, G.L. Mattingly and E.M. Yamauchi (Grand Rapids 1994) 293–316.

**Amorites** The name of tribes who occupied parts of *Canaan before the *Israelites is now also used for tribes who settled in Upper *Mesopotamia and spread east and west in the centuries around 2000 BC. The *Sumerian term *mar.du*, *Akkadian *amurrû* occurs with names of people in *Babylonia from the Early Dynastic III period onwards, showing great increase under the Third Dynasty of *Ur. Historical texts tell of *Sargon of *Akkad and later *kings fighting Amorites in Jebel Bishri west of the mid Euphrates. It is likely that drought forced them from their pastures in the steppe into the irrigated river lands. By the twenty-first century BC, Amorite pressure provoked the kings of Ur to build a wall, or chain of forts, across northern Babylonia 'to keep out the Amorites'. Sumerian *scribes characterized them as barbarians, living in tents,

eating raw meat and failing to bury their dead properly. The wall failed and Amorite tribes overran Babylonia, their own chieftains taking control in various *cities, those of *Isin and *Larsa claiming the hegemony, then *Babylon under *Hammurabi becoming the most famous. *Mari on the mid Euphrates was an Amorite centre, its texts describing many aspects of the pastoral and *agricultural life and the threat the Amorites posed to the cultivated river valley (see Nomads). Although Amorites were distinguished from *Akkadians in Babylonia as late as the seventeenth century BC, they were already merging with the local population and disappear from the records as an entity shortly afterwards. Although no Amorite artefact is identifiable in Babylonia, it is suggested that the *lex talionis* ('an eye for an eye') and the idea of a cosmic battle at creation were Amorite concepts. In Akkadian the word *amurrû* also means 'west', but whether the tribes gave their name to the direction or vice versa is unknown. A *god Amurrû occurs in personal names and on *cylinder seals, often holding a crook.

Many persons marked as 'Amorite' by Babylonian scribes bore non-Babylonian names, names now recognized as Amorite. They belong to the West *Semitic *language group rather than the East Semitic Akkadian, with distinctive features such as the verbal prefix *ya-*, the ending *-an* and non-Akkadian vocabulary, e.g. *'abdu= *'servant', *na'āmu* 'to be pleasing, gracious'. No Amorite texts survive, but the language appears to be ancestral to *Aramaic and *Hebrew, and the names of the Hebrew *Patriarchs fit into it.

In the *Levant chieftains of several towns named in the Egyptian *Execration texts of the nineteenth century BC bore Amorite names, as some did five centuries later, according to the *Amarna Letters. New dynasties of Amorite rulers were established at *Ebla, *Ugarit, *Byblos and other centres at the start of the Middle Bronze Age. Attempts by *Albright, *Kenyon and others to relate cultural changes between the Early Bronze Age and the Middle Bronze Age to immigrations by Amorites no longer find support, but it is clear that the *Hyksos invaders of Egypt were basically Amorite. During the second millennium BC a kingdom existed west of the Orontes called Amurru. It fell under Egyptian suzerainty in the fifteenth century and in the fourteenth its kings controlled much of the coast between Ugarit and Byblos, King Abdi-Ashirta and his son Aziru feuding with the Egyptians for control of Sumur, maintaining relations with them, then placing themselves under *Hittite protection, a situation which lasted until the end of the Hittite empire except for a brief period when Benteshina turned back to Egypt. The name 'Zakar-baal, king of Amurru' is engraved in early *alphabetic script on two arrowheads of about 1100 BC, the time when *Tiglath-pileser I visited the kingdom.

According to Hebrew texts, notably Numbers 13: 29, Amorites lived in the hills of Canaan east and west of the Jordan, the Canaanites in the Jordan valley and the coastal plain. They were a major population group whom the Israelites were expected to dislodge (Joshua 24: 15).                                                                ARM

G. BUCCELLATI, *The Amorites of the Ur III Period* (Naples 1966).

I.J. GELB, *Computer-aided Analysis of Amorite* (Chicago 1980).

H. KLENGEL, *Syria 3000 to 300 B.C.: A Handbook of Political History* (Berlin 1992) 160–74.

M. LIVERANI, 'The Amorites', *Peoples of Old Testament Times*, ed. D.J. Wiseman (Oxford 1973) 100–33.

R.M. WHITING, 'Amorite Tribes and Nations', *Civilizations of the Ancient Near East*, ed. J.M. Sasson (New York 1995) 1231–42.

**Amuq** This small marshy plain in southern *Anatolia, near the modern border with *Syria by the Orontes river, has been inhabited nearly continuously since *Neolithic times. An expedition from the Oriental Institute of Chicago directed by C.W. McEwan and R.J. Braidwood excavated Çatal Hüyük (not the famous site of the same name on the Konya plain in Anatolia, see Çatalhöyük), Tell Judeideh and Tell Tayinat (1933–7). Their analysis of the *pottery and *flints is still regarded as a basic framework for the early assemblages in north Syria and southern Anatolia. They divided the period into clearly defined phases: Neolithic (phases A–C), *Chalcolithic (phase F) and Early Bronze Age (phases G–J). From Judeideh also came *copper alloy figurines, three male and three female, naked except for belts and *silver hats on the males. The objects from the excavations are now in Chicago and the Hatay Museum, Antakya, Turkey.

The second millennium BC is represented by *Woolley's excavations at *Alalakh (Amuq phases K–M). The Chicago excavations revealed several *Iron Age levels at Tell Tayinat (Amuq phases N–O), with a palace of *bīt hilāni type, a *temple with two columns resting on pairs of lions and a large central room, and monumental inscriptions in *Hittite *hieroglyphs. Rectangular mud-brick buildings dating to the Iron Age were found at Çatal Hüyük and Tell Judeideh. The modern name 'Amuq' may be derived from the Neo-Hittite kingdom known as Unqi in *Assyrian records, written 'Amq' in *Aramaic. PB

R.J. BRAIDWOOD and L.S. BRAIDWOOD, *Excavations in the Plain of Antioch, I: The Earliest Assemblages, Phases A–J* (Chicago 1960).

R.H. DORNEMANN, ''Amuq', *The Oxford Encyclopedia of Archaeology in the Near East* 1, ed. E.M. Meyers (New York 1997) 115–17.

R.C. HAINES, *Excavations in the Plain of Antioch, II: The Structural Remains of the Later Phases* (Chicago 1971).

**Amurru:** see Amorites

**An:** see Anu

**Anat** Anat (also known as 'At or 'Atah) was a popular *goddess worshipped widely throughout *Syria, *Palestine and *Egypt from the mid second millennium BC until the last centuries of the first millennium BC. Portrayed as a beautiful but at the same time destructive and bloodthirsty female, she shares many characteristics with the *Mesopotamian *Ishtar. In *Ugaritic myths she is the daughter of *El and the sister of *Baal, whom she always supports and with whom she has a sexual relationship, only after having transformed herself into a cow: he mounts her as a bull, and she gives birth to a bull-calf. Although not otherwise associated with motherhood, she seems to have connections with fertility.

The island of Anat (modern 'Ana), located in the middle course of the River Euphrates, was probably called Hanat in the Old Babylonian period, and a goddess called Hanat was worshipped at *Mari at the same date. A Babylonian stela of the eighth century BC was set up on the

Cast copper figure, one of several said to come from the Jezzine area of Lebanon. Their authenticity was confirmed by the excavation of similar figures at Tell Judeideh in the Amuq. Height 25.5 cm. End of the third millennium BC. WA 135034.

Bronze figurine of a seated goddess from Ugarit, perhaps to be identified as Anat. She wears a horned cap, the symbol of divinity, and a snake is coiled around her shoulders. Mid second millennium BC (original in the Louvre, Paris).

ANATOLIA

island by a local ruler, dedicated to a goddess 'Anat, powerful queen'. But this goddess Hanat/Anat is possibly only a local deity and not the original of Anat. The name of the *Hellenistic and *Roman goddess Atargatis was a compound of '*Astarte' and 'Anat'.                                    JAB

W.F. ALBRIGHT, 'Anath and the Dragon', *Bulletin of the American Schools of Oriental Research* 84 (1941) 14–17.

V. CASSUTO, *The Goddess Anat: Canaanite Epics of the Patriarchal Age* (Jerusalem 1951).

P.L. DAY, 'Anat', *Dictionary of Deities and Demons in the Bible*, eds K. van der Toorn, B. Becking and P.W. van der Horst (Leiden/New York 1995) 61–77.

G. DEL OLMO LETE, 'Le mythe de la Vierge-Mère 'Anatu', *Ugarit-Forschungen* 13 (1981) 49–63.

J.C.L. GIBSON, *Canaanite Myths and Legends*, 2nd ed. (Edinburgh 1978).

B.K. ISMAIL et al., ''Ana in the cuneiform sources', *Excavations at 'Ana, Qala Island*, eds A. Northedge et al. (Warminster 1988) 1–5.

G. LEICK, *Sex and Eroticism in Mesopotamian Literature* (London/New York 1994).

**Anatolia**  Turkish *Anadolu*, often synonymous with the modern Republic of Turkey, more usually refers to the central highlands. Anatolia comprises several natural geographical regions: the high central plateau, the eastern massif, the *Aegean and Mediterranean coasts, the Pontic mountains and the Black Sea coast and, to the west, the Mamara region and Turkish Thrace. In *prehistory the south-east of modern Turkey should be thought of as an extension of northern *Mesopotamia and north *Syria.

The geography of Anatolia is such that the main natural routes run east–west rather than north–south, thus the Anatolian plateau can be seen as having been at different times a bridge or a barrier between Asia and Europe. More recently scholars have tended to see Anatolia as made up of diverse regions, each with its own cultural history.

Anatolia has been called the 'cradle' or 'cauldron' of civilizations since the discovery of *Çatalhöyük and subsequent research at the aceramic Neolithic sites of Ashýklý Höyük, *Çayönü and Nevali Çori which provide evidence for the origin and spread of the earliest *agriculture from Anatolia to eastern Europe. Some would see this spread as going hand in hand with the diffusion of *Indo-European languages and, by implication, Indo-European peoples, while others would hold to the older view of Indo-European infiltration into Anatolia from the north-west some time in the *Chalcolithic period or the Early Bronze Age.

From the second millennium BC the heart of the central Anatolian plateau was the core area of *Hittite civilization, which was to vie with *Egypt for control of north Syria and the east Mediterranean. The nature and extent of Minoan and then Mycenaean interaction during the rise and extension of Hittite power are hotly debated.

The end of the Late Bronze Age in Anatolia was connected with the complex series of events associated with the *Sea Peoples and the arrival of Balkan–Thracian tribes, including the *Phrygians and Ionians, which brought literate urban civilization to a close throughout much of the eastern Mediterranean and ushered in a 'Dark Age'.

By the ninth century BC new powers were emerging: Urartu in the east, Neo-Hittite states on the central plateau and in north Syria, Phrygia in the west and, soon thereafter, *Lydia, *Lycia and *Caria in the south-west. By

Map of Anatolia showing main archaeological sites.

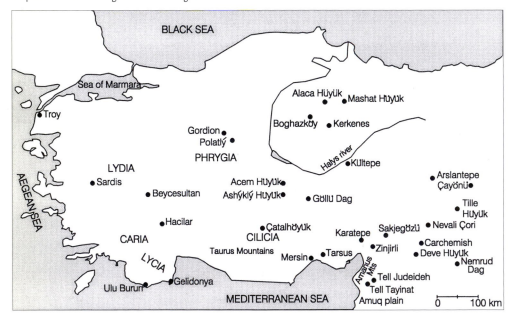

the seventh century BC *Assyria had swallowed up much of the south-east, and there is evidence for the spread of *Phoenician and *Aramaic *language and script. *Greek colonization stretched around the Mediterranean and the Black Sea.

Following the collapse of Assyria, Anatolia was subject to domination by three major powers: Lydia in the west, Cilicia in the southern centre and *Media on the north central plateau. The whole of Anatolia was incorporated into the *Achaemenid empire following the conquest of Lydia by *Cyrus II in, traditionally, 547 BC.  GDS

*Anatolia: Cauldron of Cultures* (Time Life, Lost Civilizations Vol. 23, 1995).
M.S. JOUKOWSKY, *Early Turkey: An Introduction to the Archaeology of Anatolia from Prehistory Through the Lydian Period* (Dubuque 1996).
S. LLOYD, *Ancient Anatolia* (London 1989).
C. RENFREW, 'Language Families and the Spread of Farming', *The Origins and Spread of Agriculture and Pastoralism in Eurasia,* ed. D. Harris (London 1996) 70–92.
J. YAKAR, *The Later Prehistory of Anatolia: The Late Chalcolithic and Early Bronze Age* (Oxford 1985).

**Andrae, Walter (1875–1956)** Born in Anger, near Leipzig, Germany, Walter Andrae studied architecture before beginning work with *Koldewey at *Babylon in 1898. From 1903 to 1914 Andrae directed excavations principally at *Ashur, but also at *Shuruppak, Kisurra and the *Parthian capital of Hatra. At Ashur he used his architectural training to develop stratigraphic techniques and record building levels meticulously. He brought the past to life in his publications by including imaginative watercolours and drawings of reconstructions of buildings and city views.

During the First World War Andrae served in the Near East and later worked at the Berlin Museum and taught architectural history at the university. The finds from Ashur had been confiscated by the Portuguese at the outbreak of the war, while en route to Germany. In 1926, after years of effort and intense negotiation, Andrae ransomed them for other works from the Berlin museums. He was responsible for the magnificent full-scale reconstructions in the Berlin Museum of the Processional Way and *Ishtar Gate from Babylon, and other monuments from Ashur and *Uruk.  PB

E.W. ANDRAE and R.M. BOEHMER, *Bilder eines Ausgräber: Die Orientbilder von Walter Andrae 1898–1919* (Berlin 1989).
W. ANDRAE, *Lebenserinnerungen eines Ausgräbers*, 2nd ed. (Berlin 1988).
P.O. HARPER et al. (eds), *Assyrian Origins: Discoveries at Ashur on the Tigris* (New York 1995) 17–20.

**Animal husbandry** The course of human civilization could not have developed as it did if it had not included the domestication of a variety of *animals. Indeed, the so-called '*Neolithic Revolution' was based on the domestication of *plants and animals, a process that changed the forms of the species involved and altered human history in countless ways. This process began even before the Neolithic around the edges of the *Fertile Crescent, in a widespread region often called the 'hilly flanks'.

Even after many animals had been domesticated, wild game was still an important part of the diet in antiquity. But certain species were chosen and tamed because they had much to offer their human masters; the biology of these animals changed when they were bred to enhance the more desirable traits. Pens and barns were built to control and protect this 'walking larder', and dogs and farmers took an active role in tending the domesticated species. Bones of these domesticated animals can be identified in the archaeological record, and a variety of beasts is mentioned in ancient texts and portrayed in ancient *art.

By at least 7000 BC, sheep, goat and pig had been domesticated in south-west Asia. Sheep were very important in the ancient Near East and provided wool, meat, dairy products and fertilizer – and were valuable as *sacrifices in religious ceremonies. Although *Israelite *law banned the consumption of pork, this was an

W. Andrae, 'Ashur: A View of the Festival House – A Reconstruction', 1923. Charcoal on paper (courtesy of Ernst Andrae).

important part of the diet in *Mesopotamia. Cattle were less significant than sheep, especially for the lower classes, but domesticated cattle played a vital role in the Near East beginning in the sixth millennium BC. They, too, were used for *food and animal sacrifices. Oxen were used in ploughing, harrowing and threshing; they pulled wagons and hauled *boats against the current of *rivers. Naturally, the hides of all these animals were useful, and their dung was an important fertilizer and fuel.

The use of asses, donkeys, onagers, *horses, and mules came considerably later, in the fourth and third millennia BC, but these animals served many functions. The ass, donkey, and mule were used to *transport heavy loads (on their backs or on carts) and for riding; onagers were tamed and harnessed to wagons. *Camels were used extensively in the southern *Levant and northern *Arabia by the end of the second millennium BC, but they might have been domesticated in other regions as early as the third millennium BC.

Dogs, cats and mongooses were domesticated and most useful in protecting flocks and people, controlling rodents and killing snakes, respectively. Geese, ducks and hens were important as a source of meat and eggs in Mesopotamia, and doves were raised as a sacrificial animal. The domestic chicken (*Gallus gallus*) is first attested in the thirteenth century BC and became most important in the *Persian period.

Unlike the *nomadic tribes who lived in the arid regions of the ancient Near East, the sedentary population of Mesopotamia and other regions balanced their labour with both plant and animal husbandry. The stories of Cain and Abel and Enkidu (see Gilgamesh) and *Dumuzi indicate that there must have been competition between those who managed livestock and those who tended crops. There was also conflict between the 'desert and the sown'; the nomadic peoples who lived beyond the limits of *agriculture periodically raided the *villages in better watered regions, where food and various commodities could be obtained.

The *Nuzi tablets paint a remarkable picture of the lives of *families who practised animal husbandry. The names of some ninety herdsmen are known from administrative texts. Most of the herdsmen lived away from urban centres, but they were closely linked to the social and economic life of the larger communities. Those involved in animal husbandry worked for wealthy clients who consigned their livestock to the herdsmen by means of legal documents (see Contracts). Herdsmen were responsible for missing livestock. The herding profession was hereditary, and generations of workers from the same family worked for the wealthy families who owned the flocks and herds; some herdsmen held higher status because of the social standing of the employer. These Nuzi tablets describe the sale of animals, and others deal with the exchange of grain. One text describes a lawsuit that resulted when animals were missing from the herd subcontracted from one herdsman to another. Texts that discuss herd management are most important; these include information about birth rates of lambs, culling flocks and the sheep-shearing cycle.　　　　GLM

O. BOROWSKI, *Every Living Thing: Daily Use of Animals in Ancient Israel* (Thousand Oaks, CA 1997).

J. CLUTTON-BROCK (ed.), *The Walking Larder: Patterns of Domestication, Pastoralism, and Predation* (London 1989).

B. HESSE, 'Animal Husbandry and Human Diet in the Ancient Near East', *Civilizations of the Ancient Near East*, ed. J.M. Sasson (New York 1995) 203–22.

——, 'Animal Husbandry', *The Oxford Encyclopedia of Archaeology in the Near East* 1, ed. E.M. Meyers (New York 1997) 140–3.

M.A. MORRISON, 'Evidence for Herdsmen and Animal Husbandry in the Nuzi Documents', *Nuzi and the Hurrians*, eds M.A. Morrison and D.I. Owen (Winona Lake, IN 1981) 257–96

M.A. ZEDER, *Feeding Cities: Specialized Animal Economy in the Ancient Near East* (Washington, D.C. 1991).

**Animals**  Evidence for animals in antiquity comes from three sources: references in texts, artistic representations and *bones from excavations. *Mesopotamian *scribes made lists of animal names, and there are records of *temple herds, observations of animals in *omens and lists of animals hunted or kept by *kings in special parks (see Hunting). Many real or fantastic creatures were depicted on *sculpture or *cylinder seals, particularly lions, bulls, sheep and goats in Mesopotamia, but also gazelles, elephants, horses, donkeys, dogs, vultures, crabs, flies, snakes, turtles, fish and many others.

Some animals can be domesticated and became an important part of the economy (see Animal husbandry). Sheep were probably the first to be domesticated in the tenth or ninth millennium BC, followed by goats, cattle and pigs. Cattle evolved from the now extinct aurochs; water buffalo are common on *seals in late third-millennium BC Mesopotamia, and it has been argued that they were imports from India. Although it is difficult to distinguish their bones from those of domestic cattle, wild water buffalo may have been present in *Syria during the *Halaf period, but modern stocks derive from imports of the seventh century AD. Eating of pigs is prohibited in the *Old Testament, but pig remains are common on ancient Near Eastern sites, though they became scarcer after the third millennium BC. A *Hittite *ritual against domestic quarrelling included the *sacrifice of a pig. Dogs, probably descended from wolves, are attested c.10,000 BC or earlier (perhaps even predating the domestication of sheep), and in Mesopotamia and *Anatolia they were associated with healing. Dogs were buried in the ramp of a *temple to Gula at *Isin c.1000 BC, and more than one thousand dog burials were found in *Persian levels at *Ashkelon.

Of wild animals, the most commonly hunted were deer and gazelles. Lions were regarded as the embodiment of strength and brutality, and are frequently represented as protecting *gods and kings, but were also hunted by kings, sometimes in special parks; nevertheless, lion bones are very rare on excavations. Lions did not become extinct in the Near East until after the First World War. Hippopotami and elephants, in contrast, were hunted for their *ivory and became extinct during the first millennium BC. It is unclear if elephants were native

Dogs roamed towns as scavengers and could be kept as guard-dogs, like this mastiff on a terracotta plaque of the Old Babylonian period. WA 91911.

Electrum figurine of an onager decorating a silver rein-ring from the sledge of Pu-abi, Royal Cemetery of Ur. Height 13.5 cm. c.2500 BC. WA 121348.

*Civilizations of the Ancient Near East*, ed. J.M. Sasson (New York 1995) 153–74.

H.-P. UERPMANN, *The Ancient Distribution of Ungulate Mammals in the Middle East* (Wiesbaden 1987).

E.D. VAN BUREN, *The Fauna of Ancient Mesopotamia as Represented in Art* (Rome 1939).

**Annals and chronicles** From Early Dynastic III onwards, *Babylonian *kings included in their titles phrases like 'conqueror of place *X*' and these phrases gradually grew to give more details of the conquests, as parentheses in the main sentence of records of gifts to *gods or *dedications of major building works. That remained the pattern throughout Babylonian history. In *Assyria the titles accumulated during the expansion of the fourteenth century BC and were changed into first-person narrative sentences and paragraphs in the time of *Adad-nirari I. Under *Tiglath-pileser I the narratives of royal exploits expanded so that large clay tablets could no longer contain them; instead they were written on the faces of clay prisms about 50 cm high in as many as 1300 short lines. After the introduction and genealogy of this king, a date by *eponym introduces the campaign record. The king is reintroduced with a new date before the next campaign, hence the texts are called 'annals', although they are not strictly such as years may be omitted. The prisms end with the dates when they were inscribed. This basic pattern, without the secondary introductions, was followed throughout the history of Assyria, although prisms were not made again until the time of *Sargon II, late in the eighth century BC. *Stone monuments of ninth- and eighth-century kings relate their triumphs in similar ways, paralleled by records on stone and clay tablets. *Sennacherib's reign provides clear examples of the ways 'annals' developed. His first campaign was

to Syria ('Syrian' elephant) or were transported from beyond the Indus (Indian or Asian elephant) to game reserves in north Syria where they provided ivory as well as royal *sport for *Egyptian and *Assyrian kings. Elephant remains are occasionally found on excavations. Unusual animals could be exchanged as gifts between rulers. One *Mari text records the delivery of a bear from the king of *Susa. (See Birds; Camel; Horse.)          PB

E. FIRMAGE, 'Zoology', *Anchor Bible Dictionary* 6, ed. D.N. Freedman (New York 1992) 1109–67.

A.S. GILBERT, 'The Flora and Fauna of the Ancient Near East',

Ten-sided baked clay prism with 1302 lines of cuneiform writing containing the 'annals' of Ashurbanipal down to c.644 BC. From the North Palace at Nineveh. Height 49.5 cm. WA 91026.

recorded on small clay barrels; this was compressed after the second campaign to make room for the new account and both were reduced after the third campaign. Subsequent narratives lengthened the texts so that they were written on prisms without further compression. *Esarhaddon's scribes produced less clearly organized accounts, but *Ashurbanipal's again narrated most campaigns in sequence, numbering them variously in different editions and later ones omitting some. The latest edition runs together two episodes concerning Gyges of *Lydia despite their occurrence many years apart. These 'editions' were created as needed for the *foundation inscriptions of buildings, not made annually, so some belong to successive years, other years have none. All the royal 'annals' were created to glorify the god *Ashur and his regent, the king, whether for his contemporaries or for posterity, so they never present reverses of any sort or anything that would harm his reputation. The sources of the 'annals' probably included chronicles.

The eighteenth-century BC *Eponym Chronicle from *Mari is the earliest *cuneiform example of a text listing events year by year; no others are known until the Babylonian Chronicle tablets of the sixth century BC. The main series begins in the reign of Nabu-nasir, about 747 BC, the date the *Greek writer Ptolemy gives for the start of Babylonian *astronomical records. The Babylonian Chronicle notes by years of reign of the kings of Babylon affairs in the country and also some in *Elam or relating to Assyria. The surviving tablets, which continue into the Seleucid period, with large gaps, are excerpts from more extensive records – one is labelled 'first extract'. Several tablets outside the series have comparable, even duplicate entries and one notes that two of its entries were taken from a waxed *writing tablet. Related to the Chronicles are the Astronomical Diaries, which list observations of heavenly bodies, often adding notices of notable events, political or other. All could have derived their information from a running record written on waxed tablets which could be easily kept up to date. Similar chronicles may be posited in Assyria to provide material for the royal 'annals'. The Babylonian Chronicle is distinct from the 'annals' in its third-person reporting with little evident bias, noting defeats as well as victories, interested in unusual occurrences (e.g. a lion being seen in *Babylon) as well as military and religious events.

The purpose of compiling and copying the Babylonian and similar chronicles is unknown. Beside historical curiosity and research, a desire to know what happened at a particular time, they may have been used in connection with creating *omen texts.

One chronicle has a clear purpose, the 'Weidner Chronicle' which relates that many kings suffered disasters because they failed to honour *Marduk's *temple in Babylon. It is written as a *letter of advice to an Old Babylonian king, but is known only from copies of a millennium later.

Annalistic or chronicle-like records of kings' reigns apparently existed in the *Levant in the *Iron Age (there is no evidence for earlier periods), supplying material for royal inscriptions such as the *Moabite Stone or the Tel Dan stela and for the more extensive *Hebrew books of Samuel, Kings and Chronicles in the *Bible, which, like the Babylonian Chronicle, describe military, political and religious affairs, some not falling into modern concepts of 'history'.                                                                    ARM

A.K. GRAYSON, *Assyrian and Babylonian Chronicles* (New York 1970).

A.R. MILLARD, 'Babylonian King Lists', *The Context of Scripture* 1, eds W.W. Hallo and K.L. Younger (Leiden 1997) 461–8.

A.L. OPPENHEIM, in *Ancient Near Eastern Texts*, 3rd ed., ed. J.B. Pritchard (Princeton 1969) 301–7, 563–4.

**Anshan**   Recorded as a major centre of *Elam from the third millennium BC to the *Persian period, Anshan's importance is reflected in the royal title of Elamite *kings, 'king of Anshan and Susa'. Manishtusu of *Akkad and later *Gudea claimed to have defeated Anshan. *Tin came to *Mari via Anshan, whose king's name, Siwe-pular-huhpak, gave the Mari scribes so much trouble that they recorded him as Sheplarpak. *Cyrus II claimed that his *family had ruled Anshan for generations. It has been identified with modern Tall-i Malyan, situated in a valley on the edge of the *Zagros, 43 km west of *Persepolis in *Iran. The site has been excavated by the Iranians (1961) and by William Sumner of the University of Pennsylvania (1971–8).

Tall-i Malyan is surrounded by a *city wall enclosing more than 200 ha, although the main occupation mound measures about 130 ha. Excavation and survey suggest that it was occupied from c.6000 BC to the Islamic period, with some gaps ascribed to depopulation and abandonment of the area. A series of monumental buildings dating from c.3400–1000 BC, some with painted walls and floors and associated with *cuneiform tablets and *sealings, attests to its role as an *administrative centre. A group of Middle Elamite (c.1600-1100 BC) tablets records exchanges of *metals, finished objects, grain, flour and animal products, and it is on these that the name 'Anshan' is mentioned. Bricks of an Elamite king dating to c.1120 BC, commemorating building activity, indicate its continuing royal importance. Following the Middle Elamite period there was a hiatus. No *Achaemenid occupation has been found, and later occupation is fragmentary.   PB

E. REINER, 'The Location of Anshan', *Revue d'Assyriologie* 67 (1973) 57–62.

W.M. SUMNER, 'Maljan, Tall-e (Anshan)', *Reallexikon der Assyriologie* 7 (Berlin/New York 1988) 306–20.

——, 'Malyan (Anshan)', *The Oxford Encyclopedia of Archaeology in the Near East* 3, ed. E.M. Meyers (New York 1997) 406–9.

**Anu/An**   An is the *Sumerian word for 'heaven', and An (*Akkadian Anu) is also the name of the sky-*god who is also the prime mover in creation, and the distant, supreme leader of the gods. His name is written with the same sign as that for 'god' and 'heaven'. He was regarded as a descendant of the male deity Urash, with whom he was later even identified; or else as the son of the primordial Anshar and Kishar. 'Great An' is father of all the gods. His wife is the earth-goddess Urash; in a later tradition he is married to Ki. As *Babylonian Anu he has a wife Antu. It was An who, in Sumerian tradition, took over heaven when it was separated from earth, creating the universe as we know it.

In the Babylonian cosmological theory of three super-imposed heavens, Anu occupies the topmost heaven. In Seleucid times (see Hellenistic period), An received an important cult at *Uruk together with *Ishtar.

Although in almost all periods he was one of the most important of *Mesopotamian deities, An's nature was ill-defined and, as he is seldom (if ever) represented in art, his specific iconography and attributes are obscure. In *Kassite and Neo-*Assyrian art, at least, Anu's symbol is a horned cap of the sort usually worn by gods, with several superimposed sets of bull's horns.                           JAB

D.O. EDZARD, 'Mesopotamien: Die Mythologie der Sumerer und Akkader', *Götter und Mythen im Vorderen Orient*, Vol. 1 of *Wörterbuch der Mythologie*, ed. H.W. Haussig (Stuttgart 1965) 40–1.

G. LEICK, *A Dictionary of Ancient Near Eastern Mythology* (London/New York 1991).

A. WOHLSTEIN, *The Sky-god An-Anu* (Jericho, NY 1976).

**Anunnakku**  The term Anuna (Anunnakku), which possibly means 'princely offspring', is used in earlier, especially *Sumerian, writings as a general word for the *gods, in particular the early gods who were born first and were not differentiated with individual names. They are put to work to help build the temple at Girsu, in a Sumerian *hymn, and are linked with the benign female *lama* deities. There are said to be fifty Anuna of *Eridu. The sky-god *Anu is described as king of the Anunnakku. In the *Babylonian Epic of Creation the multitude of gods are called the 'Anunnakku of heaven and earth'.

However, possibly following the use from Middle Babylonian times of the name Igigu to refer especially to the gods of heaven, the (Akkadian) term Anunnakku came to be used more for the gods of the earth and the *underworld. *Marduk and Damkina, *Nergal and Madanu – all gods associated with the underworld – are said to be powerful among them. There are 600 Anunnakku of the underworld, but only 300 of heaven, according to one text. This implies the gradual development of a detailed imagery of the underworld. (See Igigi.)     JAB

J. FALKENSTEIN, 'Die Anunna in der sumerischen Überlieferung', *Studies in Honor of B. Landsberger* (Chicago 1965) 127–40.

B. KIENAST, 'Igigu und Anunnakku nach den akkadischen Quellen', *Studies in Honor of B. Landsberger* (Chicago 1965) 141–58.

W. VON SODEN, 'Babylonische Göttergruppen: Igigu und Anunnaku: zum Bedeutungswandel theologischer Begriffe', *Comptes rendus de la onzième Rencontre Assyriologique Internationale, 1962* (Leiden 1964) 102–11.

**Anzû**  Anzû was the *Akkadian name of a monstrous bird who was probably called Imdugud in *Sumerian.

Envisaged as bird-like but having the head of a lion, and of gigantic size so that the flapping of its wings could cause whirlwinds and sandstorms, the Imdugud was probably originally a personification of an atmospheric force. Other descriptions indicate that it had a beak 'like a saw', and so presumably a bird's head. In Neo-*Assyrian art, a monster combining bird and lion elements may be the Anzû or the Asakku.

The Imdugud or Anzû steals the tablet of destinies from *Enki (in the Sumerian '*Ninurta and the Turtle') or from *Enlil (in the Akkadian 'Anzû' poem), and the bird is killed by Ninurta who eventually returns the tablet to its rightful owner. This must be a very early myth, since the Imdugud is already depicted as a heraldic animal associated with Ningirsu on a stone monument of the late Early Dynastic period known as the 'Stela of the Vultures'. The association is presumed to derive from the god Ningirsu/Ninurta's defeat of the bird.

In the Sumerian poem of 'Lugalbanda', when he is wandering in the *Zagros mountains, the hero comes upon the Imdugud fledgling in its nest, and treats it with sweetmeats. The Imdugud and its wife soon return. In '*Gilgamesh, Enkidu and the Nether World', the Imdugud and its fledgling nest in a sacred *halub* tree which *Inana has planted in the city of *Uruk.               AG/JAB

B. ALSTER, 'Ninurta and the Turtle', *Journal of Cuneiform Studies* 24 (1972) 120–5.

J.A. BLACK, *Reading Sumerian Poetry* (London 1998).

S.M. DALLEY, *Myths from Mesopotamia* (Oxford 1990) 203–27.

A. GEORGE, *The Epic of Gilgamesh* (Harmondsworth 1999).

M. VOGELZANG, *Bin šar dadmē: Edition and Analysis of the Akkadian Anzû Poem* (Groningen 1988).

C. WILCKE, *Das Lugalbandaepos* (Wiesbaden 1969).

**Aqar Quf**  Identified by *Rawlinson in 1861 on the basis of inscribed bricks, Aqar Quf is known to be the site of the *Kassite residence of Dur-Kurigalzu. Situated 30 km west of Baghdad, the whole site covers about 225 ha and comprises several hills. The highest of these is actually Aqar Quf, which was the *religious precinct, while the *palace and *administrative centre was on Tell al-Abyad. The site was excavated by *Lloyd and Taha Baqir (1942–5).

The *town was founded by the Kassite King Kurigalzu I at the end of the fifteenth or beginning of the fourteenth century BC over an older fifteenth-century BC settlement, and named 'Dur-Kurigalzu', which means 'Fort of Kurigalzu'. It was added to by later Kassite kings, but after the fall of the *dynasty in the twelfth century BC it was abandoned and never re-occupied except for occasional *burials.

The religious precinct consisted of the *ziggurat dedicated to *Enlil, the lower part of which has been restored, and *temples to Enlil, his wife Ninlil, and *Ninurta. The *palace consisted of a main courtyard, several buildings with large central halls or courtyards and three rows of rooms between, a room with *wall paintings depicting a procession of officials, and what appears to be a treasury in small vaulted rooms along a corridor. In the palace were discovered *sculptures, including a vividly modelled

The ziggurat of Dur-Kurigalzu (modern Aqar Quf), founded in the fourteenth century BC, has been eroded until only the core remains, built of mudbrick with layers of reeds at intervals. Modern reconstruction at the foot indicates the original extent of the base (courtesy of Michael Roaf).

terracotta lioness or hyena, *gold *jewellery, *glass and *cuneiform tablets.                                                   PB

T. BAQIR, *Iraq Government Excavations at 'Aqar Quf, 1942–1943* (*Iraq* Supplement, London 1944).
——, *Iraq Government Excavations at 'Aqar Quf: Second Interim Report, 1943–1944* (*Iraq* Supplement, London 1945).
——, 'Iraq Government Excavations at 'Aqar Quf: Third Interim Report, 1944–1945', *Iraq* 8 (1946) 73–93.
Y. TOMABECHI, 'Wall Paintings from Dur Kurigalzu', *Journal of Near Eastern Studies* 42 (1983) 123–31.

**Aqhat**   The Epic of Aqhat from *Ugarit recounts how *King Danel appeals for and receives a son, Aqhat. The *goddess *Anat offers Aqhat *gold and *silver, and finally immortality, in return for his bow, made by the *craftsman god. Aqhat refuses, and is killed by her henchman Yutpan, who is carried by Anat like a *bird of prey and dropped on Aqhat. Aqhat is avenged by his sister, who sets out to kill Yutpan. The remainder of the story is unclear, but there is reference to failure of crops as a result of the murder, *rituals to restore the *fertility of fields, and the recovery and burial of Aqhat's body. The purpose of this epic is obscure. It is preserved on three tablets of the thirteenth century BC written in the *cuneiform alphabet by a *priest, Elimelek.                                             PB

K.T. AITKEN, *The Aqhat Narrative* (Manchester 1990).
J.C. DE MOOR, *An Anthology of Religious Texts from Ugarit* (Leiden 1987) 224–73.
J.C.L. GIBSON, *Canaanite Myths and Legends*, 2nd ed. (Edinburgh 1978) 23–7, 103–22.
H.L. GINSBERG, in *Ancient Near Eastern Texts*, 3rd ed., ed. J.B. Pritchard (Princeton 1969) 149–55.
D. PARDEE, 'The Aqhatu Legend', *The Context of Scripture* 1, eds W.W. Hallo and K.L. Younger (Leiden/New York 1997) 343–56.
C. VIROLLEAUD, *La légende phénicienne de Danel* (Paris 1936).

**Arabia**   The Arabian peninsula is framed by high mountain ranges on its southern and western edges which catch respectively the monsoons and the rains blown off the Red Sea. This means that Yemen, in the south-western corner, and the narrow western coastal plain of the Hijaz receive relatively abundant, if seasonal, rainfall, and their populations developed sophisticated systems of *water management at a very early period. By contrast, the plateau behind the mountains consists mainly of various types of desert – sand, gravel, earth, broken lava, flint, etc. – most of which need only water to produce abundant herbage. They are criss-crossed by ancient wadi systems (dry, or seasonal, water-courses), testifying to periods of extreme rainfall in the remote past which have left vast subterranean lakes or aquifers which can often be tapped by relatively shallow wells. In addition there are numerous oases where the surface, or subsurface, waters from large catchment areas collect and where both horticulture and *agriculture have been practised for millennia.

The term 'Arabia' does not predate *Herodotus, and the peninsula has never been a single political or cultural unit. In the first half of the first millennium BC, the south-western corner, modern Yemen, saw the rise of a number of strongly individual kingdoms whose economies, though founded on agriculture, benefited hugely from the trade in frankincense, of which these states controlled the supply (see Incense and spices). The most famous of these kingdoms were Saba' (*Sheba), Ma'in, Qataban and Hadramawt. They were highly literate cultures, using the South *Semitic script, which shared a common ancestor with the Phoenicio-Aramaic *alphabet but had followed its own course of development (including its own letter-order) in both North and South Arabia since the late second millennium BC. Not until the Islamic period would the majority of the inhabitants of southern Arabia have considered themselves as in any way '*Arabs'.

From the mid first millennium BC onwards, the western two-thirds of Arabia, in both the north and the south, produced the most extensively literate societies of any in the ancient world. Although the exploration of these areas is still in its infancy by comparison with the rest of the Near East, tens of thousands of inscriptions and graffiti have already been found which attest to an almost universal ability to read and write, not only among townsmen and farmers but among the *nomads as well. On the other hand, in eastern Arabia, despite extensive excavations very little evidence has been found for the use of writing.

From at least the second millennium BC the various states in the Arabian peninsula were involved in wide-ranging commercial activities. In North-West Arabia a number of oasis towns developed distinctive societies, such as *Dedan, *Duma and *Tayma. The earliest of these so far identified is Qurayya in *Midian which flourished in the second half of the second millennium BC and seems to have had trading links with *Egypt, southern *Palestine and the Mediterranean. The oases were essential staging posts for the merchant caravans which plied between South Arabia and the *Fertile Crescent, and they grew rich on the profits. Along the Gulf coast of Arabia, states developed trading links with *Mesopotamia, *Iran and the *Indus Valley cultures, while those bordering the

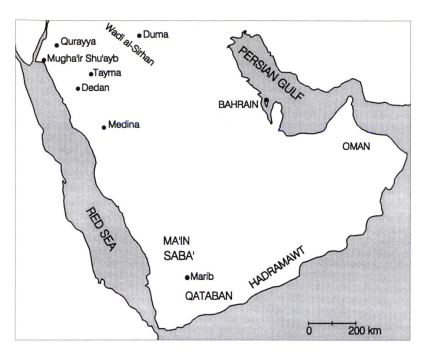

Map of Arabia showing main archaeological sites.

Indian Ocean brought goods from East Africa, India and the East Indies to Mesopotamia and the Mediterranean. There is even evidence that by the eighth century BC merchants from Arabia were acting as middlemen in the trade between *Phoenicia and *Assyria.     MCAM

A. AVANZINI (ed.), *Profumi d'Arabia* (Rome 1997).

P.J. PARR, 'Aspects of the Archaeology of North-West Arabia in the First Millennium BC', *L'Arabie préislamique et son environnement historique et culturel*, ed. T. Fahd (Leiden 1989) 39–66.

D.T. POTTS, *The Arabian Gulf in Antiquity* (Oxford 1990).

—— (ed.), *Araby the Blest: Studies in Arabian Archaeology* (Copenhagen 1988).

C. ROBIN, *L'Arabie antique de Karib'îl à Mahomet: Nouvelles données sur l'histoire des Arabes grâce aux inscriptions* (*Revue du monde Musulman et de la Méditerranée* 61) (Aix en Provence 1991).

F.V. WINNETT and W.L. REED, *Ancient Records from North Arabia* (Toronto 1970).

**Arabs** The term 'Arab' has a long and confused history and not until the fourth century AD is it found as an ethnic self-designation. In its earliest occurrences, in the *Assyrian *annals of the ninth to seventh centuries BC, it appears to mean '*nomads', rather than a specific ethnic or linguistic group. It is possible that it came into *Akkadian, *Hebrew, Sabaic and other *Semitic languages used by settled peoples from the word used by the nomads of North and Central Arabia to describe their way of life, just as this is its primary sense in bedouin Arabic today.

The term first appears in the annals of the Assyrian King *Shalmaneser III (858–824 BC), which state that 'Gindibu the Arab' contributed one thousand *camels to the alliance of twelve *kings opposing the Assyrians at the battle of Qarqar (northern *Syria) in 853 BC. Throughout the eighth and seventh centuries the Assyrians launched numerous campaigns against 'the Arabs' but also dealt with them peacefully on a day-to-day administrative and commercial basis, as shown in the royal correspondence. It has been plausibly suggested that the Assyrian attacks were motivated mainly by a desire to dominate the northern end of the very profitable frankincense trade (see Incense and spices), which was managed by the nomads and oasis-dwellers of northern Arabia. From *Tiglath-pileser III (744–727 BC) onwards, the Assyrians may have attempted to incorporate the Arabs into the *administrative system of the empire, and *Sargon II's *deportation of Arabs to *Samaria and the settlement of Arab tribes in the region south of Gaza and in *Sinai might be explained as part of this process. Certainly, the Arabs in Sinai enabled *Esarhaddon (680–669 BC) to mount the first successful *Mesopotamian conquest of *Egypt, by supplying him with large numbers of camels to carry *water for his troops and their *horses during the crossing of the desert.

The nomads of North Arabia and southern Syria in the first millennium BC were grouped in a number of tribes, several of which are mentioned in the Assyrian annals (e.g. Adbeel, Badana, Ibadidi, Marsimani, Massa', Nebaioth, Sumu(')ilu, Thamud), in the *Bible (e.g. 'Ephah, Massa', Nebayoth) and in North Arabian inscriptions (*Ms', Nbyt, S'm'l*). The most powerful confederation throughout this period was Qedar, known from both Assyrian sources and the Bible. This seems to have been led originally by *queens, some of whom were also *priestesses of the cult based at the oasis town of *Duma. We know the names of several of these: Zabibe, Samsi, Iati'e, Te'elhunu, Tabua, each called 'queen of the Arabs'

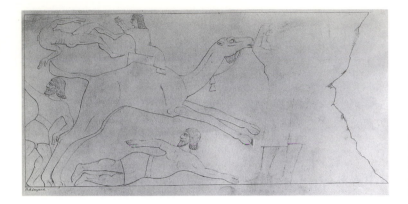

An Arab woman, perhaps Queen Samsi, is seen fleeing on her camel in Layard's drawing of a relief from the palace of Tiglath-pileser III (744–727 BC) at Nimrud. Or.Dr. vol. III, Central XIV, Slab 7b.

and clearly leaders in their own right. Later, kings of Qedar and/or 'kings of the Arabs' are mentioned alongside the queens. The term 'Arabs' (presumably meaning 'nomads') and the names of the tribe or confederation were used interchangeably by the Assyrians.

The tribes of the Qedarite confederation ranged across northern Arabia and southern and central Syria. Other tribes, such as the Nebayoth and Sumu(')ilu, seem to have been concentrated further south in the vicinity of *Tayma. *Trade played an important part in the lives and *economy of the Arabs in the first millennium BC and they seem to have developed much closer links with *Babylonia than with Assyria. A number of settlements in Babylonia bear names which are linguistically closer to North Arabian dialects than to *Akkadian or *Aramaic, and a handful of Ancient North Arabian inscriptions (possibly dating between the eighth and sixth centuries BC) have been found in southern Mesopotamia. The Arabs seem always to have sided with *Babylon in its wars with Assyria and not only fought in Mesopotamia but made diversionary attacks on the Assyrian tributary states in *Transjordan. The reasons why *Nabonidus, the last king of Babylon, spent the greater part of his reign in the North Arabian oasis of Tayma are still disputed .

The images of their *gods appear to have played a very important part in maintaining the cohesion of Arab confederations; indeed the Assyrian annals refer to one of these as the 'Confederation of Attar-samain' (one of the deities of Duma). Both *Sennacherib and *Ashurbanipal removed these images (and their priestesses) in order to weaken the tribes' ability to make trouble. However, in both cases the images and the priestesses were eventually returned and this was swiftly followed by another Arab revolt.                                                                    MCAM

I. EPH'AL, *The Ancient Arabs: Nomads on the Borders of the Fertile Crescent 9th–5th Centuries B.C.* (Jerusalem/Leiden 1982).

M.C.A. MACDONALD, 'North Arabia in the First Millennium BCE', *Civilizations of the Ancient Near East*, ed. J.M. Sasson (New York 1995) 1355–69.

——, 'Trade Routes and Trade Goods at the Northern End of the "Incense Road" in the First Millennium B.C.', *Profumi d'Arabia*, ed. A. Avanzini (Rome 1997) 333–49.

**Arad**   Arad is located in the northern *Negev in a relatively arid setting, close to the limits of the area where rain-fed *agriculture can be practised.

The site covers c.10 ha and has the largest exposure of contemporary Early *Bronze Age settlement in the *Levant. It is approximately half the size of the largest Early Bronze Age settlements in the southern Levant, but larger than most settlements of this period. It can best be characterized as a small *town and regional centre.

The site was occupied in the *Chalcolithic, Early Bronze I, Early Bronze II and possibly into Early Bronze III although this last dating is debatable. At the beginning of Early Bronze II (c.3000–2700 BC) the settlement was laid out on a new plan, coincident with the construction of a defensive perimeter wall. The defensive nature of this wall is indicated by the regularly spaced semicircular bastions projecting beyond the wall, particularly those concentrated at the weakest points where the course of the wall changes.

Most of the area within the walls appears to have been built up. Typical domestic complexes consist of a rectangular 'broadroom' entered through the long wall, with benches around the walls. This room formed the main living room, usually with a smaller ante-room; around the adjacent courtyard were a number of smaller service buildings e.g. kitchen and storage areas. These domestic complexes were arranged in blocks.

Several distinctive structures stand out from the bulk of these domestic complexes. Two sets of buildings have been labelled respectively *temple and *palace buildings. These are distinguished because of their larger size and the fact that they each consist of a set of twinned 'broadrooms'. Around a depression, the site of a later *Iron Age cistern, are clustered a series of larger structures with ground plans different from those of the 'broadroom' buildings. It is suggested that these were the setting for centralized *administrative activities that would have been located next to a large central and vital Early Bronze Age cistern, removed by the Iron Age construction. The existence of this cistern remains conjectural.

The evidence for centralized control of town planning and defensive construction, possible elite, administrative, or *religious structures argues for the interpretation of this settlement as a town. It is suggested that Arad had an

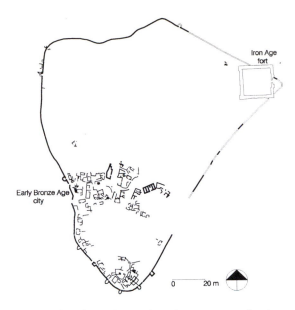

Site plan of Arad showing the Early Bronze Age wall with towers and area of excavated houses. At the right the Iron Age fort overlay the earlier town.

important regional role as a controller of the *copper supplied by sites from the south in the Arabah and *Sinai to the towns and cities to the north.

In the Iron Age a fortified 'citadel' was constructed on the site, which contained a shrine of the seventh century BC and yielded almost one hundred *Hebrew *ostraca.

DB

Y. AHARONI, *Arad Inscriptions* (Jerusalem 1981).

R. AMIRAN, *Early Arad* (Jerusalem 1978).

R. AMIRAN and O. ILAN, *Early Arad: The Chalcolithic and Early Bronze IB Settlements and the Early Bronze II City – Architecture and Town Planning* (Jerusalem 1996).

**Aram** The name was joined to other names to indicate places the *Aramaeans controlled, e.g. Aram-Beth-Rehob, Aram-Maacah, Aram-Zobah. The name was used alone especially to refer to Aram-Damascus, mainly in the historical books of the *Hebrew *Bible. Hebrew texts name one Aram as fifth son of Shem (Genesis 10: 22) and another as grandson of Abraham's brother Nahor (Genesis 22: 21) who lived in Upper *Mesopotamia, called in the Bible Aram-Naharaim, both being taken as ancestral to the Aramaeans.

The position of the *city of Aram-Damascus in a fertile plain on a major *trade route gave it great importance, and its *kings often headed alliances to attack or oppose others. The origin of the name Damascus is not known; 'the well watered place' is an attractive explanation, but involves phonetic difficulties.

Its history before the *Iron Age is obscure. The region Apum of the *Execration texts and Upe of the *Amarna Letters is thought to centre on Damascus; the town name Damascus appears in inscriptions of Tuthmosis III and of Amenophis III, in three of the Amarna Letters and in one from Kamid el-Loz, which names a king of Damascus. As the northernmost inland place under *Egypt's aegis, Damascus was subject to threat or attack by *Hittite vassals to the north and the Egyptian representative, Birya-waza, had to face them. Although Hittite power advanced southwards after the battle of *Kadesh, Ramesses II retained control of the Damascus area, a situation which continued until the *Sea People invaded.

*Israel came into conflict with Damascus frequently from 1000 BC, by which time the Aramaeans dominated it. The Bible reports that David occupied Aram-Damascus and that one Rezon took the city from Solomon's hands a few decades later (2 Samuel 8: 5, 6; 1 Kings 11: 23, 24). A King Bar-Hadad (Hebrew Ben-Hadad) had a treaty with Israel about 900 BC, but attacked the country after being bribed by Judah (1 Kings 15; 16–22), and another Bar-Hadad brought Ahab of Israel into the league which opposed *Shalmaneser III at the battle of Qarqar (853 BC), then fought him. At this point *Assyrian sources augment the biblical, naming as king Adad-idri (Hebrew Hadad-ezer) but Damascus yields no records. Hazael assassinated Bar-Hadad II in 843/2 BC and, after suffering under Assyrian attacks, which did not take the city, raised the kingdom to its greatest power during the last three decades of the ninth century BC. Hazael annexed Israelite territory in *Transjordan and subjugated both Israel and Judah (2 Kings 12: 17, 18; 13: 3, 7, 22). His son, Bar-Hadad III, c.796–775 BC, did not sustain the grip on Israel and Judah and paid heavy tribute to the invading Assyrians. He led a coalition of kings against Zakkur of *Hamath unsuccessfully. A King Hadhyan followed him, who paid tribute to Assyria, perhaps after an attack on Damascus in 773 BC. About that time, Jeroboam II of Israel (c.793–753 BC) made Damascus a vassal state (2 Kings 14; 25, 28). In 738 BC *Tiglath-pileser III records tribute from Rezin (Aramaic Radhyan) of Damascus who, allied with Israel, then threatened Ahaz of Judah, but he paid the Assyrian to relieve him (733 BC; 2 Kings 15: 37; 16: 5, 7–9). Damascus fell to the Assyrians in 732 BC and became a province (see Provincial administration). Thereafter it had importance as a commercial rather than a political centre until *Hellenistic times.

Hazael is the only king of Damascus whose inscriptions can be certainly identified; there are four short dedications or notices on *bronze *horse blinkers and *ivory plaques. The Melqart stela, found near Aleppo, was set up by a Bar-Hadad but it is not clear that he was a ruler of Damascus. Archaeological excavations have not been possible in the still occupied limits of the ancient city. At the site of the ancient *temple of Hadad-Rimmon, now the Great Mosque, a *stone slab carved in relief with a winged sphinx was unearthed, the product of a skilled sculptor working in *Phoenician style in the eighth century BC.

ARM

W. PITARD, *Ancient Damascus* (Winona Lake, IN 1987).

**Aramaeans** The *Assyrian *Tiglath-pileser I fought Ahlamu-Aramaeans, and his son Ashur-bel-kala (c.1073–1056 BC) referred to 'the land of *Aram', all in the area along the mid Euphrates and across it to Tadmor (Palmyra) and the *Lebanon mountains. During the following hundred years, Aramaeans settled in those areas, in much of Assyria and in *Babylonia. From c.930 BC onwards Assyrian *kings gradually subjugated Aramaean tribes and principalities across *Mesopotamia and *Syria until all were under their control by 700 BC. Assyrian inscriptions give much information about the Aramaeans, complemented by the *Bible and the relatively few *Aramaic inscriptions. By the ninth century BC the major groups settled between the Tigris and the great bend of the Euphrates were Bit-Adini, Bit-Bahyan, Bit-Halupe and Bit-Zaman, *bīt* 'house of' denoting the tribe, the name perhaps being that of its originator. In west Syria Bit-Agush was centred on Arpad and there were smaller kingdoms in the south, with Damascus often the leader of Aram. An Aramaean Zakkur seized *Hamath from its Neo-*Hittite rulers about 800 BC. The Aramaean states never united, forming alliances in particular political situations (e.g. to fight *Shalmaneser III at Qarqar in 853 BC) and rivalling each other. When Aramaean rulers submitted to Assyria they were left in place so long as they remained loyal, as seen at *Zinjirli and at Guzan (see Halaf, Tell) where a bilingual text calls them 'king' in Aramaic, for the benefit of the local populace, and 'governor' in Assyrian for the emperor's officials (see Fekheriyeh, Tell). Little is known of Aramaean society. Tribes might have several 'sheikhs' leading their people in a semi-*nomadic pastoral life based on the *village (*Mari texts *kaprum*, Aramaic *kepar*, as in Capernaum), raising cattle and sheep and growing various crops. The Aramaeans who settled in Babylonia continued the same lifestyle, eventually merging with the existing populace. The principal tribes there were Gambulu, Puqudu and Ru'ua.

Royal *palaces were decorated with *stone carvings, especially relief *sculptures, in Neo-Hittite style (e.g. Tell Halaf, Zinjirli), and later in Assyrian style (Tell Tayinat), and had portico entrances on the *bīt hilāni plan. *Ivory plaques which decorated *wooden *furniture were carved in *Egyptian and *Phoenician fashions by local *craftsmen, who introduced motifs of their own, and *bronze bowls with Aramaic inscriptions, found at *Nimrud, show similar designs. Aramaic *seals share patterns common throughout the Near East, only the names and script distinguishing them. In *religion the Aramaeans worshipped *Hadad in Damascus and other places, Be'el Shamem, perhaps equated with *El, and the *moon-god Shahr. They adopted *gods of the places they occupied (e.g. *Reshep, Athtar, see Ishtar) and took over Babylonian divinities (e.g. *Sîn as Si', *Nabû, Nusku as Nashuh). Their rites are unknown.

The name Ahlamu, coupled with Aram in its earliest occurrence in *cuneiform, was applied to visitors or immigrants into Babylonia as early as the seventeenth century BC and may have been borne by a related or parent tribe. That could explain the use of Aramaean in connection with Israel's *Patriarchs, otherwise treated as an anachronism or invention.

Their own migrations and Assyrian deportations carried the Aramaeans throughout the *Fertile Crescent and so rapidly spread their *language, written in their form of the *alphabet, to become the *lingua franca* of the *Persian empire and beget the Arabic, Hebrew and Syriac scripts of today.                                   ARM

P.E. DION, *Les araméens à l'âge du fer* (Paris 1997).
A.R. MILLARD, 'Arameans', *Anchor Bible Dictionary* 1, ed. D.N. Freedman (New York 1992) 345–50.

**Aramaic** Aramaic belongs to the West Semitic branch of the *Semitic *languages and is attested from the ninth century BC until the present day (as Syriac); this entry summarizes only the earliest phase, Old Aramaic, current from the ninth to the sixth centuries BC. The earliest examples are engraved on *stone monuments erected by local *kings in *Syria, at Tell *Fekheriyeh in the east, in the north-west at *Zinjirli and south of Aleppo (notably the Melqart stela, the Zakkur stela at Afis, the Sefire *treaties, the Tel Dan stela). In addition there are some brief dedicatory inscriptions on *metal and *ivory (of Hazael and others), *seal legends, *ostraca from *Nimrud and *Ashur and fifty or more clay tablets with annotations or complete texts scratched on them in Aramaic. They present some differences of dialect.

Old Aramaic preserved more phonemes than the *Canaanite–*Phoenician *alphabet could distinguish, so, for example, *th* is represented by *š* (at Tell Fekheriyeh by *s*). Like *Hebrew and Phoenician, Aramaic has prefixed and suffixed forms in verbal conjugations and simple, reflexive/passive (prefix *t-*), factitive (doubled second root letter), causative (prefix *h*) stems, with jussive marked by *l-* in some areas. Most distinctive is the definite article, which is suffixed to the defined word, rather than prefixed as in other Semitic languages (e.g. *mlk* 'a king', *mlk'* 'the king'). The suffix for 'his' on plural nouns is *-wh*.

The name of Bar-Rakkab, son of Panammuwa, is incised in clear Aramaic script of the eighth century BC on this silver ingot found at Zinjirli. Present weight 402.9 g, originally about 500 g. WA 134918.

Old Aramaic shared much vocabulary with other West Semitic languages, borrowed freely from *Akkadian and maintained its own distinctiveness (e.g. *'ty* 'to come', *mlh* 'word'). Akkadian affected the language in the east and, probably, Canaanite in the west.

Fragments of a lengthy prose narrative, referring to Balaam son of Beor, painted on a plaster wall at Tell *Deir Alla late in the ninth century BC preserve the earliest specimen of Aramaic *literature, in a local dialect. Among papyri of *Persian date found at Elephantine in Egypt are parts of a copy of the 'Wisdom of Ahiqar', a tale and collection of proverbs, which may date back to the seventh century BC.

The spread of Imperial Aramaic as the *lingua franca* under *Achaemenid rule resulted in the loss of some Old Aramaic features, while others, especially those seen in texts from the east, became part of the new form from which other dialects developed. ARM

F.M. FALES, *Aramaic Epigraphs on Clay Tablets of the Neo-Assyrian Period* (Rome 1986).

J.A. FITZMYER and S.A. KAUFMAN, *An Aramaic Bibliography, Part I* (Baltimore 1992).

J.C.L. GIBSON, *Textbook of Syrian Semitic Inscriptions II: Aramaic Inscriptions* (Oxford 1975).

J. HOFTIJZER and G. VAN DER KOOIJ, *Aramaic Texts from Deir 'Alla* (Leiden 1976).

J. HUEHNERGARD, 'What is Aramaic?', *Aram* 7 (1995) 261–82.

S. SEGERT, *Altaramäische Grammatik* (Leipzig 1975).

## Archaeology

**Archaeology** Archaeology is the recovery and understanding of humankind's history through the study of physical remains and material culture, such as *bones, *pottery, ornaments, *weapons and architecture. Near Eastern archaeology is particularly distinctive because of the abundance of written documents, mostly on clay and largely from *Mesopotamia (see Writing). Their subject matter covers the whole spectrum of human experience and provides a level of detail and insight which is a useful complement to archaeological evidence.

In the Near East, archaeology can properly be said to have begun only in the early nineteenth century. Earlier travellers tended to be Christian pilgrims looking for sites with *biblical connections, especially in *Palestine. The pioneer excavators of the nineteenth century were diplomats, scholars, soldiers and colonial administrators, who are often accused of being interested only in the recovery of treasures for European museums, but many of whom carefully recorded what they found. *Rich published the first detailed study of *Babylon in 1815, and in the 1840s *Botta, *Layard and *Rassam excavated the principal *Assyrian *palaces. The accounts of this work, especially that of Layard and of *Schliemann at *Troy in the 1870s, were immensely popular with a wide public. The biggest single step towards turning archaeology away from a scramble for antiquities and into a proper discipline was *Petrie's work at Tell el-*Hesi in 1890, when he inaugurated stratigraphic excavation by cutting a vertical section through the *tell. This fundamental methodology was later improved by *Reisner and *Kenyon, and by

particular attention to pottery typology by *Albright at Tell *Beit Mirsim and by Pinhas Delougaz at the Diyala sites in eastern *Mesopotamia. Tracing of mudbrick walls was developed by German archaeologists in Mesopotamia.

Modern archaeology as a professional discipline depends on careful recording of the maximum information possible from surveys and excavations, often now on computer, and combines the skills of many non-archaeological specialists from the natural and social sciences, including botanists, chemists, geomorphologists, metallurgists and statisticians. Archaeological excavation now is invariably stratigraphic, based on carefully removing the layers of a site in reverse order of deposition. Individual sites are often subsumed in wider landscape studies in which the story of regional settlement can be reconstructed. Two major problems are the slow pace of publication of archaeological excavations (although many reports are now available with minimal delay on the Internet), and the pace of agricultural and industrial development which has led to the destruction of many sites. The building of major dams in recent years in many Near Eastern countries has sometimes been accompanied by large-scale rescue archaeology projects which have systematically recorded previously unknown regions. (See Chronology; Euphrates–Tigris rescue sites.) PB

S. LLOYD, *Foundations in the Dust: The Story of Mesopotamian Exploration*, 2nd ed. (London 1980).

P.R.S. MOOREY, *A Century of Biblical Archaeology* (Cambridge 1991).

C. RENFREW and P. BAHN, *Archaeology: Theories, Method and Practice* (London 1991).

## Archives

**Archives** Documents were stored together already in the *Uruk period, but the very early archives, presumably out of date, were found discarded as rubbish. *Ebla has provided the earliest archive *in situ*. Over two thousand tablets lay in a specially constructed room of the *palace, originally lined with *wooden shelves from which many tablets had slipped to the floor in a fire and lay in the order they had been shelved. Special rooms, securely sealed, served for storing large archives, with other valuables. Tablets could also be kept on benches or shelves in rooms of *houses, in pigeon-holes in walls, or, most commonly, in baskets, boxes or pots. Clay tags which once secured such containers survive, listing the contents, often by category. In the last third of the third millennium BC, individual tablets reveal signs of organization with the days of the month noted on the edges (Akkadian period) or the main content (Ur III), which, in the first millennium BC, might be in *Aramaic for the benefit of non-*cuneiform-reading clerks. *Pottery jars were sometimes specially made with a notice of what they were to cointain inscribed on them before firing (e.g. at *Ashur). Archives from private houses identify the owners, enabling their activities to be traced in business, *administration and *family affairs (e.g. at *Ur – Old Babylonian, *Nuzi – Middle Babylonian, *Ugarit – Late Bronze Age, and *Nimrud – Neo-Assyrian). Some belonged to staff of *temples or palaces who did not always separate private documents from official ones. Archives of papyrus and leather in Egypt show a similar situation, and that may be adduced for the *Iron Age in the *Levant where only *ostraca and the sealings of the papers survive. Common to all the archives found is a time span of, usually, three generations or less, the earlier texts having been discarded as out of date and the last texts being written shortly before the site was abandoned or destroyed (as at Ugarit, *Hattusas). If the occupants left voluntarily, they will have taken their current files, leaving only 'dead' ones to posterity (as with the *Amarna Letters).                    ARM

K.R. VEENHOF (ed.), *Cuneiform Archives and Libraries* (Leiden 1986).

## Ark of the Covenant

According to Exodus 25: 10–22; 37: 1–9, the Ark was a box about 1.22 by 0.76 by 0.76 m, made of acacia *wood and entirely plated with *gold. It was intended basically as a container for the two *stone tablets bearing the terms of God's covenant with *Israel given to Moses at Mount Sinai (Exodus 40: 20; Deuteronomy 10: 1–5). The box had hoops at each corner to hold poles so that two men could carry it on their shoulders. In that it was like a chest found in Tutankhamun's tomb, although that had a more sophisticated means of storing the carrying-poles. The gold-plated lid of the Ark, the Mercy-Seat, was flat, with a rim, and on it two golden cherubim stood facing each other, with their wings spread over the lid to guard it.

The *biblical texts set the creation of the Ark in the period of Israel's *Exodus from *Egypt when Israel had no permanent *temple, so where in other cultures *covenant or treaty documents were kept for safety in shrines, sometimes at the foot of a *god's statue, here Israel needed a box. Various terms denote the Ark, notably 'Ark (of the covenant) of God' or 'of *Yahweh' and 'Ark of the Testimony (=Covenant)'. It was viewed as God's footstool where he was enthroned, it was the place where he appeared and consequently became a symbol of his presence (Numbers 10: 35), functioning to some extent in the same way as images in other *religions. The Ark was the holiest of all the sacred *furniture, standing in the innermost part of the Tabernacle and later of the Temple. Annually the High *Priest approached it and poured the blood of the Atonement *sacrifice upon it, as a substitution for the death of every Israelite who had broken the terms of the treaty during the previous year (Leviticus 16).

Once Israel was established in *Canaan, the Ark was based at Shiloh and, after being captured by the *Philistines and returned, was eventually taken by David to *Jerusalem where Solomon placed it in his temple. It was probably destroyed when *Nebuchadnezzar II's forces sacked the temple, but legends assert that it was hidden in Mount Nebo in *Jordan (2 Maccabees 2: 4–8), in a cave beneath Jerusalem, or was taken, much earlier, to Ethiopia.                    ARM

C.L. SEOW, 'Ark of the Covenant', *Anchor Bible Dictionary* 1, ed.

D.N. Freedman (New York 1992) 386–93.

R. DE VAUX, *The Bible and the Ancient Near East* (London 1972) 136–51.

**Army:** see Military organization

## Arpachiyah

Arpachiyah was excavated in 1933 by *Mallowan, with a small sounding in 1976 by I. Hijara. The site is located just to the east of the Tigris and northwest of *Nineveh. It is therefore in the *Assyrian steppe, an area suitable for dry farming.

The site is less than a hectare in area. Despite its size it has interesting evidence that might indicate its role as a central place in an early redistribution system. The site dates to the *Halaf period some time between 6000 and 5000 BC.

The most prominent features on the site, quite literally, were two large structures on the crown of the mound. The earlier of these was a large circular building with a large rectangular antechamber. This sort of structure has been christened by archaeologists a 'tholos' and is typical of other Halaf sites. Most of these buildings appear to be domestic dwellings. This particular example was one of the most substantial on the site with walls over 1 m thick. Its location and size might well prompt a view that it was the dwelling of a powerful individual.

Immediately over this dwelling, a more complex multi-roomed rectilinear building was constructed. This building was burned down. In a room that lay directly over the ante-chamber of the earlier *tholos*, and may have represented a rebuild of that room, was found a mass of material in the debris, including a large quantity of elaborately painted multi-coloured *pottery. Because of the precision shown in manufacture, painting and firing control, this sort of pottery was almost certainly a specialist product. A palette with red ochre on it found in the room might be related to such pottery production. *Obsidian and *flint cores were found in the room, suggesting that production of obsidian *tools and possibly *jewellery took place in association with the use of the structure. Obsidian and *stone vessels and obsidian jewellery were also found. Also in the burnt house was a mass of burnt clay *seal impressions showing the sealing of containers, one of the earliest examples of the administrative use of seals. Such containers may have held some of the other material recovered or possibly organic materials that did not survive.

Analysis of the ceramics has suggested that Arpachiyah was a production centre for fine ceramics which were then distributed quite widely in north-east *Mesopotamia. The presence of obsidian blades and other obsidian material on a number of sites, but no cores, from which they would have been knapped, suggests that production of obsidian tools and jewellery took place at a limited number of centres and Arpachiyah may have been one. It is intriguing to find a range of such specialist products concentrated in one setting. As a result the burnt house has been interpreted variously as chief's house,

*temple or specialists' workshop. Whichever is appropriate, it was clearly the setting for the storage and possibly manufacture of goods involved in a redistribution system with some administrative control.     DB

I. HIJARA, 'Arpachiya 1976', *Iraq* 42 (1980) 131-54.
M. MALLOWAN and J.C. ROSE, 'Excavations at Tell Arpachiyah, 1933', *Iraq* 2 (1935) 1–178.

**Arslan Tash** This low-lying site in the fertile plain of Suruj (ancient Serug) in north Syria was excavated by a French team in 1928. It is identified from eighth-century BC inscriptions on basalt lions as *Assyrian Hadatu, and was probably founded by the Assyrians, perhaps in the ninth century BC, close to a *town now represented by the large mound of Tell Hadjib. Town *gates were guarded by monumental basalt lions and faced with stone relief *sculptures showing scenes of military parades and animal *hunts. A *temple compound was approached through a gate guarded by basalt lions, and the temple was entered by a door flanked by basalt bulls. Some of the gateway lions were inscribed in *Akkadian, *Aramaic and Luwian by Ninurta-belu-usur, a subordinate of Shamshi-ilu, governor of Til Barsip in the early eighth century BC.

Excavations uncovered an Assyrian *palace of mudbrick, and the *Bâtiment aux ivoires* built in basalt and mudbrick which contained a black-and-white pebble courtyard as now found also at *Til Barsip and Tille Hüyük, as well as *ivories in *Syrian, *Phoenician and Assyrian styles, conceivably loot or tribute from *Damascus. Over the Assyrian palace was built a *Hellenistic temple in which was re-used an Assyrian basalt statue of a divine attendant (of *Nabû?) holding a box (containing the

Late Halaf-period painted pottery from Arpachiyah, c.5000 BC. WA 127560, 127582.

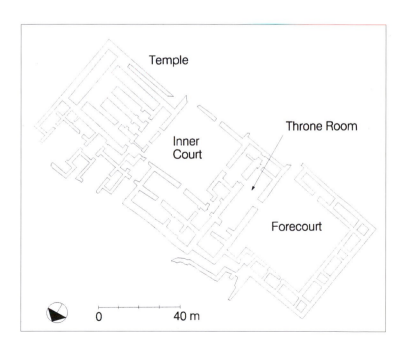

The Neo-Assyrian palace at Arslan Tash, with adjacent temple.

tablet of destinies?), similar to a pair of statues from *Nimrud. *Greek letters were carved on one of the Assyrian basalt bulls.

Two clay amulets inscribed with incantations in Aramaic are probably authentic.    SMD

F. THUREAU-DANGIN *et al.*, *Arslan-Tash* (Paris 1931).
J. VAN DIJK, 'The Authenticity of the Arslan Tash Amulets', *Iraq* 54 (1992) 65–8.

**Arslantepe (Malatya)**   Arslantepe, a large mound 30 m in height, is located west of the Euphrates river in eastern *Anatolia. The site controls the most important Euphrates crossing north of the Anti-Taurus mountains. Its material culture reflects varied influences through its occupation from the *Chalcolithic to Neo-*Hittite periods, c.5000–700 BC. Initial excavations were conducted by Louis Delaporte (1932–9) and Claude Schaeffer (1950s) before the start of an ongoing programme directed successively by Piero Meriggi, Salvatore Puglisi, Alba Palmieri and Marcella Frangipane (1961–).

Settlement at the site goes back to the *Ubaid period, c.4500 BC. During the early to mid fourth millennium BC the settlement took on major proportions, with buildings on a monumental scale and domestic dwellings. These Chalcolithic developments foreshadow the onset of urbanism in the later fourth millennium BC, and suggest that the origins of sophisticated urban society may be sought as much in Anatolia or northern *Mesopotamia as in the south.

By 3300 BC Arslantepe was in contact with the urban civilization of Late *Uruk south Mesopotamia. Immense public buildings, comprising a series of *temples and administrative structures, were built on the summit of the mound. Of particular note are the decorations, stamped and painted, which adorn the outer temple walls, depicting stylized humans and animals in black and red. Plastered *altars, benches and tables were found inside the temples. Great quantities of clay sealings with impressions of *stamp and *cylinder seals indicate the role of the temples within economic and social *administration.

The Late Uruk-related civilization of Arslantepe was brought to a sudden end around 3000 BC with the violent destruction of all the public buildings. The new settlement built on the ruins showed affinities with cultures of eastern Anatolia and the *Caucasus region. The continuing significance of the site is vividly demonstrated by a spectacular *tomb of about 2900 BC, of a *king or prince buried with his retainers – possibly as human *sacrifices – and large amounts of high-quality *metal items. The site remained important and was destroyed by fire at the end of the Late Bronze Age.

During the Neo-Hittite period (twelfth to eighth centuries BC) Arslantepe, or ancient Melid, had a *palace with *stone reliefs, the earliest Neo-Hittite reliefs known. Recent textual evidence has shown that there was a resurgence of Hittite power along the Euphrates, based at *Carchemish, extending from *Emar to Melid, at this time. The settlement declined thereafter, with small-scale *Roman occupation before final abandonment. The name Melid lives on in the name of the nearby towns of Eski Malatya and Malatya itself.    RM/GDS

L. DELAPORTE, *Malatya, Arslantepe* (Paris 1940).
M. FRANGIPANE, 'Dipinti murali in un edificio "palaziale" di Arslantepe–Malatya: aspetti ideologici nelle prime forme di centralizzazione economica', *Studi Micenei ed Egeo-Anatolici* 30 (1992) 143–54.
——, 'Arslantepe – Melid – Malatya', *Arslantepe, Hierapolis, Iasos, Kyme*, ed. C. Carratelli (Venice 1993) 30–103.
——, 'Arslantepe', *The Oxford Encyclopedia of Archaeology in the Near East* 1, ed. E.M. Meyers (New York 1997) 212–15.
——, 'A 4th-Millennium Temple/Palace Complex at Arslantepe–Malatya: North-South Relations and the Formation of Early State Societies in the Northern Regions of Greater Mesopotamia', *Paléorient* 23 (1997) 45–73.
M. FRANGIPANE and J.D. HAWKINS, 'Melid', *Reallexikon der Assyriologie* 8 (Berlin/New York 1993–7) 35–52.
A. PALMIERI, 'Excavations at Arslantepe (Malatya)', *Anatolian Studies* 31 (1981) 101–19.

One of several nearly identical human figures painted on the walls of an access room leading to the interior of the Late Chalcolithic palatial complex at Arslantepe (courtesy of Roger Matthews).

**Art, artists**   There was no distinction in the ancient Near East between art and craft, or artist and *craftsman. Our modern conception of 'art' often implies something made for its own sake, not necessarily practical. In the ancient Near East, all objects were made – and usually commissioned – for a specific purpose. Craftsmen never signed their work, and, apart from a few *tombs and names in administrative documents, we cannot identify them as individuals. There was not even a word for 'artist': craftsmen of various kinds in *palace or *temple workshops were grouped together as artisans with singers, *scribes, brewers, cooks, barbers and so on. There was no language for discussing art. The value of an item was most often expressed in relation to its expense, not its aesthetic quality, although there are occasional texts which praise the skill with which something was made, and a very few which record a viewer's pleasure on seeing an object (e.g. *Shalmaneser III in a dedicatory inscription on a royal statue). Function certainly took precedence over form: for example, at *Mari woodworkers were commissioned to sculpt statues, but also to build chariots. They were artisans, not artists.

If we accept the modern distinction between art and craft, strictly speaking we should not refer to ancient Near Eastern 'art' and 'artists' at all, but to 'crafts' and 'craftsmen'. At most, ancient craft can be appreciated as art in the modern sense when it transcends the strict purpose for which an object was produced by arousing an emotional reaction in the viewer, and goes beyond a standardized design by exhibiting a craftsman's individual inspiration. An example might be the lion-hunt reliefs of *Ashurbanipal's palace at *Nineveh, where the purpose of the scene is to show the *king's bravery and mastery over fierce *animals: but the craftsman has so poignantly depicted the agony of the dying lions that the (modern) viewer empathizes with the animals.

Unlike *Egyptian art, ancient Near Eastern arts and crafts have no stylistic unity and there is a lack of continuity over time. Each region and period had its own characteristics and development, often conditioned by the environment and resources, although in most periods each area was open to external influence through *trade in craft items, movement of patrons and craftsmen, and conquest. In general, the systems of representation were not naturalistic but idealized, and used narrow stylistic conventions and attributes which had particular meanings and sent special messages to the intended audience. Some scholars argue that systems of proportion in figural representation were used, particularly in *Mesopotamia and *Iran, but this remains unproved. Not all materials have survived equally: our knowledge of arts and crafts made of organic materials – *textiles, *wood, leather – is almost non-existent, except for references to such objects in economic texts. (See Cylinder seal; Ivory carving; Sculpture; Seals; Stamp seal; Wall painting.)    PB

H. FRANKFORT, The Art and Architecture of the Ancient Orient, 5th ed. revised by M. Roaf and D. Matthews (London 1997).

A.C. GUNTER (ed.), Investigating Artistic Environments in the Ancient Near East (Washington, D.C. 1990).

D. MATTHEWS, 'Artisans and Artists in Ancient Western Asia', Civilizations of the Ancient Near East, ed. J.M. Sasson (New York 1995) 455–68.

I.J. WINTER, 'Aesthetics in Ancient Mesopotamian Art', Civilizations of the Ancient Near East, ed. J.M. Sasson (New York 1995) 2569–80.

**Arvad**  The most northerly of *Phoenician cities, Arvad (or Arwad, modern Ruad) is on an island measuring

Among the remarkable sculptures of animal hunts in Ashurbanipal's palace at Nineveh none has caught modern attention so strongly as the 'Dying Lioness'. The sculptor has transcended simple representation to portray the animal's agony in a manner which foreshadows classical Greek sculpture. c.650 BC. WA 124856.

800 by 500 m, c.2.5 km from the Mediterranean coast between *Ugarit and *Byblos. The name 'rwd in Phoenician means 'refuge', and the *Assyrians described it as 'in the midst of the sea'. Strabo in the first century BC/AD wrote that it was so small that houses had to be built several storeys high. It has not been excavated and only *Roman remains are visible. It was probably connected with the mainland sites of Amrit (port, cemetery) and Tartus (cemetery).

Arvad is mentioned in second-millennium BC texts from *Ebla, *Alalakh, *Amarna and *Egypt, and in the *Old Testament. These portray the inhabitants as seafarers, travelling to various coastal cities and to Egypt, and involved in the intrigues described in the Amarna Letters. Arvad paid tribute to *Tiglath-pileser I and appeared frequently in later Assyrian records. The king of Arvad sent 200 soldiers to the battle of Qarqar against *Shalmaneser III in 853 BC, but this compares with 10,000 soldiers from other cities, reflecting Arvad's modest size. Arvad continued to pay tribute to *Nebuchadnezzar II, and some of its inhabitants were deported: men of Arvad are listed in *Babylonian ration lists as receiving provisions. The *Persian *king later owned a *palace on the island.    PB

L. BADRE, 'Arwad', The Oxford Encyclopedia of Archaeology in the Near East 1, ed. E.M. Meyers (New York 1997) 218–19.

**Ashdod**  The *Philistine *city of Ashdod, mentioned many times in the *Bible, is identified with Tel Ashdod on the coast of *Palestine north of *Ashkelon. People from Ashdod are first mentioned in texts from *Ugarit as *textile and *tin merchants, and the city was prominent in later *Assyrian inscriptions. After its revolt against *Sargon II, Ashdod was conquered and sacked and its territory annexed under an Assyrian governor, although later kings ruled as Assyrian vassals. After Assyria's fall,

Pottery stand depicting musicians, from Ashdod. Eleventh century BC (© The Israel Museum, Jerusalem).

**Asherah** The term 'Asherah' was used as the name of a popular *goddess and to designate images associated with her. Asherah is the *Hebrew name for this deity, *Akkadian and *Hittite equivalents are well-attested in the second millennium BC and she is named in a South *Arabian inscription from the middle of the first. Her nature is often difficult to discern in some places as she acquired attributes of *Astarte, *Anat and *Ishtar-Inana.

The goddess Ashratu is the *Babylonian version of Asherah and shares her attributes. Ashratu reached *Babylonia as the consort of the god Amurru, with the *Amorites. In god lists she appears as daughter-in-law of *Anu, but is known as 'lady of the steppes' and associated with mountains, pointing to her *Syrian origin.

The Babylonian epithet 'lady of voluptuousness' alludes to Ashratu's erotic character, and this appears to some extent in the *Ugaritic *myths. She was wife of *El and mother of the gods, received offerings beside El and is sometimes called Elat, 'goddess'. In the *Baal myths she is estranged from her husband, but intercedes for Baal and Anat. Asherah was associated with *fertility and is described as suckling the *king. Her *sexual appetite is the main theme in the tale of Elkunirsha, preserved in Hittite, while her title 'lady of the sea' discloses her marine connections, explaining her importance for ports like Ugarit, *Tyre and *Sidon.

The *Bible warns the *Israelites against worshipping Baal and Asherah, apparently as Baal's wife, and Baals and Asheroth (the feminine plural form in Hebrew), in part because of the aspects of fertility and *prostitution linked with her cult. In Hebrew the masculine plural form of her name, *asherim*, designated symbols of the goddess which were probably *wooden poles or images. The Israelites were instructed to burn them. Hebrew inscriptions found at Kuntillet Ajrud in northern *Sinai and at Khirbet el-Qom, near Hebron, mention 'Yahweh and his Asherah', evidence that these cults continued in Israel, as the prophetic denunciations in the Bible imply. GLM

J. DAY, 'Asherah', *Anchor Bible Dictionary* 1, ed. D.N. Freedman (New York 1992) 483–7.

R.S. HESS, 'Asherah or Asherata', *Orientalia* 65 (1996) 209–19.

S.M. OLYAN, *Asherah and the Cult of Yahweh in Israel* (Atlanta, GA 1988).

S.A. WIGGINS, *A Reassessment of 'Asherah': A Study According to the Textual Sources of the First Two Millennia B.C.E.* (Kevelaer 1993).

N. WYATT, 'Asherah', *Dictionary of Deities and Demons in the Bible*, eds K. van der Toorn, B. Becking and P.W. van der Horst (Leiden 1995) 183–95.

according to *Herodotus, the Egyptian King Psamtik I besieged Ashdod for twenty-nine years. Subsequently it became a *Babylonian and then a *Persian province.

Tel Ashdod consists of an acropolis of 8 ha and a lower city of 28 ha. Excavations by Moshe Dothan (1962–72) uncovered a total of twenty-three strata. *Chalcolithic and Early *Bronze Age sherds were found on the mound, but the acropolis was first settled at the end of the Middle Bronze Age, from which a pilastered brick city *gate survives. The Late Bronze Age town may have been the residence of an Egyptian official whose name is inscribed on a stone door post.

Following a destruction, probably by the *Sea Peoples, eight *Iron Age strata reveal the gradual expansion of the Philistine city, with walls, towers, residential, cult and *potters' quarters. A figurine of a seated woman forming part of a throne may represent a Philistine goddess. The lower city was first settled in the eleventh century BC. From this period comes a pottery *incense stand showing five figurines of *musicians playing different instruments, and above an incised procession of domestic *animals. About 3000 human *burials beneath the floors come from a later stratum probably destroyed by *Sargon II in 712 BC. Three basalt fragments inscribed in *cuneiform are part of an Assyrian victory stela erected by Sargon. The city declined after the destruction, but continued to be occupied until the Byzantine period. PB

M. DOTHAN *et al.*, *Ashdod* 1–5 (Jerusalem 1967, 1971, 1982, 1983).

——, 'Ashdod', *The New Encyclopedia of Archaeological Excavations in the Holy Land*, ed. E. Stern (Jerusalem 1993) 93–102.

**Ashkelon** Located on the coast of *Palestine, 60 km south of modern Tel Aviv, Ashkelon is founded on an underground *river tapped by wells, the oldest dating to c.1000 BC. The fresh *water and fertile soils enhanced its importance as a seaport. It appears in the *Execration texts and the *Amarna Letters, and was under *Egyptian control in the Late *Bronze Age; a siege by the Pharaoh Merneptah is depicted on a relief at Karnak in Egypt.

The *Bible records Ashkelon as a major *city of the

The earliest occupation on the mound of Ashkelon, which covers 60 ha, dates from the Early Bronze Age, although some *Chalcolithic pottery has been found and there is a *Neolithic settlement nearby. The first *fortifications were built in the Middle Bronze Age, followed by a continuous sequence up to the Crusader period, including rich Persian-period remains with warehouses and the largest dog *cemetery known from antiquity.

Its location was never forgotten, and in 1815 the eccentric Lady Hester Stanhope, who lived in a fortified village on Mount Lebanon, led an expedition to Ashkelon in search of buried treasure. The first excavations were by *Garstang and W.J. Phythian-Adams (1921–2), and since then much work has been carried out, notably large-scale excavations by L.E. Stager since 1985. The latter discovered a *silver-coated *bronze figurine of a calf inside a model shrine within a Middle Bronze Age *temple. The silver calf was a *religious symbol linked with the worship of *El or *Baal and later of *Yahweh, and this example is one of the finest surviving pieces of *Canaanite *metalwork.                                                          PB

L.E. STAGER, 'Ashkelon', *The New Encyclopedia of Archaeological Excavations in the Holy Land*, ed. E. Stern (Jerusalem 1993) 103–12.

This model calf lay inside the pottery vessel, which was once fitted with a door, in a late Middle Bronze Age shrine at Ashkelon. The calf is 10.5 cm high, 11 cm long (courtesy of L.E. Stager and the Leon Levy Expedition, photographed by Carl Andrews).

*Philistines. *Assyrian inscriptions note that Ashkelon paid tribute from the eighth century BC on, although *Sennacherib had to quell a rebellion by a usurper. In 604 BC *Nebuchadnezzar II destroyed the city and *deported its last Philistine king to *Babylon, where administrative documents record distribution of rations to exiles from Ashkelon. The city recovered and flourished during the *Persian period, under the control of *Tyre.

**Ashur (city)**   Ancient site on the west bank of the Tigris river, close to the modern village of Qal'at Sherqat, 100 km south of Mosul, northern Iraq. Ashur (sometimes written 'Assur') has been extensively investigated, in the nineteenth century by soundings for the British Museum, then by a series of major excavations by *Andrae (1903–14), by an Iraqi programme of excavation and restoration (1978–86) and by renewed German expeditions (1988–90). There is currently a major German project of research and publication.

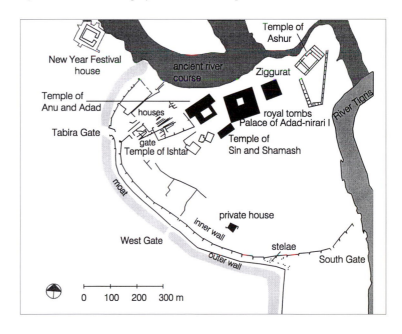

Diagrammatic plan of the city of Ashur.

The first settlement began c.2500 BC. Early in the second millennium BC, Ashur was the centre of a major *trade network reaching across *Anatolia, then the *city-state was a dependency of *Babylonia or of the kingdom of *Mitanni, whose *King Saussatar (reigned c.1500–c.1450 BC) is said to have looted the *palace at Ashur. At some time in the fourteenth century BC, Ashur won independence, subsequently becoming a regional military and commercial power. In the ninth century BC the capital of the expanding state was moved to the strategically better situated *Nimrud (later to *Khorsabad, then *Nineveh). Nevertheless, as the original homeland and throughout *Assyrian history the religious capital, Ashur's continued importance was ensured. The city apparently remained the place of *burial for all Assyrian kings. New palaces, *temples and affluent housing developments, including priestly quarters, continued to be built there. Three palaces have been identified by excavations, beginning with that of *Shamshi-Adad I. A list of buildings at the city made during the reign of *Sennacherib names thirty-four temples, of which fewer than a third have been located. Around the inner city was constructed a defensive wall, some 4 km long. On its eastern side ran the Tigris, with quays originally built under *Adad-nirari I (reigned c.1305–c.1274 BC). To the north, where a branch of the river ran by a high natural eminence, Sennacherib built a system of buttressed defensive walls and a semi-circular stone watch-tower. Ashur was destroyed by the *Medes and Babylonians in 614 BC. An area of the city enjoyed a limited revival in the *Parthian period.          AG

P.O. HARPER et al. (eds), Assyrian Origins: Discoveries at Ashur on the Tigris (New York 1995).

R.W. LAMPRICHS, 'Assur', The Oxford Encyclopedia of Archaeology in the Ancient Near East 1, ed. E.M. Meyers (New York 1997) 225–8.

J. RENGER, 'Das Assurprojekt der Deutschen Orient-Gesellschaft und des Vorderasiatischen Museums zu Berlin', Assyria 1995, eds S. Parpola and R.M. Whiting (Helsinki 1997) 261–79.

J.M. RUSSELL, 'Assur', The Dictionary of Art 2, ed. J. Turner (New York/London 1996) 636–8.

## Ashur (god)

Ashur was the *god of the *Assyrian nation. Originally he may have been the local deity of the *city of the same name, or merely a personification of the city itself. *Oaths were sworn by the name of the city as if it were itself a god. As the extent and power of Assyria spread, Ashur became the supreme god of the emergent state and empire.

Eventually, with the growth of Assyria and the increase in cultural contacts with southern *Mesopotamia, there was a tendency to assimilate Ashur to certain of the major deities of the *Sumerian and *Babylonian pantheons. From about 1300 BC there were attempts to identify him with Sumerian *Enlil, probably in an effort to cast him as the chief of the gods. Ninlil thus became Ashur's wife, and was worshipped in Assyria under the name Mullissu. Later, Ashur was identified with Anshar, the father of *Anu in the Babylonian Epic of Creation,

The god Ashur is shown as a human figure in a winged disk hovering over his subjects on Assyrian reliefs and seals. Relief carving from the palace of Ashurnasirpal II (883–859 BC) at Nimrud. WA 124551.

presenting Ashur as a god of long standing, present from the creation of the universe: an identification may have been suggested by nothing more than the similarity of the names. Under *Sennacherib (reigned 704–681 BC), an attempt was made, at an official level, to reattribute to Ashur the mythology of the Babylonian national god *Marduk, as well as the rituals of the *New Year ceremonies at *Babylon itself. Ashur's cult outlived the Assyrian empire and survived in northern Mesopotamia until the third century AD.

Even the emblems of Ashur were adopted from Babylonian gods. His animal, the snake-dragon, was taken over from Marduk. In collections of symbols of the gods, Ashur seems to be represented by a horned cap, inherited from Anu and Enlil.

Ashur remains an indistinct deity with no clear character, tradition or iconography of his own. It was said to be solely within his power to grant (or to remove) the *kingship over Assyria, and the Assyrian king was his chief *priest and lieutenant on earth. It was particularly common for the names of Assyrian kings to contain the god's name as an element (e.g. *Ashurnasirpal, *Ashurbanipal, *Esarhaddon (Ashur-ahhe-iddina)).          JAB

D.O. EDZARD, 'Mesopotamien: Die Mythologie der Sumerer und Akkader', Götter und Mythen im Vorderen Orient, Vol. 1 of Wörterbuch der Mythologie, ed. H.W. Haussig (Stuttgart 1965) 43–4.

G. LEICK, A Dictionary of Ancient Near Eastern Mythology (London/New York 1991).

G. VAN DRIEL, The Cult of Aššur (Assen 1969).

## Ashurbanipal

'Ashur is creator of the son', *king of *Assyria, 668–c.627 BC.

At *Esarhaddon's *death, his arrangements for the succession were followed: Ashurbanipal became king of Assyria and ensured the installation of his brother Shamash-shum-ukin as king of *Babylon the next year. Ashurbanipal's reign is better documented than any of his predecessors', for the first thirty years, with building inscriptions, '*annals', *letters and oracular inquiries. He continued Esarhaddon's policies of reconstruction at *Babylon, returning the statue of *Marduk in 668 BC, and attack on *Egypt, resuming the campaign halted by his father's death in 667 BC. *Levantine rulers paid tribute and, as the Assyrians advanced on Memphis, Pharaoh Tirhakah fled south to Thebes. Assyria's control was not secured, a rebellion followed and was crushed, with one prince, Necho, reinstated as ruler of the north. In 663 BC further revolt drew Ashurbanipal's troops up the Nile to Thebes, which was captured and its wealth looted. Necho and his son Psamtik were left in charge of the country, eventually asserting their independence about 656 BC. Early in his reign another distant region came to Ashurbanipal's notice as Gyges, king of *Lydia, asked his help in combating *Cimmerian invaders. Successful Gyges sent captured chiefs to *Nineveh, but years later allied himself with Psamtik, by then Assyria's enemy, and fell before another Cimmerian onslaught (c.645 BC). His son submitted again to Ashurbanipal. Military actions in various areas dealt with revolts and frontier incursions (e.g. *Urartu, Mannai). Relations with *Elam fluctuated as its rulers took positions for or against Assyria and Assyria responded with support or attack. One Elamite king, Teumman, entered *Babylonia, was chased back and executed. His head was hung in the trees of the arbour where Ashurbanipal and his *queen *feasted, as shown on a *palace relief at Nineveh. In 652 BC Ashurbanipal's brother sided with the Babylonians and rejected Assyria's overlordship, gaining support from *Chaldaeans, *Arabs and Elamites. The war lasted four years in Babylonia, some places changing hands more than once. Eventually Assyrian forces besieged Babylon, taking the city after two years. Shamash-shum-ukin perished in his burning palace. Ashurbanipal did not take vengeance as *Sennacherib had done: he continued his father's plan and installed Kandalanu as king. Who he was is not clear; he may have been another brother or even Ashurbanipal himself. Assyrian garrisons were posted in various *towns. A Chaldaean leader Nabu-bel-shumate was

particularly troublesome, harrying Assyrian troops and finding refuge in Elam. Partly to end this nuisance, partly to secure compliant rulers, Ashurbanipal attacked Elam in 648 and in 647 BC, the final assault culminating in the sack of *Susa. Soon afterwards, Nabu-bel-shumate and his squire killed each other and the rebel's body was sent to Nineveh pickled in salt. These victories led other distant kings to send envoys to gain Ashurbanipal's favour, including the king of *Bahrain and *Cyrus I, king of the then small state of *Persia. By 639 BC Ashurbanipal held sway from southern *Anatolia to northern *Arabia, from western *Iran to the Mediterranean; only Egypt had been lost. After that date there are no more inscriptions, the most likely explanation being that Ashurbanipal moved his court away from Nineveh. The war with Shamash-shum-ukin and subsequent need to hold Babylonia, threats from Cimmerians and *Medes in the north-east, coupled, maybe, with slacker control by the king and loss of national identity, combined to cloud his last years.

Ashurbanipal is famous for his *library of *cuneiform tablets which he collected at Nineveh, and which he claimed to be able to read, and for the relief *sculptures in his North Palace at Nineveh. These show military action and, most notably, the royal *hunt of wild *animals, with great verve, highlighting the king in hand-to-hand combat with a wounded lion, a scene demonstrating royal power, but unlikely ever to have happened. Although his reign ended in decline and Assyria disappeared soon afterwards, Ashurbanipal raised it to a great height in power and in culture. ARM

R. BORGER, *Beiträge zum Inschriftenwerk Assurbanipals* (Wiesbaden 1996).

A.K. GRAYSON, 'Assyria 668–635 B.C.: The Reign of Ashurbanipal', *Cambridge Ancient History* 3.2, 2nd ed. (Cambridge 1991) 142–61.

D.D. LUCKENBILL, *Ancient Records of Assyria* 2 (Chicago 1927) 290–407.

M. STRECK, *Assurbanipal und die letzten assyrischen Könige* 1–3 (Leipzig 1916).

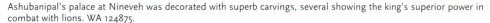

Ashubanipal's palace at Nineveh was decorated with superb carvings, several showing the king's superior power in combat with lions. WA 124875.

**Ashurnasirpal** Two *kings named Ashurnasirpal, '*Ashur guards the heir', ruled *Assyria. Ashurnasirpal I, son of *Shamshi-Adad IV and grandson of *Tiglath-pileser I, ruled c.1050–1031 BC. Apart from the *Eponym List, the Assyrian *King List, and a brick from his *palace at *Ashur, his reign is known only from *hymns to *Ishtar of *Nineveh in later copies. In them he mentions his birth and upbringing outside Assyria, then his rich gifts to the *goddess while praying for healing from a severe *disease. A monument known as the White Obelisk, found at *Nimrud, has been attributed to this king, but is better assigned to his later namesake.

Ashurnasirpal II (883–859 BC), son of *Tukulti-Ninurta II, has left many inscriptions, especially at Nimrud where he built his new capital city with a major palace. He also built at Nineveh, *Ashur, *Balawat and Apqu (Tell Abu Marya). His '*annals' tell of fourteen major campaigns prior to 866 BC, when the records end. He extended Assyrian power further than his father, crossing the Euphrates, reaching the Mediterranean and receiving tribute from states as far south as *Tyre. Ashurnasirpal reports little opposition in the *Levant, but some places in eastern *Syria which had submitted to his father were encouraged to revolt by Bit-Adini, on the Euphrates below *Carchemish, and the *Babylonians. He suppressed the rebels pitilessly, plundering the *towns and erecting inscribed stelae in some. His forces also entered the *Zagros and marched up the Tigris and along the Turkish foothills; they did not enter Babylonia.

In Nimrud Ashurnasirpal built the North-West Palace discovered by *Layard. This is the earliest Assyrian palace known with carved stone reliefs along the walls as well as colossal guardian figures of lions and human-headed winged bulls at the *doorways (see Sculpture). The sculptors depicted scenes of *ritual, *war and *hunting, with the king always majestic, victorious, the enemies cowed, tortured and executed. The ferocious treatment of rebels pictured, and described in the 'annals', led one historian to speak of 'the calculated frightfulness of Ashurnasirpal'. The purpose of this display was to exalt the king and his god Ashur, to demonstrate the king's claim to be 'king of the universe'. Ashurnasirpal seems to have set a model for

his successors. Politically he tried to control his large realm by allowing local rulers to remain so long as they were loyal and paid regular tribute, or by placing his own governors in conquered towns (see Provincial administration). He created storehouses in the provinces to supply his troops.

Later cleaning of the palace and lack of excavations at other sites of his reign mean that, so far, hardly any administrative or legal documents are available to broaden the picture of life and society.　　ARM

Ashurnasirpal I:
B. FOSTER, *Before the Muses* 1 (Bethesda 1993) 239–45 (hymns).
A.K. GRAYSON, *Assyrian Royal Inscriptions* 2 (Wiesbaden 1976) 66–8.
——, *Assyrian Rulers of the Early First Millennium* BC 1 *(1114–859 BC)* (Toronto 1991) 122–3.
D.J. WISEMAN, 'Assyria and Babylonia c.1200–1000 B.C.', Cambridge *Ancient History* 2.2, 2nd ed. (Cambridge 1975) 469–70.

Statue of Ashurnasirpal II from a temple at Nimrud. Height 1 m. WA 118871.

Relief from Nimrud showing Ashurnasirpal II hunting lions. WA 124534.

Ashurnasirpal II:

A.K. GRAYSON, *Assyrian Royal Inscriptions* 2 (Wiesbaden 1976)
66–8.
——, *Assyrian Rulers of the Early First Millennium* BC 1
*(1114–859 BC)* (Toronto 1991) 189–397.
——, 'Assyria: Ashur-dan II to Ashur-nirari V (934–745 B.C.)',
*Cambridge Ancient History* 3.1, 2nd ed. (Cambridge 1982)
253–9.

**Ashur-nirari** Five kings are listed in the *Assyrian
*King List with this name, meaning '*Ashur is my help'.
Almost nothing is known about any of them except for
the last.

Ashur-nirari I was the son of Ishme-Dagan II, and
reigned for twenty-six years in the mid second millennium BC when *Ashur was essentially still a *city-state,
but his exact dates are uncertain. Little is known of him:
his inscriptions on bricks and clay cones from Ashur
concern work on *temples, a *gate and the city wall.

Ashur-nirari II (c.1426–1420 BC) was the son of Enlil-
nasir II. No contemporary inscription of his has been
preserved.

Ashur-nirari III (c.1203–1198 BC) was the son of
Ashur-nadin-apli. He is best known from a *letter sent by
a *Babylonian king, preserved in a copy in the *library of
*Ashurbanipal, in which the Assyrian ruler is scolded,
abused and insulted. Clearly at this period the Assyrian
king was in an inferior position with regard to the Babylonian king.

Ashur-nirari IV (1019–1014 BC) was the son of *Shalmaneser II, and appears only in the king lists and
*eponym lists.

Ashur-nirari V (754–745 BC) was the son of *Adad-
nirari III. In his second year he campaigned against Arpad
in north *Syria and negotiated a *treaty with its King
Mati'ilu. The surviving fragments of this treaty curse
Mati'ilu, who is represented by a *sacrificial lamb in the
accompanying *ritual, in case he violated the treaty.
Ashur-nirari also campaigned on Assyria's northern
*border against *Urartu, whose King Sarduri II claimed
to have defeated him.                                    PB

A.K. GRAYSON, *Assyrian Royal Inscriptions* 1 (Wiesbaden 1972)
33–4, 37–8, 137–8.
——, *Assyrian Royal Inscriptions* 2 (Wiesbaden 1976) 70.
——, 'Assyria: Ashur-dan II to Ashur-nirari V (934–745 B.C.)',
*Cambridge Ancient History* 3.1, 2nd ed. (Cambridge 1982)
238–81.
——, *Assyrian Rulers of the Third and Second Millennia* BC *(to
1115 BC)* (Toronto 1987) 83–9.
——, *Assyrian Rulers of the Early First Millennium* BC II
*(858–745 BC)* (Toronto 1996) 246–7.
D.D. LUCKENBILL, *Ancient Records of Assyria and Babylonia* 1
(Chicago 1926) 17–18, 265–8.

**Assyria, Assyrians** From the *Anatolian foothills the
Tigris *river flows south for some 200 km then breaks
through a range of hills, the Jebel Makhul and Jebel
Hamrin, into *Babylonia. That stretch of river is the heart
of Assyria. From the *Zagros foothills in the east two tributaries join the Tigris, the Upper Zab and the Lower Zab.

On the west side, the Wadi Tharthar lies parallel to the
Tigris, watering the oasis of Hatra. Beyond, the steppe
land of the Jazira extends to the *Khabur river, relieved
only by the steep Jebel Sinjar. Much of Assyria is fertile,
receiving adequate rainfall for *agriculture in most years
and so not demanding the enormous expenditures of
labour the Babylonian *irrigation systems consumed,
with various fruit-trees growing in the northern area and
good grazing. Settlements in the earliest periods demonstrate the attractiveness of the area for incipient farmers,
among them Umm Dabaghiyah, *Hassuna, *Arpachiyah.
In due course the *Halaf culture spread across the whole
of north *Mesopotamia and *Syria, and in the fifth
millennium BC the *Ubaid culture dominated, with large
occupations at major sites such as *Nineveh, as yet hardly
explored, followed by the *Uruk. Local independence
then appears in the *Ninevite V *pottery before Early
Dynastic features spread from Babylonia. *Kings of
*Akkad built at Nineveh and it is near the end of the third
millennium BC that the earliest building inscriptions
from *Ashur record work there and name local rulers.
Besides Ashur and Nineveh, the major *towns were
*Nimrud and Arbela (modern Erbil). In the twentieth
and nineteenth centuries BC the kings included Ilushuma,
who claimed to have made some impact in Babylonia,
but, apart from the imperial interlude of *Shamshi-Adad
I, Assyrian kings were occupied with local affairs and the
*trade that flourished with *Kanesh and associated
centres. In the mid second millennium BC, *Mitanni
made Assyria's kings its vassals, a situation eventually
ended by Ashur-uballit I, about 1350 BC. The Middle
Assyrian kingdom now grew as a major power (see Adad-
nirari I; Shalmaneser I; Tiglath-pileser I; Tukulti-Ninurta
I), controlling territory as far west as the Euphrates below
*Carchemish. In the decades after 1100 BC, pressures from
*Aramaean and other tribes reduced Assyria to little
more than the land on the immediate banks of the Tigris.
Although in eclipse, the line of kings continued and all
but two are known from their own building inscriptions.
About 930 BC, Assyria renewed its strength under Ashur-
dan III, who began to conquer some of the nearest
Aramaeans and restore Assyrians to lands they had previously held. The ensuing Neo-Assyrian empire saw
Assyrian power expanding ever wider until Egypt was
conquered briefly in the seventh century BC (see Ashurnasirpal; Shalmaneser III; Tiglath-pileser III; Sargon;
Sennacherib; Esarhaddon; Ashurbanipal). And then, in
two decades, the whole edifice collapsed, with Nineveh
falling in 612 BC to the Babylonians and the *Medes.

'Assyrians' can be identified from about 2000 BC
onwards through their dialect of *Akkadian. However, no
ancestral or tribal name Ashur is mentioned, so Assyrians
were probably named from their location, around Ashur.
East *Semites were joined by *Amorites, Shamshi-Adad's
line being grafted into the Assyrian *King List. Some
*Hurrians were also in the population and doubtless
others from the mountains to the east and north and
some from Babylonia. With no natural frontiers, Assyria
was open to such immigrants and to raiders drawn to
the productive terrain. Toughened by fighting off such

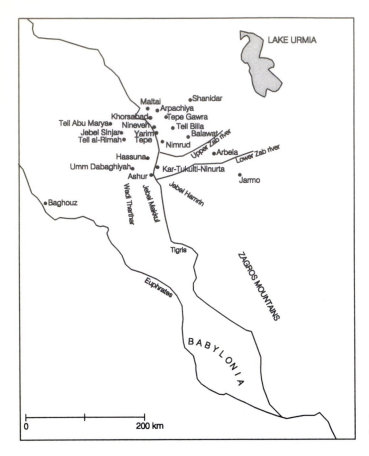

Map of Assyria showing main archaeological sites.

attacks, the Assyrians had the core for an effective army. Their king stood in particularly close relationship to the national *god Ashur as his viceroy. These were contributory factors in Assyria's national career.                    ARM

H.W.F. SAGGS, *The Might that Was Assyria* (London 1984).

**Astarte**  This is the Greek form of the *goddess's name, as written by Philo of *Byblos in the first century AD, equating her with Aphrodite. It is 'Athtartu in *Ugaritic, 'Ashtoreth in *Hebrew, both feminine forms. *Akkadian *Ishtar and South *Arabian 'Athtar are masculine in form (although Akkadian *ishtarātu* is feminine, 'goddesses'). She often occurs at Ugarit, paired with *Anat, who takes a more active role in the *myths, and eventually the two merged as Atargatis in the *Persian period. Astarte was important in *Phoenicia, notably at Sidon, and the *Bible mentions her as Ashtoreth of the Sidonians whose shrine Solomon built in *Jerusalem (1 Kings 1: 5, 33), although no details are known about her cult there or in other *towns. The biblical expression 'queen of heaven', found in Jeremiah's prophecy, probably refers to her. Place names incorporating her name indicate her importance. Her character seems to be connected with *war (see Ishtar) in Egyptian inscriptions which, in the late period, call her 'Mistress of *horses, lady of the *chariot'. One Egyptian myth makes her daughter of Re, married to Seth

(=*Baal), but the fragmentary *story 'Astarte and the Sea' makes her daughter of Ptah. Several biblical references link Ashtoreth, perhaps as plural, 'goddesses', with Baal, to be avoided at all costs by the *Israelites. Over the length of time involved and the geographical range, the characteristics of the goddess and her cult evidently varied considerably.                    GL/ARM

A.L. PERLMAN, *Asherah and Astarte in the Old Testament and in Ugaritic Literature* (Berkeley, CA 1978).
N. WYATT, 'Astarte', *Dictionary of Deities and Demons in the Bible*, eds K. van der Toorn, B. Becking and P.W. van der Horst (Leiden 1995) 204–13.

**Astronomy and astrology**  There was little distinction in the ancient Near East between what we today classify as astronomy and astrology. The observation and recording of celestial phenomena were largely for the purpose of gathering data for the prediction of events, and were a form of *divination. A belief in divine signs was linked with objective observation, *mathematical calculation and the correct prediction of the movement of celestial bodies.

The earliest known systematic interest in celestial events appears in the Old *Babylonian lunar and solar omens c.1700 BC. The compilation of astrological *omens peaked in the first millennium BC. These omens concerned observations of the moon, sun (especially eclipses), planets and stars, as well as earthquakes and weather patterns, and they were linked to predictions about the *king and the state. They usually took the form 'If x occurs (in the sky) then y will occur (on earth)' (e.g. the king will die, or there will be peace, and so on). The Neo-*Assyrian version of the standard series of celestial omens, found in the library of *Ashurbanipal at *Nineveh, is entitled Enūma Anu Enlil, the title coming from the first three words, 'When *Anu and *Enlil', the introduction describing the creation of the universe. Earlier versions of the series have been found in *Hittite and *Akkadian texts from *Boghazköy, at *Susa and in *Syria.

In the Neo-Assyrian period, scholars in various Assyrian and *Babylonian *cities regularly observed the heavens and made reports and predictions about political and economic events. The purpose of the reports was to inform the king of propitious times for certain activities, and to protect him against evil portents. For example, a lunar eclipse might lead to the application of the substitute king ritual (see Kings and kingship), as in the reigns of *Esarhaddon and *Ashurbanipal. The specialists compiled reference texts focusing on the visibility of the moon and the variation in the length of daylight throughout the year, but also including dates of stellar risings and periods of the planets. A comprehensive work written on two tablets, entitled MUL.APIN ('Plough Star') and dating to the seventh century BC, is a summary of early astronomical knowledge concerning the stars, sun, moon and planets.

Later developments, in the *Achaemenid period and after, included the development of personal predictions from celestial phenomena (horoscopes), the invention of the zodiac in Babylonia c.500 BC, and the practice of keeping astronomical diaries recording lunar, planetary, meteorological, economic, political and other events. Although the earliest known such diary dates to 652 BC, most surviving examples date after c.400 BC. They may have been used as raw data for predictions. '*Chaldaean' (i.e. Babylonian) astronomy was famous in the *Greek world, and influenced *Indian and medieval European science.                                                    PB

H. HUNGER (ed.), Astrological Reports to Assyrian Kings (Helsinki 1992).

O. NEUGEBAUER, The Exact Sciences in Antiquity, 2nd ed. (Providence 1957) 97–144.

F. ROCHBERG, 'Astronomy and Calendars in Ancient Mesopotamia', Civilizations of the Ancient Near East, ed. J.M. Sasson (New York 1995) 1925–40.

F. ROCHBERG-HALTON, Aspects of Babylonian Celestial Divination: The Lunar Eclipse Tablets of Enuma Anu Enlil (Vienna 1988).

**Autobiographies** There were no autobiographies in the ancient Near East in the modern sense, meaning a retrospective and introspective review of the author's own life. Some texts purport to be autobiographical, such as royal inscriptions commemorating a *king's achievements or chronicling a campaign. In these, a first-person narrator recounts parts of his own life, but probably without exception these were written and composed by scribes and not by the subjects themselves.

A characteristic of modern autobiographies is inner thought, disclosing the motives and intentions of the subject. A few ancient Near Eastern texts show this, particularly the inscription of Idrimi of *Alalakh, carved across his statue, in which he describes how he regained his throne against all manner of setbacks, mostly adventures in exile. Nevertheless, it is likely that even this unique text, which reveals Idrimi's inner thoughts, was composed after his death. It has been grouped with other *Akkadian so-called fictional autobiographies, which can legitimize messages by ascribing them to authoritative figures, often long dead, and occasionally to gods.     PB

M. DIETRICH and O. LORETZ, 'Die Inschrift der Statue des Königs Idrimi von Alalah', Ugarit-Forschungen 13 (1981) 201–69.

E.L. GREENSTEIN, 'Autobiographies in Ancient Western Asia', Civilizations of the Ancient Near East, ed. J.M. Sasson (New York 1995) 2421–32.

E.L. GREENSTEIN and D. MARCUS, 'The Akkadian Inscription of Idrimi', Journal of the Ancient Near Eastern Society of Columbia University 8 (1976) 59–96.

T. LONGMAN III, Fictional Akkadian Autobiography: A Generic and Comparative Study (Winona Lake, IN 1991).

G.H. OLLER, The Autobiography of Idrimi (University Microfilms International, Philadelphia, PA 1977).

# B

**Baal** 'Baal' is a common *Semitic noun that means 'lord' or 'owner', but it also occurs quite frequently in ancient texts as the proper name of an important *god. Baal was, in fact, one of the most widely known deities in the West Semitic pantheon, and he was associated with aspects of the natural world that were central to *agriculture and society. The name was associated specifically with the deity Hadad, and he could be known as Baal Hadad or just Baal. Sometimes the term 'Baal' was used with reference to local manifestations of this god (e.g. Baal-Sidon, Baal-Hermon, Baal-Peor), but it was also used in its general sense to refer to other deities altogether. The list of toponyms that contain the name 'Baal' reflects the widespread nature of this cult, but such ambiguity also means that iconography associated with Baal is often difficult to identify with certainty.

Baal appears in Near Eastern texts beginning in the third millennium BC, but he was best known from his prominent role in *Ugaritic literature (c.1250 BC). The latter contains over five hundred references to Baal, who was said to live on Mount Sapanu/Zaphon (Jebel el-Aqra'), north of Ugarit. The so-called 'Baal cycle' is told on six tablets (and fragments) that were found on the acropolis at Ras Shamra; some 1830 lines survive out of a much longer original *epic, which developed over a long period of time. Baal was identified as the son of Dagon (see Dagan) but was also known as the son of *El, the head of the Semitic pantheon. His consort and sister was *Anat (in the Ugaritic texts), but the *Bible links Baal with the goddesses *Asherah (Athirat) or Ashtaroth.

Throughout the ancient Near East, Baal was viewed as a storm-god and was associated with clouds, thunder, lightning and rain (see Weather-gods). Among the peoples who practised agriculture in relatively dry climates, he was understood as a god of *fertility. Baal was the principal actor in Ugaritic mythology, but he had to struggle for his supremacy, especially against his brothers *Yam (sea) and *Mot (death). This conflict is the major theme of the Baal epic. As the *Canaanite deity of weather and fertility, he was linked with the annual return of vegetation.

In numerous passages the Bible records a long-term, intense animosity towards Baal and those who worshipped this deity (e.g. Numbers 25; Judges 6; 1 Kings 18; Hosea 2). On the other hand, it is clear that titles and attributes applied to Baal were also assimilated into the *Israelite understanding of *Yahweh. For example, the latter was said to ride on the clouds (Psalm 68: 4) and to manifest his power in the thunderstorm (Psalm 29), concepts also associated with Baal. Near Eastern texts, including the Bible, mention many features of the worship of Baal (e.g. *festivals, *sacrifices, *altars, *temples, *priests, prophets (see Prophecies and oracles), images).

GLM

J. DAY, 'Baal (Deity)', *Anchor Bible Dictionary* 1, ed. D.N. Freedman (New York 1992) 545–9.

W. HERRMANN, 'Baal', *Dictionary of Deities and Demons in the Bible*, eds K. van der Toorn, B. Becking and P. W. van der Horst (Leiden 1995) 249–63.

J.C. DE MOOR and M.J. MULDER, 'ba'al', *Theological Dictionary of the Old Testament* 2, eds G.J. Botterweck and H. Ringgren (Grand Rapids, MI 1975) 181–200.

D. PARDEE, 'The Ba'lu Myth', *The Context of Scripture* 1, eds W.W. Hallo and K.L. Younger (Leiden/New York 1997) 241–74.

S.B. PARKER (ed.), *Ugaritic Narrative Poetry* (Atlanta, GA 1997).

M. SMITH, 'Interpreting the Baal Cycle', *Ugarit-Forschungen* 18 (1986) 313–39.

——, *The Ugaritic Baal Cycle* 1 (Leiden 1994).

L.E. TOOMBS, 'Baal, Lord of the Earth: The Ugaritic Baal Epic', *The Word of the Lord Shall Go Forth*, eds C.L. Meyers and M. O'Connor (Winona Lake, IN 1983) 613–23.

**Babel:** see Tower of Babel

**Babylon** The most famous *city of the Near East in antiquity, symbolizing the whole of *Mesopotamian civilization, Babylon lies on the bank of the Euphrates river 90 km south-west of modern Baghdad in Iraq. Its name derives from the *Hellenized form of the *Akkadian *Bab-Il* ('the gate of *god') which appears in the *Bible as 'Babel' (see Tower of Babel). Interest in rediscovering Babylon was stimulated by the biblical stories and by the account of *Herodotus.

The present-day ruins comprise many scattered *tells extending for about 2 km north–south and 1.2 km east–west. Babylon was visited by Islamic and European travellers from the tenth century AD on, and first investigated in 1616 by the Italian Pietro della Valle, who brought back to Europe the first *cuneiform inscriptions on bricks. *Rich began a systematic survey in 1811, and some of the objects he brought back are now in the British Museum. Thereafter the site was visited and excavated on a small scale many times, among others by *Layard, *Rawlinson and *Rassam, until the major German excavations of 1899–1917, eventually directed by *Koldewey. In recent years the Iraqi Department of Antiquities has undertaken a programme of excavation and restoration.

The major result of the German excavations was the exposure of the Neo-*Babylonian levels, revealing a *fortified city with an outer ring of walls 18 km long, according to Herodotus with enough space to enable a four-horse *chariot to turn around. The city was divided by the Euphrates (which has since changed its course) into unequal halves, connected by a bridge resting on stone boat-shaped piers. The most famous, and the only one excavated, of the city's nine gates, all named after

Plan of the main city of Babylon, east of the Euphrates, in the Neo-Babylonian period.

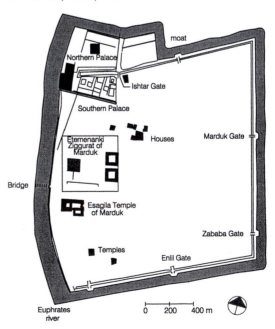

The Ishtar Gate at Babylon was covered with blue-glazed bricks and moulded reliefs. The reconstruction in Berlin is almost 15 m high (photograph courtesy of the Vorderasiatisches Museum, Staatliche Museen, Berlin).

A boundary stone (*kudurru*) bearing the figure of King Marduk-nadin-ahhe of Babylon (c.1090 BC), recording a purchase of land by a royal official. Height c.60 cm. WA 90841.

deities, is the *Ishtar *Gate, decorated with figures of *animals moulded in relief in glazed and unglazed bricks. It has been reconstructed in the Berlin Museum. A processional way ran from the *temple of Marduk through the Ishtar Gate to the *akitu* (*New Year festival) temple. This avenue was bordered by high walls, which formed the limit of the southern citadel on the west. This was built round five courtyards with reception rooms on the south side. It was created by *Nebuchadnezzar II, who called it 'the marvel of mankind, the centre of the land, the shining residence, the dwelling of majesty'; it was later used by the *Achaemenid kings, and was the scene of Alexander the Great's death. The centre of the city was the temple precinct Esagila, with the cult centres of *Marduk and other gods. To the north was another temple precinct, Etemenanki, where the remains of the *ziggurat are found. Although little now survives, originally this consisted of six stepped platforms, with a shrine to Marduk on top, reached by a monumental staircase and two side stairways. The Hanging Gardens of Babylon were one of the Seven Wonders of the Ancient World, but their location is uncertain (see Gardens).

Partly as a result of the rising water table, settlements of earlier periods at Babylon are not well known and can mostly be reconstructed only from literary sources,. *Sargon of *Akkad is said to have destroyed Babylon; two temples are known from the time of one of his successors, Shar-kali-sharri. Babylon rose to prominence as a provincial capital during the Third Dynasty of *Ur, and from the time of *Hammurabi became the most important political, cultural and religious centre of southern Mesopotamia. The city is described on a series of tablets dating to the late twelfth century BC. At that time it was divided into ten districts, with eight gates, and at least fifty-three temples, as well as other shrines and buildings.

Babylon continued to be a royal residence after its fall to the *Persians in 539 BC, and was to have been the capital of Alexander the Great's world empire. It lost its pre-eminence with the founding of Seleucia on the Tigris (see Hellenistic period), and by the second century AD seems to have been deserted, though by the ninth century AD it was re-occupied and once more a provincial capital.

PB

W. ANDRAE, *Babylon: Die versunkene Weltstadt und ihr Ausgräber Robert Koldewey* (Berlin 1952).

E. KLENGEL-BRANDT, 'Babylon', *The Oxford Encyclopedia of Archaeology in the Near East* 1, ed. E.M. Meyers (New York 1997) 251–6.

K. KOHLMEYER, *Wiedererstehendes Babylon: Eine antike Weltstadt im Blick der Forschung* (Berlin 1991).
R. KOLDEWEY, *The Excavations at Babylon* (London 1914).

**Babylonia, Babylonians** Babylonia is the name given to ancient southern *Mesopotamia, approximately from modern Baghdad to the Persian Gulf, and from the *Syrian and *Arabian deserts to the *Zagros mountains. The name comes from the place name '*Babylon', and is used as both a geographical and a political term. In ancient times, the north was called *Akkad and the south *Sumer, and the phrase 'lands of Sumer and Akkad' was still used centuries after these terms ceased to have any meaning.

An urban culture based on *irrigation had already developed by the fourth millennium BC, and by the third millennium BC there is evidence for city-states populated by Sumerians, who invented the *cuneiform system for writing their language. Akkadians immigrated into the area during the third millennium BC, eventually becoming the dominant population or ethnic group, and henceforth *Akkadian was the main language of Babylonia, written in the cuneiform script borrowed from the Sumerians.

The political structure was always basically that of the *city-state, with power and resources vested in the twin pillars of *palace and *temple. The area was a unified political unit only in certain periods. Occasionally particular cities expanded into territorial states and ruled over part or all of Babylonia and sometimes beyond, e.g.

Akkad, the Third Dynasty of *Ur, the First Dynasty of Babylon, the *Kassites, and the Neo-Babylonian empire. A characteristic of Babylonian history was the frequent infiltration and eventual assimilation of new ethnic groups, often originally *nomadic, whose descendants sometimes ended up ruling the area, e.g. *Amorites, Kassites and *Aramaeans. The Aramaeans infiltrated into Babylonia in the late second millennium BC, and Aramaic increasingly became the language of everyday life, Akkadian remaining the language of official inscriptions and literature.

From the ninth century BC, Babylonia was the object of systematic *Assyrian interest and eventually part of its empire. With the fall of Assyria, the Neo-Babylonian empire founded by *Nabopolassar and extended by *Nebuchadnezzar II, with its capital at Babylon, became the dominant power in Mesopotamia, ruling over most of the area of the former Assyrian empire, until the conquest of Babylon by *Cyrus II in 539 BC which ushered in the *Persian empire.

Babylonia is an alluvial plain with a small amount of rainfall, and *agriculture was possible only by irrigation using the waters of the Tigris and Euphrates rivers, which flood in spring, and of canals. The southern part of Babylonia consists of marshes where people lived on *boats as well as on land. Babylonia was poor in raw materials: *metals, *stone and *wood had to be imported. Local trees, such as palm and tamarisk, were not suitable for constructing large buildings. Buildings were largely constructed of sun-dried mudbrick, which was freely available, stone being used only for the foundations (see

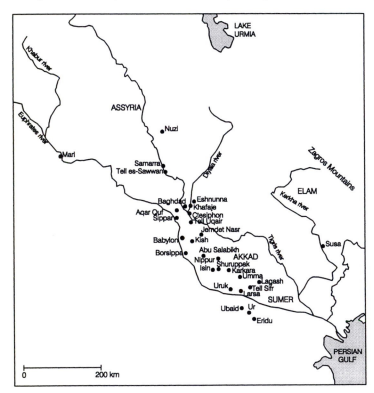

Map of Babylonia showing main archaeological sites.

Building materials). Already in the third millennium BC, Babylonians specialized in crafts, especially *textile and leatherwork, *pottery, metalworking and stoneworking, using imported materials. PB

A.K. GRAYSON, 'History and Culture of Babylonia', *Anchor Bible Dictionary* 4, ed. D.N. Freedman (New York 1992) 756–77.

J.N. POSTGATE, *Early Mesopotamia: Society and Economy at the Dawn of History* (London 1994).

H.W.F. SAGGS, *The Greatness that was Babylon* (London 1962).

——, *Babylonians* (London 1995).

## Bahrain

Lying in the Persian Gulf off the east coast of *Arabia, the Bahrain archipelago did not separate from the mainland until the sixth or fifth millennium BC. It is now identified with ancient Dilmun, together with Failaka Island to the north which has similar remains, although it is likely that the name referred to eastern Arabia until the third millennium BC. Dilmun appears in *Mesopotamian literary texts as a virtual paradise. Its main role was as an intermediary in the *copper trade between *Oman (ancient Magan) and *Mesopotamia from the third millennium BC on.

A few sites containing imported *Ubaid *pottery show links with Mesopotamia by the fourth millennium BC, but settlement peaked with the Gulf trade in the late third and early second millennia BC. Saar was a city with a network of streets and small buildings with L-shaped rooms, and *temples have been found there and at Barbar and Diraz. A large walled area at Qal'at Bahrain enclosed a storeroom, private *houses and a workshop for *stamp seals. Circular stamp seals (called Dilmun or Persian Gulf seals) were characteristic of Dilmun, often depicting two men drinking through straws, or prancing gazelles.

Tens of thousands of *burial mounds dating to this period cover Bahrain. Most of them have a single burial chamber, either above or below ground. The pottery and *seals are mostly of local production, and these were clearly the graves of a local population. Although Bahrain has a fertile north coast, its *agricultural potential is limited, though some cereals may have been grown; Mesopotamian texts record huge shipments of barley to Dilmun, presumably to feed the population.

The Gulf trade was severely reduced in the eighteenth century BC, but Qal'at Bahrain continued as an important site. A storage building destroyed by fire yielded *cuneiform inscriptions dating to the fourteenth century BC, which mention a temple, the *palace of a local ruler, and the *Kassite king; a *Babylonian official stationed in Dilmun reported back on threats to the date crop, perhaps indicating Kassite control. A large residence, perhaps the palace of Uperi, a king of Dilmun mentioned as a tributary of *Sargon II, has been partially excavated. Later burials in clay *coffins beneath the floors of the building contained *bronze *wine sets, bowls with the skeleton of a snake coiled around a precious stone, and a hoard of *silver, dating to the sixth or fifth century BC. PB

H.A. AL KHALIFA and M. RICE (eds), *Bahrain through the Ages: The Archaeology* (London 1986).

A Dilmun (or Persian Gulf) stamp seal from Saar, showing a man with a prancing gazelle. Late third millennium BC (courtesy of the London–Bahrain Archaeological Expedition).

H. CRAWFORD, 'The Site of Saar: Dilmun Reconsidered', *Antiquity* 273 (1997) 701–08.

——, *Dilmun and its Gulf Neighbours* (Cambridge 1998).

D.T. POTTS (ed.), *Dilmun: New Studies in the Archaeology and Early History of Bahrain* (Berlin 1983).

——, *The Arabian Gulf in Antiquity* (Oxford 1990).

——, 'Bahrain', *The Oxford Encyclopedia of Archaeology in the Near East* 1, ed. E.M. Meyers (New York 1997) 266–8.

## Balawat gates

The finest surviving examples of a type of *gate that was used in many *Assyrian official buildings are those erected by *Shalmaneser III (858–824 BC) in his palace at Balawat (ancient Imgur-Enlil), 16 km north-east of *Nimrud, in the ninth century BC. The original *wooden gates were 6.8 m high and 2.3 m wide. The wood has not survived, but a foundation inscription of *Ashurnasirpal II (883–859 BC) specifies that the doors he erected earlier were made of cedar. Shalmaneser's doors were not hinged, but hung on vertical trunks, capped with *bronze, which turned in *stone sockets set into the floor. The edges of each leaf were sheathed in bronze and eight bronze bands were nailed across the faces and around the door-posts.

The bronze bands are what has survived. They are decorated in relief by hammering from behind, with details engraved on the front. Each band is about 27 cm high with two registers showing incidents from the campaigns of Shalmaneser's first ten years. The campaigns are identified by a line of *cuneiform text above each scene, and are described more fully on the duplicated 'Gate Inscription' on the edge of each leaf and in Shalmaneser's *annals. The workmanship and subject matter on the bronze bands are varied – camp life, siege warfare, tribute payment, *animal *sacrifice, as on the stone palace reliefs – and it is clear that this was not all the work of a single *craftsman.

Originally, fragments of the bands appeared on the antiquities market, but *Rassam discovered the rest at Balawat although he was unjustly accused of pilfering them from *Nimrud. Rassam and later *Mallowan found sets of bronze bands from two gates erected by Ashurnasirpal II at Balawat, but these are less well preserved. These were found in a temple, but their inscriptions refer to the palace where presumably they were originally erected. PB

J.E. CURTIS, 'Balawat', *Fifty Years of Mesopotamian Discovery*, ed. J.E. Curtis (London 1982) 113–19.

Reconstruction of the Balawat gates. WA 124656–124662.

L.W. KING, *Bronze Reliefs from the Gates of Shalmaneser* (London 1915).

J.N. POSTGATE, 'Imgur-Enlil', *Reallexikon der Assyriologie* 5 (Berlin/New York 1976) 66–7.

**Balikh**  The Balikh river is a small tributary of the Euphrates in north *Syria, which together with the *Khabur waters the area known as the Jazira. Even over a distance of only 100 km, the rainfall in the Balikh region decreases measurably, so that the north is a fertile *agricultural area while the south is steppeland more suitable for grazing. The region is extremely rich in sites of all periods. Three of the most important are Tell Chuera, which has important remains from the third millennium BC, including a number of *Sumerian statues; Tell Hammam et-Turkman, a multi-period site occupied from the

*Ubaid to the *Roman periods; and Tell *Bi‘a (ancient Tuttul) with significant Middle Assyrian texts.       PB

N. LEWIS, 'The Balikh Valley and its People', *Hammam et-Turkman* 1, ed. M.N. Van Loon (Leiden 1988) 683–95.

W. ORTHMANN, *Tell Chuera: Ausgrabungen der Max Freiherr von Oppenheim-Stiftung in Nordost-Syrien* (Damascus 1990).

**Banat, (Tell)**  Now known primarily for its 'royal grave' discovered in 1996, Tell Banat is part of an extended settlement complex, with Tell Kabir and Tell Banat North, on the Euphrates river in *Syria south-east of *Carchemish. Excavations since 1989 by Thomas McClellan and Anne Porter have unearthed occupation dating to two periods, the mid and late third millennium BC. Tell Kabir has a building identified as a long-room *temple, Tell Banat North has monuments of both periods (White Monument I and II), while Tell Banat itself has an artificial gravel platform extending underneath a series of public buildings and a *burial complex, and an area of kilns and buildings associated with *pottery production.

The Tell Banat public building of the third millennium BC comprises three descending terraces dug into the platform. Two column bases still remain on the highest terrace. On the second terrace a series of rooms is arranged around a tiled floor with steps leading to the third terrace; originally there was a columned portico from which a stepped revetment led to the lower terrace.

To the south-east of the Banat building is the magnificent Tomb 7, around which is a series of burials, including *horse burials, dating to both periods of occupation. Tomb 7 was perhaps a burial place for a high-ranking person or family. It consists of five chambers with connecting corridors, roofed with nine large limestone slabs. Each chamber has a series of wall niches containing pottery and other objects, including a decorated ostrich egg with a stopper inlaid with lapis lazuli and mother-of-pearl; in one corner were two lapis lazuli bottle stoppers inlaid with *gold florettes. In the largest chamber, a *wooden *coffin contained traces of a human skeleton covered with beads, including gold beads paralleled by *Schliemann's treasure at *Troy.       PB

T. McCLELLAN and A. PORTER, 'Banat', *American Journal of Archaeology* 101 (1997) 106–8.

A. PORTER, 'The Third Millennium Settlement Complex at Tell Banat: Tell Kabir', *Damaszener Mitteilungen* 8 (1995) 125–63.

——, 'Tell Banat – Tomb 1', *Damaszener Mitteilungen* 8 (1995) 1–50.

**Banquets and feasts**  Feasting marked *religious, state and private celebrations. The *Sumerian logogram for 'feast' means '*beer-pouring', and consumption of beer and *wine played a major part. Brewing in *Mesopotamia was a *temple activity connected especially with the cult of *Ishtar. Drinking scenes feature on *seals and *sculptures of various periods. Drinking sets of precious materials confirm that alcohol was important; texts and material finds of several periods record a variety of communal jars, pouring jugs, personal drinking bowls or animal-headed drinking vessels, and long 'straws'. The legend of *Aqhat shows that inebriation was to be expected.

The *New Year festival was also called the time of feasting, for which the *gods issued invitations and fixed destinies for the coming year. Feasts of assembly were the occasion for making decisions and swearing *oaths of loyalty, as when *Marduk was elected to power in the Epic of Creation. At the Old Babylonian military census, the *tēbibtum* *ritual included a feast at which loyalty oaths were sworn. Betrothal was another occasion for feasting (see Marriage), and funerary banquets are shown on *Iron Age stelae from *Syria. A seven-day repast at the *death of *Nabonidus' mother was part of officially declared mourning. An *Assyrian national feast attended by the gods of all major *cities was the *tākultu*, at which the *king offered *food and drink to the gods in return for their blessing on king and country.

Feasts of consecration were held when, for instance, Marduk finished building *Babylon in the Epic of Creation, when *Baal's new *temple at *Ugarit was completed, and when *Ashurnasirpal II (883–859 BC) finished his North-West Palace at *Nimrud, inviting 69,574 people and listing a great quantity and variety of foods and drinks, including wine and beer, recorded in a formal inscription. *Gardens were sometimes the setting for such events.

The Nimrud Wine Lists probably refer to triumphal banquets held after campaigns, at which tribute and booty were displayed in the presence of foreign envoys. Royal women, singers (see Songs), *dancers and *musicians attended. An Assyrian *sculpture shows *Ashurbanipal (668–c.627 BC) reclining in a garden, drinking with his *queen, surrounded by trophies and musicians; this is the earliest dated representation of a banquet with a reclining posture. A much earlier triumphal feast is shown on the Standard of *Ur, with banqueters seated upright in the traditional way, also accompanied by musicians.                                                    SMD

J.-M. DENTZER, *Le motif du banquet couché dans le Proche-Orient et le monde grec du VIIe au IVe siècle avant J.-C.* (Rome 1982).

J.J. GLASSNER, A. ÜNAL and P. CALMEYER, 'Mahlzeit', *Reallexikon der Assyriologie* 7 (Berlin/New York 1987–90) 259–71.

A.K. GRAYSON, *Assyrian Royal Inscriptions* 1 (Wiesbaden 1972) 172–6.

R. GYSELEN (ed.), *Banquets d'Orient* (Burre-sur-Yvette 1992).

F. PINNOCK, 'Considerations on the "Banquet Theme" in the Figurative Art of Mesopotamia and Syria', *Drinking in Ancient Societies: History and Culture of Drinking in the Ancient Near East*, ed. L. Milano (Padua 1994) 15–26.

**Beer**  Many types of beer, each with its own name, were brewed at least from the third millennium BC in *Mesopotamia, from where most of the evidence comes; the principal beverage in the *Levant appears to have been *wine, although beer is also mentioned in *Bronze Age texts from *Syria. Details of brewing techniques are known from texts, particularly a *Sumerian *hymn to Ninkasi, 'The Lady Who Fills the Mouth', the patron goddess of beer. Being hard to keep, beer was probably made daily. Malted *bread made from barley or emmer wheat, and flavoured with herbs, spices, dates and honey, was mixed with hulled grains, warmed and then cooled. Fermentation was assisted by the addition of honey or dates. The mash was mixed with *water and filtered. The cheapest beer was diluted with water, and an alcoholic drink made from fermented date palm juice was also called beer. The *Hittites drank 'beer-wine' and 'beer-

On the 'Royal Standard' from Ur a king and his courtiers drink to celebrate a victory. Shell inlay on lapis lazuli. Early Dynastic III period, c.2500 BC. WA 121201.

Ashurbanipal (668–c.627 BC) drinks with his queen in an arbour, cooled by fans and entertained by musicians; the head of an Elamite enemy hangs in a tree. Relief carving from the North Palace at Nineveh. WA 124920.

Impression of a cylinder seal from Ur showing figures drinking beer from a jar through long straws. Height 4.4 cm. Early Dynastic IIIa, c.2500 BC. WA 121545.

honey', which was either mead or regular beer made from barley and sweetened with honey. Some of the vessels used in brewing form the basis of a Sumerian drinking *song.

Drinking beer was one of the blessings of civilization, according to the *Epic of *Gilgamesh. *Gods are mentioned as drinking beer to feel happy, and beer was included in the food offerings in Mesopotamian *temples. Brewers are listed as personnel of temple and *palace households. Beer was among the products delivered to *Assyria as tribute from conquered lands. At the inauguration of his new capital of *Nimrud, *Ashurnasirpal II supplied his 69,574 guests with 10,000 jars of beer and 100 containers of fine mixed beer.

Beer was regarded as so important that during part of its production it was protected by guard dogs. It is nutritious and was an important part of the diet, and *Babylonian lists record that a man could receive between one and four litres of beer as part of his daily ration. Texts from *Mari reveal that beer was drunk warm (while wine was chilled). Spouted jars and bowls thought to have been for beer are known from the *Uruk period; the *cuneiform sign for 'beer' is a tall jar, sometimes with a spout. Vessels with sieves from *Gordion may have been for beer, which the *Phrygians were known for drinking. Communal drinking of beer from one vessel through straws made of reeds or metal, long enough to reach beneath the froth, is depicted on Sumerian *cylinder seals. Beer was also used in *medical prescriptions, often mixed with other substances to make them palatable, and in *Hittite and Babylonian cult ceremonies.          PB

M. CIVIL, 'A Hymn to the Beer Goddess and a Drinking Song', *Studies Presented to A. Leo Oppenheim*, eds R.D. Biggs and J.A. Brinkman (Chicago 1964) 67–89.

L. MILANO (ed.), *Drinking in Ancient Societies: History and Culture of Drinking in the Ancient Near East* (Padua 1994).

A.L. OPPENHEIM and L.F. HARTMAN, *On Beer and Brewing Techniques in Ancient Mesopotamia* (Baltimore, MD 1950).

J.M. RENFREW, 'Vegetables in the Ancient Near Eastern Diet', *Civilizations of the Ancient Near East*, ed. J.M. Sasson (New York 1995) 191–202.

W. RÖLLIG, *Das Bier im Alten Mesopotamien* (Berlin 1970).

**Beer Sheba** The major southern *Israelite town in the *Old Testament, Beer Sheba is normally identified with Tell es-Saba', but occasionally with nearby Bir es-Saba' which has *Iron Age and *Roman–Byzantine remains. Beer Sheba/Tell es-Saba', whose summit covers one hectare, lies in the northern *Negev in a valley of freshwater springs and rich soil. It was excavated by Yohanan Aharoni (1969–75) and Ze'ev Herzog (1976).

Nearby are *Chalcolithic settlements consisting of subterranean dwellings, similar to *Shiqmim, and some *pottery from this period has been found on the mound. It was not re-occupied until the beginning of the Iron Age. The nine Iron Age strata show the development of the *town from caves and pits into a major *fortified *administrative centre. The Iron II *city was built and destroyed four times, although there are still chronological uncertainties.

The development culminated in the Iron II period in an oval city surrounded by a casemate wall, one of the best preserved plans of an Israelite city, of which approximately two-thirds has been excavated. All the streets converge on a town square just inside the gate, which was probably a meeting place and *market. The streets have drainage channels below them, and are flanked by buildings, mostly four-room houses. Near the gate are administrative buildings and storehouses. Some of the *stones used in the storehouses appear to come from a dismantled horned *altar, which has stimulated a lively debate about the original location of the *temple. There is also debate about the date of the destruction of this city, which is put anywhere between 701 (*Sennacherib) and 586 BC (*Nebuchadnezzar). The site was resettled after the destruction, still within the Iron Age, but apparently no longer as an administrative centre. After a gap, Beer Sheba was occupied from the *Persian until the Roman periods, and finally as a way station in the eighth to ninth centuries AD.          PB

Y. AHARONI (ed.), *Beer-sheba* 1 (Tel Aviv 1973).
Z. HERZOG, *Beer-sheba* 2 (Tel Aviv 1984).

Sketch plan of Beer Sheba c.700 BC.

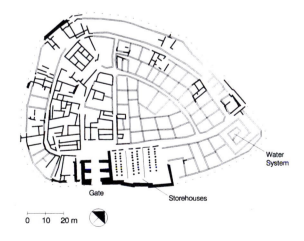

Water System

Gate          Storehouses

0   10   20 m

Z. HERZOG et al., 'Beersheba', *The New Encyclopedia of Archaeological Excavations in the Holy Land*, ed. E. Stern (Jerusalem 1993) 161–73.

**Beidha** Beidha, in the southern Jordanian highlands near Petra, was one of the earliest extensively excavated *Neolithic sites. The main excavations were conducted by Diana Kirkbride in the 1960s. The site is small, covering less than one hectare. There is enough rainfall in this area today for dry farming; springs and a major wadi attest to the presence of significant quantities of the key resource – *water. At the same time the site is close to areas of dry steppe where today, and in the past, *agriculture would have been a more risky venture.

A *Natufian occupation was located on the site and represents a relatively short-term settlement without substantial structures and with a chipped stone assemblage that suggests a contrast in the nature of activities compared to the classic Natufian '*village' settlements of the moister areas such as Ain Mallaha.

Three broad periods of occupation identified by Kirkbride as belonging to the later aceramic Neolithic (Pre-Pottery Neolithic B) were exposed over a broad area on the site. The earliest of these broad exposures revealed circular and sub-circular structures. *Wooden posts ringed or were built into the walls to support the superstructures. The evidence of these constructions, investment in site facilities and subsistence evidence points to a relatively sedentary component to the community at Beidha at this time. On the other hand these circular structures contrast with contemporary structures of other sedentary communities at sites like *Ain Ghazal and *Jericho and might be seen as relating to the curvilinear structures of more mobile communities in more arid areas in the *Negev, *Sinai, and eastern Jordan. Perhaps here we have evidence of a mobile community undergoing sedentarization.

The second broad phase of occupation, less clearly documented, consists of more typical Pre-Pottery Neolithic B rectilinear architecture. The third phase consists of relatively standardized buildings that contrast with those of the earlier phases. These 'corridor' buildings had basements sunk into the ground with a room above. Little evidence for the room survives but the basements were divided into six compartments, three along each side of a corridor. Manufacturing debris and toolkits suggest that these basements were used for storage and possibly craft activities.

*Radiocarbon dates suggest that the two earliest of these broad phases belong to the Middle Pre-Pottery Neolithic B (c.8000-7500 BC). Only three dates come from the corridor building phase and these may be on residual material. Differences in the lithics (stone tools) between earlier and later phases hint that the corridor buildings may date to the later Pre-Pottery Neolithic B or beginning of the seventh millennium BC as at Ain Ghazal.

Two buildings point to intriguing features of social organization in even a small aceramic Neolithic community. In the corridor buildings phase is a large structure contrasting with its corridor building neighbours. In this building an L-shaped corridor or room flanks a very large rectangular room (9 by 7 m). A red painted line borders the large room. A large *stone basin is found in one corner of the room. The lack of similarity with contemporary domestic structures and lack of fixtures do not suggest a straightforward domestic structure. It is probable that we must see this building not as the dwelling of some distinguished *family but rather as a special-purpose building dedicated to community functions (its large size suggests it may be a meeting room), *religious or secular, or quite plausibly a combination of both. Approximately 50 m from the main area of settlement is an oval structure joined by a path to the main area of the site. This building is unique because of its oval floor plan, since in one phase of its life it was paved with exotic and dramatically coloured stones and in its centre was set a large upright stone. The potential symbolic significance of such fixtures is clear even if a precise interpretation eludes us. Again we may see here evidence for a community structure serving a symbolic and possibly religious role.

The evidence for *food acquisition is interesting. Wheat and barley were probably cultivated, terebinth and other nuts and *plants collected. Goat and ibex played a role in the diet, but different views exist as to whether the goat was herded or hunted.                                    DB

B. BYRD, *The Natufian Encampment at Beidha: Late Pleistocene Adaptation in the Southern Levant* (Aarhus 1989).

D. KIRKBRIDE, 'Beidha: Early Neolithic Village Life South of the Dead Sea', *Antiquity* 42 (1968) 263–74.

**Beit Mirsim, (Tell)** *Albright's excavations (1926–32) at this 3-ha site in the hill country of *Palestine made it the type site for Palestinian *pottery and chronology for over half a century. More recent work has amended some of Albright's conclusions. He identified the site with *biblical Debir, but that is now proposed as Khirbet Rabûd, and the ancient name of Tell Beit Mirsim is unknown.

The earliest occupation dating to Early Bronze II–IV is poorly preserved, but the Middle Bronze Age town was fortified, with a well laid out plan including several large *houses which have been called 'patrician villas'. After a destruction and a gap in occupation, the Late Bronze II town included a large building with a collapsed roof, numerous grain pits between the houses, and imported Mycenaean and Cypriot pottery. After another destruction, probably c.1150 BC, remains of large grain pits and some houses represent a typical *Iron Age *Israelite site, *fortified by a casemate city wall in the final phase and perhaps destroyed by the *Egyptian Pharaoh Shoshenq I (Shishak) in c.924 BC. The final Iron Age stratum has a large *town plan with many 'four-room' *houses, a casemate wall with *gate, another gate and tower structure resembling a *bīt hilāni, and buildings with pierced stone drums possibly for pressing olives (not dye-vats as the excavator thought). Albright dated the destruction of the final Iron Age town to the *Babylonian conquest of 587 BC, but it is now attributed to *Sennacherib in 701 BC.

There is some evidence for slight re-occupation in the seventh or early sixth century BC.

The site's *cemetery was discovered and thirty tombs dating between Early Bronze IV and Iron II were excavated in 1978–82 by D. Alon and E. Braun. PB

W.F. ALBRIGHT, *The Excavation of Tell Beit Mirsim I: The Pottery of the First Three Campaigns* (New Haven, CN 1932).

——, *The Excavation of Tell Beit Mirsim IA: The Bronze Age Pottery of the Fourth Campaign* (New Haven, CN 1933).

——, *The Excavation of Tell Beit Mirsim II: The Bronze Age* (New Haven, CN 1938).

——, *The Excavation of Tell Beit Mirsim III: The Iron Age* (New Haven, CN 1943).

W.F. ALBRIGHT and R. GREENBERG, 'Beit Mirsim, Tell', *The New Encyclopedia of Archaeological Excavations in the Holy Land*, ed. E. Stern (Jerusalem 1993) 177–80.

W.G. DEVER, 'Beit Mirsim, Tell', *Anchor Bible Dictionary* 1, ed. D.N. Freedman (New York 1992) 648–9.

**Berossus** A scholar/*priest living in *Babylon in the third century BC, Berossus wrote a three-volume history of *Babylonia in *Greek called the *Babyloniaca*. Only parts of it have survived, quoted by later historians such as Eusebius in the fourth century AD.

Berossus' sources included the *Sumerian *King List, the Babylonian *Chronicle and other ancient works. His first book contained a geography of Babylonia and described the creation; the second recounted the *Flood and the *dynasties which ruled before and after down to Nabonassar; the third dealt with the period from *Assyrian rule probably to Alexander the Great's conquest. Some material under Berossus' name concerns *astronomy and astrology – more Greek than Babylonian – and it is still disputed whether this was authentically written by Berossus, or by someone else later but attributed to him.

Berossus presented his history to the Seleucid King Antiochus I, who was rebuilding Babylonian *temples, perhaps in gratitude and to demonstrate the long human and religious legacy of his land. It appears that the *Babyloniaca* was read for at least two hundred years, and from the first century BC in summary form as part of a compilation on eastern history by the Greek Alexander Polyhistor, which has also not survived. PB

S.M. BURSTEIN, *The Babyloniaca of Berossus* (Malibu, CA 1978).

A. KUHRT, 'Berossus' *Babyloniaka* and Seleucid Rule in Babylonia', *Hellenism in the East: The Interaction of Greek and Non-Greek Civilizations from Syria to Central Asia after Alexander*, eds A. Kuhrt and S. Sherwin-White (London 1987) 32–56.

——, 'Ancient Mesopotamia in Classical Greek and Hellenistic Thought', *Civilizations of the Ancient Near East*, ed. J.M. Sasson (New York 1995) 62–3.

**Beth Shan** Tel Beth Shan (also spelled Beth-Shean, Arabic Tell el-Husn) is an imposing mound that sits at the intersection of the north–south Jordan Valley road and a route that crosses the Jordan river, between the Jezreel Valley and *Transjordan. This mound covers c.4 ha, but is surrounded by a much larger settlement from the *Hellenistic and later periods, when the site was known as Scythopolis and, still later, as Beisan. Extensive excavations on Tel Beth Shan have revealed evidence from *Neolithic to medieval times.

Beth Shan has been excavated by C.S. Fisher, A. Rowe and G.M. FitzGerald (1921–33) and Y. Yadin and A. Mazar (1989–95). Remains from the Neolithic, *Chalcolithic and Early *Bronze Age formed a deep layer on the mound. The small settlement remained unfortified during the Middle Bronze Age. During the Late Bronze Age Beth Shan was an important city in the *Egyptian administrative system of *Canaan (sixteenth to twelfth centuries BC). Its name appears in numerous sources from Egypt, including accounts of military campaigns and one *Amarna Letter. In 1993, excavators discovered a small clay cylinder in one of the site's excavation dumps; it contained an *Akkadian *letter written by Tagi, governor of a *town near the Carmel range, to Lab'aya of Shechem, one of the best-known characters in the Amarna correspondence. A series of five successive *temples, from Late Bronze I to Iron I, was also unearthed on the summit; this sacred area has a unique plan associated with Egyptian and Canaanite artefacts. Finds from this era include basalt stelae of Seti I and Ramesses II, and the Late Bronze to Iron I transition also yielded remains of over fifty anthropoid *coffins, often identified as the burial containers for *Sea People mercenaries serving with the Egyptian army.

Towards the end of twelfth century BC, the Egyptian administrative control at Beth Shan came to an end; it is unclear whether the Sea Peoples played any part in this transition, since their characteristic *pottery has not been found here. The *Bible reports the failure of the Hebrews to dislodge the Canaanites from Beth Shan, and later the demise of Saul and his sons – at the hands of the *Philistines – and the display of Saul's body on the wall of Beth Shan. Two temples from upper stratum VI (eleventh century BC) have been linked with the two temples at Beth Shan mentioned in the *Bible; these temples contained a rich assemblage of cultic vessels. A destruction layer from the end of the tenth century BC probably dates to the Pharaoh Shishak's invasion of c.924 BC, and later Iron II occupation (reflected in complicated stratigraphy) came to an end with the *Assyrian conquest in 732 BC. Significant occupation at Beth Shan did not resume until the Hellenistic period. GLM

F.W. JAMES, *The Iron Age at Beth Shan: A Study of Levels VI–IV* (Philadelphia, PA 1966).

F.W. JAMES and P.E. McGOVERN, *The Late Bronze II Egyptian Garrison at Beth Shan: A Study of Levels VII and VIII* (Philadelphia, PA 1986).

A. MAZAR, 'The Excavations at Tel Beth Shean during the Years 1989–94', *The Archaeology of Israel: Constructing the Past, Interpreting the Present*, eds N. A. Silberman and D. Small (Sheffield 1997) 144–64.

——, 'Four Thousand Years of History at Tel Beth-Shean: An Account of the Renewed Excavations', *Biblical Archaeologist* 60 (1997) 62–76.

E. OREN, *The Northern Cemetery at Beth Shan* (Leiden 1973).

Y. YADIN and S. GEVA, *Investigations at Beth Shean: The Early Iron Age Strata* (Jerusalem 1986).

**Beycesultan** Beycesultan is the modern name of one of the largest mounds in western Turkey, on a former course of the Meander river c.5 km south of Çivril in Denizli province. It was excavated by *Lloyd (1954–9) in the expectation that it was a major *city in the *Bronze Age kingdom of Arzawa. The double mound measures some 600 by 400 m. Forty building levels were recognized in 40 m of occupation deposits spanning the late *Chalcolithic to the end of the Late Bronze Age, with some Byzantine levels on the flat-topped southern area. Levels XL–XX are Late Chalcolithic, XIX–XVII Early Bronze Age I, XVI–XIII Early Bronze Age II, XII–VI Early Bronze Age III, V–III Middle Bronze Age, II–I Late Bronze Age.

The Chalcolithic, with twenty-one building levels forming a mound some 11 m in height, was only reached in a deep sounding. Rectangular mudbrick buildings with benches and hearths were precursors of later structures. The Early Bronze I settlement yielded what were thought by the excavators to be pairs of shrines, central hearths, horns of consecration and remains of offerings. More recent opinion favours interpretation of these structures as *houses. Early Bronze II sees the first introduction of wheel-made *pottery alongside the local hand-made tradition. There is strong continuity through the Late Chalcolithic to the end of the Early Bronze Age.

Beycesultan reached its apogee in the early Middle Bronze Age when level V yielded a great burnt *palace. The two-storeyed timber and mudbrick architecture, skilfully excavated by Lloyd, bore traces of painted murals on the fallen upper walls. The construction techniques, the materials and the general concept of the plan resemble contemporaneous central *Anatolian construction techniques at Kültepe and Acem Höyük, and the later *Hittite palace at Mashat Höyük. Some have also seen parallels with Minoan Crete. Also excavated in level V were a *temple and a portion of the city defences. The palace was presumably the seat of a provincial ruler in Arzawa, but no inscriptions were found. In level IV, following the fire, there was a long sequence of *village dwellings.

On the eastern summit was a major Late Bronze Age complex which, according to Mellaart, was also a palace.

GDS

S. LLOYD, *Beycesultan* 3.1 (London 1972).

S. LLOYD and J. MELLAART, *Beycesultan* 1 (London 1962).

——, *Beycesultan* 2 (London 1965).

J. MELLAART, 'Beycesultan', *Ancient Anatolia,* ed. R. Matthews (London 1998) 61–8.

J. MELLAART and A. MURRAY, *Beycesultan* 3.2 (London 1995).

K. WERNER, *The Megaron during the Aegean and Anatolian Bronze Age* (Jonsered 1993).

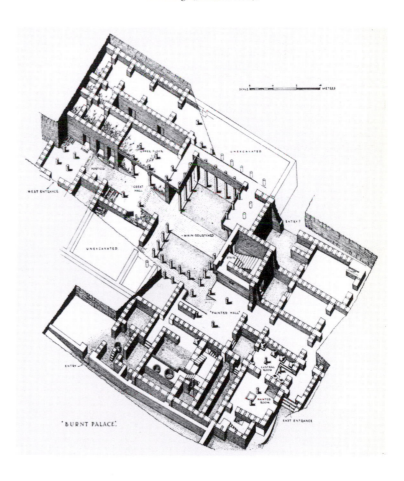

Perspective reconstruction by Seton Lloyd of the level V burnt palace at Beycesultan (from S. Lloyd and J. Mellaart, *Beycesultan* 2 (London 1965) fig. A13, courtesy of the British Institute of Archaeology at Ankara).

**Beydar, (Tell)** A European and Syrian expedition excavating at Tell Beydar on a tributary of the *Khabur in 1993–4 found 147 *cuneiform tablets of the late Early Dynastic III period. Although they are the only documents from the Khabur region contemporary with the *Ebla tablets, they follow *Mari and *Babylonian *scribal practices more closely, with local variations. The *language is *Akkadian and most of the personal names are *Semitic. The texts deal with *administrative affairs, workers from different '*gates' of the *town and from villages, distribution of *animal products, repair of carts, etc. Most of the tablets lay in a *house, two in a large official building in which were many broken sealings (see Seals), and four in a *palace on the top of the *tell. Further excavations show that the site was a regional centre, apparently part of the kingdom of Nagar (see Brak, (Tell)). ARM

F. ISMAIL et al., *Administrative Documents from Tell Beydar*, Subartu 2 (Turnhout 1996).

M. LEBEAU and A. SULEIMAN, *Tell Baydar: Three Seasons of Excavations (1992–1994). A Preliminary Report*, Subartu 3 (Turnhout 1997).

**Bi'a, (Tell)** Ancient Tuttul, modern Tell Bi'a, stood at the important crossroads at the confluence of the *Balikh and the Euphrates. There *Sargon of *Akkad reported he worshipped the local *god, *Dagan. German excavators in the 1990s uncovered occupation of the third millennium BC, including royal *tombs and a *palace of Early Dynastic III date, some finds showing similarities to contemporary *Ebla. An extensive later palace contained *cuneiform tablets from the reign of *Shamshi-Adad I, mostly *administrative, but including three *letters, *mathematical calculations and a piece of *Hurrian *magic. In two areas of that palace lay scores of skeletons, not formally buried, the result of either an epidemic or an enemy attack. ARM

K. KOHLMEYER and E. STROMMENGER, 'Die Ausgrabungen in Tall Bi'a 1994 und 1995', *Mitteilungen der Deutschen Orient-Gesellschaft* 127 (1995) 43–55.

M. KREBERNIK, 'Schriftkunde aus Tall Bi'a', *Mitteilungen der Deutschen Orient-Gesellschaft* 123 (1991) 41–70 and 125 (1993) 51–60.

——, 'Tall Bi'a 1993: Die Schriftfunde', *Mitteilungen der Deutschen Orient-Gesellschaft* 126 (1994) 33–6.

E. STROMMENGER, 'Die archäologischen Forschungen in Tall Bi'a 1980', *Mitteilungen der Deutschen Orient-Gesellschaft* 113 (1981) 23–34.

——, 'Die Ausgrabungen in Tall Bi'a 1990', *Mitteilungen der Deutschen Orient-Gesellschaft* 123 (1991) 7–34.

——, 'Die Ausgrabungen in Tall Bi'a 1993', *Mitteilungen der Deutschen Orient-Gesellschaft* 126 (1994) 11–31.

**Bible** The twenty-two books of the *Hebrew Bible are the only ancient Near Eastern writings which have a continuous history to the present day. The content of the collection ('canon') was fixed by the first century AD in Judaea. From the third century BC onwards the books were translated into Greek (the Septuagint), and, when the Christians adopted that version, they included other writings now known as the Apocryphal or Deutero-canonical books. Christian writings of the first century AD in Greek were assembled as a second collection in due course, known as the New Testament, the Hebrew books being the Old Testament.

The Hebrew books are divided into three sections, the Law, the Prophets and the Writings. The five books of the Law (Torah) contain the accounts of the *creation of the world, the *Flood and the Patriarchs Abraham, Isaac, Jacob and Joseph, *Israel's ancestors, and the escape of their descendants from Egypt (the Exodus), led by Moses, to occupy the land of *Canaan. The laws, Israel's constitution, occupy much of the Torah. The Prophets fall into two parts. The Former Prophets continue the history of Israel from the conquest of Canaan under Joshua through the turbulent times of the Judges to the Monarchy. From the glory of David and Solomon the national decline is traced until the Exile to *Babylon and the return. The Latter Prophets present the *oracles of Isaiah, Jeremiah and others, mostly directed against Israel and Judah, many in majestic *poetry. The Writings opens with the Psalms (the *hymn-book of Israel), followed by *wisdom literature (a love *song), Ruth (a romance), and laments and narratives from post-exilic times.

The Dead Sea Scrolls preserve the oldest manuscripts, all except one (Isaiah) incomplete, copied from the second century BC to AD 67, so the earlier history of the books is conjectural. Internal examination led nineteenth-century scholars to distinguish periods of composition and sources on the basis of lexical differences, supposed inconsistencies and hypothetical religious developments. Although these views are widely taught, increased knowledge of ancient culture, especially *scribal habits, makes them highly dubious. From the first century AD the text was preserved with little variation down to the Middle Ages (Massoretic Text) and the invention of printing. ARM

B.M. METZGER and M.D. COOGAN (eds), *The Oxford Companion to the Bible* (Oxford 1993).

**Birds** Birds appear frequently in ancient Near Eastern *art, for example on *cylinder seals of all periods and on *Kassite *kudurrus, usually as symbols of *gods (see Divine symbols), but little is known of how they were exploited in antiquity. This is largely due to the fragility of their skeletons, which do not survive *food preparation, consumption and burial as well as those of other animals, and so their remains are not so often recovered by *archaeology. Among the birds known from excavations are the chukar, mallard, white stork and quail. Ostriches were hunted and ostrich eggs were occasionally used as containers. *Wooden and *ivory boxes are known in the shape of ducks or geese, especially from the Late Bronze Age *Levant, though the birds themselves were kept from at least the third millennium BC. Chickens, attested from the thirteenth century BC, became common in the Near East only in the late *Persian and *Hellenistic periods (see Animal husbandry; Food).

Birds were an important component of *Hittite *magic. A bird observer or enchanter carried out rituals against 'evil' birds, observed signs given by birds, and was responsible for the capture and breeding of birds used for *rituals and *divination. The flights of at least twenty-six different types of birds were also interpreted for the purpose of *oracles, though only the eagle and rock partridge have been positively identified. The birds' movements and other behaviour were noted as giving particular signs which established a result.

Exotic birds formed part of the tribute offered to the *Assyrians, e.g. 'flying birds whose wings are dyed blue purple'.                                                                              PB

A. ARCHI, 'L'ornitomanzia ittita', *Studi Micenei ed Egeo-Anatolici* 16 (1975) 119–80.

A.S. GILBERT, 'The Flora and Fauna of the Ancient Near East', *Civilizations of the Ancient Near East*, ed. J.M. Sasson (New York 1995) 153–74.

A. SALONEN, *Vögel und Vogelfang im alten Mesopotamien* (Helsinki 1973).

**Bīt hilāni** When *Sargon II built a new *palace at *Khorsabad, he copied elements used in north *Syrian architecture. His texts specifically refer to 'a portico patterned after a *Hittite palace, which they call a *bīt hilāni* in the *Amorite tongue'. Here, 'Hittite' referred to the population of north Syria, and the term *bīt hilāni* was probably the name just for a portico built in front of the palace gates, although exactly what architectural features were considered to comprise a *bīt hilāni* remains unclear: other references to the *bīt hilāni* are found in inscriptions of *Tiglath-pileser III and *Sennacherib. The *Assyrians did not use the complete plan of the north Syrian buildings, only the portico, but this is a constituent part of a typical building type found in north Syria in the first millennium BC, and the term *bīt hilāni* is normally now applied to this whole building. It consisted of a portico with one to three columns (often in the shape of human figures on animal bases, which are specifically mentioned by Sennacherib) giving access to a broad room, probably the throne room, with rooms or stairs to one side of the portico. It is found at *Zinjirli, *Carchemish and Tell *Halaf, but elements of it are present already in the eighteenth- and fifteenth-century BC palaces at *Alalakh.                                                                              PB

H. FRANKFORT, 'The Origin of the bît-hilani', *Iraq* 14 (1952) 120–31.

——, *The Art and Architecture of the Ancient Orient* (Harmondsworth 1969) 167–75.

R. NAUMANN, *Architektur Kleinasiens von ihren Anfängen bis zum Ende der Hethitischen Zeit* (Tübingen 1955) 360–78.

J. RENGER and B. HROUDA, 'Hilani, bit', *Reallexikon der Assyriologie* 5 (Berlin/New York 1972–5) 405–9.

H. WEIDHAUS, 'Der bit-hilani', *Zeitschrift für Assyriologie* 45 (1939) 108–68.

I. WINTER, 'Art as Evidence for Interaction: Relations between the Assyrian Empire and North Syria', *Mesopotamien und seine Nachbarn*, eds H.J. Nissen and J. Renger (Berlin 1982) 355–82.

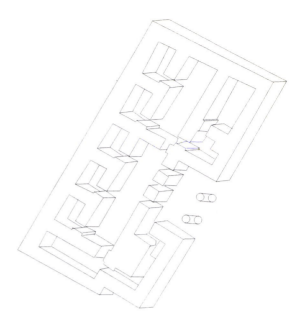

Typical plan of a *bīt hilāni*.

The entrance to the Aleppo Museum is a reconstruction of the portico of the *bīt hilāni* at Tell Halaf (courtesy of Alan Millard).

**Boats and ships** In the ancient Near East, boats and ships can be divided into those used on the major *rivers and canals of *Mesopotamia, and seagoing ships used in the Mediterranean and Persian Gulf.

River and canal traffic was important for commerce and warfare in Mesopotamia, and texts from the *Ur III period refer to 600 transport vessels carrying grain, and a fleet of 240 enemy ships attacking *Kish. Many types of river craft used on the Tigris and Euphrates rivers in ancient times, known from models and depictions, have continued to the present day: inflated animal skins either for people or in large numbers to form a raft for heavy cargoes; round baskets of wicker covered with hides; and boats, especially for the marshes, made of reed bundles tied together. *Sumerian documents also refer to plank-built boats, in which the vessel shell was probably constructed first without any interior framework. Sailboats were not common and there is little evidence for their use on the Tigris and Euphrates. Boats were sometimes

A relief found in Sennacherib's palace at Nineveh illustrates Phoenician warships with curved prows and sharp rams and ships for trade and transport. The drawing was made when the reliefs were found, in bad condition. Or. Dr. IV,7, detail.

towed: large *wooden barges are depicted being towed in *Assyrian reliefs. Barges and boats also served as pontoons for floating bridges. *Laws governed waterborne traffic, including rights of way, salvage, boat hire rate and pay scales for crews.

Mesopotamian texts record ships *trading with distant lands, or attacking them by sea, from the third millennium BC on, and *Egyptian reliefs record *Syrians as crewmen on the *Byblos route, but the best evidence for seagoing ships are the Late Bronze Age shipwrecks at *Gelidonya and *Ulu Burun. Contemporary texts and depictions supplement this evidence: the *king of *Ugarit was asked to outfit 150 ships; and Egyptian tomb paintings illustrate *Canaanite *merchant ships with single masts, with yards and booms, the earliest evidence for a crow's nest, and wicker fencing along the sides, perhaps to keep the spray off the deck. The slightly later ships of the *Sea Peoples are shown on Egyptian temple reliefs as double-ended vessels with birds' heads on their bows and sterns.

*Phoenician ships are known mainly from *Assyrian reliefs, and indeed the Assyrians used them in their military campaigns. Several types are known: double-ended vessels with high stem and sometimes stern shaped like a *horse's head, using between two and five standing rowers; warships with a ram protruding from the bow, with rowers protected inside the hull; and double-banked warships with rams, adopted from Greece, and a row of shields on either side of the hull. The Phoenicians became the most renowned sailors of the ancient world, and *Herodotus records, sceptically, that they circumnavigated Africa about 600 BC. (See Navigation.)    PB

G.F. BASS, 'Sea and River Craft in the Ancient Near East', *Civilizations of the Ancient Near East*, ed. J.M. Sasson (New York 1995) 1421–31.

L. CASSON, *Ships and Seamanship in the Ancient World*, rev. ed. (London/Baltimore 1995).

M.-C. DE GRAEVE, *The Ships of the Ancient Near East (c.2000–500 B.C.)* (Louvain 1981).

S. WACHSMANN, *Seagoing Ships in the Bronze Age Levant* (London 1998).

**Boghazköy**  Boghazköy is the modern Turkish village adjacent to Hattusas, the *Hittite capital, in north-central *Anatolia. First recorded by Texier in 1834, and excavated by the German Archaeological Institute since 1907, it is now a National Park and UNESCO World Heritage site. At its greatest extent the *city covered some 2 sq km.

It was a *Hattian city in the early second millennium BC, with an *Assyrian *merchant colony. Destroyed and cursed by King Anitta of Kussara, it was refounded by *Hattusilis I as the first capital of the Hittite Old Kingdom. Although strongly fortified, the city fell to the northern Kaska peoples on several occasions and was briefly abandoned when King Muwatalis moved the capital to Tarhuntassa. Hattusas reached its greatest extent in the thirteenth century BC, when the addition of the ceremonial upper or southern city doubled its size. About the same time the extramural rock shrine at Yazýlýkaya was completed. Finally, the Hittite city was destroyed in widespread events that ended the *Bronze Age in the eastern Mediterranean about 1180 BC. Evidence for village occupation in the Dark Age (early Iron Age, c.1200–900 BC) on the Büyük Kaya has emerged since 1993. The strongly defended middle and late Iron Age settlement was restricted in size.

The older city comprises *palaces on Büyük Kale and the lower city, with the Great *Temple (Temple 1) dedi-

Relief at Yazýlýkaya of King Tudhaliyas IV (c.1250–1220 BC) being embraced by the god Sharruma (courtesy of Dominique Collon).

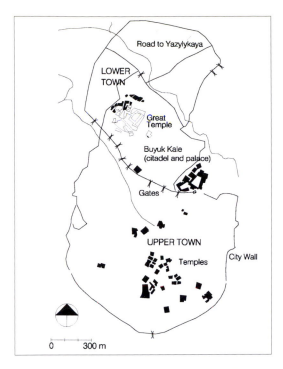

Diagrammatic plan of Boghazköy during the Hittite New Kingdom.

**Bone** Archaeologists give much attention to the collection of human skeletal remains and to animal bones. The former provide numerous insights into population statistics, diet and health of ancient peoples, while the latter offer unique information on *animal husbandry and diet. Because *animal bones are among the most ubiquitous and inexpensive raw materials, it comes as no surprise that artefacts made out of bone appear in the archaeological record at an early date. Strangely enough, archaeologists have not made many detailed studies of their use in antiquity. This is probably because bone is rarely mentioned in ancient written sources, and most attention has been given to more expensive, exotic materials, especially *ivory.

Boneworking was a well established craft in many parts of the Near East by the Late *Palaeolithic period, and a standard repertoire of bone objects was known

Carved bone handle from Tell Abu al-Kharaz in Jordan, decorated with two sphinxes. Height 12.5 cm. c.800 BC (courtesy of Peter Fischer, drawing by Richard Holmgren).

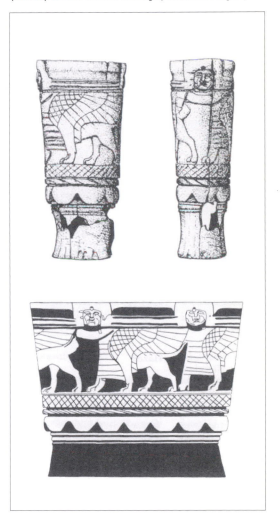

cated to the *weather-god of Hatti and the sun-goddess of Arinna. Extensions northwards encompassed the Büyük Kaya with a processional route to Yazýlýkaya. The southern defences included several gates, decorated with lions, sphinxes and a warrior god, posterns and tunnels through the fortifications, a pair of stone-lined pools associated with two built chambers (one inscribed) and numerous temples.

Yazýlýkaya comprises two natural chambers bearing some of the finest Hittite relief *sculpture. Chamber A has the pantheon of the empire, processing in hierarchical order on opposing walls: male deities at left, female at right, converging on a central tableau where the Hurrian weather-god Teshup meets the Hurrian goddess Hepat. Behind the *goddess is Sharruma, the sun-god. The deities hold their names in Hurrian, but written in Luwian hieroglyphs. Behind the goddesses *Tudhaliyas IV strides over mountains and is identified by hieroglyphs. Chamber B originally had a larger than life statue of Tudhaliyas; reliefs include a sword-*god and the sun-god Sharruma escorting Tudhaliyas into the next world. Niches contained *cremated royal remains.          GDS

R.L. ALEXANDER, *The Sculpture and Sculptors of Yazýlýkaya* (Newark, NJ 1986).

K. BITTEL, *Hattusha: The Capital of the Hittites* (Oxford 1970).

P. NEVE, *Hattusa: Stadt der Götter und Tempel*, 2nd ed. (Mainz 1996).

J. SEEHER, 'The Early Iron Age Settlement on Büyükkaya, Bögazköy', *Thracians and Phrygians: Problems of Parallelism*, eds N. Tuna, Z. Aktüre and M. Lynch (Ankara 1998) 71–8.

when *village life emerged in *Mesopotamia (e.g. awls, blades, scrapers). Bone was the most commonly used material that was fashioned into artefacts; most worked bone was from mammals. Once the basic techniques for working bone had been developed, they were used over the course of thousands of years. By c.3000 BC, *metal began to replace bone as the raw material for certain *tools and implements, and metal tools replaced *stone as the principal means by which the bone was worked. These tools were similar to those used for cutting, shaping and finishing wood. According to the *Bible, Samson used the 'fresh jawbone of an ass' as a weapon without benefit of any craftsmanship!

Bone was used to manufacture simple tools and more elaborate decorative objects. By c.10,000 BC, inhabitants of Zawi Chemi in the *Zagros mountains possessed a basic 'toolkit' of bone. In the *Natufian period, by c.9000 BC, artisans carved animal shapes into bone sickle hafts. Bone was not used as widely in *Mesopotamia as it was in Turkey and the *Levant, where bone objects became standard from the *Neolithic period on down.

*Craftsmen added the lathe to their toolkit c.1500 BC, and bone was used to make decorations for *furniture and *wooden boxes, *jewellery, and hairpins. Decorated bone pins have been found at *Ashur and *Nippur and on numerous sites in *Palestine. From Middle Bronze II until the *Persian period, *Ashkelon became a centre of boneworking. At *Nuzi bone was cut into geometric shapes and used in inlays; bone pieces of various shapes were used in a similar way on wooden boxes found in *Jericho's Middle Bronze Age tombs.

Bone was used for the production of needles, gaming pieces (see Toys and games), whistles, spindle-whorls, spatulae, fishhooks, pegs and handles. At Tell Abu al-Kharaz, in north-western Jordan, archaeologists found a carved bone handle that was decorated with two sphinxes and a band with criss-cross lines. This piece, which dates to c.800 BC, is similar to a group of handles discovered in *Nimrud's Burnt *Palace and to one found at *Hazor. Since the handles from Nimrud are not carved in *Assyrian style, they were probably taken as loot and may have originated in a Palestinian production centre. GLM

P.M. FISCHER and G. HERRMANN, 'A Carved Bone Object from Tell Abu al-Kharaz in Jordan: A Palestinian Workshop for Bone and Ivory?', *Levant* 27 (1995) 145–63.

H.A. LIEBOWITZ, 'Bone, Ivory, and Shell: Artifacts of the Bronze and Iron Ages', *The Oxford Encyclopedia of Archaeology in the Near East* 1, ed. E.M. Meyers (New York 1997) 340–3.

P.R.S. MOOREY, *Ancient Mesopotamian Materials and Industries: The Archaeological Evidence* (Oxford 1994).

E.E. PLATT, 'Bone Pendants', *Biblical Archaeologist* 41 (1978) 23–8.

P. WAPNISH, 'Bone, Ivory, and Shell: Typology and Technology', *The Oxford Encyclopedia of Archaeology in the Near East* 1, ed. E.M. Meyers (New York 1997) 335–40.

**Books** The book with pages (codex) did not come into use until the first Christian centuries. However, already in the Early Dynastic III period *scribes were copying legends, *hymns, proverbs and other literary texts at

*Lagash, *Shuruppak, the modern Abu Salabikh and other sites. Slight hints imply that prayers or spells were copied earlier. Several of those *Sumerian 'books' continued to be copied over the next eight centuries, but few examples made between Early Dynastic III and the Old *Babylonian period survive. In Old Babylonian times Sumerian *literature was copied extensively, so that some works are known from dozens of manuscripts. At the same time, *Akkadian literature flourished and supplanted Sumerian to a large extent. Very long compositions were divided over several tablets, the last line of one becoming the first of the next (the 'catch-line'). For example, the Old Babylonian *Epic of Atrahasis (see Cosmogonies; Flood) occupied three large tablets, in the work of one pupil-scribe, each holding some four hundred lines in four columns on either face. Every tenth line was marked and the total in each column noted at its foot, with the overall total at the end. The scribe added the title of the work, its opening words, the number of the tablet, his name and the date, the whole forming the colophon, equivalent to a title-page. These practices helped accuracy in copying and noted responsibility; many of them continued into the last centuries BC and probably influenced Jewish scribes. Books were made as scribal exercises, for use in *rituals and some, probably, for reading aloud to entertain. Some were collected in *libraries. Authors were rarely named; some books were attributed to *gods or ancient rulers and there are a few cases where acrostics of the initial signs of lines read consecutively spell the names of the authors.

Where *cuneiform writing spread, similar books are found, especially in the second millennium BC in *Elam, in *Hurrian and *Hittite *towns and in the *Levant. At *Ugarit scribes copied local myths and legends in the cuneiform *alphabet on tablets set out in Babylonian style, occasionally with colophons. Wax-covered tablets could also make books. A high-class set of twelve *ivory leaves, with *gold hinges at alternate edges, was prepared for *Sargon II of *Assyria and recovered from a well

Three panels from a set of ivory writing-boards originally joined by hinges. Wax filling the panels was impressed with the cuneiform text of a series of omens. Made for Sargon II, c.710 BC, found with fragments of wooden writing-boards in a well at Nimrud. Height 33.8 cm. WA 131952.

at *Nimrud. Enough wax remained to reveal that the book had apparently contained over 7500 lines of an encyclopaedia of *omens. Simultaneously, no doubt, *Egyptian-trained scribes in the Levant wrote books on papyrus rolls and *Canaanites followed them, using their simple alphabet. As that alphabet replaced cuneiform, so books were written on perishable leather or papyrus rolls. The text painted on wall-plaster uncovered at Tell *Deir Alla represents a column of such a roll from the ninth century BC. The earliest *Semitic book rolls extant are the fragmentary *Aramaic papyri of the fifth century BC from Elephantine, near Aswan in Egypt, containing the texts of Darius I's 'Behistun inscription', the 'Wisdom of Ahiqar' and another very incomplete story.                                    ARM

A. MILLARD, 'Books in the Late Bronze Age in the Levant', *Israel Oriental Studies* 18: *Past Links: Studies in the Languages and Cultures of the Ancient Near East*, eds S. Izre'el, I. Singer and R. Zadok (Winona Lake, IN 1998) 171–81.

**Borders:** see Boundaries and frontiers

**Borsippa** The ruins of modern Birs Nimrud, southwest of *Babylon, were considered by early travellers to be the *Tower of Babel. *Rawlinson's discovery of foundation cylinders (see Foundation deposits) proved that its ancient name was Borsippa, although it was also occasionally known by other names. It was excavated by *Layard (1850), F. Fresnel (1852), Rawlinson (1854), *Rassam (1879–82), *Koldewey (1901–2), and an Austrian team (1980–).

Borsippa was renowned in antiquity as the cult centre of *Nabû, whose *temple precinct was called Ezida. The site was occupied from the late third millennium BC until the Islamic period. The plan of the *city can be schematically delineated. It was square in plan and approximately 1500 sq m in area, surrounded by city walls; eight named city *gates are known. The city was divided into four named quarters. In one corner was a *palace, but this possibly dates only from the *Persian period. There were several temples to different *gods, but at the centre was the Ezida precinct, surrounded by its own buttressed wall with eight named gates. The Ezida precinct is first mentioned in the prologue to *Hammurabi's code, although most of the evidence for rebuilding dates to the first millennium BC. The original date of the *ziggurat, within the precinct, is unclear, although it was at least renewed by *Nebuchadnezzar II whose cylinders were discovered in the foundations. The Processional Way of Nabû led from the Ezida precinct to the Lapis Lazuli Gate, the main exit leading to the road to Babylon.                         PB

W. ALLINGER-CSOLLICH, 'Birs Nimrud I: Die Baukörper der Ziqqurrat von Borsippa. Ein Vorbericht', *Baghdader Mitteilungen* 22 (1991) 383–499.
——, 'Birs Nimrud II: "Tieftempel" – "Hochtempel". Vergleichende Studien Borsippa-Babylon', *Baghdader Mitteilungen* 29 (1998) 95–330.
E. UNGER, 'Barsippa', *Reallexikon der Assyriologie* 1 (Berlin 1932) 402–29.

**Botta, Paul-Émile (or Paolo Emilio) (1802–70)** French doctor, traveller, writer, career diplomat, zoologist, archaeologist and *cuneiformist, Botta was the first European excavator in *Mesopotamia. His discovery in 1843 of *Sargon II's palace at *Khorsabad was the beginning of large-scale field *archaeology in the Near East.

Born in Turin, the son of Carlo Botta, the Piedmontese doctor and historian, Botta emigrated with his father to France, where they took citizenship in 1814. He studied medicine and travelled as ship's surgeon in 1826–9. After qualifying in 1830, he was military doctor to Muhammed Ali, Khedive of Egypt, seeing action in Libya and the Arabian Peninsula. In 1836–7 he explored the Yemen for the Musée d'Histoire Naturelle de Paris. Returning to France in 1838, he was in 1841 appointed Consular Agent in Mosul, then in the Ottoman province of Mesopotamia. This position had been created specially for Botta, and was linked to a secret project of Julius Mohl, Secretary of the Société Asiatique, for the rediscovery of *Nineveh.

Botta soon commenced excavations in the Kuyunjik mound of Nineveh, which, however, he found unproductive. Transferring to Khorsabad (then believed to be another part of Nineveh), he quickly discovered the remains of the *palace. The French Ministry of the Interior then financed further work, on a larger scale, and sent out Eugène Napoléon Flandin (1809–89) to draw the *sculptures. By the end of 1845, Botta had unearthed the greater part of the royal palace.

One shipment of antiquities, mostly *Assyrian reliefs, was lost at sea, but another formed the beginnings of the Musée des Antiquités Orientales at the Louvre, the first museum of Near Eastern antiquities in the world, inaugurated by King Louis-Philippe on 1 May 1847. The state-financed *Monuments de Ninive* appeared in 1849–50, five lavishly produced folio volumes, one of Botta's text and four of drawings by Flandin.

Thereafter Botta, while still finding time for cuneiform studies, continued his diplomatic career, holding senior posts in Jerusalem, Baghdad and Tripoli, before returning to France in 1869. He died at Achères. Botta's successor as Consular Agent in Mosul, *Place, completed the excavation of the palace at Khorsabad, and made a plan of the *city.                                    AG

G. BERGAMINI, 'Paolo Emilio Botta e la scoperta della civiltà assira', *Bollettino della Società Piemontese di Archeologia e Belle Arti* 38–41 (1984–7) 5–16.
P.-É. BOTTA, with E.N. Flandin, *Monuments de Ninive*, 5 vols (Paris 1849–50).
E.C. KNOWLTON, 'Paul-Émile Botta, Visitor to Hawaii in 1828', *Hawaiian Journal of History* 18 (1984) 13–37.
J. VIAU, *Botta et la découverte de Ninive* (Paris 1914).

**Boundaries and frontiers** Each *village, town and state in the ancient Near East had an area which it claimed as its own and which in principle belonged to the local *god. Often the boundaries of these areas were marked in some way, for example by stelae or sometimes by dikes or canals, and crossing of them by outsiders frequently led to conflict.

The best description of national frontiers and the conflicts that arose from them results from the long-standing border dispute between *Lagash and Umma in the Early Dynastic period, documented in detail in the records of Lagash. Originally, Ningirsu and Shara, the gods of Lagash and Umma, had agreed on the boundary between their estates. Following a quarrel between the mortals of Lagash and Umma, Mesalim, *king of *Kish, acted as mediator and fixed the frontier at a dike, erecting a stela to mark the spot. This new frontier also required divine sanction and was witnessed by the gods. The men of Umma later removed Mesalim's stela, crossed the border dyke and invaded the lands of Lagash: King Eannatum of Lagash defeated Umma, commemorating his victory with a new stela, now known as the 'Stela of the Vultures'.

Kings and governors often mediated in boundary disputes between tributary states. A vassal *treaty between the *Hittite King *Tudhaliyas IV and Ulmi-Teshup of Dattasa describes the borders of the land, including landmarks which belonged to other lands. Texts from *Ugarit describe the borders between city states, confirmed by Hittite kings, and the *Hebrew *Bible contains descriptions of the borders of *Canaan and between the territories of the *Israelite tribes. Boundaries of city-states were well defined, and so were the boundaries of the villages which belonged to them. Within the specified village boundaries, the mayor and village elders took responsibility for *law, *water rights and *agricultural matters. *Babylonian and Hittite *contracts describe borders between properties owned by individuals, e.g. houses, fields and vineyards.

As soon as a polity expanded beyond its existing boundaries, a form of *provincial administration was required. Provincial boundaries were based on previous boundaries of separate city-states, and from the *Ur III period there are detailed records of the exact boundaries of provinces, based on features such as settlements, buildings, hills and canals. A stated aim of *Assyrian kings was to expand the frontiers of Assyria, and they made a systematic distinction between new provinces, which were regarded as part of Assyria proper and their inhabitants as Assyrian citizens, and tributary states, which remained independent and paid tribute to Assyria but were regarded as outside the borders of Assyria.

Unless inscriptions specify the location of a frontier between states, it can be difficult to establish from *archaeological evidence, since frequent border conflicts meant that frontiers were constantly changing. Occasionally neighbouring states have distinctively different elements in their material culture which may help to locate their common frontier. An example might be the border between *Moab and *Ammon in *Transjordan. The two areas have distinctively different pottery, which changes abruptly across the Wadi eth-Thamad, and the presence of a series of forts along the same wadi may be further evidence that Moab's northern border is to be located there.

*Kassite *kudurrus are often called boundary markers, but in fact they were records of royal land grants to private individuals, which detail the plot of land and any accompanying duties and put *curses on whoever tampers with the stela or deprives the owner of his land.

PB

J.S. COOPER, *Reconstructing History from Ancient Inscriptions: The Lagash–Umma Border Conflict* (Malibu, CA 1983).

P.M.M. DAVIAU, 'Moab's Northern Border: Khirbat al-Mudayna on the Wadi ath-Thamad', *Biblical Archaeologist* 60 (1997) 222–8.

R.H. HESS, 'Late Bronze Age and Biblical Boundary Descriptions of the West Semitic World', *Ugarit and the Bible*, eds G.J. Brooke, A.H.W. Curtis and J.F. Healey (Münster 1994) 123–38.

R. KLETTER, 'Pots and Polities: Material Remains of Late Iron Age Judah in Relation to its Political Borders', *Bulletin of the American Schools of Oriental Research* 314 (1999) 19-54.

M. LIVERANI, *Prestige and Interest: International Relations in the Near East ca.1600–1100 B.C.* (Padua 1990) 33–112.

**Brak, (Tell)** Tell Brak is a large multi-period mound in north-eastern *Syria, close to the modern borders with Turkey and Iraq. The site lies on the margins of the rain-fed *agriculture zone at the northern limits of the north *Mesopotamian plain. The ancient name of the settlement is probably Nagar or Nawar. Excavations at Brak have been conducted by *Mallowan (1937–8), David Oates (1976–93) and Roger Matthews (1994–6), and are continuing.

Late third-millennium BC hoard of objects made of gold, silver and precious stones, from area HS3 at Tell Brak (courtesy of Roger Matthews).

Alabaster head for a statue from the Eye Temple at Tell Brak. Two similar, broken, heads were also found. Height 17 cm. Late Uruk period, c.3300–3000 BC. WA 126460.

Earliest occupation belongs to the *Ubaid period and there is then a long sequence of continuous settlement through the fourth and third millennia and into the late second millennium BC. During the Early to Middle *Uruk period (c.4000–3300 BC) the site was extensively occupied, as were several satellite mounds nearby. From these levels there is evidence for the use of some of the earliest *cylinder seals. In the Late Uruk period (c.3300–3000 BC) there were extensive contacts with south Mesopotamia at the time of the evolution of urban civilization. Especially important at Brak is the Eye *Temple, where large quantities of stone *eye idols were found.

In the early third millennium Brak lost contact with the literate civilization of the south and evolved its own brand of complex society, in the so-called Ninevite 5 period. A small temple and other buildings of this period have been excavated. By 2500 BC Brak had become a major urban centre, controlling much of the region, as attested by tablets from the nearby site of *Beydar. During this period Brak was at its most extensive and wealthiest, and several rich hoards of precious *metals and artefacts have been recovered. Extensive finds of *cuneiform texts have not so far been made. By 2300 BC Brak had been conquered by the *Akkadian *kings of south Mesopotamia who used the site as their regional centre, constructing several massive buildings, including a *palace of the king *Naram-Sin.

Following the collapse of Akkadian rule in north Mesopotamia, much of the site was abandoned. During the middle of the second millennium the site revived with the construction of a *Mitannian palace on the summit of the mound, but by 1200 BC the settlement was completely deserted. RM

Regular excavation reports in the journal *Iraq* from 1977 onwards.

M.E.L. MALLOWAN, 'Excavations at Brak and Chagar Bazar', *Iraq* 9 (1947) 1–266.

D.M. MATTHEWS, *The Early Glyptic of Tell Brak* (Fribourg/Göttingen 1997).

D. OATES, J. OATES and H. McDONALD, *Excavations at Tell Brak I: The Mitanni and Old Babylonian Periods* (Cambridge 1998).

**Bread** Eating bread (and drinking *beer) are the blessings of civilization, Enkidu is told in the *Epic of *Gilgamesh. Bread was the staple *food across the whole Near East, from the schoolboy given two bread rolls for lunch by his mother, to the *gods for whom bread is listed among food offerings (although in practice most of it was redistributed to feed *temple dependants). Bread appears allegorically in epics: the 'bread and water of life' offered to *Adapa would have given him immortality. *Nomads were despised because they 'know no barley'.

Bread was usually made from barley or emmer wheat. Most bread was unleavened and flat, shaped by hand and cooked directly on a flat stone or dish over a fire or in an oven (like the bread the *Israelites made at the first Passover). Examples of flat bread were found in the tomb of Puabi at *Ur; bread may also have survived in the Middle Bronze Age *tombs at *Jericho, but the identifica-

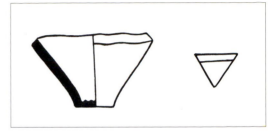

A bevelled-rim bowl (left) was perhaps the origin of the picture which became the cuneiform sign for 'bread' (right). With a change of direction and rapid writing, the sign changed shape over 2500 years (courtesy of Alan Millard).

tion is not certain. Leavened bread, using sour dough or yeast (probably obtained from brewers), was made in moulds of different shapes, some of which have survived. Bowls with a bevelled rim, very common in the *Uruk period in the fourth millennium BC, may have been moulds for lightly baked leavened bread; the *cuneiform sign for 'bread' resembles the shape of a bevelled rim bowl.

At least four different kinds of bread are known from the *Mari texts. The *Hittites used many types of bread in cult ceremonies, differentiated by size, weight, geographic origin, ingredients, intended use, techniques of preparation, and shape. Hittite bread could be geometric, or modelled after animals, anatomical features (teeth, tongues, ears, and a masterpiece representing the mouth, tongue and twelve teeth) or celestial bodies (sun, moon and stars). Other shapes are known from *Mesopotamia, including hearts, hands, fingers and teats.

In Mesopotamia and *Hatti, 'bread-makers' were employees of *palaces and *temples, under the supervision of a 'head baker'. Private citizens made their own bread. Hittite bakers who prepared bread as offerings to gods had to be deloused, then shave, bathe, clean their fingernails and wear clean clothes. Their kitchen had to be swept and sprinkled before bread could be made. A Hittite *ritual consisted of a *priest mixing dough with yeast to promote fermentation, while uttering a *curse. PB

H.A. HOFFNER, Jr, *Alimenta Hethaeorum: Food Production in Hittite Asia Minor* (New Haven, CN 1974) 129–220.

A.R. MILLARD, 'The Bevelled-rim Bowls: Their Purpose and Significance', *Iraq* 50 (1988) 49–57.

J.M. RENFREW, 'Vegetables in the Ancient Near Eastern Diet', *Civilizations of the Ancient Near East*, ed. J.M. Sasson (New York 1995) 191–202.

J. SCHAWE, 'Backen, Bäcker(ei)', *Reallexikon der Assyriologie* 1 (Berlin 1932) 387–8.

**Bronze** Bronze is an alloy of *copper and *tin, stronger than unalloyed copper. It first appeared during the first half of the third millennium BC. Third-millennium BC texts from *Ur and *Ebla indicate the production of bronze with tin contents varying between 9 and 17 per cent, although higher contents are recorded. Analytical data is not yet available for copper objects from Ebla, but analysis of artefacts from contemporary sites in *Syria shows that few contained tin at the levels recorded in the texts. Many were made from low-tin bronze, unalloyed, or low-arsenic coppers. A high proportion of the artefacts from the Royal Cemetery at *Ur were bronzes, although a substantial number were not. These contrasts highlight the complex range of alloys in use and the existence of real variations in metallurgical practices. Tin contents in the range 1–4 per cent are quite common, and may represent the mixing of high-tin bronzes with other copper alloys during recycling.

During the second millennium BC bronze became more widely available. There is evidence from *Hama in the early second millennium BC for the deliberate addition of several per cent lead to bronze, probably to improve the flow of the molten metal, and thus ease the filling of complex moulds. However, there is little evidence for the widespread, systematic production of leaded-bronze at this time. In fact, many weapons from Tell ed-Dab'a in the Nile Delta (probably ancient Avaris, the *Hyksos capital) were made from unalloyed copper.

Bronze usage did not cease with the adoption of *iron as the preferred medium for *tools and weapons. Rather, the two metals assumed complementary roles. Bronze continued in use for those items requiring casting or extensive sheet working, or for which a good, polished surface was desirable. Bronze *wine sets, including jugs, bowls and strainer vessels, appeared during the *Iron Age, together with an extensive repertory of large bronze artefacts such as cauldrons with cast attachments in the shape of griffins, bulls or sirens, tripod stands and fine bowls. Similar material occurs throughout the Near East and the Mediterranean and is associated with drinking, entertaining and other aspects of high status behaviour. It is

Bronze cauldron with siren attachments, from a grave at Gordion, eighth century BC (University of Pennsylvania Museum, neg. R351:21).

probably for this reason that large quantities of such material were recovered from the major *Assyrian cities, much taken as tribute or booty.

Sheet bronze was also much used in architectural decoration, for example in the *Balawat gates.　　GP

J.E. CURTIS (ed.), *Bronzeworking Centres of Western Asia, c.1000–539 BC* (London 1988).

P.R.S. MOOREY, *Ancient Mesopotamian Materials and Industries: The Archaeological Evidence* (Oxford 1994).

O.W. MUSCARELLA, *Bronze and Iron: Ancient Near Eastern Artifacts in the Metropolitan Museum of Art* (New York 1988).

J.D. MUHLY, *Copper and Tin: The Distribution of Mineral Resources and the Nature of the Metals Trade in the Bronze Age* (New Haven, CN 1973).

D.T. POTTS, *Mesopotamian Civilization: The Material Foundations* (New York 1997).

**Bronze Age** The Bronze Age is the second age of the 'three age system' of Stone, Bronze and *Iron Ages devised by Christian Thomsen in 1816–19 as a way of classifying the collections of the National Museum of Denmark. He argued that the ages must have followed in that order, because *stone would not have been used if *bronze were available for *tools, nor bronze after the introduction of *iron. The scheme eventually became very elaborate by sub-dividing the ages further and by the insertion of a Copper Age (*Chalcolithic) between Stone and Bronze (while the Stone Age is now divided into *Palaeolithic, *Epipalaeolithic, and *Neolithic; see also Mesolithic). This system was applied to most of the world, including parts but not all of the ancient Near East. Now it is largely an abstract terminology unrelated to technological change, since it is clear that the use of stone, bronze and iron was not restricted to their respective ages.

In the ancient Near East, the Bronze Age is divided into Early, Middle and Late Bronze Ages, which are further subdivided, but the terminology is used systematically only in the *Levant and *Anatolia. In *Mesopotamia and *Iran periods are denoted by 'phases' or 'cultures' named either after type sites (e.g. *Halaf, *Ubaid) or after political units (e.g. Early Dynastic period, Akkadian period in Mesopotamia, or Proto-, Old and Middle *Elamite periods in Iran). In Anatolia, part at least of the Middle Bronze Age is more usually called the *Hittite Old Kingdom, while the Late Bronze Age is the period of the Hittite Empire. In the Levant, the Early Bronze Age starts c.3600 BC and the Late Bronze Age finishes c.1200 BC (see Chronological Chart for subdivisions, dates and correlations between areas).　　PB

I. FINKELSTEIN, 'Toward a New Periodization and Nomenclature of the Archaeology of the Southern Levant', *The Study of the Ancient Near East in the Twenty-first Century*, eds J.S. Cooper and G.M. Schwartz (Winona Lake, IN 1996) 103–23.

B.G. TRIGGER, *A History of Archaeological Thought* (Cambridge 1989) 73–9.

H. WEIPPERT, 'Metallzeitalter und Kulturepochen', *Zeitschrift des Deutschen Palästina-Vereins* 107 (1991) 1–22.

**Building materials** The building material most characteristic of the ancient Near East was mudbrick, a mixture of soil, *water and straw shaped either by hand or later in a mould, and bonded by mud mortar. Mudbrick is first documented during the Aceramic (Pre-Pottery) *Neolithic, deriving from the earlier practice of building in pisé (irregular blocks of clay). Brick size and shape was highly variable, although a few forms such as *riemchen* (oblong bricks, square in cross-section) and plano-convex bricks were characteristic of particular regions or periods. Baked brick was used in *Mesopotamia, but usually only to provide a waterproof foundation course or the outer skins of important buildings such as *ziggurats. Glazed brick friezes appeared during the mid second millennium BC.

Defensive walls were generally made of mudbrick. These could be placed atop an earthen rampart, supported by stone revetments, and faced with a white plaster glacis to provide stability and a slippery surface against attack, and to enhance appearance (see Fortifications).

*Wood was used for a variety of functions, including roofs, lintels and doors. While mud plaster was used as a weatherproof coating for mudbrick walls, a harder white lime plaster was favoured for the coating of internal walls and floors in many areas during the Aceramic Neolithic. Preparation was a costly procedure, which involved burning limestone at 900°C in order to produce lime, which was then mixed with water to form plaster. In *prehistoric Mesopotamia, gypsum and mud plasters were preferred, with bitumen employed for water conduits during later periods. Reeds were used for roofs and in ziggurats.

In the basalt areas of south *Syria, entire structures were built from stone. The widespread adoption of *stone architecture is a characteristic of the *Hellenistic period. In Mesopotamia, with the exception of its use for door-sockets, stone when used in building had a decorative rather than a structural role. The Neo-*Assyrian reliefs which decorated the walls of *palaces were frequently, though not exclusively, carved in local gypsum. The same applies to the use in second-millennium BC public buildings in the *Levant of a row of dressed limestone and basalt orthostats (standing stone slabs) to provide a frieze of contrasting colours along the lower face of mudbrick walls. Defences at major Assyrian sites included sections built of dressed stone.

Outside Mesopotamia fieldstones were also employed structurally, as foundation courses for mudbrick walls and as actual walls. Ashlar masonry, stone blocks dressed so that they could be fitted together without mortar, appeared at Late Bronze Age *Ugarit, and was particularly characteristic of *Iron Age architecture in the southern Levant. Larger buildings in this area featured carved stone capitals, a technique which was to become particularly associated with Greek architecture.　　　GP

O. AURENCHE, *La maison orientale: L'architecture du Proche Orient ancien des origines au milieu du quatrième millénaire* (Paris 1981).

H. FRANKFORT, *The Art and Architecture of the Ancient Orient*, 5th ed. (New Haven, CN 1996).

A. KEMPINSKI and R. REICH (eds), *The Architecture of Ancient Israel from the Prehistoric to the Persian Periods* (Jerusalem 1992).

P.R.S. MOOREY, *Ancient Mesopotamian Materials and Industries: The Archaeological Evidence* (Oxford 1994).

G.R.H. WRIGHT, *Ancient Building in South Syria and Palestine* (Leiden 1985).

**Bureaucracy:** see Administration

**Burial:** see Death and funerary beliefs and customs

**Busayra** Modern Busayra (or Buseirah) in Jordan is generally identified with Bozrah, mentioned in the *Bible as a *city of *Edom, and was probably the kingdom's capital. The site, 25 km south-east of the Dead Sea, is a natural stronghold on a high spur surrounded on three sides by deep ravines and connected to the main land mass only on the south side. To the south-west lies Faynan, the largest *copper-production centre in the southern *Levant, heavily exploited during the *Iron Age and undoubtedly a factor in Busayra's importance.

Busayra was first surveyed by *Glueck (1933) and excavated by Crystal-M. Bennett (1971–4, 1980). The ancient site is dominated by a mound about 3200 sq m in area, the rest being hidden under the modern town to the south. Bennett's excavations revealed a fortified *administrative centre dating to the seventh century BC, within the Iron II period, possibly continuing into the *Persian period; there is some evidence of re-use in the *Nabataean and *Roman periods. Two large buildings, probably a temple and palace, were constructed on stone and earth platforms to raise them above the surrounding residential houses. The temple had an impressive columned entrance and next to it a possible purification room with a drain. The palace included a large plastered courtyard and a bathroom with a stone toilet and bath.

Few luxury items were excavated and only a small number of inscribed *ostraca, *seals, *weights and seal

Two plano-convex bricks with deep thumb-holds, from Ubaid, Early Dynastic period. WA 115324–6.

The natural stronghold of Busayra, probably biblical Bozrah, the capital of Edom (courtesy of Piotr Bienkowski).

impressions on *pottery. The distinctive painted pottery from Busayra is particularly fine and certainly has the widest repertoire of forms in Edom.                    PB

C.-M. BENNETT, 'Excavations at Buseirah (Biblical Bozrah)', *Midian, Moab and Edom: The History and Archaeology of Late Bronze and Iron Age Jordan and North-West Arabia*, eds J.F.A. Sawyer and D.J.A. Clines (Sheffield 1983) 9–17.

P. BIENKOWSKI, 'Buseirah', *The Oxford Encyclopedia of Archaeology in the Near East* 1, ed. E.M. Meyers (New York 1997) 387–90.

**Byblos**   An important port in *Lebanon, on a promontory with two harbours 60 km north of Beirut, Byblos was the main *Levantine centre for *trade with *Egypt in ancient times. The Greek word *bublos* ('papyrus scroll') originated from the name of Byblos, from its principal role in the papyrus trade between Egypt and the Aegean, especially in the *Iron Age. There are several variants on the name in different languages, including *Gubla* (*Akkadian) and *kbn* (Egyptian). Soundings were first carried out by Ernest Renan (1860), and excavations by Pierre Montet (1921–4) and Maurice Dunand (1928–75). Most of the visible remains are Crusader, but the site has been particularly affected by re-use of building materials and quarrying, making the ancient stratigraphy difficult to interpret.

According to Greek legends, Byblos was founded at the beginning of time by the god *El, identified by the Greeks with Kronos. Occupation has been continuous since the *Neolithic period. From the Early Bronze Age to the Iron Age, Byblos was an important *fortified *city-state, although local *dynasts were often dependent on Egypt. Numerous *hieroglyphic inscriptions testify to Egyptian presence there in all periods to acquire *wood for *ships, *coffins, and *tomb and *palace construction. The *temple to Baalat Gebal ('the lady of Byblos'), associated with the Egyptian goddess Hathor, was first constructed in the Early Bronze Age. Over its ruins in the Middle Bronze Age was erected the Obelisk Temple, with over twenty-six obelisks in its courtyard. To the same period date nine royal sarcophagi found in underground chambers, and the use of a syllabic script, Byblos *hieroglyphic, consisting of about eighty signs known from texts engraved on stone slabs and copper plates. Later, the *Amarna Letters include requests for Egyptian military assistance from Ribaddi, king of Byblos; however, no remains of the city of his time have been discovered.

During the Iron Age, Byblos was an important *Phoenician city, referred to in *Assyrian and Egyptian texts. It appears in the Egyptian story of Wenamon, set in c.1100 BC, in which the *king of Byblos is accused of being impolite to an Egyptian official seeking wood. An important find was the sarcophagus of King Ahiram, decorated with Egyptian-influenced scenes, inscribed with the earliest Phoenician *alphabetic text dating to c.1100 BC.          PB

M. DUNAND, *Fouilles de Byblos*, 5 vols (Paris 1937–58).

——, *Byblos: Its History, Ruins, and Legends*, 2nd ed. (Beirut 1968).

N. JIDEJIAN, *Byblos through the Ages* (Beirut 1968).

P. MONTET, *Byblos et l'Égypte: quatre campagnes de fouilles à Gebeil 1921–1924* (Paris 1929).

E. RENAN, *Mission de Phénicie* (Paris 1864).

M. SAGHIEH, *Byblos in the Third Millennium B.C.* (Warminster 1983).

A view of the Middle Bronze Age Obelisk Temple at Byblos, with stelae up to 2 m high re-erected on their original bases (courtesy of Alan Millard).

# C

---

**Calendar** In *Babylonia, time was regulated by a civil calendar, based on the intervals produced by the motion of the sun and moon. The three basic time intervals were the solar year, the lunar month and the solar day. The year began in spring with the month *Nisannu* (March/April). A month began with the first sighting of the lunar crescent.

The motions of the sun and moon are not connected or uniform, so twelve lunar months do not make one solar year, but 354 days, about eleven days less than the average year. The months therefore fall eleven days behind each year. To compensate for this, from the third to the end of the first millennia BC the Babylonian calendar, by royal decree, intercalated an extra thirteenth month. This was not done regularly, but whenever necessary to maintain a month in its proper place, normally an extra sixth or twelfth month being intercalated. A regular cycle was introduced in the *Achaemenid period, intercalating seven months at fixed intervals within a nineteen-year period (later known as the Metonic cycle, after the fifth-century BC Greek astronomer Meton).

Month names first appeared in the Early Dynastic period. In the north and west local month names continued in use (e.g. at *Nuzi, *Ugarit). Months were divided into halves, or into seven-day units for cultic purposes, although a continuous seven-day cycle (a week) was unknown in *Mesopotamia (the seven-day week was officially introduced within the *Roman empire by the emperor Constantine in AD 321). The day was divided in several ways: into twelve 'double-hours' in *astronomy, or into four divisions between sunsets in Late Babylonian astronomical texts.

The *Assyrian calendar in the second millennium BC began in the autumn and had no intercalary month, resulting in the slipping of the seasons backwards through the months. The Assyrians adopted the Babylonian calendar in the time of *Tiglath-pileser I and in the *Persian period it spread across the Near East, replacing the systems in use in *Syria and *Israel (where the months were often simply numbered). Traditional Jewish and Arab calendars keep it alive.　　　PB

E.J. BICKERMAN, *Chronology of the Ancient World* (London 1980).

M.E. COHEN, *The Cultic Calendars of the Ancient Near East* (Bethesda, MD 1993).

H. HUNGER, 'Kalender', *Reallexikon der Assyriologie* 5 (Berlin/New York 1980) 297–303.

F. ROCHBERG-HALTON, 'Calendars: Ancient Near East', *Anchor Bible Dictionary* 1, ed. D.N. Freedman (New York 1992) 810–14.

R.A. PARKER and W. DUBBERSTEIN, *Babylonian Chronology*, 3rd ed. (Chicago 1956).

The month names of the major calendars of the ancient Near East.

| Modern | III Dynasty of Ur | Nippur | Babylonia | Hebrew | Arabic |
|---|---|---|---|---|---|
| March / April | še-kin-ku₅ | bára-zag-gar | nisannu | nîsan | nîsăn |
| April / May | màš-da-gu₄ | gu₄-si-sá | ayau | 'ayar | 'ayār |
| May / June | zahₓ-da-gu₇ | sig₄-ga | simānu | sîvān | ḥasirān |
| June / July | u₅-bí-gu₇ | šu-mumun-na | du'uzu | tammûz | tamûz |
| July / August | ki-síg-ᵈnin-a-zu | ne-IZI-gar | abu | 'ab | 'ab |
| August / September | ezem-ᵈnin-a-zu | kin-ᵈinna | ulūlu/elūlu | 'elûl | 'êlûl |
| September / October | á-ki-ti | du₆-kù | tašritu | tishrî | tishrîn 'awwal |
| October / November | ezem-ᵈšulgi | apin-du₈-a | araḥsamma | marchešvan | tishrîn thanî |
| November / December | ezem-ᵈšu-dsuen | gan-gan-na | kislimu | chislev | kanun 'awwal |
| December / January | ezem-maḥ | ab-ba-è | ṭabētu | ṭebet (Ass. kanunu) | kanûn thanî |
| January / February | ezem-an-na | udra | šabāṭu | shebt | shabāṭ |
| February / March | ezem-ᵈme-ki-gál | še-kin-ku₅ | addaru | 'adãr | 'adhār |

**Camel** The family *camelidae* (order *Artiodactyla*) is thought to have originated in North America but to have crossed into Asia over two million years ago. The relationship between the two Asiatic species, the Bactrian camel (two-humped) and the dromedary (one-humped), is disputed. A camel bone from the Red Sea coast of *Arabia has produced a radiocarbon date of around 7000 BC, and rock-drawings in Arabia, speculatively dated to between the seventh and fifth millennia BC, show dromedaries being hunted by men on foot with spears, though these compositions should not be confused with much later pictures showing horsemen *touching* domesticated camels with their lances to establish their claim on them during a raid.

It seems likely that the Bactrian camel had been domesticated in Turkmenistan, and possibly *India, by the early third millennium BC, but it is not until the late second millennium BC that there is any firm data for the domestication of the dromedary. However, this is partly due to the difficulty of distinguishing between the bones of wild and domesticated camels. The best early evidence for the domestication of the dromedary comes from south-eastern Arabia.

The camel was almost certainly bred originally for its milk, which is extremely rich and nutritious. Only later was it used as a pack animal, and later still as a mount. Its willingness to eat shrubs, which even goats disdain, and its famed ability to go for days without water, enabled its owners to exploit ever greater tracts of arid land, unsuitable for other animals. When used as a pack animal it enabled *merchants to open up previously impassable routes and permitted the *Assyrian King *Esarhaddon (680–669 BC) to undertake the first successful *Mesopotamian invasion of *Egypt. Curiously, there is no evidence of the use of the camel in Egypt before the *Roman period.

The camel thus enabled the *Arabs on land to rival the *Phoenicians on the sea as the long-distance traders *par excellence* of the ancient Near East and gave them a mobility in peace and war which enabled them to live in places in which their enemies could not long survive. It

was for this reason that all ancient conquests of the Arabs were short-lived.

Contrary to a widely held misconception, the camel was never used as a fighting mount. The camel was used to transport warriors to the battle, where they dismounted and went into battle on foot or, towards the end of the first millennium BC, on horseback. It was also used to permit the warriors to make a speedy escape in the event of defeat. Both these aspects are shown on the reliefs from *Ashurbanipal's palace at *Nineveh where the Arabs can be seen with their camels couched, going into battle on foot brandishing their swords and bows and, later, fleeing from the victorious Assyrian soldiers, often riding two to a camel with the pillion-rider trying ineffectively to ward off the pursuit.    MCAM

J. CLUTTON-BROCK and C. GRIGSON (eds), *Animals and Archaeology 3: Early Herders and their Flocks* (Oxford 1984).
M.C.A. MACDONALD, 'Camel Hunting or Camel Raiding?', *Arabian Archaeology and Epigraphy* 1 (1990) 24–8.
J. ZARINS, 'Camel', *Anchor Bible Dictionary* 1, ed. D.N. Freedman (New York 1992) 824–6.

**Canaan, Canaanites** From the ancient Near Eastern perspective, Canaan was an important region that bordered the Mediterranean Sea between *Anatolia and *Egypt. This was the land that stood between *Mesopotamia and the 'Upper Sea'; it was distant but eventually came into the Mesopotamian political and cultural sphere. The name 'Canaan' appears with variant spellings and its exact derivation is not certain. The earliest literary reference to the Canaanites comes from *Mari, in the eighteenth century BC, but some have claimed that Canaan is mentioned in the much older *Ebla tablets. Canaan appears in a number of Egyptian texts, first in the fifteenth century BC and later in the *Amarna Letters. The land of Canaan was frequently the objective of Egyptian military campaigns, including one referred to in the Merneptah stela. Towards the end of the thirteenth century BC, this pharaoh claims to have conquered Canaan, along with '*Israel' and other peoples. Of course, Canaan and the Canaanites play a prominent role in the *Bible, especially in the Pentateuch and conquest narratives. Of all the ethnic groups who opposed the Hebrew settlement in a new territory, the Canaanites were regarded as the leading adversaries of fledgling Israel.

Several scholars have suggested that it is difficult to know exactly what the other Near Eastern peoples understood when they heard the term 'Canaanite'. In terms of historical geography, the maximum range of Canaan is clear, but it is often difficult to distinguish Canaanites from, say, the *Amorites and Jebusites. Modern scholars use the term Canaanite to mean different things at different times. At what point in the flow of *Bronze Age civilization did the Canaanites emerge as a distinct group? What is their genetic and cultural relation to the *Phoenicians, the kingdom of *Ugarit, and the Bronze Age population of *Transjordan? These questions are compounded by the lack of certainty regarding Canaanite origins.

While there were urban centres in the Early Bronze

An Assyrian sculptor's vivid rendering of Arabs trying to escape on camels decorated a room in Ashurbanipal's palace at Nineveh. WA 124926.

Age *Levant, the rapid growth of *fortified *city-states that began in Middle Bronze II is attributed to the Canaanites. The classic Canaanite culture took shape in major towns like *Hazor, Dan, *Megiddo, Shechem, *Jericho, *Lachish and *Gezer. The Canaanite civilization flourished during the Late Bronze Age, as it interacted with other regions – including Egypt, the *Aegean and *Cyprus – economically and culturally. Canaanite *agriculture and industry attracted the attention of the Egyptian New Kingdom. When the Late Bronze Age civilization declined and the Egyptians withdrew from their long-term occupation of Canaan, new groups emerged on the scene. Along the way, the Canaanite language (itself part of the North-West *Semitic group) split into a number of regional dialects (e.g. *Hebrew, Phoenician, *Ammonite, *Moabite, *Edomite). The Canaanites are credited with inventing the *alphabet that lies at the foundation of Western civilization.

Any student of the Bible is familiar with the negative picture of Canaanite society and *religion that was painted by the Hebrew authors. The primary source for the study of Canaanite religion is the large collection of *cuneiform tablets from Ugarit, which lay north of Canaan proper. These texts provide the Canaanite vantage point on their religious practices and their pantheon, which includes *El, *Baal and *Asherah. Excavations at Canaanite sites in the Levant have shed much light on their *burial practices and most aspects of their material culture. The terms Canaan and Canaanite dropped out of use when the *Iron Age kingdoms that had absorbed so much of Canaanite culture created a new configuration of power.                    GLM

J.A. HACKETT, 'Canaanites', The Oxford Encyclopedia of Archaeology in the Near East 1, ed. E.M. Meyers (New York 1997) 409–14.

N.P. LEMCHE, The Canaanites and Their Land: The Tradition of the Canaanites (Sheffield 1991).

A.R. MILLARD, 'The Canaanites', Peoples of Old Testament Times, ed. D.J. Wiseman (Oxford 1973) 29–52.

A.F. RAINEY, 'Who Is a Canaanite? A Review of the Textual Evidence', Bulletin of the American Schools of Oriental Research 304 (1996) 1–15.

K.N. SCHOVILLE, 'Canaanites and Amorites', Peoples of the Old Testament World, eds A.J. Hoerth, G.L. Mattingly and E.M. Yamauchi (Grand Rapids, MI 1994) 157–82.

J.N. TUBB, Canaanites (London 1998).

## Carchemish

Ancient Carchemish (also known as Karkamish) is located at the modern village of Jerablus (formerly Jerabis) on the west bank of the Euphrates river, on the Turkish side of the modern border with *Syria. The strategic location is emphasized by the river crossing of the Berlin–Baghdad railway at this point.

The identification has been certain since 1876 when G. Smith from the British Museum was taken to the site by W.H. Skene, British consul at Aleppo. The next consul, P. Henderson, excavated for the Museum between 1878 and 1881. Work resumed in 1911 under D.G. Hogarth, taken over by Campbell Thompson the following year and continued thereafter by *Woolley until the outbreak of war in 1914. T.E. Lawrence was assistant for all five campaigns. Woolley returned in 1920 but his efforts were frustrated by new hostilities.

At the nearby site of Yunus, Woolley excavated kilns, now known to belong to the early *Chalcolithic *Halaf culture, which produced distinctive painted *pottery.

Carchemish was of considerable importance in later periods, as textual references from *Ebla and *Mari attest, and was later the seat of the *Hittite viceroy. Apart from the second-millennium BC defences of the inner *town, little is known archaeologically before the *Iron Age. The site comprises three elements: a high citadel, an inner or lower town and an outer town. The *fortifications of the citadel and the lower town, including the west and south gates, and *houses and *gates in the outer town were excavated. But of greatest importance were the monumental sculpted and inscribed façades associated with the *temple of the storm-god, the gatehouse and the great staircase leading to the citadel. The most important façades are known as the Herald's Wall, with alternating white limestone and black basalt orthostats, some of which are thought to have come from earlier monuments; the long wall of sculpture; the Kubaba and Karhuha procession; and the later modification to the gate known as the royal buttress. The majority of these reliefs are on display in the Museum of Anatolian Civilizations at Ankara. Their study reveals the development of *sculptural style in association with changes in fashion and even in language, with Luwian *hieroglyphic and the introduction of *Aramaic.

Carchemish fell to *Sargon II in 717 BC and was the locale for the battle that finally destroyed the Neo-*Assyrian empire when, in 605 BC, the Neo-*Babylonians under *Nebuchadnezzar II defeated the Assyrians' *Egyptian allies led by the Pharaoh Necho.                    GDS

J.D. HAWKINS, 'Karkamiš', Reallexikon der Assyriologie 5 (Berlin/New York 1980) 426–46.

——, Corpus of Hieroglyphic Luwian Inscriptions (Berlin, in press).

D.G. HOGARTH, Carchemish: Part I, Introductory (London 1914).

C.L. WOOLLEY, Carchemish: Part II, The Town Defences (London 1921).

——, Carchemish: Part III, The Excavations in the Inner Town (London 1952).

## Caria, Carians

A region of south-west Turkey, south of *Lydia, Caria was first settled in the *Neolithic but became a distinctive culture only in the first millennium BC. Carians may originally have been of *Aegean origin and settled in the area in the second millennium BC. The earlier first-millennium BC communities seem to have been independent, mainly *temple centres for native deities, and Caria came under Lydian control. There was considerable *Hellenistic influence, and already the *pottery of the eighth and seventh centuries BC had a geometric tradition similar to that of east Greece. In 546 BC, Caria was brought under *Persian rule and placed under the Lydian satrapy. By the fourth century BC, its culture was similar to that of a *Greek city-state.

The Carian *language is related to Luwian (*Hittite) and is known from inscriptions written in a local form of the Greek *alphabet discovered in Caria and others left in Egypt by Carian mercenaries.                                    PB

L. and J. ROBERT, *La Carie* (Paris 1954).

R.T. MARCHESE, *The Historical Archaeology of Northern Caria* (Oxford 1989).

J. RAY, 'An Outline of Carian Grammar', *Kadmos* 29 (1990) 54–73.

**Carmel caves**  The Carmel mountain range is found in the north-west of Israel immediately adjacent to the modern coastline and indeed projecting out into the sea close to modern Haifa. With lower sea levels at different times in the *Palaeolithic the coastal plain would have been wider and an important resource area. The most important *prehistoric sites currently excavated are located along the western side of the range at the junction between coastal plain and hills behind, and the ancient inhabitants could exploit both areas easily. These sites are the caves of Tabun, Skhul, El Wad and Kebara. Other important sites are Nahal Oren and Sefunim.

Tabun, Kebara, and Skhul are particularly important for their Middle Palaeolithic remains. At Tabun, a large three-chambered cave, there are 20 m of deposits spanning the Lower and Middle Palaeolithic. This site is therefore particularly important for the sequence of *flint industries and the evidence for environmental and economic changes it provides over a long time span. Human remains have been recovered at these three sites which have been the basis of a controversy about the origins of our species of humanity – 'modern humans', *Homo sapiens* – that spans the past fifty years. At Tabun in the Middle Palaeolithic layers was recovered a skeleton of an adult female Neanderthal. In Kebara cave a complete Neanderthal infant and substantially complete adult have been recovered. The indications are that both the Kebara bodies represent deliberate *burials. Yet at Skhul, only a short distance from Tabun, in Middle Palaeolithic layer B the remains of ten burials and fragmentary remains of other individuals were recovered. These skeletons from Skhul have many of the features of modern humans, *Homo sapiens*.

Broadly speaking we can date these two forms of hominid by associated archaeological materials to the Middle Palaeolithic between 150,000 and 40,000 bp ('before present') but the evidence for more precise dating is disputed. What can this evidence tell us about the relationships between modern and archaic humans and the origins of our species? Given the time span involved, it is difficult to demonstrate the presence of modern humans and Neanderthals in the area at the same time. In fact it is likely that the earliest Neanderthals from Tabun may predate the modern humans at Skhul dated to c.92,000 bp and that the Kebara Neanderthals postdate the *sapiens* at Skhul, being dated to c.58,000–42,000 bp. It has been suggested that modern humans shifted out of Africa in warm phases and Neanderthal populations shifted north and south owing to climate change as well.

Less contentiously but equally significant, it is clear that the modern humans of Skhul almost certainly used a Middle Palaeolithic toolkit similar to that of Neanderthals. Further, their burial practices were not dissimilar. Whatever anatomical and related behavioural differences in certain aspects of culture, there was little to distinguish Neanderthals and early modern humans. Changes in behaviour in the Upper Palaeolithic long postdate the appearance of modern humans in the Levant and are not intrinsic to our species but may have benefited or been associated with our species more than Neanderthals.

The cave of El Wad is important because of the typical large *Natufian settlement excavated there.          DB

T.E. LEVY (ed.), *The Archaeology of Society in the Holy Land* (London 1995).

C. STRINGER and C. GAMBLE, *In Search of the Neanderthals* (London 1993).

**Çatalhöyük (Çatal Hüyük)**  Çatalhöyük is located in south-central *Anatolia on the Konya plain at 1000 m above sea level. It is to be distinguished from the Çatal Hüyük of the *Amuq plain. The Konya basin is a flat plain covering 11,000 sq km. Rainfall ranges from 200 to 100 mm a year from the edge of the plain to its centre, and *rivers drain from the surrounding mountains to create marshy areas and small lakes. The environment provides intriguing contrasts: general aridity, but waterlogged areas and spring flooding, considerable cold in winter and heat in summer. Given this, the distinctive features revealed by excavation at the site are particularly intriguing.

Çatalhöyük was first excavated by James Mellaart in 1960–4. Excavations have been renewed by Ian Hodder since 1993 as part of a twenty-five-year project. The site consists of two adjacent mounds, east and west, on either side of an ancient river course. The east mound is *Neolithic and dates to c.7000 BC. The west mound dates to the Early *Chalcolithic period (c.6000 BC). Occupation shifted from one site to the other through time, and the site was probably not abandoned during this period.

Given its period of occupation, the site can be regarded as significant in a number of ways: its relatively large size, extremely elaborate buildings, the importing to the site of large quantities of exotic materials, and the evidence for elaborate and sophisticated craft activities.

This is one of a very few large Neolithic sites in the Near East (east mound c.13 ha, west mound c.8 ha; see also Ain Ghazal). Excavation and surface scraping have revealed that buildings were densely packed, and for substantial periods different areas of the site were occupied contemporaneously. Buildings were so densely packed, giving extra insulation against summer heat and winter cold, that access to the interiors was over roofs rather than by paths between structures. Given the average size of buildings at c.24 sq m it is likely that between two and six thousand people lived at Çatalhöyük when it was at its greatest extent, making it an unexpectedly large community for this early period. One is forced to ask the question: was Çatalhöyük a central site supplying goods and services to surrounding communities, thus defining

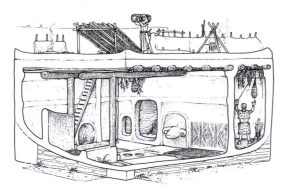

Reconstruction of Neolithic house at Çatalhöyük, c.7000 BC.

expeditions and exchange governed this acquisition. Within the chipped stone industry there is evidence for elaborate production of large points by pressure flaking. Large quantities of long obsidian blades were produced by pressure debitage. Given the skills and efficiencies involved it is likely that only a few in the community were involved in such production, but whether this was family-based or more specialized involving exchanges in the community is the subject of further research.　　DB

I. HODDER, *On the Surface: Çatalhöyük 1993–1995* (Cambridge 1997).

J. MELLAART, *Çatal Hüyük: A Neolithic Town in Anatolia* (London 1967).

I. TODD, *Çatal Hüyük in Perspective* (London 1976).

it as one of the earliest *towns and helping to explain its large size? Survey by Douglas Baird in the vicinity of Çatalhöyük has documented a number of small Neolithic communities which contrast markedly with Çatalhöyük in terms of their size and may allow this possibility.

The buildings demonstrate a remarkably uniform rectangular ground plan across the site and from earlier to later levels, consisting of a main room with a single or compartmentalized side chamber. Buildings were often reconstructed on the same spot with virtually identical features. Hearths or ovens and ladder were on the southern wall, platforms for sleeping, eating and socializing on the northern and eastern walls, side chambers with storage elements at the western end. *Burials were placed under platforms, *women and *children in the north-west, adult men under the eastern platform. This may indicate gender distinctions in the use of the buildings and platforms and activities in life. Buildings were replastered frequently, many over one hundred times. These apparently annual plasterings may indicate the lifespan of individual buildings.

Many such plasterings were decorated with *wall paintings. Most are geometric designs but a few paintings show naturalistic groups of people surrounding *animals like stag, boar and cattle. These may be *hunting scenes. In a few cases vultures are depicted flying over headless corpses. Relief figures and horns adorned walls, and horns adorned benches and small pilasters within buildings. The degree of elaboration varies from building to building, and Mellaart felt that the most elaborate might be shrines and Çatalhöyük a *religious centre. These buildings changed their appearance frequently, and the domestic and uniform features of most buildings make it likely that these were not distinct shrines, but that a complex symbolism and sets of *ritual guided many areas of activity, achieving material expression in varying ways in many *families' lives and homes.

Since the site is in an alluvial plain, raw materials like *stones and *wood are rare locally. *Copper, turquoise, *obsidian, *flint, basalt, marine shells and carnelian were imported from distances of between 40 and 250 km. It is likely that complex procurement patterns involving

**Caucasus** A mountain range stretching from the Black Sea to the Caspian Sea, the Caucasus defines the northern limits of the ancient Near East. The northern Caucasus had closer connections with southern Europe, and its *Bronze Age is known best for its earthen *burial mounds or '*kurgans' at *Maikop and elsewhere. The southern Caucasus (Transcaucasia) had close political and historical interaction with the Near East especially in the Bronze and *Iron Ages. In the third millennium BC the Early Transcaucasian (Kura-Araxes) culture spread far south to north-west *Iran and down to *Palestine, where its distinctive ceramics are given the name Khirbet Kerak Ware. Whether this involved the actual movement of people is still disputed, although some scholars have linked this movement with the arrival of *Hurrian groups. In the Transcaucasian heartland, this culture is characterized by small sites associated with extensive *agricultural terraces, dams and cyclopean stone *fortifications.

In the late third millennium BC these sites were suddenly abandoned, an event perhaps associated with the appearance of large and rich earth and *stone burial mounds or kurgans, containing *gold and *silver *jewellery and vessels and elaborate *tools and weapons, including early *tin *bronzes. The Caucasus mountains are rich in *copper ores, and the region became an important centre for the development of metallurgy in the second

Principal sites in the Caucasus.

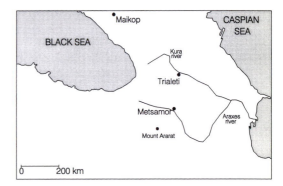

and first millennia BC, perhaps influenced from southern *Anatolia.

Large *fortified settlements reappeared only in the mid second millennium BC, though kurgans continued to be built. In the areas bordering Anatolia and northern *Mesopotamia, these sites may have been part of a Late Bronze/Early Iron Age state which was a precursor of the historically documented *Urartu. From burials at the huge site of Metsamor come two inscriptions with the names of *Kassite *kings. The tombs were clearly of important people, one containing two principal burials, fifty accompanying human burials, mainly *women, with *horses, bulls, sheep and dogs.

By the late second millennium BC the settlement pattern was essentially based on heavily fortified sites on impregnable natural outcrops along major communication routes, a pattern which has continued almost to the present day. The area also attracted pastoral *nomadic groups, such as the *Scythians, who drove the indigenous peoples into the mountains and occasionally themselves left their mark on history.                    PB

C. BURNEY and D.M. LANG, *The Peoples of the Hills: Ancient Ararat and Caucasus* (London 1971).

P.L. KOHL, 'Central Asia and the Caucasus in the Bronze Age', *Civilizations of the Ancient Near East*, ed. J.M. Sasson (New York 1995) 1051–65.

B.A. LITVINSKY, 'Archaeology and Artifacts in Iron Age Central Asia', *Civilizations of the Ancient Near East*, ed. J.M. Sasson (New York 1995) 1067–83.

V.A. TRIFONOV, 'The Caucasus and the Near East in the Early Bronze Age (Fourth and Third Millennia BC)', *Oxford Journal of Archaeology* 13 (1994) 357–60.

**Çayönü**  The site of Çayönü Tepesi is located in eastern Turkey on the headwaters of the Tigris *river, but also close to the area where the Euphrates rises and to the copper mines at Ergani Maden. The site covers c.3–4 ha. It has been excavated since the 1970s first by R. Braidwood and H. Çambel, later by a team led by the Özdogans. The site has a long sequence of occupation spanning the aceramic and ceramic *Neolithic periods.

The earliest phases, dating to the ninth millennium BC, have features similar to those encountered elsewhere in the Near East at this period when crop cultivation was first being established. Typical are a series of round structures cut down into earlier deposits.

The architecture of the succeeding phases undergoes distinctive developments. In the later ninth millennium BC, as elsewhere in the Near East, rectilinear architecture appears. The earliest such buildings belong to the grille plan type: at one end of the structure a series of low, closely spaced, parallel walls formed a grill-like foundation, with channels, which were open at least at one end, between the walls. This area probably supported a raised floor. The other end of the building had a single large room with three small cells, probably for storage, at the end of the room.

These buildings were succeeded by 'cell plan' buildings. The foundations of these rectilinear buildings were divided into eight to twelve cells. The presence of paving and communication ways between these cells suggests that they served specific purposes. The absence of hearths suggests that they may have been a basement level for storage and/or other activities.

The 'cell plan' buildings were succeeded by a phase of so-called 'large room' buildings. These buildings were again rectangular but were not divided into distinct areas like the earlier structures nor did they seem to have basement or raised floor levels. This phase probably belongs to the beginning of the seventh millennium BC, just before the appearance of pottery in the region.

There are also less well preserved Pottery Neolithic levels on the site.

Contemporary with the cell and grille plan structures, at the eastern end of the site stood an open space. At one time this may have had a series of upright monoliths in it. To the south and east of this area was a series of buildings whose ground plans and contents singled them out from their domestic contemporaries. These buildings shared certain features including the basic element in their plan, a large rectangular single room. They also had distinctive floors often decorated – the 'terrazo' building had ochre-covered pebbles set into the floor marking two sets of parallel red lines; the 'flagstone' building had a floor paved with large slabs and an orthostat (standing stone slab) set into the floor. One version of these buildings, the so-called skull building, had an apsidal end and compartments at that end of the building that contained human skulls and some long bones. There were also benches along the walls in the skull building. These distinctive features suggest buildings devoted to community practices which included at least on occasion aspects of mortuary cult.

An important assemblage of hammered and annealed *copper artefacts has been recovered from the site, documenting the earliest extensive use of copper.                    DB

L.S. and R.J. BRAIDWOOD (eds), *Prehistoric Village Archaeology in South Eastern Turkey* (Oxford 1982).

J. YAKAR, *Prehistoric Anatolia: The Neolithic Transformation and the Early Chalcolithic Period* (Tel Aviv 1991).

**Cemeteries**  Since a society's treatment of the dead reflects some of its cultural values, scholars have learned much about ancient Near Eastern cultures through studying *funerary practices and *tombs. In the earliest *prehistoric periods, burials were often placed near *houses or even beneath floors of occupied dwellings (as at *Çatalhöyük). A major shift from these so-called intramural burials took place in the *Chalcolithic period, when the *families of the dead began to bury their deceased relatives in formal cemeteries outside the settlement, although house burials continued in *Mesopotamia and *Ugarit. The practice of extramural burial gradually evolved into formal cemeteries, i.e. the kind of burial plots that are familiar to inhabitants of modern Western cultures.

There were many variations in the funerary practices from region to region, but the preference for cemeteries probably reflected a number of common values. Firstly, they were communal in nature, intended for members of the same tribes, clans or families. Cemeteries fostered a group identity, and multiple burials – often of members from the same clans or extended families – were common in some periods and regions. This meant that communal or family burial plots allowed a deceased patriarch or *king to be 'gathered to his people' (cf. Genesis 25: 8; 49: 33). Secondly, the adoption of extramural cemeteries brought more uniformity to the treatment of the dead. Perhaps the rites and burial procedures had more of a public nature. Thirdly, the preference for proper burial in a necropolis could reflect more concern for the dead and an awareness of ancestral traditions. Fourthly, the steady use of a cemetery meant that it grew in size. After the Chalcolithic period, most large permanent settlements had cemeteries, which reflected the sedentary nature of a particular population. Fifthly, the communal cemetery represented another place where socio-economic status was displayed, though this was not true in all cases.

Many ancient Near Eastern cemeteries have been excavated, usually in connection with the excavation of a settlement site. The spectacular Royal Cemetery at *Ur represents the necropolis of *Sumer's ruling class. The royal or priestly burials illustrate the funerary *rituals, including human *sacrifice, that accompanied the deaths of such powerful individuals. (See also Kurgan.)    GLM

M.-TH. BARRELET, 'Les pratiques funéraires de l'Iraq ancien et l'archéologie: état de la question et essai de prospective', *Akkadica* 16 (1980) 2-27.

R. GONEN, *Burial Patterns and Cultural Diversity in Late Bronze Age Canaan* (Winona Lake, IN 1992).

K.M. KENYON, *Excavations at Jericho 1: The Tombs Excavated in 1952–4* (London 1960).

——, *Excavations at Jericho 2: The Tombs Excavated in 1955–8* (London 1965).

R.T. SCHAUB and W.E. RAST, *Bab edh-Dhra': Excavations in the Cemetery Directed by Paul W. Lapp (1965–67)* (Winona Lake, IN 1989).

D. USSISHKIN, *The Village of Silwan: The Necropolis from the Period of the Judean Kingdom* (Jerusalem 1993).

C.L. WOOLLEY, *Ur Excavations, Volume II: The Royal Cemetery* (London 1934).

**Ceramics:** see Pottery

**Chagar Bazar**   Chagar Bazar is located in the *Khabur river basin area of northern *Syria, close to the border with Turkey. The site was excavated by *Mallowan in the 1930s, with renewed work beginning in 1999 by joint British-Belgian and Spanish teams. It has remains spanning almost four thousand years of the *prehistory and early history of north *Mesopotamia.

The earliest evidence for occupation at Chagar Bazar comes from Pit M in the form of painted pottery of *Samarra type, related to material of seventh-millennium BC date from central Iraq. Also from Pit M comes considerable evidence of a long-lived *Halaf occupation. Architectural remains included a *tholos* (a circular building) and other structures. Painted Halaf *pottery was found in

A type of pottery distinguished by monochrome decoration in geometrical patterns was called 'Khabur Ware' by Mallowan when he found quantities of it at Chagar Bazar. It was widespread in Upper Mesopotamia c.1900–1600 BC. WA 125351.

some quantities and indicates an occupation through almost all of the Halaf period, c.6000–4500 BC, as well as into the Halaf–*Ubaid Transitional period when new influences from southern Mesopotamia were being felt. Scientific study of the Halaf pottery from Chagar Bazar has shown that vessels were traded between the site and nearby Tell Halaf as well as amongst local communities.

Following the Halaf period, there appears to have been limited occupation at Chagar Bazar, if any, during the Ubaid and *Uruk periods. There is a major reoccupation of the site at the start of the Early *Bronze Age, c.3000 BC. Painted and incised pottery of Ninevite 5 type, early third millennium BC in date, is common and there is much evidence of Early Dynastic and *Akkadian presence, including bullae (clay tags) with *seal impressions and short *cuneiform inscriptions in the Akkadian language. There are indications that the entire site may have been abandoned, perhaps as part of a wider regional abandonment in north-eastern Syria, for a few centuries around 2000 BC.

Chagar Bazar next comes to the fore at the time of *Shamshi-Adad I of *Assyria, c.1813–1781 BC. A large *palace or storehouse was constructed, and an archive of about a hundred cuneiform tablets includes names of Akkadian, *Amorite and *Hurrian origin, attesting the ethnic mix of the settlement at this time. Following the destruction of the palace by fire, domestic *houses were constructed and many graves deposited within the mound. The site was finally abandoned c.1500 BC.    RM

J. CURTIS, 'Chagar Bazar', *Fifty Years of Mesopotamian Discovery*, ed. J. Curtis (London 1982) 79–85.

M.E.L. MALLOWAN, 'The Excavations at Tall Chagar Bazar, and an Archaeological Survey of the Habur Region, 1934–5', *Iraq* 3 (1936) 1–86.

## Chalcolithic

**Chalcolithic** This period dates between c.6000 BC and 3000 BC. However, the way the term has been applied to different local cultural sequences means that in different parts of the Near East the period covers slightly different time ranges. Thus in *Anatolia the Early Chalcolithic begins c.6000 BC, in the southern *Levant c.5000 BC. The term is eschewed in *Mesopotamia, although the north Mesopotamian *Uruk period is also called Late Chalcolithic, especially where local material culture is not classically Uruk. In the southern Levant it ends c.3600 BC.

Literally the term means 'copper-stone' age. It was initially conceived as a period when *copper metallurgy (see Metalworking) appeared alongside more traditional aspects of *Neolithic material culture. The archaeologist Gordon Childe gave the term its classic socio-economic expression in suggesting that the appearance of copper metallurgy resulted in the development of specialist producers and exchange. These, he argued, would need to be supported by production of surplus food. Limited social hierarchy would have developed to control surplus and redistribution. These insights still permeate views of the Chalcolithic.

We now know that metallurgy appeared during the period termed Neolithic in Anatolia at sites like * Çayönü, Ashýklý Höyük and *Çatalhöyük. Annealing and hot hammering of copper are suggested at the first two of these sites. The Çatalhöyük copper may have been smelted, but was certainly melted. Metallurgy became widespread outside Anatolia during the Chalcolithic period. Whilst copper not *bronze was used for both utilitarian and prestige items (see Shiqmim), *gold, *silver and lead metallurgy is also documented.

Chalcolithic communities have evidence of specialization in the manufacture of *ceramics, chipped stone (see Flint-working; Obsidian), metal items, *stone bowls and *ivory figurines. Movement of such finished goods and raw materials is clearly attested as part of both local and extra-regional exchange. In Mesopotamia such production and exchange is complicated enough to warrant use of *seals, presumably to identify owners, controllers, producers or recipients, or perhaps to convey more esoteric information. Exceptional structures point to elite dwellings, communal activities or public rituals. Walled settlements in Anatolia (*Mersin, *Hacilar) and the proliferation of maceheads in stone and copper suggest increases in the scale and frequency of conflict.

The widescale exploitation of metals may not necessarily be the key factor behind such developments, but it was obviously bound up in the increasing diversity of roles within society and an increasing complexity of interactions within and between communities almost certainly involving more elaborate political systems.    DB

## Chaldaeans

**Chaldaeans** *Assyrians first record the presence of Chaldaeans in southern *Babylonia in 878 BC. Chaldaean tribes apparently entered Babylonia between 1000 and 900 BC beside *Aramaean tribes. There were three principal groups: Bit-Amukanni, settled near *Uruk, Bit-Dakkuri, near *Babylon, and Bit-Yakin, near *Ur and the marshland, each with its own ruler, many occupying major *towns. During the eighth century BC incessant warfare within Babylonia led to three Chaldaeans taking the throne, but none lasted long until Merodach-Baladan of Bit-Yakin came to the fore in 731 BC. He managed to remain alive to trouble the Assyrians for three decades. *Sargon II and *Sennacherib mounted campaigns against him, constantly frustrated by his ability to withdraw into the marshes or find sanctuary in *Elam. After two spells of *kingship (721–710, 703–702 BC) he was harried out of Babylonia and died in Elam. Thereafter various Chaldaean leaders attacked Assyrian garrisons and centres as well as Babylonian and Aramaean interests until there was a brief unity in the Shamash-shum-ukin rebellion against *Ashurbanipal (652–648 BC). The Chaldaean leader at that time was Nabu-bel-shumate. He never managed to do more than irritate the Assyrians, although his actions cost them dear and led to Ashurbanipal mounting a devastating attack on Elam where he had sanctuary. However, as Assyria weakened, the Chaldaeans took their opportunity. In 626 BC the Chaldaean *Nabopolassar seized the throne of Babylon and established the Chaldaean *dynasty which lasted until *Cyrus II of *Persia captured Babylon in 539 BC. Nabopolassar, in alliance with Cyaxares of *Media, brought the downfall of Assyria and took over most of Assyria's empire, his son *Nebuchadnezzar moving westwards several times to establish control in the *Levant. Although the Chaldaean kings maintained and renewed Babylonian religious and cultural traditions, writing their monumental inscriptions in *Akkadian *language and *cuneiform script, their native language was a form of *Aramaic. In the *biblical Book of Daniel, Aramaic is described as the 'language of the Chaldaeans' and so for a long time was called Chaldee by western writers.    ARM

J.A. BRINKMAN, *A Political History of Post-Kassite Babylonia 1158–722 B.C.* (Rome 1968) 260–7.

——, *Prelude to Empire: Babylonian Society and Politics, 747–626 BC* (Philadelphia, PA 1984).

## Chariots

**Chariots** Ancient Near Eastern chariots were essentially mobile firing platforms for archers, made of *wood, leather strips and *metals, which needed to be stable, fast and manoeuvrable. Early wheeled vehicles in *Mesopotamia, dating to the third millennium BC, had two or four disk wheels, were pulled by asses or onagers, and may have been difficult to manoeuvre. The turning point in the development of the chariot came primarily with the introduction of the light, spoked wheel and the shifting of the axle to the back to give manoeuvrability. The first proper chariots appear on *Anatolian and *Syrian *seals in the early second millennium BC and are mentioned in the *Mari texts. These were light, open vehicles with two

A Sumerian chariot depicted by engraved and painted shell inlay on the 'Standard' from the Royal Cemetery at Ur, c.2500 BC. The four animals, heavy frames and solid wheels make it hard to gauge their effectiveness in battle. WA 121201.

spoked wheels, drawn by *horses yoked on either side of a draught pole, and with fittings for *weapons. They were used primarily in *warfare, but also in *hunting and processions.

The chariot was introduced to *Egypt from the *Levant. Asiatic and Egyptian chariots are illustrated on Egyptian reliefs and paintings of the late second millennium BC, and actual examples have survived in Egyptian tombs. Two-man Asiatic chariots carried archers, but three-man *Hittite chariots with driver, shield-bearer and spearman may have been simple transports rather than shock attack vehicles. The Hittite army at Kadesh had 2500 chariots, composed of much smaller units supplied by the Hittite king's allies; the *Amarna Letters refer to units of ten, thirty or fifty chariots.

*Assyrian *palace reliefs of the ninth to seventh centuries BC depict the changing design of chariots as they became bigger to accommodate four men, heavier and drawn by four horses, and so less mobile. An earlier Egyptian relief had shown a single Libyan carrying a light chariot on his shoulders, while an Assyrian relief shows two Assyrian soldiers carrying a chariot, giving an indication of the increasing weight. The side of the Assyrian chariot became solid and often armed with metal plates, while crew and horses sometimes wore protective armour. A thrusting spear kept in the rear was for use dismounted. The reliefs also depict *Urartian, Neo-Hittite and Levantine chariots which resemble Assyrian models.

Depictions of the turreted and scythed *Achaemenid chariots mentioned by classical authors have not survived, but the sources show that they were useless against *Greek infantry. By the late first millennium BC, military chariots were largely replaced by mounted troops who had greater mobility, though hunting and processional chariots remained in use.

The ancient vocabulary concerning chariots is documented in *Sumerian and *Akkadian texts, and about one hundred terms describe types of chariots, materials, and chariot parts including platform, body, dust-shield, front, tail, pole, yoke, axle and wheels. Parts of chariots

have been excavated, including Early Dynastic ones in tombs at *Kish, and there are also models in clay and metal from various periods and places.  PB

J.H. CROUWEL and M.A. LITTAUER, 'Chariots', The Oxford Encyclopedia of Archaeology in the Near East 1, ed. E.M. Meyers (New York 1997) 485–7.
M.A. LITTAUER and J.H. CROUWEL, Wheeled Vehicles and Ridden Animals in the Ancient Near East (Leiden 1979).
S. PIGGOTT, The Earliest Wheeled Transport (London 1983).
Y. YADIN, The Art of Warfare in Biblical Lands in the Light of Archaeological Discovery (London 1963).

**Childbirth**  Childbirth was a risky activity in the ancient Near East. Texts often mention mothers and children dying in childbirth, and infant mortality must have been high. Pre-natal care was essentially *magical, using amulets, *rituals and incantations.

*Mesopotamian incantations depict the unborn child as a *ship with an unknown cargo on a dark sea. *Hittite documents describe restrictions on a *woman's diet and *sexual relations prior to giving birth, and whether she must be separated from her *family. There are *oracles for assessing a woman's condition and foretelling the outcome of a birth, and one Mesopotamian text dealing with the treatment of a woman ill during pregnancy, which prescribes vegetable drugs, anointing, bandaging and finally magic.

A woman delivered the baby in a crouching position, sometimes on two stones, cushions or a special stool, assisted by a midwife. If the birth was difficult, an incantation called 'The Cow of Sîn' was recited in Mesopotamia, recalling the cow impregnated by *Sîn who had an easy delivery with the help of the *god. Drugs sometimes assisted childbirth, for example the bark of a certain tree which the woman chewed; she might also have her stomach massaged with an ointment. Labour pains are often used in literature to describe extreme anguish.

In Hittite stories, the midwife presents the child to the father, the baby is acknowledged and given a name and its destiny is foretold. Hittite rituals are concerned with the continued *fertility of the mother and a favourable destiny for the baby. A ceremony three to four months after the birth celebrated the re-entry of the mother into the community and the initial entry of the child. In Mesopotamia too the baby was named soon after birth.

Baked clay plaque of goddess holding babies and flanked by newborn babies, possibly miscarried foetuses. Isin-Larsa/Old Babylonian period (© Pierre et Maurice Chuzeville, Département des Antiquités Orientales, Musée du Louvre AO 12442).

Children were nursed by their mother or a wet nurse for two to three years.

Abortions and miscarriages are discussed in legal texts. *Hammurabi's *Laws and *biblical laws prescribe penalties for injuring a pregnant woman so that she miscarried and in the Hittite Laws the fine varied according to the month of the pregnancy. Abortion was also a crime, but the penalty depended on the circumstances and the social status of the woman (see Social classes). However, one Mesopotamian *medical text apparently gives a prescription for stimulating abortion, which consisted of eight ingredients mixed in *wine and drunk on an empty stomach.

A malformed foetus or an unburied stillborn child was believed to become a restless ghost. The birth of a malformed baby in Mesopotamia was followed by a ritual to avert evil, after which the body was thrown into the river. Clay plaques from the early second millennium BC in Mesopotamia depict a goddess with newborn babies, and it has been suggested that these represent stillborn foetuses. Abnormalities were often reported in *omen texts, for example Siamese twins, a hermaphrodite or quadruplets.                                                PB

Stela of Urnanshe of Lagash and his sons, commemorating the construction of a religious building. Early Dynastic period, c.2500 BC (© Photo RMN. Louvre AO 2344).

G. BECKMAN, *Hittite Birth Rituals* (Wiesbaden 1983).

H.W.F. SAGGS, *The Might that Was Assyria* (London 1984) 138–40.

M. STOL, 'Private Life in Ancient Mesopotamia', *Civilizations of the Ancient Near East*, ed. J.M. Sasson (New York 1995) 485–501.

M. STOL and F.A.M. WIGGERMANN, *Zwangerschap en geboorte bij de Babyloniërs en in de Bijbel* (Leiden 1983).

## Children

There can be no doubt that the social value of children is culturally conditioned. This makes it difficult, if not impossible, for modern scholars to determine the status and worth of infants and young people in the ancient Near East. Ancient texts, art and artefacts indicate that children were viewed in ways that are quite familiar to Western families. It should be noted that the nature and amount of evidence on children in antiquity is meagre. The scarcity of artistic portrayals of children outside Egypt has led at least one authority to hazard a guess that childhood along the Nile was happier than it was in Mesopotamia. Even if the profile of children is not high in the ancient literary and archaeological record, they were certainly present in large numbers – and they played an important role in family and economic life.

Children were one of the dependent groups in ancient Near Eastern households. In an age of high infant mortality their birth was a sign of divine favour and a source of joy (cf. Psalms 127–8). The primary role of parents was that of care-giver and educator. Like widows and the poor, orphans had few rights, and the most humane aspects of ancient law codes made provisions for children who had no parents to protect them, and *kings boasted that they did so. Near Eastern wisdom literature also set high ethical standards for treatment of orphans, since it was believed that the gods took pity on them. In the Ugaritic Epic of Aqhat, Danel was praised because he protected the widow and adjudicated the case of the fatherless. The Hebrew prophets roundly condemned those who oppressed the poor and took advantage of widows and orphans.

Deities were thought of as parents of human beings, and these groups were bound together by love and obedience. If mothers and fathers were responsible for the care of their children, children were obliged to 'honour' their parents (cf. Exodus 20: 12), which included taking care of them in their old age. This need led some Near Eastern societies to allow adoption of an adult, if there were no children to cover this duty.

The bearing and raising of children were regarded as a primary purpose of women and a rationale for marriage. If a woman was barren, her husband could take a second wife. In Assyrian, Hittite and Israelite society, the widow of a man who died before he fathered children should marry her brother-in-law ('levirate marriage'). Sons were preferred over daughters, but laws provided for the inheritance of property by daughters if necessary. In most societies primogeniture was the norm.

The life of some children was luxurious, while the offspring of peasants and slaves worked hard. When parents were desperate, children were forced into debt slavery. The sacrifice of children, which was widely practised at times of crisis in the Phoenician colony of Carthage from c.750 to 146 BC, resulted from parental vows. Even if this ritual infanticide was practised as a form of population control, it illustrates the status that infants held in certain times and places. (See Education.)
                                                GLM

J.S. DEREVENSKI, 'Where Are the Children? Accessing Children in the Past', *Archaeological Review from Cambridge* 13 (1994) 7–20.

F.C. FENSHAM, 'Widow, Orphan, and the Poor in Ancient Near Eastern Legal and Wisdom Literature', *Journal of Near Eastern Studies* 21 (1962) 129–39.

J. HAWKES, *The First Great Civilizations: Life in Mesopotamia, the Indus Valley, and Egypt* (New York 1973).

L.E. STAGER and S.R. WOLFF, 'Child Sacrifice at Carthage – Religious Rite or Population Control?', *Biblical Archaeology Review* 10 (1984) 30–51.

C.J.H. WRIGHT, 'Family', *Anchor Bible Dictionary* 2, ed. D.N. Freedman (New York 1992) 761–9.

C. ZACCAGNINI, 'Feet of Clay at Emar and Elsewhere', *Orientalia* 63 (1994) 1–4.

**Chogha Zanbil** The *Elamite royal *city and religious centre of *āl Untash-Napirisha* ('city of Untash-Napirisha'), identified with modern Chogha Zanbil, lies 40 km south-east of *Susa in *Iran. The city was built by King Untash-Napirisha (c.1275-1240 BC) as a new capital but never completed. It was largely abandoned after his death, and his twelfth-century BC successors moved the capital back to Susa.

The site was discovered and excavated by Roland de Mecquenem (1935–9, 1946) and later systematically by *Ghirshman (1951–62). It covers c.100 ha and has two parts: a walled sacred precinct with a *ziggurat and several *temples, and a fortified royal city. The ziggurat was originally a monumental square building, later changed into a ziggurat, unusually with internal rather than external stairways. At the top was a temple, decorated with *silver- and *gold-coloured glazed bricks, dedicated to Napirisha and Inshushinak, the gods of *Anshan and Susa. The royal city consisted of the main city *gate and three *palaces. The most elaborate, Palace I, had vaulted *tombs under the floors of rooms, all but one with *cremation *burials, the only example of this funerary practice in Elam. South-west of the palaces was the temple of Nusku, sometimes interpreted as a fire temple.

PB

R. GHIRSHMAN, *Tchoga Zanbil (Dur Untash) 1: La ziggurat, 2: Téménos, temples, palais, tombes* (Paris 1966, 1968).

R. DE MECQUENEM and J. MICHALON, *Recherches à Tchoga Zembil* (Paris 1953).

P. DE MIROSCHEDJI, 'Chogha Zanbil', *The Oxford Encyclopedia of Archaeology in the Near East* 1, ed. E.M. Meyers (New York 1997) 487–90.

E. PORADA, *Tchoga Zanbil (Dur Untash) 4: La glyptique* (Paris 1970).

M.J. STÈVE, *Textes élamites et accadiens de Tchogha Zanbil* (Paris 1967).

**Chronicles:** see Annals and chronicles

**Chronology** There are two types of chronologies, relative and absolute. Relative dates of archaeological layers and the objects in them can be inferred from the stratigraphy of ancient *tells; stratigraphy also helps with establishing typologies of objects, since the shape of artefacts changes over time and one can arrange them in a relative chronological sequence, comparing similar objects from different sites. Absolute chronology provides actual dates BC or AD, inferred from ancient written sources which refer to *astronomical events, or link to the known systems of Greece and Rome, or from scientific techniques such as tree-ring or *radiocarbon dating which can give an estimate of the date of an object.

Ancient Near Eastern societies measured time by arbitrary fixed points, particularly the accession year of a *king. Lengths of kings' reigns were recorded in *king lists, *annals, *chronicles and royal inscriptions. In order to tie in the ancient chronologies with our modern system we require anchors: ancient dated descriptions of events such as astronomical phenomena to which we can give an absolute date and thus tie in the remainder of the ancient chronology. For *Babylonia for most of the first millennium BC there are regular records of astronomical phenomena linked to other events, while for *Assyria there are the *eponym lists. The Assyrian and Babylonian dates for the first millennium BC are accurate enough to allow dating of other events in the ancient Near East, where there is some correlation.

Earlier dates are more conjectural, and *Hittite chronology is very uncertain. The absolute chronology of the second millennium BC is based on just a few fixed points. In *Mesopotamia the key is a group of *cuneiform tablets known collectively as the 'Venus Tablet of Ammisaduqa' which appear to record a sequence of first and last visibilities of Venus during the early years of the reign of Ammisaduqa of the First Dynasty of *Babylon. This evidence suggests three possible dates for the accession year of Ammisaduqa: 1702, 1646 and 1582 BC ('high', 'middle' and 'low' dates). Often the 'Middle Chronology' is used for convenience, although it has been shown that this is no longer plausible, some now preferring the 'High Chronology'. Lately a fourth system has been proposed, arising from a study of Old Babylonian and *Kassite *ceramics, with Ammisaduqa year 1 about 1550 BC. However, from about 1300 BC onwards the maximum variation possible is about twenty years; there are certainly no grounds for shortening the chronology by as much as a hundred years as some have attempted.

Since absolute dates are still uncertain, for many areas chronological designations are broadly based on technological stages: Stone Age (*Palaeolithic, *Epipalaeolithic (*Mesolithic), *Neolithic), *Chalcolithic, *Bronze Age and *Iron Age. These terms are not descriptive; for instance *iron was in use before the beginning of the Iron Age proper. In some areas, such as the *Levant, these are the only chronological terms used, since written material is so sparse. For *prehistoric phases in Iraq and *Iran, a relative chronology is denoted by 'phases' or 'cultures' such as *Hassuna or *Halaf, which are characterized by a distinctive material culture.

PB

P. ASTRÖM (ed.), *High, Middle or Low? Acts of an International Colloquium on Absolute Chronology*, 3 vols (Gothenburg 1987–9).

J.A. BRINKMAN, 'Mesopotamian Chronology of the Historical Period', *Ancient Mesopotamia*, 2nd ed., by A.L. Oppenheim (Chicago 1977) 335–48.

F.H. CRYER, 'Chronology: Issues and Problems', *Civilizations of the Ancient Near East*, ed. J.M. Sasson (New York 1995) 651–64.

R.W. EHRICH (ed.), *Chronologies in Old World Archaeology*, 3rd ed. (Chicago 1992).

H. GASCHE *et al.*, *Dating the Fall of Babylon: A Reappraisal of Second-millennium Chronology* (Ghent/Chicago 1998).

C. RENFREW and P. BAHN, *Archaeology: Theories, Method and Practice* (London 1991) 101–48.

M.B. ROWTON, 'Chronology: Ancient Western Asia', *Cambridge Ancient History* 1.1, 2nd ed. (Cambridge 1970) 193–239.

**Cimmerians** *Assyrian texts report conflicts with the Cimmerians in the reigns of *Esarhaddon and *Ashurbanipal and that they had defeated an *Urartian *king late in the eighth century BC. They were listed with other enemies beyond Assyria's frontiers when its kings asked the *god *Shamash for advice on their tactics. The Cimmerians advanced westwards across *Anatolia to *Lydia where King Gyges defeated them with Assyrian help, then, after he had broken his *treaty with Assyria, the Cimmerians defeated him, to Ashurbanipal's glee, an event recorded also by the *Greek historian *Herodotus (I.15). Other Greek sources tell of havoc wrought by the Cimmerian chieftain Lygdamis, with little doubt the Tugdamme who, Ashurbanipal reports, twice attempted to invade Assyrian territory, thwarted at first by a thunderbolt striking his camp, later by a mortal disease, c.640 BC. *Hebrew authors knew the Cimmerians as a remote people in the north, associated with other Anatolian groups (the Gomer, in Genesis 10: 2, 3; Ezekiel 38: 6).

The Cimmerians were apparently of Indo-Iranian stock, perhaps related to the *Scythians, but information about them is second-hand and fragmentary. No material remains can be labelled 'Cimmerian'. ARM

A. IVANTCHIK, *Les Cimmeriens au Proche-Orient* (Fribourg 1993).

G.B. LANFRANCHI, *I Cimmeri: Emergenza delle elites militari iraniche nel Vicino Oriente (VIII–VII sec. a.C.)* (Padua 1990).

**Cities, towns and villages** It is difficult to define the terms village, town and city in the ancient Near East, and they are often used interchangeably. Villages originated with the first sedentary settlements in the *Epipalaeolithic period. From the beginning they had a characteristic form and structure that has continued almost to the present day. Villages were always nucleated, with a tight cluster of *houses with only narrow lanes between them and few open public spaces, usually unwalled and located near a water source. The development of *agriculture provided a firm *economic base, and village life remained the predominant form of settlement for thousands of years. In some areas, such as *Anatolia and *Iran, towns of any size were comparatively few in number at most periods: cities such as *Boghazköy or *Susa were exceptional, and the former seems to have been a religious and administrative centre for a rural population. In the second millennium BC, *cuneiform texts use a determinative sign usually translated 'town' or 'city' before names of settlements, but it applied to any collection of houses, however small, and most 'towns' were in fact only villages on average 1 ha in size. From texts we know that villages were often governed by a body of elders. Sometimes they were subject to an external political authority in a town or city, and provided towns with their surplus of *food

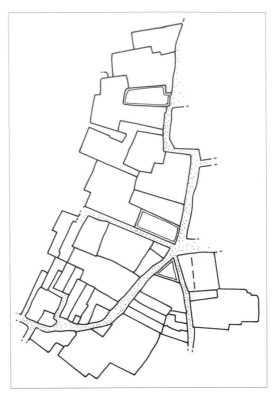

Plan of Old Babylonian house area at Ur, c.1800 BC.

and craft products. In return, villages received goods not made in the village, or the use of services such as *temples which might be available only in towns.

In *Mesopotamian *myths, towns were regarded as a creation of the *gods, dating almost to the beginning of the world. In reality, the first cities (or large towns) emerged by c.3500 BC in southern Mesopotamia and were slowly developed in other areas, as isolated settlements grew into regional centres ('city-states'). This process was probably linked to the growing economic and social power of the temples. The essential characteristics of these first cities were the development of *social classes, hierarchical *administrative systems and a highly centralized economy headed by the temples. Most cities were not self-sufficient, but dependent on outlying towns and villages to produce the surplus which supported their populations and institutions. Later texts from *Ugarit in *Syria record the precise contributions of outlying settlements to the centralized city economy. Most archaeologists would agree that such outlying settlements define the difference between towns and cities: towns were not centres of settlement systems and so required less complex administrative mechanisms.

*Uruk became the largest early city, with a population estimated at forty to fifty thousand, its walls enclosing an area of 400 ha by c.2700 BC. Around it lay several small towns and villages. Most southern Mesopotamian cities, composed of several sectors divided by ancient watercourses, had a similar structure. They comprised the main temple, always the highest part of the settlement, though not in the centre; a *palace often located some distance from the temple; canals which provided *water, but also divided the city into *religious, administrative, residential, *craft and *burial sectors; *roads running parallel to the canals or at right angles; and *fortifications surrounding the city.

The cities of northern Mesopotamia were quite different, and often paralleled in the *Levant and Anatolia. In the third and second millennia BC, the *tells accumulated from centuries of settlement became raised citadels for temples, and new large lower towns were created, encircled by fortifications. It is not clear if the lower towns were fully occupied, and there may have been extensive open areas. Palaces have been found in some lower towns, repeating the separation between temple and palace in southern Mesopotamia. The *Assyrians systematically united palace and temple on a citadel, located by the city walls, although the earliest example is known at *Alalakh in the eighteenth century BC. Assyrian cities included areas reserved for the *army, as well as extensive *gardens, orchards and parks. *Nineveh, at 700 ha the largest city yet known, was described by *Sennacherib as divided into an administrative and urban centre in the north, and a military camp in the south.

The best-recorded settlement hierarchy is that in *Israel and Judah during the *Iron Age, when an urban administrative system was centrally planned by a monarchy. The settlements can be divided into royal capitals (*Samaria and *Jerusalem), major and secondary administrative centres, fortified provincial towns, fortresses, and later Assyrian provincial capitals, as well as scores of surrounding agricultural villages. The administrative centres were inhabited not by farmers but by elite families linked to the monarchy with numerous administrative and service personnel.　　　　　　　　　　　　PB

F.S. FRICK, 'Cities: An Overview', The Oxford Encyclopedia of Archaeology in the Near East 2, ed. E.M. Meyers (New York 1997) 14–19.

M. HELTZER, The Rural Community in Ancient Ugarit (Wiesbaden 1976).

J.-L. HUOT, J.-P. THALMANN and D. VALBELLE, Naissance des cités (Paris 1990).

A.M.T. MOORE, 'Villages', The Oxford Encyclopedia of Archaeology in the Near East 5, ed. E.M. Meyers (New York 1997) 301–3.

E.C. STONE, 'The Development of Cities in Ancient Mesopotamia', Civilizations of the Ancient Near East, ed. J.M. Sasson (New York 1995) 235–48.

M. VAN DE MIEROOP, The Ancient Mesopotamian City (Oxford 1997).

**Climate** In most of the Near East today, the climate is hot and dry during the summer and cooler and generally wetter during the winter, although some areas hardly ever get any rain at all. Of course there is a difference in climate between mountains, plains and coastal areas, and between different regions. Average summer temperatures are normally between 20° and 30° C but can go higher; average winter temperatures can go down to –10°C or

lower in the Taurus mountains, but can stay between 10° and 20°C in southern *Iran or near the Red Sea. In winter, especially in the mountains and upland plains, snow can occasionally lie for about one hundred days in a year. As regards rain, successful *agriculture without artificial *irrigation requires a reliable annual rainfall of at least 200 mm. This 200-mm rainfall line, called an isohyet, more or less corresponds to the arc of the *Fertile Crescent. North of the line, the *Syrian and *Mesopotamian plains receive sufficient rainfall for agriculture; south of the line there has never been an average annual rainfall of 200 mm.

Archaeologists are interested in measuring changes in climate in antiquity in order to understand its effect on human behaviour and settlement patterns. A record of ancient climate in a particular area can be established by analysis of pollen from stratified cores taken from geological deposits or sediments of rivers, lakes and inland seas, and dendrochronology (tree-ring studies) can also detect variations in rainfall. However, these analyses are time-consuming, and large areas of the Near East have still not been covered by such studies.

Current evidence shows that there was a dramatic change in the climate of the Near East at the end of the last Ice Age, c.10,000 bp ('before present'). The climate, which had been cold and dry, became warmer and slightly moister and more attractive for human settlement, and within a thousand years or so it was similar to that of today. Drier periods can be detected c.3000, 2200 and 1300 BC, but these are the only major changes in climate which appear to have affected the entire Near East over the last ten thousand years. Of course there were other minor variations, but these were localized and normally of short duration.　　　　　　　　　　PB

K.W. BUTZER, 'Environmental Change in the Near East and Human Impact on the Land', Civilizations of the Ancient Near East, ed. J.M. Sasson (New York 1995) 123–51.

J.M. WAGSTAFF, The Evolution of Middle Eastern Landscapes: An Outline to A.D. 1840 (London 1985) 9–25, 219–23.

**Clothing** Most of our knowledge about clothing in the ancient Near East comes from *Mesopotamia. There is also representational, especially sculptural, evidence from *Anatolia, and *Syrians are shown on Egyptian reliefs and paintings of the second millennium BC. The earliest *textile fragments identified as clothing are cloth rectangles of flax interpreted as the remains of headdresses or string skirts from Nahal Hemar in the Judaean desert, dating to c.8000 BC. Slightly later are *wall paintings from *Çatalhöyük depicting males with leopardskin clothes around their waists.

Mesopotamian clothing was relatively uncomplicated. Typically, a main garment was a rectangle of loosely woven wool (or linen, less common until the first millennium BC), bleached white or dyed red or blue, simply wrapped around the body. *Art rarely shows details of the folds, so the best indication of the draping is the borders. Men seem normally to have wrapped their garments around in an anticlockwise direction, *women the reverse.

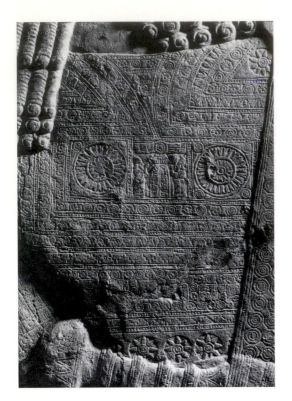

(*left*) Assyrian sculptors took care to represent kings' robes as accurately as possible. This dress of Ashurbanipal (668–c.627 BC) was embroidered and adorned with decorative gold plaques. WA 124867.

(*right*) Cast bronze votive figure from the Old Babylonian period, wearing a long robe with heavy borders. Height 35 cm. c.1950 BC. WA 91145.

Along the shorter sides the warp formed a straight fringe, sometimes knotted into tassels. On the longer sides, the weft might be left as long loops. Coloured garments were normally fringed in white, white ones often in colour. *Military and working dress was usually short and unrestrictive, while longer attire was the norm for leisure, ceremonial, *ritual and non-manual work.

Early Dynastic menswear consisted of a short cloth, knotted or belted behind the left hip. (In the *Uruk period a similar dress was usually knotted at the front.) Early Dynastic carvings show this kilt made of fleece, with hanging locks of wool. Later, men wore a larger cloth, wrapped around the body so as to restrain the left arm while leaving the right free. Women always wore a long-length cloth. There were two main forms, one wrapped around and pinned or stitched at the left breast, the other with the cloth stretched across the bosom, crossed at the back and with the ends passing over the shoulders and hanging down free at either side at the front. The first style was the more common in the Early Dynastic period, the second afterwards. The two styles might therefore represent the traditional dress of *Sumerian and *Akkadian womenfolk. Before the first millennium BC, people are usually depicted barefoot.

*Assyro-*Babylonian menswear seems to have involved an ankle- or knee-length rectangular tunic, often with embroidered neck and arm borders (full embroidery for royal dress), occasionally with tasselled lower fringe, and girt by a cummerbund, sometimes with a narrower belt over it. Courtiers wore a sash down the right side of the skirt, while the king had a shawl. Sandals were the

usual footgear. Assyrian women wore a similar tunic, with a large shawl enveloping the shoulders. The Assyrian *king wore a headband with rosette decoration, usually wrapped around a fez. The Neo-Babylonian royal headdress, which continued into the *Persian period, was a pointed cap with streamer.

The basic clothing for Syrian men in the second millennium BC was a long-sleeved, close-fitting top and a simple wraparound kilt, of brightly patterned linen or wool and often with coloured fringes. Women wore a caped garment with a tiered skirt, and *children were depicted naked. In Anatolia and the *Levant, local kings were shown in sculpture wearing variations of Assyro-Babylonian dress, usually a long robe with a draped or pleated shawl over the right shoulder. The Neo-Hittite royal family at *Carchemish wore long tunics, pleated at the back, with short sleeves and round necklines, a royal shawl or a cummerbund, and shoes with ornamented heels.                                                           AG

D. COLLON, 'Clothing and Grooming in Ancient Western Asia', *Civilizations of the Ancient Near East*, ed. J.M. Sasson (New York 1995) 503–15.

D. COLLON, M. ROAF and V.S. CURTIS, 'Ancient Near East, §II, 7. Dress', *The Dictionary of Art* 1, ed. J. Turner (New York/London 1996) 883–8.

A. GREEN, 'Nadel', *Reallexikon der Assyriologie* 9 (Berlin/New York 1998) 68–73.

D. IRVIN, 'Clothing', *The Oxford Encyclopedia of Archaeology in* the Ancient Near East 2, ed. E.M. Meyers (New York 1997) 38–40.

W. REIMPELL, Geschichte der babylonischen und assyrischen Kleidung (Berlin 1921).

H. WAETZOLDT and E. STROMMENGER, 'Kleidung', Reallexikon der Assyriologie 6 (Berlin/New York 1980–3) 18–37.

H. WAETZOLDT and R.M. BOEHMER, 'Kopfbedeckung', Reallexikon der Assyriologie 6 (Berlin/New York 1980–3) 197–210.

**Coffins** A variety of containers of different shapes and materials was used as coffins in the ancient Near East, although the use of coffins was not common in all areas and periods. *Burial in pots was popular in *Mesopotamia, *Anatolia and the *Levant. Often, two storage jars had their rims and necks removed and were placed shoulder to shoulder with the deceased inside. In the first millennium BC in Mesopotamia, a single large jar was used, either laid on the ground on its side or standing vertically in a grave shaft, sometimes with a *wooden lid. A single jar was also often used for infants in the Levant.

Anthropoid coffins – clay coffins in human form with modelled lids depicting a human face and upper body – were used in the Levant in the Late *Bronze and *Iron Ages, and probably derived from *Egyptian prototypes. The earliest examples may have been burials of Egyptians stationed in *Canaan. Each coffin could hold more than one individual, usually between two and six. Although one example from Deir el-Balah in *Palestine was made of limestone, *stone is little attested for coffins. Two limestone coffins dating to the Middle Bronze Age were found at Tell ed-Daba, probably the *Hyksos capital of Avaris, while the tenth-century BC stone sarcophagus of Ahiram from *Byblos is decorated with friezes depicting the *king, funerary ceremonies and lions.

The bathtub coffin was typically *Assyrian, and introduced into the Levant and even *Bahrain. This was a deep ceramic vessel, about one metre long, with one rounded and one straight end, decorated with bands, with handles around the sides. Bathtub coffins were often covered with a lid of palm-wood planks or bricks, and occasionally coated with bitumen. The earliest examples come from *Ashur, dating to the late second millennium BC, were used there for royal burials in the first, and may have continued into the *Persian period. *Bronze examples are also known from many parts of the Near East, with wood or bronze covers, dating to the eighth and seventh centuries BC. The bodies were in contracted positions on their sides, although at *Babylon and *Carchemish *cremated remains have been found inside them. Mesopotamian sites also yielded hundreds of other clay coffins of different types, from oval terracotta sarcophagi in the Early Dynastic period, and *house-shaped coffins at Old Babylonian *Ur, to longer coffins in which the bodies were almost extended, though these probably date to the Persian period if not later. In Ashur smashed stone coffins were unearthed, prepared for named Assyrian kings, and at *Nimrud stone coffins of Assyrian *queens have been found buried beneath rooms in the *harem part of the *palace.

Wooden coffins have not usually survived, although two Iron Age carbonized examples were preserved at Sahab in *Jordan. Perhaps surprisingly, there is only one occurrence of the word 'coffin' in an *Akkadian *cuneiform text, in which an unnamed Assyrian king describes the burial of his father and mentions a stone coffin, its lid sealed with *copper and secured with tags.    PB

H. BAKER, 'Neo-Babylonian Burials Revisited', The Archaeology of Death in the Ancient Near East, eds S. Campbell and A. Green (Oxford 1995) 209–20.

E. BLOCH-SMITH, Judahite Burial Practices and Beliefs about the Dead (Sheffield 1992).

R. GONEN, Burial Patterns and Cultural Diversity in Late Bronze Age Canaan (Winona Lake, IN 1992).

D. MARCUS, 'The Term "Coffin" in the Semitic Languages', Journal of the Ancient Near Eastern Society of Columbia University 7 (1975) 85–94.

E. STROMMENGER, 'Grabformen in Babylon', Baghdader Mitteilungen 3 (1964) 157–73.

J.R. ZORN, 'Mesopotamian-style "Bathtub" Coffins from Tell en-Nasbeh', Tel Aviv 20 (1993) 216–24.

An Assyrian bronze coffin made for an important person, perhaps a priestess. Other coffins were made in clay. Length 1.23 m. From Ur, c.700 BC. WA 118604.

**Coinage** Pieces of *metal of consistent weight, stamped with a mark guaranteeing their standard, appeared in western *Anatolia in the first half of the sixth century BC. Following *Greek tradition, they are commonly associated with *Lydia, a source of electrum of which the first examples are made, and its wealthy *King *Croesus, but there is no definite connection. They were made by hammering the metal lump on to an engraved die with punches, at first unengraved. The earliest specimens have a lion's head on one side and punch marks on the other. The idea spread, so that cities in Asia Minor, Greece, *Cyprus, Cyrene and Italy were issuing *silver coins by 500 BC and many more throughout the *Levant soon thereafter. Even in the earliest stage, a variety of denominations was coined, from the stater of about 14 g to the minute one-ninety-sixth of a stater, weighing about

Electrum stater, the earliest inscribed coin, probably minted in Halicarnassus in Caria. The legend is usually translated 'I am the badge of Phanes'. Diameter 2.1 cm, weight 14.02 g. Sixth century BC. BMC 1 (Bank Collection 950).

0.15 g and about 4 mm in diameter. *Persia's emperors minted *gold darics and silver shekels (sigloi) from about 520 BC until Alexander's conquest, carrying a single design of the king, kneeling with bow, on one side and punch marks on the other. However, they allowed their governors and some *cities to strike coins in their own names. *Sennacherib boasts of casting *bronze figures for his *palace at *Nineveh in clay moulds 'as in casting half-shekel pieces', but no examples of such pieces are known from his time and it is not certain that they were coins. Early coin hoards often include lumps of bullion, cut pieces of plate and *jewellery and broken coins, indicating the continuing use of weighing and barter, but coinage gradually removed the need for those complexities, although many early coins bear cuts made to test their purity, perhaps revealing some scepticism over the worth of the issuing authorities' marks in circumstances where coins of many cities and rulers mingled. Coinage may have been stimulated by the need to pay mercenary soldiers and by the growth of *market exchange as the Greek cities developed.                ARM

I. CARRADICE (ed.), *Coinage and Administration in the Athenian and Persian Empires* (Oxford 1987).

C. HOWGEGO, *Ancient History from Coins* (London 1995).

D.D. LUCKENBILL, *The Annals of Sennacherib* (Chicago 1924) 109 vii.16–18.

**Contracts**  In the ancient Near East, formal agreements between parties were recorded in contracts written on *cuneiform tablets or other materials, although a written agreement was not essential. In the case of an oral agreement, there must have been symbolic acts, witnesses and a prescribed form of words to render the agreement valid, but the evidence for these has not survived. Legal documents refer to symbolic acts even in the case of written agreements, but over the centuries these were referred to less and less, perhaps because the written record was regarded as valid on its own.

Written contracts are best attested from *Mesopotamia. Their wording changed over time, and some clauses were peculiar to particular localities (such as *Nuzi), but they always recorded essentially the same information: the nature of the agreement between the parties or the job to be done; the conditions, i.e. in the case of a work contract, payment (normally in *silver, wool, barley or sheep), *clothing and ration allowances if appropriate, penalties for non-fulfilment or withdrawal from the contract, sometimes special clauses regarding holidays, in land-lease contracts clauses covering allocation of losses sustained by storm or flood; the names of the parties and of witnesses (sometimes only two or

three, occasionally thirteen or so); the date (day, month and year of a *king's reign); and often the name of the *scribe (sometimes appended as a final witness). Sometimes the personal *seal of a witness was impressed in the wet clay, and a clay envelope wrapped around the tablet repeating the contents.

Contracts were drawn up for loans, sales, land leases, apprenticeships, hired labour, manufacturing work, *adoptions, *marriages, divorces – some contracts were essentially prenuptial agreements, for example delineating the rights and responsibilities of a future son-in-law in return for cancelling his debts and giving him inheritance rights. Marriage contracts were kept indefinitely, but loan and debt contracts were usually destroyed when the debt was paid. Some surviving examples were model contracts prepared as scribal exercises. By the seventh century BC, commodity contracts, e.g. for grain, may have been primarily in Aramaic on papyrus, but currency loans remained in Akkadian on cuneiform tablets.

A typical herding contract between the owner of a flock and a shepherd included the composition of the flock and the conditions of employment, i.e. that the shepherd was liable for replacing any lost animal, and the amount and nature of payment. The shepherd normally kept all the milk products and a fixed amount of wool per adult animal, a food ration and a clothing allowance, and also received the pay for a subordinate. The contract might specify that if the shepherd's shepherd boy ran away, the shepherd was responsible for the loss. *Palaces and *temples, with larger flocks, made contracts with herding contractors, who in turn employed shepherds.

Labour or work contracts which specified work to be carried out in return for a stated payment were not common, and may have been based on oral agreements. None at all have been found from *Hittite *Anatolia. Some labour contracts from the Neo-*Babylonian period stipulated that during the period of the contract the hired labourer had no right to leave his job and seek another. If the labourer missed a certain number of workdays, he had to hire a replacement, pay him the appropriate wage and supply the normal food ration.                PB

Document defining the division of property between a brother and sister. The tablet was enclosed in a clay envelope on which the text was repeated and the seals of witnesses impressed. From Alalakh, eighteenth century BC. WA 131449.

M.A. DANDAMAYEV, 'Free Hired Labor in Babylonia during the Sixth through Fourth Centuries BC', *Labor in the Ancient Near East*, ed. M.A. Powell (New Haven, CN 1987) 271–9.

G. DOSCH, 'Non-slave Labor in Nuzi', *Labor in the Ancient Near East*, ed. M.A. Powell (New Haven, CN 1987) 223–35.

S. GREENGUS, 'The Old Babylonian Marriage Contract', *Journal of the American Oriental Society* 89 (1969) 505–32.

J.N. POSTGATE, *Fifty Neo-Assyrian Legal Documents* (Warminster 1976) 4–5, 32–55.

——, 'Middle Assyrian to Neo-Assyrian: The Nature of the Shift', *Assyria im Wandel der Zeiten*, eds H. Waetzoldt and H. Hauptmann (Heidelberg 1997) 159–68.

J.N. POSTGATE and S. PAYNE, 'Some Old Babylonian Shepherds and their Flocks', *Journal of Semitic Studies* 20 (1975) 1–21.

C. ZACCAGNINI, 'On the Juridical Terminology of Neo-Assyrian and Aramaic Contracts', *Assyria im Wandel der Zeiten*, eds H. Waetzoldt and H. Hauptmann (Heidelberg 1997) 203–8.

**Copper**  Copper lay at the heart of *metalworking prior to the appearance of *iron. There are good sources of copper ores in *Anatolia and *Iran, and at Faynan and Timna in the southern *Levant. *Cyprus was a substantial exporter during the second millennium BC, while Magan, now identified with *Oman, was a major supplier of copper to *Mesopotamia during the third and early second millennia BC.

The earliest copper artefacts were made from native copper, nuggets of which can be cold hammered to make simple pins and rings, a practice documented at Çayönü in eastern Anatolia by 8000 BC. This initial phase is sometimes described as 'trinket metallurgy'. The process of smelting, that is the extraction of metal from its ore through heating, is first documented by the discovery of a lead bracelet from *Yarim Tepe dating to the early seventh millennium BC.

Copperworking debris is known from a number of fifth-millennium BC contexts including Tepe Ghabristan in Iran and several *Chalcolithic settlements in Anatolia and southern *Palestine. The first large groups of artefacts survive from the fourth millennium BC at Nahal Mishmar west of the Dead Sea (316 objects) and at *Arslantepe in eastern Anatolia, and mark the emergence of large-scale copper metallurgy.

Two distinct copper industries are documented in Chalcolithic Palestine. One used low-impurity copper, probably from Faynan, to produce utilitarian artefacts. The other used an alloy high in arsenic and antimony to produce a range of elaborate 'prestige' artefacts, many made using the sophisticated technique of lost-wax casting. Also appearing throughout the ancient Near East at this time was copper with several per cent of arsenic, an alloy superior to copper in both hardness and working properties. The alloy of copper and *tin (*bronze) was developed in the third millennium BC. During the Late Bronze Age copper was transported around the eastern Mediterranean in the form of distinctive oxhide ingots, a large number of which were found on the *Ulu Burun *shipwreck.

In addition to *tools and weapons, copper was used for the production of statuary. Large, complex statues were made in several pieces, and hollow-cast for economy. Copper was also employed as a decorative element in public architecture, for example in the frieze of the third-millennium BC *temple at *Ubaid, or the lion statues at the entrance to the Temple of *Dagan at *Mari.

GP

P.T. CRADDOCK, *Early Metal Mining and Production* (Edinburgh 1995).

P.R.S. MOOREY, *Ancient Mesopotamian Materials and Industries: The Archaeological Evidence* (Oxford 1994).

J.D. MUHLY, 'Mining and Metalworking in Ancient Western Asia', *Civilizations of the Ancient Near East*, ed. J.M. Sasson (New York 1995) 1501–21.

M. TADMOR *et al.*, 'The Nahal Mishmar Hoard from the Judean Desert: Technology, Composition, and Provenance', *Atiqot* 27 (1995) 95–148.

Copper objects from the Chalcolithic hoard in the 'Cave of the Treasure' at Nahal Mishmar: crown; sceptre decorated with ibexes; macehead decorated with double ibex (© The Israel Museum, Jerusalem. IAA 61-177, 61-88, 61-119).

**Cosmetics** Compared with the copious artistic evidence from *Egypt, relatively little is known about cosmetics in the ancient Near East. On most relief and *sculpture, the colour has not survived so there is no indication of how the eyes and faces of men and *women might have been highlighted with cosmetics. Objects which contained or applied cosmetics have been found on excavations, and sometimes these contain a residue of the original cosmetic which can be analysed. Textual evidence is scanty. Certainly women – and *goddesses in *myths – used cosmetics for eyes and for the complexion. Eye-shadow was mainly made of antimony paste, and in *Assyria applied with a carved *ivory pin. Rouge for the face is mentioned in one text. In one of the *Amarna Letters, King Tushratta of *Mitanni mentions sending a scent container full of 'sweet oil' to his sister at the Egyptian court. In the *Mari texts, a perfume-maker is known, in charge of essences of cypress, storax, myrtle, cedar and juniper. Recipes for perfume from late second-millennium BC *Ashur include myrtle and other aromatic plants, steeped and simmered in water for several days, after which oil was added.

Cosmetic palettes made of ivory, *stone or occasionally *metal were widely used in most periods. Usually these have a saucer-shaped indentation in the middle where the cosmetic was kept and possibly mixed. Sometimes the palettes have engraved decoration, or were made in the shape of *animals, perhaps indicating that they were toilet items of value. It is possible that in addition to holding cosmetic pastes for use as make-up, these palettes were also used for *medicinal pastes and unguents. Small stone pestles and *copper or *bone sticks or rods, also found on excavations, may have been used to crush and mix raw materials into cosmetics.

Chemical analysis of the remains of pastes found on palettes, some from the 'Royal Cemetery' at *Ur, shows that they were often derived from natural dyes, such as flowers, roots, berries and invertebrate animals, or from minerals. Blue paste came from cobalt, green from malachite or turquoise, and red probably from ochre.    PB

M. BIMSON, 'Cosmetic Pigments from the "Royal Cemetery" of Ur', *Iraq* 42 (1980) 75–9.

M. DAYAGI-MENDELS, *Perfumes and Cosmetics in the Ancient World* (Jerusalem 1989).

E. EBELING, 'Mittelassyrische Rezepte zur Herstellung von wohlriechenden Salben', *Orientalia* 17 (1948) 129–45, 299–313; 18 (1949) 404–18; 19 (1950) 265–78.

E. PASZTHORY, *Salben, Schminken und Parfüme im Altertum* (Mainz am Rhein 1992).

**Court:** see Royal court

**Covenants:** see Treaties and covenants

**Craftsmen** In ancient Near Eastern sources, the phrase we translate as 'craftsman' or 'artisan' meant any practitioner of a specialist skill. What we today call 'craftsmen'

or even '*artists' – sculptors, carpenters, potters, metalworkers – appear collectively in administrative texts together with musicians, *scribes, cooks, diviners and so on.

The training of craftsmen is not often documented, but skills could be either acquired through apprenticeships or passed on within families – some dynasties of carpenters, metalworkers and goldsmiths are documented over centuries. There is debate as to whether there were guilds of craftsmen, but this is unlikely before the fifth century BC, although Neo-*Babylonian craftsmen at *Uruk collectively bargained with their *temple employer over working conditions.

Virtually all the extant written documentation concerns state workshops or employees. The organization of royal workshops is well documented at *Mari, where the Old Babylonian *palace was a centre of production of articles made from *metals, wool, *stone, *wood and leather. Texts include lists of goods, names of craftsmen and their rations, and *letters which give orders, accept deliveries and record complaints, including a strike by craftsmen against an unpopular foreman. Craftsmen employed by the palace were provided with accommodation in a craft quarter and given payment, clothing, rations and *slaves and employed for life (although Neo-Babylonian Uruk used contract staff). Blind people are listed among craftsmen in palace workshops at *Chagar Bazar, receiving the same rations as others. Palace workshops used both free men and prisoner-of-war slaves, and new influxes of prisoners from *military campaigns were quickly absorbed. The Mari texts record craftsmen escaping from one *city to another and being returned in chains. Craftsmen were also expected to help with the harvest, and the *Hittite Laws list the military and *agricultural duties of metalworkers. Sometimes craftsmen were sent from one royal court to another, for example when a Hittite *king requested a sculptor from the king of *Babylon. There is some evidence for itinerant craftsmen travelling with extensive trains, including slaves.

*Work was normally organized by material: stone-cutters made *seals, reliefs and vases, while carpenters made lyres, statues or wagons. Single workshops did not always complete an item: at *Isin, carpenters made *furniture which was sent to another workshop for inlaying. Workshops are difficult to identify archaeologically: among those known are ones for seals at *Ugarit,

Terracotta of a craftsman, probably a carpenter, at work on a furniture leg. Old Babylonian period, c.1800 BC (© Pierre et Maurice Chuzeville, Département des Antiquités Orientales, Musée du Louvre AO 12450).

stone vessels at *Alalakh, and a sculptor's workshop at *Eshnunna. Craftsmen of the same type often worked in the same quarter, within or outside a town. *Textiles often appear to have been made at home, although texts from the Third Dynasty of *Ur refer to textile factories in outlying *villages which employed up to two hundred female weavers. Craft quarters situated outside or at the edge of *towns were usually those with facilities such as furnaces or which produced pungent odours, or required large amounts of raw materials, for example late third-millennium BC *copper and *pottery production quarters at Altintepe in Turkestan. Craftsmen sometimes lived in their craft quarters, as with metalworkers at *Shahr-i Sokhta in *Iran in the third millennium BC, though at Sarepta in *Phoenicia and at Tepe *Hissar the craft quarters were not residential.

Possible *tombs of craftsmen are known, for example one at Tello containing weighing equipment perhaps belonging to a *jeweller, and a possible leatherworker's tomb at Ur. Depictions of craftsmen are rare: one of the few is on the *Balawat gates, showing a mason carving the rock relief of *Shalmaneser III.                                    PB

S. DALLEY, *Mari and Karana: Two Old Babylonian Cities* (London 1984) 50–77.
A.C. GUNTER (ed.), *Investigating Artistic Environments in the Ancient Near East* (Washington, D.C. 1990).
D. MATTHEWS, 'Artisans and Artists in Ancient Western Asia', *Civilizations of the Ancient Near East*, ed. J.M. Sasson (New York 1995) 455–68.
P.R.S. MOOREY, *Ancient Mesopotamian Materials and Industries: The Archaeological Evidence* (Oxford 1994) 13–19.

## Creation legends and cosmogonies

The two most famous accounts of the creation of the world and humankind surviving from the ancient Near East are the *Hebrew in Genesis 1, 2 and the *Babylonian Epic of Creation ('*Enūma eliš*'). The latter was written to glorify *Marduk, perhaps when his statue was recovered from *Elam by *Nebuchadnezzar I (c.1120 BC). It explains how nothing existed at first except Apsû and Tiamat, the watery mass of fresh water and ocean. Four generations of *gods were born within them and disturbed them by their antics, so Anzû proposed to destroy them. *Ea, the youngest, cast a spell on Anzû, took his regalia and killed him, making the fresh water (Apsû) his abode. There Marduk was born. The rumbustuous gods still disturbed Tiamat, and her supporters encouraged her to fight them, with Qingu as her champion and a gang of *monsters. Ea failed to overcome them, so called on Marduk. Discovering their danger, the gods summoned Marduk, held a *banquet and endowed him with supreme power, proved by his ability to destroy a constellation by his command, then call it back into existence. In single combat, Marduk killed Tiamat and conquered her allies, taking as his prize the Tablet of Destinies, the control of the future. Tiamat he split, half becoming the sky, its waters contained above it, setting the stars in their places, the moon to regulate the *calendar. From her eyes he drew the Tigris and Euphrates; her udders became moun-

The design on this cylinder seal is thought to depict Marduk defeating Tiamat, as described in the Babylonian Epic of Creation. Height 3.4 cm. Assyrian, c.700 BC. WA 89589.

tains. All the gods hailed Marduk as king and he proposed to create man to work the land, allowing the gods to rest. Ea suggested a defeated god be killed to provide the raw material, so Qingu was executed and man made from his blood. Finally *Babylon was built as Marduk's sanctuary and, in another banquet, Marduk's status was fixed in fifty ceremonial names. In its surviving manuscripts, all of the first millennium BC, the epic was written on seven tablets.

In Genesis God creates by command in six days, in sequence, light and darkness, the atmosphere, land and plants, heavenly bodies and time-keeping, marine creatures and birds, land animals and humankind, resting on the seventh day. Comparison with *Enūma eliš* has led to assertions of dependence. Genesis 1: 2 speaks of 'the face of the deep', the *Hebrew word *tehom* being taken as the same as Tiamat, but it is now clear that there is only a linguistic link rather than any real connection. The seven days were compared to the seven tablets, but the latter are the fortuitous result of the division of the text for convenient copying. Splitting Tiamat to make heaven and earth is like the dividing of the two in Genesis 1, 3–5, but this idea is found in creation stories from other societies, too. In the creation of man with a divine element to care for the earth and the consequent divine rest there is a general similarity.

The Hebrew narrative has more in common with the older Babylonian poem, the Epic of Atrahasis (see Flood). This begins with the gods wearied through toiling to dig canals and raise food, striking in protest. Eventually Ea proposes the creation of a substitute. With the Mother goddess, he mixes clay with the flesh of an executed god, the gods spit on the mixture, wombs are prepared and seven pairs of humans born. The gods rest as man works the land. The story continues to the Flood. *Enūma eliš* clearly draws on parts of this story, and of others.

Other *Sumerian and Babylonian accounts present various ideas. The gods themselves arose from the earth, or were self-generated, or there was an original pair, variously the horizons of heaven and earth, earth and water, or eternity. As for humanity, a god dug in the ground with his hoe for clay to make them in a mould, like a brick, or they sprouted from the ground like a plant. A unique Babylonian composition, centred on the *town of

Dunnu, tells of the earth and her spouse producing the sea and the cattle-god, the latter marrying his mother and killing his father, a sequence repeated by successive generations.

The last myth is comparable to the *Hurrian *Kumarbi story in which Kumarbi leads the *underworld gods against the gods of heaven, in the process emasculating his father *Anu and becoming pregnant with the *weather-god and other gods. Echoes of these ideas are seen in the Olympic creation story of ancient Greece and the *Phoenician story of Elyon and Uranus reported in *Roman times.

The threat of the uncontrollable ocean lies behind Enūma eliš's picture of Tiamat and that aspect appears in the *Ugaritic *Baal myth as he conquers Yam, the sea, although that is not a creation story. In a *letter from *Mari, the god *Adad mentions the weapons with which he fought the sea. Echoes of this picture are seen in *Yahweh's defeat of Leviathan, Rahab and sea monsters in the Hebrew *Bible and in references to setting *boundaries for the ocean. That these are all references to a cosmic battle at creation may be questioned; Babylonia has a myth about the god *Ninurta defeating waters threatening the created world.               ARM

S. DALLEY, Myths from Mesopotamia (Oxford 1989).

A. HEIDEL, The Babylonian Genesis (Chicago 1951).

R. S. HESS and D. T. TSUMURA (eds), I Studied Inscriptions from Before the Flood (Winona Lake, IN 1994).

H.A. HOFFNER, Jr., Hittite Myths (Atlanta, GA 1990) 38–61 (Kumarbi).

W.G. LAMBERT, 'The Cosmology of Sumer and Babylon', Ancient Cosmologies, eds C. Blacker and M. Loewe (London 1975) 42–65.

——, 'Myth and Mythmaking in Sumer and Akkad', Civilizations of the Ancient Near East, ed. J.M. Sasson (New York 1995) 1825–35.

D.T. TSUMURA, The Earth and the Waters in Genesis 1 and 2: A Linguistic Investigation (Sheffield 1989).

## Cremation

In the ancient Near East, cremation did not normally result in complete destruction of the body, and the burned bones were collected and buried, often in a *pottery container. It is sporadically attested in all areas from the sixth millennium BC on. Isolated instances of cremation, among the more usual inhumation, are sometimes interpreted as *burials of foreign residents or individuals somehow distinguished from the rest of the population, for example prisoners, lepers or *criminals. Textual evidence hints at the cremation of the dead *king in the *Ur III period, and of the dead substitute king in the Neo-*Assyrian period.

Cremation was first practised systematically by the *Hittites in the second millennium BC. At the cemetery of Osmankayasi, the burned remains were put in small vessels inside storage jars laid in pairs mouth to mouth, and placed in a grotto. Several Hittite cremation *rituals describe the treatment of royal corpses, the best preserved being a fourteen-day ritual. This took place at the capital, *Hattusas, and the royal dead were brought there even if they normally resided in the provinces and had died far

away. The corpse was burned in a special location, and the burnt bones were wrapped in a linen cloth and placed in a grave chamber. As part of the ritual, heads of *horses and oxen, and picks, spades and ploughs were also burned and the ashes scattered.

Cremation remained common in *Syria and *Anatolia in the first half of the first millennium BC, at *Carchemish, *Deve Hüyük, *Hama and in *Phrygia, possibly attesting to a lingering Hittite tradition. It was also known in *Palestine and especially *Phoenicia, often practised alongside inhumation. However, there was no uniformity in the treatment of cremated remains, which ranged from burial in urns in built tombs to placement of burnt bodies in sandpits.                                                    PB

P. BIENKOWSKI, 'Some Remarks on the Practice of Cremation in the Levant', Levant 14 (1982) 80–9.

W. HOROWITZ and P.J. WATSON, 'Further Notes on the Birmingham Tablets Volume I', Acta Sumerologica (Japan) 13 (1991) 409–17.

H. OTTEN, Hethitische Totenrituale (Berlin 1958).

## Crime and punishment

The evidence for crime comes from *Mesopotamian and *Hittite *law codes and a few surviving records of court cases. Murder, rape, wounding, theft, *adultery and negligence causing injury or damage were recognized as crimes. Each law code contains slightly different cases and punishments, but there are many similarities.

In cases of murder, the victim's *family could choose between the death penalty and compensation, though a lighter penalty might be set where there was no premeditation. For rape, the status of the victim – whether she was married or not – and her lack of consent were taken into account. If the rapist was married, his wife might be assigned to the father of the victim for *sexual abuse. If the act took place in the *city, consent was presumed; if in the country, it was not, and it was classed as rape. This test, from the Code of *Hammurabi, is explained in the *Old Testament book of Deuteronomy, since in the city the girl's cries for help would be heard, so if she did not cry out consent was presumed. Wounding of parts of the body could be punished by reciprocal wounding of the offender, or sometimes by payment of the doctor's fee and even nursing the victim and compensating him. The Middle *Assyrian laws were particularly draconian, and, if a *woman intervened in a fight and crushed a man's testicles, her nipples were torn out. In cases of aggravated theft, the victim was entitled to the death penalty as revenge, but for simple theft compensation was imposed. If a householder killed a burglar at night on his premises, he was not guilty of murder. Negligence was recognized as potentially a serious crime: a builder whose construction collapsed on a houseowner and killed him could be executed, but in less aggravated cases compensation sufficed. If the houseowner's son died, it was the offender's son upon whom revenge was exacted. The killing of a *slave normally resulted in a payment to his master.

The punishment meted out by a court was essentially on behalf of the victim or his family: the punishment set the limit on revenge against the offender or his family, or set the level of compensation in lieu of revenge. The way in which the death penalty was carried out was not usually stated, but drowning, stoning, burning, impalement and dismemberment by ox teams are mentioned. Occasionally, an example was set by beheading a criminal and displaying his head. Mutilation was used as a tit-for-tat punishment, such as cutting off a hand for wounding, a lip for unlawful kissing, castrating an adulterer, or stinging by bees for stealing a hive. Flogging was used, the Middle Assyrian laws specifying between twenty and one hundred strokes.

There is some evidence for incarceration in prisons for short periods, for those awaiting trial or the death penalty. The *Mari archives suggest that prisoners were put to work, and that a prisoner could negotiate a payment for his release, while Old Assyrian texts from *Kanesh suggest that a prisoner could continue his business activities through visitors. Locations of prisons are uncertain. There are indications that the temple of *Enlil at *Nippur contained a prison, and a remote Hittite outpost had its own prison. It is possible that in the Old Hittite period, a family or tribe could apprehend a criminal and hold him in its own house until trial.    PB

J.J. FINKELSTEIN, 'Sex Offenses in Sumerian Laws', *Journal of the American Oriental Society* 86 (1966) 355–72.

H.A. HOFFNER, JR, 'Legal and Social Institutions of Hittite Anatolia', *Civilizations of the Ancient Near East*, ed. J.M. Sasson (New York 1995) 555–69.

T. JACOBSEN, 'An Ancient Mesopotamian Trial for Homicide', *Toward the Image of Tammuz*, ed. W.L. Moran (Cambridge, MA 1970) 193–213.

M. ROTH, 'Homicide in the Neo-Assyrian Period', *Language, Literature, and History: Philological and Historical Studies Presented to Erica Reiner*, ed. F. Rochberg-Halton (New Haven, CN 1987) 351–65.

J.M. SASSON (ed.), *The Treatment of Criminals in the Ancient Near East* (Leiden 1977).

R. WESTBROOK, 'Punishments and Crimes', *Anchor Bible Dictionary* 5, ed. D.N. Freedman (New York 1992) 546–56.

**Croesus** In Greek and Roman tradition, Croesus, the last king of *Lydia (c.560–547 BC), was the classic tragic figure: a king with wealth and power who lost everything. He has remained a common theme for painting and drama up to the present. The most important source for his life is *Herodotus, who wrote well after his death. The only contemporary written evidence for Croesus appears to be fragmentary dedications on column bases of the Temple of Artemis at Ephesus.

According to Herodotus, Croesus conquered all the nations west of the Halys river in *Anatolia except the Cilicians and *Lycians. Although he fought against *Greek states on the coast, he made numerous lavish dedications to Greek sanctuaries of precious vessels, columns and statues. A *silver krater (large bowl) he donated to Delphi, used annually as a container in a public *festival, had a capacity of between 15,000 and 22,800 l. In *Greek tradition, Croesus was associated with the minting of the earliest *coins.

Croesus of Lydia is credited with some of the earliest coins. Gold and silver pieces show a lion confronting a bull with shapeless punch marks on the reverse. Gold stater, diameter 1.65 cm, weight 8.05 g. BMC 31.

Croesus on his pyre, depicted on a fifth-century BC Greek vase found in Italy (original in the Louvre; from S. Lloyd, *Ancient Turkey* (London 1989) fig. 37).

Croesus was eventually defeated by *Cyrus II, using *camels whose smell disrupted the *horses of the Lydian cavalry and then capturing *Sardis. There are contradictory accounts concerning Croesus' subsequent fate. The *Babylonian *Nabonidus *Chronicle might imply that the Lydian king was killed, but he is not named, nor is the reading of the name of the land certain. Herodotus describes two incidents, usually dismissed as legends, which saved the life of Croesus. A *Persian soldier was about to strike him when the king's son, hitherto deaf and dumb, shouted 'Man, do not kill Croesus', and he was brought before Cyrus. Then, when Croesus was about to be burned alive on a pyre, a sudden storm extinguished the flames. According to Herodotus, Croesus later became a counsellor to Cyrus and to his successor, Cambyses.   PB

C.H. GREENEWALT, 'Croesus of Sardis and the Lydian Kingdom of Anatolia', *Civilizations of the Ancient Near East*, ed. J.M. Sasson (New York 1995) 1173–83.

G.M.A. HANFMANN, *From Croesus to Constantine* (Ann Arbor, MI 1975) 1–21.

**Crowns and royal regalia** When kingship was brought to earth by the *gods, according to *Sumerian mythology, it was represented by three symbols: a hat, a stick and a stool. These are essentially the same as royal regalia in the millennia since: crown, sceptre and throne.

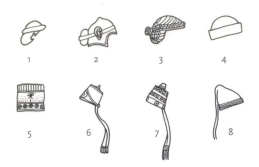

The changing shape of crowns in different periods (after W. Waetzoldt and R.M. Boehmer, 'Kopfbedeckung', *Reallexikon der Assyriologie* 6 (Berlin/New York 1980–3)):
1. Uruk–Jemdet Nasr, 2. Early Dynastic III, 3. Akkadian, 4. Old Babylonian, 5. Kassite, 6. Middle Assyrian, 7. Neo-Assyrian, 8. Neo-Babylonian.

These three symbols are often mentioned in *hymns addressed to *kings, together with other royal regalia, for example a mace.

Depictions of rulers in *sculpture and on *seals sometimes show them sitting on special thrones and holding a mace or sceptre. Sometimes kings hold a lotus flower, which was a royal symbol among the *Aramaeans and *Ammonites. *Hittite kings are often depicted with a curved staff of office, sometimes interpreted as a symbol derived from a shepherd's crook and reflecting the concept of the king as shepherd.

Particular forms of headgear seem to have distinguished rulers, and some texts refer to a 'golden crown'. What may be a real *gold crown came from the Royal Tombs at *Ur, a gold helmet in the shape of a hairstyle then associated with royalty, decorated with a thick plait wrapped round the head and looped in a bun at the nape of the neck. This royal 'bun' could be strapped to a helmet to denote royalty, as worn by King Eannatum of *Lagash on the Stela of the Vultures commemorating his victory over Umma, by Lamgi-Mari at *Mari and possibly by *Sargon of *Akkad.

The statues of *Gudea of *Lagash depict him wearing a new type of crown that was to become traditional attire of royalty for several centuries and was also worn by kings of neighbouring lands. This was a close-fitting cap with a vertical brim decorated with little curls that probably indicated fur. This brimmed crown was part of the dress of the king as a warrior, at least on ceremonial occasions. In *Syria in the early second millennium BC, kings wore a tall, round-topped headdress or a version of the *Babylonian brimmed crown. Hittite kings wore a close-fitting cap.

The crown of Neo-Assyrian kings was a pointed cone around which was a turban, shaped like a truncated cone, with one end hanging down. *Ashurbanipal wore either a hairband studded with rosettes – a version of everyday Assyrian wear – or a taller form of the turban, also with rosettes. His *queen had a crenellated crown that was later adopted by the *Achaemenids, and which is much

closer to what we imagine today as a 'crown'. Eighth-century BC queens' burials from *Nimrud under the floors of the *palace included an intricate gold crown or headdress and a headband with a tasselled fringe. Neo-Babylonian kings had a crown in the shape of a helmet. In the same period, *Elamite kings wore a domed crown with a feather hanging down behind. Earlier Aramaean rulers wore a distinctive domed hat with a point, perhaps a version of the Assyrian turban, later ones a variety of headdresses. PB

D. COLLON, 'Clothing and Grooming in Ancient Western Asia', *Civilizations of the Ancient Near East*, ed. J.M. Sasson (New York 1995) 503–15.

J.N. POSTGATE, *Early Mesopotamia: Society and Economy at the Dawn of History* (London 1992) 260–3.

E. UNGER, 'Diadem und Krone', *Reallexikon der Assyriologie* 2 (Berlin 1938) 201–11.

W. WAETZOLDT and R.M. BOEHMER, 'Kopfbedeckung', *Reallexikon der Assyriologie* 6 (Berlin/New York 1980–3) 197–210.

**Cuneiform script** As the very early *writing came to be a matter of course in *Babylonia, *scribes wrote faster and the original pictorial signs were simplified. The reed stylus was cut to impress either a straight line or a corner into the clay tablets which were held in the hand for use as writing material. Pressure by the scribe's hand pushed one end of the stylus deeper into the clay, characteristically producing the wedge shape that has given the script its name (Latin *cuneus*, 'wedge'). The earliest inscriptions on *stone do not reproduce the wedge shapes. At first writers manipulated the stylus to produce wedges with their heads at any point in a circle, but for ease and rapidity they gradually stopped making any in the degrees between 12 and 7 o'clock. By the mid second millennium BC the pictorial forms had disappeared, and the signs were conventional groups of wedge-shaped strokes. Speed of writing brought continuing simplification in documents of daily life over the next two millennia, monuments and *seal inscriptions often presenting older forms.

The signs stood for words (logograms) and were written in sense groups within ruled compartments until the *dynasty of *Akkad when the wider writing of *Akkadian required the sequence of signs to be clearer so they were written in horizontal lines reading from left to right, according to common opinion, although it is possible that the signs were read in columns from top to bottom and right to left for some time.

The earliest tablets (*Uruk IV) show about 1,200 logograms in use, but the introduction of the 'rebus principle' (see Writing), which permitted the syllabic spelling of words, allowed the number to drop to about six hundred. Whether the stimulus for that principle arose within the native use of the system or from the need to write foreign words is uncertain. By the middle of the third millennium BC cuneiform was being adopted for *Semitic Akkadian. While common nouns might still be shown by logograms, syllabic signs were added to mark Semitic case endings and suffixes and most words were

The picture of a fish as it developed in the third millennium BC, the early second millennium BC (Hammurabi's Laws and cursive form), the Neo-Assyrian period and the Persian period. The sign retained its value *ha*, the Sumerian word for fish, as a syllabic sign, but could also be read in Akkadian *nunu*, 'fish'.

An example of the use of cuneiform signs. Transliterated as [md]EN-*ib-ni ina* GIŠ.GU.ZA *ú-šib*, the signs are:
   [m] determinative sign for man,
   [d] determinative sign for god,
   EN Sumerian logogram for 'lord', with the determinative before it, therefore, the Akkadian god Bel,
   *ib-ni* syllabic spelling of an Akkadian verbal form, *ibni*, 'he created',
   *ina* logogram for 'in, on',
   GIŠ Sumerian determinative sign for a wooden object,
   GU.ZA Sumerian logogram 'throne', Akkadian *kussî*,
   *ú-šib* syllabic spelling of an Akkadian verbal form, *ûšib*, 'he sat'.
The sentence means 'Bel-ibni sat on the throne'.

written syllabically. The stock of signs needed for daily business in the Old *Babylonian period fell to about two hundred, when it was usual to write most words syllabically. In subsequent centuries there was a tendency to use more logograms, especially in technical cultic and *omen compositions. To counter the ambiguity inherent in the mixture of logographic and syllabic values, a small number of logograms were placed before or after nouns to show their classification. Thus the sign for '*wood' preceded names of *trees or wooden objects (e.g. a chair, a *boat), the sign for plurality after a noun marked it accordingly. The Sumerian language was apparently tonal, but since the sounds cannot be recovered, modern transcriptions give the language many words which look the same, although they are written with different signs and it is conventional to distinguish them numerically, thus *sá* 'to be equal' is not the same as *sa₄* 'to name' or *sa₁₀* 'to buy, sell'. The language did not have the same phonetic stock as Akkadian and other languages written in cuneiform, so many signs had to do double duty, for example *ga* serving also for *qa*, *az* for *as*. Despite these seemingly clumsy aspects, the script was used across the *Fertile Crescent and beyond for two thousand years and had a major role in spreading Babylonian culture, facilitating *trade, *administration and imperialism and preserving history and tradition. ARM

D.O. EDZARD, 'Keilschrift', *Reallexikon der Assyriologie* 5 (Berlin/New York 1976–80) 544–68.
H.J. NISSEN, P. DAMEROW and R.K. ENGLUND, *Archaic Bookkeeping: Writing and Techniques of Economic Administration in the Ancient Near East* (Chicago/London 1993).
C.B.F. WALKER, *Cuneiform* (London 1987).

A brick inscribed with the titles and conquests of Eannatum of Lagash illustrates the wedge-shaped strokes and angular forms which the cuneiform script had taken after several centuries of use. From Lagash, c.2400 BC. WA 85979.

**Curses:** see Oaths and curses

**Cylinder seal** The earliest archaeological evidence for cylinders carved with designs comes from impressions found at the small site of Sharafabad in south-west *Iran dating to the Middle *Uruk Period (c.3600 BC). Recently impressions of a similar date have been discovered at Tell *Brak in north *Syria. Cylinder seals appear slightly later at Uruk and *Susa, where they are used to mark clay which covered cords securing doors and containers. By the Late Uruk period (3300-3000 BC) cylinder seals are rolled over hollow clay balls containing 'tokens' as well as impressing clay tags and tablets marked with tally signs. Often up to three different cylinder seals were impressed on each piece of clay with scenes showing economic activities, food production, processions or *ritual acts. These may reflect different 'departments' within the central authority. With the development of *cuneiform writing in southern *Mesopotamia, *stamp seals were largely replaced here with cylinders, although impressions on cuneiform tablets did not appear until the end of the third millennium BC. Cylinders were then used wherever cuneiform was adopted, for example by the *Hittites, *Elamites and *Urartians. The designs on

Lapis lazuli cylinder seal showing two banquet scenes, the principal figure in the upper register being the female seated at the left, perhaps the owner of the seal named in the inscription 'Pu-abi, queen'. Height 4.9 cm. From Pu-abi's tomb at Ur, Early Dynastic IIIa, c.2500 BC. WA 121544.

Around the surface of this cylinder the engraver has cut a spirited rendering of a lion fighting a winged horse while another horse sits peacefully. Height 4.1 cm. Middle Assyrian, thirteenth century BC. WA 129572.

cylinder seals varied from region to region and over time, and often individual seals can be quite closely dated according to their design or inscription.

In Mesopotamia cylinder seals fell out of favour only when the *Aramaic script, using ink on papyrus, parchment or leather began to replace cuneiform towards the middle of the first millennium BC. The writing material was rolled and tied with a string or cord, whose knot was kept secure by stamping a seal on wax or clay.     PTC

D. COLLON, *First Impressions: Cylinder Seals in the Ancient Near East* (London 1987).

E. PORADA (ed.), *Ancient Art in Seals* (Princeton, NJ 1980).

**Cyprus** Cyprus is one of the largest Mediterranean islands (area 9282 sq km), located at the northern end of the eastern Mediterranean. It lies 122 km from the *Syrian coast and 69 km to the south of the Turkish coast. In winter, in clear weather with snow on the mountains, Cyprus and Turkey are intervisible.

Geographically, topographically and environmentally Cyprus can be divided into three distinct areas. The centre and west of the island are dominated by a volcanic massif, the Troodos mountains, fringed in the south by a narrow and in the west by a wider set of heavily dissected limestone plateaux. The Troodos and the adjacent plateaux receive more rainfall than other parts of the island. The northern coast of the island is dominated by a linear ridge of mountains, the Kyrenia range, which also creates the distinctive finger of the Karpass peninsula pointing towards Syria. Between the Troodos and Kyrenia ranges and to the east of the Troodos is lower-lying relatively arid land, most of which is known as the Mesaoria. The Troodos is dominated by forest. The southern and western plateaux and Kyrenia range have a mixture of woodland, tree and fruit crops (especially olive and vine) and cereal or legume cultivation. The Mesaoria was the breadbasket of Cyprus.

It now seems likely that initial subsistence settlement by expanding agricultural communities occurred in the aceramic *Neolithic. Much of the interaction between Cyprus and the rest of the ancient Near East may relate to the presence of large quantities of *copper on the island. The copper ores are located in a ring of rocks around the lower elevations of the Troodos massif. On Cyprus the earliest evidence for the exploitation of copper comes from the fourth millennium BC, somewhat later than in neighbouring areas, which may relate to the relative isolation of populations on the island in earlier *prehistory. A degree of intense contact between Cyprus and the surrounding mainlands is indicated by material culture and some evidence of exchange in the second part of the third millennium BC (Early Cypriot period). At this period a mass of copper-based *weapons and other *metalwork is found in Cypriot tombs and it is at this period we might imagine the first significant export of Cypriot copper. Chemical analyses suggest, by the Late *Bronze Age, the extensive export of large quantities of Cypriot copper through thriving emporia on the coasts of the island. During the second millennium BC Cyprus, or part of it, was probably known as *Alashiya, and texts referring to this state mention the exchange of large quantities of copper and indicate the relative importance of Alashiya's ruler.

Destructions at the end of the Late Bronze Age may have been connected with the *Sea Peoples, although there was continuity of occupation. After a so-called 'Dark Age' between c.1050 and 850 BC, when *jewellery and metalwork are nevertheless evidence of prosperity and foreign contacts, the *Phoenicians colonized the *city of Kition. Cyprus was conquered by the *Assyrians in the late eighth century BC, and in the sixth century BC by the *Egyptians and then the *Persians. During this time (Archaic period), Cyprus was organized into independent cities mentioned in Assyrian texts.     DB

V. KARAGEORGHIS, *Cyprus* (London 1982).

Map of Cyprus.

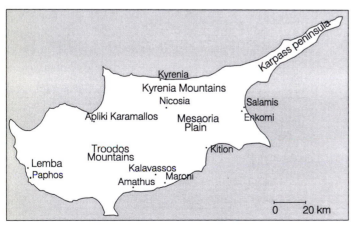

**Cyrus**  Name of the first *Achaemenid king (Cyrus II), his grandfather (Cyrus I), and a brother of Artaxerxes II (Cyrus the Younger). According to Josephus, Xerxes I's son was also called Cyrus, but took the throne name Artaxerxes (I, 465–424 BC).

Cyrus I (mid seventh century BC?): Little is known for certain of this person. In the genealogies of Cyrus II he is recorded as the 'great king, king of *Anshan', descendant of Teispes, father of Cambyses I and grandfather of Cyrus II. He does not appear in the genealogy of Darius I at Bisitun, where Teispes' son is named as Ariaramnes. It is normally considered that Teispes was father of both Cyrus I and Ariaramnes, who after his death ruled respectively in Anshan and *Persia, although it is not certain that Anshan and Persia were ever separate kingdoms. Cyrus I is sometimes equated with 'Kurash, king of the land of Parsuash', who sent tribute to *Ashurbanipal in about 640 BC, but the identification is not proved. *Seal impressions on tablets from *Persepolis are inscribed 'Cyrus, the Anshanite, son of Teispes', but it is not clear whether they refer to the royal Cyrus I, and they may be later.

Cyrus II (559–530 BC): Cyrus' early life is narrated by *Herodotus, partially corroborated by the *Babylonian *Nabonidus *Chronicle. Born about 600 BC, in 559 BC Cyrus became king of Anshan, then under the control of the *Medes. He deposed the Median king Astyages in 550 BC, seizing his capital *Ecbatana and establishing himself as king of the Medes and Persians with his capital at *Pasargadae. In 547 BC he conquered Asia Minor, including the *Greek cities, and *Lydia, with its King *Croesus. In 539 BC Cyrus' army entered *Babylon without a fight and inherited the Neo-*Babylonian empire, as described on the so-called Cyrus Cylinder. Cyrus then campaigned in the east; Herodotus describes his death at the hands of the *queen of the Massagetae in central Asia, with Cyrus' decapitated head put into a skin with human blood so that he could quench his thirst for blood, although

Tomb of Cyrus II at Pasargadae: watercolour by Sir Robert Ker Parker (British Library Add. MS 14758(i) 47/57).

different accounts of his death exist. The Roman historian Arrian records that Alexander the Great ordered the restoration of Cyrus' tomb at Pasargadae after reading its inscription: 'O man, I am Cyrus the son of Cambyses, who founded the empire of Persia, and was king of Asia. Grudge me not therefore this monument.' The tomb survives, although there is no trace of any inscription.

Cyrus the Younger: Appointed satrap of Asia Minor in 408 BC by his father, Darius II, he revolted against his brother Artaxerxes II in 401 BC using Greek mercenaries and was killed in battle. The return of his army to Greece was chronicled by Xenophon in his *Anabasis*.     PB

M.A. DANDAMAEV, *A Political History of the Achaemenid Empire* (Leiden 1989).

W. EILERS, 'Kyros – eine namenkundliche Studie', *Beiträge zur Namenforschung* 15 (1964) 180–236.

T.C. YOUNG, 'The Early History of the Medes and the Persians and the Achaemenid Empire to the Death of Cambyses', *Cambridge Ancient History* 4, 2nd ed. (Cambridge 1988) 24–46.

# D

**Dagan**  Dagan (*Hebrew Dagon) was a West *Semitic *god worshipped throughout the Near East, and especially in the region of the middle Euphrates. The original meaning of the name is unknown, although it has been interpreted as signifying either 'rain' or else 'corn', and Dagan appears to have been a *weather and perhaps *fertility deity. Additionally, he was regarded as a god of the dead at *Mari, where his cult is attested from c.2500 BC, and at *Ugarit, where he was known from about 1300 BC as the father of the god *Baal and second in rank only to the supreme god *El, although he does not

feature as a prominent character in the corpus of Ugaritic *myths. At *Ebla, where his cult was established about 2300 BC, he was the principal deity, and was also an important god at Tuttul (modern Tell *Bi'a) and at Mari. At some uncertain date Dagan became the chief deity of the *Philistines. The *Akkadian kings credited him with much of their military success. The kings of the Third Dynasty of *Ur established for Dagan an official state cult, and a sanctuary to him was constructed at *Nippur. In the Old Babylonian period, there was a temple to the god at *Isin.

The tradition going back at least to the fourth century AD of Dagan as a fish-god is erroneous. JAB/AG

J.F. HEALEY, 'The Underworld Character of the God Dagan', *Journal of North-West Semitic Languages* (1977) 43–51.

——, 'Dagon', *Dictionary of Deities and Demons in the Bible*, eds K. van der Toorn, B. Becking and P.W. van der Horst (Leiden 1995) 408–13.

K. ICHIRO, *Deities in the Mari Texts* (Ann Arbor, MI 1979) 111–51.

H. SCHMÖKEL, *Der Gott Dagan: Ursprung, Verbreitung und Wesen seines Kultes* (Borna/Leipzig 1928).

N. WYATT, 'The Relationship of the Deities Dagan and Hadad', *Ugarit-Forschungen* 12 (1980) 375–9.

**Damascus:** see Aram

**Dance** Dancing is frequently mentioned in *Meso-potamian and *Hittite texts accompanying *music and singing (see Songs), often as part of *rituals and processions; dances are depicted on *cylinder seals. The closest we get to choreography is a Hittite text describing a series of dance steps in order, but without providing the context for the dance. Dancers performed solo, in pairs and in groups in a row or circle. No dancing by men and *women together is attested; different groups of women, young men and old men took turns. Dance positions included spread, crossed and squatting legs, foot clutches and leaps. Only men performed the whirl, squat and acrobatic dances. Hittite dances included parallel rows or circles catching up with the row in front, animal movements and folk dances named after *cities and countries. Dancing was performed on platforms or tables, and in one scene on a kettledrum laid on its side. Dancers sometimes performed while playing musical instruments and singing.

In cult *festivals performers danced, sang and acted in costumes and masks, or in the nude, and sometimes wrestled and acted out mock battles using stage *weapons. Cult activities, probably of the goddess *Ishtar (Inana), included dancing around a copulating couple and transvestite dancing – the latter dancers emitted 'twitters' and 'chirps'. Hittite texts give instructions for group dances performed for the gods or royalty,

Cylinder seal design of the eighteenth century BC including three dancing figures at the left end of the upper register. Height 2.5 cm. WA 86269.

especially during cult processions at festivals, which included a nude solo acrobatic dance. Some Hittite dances involved mime and recreated scenes from the hunt connected with Teteshkhapi, a nature-god.

Not all dancers were professionals employed by *palaces and *temples. Ordinary people danced on social occasions, and officials, *priests and even a Hittite *queen danced during rituals. *Magic and healing rituals were accompanied by dancers, sometimes in animal costumes, chasing away the disease or *demons. PB

Y. GARFINKEL, 'Dancing and the Beginning of Art Scenes in the Early Village Communities of the Near East and South East Europe', *Cambridge Archaeological Journal* 8 (1998) 207–37.

A.D. KILMER, 'Music and Dance in Ancient Western Asia', *Civilizations of the Ancient Near East*, ed. J.M. Sasson (New York 1995) 2601–13.

S. DE MARTINO, *La danza nella cultura ittita* (Florence 1989).

——, 'Music, Dance, and Processions in Hittite Anatolia', *Civilizations of the Ancient Near East*, ed. J.M. Sasson (New York 1995) 2661–9.

**Dating:** see Chronology

**Death and funerary beliefs and customs** All people die, and concern about what happens to the person after death has been an important factor of belief systems and practices in many cultures. In the ancient Near East, as in other cultures, there was a range of different methods of disposing of corpses and of accompanying funerary *rituals. Sometimes bodies were simply exposed to nature, or were *cremated (burnt). The most common practice, however, or at least most detectable in the archaeological record, was inhumation (burial). Differing customs and frequently beliefs are reflected in the variables of burial, such as the construction and degree of elaboration of the *grave architecture, the nature and position of any accompanying grave goods (or lack of them), the position and orientation of the body, the presence or absence of secondary deposits or offerings associated with the funeral and so forth. It is a complex study, which for the ancient Near East has only comparatively recently started to receive serious treatment.

We have some understanding of ideas about the afterlife from *Mesopotamian inscriptions. There was generally a belief in survival of the person in the form of a ghost (*gidim* or *eṭemmu*) who lived in the *underworld. An obligation of the surviving relatives was to make funerary offerings (*kispu*) of *food, drink and oil. Without these offerings, or worse, without proper burial, or if the deceased were disinterred, the ghost would be forced to wander around and might haunt the living. Yet conditions in the underworld were also dismal. In *Sumerian belief, the dead were in utter darkness, feeding on dust and scraps. In the *Assyro-*Babylonian underworld the dead resided among an array of horrifying *demons. A Sumerian poem suggests that on entering the afterlife the dead were expected to present gifts to the *gods of the underworld, while a poem of the Third Dynasty of *Ur refers to differing treatment of the dead in the afterlife according to their condition of burial. To the archaeologist the study of burials is important for what it reveals not so much about death and funerary practices as about life and social status. It has long been appreciated that, notwithstanding certain exceptions, in death it has been usual for persons to maintain the ranking that they enjoyed in life: at its simplest, expensive and labour-intensive burials for the rich, quick and simple burial for the poor.

JAB/AG

J. BOTTÉRO, 'La mythologie de la mort en Mésopotamie ancienne', *Death in Mesopotamia*, ed. B. Alster (Copenhagen 1980) 25–52.

S. CAMPBELL and A.R. GREEN (eds), *The Archaeology of Death in the Ancient Near East* (Oxford 1995).

I.L. FINKEL, 'Necromancy in Ancient Mesopotamia', *Archiv für Orientforschung* 29/30 (1983–4) 1–17.

A.R. GREEN, 'Hell's Angels: Die Ikonographie des Todes in der neuassyrischen und der neubabylonischen Kunst', *Altorientalische Forschungen* 26 (1999) in press.

B. GRONEBERG, 'Zu den mesopotamischen Unterweltsvorstellungen: Das Jenseits als Fortsetzung des Diesseits', *Altorientalische Forschungen* 17 (1990) 244–61.

D.T. POTTS, *Mesopotamian Civilization: The Material Foundations* (London 1997) 220–35.

A. TSUKIMOTO, *Untersuchungen zur Totenpflege (kispum) im alten Mesopotamien* (Neukirchen/Vluyn 1985).

**Decipherment** Knowledge of *Hebrew and *Aramaic in various forms alone survived into modern times from the *languages of the ancient Near East. Forgotten scripts had to be deciphered before other languages could be understood. The local Aramaic *alphabet of Palmyra was decoded first (J.J. Barthélemy, J. Swinton, 1754), with Barthélemy reading the *Phoenician and *Achaemenid Aramaic alphabets soon after. The Old South *Arabian alphabet and dialects were unlocked by E. Rödiger and W. Gesenius in 1842 through the discovery of medieval Arabic books which gave equivalents for the letters. More difficult were the *cuneiform scripts which the numbers of signs implied were not simple alphabets. In 1802 G. Grotefend began to unravel them by establishing the values for most of the thirty-six syllabic signs and some word signs used for Old *Persian on the basis of comparison with later Persian texts. More complicated systems standing in parallel with Old Persian on rock inscriptions in *Iran, notably at Bisitun, attracted *Rawlinson. He made his own translation of the Old Persian (1835–7) and worked on one of two parallel texts. Shortly afterwards *Botta and *Layard unearthed many cuneiform inscriptions in *Assyria and rapidly published copies of them. The publications reached E. Hincks, an Anglican clergyman in Ireland, who advanced Grotefend's work in Old Persian and made the major breakthrough in recognizing that the parallel script, also found in Assyria, comprised syllabic and word signs for writing the *Semitic language of Assyria and *Babylonia. The Royal Asiatic Society invited four scholars who had been working on the Assyrian texts to submit their translations of a previously unseen text. When the versions were compared in

Lines from one of Henry Rawlinson's notebooks with attempts at deciphering the cuneiform syllabary of the Elamite language (British Library MS 47620).

1857, they were found to be sufficiently similar to demonstrate that the cuneiform script had been deciphered, although much was not fully understood until decades later.

A variety of other scripts used in the Near East have been deciphered since cuneiform. E. Hincks pioneered the understanding of the cuneiform syllabary used for inscriptions in *Urartu between 1000 and 600 BC. Monuments from *Syria and *Anatolia bearing *Hittite *hieroglyphic signs defied extensive interpretation until a bilingual Phoenician–Hittite inscription was found at *Karatepe. That allowed values to be ascertained for many signs, but some uncertainties still remain. In *Iron Age *Cyprus inscriptions in a syllabary derived from Cypro-Minoan (see below) occur on some monuments beside *Greek texts. G. Smith established its reading in 1871. In Anatolia the *Carian, *Lycian, *Lydian and *Phrygian languages were written with forms of the Greek alphabet, sometimes augmented, the languages becoming understood through the discovery of parallel Greek texts, although many points have yet to be clarified.

For all of these scripts, the availability of bilingual texts of some sort gave the key. Other scripts have lacked that benefit. The Proto-Sinaitic inscriptions from Serabit el-Khadem present the outstanding example. The limited number of signs suggests a type of alphabet and, reasoning back from Hebrew and Phoenician, Sir Alan Gardiner was able to identify some of the signs as ancestral to the *Canaanite alphabet in 1916. In 1929 excavations at *Ugarit yielded clay tablets inscribed with an unknown cuneiform script of thirty characters. C. Virolleaud, H. Bauer and E. Dhorme quickly deciphered it as an alphabetic writing by initially guessing that it represented a Semitic language, now called Ugaritic. Yet to be deciphered are the few 'pseudo-hieroglyphic' inscriptions from *Byblos from the mid second millennium BC, a system using 114 signs, so probably syllabic, and the half-dozen clay tablets from Tell *Deir Alla bearing deeply incised characters, superficially similar to Mycenaean Greek Linear B. Also related to that is the Cypro-Minoan writing found on clay tablets and tags in Cyprus and on a few tablets and other objects at Ugarit.       ARM

P.T. DANIELS and W. BRIGHT (eds), *The World's Writing Systems* (Oxford 1996) 139–88.

C.H. GORDON, *Forgotten Scripts: The Story of their Decipherment* (Harmondsworth 1971).

M.H. POPE, *The Story of Archaeological Decipherment: From Hittite Hieroglyphs to Linear B* (London 1975).

## Dedan

**Dedan**   Dedan (now called Khirbat al-Khurayba, c.3 km north of modern al-'Ula) was one of the largest oases in north-west *Arabia. It had extensive *irrigated fields as well as palm groves and controlled a narrow passage between high mountains and broken-up lava-flows at a strategically important point on one of the major routes between South Arabia and the *Fertile Crescent. In the *Old Testament, Dedan is often associated with Sheba, reflecting the fact that it was via this route that much of the merchandise travelled from *Saba' to *Transjordan, *Palestine and the Mediterranean (cf. the association of *Tayma and Saba' in the *cuneiform sources).

*Nabonidus, *king of *Babylon (555–539 BC), claimed to have killed a king of Dedan during his ten-year sojourn in Arabia, but at present we have no way of knowing how long the kingdom existed before and after this event. The oasis had its own *alphabet, and one of the inscriptions found there is the epitaph of a certain Kbr'l son of Mt''l king of Dedan. Other texts in this, or a very closely related, script have been found in southern *Mesopotamia. Minaean *merchants from South Arabia set up a *trading station at the oasis in the second half of the first millennium BC, probably because of its links with *Egypt and the Mediterranean, and the kingdom of Dedan was succeeded in the oasis by that of Lihyan. It also seems to have had close links with *Edom. The chief Edomite deity, Qos, is found in a number of theophoric names borne by inhabitants of the oasis, and Ezekiel and Jeremiah in the Old Testament both treat it as the furthest point of Edom.       MCAM

G. BAWDEN, 'Khief Il-Zahrah and the Nature of Dedanite Hegemony in the al-'Ula Oasis', *Atlal* 3 (1979) 63–72.

M.C.A. MACDONALD, 'North Arabia in the First Millennium BCE', *Civilizations of the Ancient Near East*, ed. J.M. Sasson (New York 1995) 1355–69.

——, 'Trade Routes and Trade Goods at the Northern End of the "Incense Road" in the First Millennium B.C.', *Profumi d'Arabia*, ed. A. Avanzini (Rome 1997) 333–49.

A.A. NASIF, *Al-'Ula: An Historical and Archaeological Survey With Special Reference to Its Irrigation System* (Riyadh 1988).

## Dedications and votive gifts

**Dedications and votive gifts**   Recognizing a superior power leads human beings to try to gain favour or to acknowledge and sustain it with presents. The more costly the gift to the giver, the more readily the superior might be expected to comply. At many sites of *temples and shrines bowls, clay figures and more valuable objects are sometimes found where they were set before the *gods or, more often, in pits or trenches (*favissae*) where they were deposited when they had served their purpose, for, having been presented to the deity, they could not be put in a secular dump. The dedication could extend to *slaves and *family members devoted to the service of the

Pale blue chalcedony pebble, polished and pierced as a bead, 4 by 3 by 2.8 cm. The inscription proclaims that the Elamite King Shilhak-Inshushinak had it made and gave it to his daughter, as the picture shows. Twelfth century BC. WA 113886.

gods. Thus *Sargon of *Akkad installed his daughter as *priestess of *Sîn at *Ur and *Nabonidus of *Babylon did the same centuries later. *Phoenicians dedicated their *children to Molech, as did some *Israelites, possibly through fire.

The piety of royal donors was recorded in *Babylonia from Early Dynastic times onward. The notice might be brief, '*King X gave this to god Y', or very long, with praise for the god, rehearsal of the monarch's devotion and prayers for his welfare. After war a portion of the booty might be given to the appropriate god or gods (cf. David of Israel, 2 Samuel 8: 11, 12). *Scribes might copy these notices at later dates and their copies may survive when the valuable originals have disappeared, giving important information (see Sargon; Naram-Sin).

Similar gifts might mark the making or fulfilment of a vow. Occasionally inscriptions are specific, such as the 'Melqart Stela' erected by an *Aramaean King Bar-Hadad near Aleppo, 'because Melqart heard my plea', or many Phoenician and Punic stelae recording offerings made to fulfil vows.       ARM

J. DAY, *Molech: A God of Human Sacrifice in the Old Testament* (Cambridge 1989).

F. ROSENTHAL, in *Ancient Near Eastern Texts*, 3rd ed., ed. J.B. Pritchard (Princeton, NJ 1969) 655.

**Defences:** see Fortifications

**Deification** Deification is the act or process of nominating and treating human beings as if they were deities. In the ancient Near East, it was restricted to *kings, and the deification of kings during their own lifetime was confined to a limited period of *Mesopotamian history. The first king to become a living god was *Naram-Sin, king of *Akkad (reigned c. 2260–2223 BC), and the practice continued with the subsequent kings of Akkad and of the Third Dynasty of *Ur, and with those of the dynasties of *Isin, *Larsa and *Babylon down to Samsu-ditana (reigned c.1625–1595 BC).

Kings who were deified often claimed to be sons or brothers of *gods or heroes (for example, of Lugalbanda). A cult was offered to deified kings in *temples throughout their kingdoms, sometimes continuing after their death, and an extensive literature of *Sumerian praise *poetry was composed and performed in their honour.        JAB

J.-J. GLASSNER, *La chute d'Akkadé: L'évènement et sa mémoire* (Berlin 1986).

J. KLEIN, *Three Šulgi Hymns: Sumerian Royal Hymns Glorifying King Šulgi of Ur* (Ramat-Gan 1981).

M.-C. LUDWIG, *Untersuchungen zu den Hymnen des Išme-Dagan von Isin* (Wiesbaden 1990).

W.H.P. RÖMER, *Sumerische 'Königshymnen' der Isin-Zeit* (Leiden 1965).

J. WESTENHOLZ, *Legends of the Kings of Akkade* (Winona Lake, IN 1996).

**Deir Alla, (Tell)** The 4-ha mound of Deir Alla is located in the eastern Jordan Valley. It was first described by Selah Merrill (1881), surveyed by *Glueck (1940), and has been excavated by the Dutch since 1960. It has been tentatively identified with biblical Succoth or Penuel, but this is not certain.

Deir Alla was first occupied in the Middle Bronze Age, from which rooms and part of a *fortification wall have been found. A Late Bronze Age sanctuary built on an artificial platform contained inscribed rectangular clay tablets, still undeciphered, and a faience vase inscribed with the name of the *Egyptian Queen Tawosret (c.1180 BC). Twenty strata represent the whole of the *Iron Age and the *Persian period. The earliest Iron Age levels may reflect use by itinerant bronzesmiths; this period ended with an earthquake, one victim being found squashed in a crack in the earth. In a later Iron II room was found plaster, fallen from a wall, inscribed in black and red ink. The *Aramaic text concerns the prophet Balaam, known from the Bible, and imitates a column from a scroll, one metre high, probably dating to the ninth century BC.   PB

H.J. FRANKEN, *Excavations at Tell Deir 'Alla 1: A Stratigraphical and Analytical Study of the Early Iron Age Pottery* (Leiden 1969).

——, *Excavations at Tell Deir 'Alla: The Late Bronze Age Sanctuary* (Louvain 1992).

J.A. HACKETT, *The Balaam Text from Deir 'Alla* (Chico, CA 1984).

J. HOFTIJZER and G. VAN DER KOOIJ, *Aramaic Texts from Deir 'Alla* (Leiden 1976).

G. VAN DER KOOIJ, 'Deir 'Alla, Tell', *The New Encyclopedia of Archaeological Excavations in the Holy Land*, ed. E. Stern (Jerusalem 1993) 338–42.

G. VAN DER KOOIJ and M.M. IBRAHIM, *Picking Up the Threads … A Continuing Review of Excavations at Deir Alla, Jordan* (Leiden 1989).

**Demons and monsters** In most religions there is a belief in various kinds of supernatural beings ranking between the level of *gods and humans. 'Demon', in its original *Greek sense (*daimōn* 'supernatural being', 'spirit') serves as an approximate translation of *Akkadian terms like *rābiṣu* (*Sumerian *maškim*), which can refer to, and be qualified as, a good or bad 'demon'. However, in modern studies of ancient *Mesopotamian *art and iconography, the term 'demon' has generally been applied to any upright human-bodied hybrid creature, while 'monster' has been applied to an animal combination on all fours.

Demons only rarely figure in *mythology. The scores of demons whose names are known to us are mentioned mainly in *magical incantations. Generally, 'evil' demons seem to have been conceived as mere agents and executors of the will of the gods; their role was to implement divinely ordained punishment for sin. They were often imagined as spirits of the wind or storms. Their usual method of attacking humans was by inflicting diseases. Evil gods and demons are only very rarely depicted in art, perhaps because it was thought that their images might endanger people.

In the earliest periods, the features of different animals were combined into unnatural composite beings. In

Part of an Aramaic text written on a plastered wall at Tell Deir Alla, late ninth century BC. In the first two lines the scribe omitted a word which he then wrote above the line (courtesy of Gerrit van der Kooij).

The hero Gilgamesh faced the giant Humbaba in the Cedar Forest. A Babylonian diviner thought the giant's face might be seen in this formation in the entrails of a sacrificed sheep. Clay, height 7 cm, c.1700 BC. WA 116624.

the Akkadian period, scenes on *seals show the capture and punishment of nefarious demons. In the Old *Babylonian period, *cylinder seal designs often mix images (gods, symbols and other motifs) of good and bad associations with respect to mankind. In *Mitannian, *Kassite and Middle *Assyrian art of the fourteenth to eleventh centuries BC, the human-centred imagery of the Old Babylonian period gave way to a preponderance of animal-headed hybrids. In Neo-Assyrian and Neo-Babylonian art, individual demons were depicted in their full horror; in *palaces and *temples, monumental statues and reliefs of magically protective beings were erected, and small clay images of them were buried in the foundations.                                                    AG/JAB

J.A. BLACK and A.R. GREEN, *Gods, Demons and Symbols of Ancient Mesopotamia: An Illustrated Dictionary*, 2nd ed. (London 1998).

A. FALKENSTEIN, *Haupttypen der sumerischen Beschwörung* (Leipzig 1931).

M.J. GELLER, *Forerunners to Udug-hul: Sumerian Exorcistic Incantations* (Stuttgart 1985).

K. VAN DER TOORN, B. BECKING and P.W. VAN DER HORST (eds), *Dictionary of Deities and Demons in the Bible* (Leiden 1995).

F.A.M. WIGGERMAN, *Mesopotamian Protective Spirits: The Ritual Texts* (Groningen 1992).

**Deportation**  The practice of uprooting large groups of people and resettling them elsewhere was first practised in the second millennium BC by the *Egyptians, the *Hittites and the Middle *Assyrian *kings; however, the earlier Code of *Hammurabi contains a clause warning that any king ignoring the *laws would be punished by the deportation of his people. The most detailed information comes from the Neo-Assyrian period, from the time of *Tiglath-pileser III and his successors, when

As Chaldaeans are deported, a mother gives her child a drink from a skin bottle. Detail from a relief in Sennacherib's palace at Nineveh. WA 124954.

deportation became a systematic part of imperial policy. Assyrian royal inscriptions describe in some detail the numbers of people they deported and their destinations, and deportees also appear in administrative, business and legal texts, undertaking various transactions in their new lives.

The reasons why the Assyrian kings deported populations included punishment for rebellion against Assyrian rule, liquidation of rival powers, enlarging the Assyrian *army, acquiring *craftsmen and unskilled labourers, and populating other *cities or regions. Populations were deported from all corners of the empire, the majority to Assyria proper, although sometimes populations were exchanged. In the Neo-Assyrian period alone, 157 cases of wholesale deportation are recorded, affecting a total of 1,210,928 people, the largest single number in one deportation being 208,000 that *Sennacherib deported from *Babylonia to Assyria. The majority of deportees were civilians, but sometimes included members of the royal family, high officials, soldiers or craftsmen.

Deportees are depicted on Assyrian reliefs, carrying only a few belongings and probably some *food and water. Most went on foot, but occasionally women and children travelled on donkeys, on *horses or in carts. The hands and feet of men were often chained, but perhaps this applied only to men of rank and status. Assyrian *provincial governors through whose territories the deportees travelled had written instructions to supply them with provisions. Officials responsible for the deportees had to send regular *letters to the king reporting on their condition during the march to their destination. One letter reports that whole *families had managed to escape while being transported.

Deportees were classified according to sex, trade and number of dependants. The Assyrians kept families and communities together, and transported and resettled them in geographical, national or cultural groups. The status of deportees in their new areas is arguable, and there is some evidence from Assyrian inscriptions that until about the reign of Sennacherib they were considered free men, literally inhabitants of Assyria, liable to various *taxes and services; but afterwards, particularly under *Esarhaddon, they were '*slaves of the king' and could be distributed along with other booty among private individuals. Very rarely there is evidence that some deportees were allowed to return to their homeland.                PB

B. ODED, *Mass Deportations and Deportees in the Neo-Assyrian Empire* (Wiesbaden 1979).

J.N. POSTGATE, Review of B. Oded, *Mass Deportations and Deportees in the Neo-Assyrian Empire*, *Bibliotheca Orientalis* 38/5–6 (1981) 636–8.

**Deve Hüyük**  In 1913, *Woolley and T.E. Lawrence (later 'Lawrence of Arabia') investigated this *cemetery site west of *Carchemish on the border between modern *Syria and Turkey. The objects they recovered were largely purchased from local peasants who plundered the *graves, often at night and in the presence of the British archaeologists.

The site has cemeteries of three periods. Deve Hüyük I was a *cremation cemetery dating to the eighth century BC. Deve Hüyük II was a *military inhumation cemetery dating to the fifth century BC, used for *Achaemenid troops, probably from *Persia rather than local conscripts. The soldiers were buried with *weapons and *pottery, the *women with personal ornaments and *cosmetic articles. Deve Hüyük III is the name given to fragmentary evidence for intrusive graves of the *Parthian period cut into the Deve Hüyük II cemetery.

PB

P.R.S. MOOREY, *Cemeteries of the First Millennium B.C. at Deve Hüyük* (Oxford 1980).

**Dilmun:** see Bahrain

**Diplomacy** Much information on the use of diplomats is available from major archives like those of the Old *Babylonian palace of *Mari and the short-lived *Egyptian capital at Amarna (Akhetaten). A further source is the surviving documents of the *Assyrian empire. Envoys often travelled with *merchants. Passports were issued to envoys together with *letters of introduction, and allied diplomats were allowed entrance to the *palace. Formal relations were cultivated through enquiries after the health and well-being of the monarch and by the exchange of valuable gifts between rulers. Relationships were often cemented by the marrying of each other's daughters, and some letters reflect the continued concern for the girl's well-being after the *marriage had taken place. The diplomats were often maintained at state expense. However, permission was often required to leave the court of a host, and some envoys were kept as virtual hostages. Letters and oral reports of diplomats are mentioned in the texts, and they were clearly expected to gather as much information as possible about the court and country they were visiting. Reliability of the envoys was often checked with other officials and rulers, while translators were employed on the court staff.

Elamite ambassadors, on the right, meet Urartian envoys wearing pointed caps, under the gaze of Assyrian soldiers, to learn how Assyria treated insolent neighbours. Relief from the North Palace of Ashurbanipal at Nineveh. WA 124802.

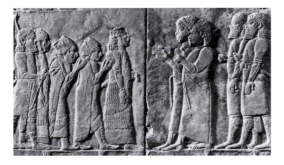

Texts make it clear that vassals were not permitted by their overlords to accept messengers from the latter's enemies, and envoys could be turned back at the borders. In one of the *Amarna Letters, the Babylonian *King Burnaburiash complains about the Assyrians (allegedly his vassals) sending a delegation to the Egyptian court. Diplomacy in times of *war could involve the most important officials. When the Assyrian armies under *Sennacherib attacked the kingdom of *Judah, his chief butler, a senior official, had to shout to the officials of Hezekiah who were standing on the walls of *Jerusalem (2 Kings 18: 17–35). Diplomatic moves could also include sending specialists: a letter from the *Hittite King *Hattusilis III to the Babylonian ruler Kadashman-Enlil II assures the latter that the Babylonian doctor who had been sent to his court had died of natural causes.      PTC

S.A. MEIER, *The Messenger in the Ancient Semitic World* (Atlanta, GA 1988).

G.H. OLLER, 'Messengers and Ambassadors in Ancient Western Asia', *Civilizations of the Ancient Near East*, ed. J.M. Sasson (New York 1995) 1465–73.

J.N. POSTGATE, *Taxation and Conscription in the Assyrian Empire* (Rome 1974).

**Disease:** see Medicine

**Divination:** see Omens and divination

**Divine cult** A divine cult is defined as a system of religious worship, especially as expressed in *ritual, a devotion or homage to one or more deities. Religious worship took both public and private forms in the ancient Near East. The scale and nature of public divine cult is clear from the remains of *temples and associated buildings. The plans of these can often give a lot of information about the nature of the cult. For example, the survival until the end of the Early Dynastic period in *Mesopotamia of the so-called bent-axis approach, whereby the main *altar and cult statue are not visible from outside the doorway, suggests strongly the more ancient practice of a cult administered by *priests without the direct participation of the people. Written descriptions of, or prescriptions for, many ceremonies and rituals are preserved, which give very precise information about what happened. Stemming from a basic belief that humankind had been created to serve and, in particular, to feed the *gods, frequent and regular *sacrifice and offering were considered necessary. *Animal sacrifice, most frequently of sheep, in early times in Babylonia also of fish, was performed, with the roast meat redistributed to the temple clergy after being 'offered' to the god. In certain special rituals, goats, puppies, equids and *birds were also sacrificed. However, most regular offerings consisted of grain, cream, honey, cakes, *beer and *wine: the same as human *food, with an emphasis on the luxury items. Garments, *furniture, *boats, military booty and *jewellery were also offered. At certain periods, human beings were dedicated for service in the temples.

Elaborate temple *music was performed during ceremonies. *Incense and other aromatics were burned in purification rites, which might also involve sweeping, water sprinkling and washing by the participants.

The evidence for the private forms of cult is mostly archaeological, in the form of votive objects which represent an essentially private vow or promise on the part of the worshipper in exchange for alleviation of some ill, or satisfaction of some desire, which it was believed the deity would provide. For example, small models of sexual or other bodily organs, of pregnant women or of copulating couples are considered to represent requests for cures or thanksgiving for benefits received.

The daily attentions divinities required were much the same in the *Levant as elsewhere: the statue had to be awakened and fed, *clothing sometimes changed, furnishings and equipment renewed. *Metal, clay and, rarely, *stone statues illustrate the forms of deities conceived. West Semitic *hymns of praise are preserved in the biblical Psalms (Psalm 29 may echo a *Canaanite poem) and snatches occur in other texts. In orthodox *Israelite cult there were morning and evening sacrifices but no statue that needed attention. Indeed, *Hebrew writers mocked the futility of idolatrous cults (Isaiah, the *Hellenistic 'Bel and the Dragon'). JAB/ARM

D.O. EDZARD, 'Private Frömmigkeit in Sumer', *Official Cult and Popular Religion in the Ancient Near East*, ed. E. Matsushima (Heidelberg 1993) 195–208.

B. MENZEL, *Assyrische Tempel* (Rome 1981).

H.I.H. PRINCE TAKAHITO MIKASA (ed.), *Cult and Ritual in the Ancient Near East* (Wiesbaden 1992).

F.A.G. WIGGERMAN, 'Theologies, Priests and Worship in Ancient Mesopotamia', *Civilizations of the Ancient Near East*, ed. J.M. Sasson (New York 1995) 1857–70.

**Divine symbols**  Most deities in the ancient Near East had their associated symbols (*Akkadian *šurinnu*) – *animals, *monsters, *plants, heavenly bodies, items of daily life – each usually, though not always, specific to a deity, though most deities had more than one symbol. *Gods and goddesses could be depicted together with their distinctive natural or hybrid animals, as, e.g., on the *Assyrian rock reliefs at Maltai, or could be represented by their symbols, as, e.g., in miniature on *seals or on large-scale *sculptures. A good illustration is given by the *kudurrus*, or ancient stone records of land grants, found in *Babylonia from the *Kassite to the Neo-*Babylonian period. The top of the stone was usually carved with symbols of gods, such as a sun for the solar god *Shamash, a crescent for the moon-god *Sîn, an eight-pointed star for *Ishtar (the goddess of the planet Venus), a turtle or capricorn for the water-god *Ea.

An interesting case of the special use of a divine symbol is instanced during the restoration of the temple of Shamash at *Sippar by the Babylonian King Nabû-apla-iddina in c.870 BC. The cult statue of the god had been lost, and a large sun-disk was erected in its place pending the fashioning of a new statue, allegedly modelled on a clay copy of the original. (See also Sacred animals.) JAB/AG

In front of the Assyrian King Ashurnasirpal II (883–859 BC) are the symbols of his gods: (left to right) the star for Ishtar, the lightning for Adad, the moon crescent for Sîn, the winged disk for Shamash and the horned helmet for Ashur. Stela from the temple of Ninurta at Nimrud. WA 118805.

A. GREEN, 'Mesopotamian Religious Iconography', *Civilizations of the Ancient Near East*, ed. J.M. Sasson (New York 1995) 1837–55.

U. SEIDL, 'Göttersymbole und -attribute', *Reallexikon der Assyriologie* 3 (Berlin/New York 1957–71) 483–90.

——, *Die babylonischen Kudurru-Reliefs: Symbole mesopotamischer Gottheiten* (reprint, with added appendix and table, of *Baghdader Mitteilungen* 4 (1968) 7–220) (Fribourg/Göttingen 1989).

E.D. VAN BUREN, *Symbols of the Gods in Mesopotamian Art* (Rome 1945).

**Domuztepe:** see Karatepe and Domuztepe

**Doors:** see Gateways and doors

**Dorak treasure**  The Dorak treasure is an infamous group of objects published in coloured drawings in 1959 by the archaeologist James Mellaart, but whose actual existence has never been confirmed, leading to speculation about their authenticity.

The material was described as a rich collection of objects from an unpublished clandestine excavation of two royal *tombs of the Yortan culture, undertaken 'at about the time of the Turco-Greek war', rediscovered by Mellaart in private possession in Izmir in Turkey. He reported that the objects came from a small *cemetery consisting of two royal cist graves and two pithos burials

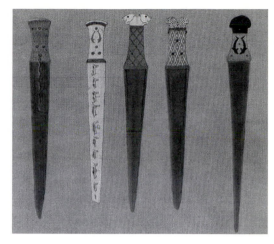

Figurines in silver (left) and electrum (right) with gold ornaments, from Dorak. Height c. 15 cm, c.2300 BC.

Swords from the Dorak tombs, c.2300 BC. The second on the left is of silver engraved with ships, the one on the far right is of bronze with lapis lazuli dolphins on a gold hilt (from *Illustrated London News* (28 November 1959) 754, pls I and III; courtesy of James Mellaart).

J. MELLAART, 'The Royal Treasure of Dorak', *Illustrated London News* (28 November 1959) 754, pls I–III.
——, 'Anatolia c. 4000–2300 B.C.', *Cambridge Ancient History* 1.2, 2nd ed. (Cambridge 1971) 390–5.

of servants (i.e. burials in large pottery jars), found high up on a hill slope near the village of Dorak in north-west Turkey, inland from the southern shore of the Sea of Marmora between the Dardanelles and the Bosphorus. Tomb I measured 1.80 by 0.83 m, with the '*king' stretched out on his back surrounded by ceremonial objects, *weapons and vessels of precious metals, as well as *pottery and *stone. Tomb II measured 3.10 by 2 m and contained two burials: a 'king' and a '*queen'. At the king's feet lay the skeleton of a dog. The grave goods were similar to Tomb I, although the queen was provided with *jewellery and *cosmetic items.

Among the magnificent objects reported were a dismantled chair or throne plated with thick sheet *gold, some strips embossed with the name and titles of Sahure, second king of the *Egyptian Fifth Dynasty; five figurines of electrum, *silver and gold; a silver sword engraved with *ships; swords and daggers with *ivory hilts covered with gold sheet with lapis lazuli rivets and rock crystal pommels; and a *bronze sword with a lapis lazuli pommel, and lapis lazuli dolphins on a gold hilt. Possible comparisons can be made with material from *Troy II, dated to c.2300 BC.

The promised publication of this material never appeared, no photographs are available, and nothing more has ever been heard of the objects or tombs. A formal enquiry by the Institute of Archaeology in London cleared Mellaart of forgery, and he remains convinced that the material was genuine. PB

**Dreams** According to texts from *Mesopotamia dreams were seen as channels for divine messages. *Gudea, ruler of the *Sumerian city of *Lagash, describes how the god Ningirsu appeared to him in a dream and gave instructions for the building of a *temple. Similarly, in the *Mari *archive people who fell asleep in a temple are described as receiving divine messages which were reported directly to the *king. In the Epic of *Gilgamesh, the hero receives notice of the appearance of his companion Enkidu in a series of dreams. In addition, dreams were also seen as a method (though not extensively used) among the wider techniques of *divination, and were occasionally deliberately solicited. Several dream omen lists survive but it is possible that foretelling the future through dreams became more important in Mesopotamia during the first millennium BC when closer contact was established with the *Levant and *Egypt where the technique of interpreting dreams was more popular, although there is no evidence of external influence. In the *Old Testament, for example, the dreams of Pharaoh are famously interpreted by Joseph, and Solomon received a message from God in a dream (1 Kings 3: 5). Large fragments of a 'dream book' were found in the library of *Ashurbanipal at *Nineveh. In this text, the associations that link the dream to the prediction are rarely understandable and cover all sorts of dreams: losing teeth, receiving gifts, flying. Ashurbanipal himself describes how he had a dream in which the goddess

*Ishtar appeared to him and it is possible that he is the prince, described in another text, who had a dream revealing the *underworld filled with demonic creatures. The Mesopotamian god Mamu was associated with dreams and had a temple at Imgur-Enlil (modern *Balawat).                                        PTC

J.A. BLACK and A.R. GREEN, *Gods, Demons and Symbols of Ancient Mesopotamia: An Illustrated Dictionary*, 2nd ed. (London 1998).

A.L. OPPENHEIM, *The Interpretation of Dreams in the Ancient Near East* (Philadelphia, PA 1956).

**Dress:** see Clothing

**Drunkenness**  The use of substances that alter mood and consciousness has been part of human life since the *Palaeolithic period. In the ancient Near East, the most widespread intoxicant was alcohol, initially derived from fermenting cereals. *Beer, in various degrees of strength, was the main beverage in *Mesopotamia, forming part of subsistence rations and payments. Fermented fruit juices, particularly of dates, were another source for alcoholic drink in the southern regions. Grape-based *wine seems to have been produced in the *Syrian coastal regions from a very early period and was circulated widely throughout the Near East as an elite product for feasts and *banquets.

The effects of alcohol are described in various literary texts and *medico-*magical sources. It was known to be effective as an aphrodisiac (a frequent theme in *Canaanite *poetry, as in the Song of Songs), to produce euphoria and to be conducive to social ease (the banquet). The 'morning-after' symptoms were treated with various substances, including 'the hair of the dog', as described in an *Ugaritic text where the god *El suffers from the effects of excessive consumption. The negative consequences of too much drink can be more serious than a headache: in the Sumerian *myth '*Enki and Ninmah' a competition between the creator deities, triggered by drunken rivalry, results in the creation of damaged and malformed human beings. *Inana manages to take the *me* (divine powers) from the intoxicated Enki. In a *Hurrian myth the sea-monster and all his brood are overcome when they succumb to drunken slumber, and in the *biblical story of Lot, his daughters give him wine to make love to him and thus perpetuate their race.        GL

K.J. CATHCART, 'Ilu, Yarihu and the One with Two Horns and a Tail', *Ugarit, Religion and Culture*, eds N. Wyatt, W.G.E. Watson and J.B. Lloyd (Edinburgh 1990) 1–6.

S.N. KRAMER and J. MAIER, *Myths of Enki, the Crafty God* (New York 1989).

**Duma**  The name appears as *Dûmâ* in the *Old Testament and ᵘʳᵘ*A-du-um-ma-tu* or ᵘʳᵘ*A-du-mu-u* in the *Assyrian *annals. It refers to the large oasis, known in medieval Arabic sources as Dumat-al-Jandal, modern Al Jauf, which lies at the southern end of the Wadi al-Sirhan in north-west *Arabia. It dominated a major bifurcation of the *trade route from southern Arabia to the north,

one branch going up the Wadi al-Sirhan to *Transjordan, *Syria, *Palestine and the Mediterranean and the other running north-east to *Babylonia and *Assyria. It was therefore of crucial importance to the Neo-Assyrians in their attempts to dominate the frankincense trade (see Incense and spices) in the mid first millennium BC.

At that period Duma was the cult centre of the confederation of nomadic tribes called Qedar. In the earliest references, this group seems to have been led exclusively by '*queens' who were more probably the *priestesses of the cult at Duma, though later 'kings' are also mentioned. These *women led the Qedarite *Arabs into battle and took the images of their *gods to war. At one point the Assyrian annals describe these tribesmen as the 'confederation of Atarsamain', one of the deities of Duma to whom prayers are addressed in inscriptions carved on the rocks not only around the oasis but in other parts of north Arabia and even southern Syria, which was also within Qedarite territory. Among the other deities of Duma listed by the Assyrians were Ruldaiu and Nuhai, who in their north Arabian forms *Rdw* and *Nhy* are very often invoked in the so-called 'Thamudic' inscriptions of the *nomads, and are found in prayers in the specific script of the oasis.                                MCAM

I. EPH'AL, *The Ancient Arabs: Nomads on the Borders of the Fertile Crescent 9th–5th Centuries B.C.* (Jerusalem/Leiden 1982).

M.C.A. MACDONALD, 'North Arabia in the First Millennium BCE', *Civilizations of the Ancient Near East*, ed. J.M. Sasson (New York 1995) 1355–69.

——, 'Trade Routes and Trade Goods at the Northern End of the "Incense Road" in the First Millennium B.C.', *Profumi d'Arabia*, ed. A. Avanzini (Rome 1997) 333–49.

**Dumuzi (Tammuz)**  The *god Dumuzi is a shepherd god. In a disputation with Enkimdu, the god of *irrigation and cultivation, Dumuzi represents the conflicting interests of the pastoralist. When *Inana visits the *underworld, and cannot return without a substitute to take her place, *demons come to fetch her beloved young husband Dumuzi to replace her. In this way, Dumuzi died and became a god of the Underworld. In the *Sacred Marriage, in which *Sumerian *kings were ritually married to Inana, the king was identified with Dumuzi. In a later literary tradition, Dumuzi and Ningishzida are represented as the gatekeepers of the heaven of *Anu.

The early history of the various cults of Dumuzi and related deities is complex and bewildering. The Dumuzi worshipped at Bad-tibira was later thought to have been an antediluvian king of the *town (described as a 'shepherd'). The Dumuzi worshipped at *Uruk as the husband of Inana was connected with nearby Kuara and was also, in one account, thought to have been an early king of Uruk. The god Ama-ushumgal-ana, later identified with Dumuzi, was originally worshipped at a village near *Lagash and in one cult *song is described as a warrior hero. In some *Sumerian *poetry, Dumuzi is also referred to as 'my Damu' (possibly not the same as Damu the god of healing).

*Ritual *lamentation for the death of Dumuzi seems

to have been widespread, and is mentioned in the *biblical Book of Ezekiel (8: 14). Tammuz is a *Hebrew form of the *Mesopotamian name. In Early Dynastic Lagash the sixth month of the year was named after the *festival of Dumuzi, and in a later north Mesopotamian calendar one of the months is called Dumuzi. The fourth month of the Standard Babylonian calendar was called *Du'uzu* or *Dûzu*, and *Tammuz* is still used in Arabic and Hebrew as the name for July.

The god Dumuzi and the *stories concerning him do not seem to be depicted in Mesopotamian *art.　JAB

B. ALSTER, *Dumuzi's Dream* (Copenhagen 1972).

T. JACOBSEN, 'Toward the Image of Tammuz', *Toward the Image of Tammuz and Other Essays on Mesopotamian History and Culture*, ed. W. Moran (Cambridge, MA 1970) 73–101.

——, *The Treasures of Darkness* (New Haven/London 1976) chapter 2.

W. SLADEK, *Inanna's Descent to the Netherworld* (University Microfilms International, Philadelphia, PA 1974) 225–39.

J.J.A. VAN DIJK, *La sagesse suméro-akkadienne* (Leiden 1953) 65–85.

**Dur-Katlimmu:** see Sheikh Hamad, (Tell)

**Dur-Kurigalzu:** see Aqar Quf

**Dynasty** Inheritance and the *family line were important to all people of the ancient Near East, especially to ruling families. In the *Sumerian *King List succession from father to son is noted in several *towns as the hegemony moved from place to place. The concept is explicit in the Old *Babylonian document 'The Genealogy of the *Hammurabi Dynasty', a text written for a *funerary *ritual to ensure that all the dead were pacified. This lists the kings of the 'dynasty of *Amorites' down to the time of composition, naming nineteen ancestors before the first *king, names two other dynasties (of Hana and *Guti) and then embraces any not mentioned by name. *Scribes who composed Babylonian King List A labelled distinct lines of kings as 'dynasty of *X' (*Sumerian *bala*, *Akkadian *palû*). The *Assyrian King List is the most impressive example of the ancient attitude, although 'dynasty' is not specified, purporting to display a continuous line of kings from *Shamshi-Adad I's ancestors to *Shalmaneser V, explaining what happened where the succession was broken and noting usurpers. Late Assyrian kings claimed that their lineage reached back to the last of seven usurpers in the eighteenth century BC. Inscriptions set up by governors of Suhu on the mid Euphrates around modern Haditha in the eighth century BC give their genealogy back for six or seven generations and claim 'an enduring lineage' stemming from a son of *Hammurabi a millennium earlier.

In the west, Late Bronze Age rulers of several towns traced their families back to the start of the Middle Bronze Age. *Ugarit gives the clearest example with a King List compiled for funerary rites, naming rulers in reverse order from, perhaps, the last to the founder, Yaqarum, whose Old Babylonian-style *seal continued to be used by his last descendants. The *Hittites produced similar lists in ritual texts, covering shorter spans, and Neo-Hittite princes of the early first millennium BC traced their ancestry to the great rulers of the Hittite empire. In *Israel no enduring dynasty emerged, whereas the family of David held the throne of Judah from c.1000 to 586 BC.　ARM

G. FRAME, *Rulers of Babylonia from the Second Dynasty of Isin to the End of Assyrian Domination (1157–612 BC)* (Toronto 1995) 275–319 (rulers of Suhu).

J.D. HAWKINS, 'Kuzi-Tešub and the "Great Kings" of Karkamiš', *Anatolian Studies* 38 (1988) 99–108.

K.A. KITCHEN, 'The King List of Ugarit', *Ugarit-Forschungen* 9 (1977) 131–42.

# *E*

**Ea** Ea (Enki) was the *Mesopotamian *god of the subterranean freshwater ocean (*abzu*), and was especially associated with wisdom, *magic and incantations, and with the arts and crafts of civilization. He is sometimes called by the names Nudimmud or Ninshiku or by the title 'Antelope of the *abzu*'. Enki/Ea was a son of *Anu/An, or else of the goddess Namma, and a twin brother of the god Ishkur/*Adad. His wife was Damgalnuna/Damkina, and their offspring included the gods *Marduk, Asarluhi, Enbilulu, the sage *Adapa and the goddess Nanshe. His minister was the two-faced god Isimud/Usmû. This Enki (whose name is Enkig in full) is not the same as *Enlil's ancestor Enki ('Lord Earth').

Enki's most important cult centre was the E-abzu ('Abzu House') at *Eridu. As a provider of fresh water and a creator god and determiner of destinies, Enki was always seen as favourable to mankind. In the *Epics of Atrahasis and *Gilgamesh, especially, he takes the part of man against the other gods and helps mankind to escape the *Flood sent by their decision. In the *Sumerian poem '*Inana and Enki' he controls the *me* concerned with every aspect of human life, and in 'Enki and the World Order' he has the role of organizing in detail every feature of the civilized world. He also appears as a powerful and cunning deity in a number of *Hittite myths of *Hurrian origin.

Ea, god of the fresh water, is portrayed in a watery shrine, its door-posts guarded by bull-men. Height 2.7 cm. Cylinder seal, Akkadian period, c.2200 BC. WA 89771.

In *art Enki is represented as a seated god with long beard, wearing a cap with many horns and a long, pleated robe. Streams of water flow from his arms to the ground, sometimes with little fish swimming along the flow. Often the god is seen receiving worshippers or bearers of offerings, or else he receives the bird-man, brought before him as a prisoner under guard, or the lion-demon. These may be introduced by other gods, most commonly by Enki's minister Isimud. Sometimes Enki is shown seated within a structure, the *abzu*, or else his E-abzu shrine, surrounded by channels of water.

In the symbolism of the *Kassite, *Babylonian and *Assyrian periods, Ea's beast was the goat-fish. The god's other symbols were a curved stick terminating in a ram's head, and a turtle. AG/JAB

C.A. BENITO, 'Enki and Ninmah' and 'Enki and the World Order' (University Microfilms International, Philadelphia, PA 1969).

G. FARBER-FLÜGGE, Der Mythos 'Inanna und Enki' unter besonderer Berücksichtigung der Liste der me (Rome 1973).

H. GALTER, Der Gott Ea/Enki in der akkadischen Überlieferung (Graz 1981).

S.N. KRAMER and J.R. MAIER, Myths of Enki, the Crafty God (Oxford 1989).

W.G. LAMBERT and A.R. MILLARD, Atra-hasis:The Babylonian Story of the Flood (Oxford 1969).

H.L.J. VANSTIPHOUT, 'Why Did Enki Organise the World?', Sumerian Gods and their Representations, eds I.L. Finkel and M.J. Geller (Groningen 1997) 117–34.

**Ebla** An Italian expedition led by Paolo Matthiae began excavations at Tell Mardikh 55 km south-south-west of Aleppo, in 1964, attracted by the size of the site and signs of Early and Middle Bronze Age occupation. The site is surrounded by an enormous rampart of earth and stones, penetrated by four *gateways, one of them lined with blocks of black and white *stone, built in the Middle Bronze Age (level IIIA). In the centre of the enclosure is the *tell; on top, Middle Bronze Age basalt basins, carved in relief in styles related to 'Cappadocian' *seals, drew attention to a large *temple (D) of the 'migdol' (tower) type. Part of a statue found in 1968 bears a *cuneiform inscription indicating that Ibbit-Lim, ruler of Ebla, dedi-

cated it to *Ishtar. Two *palaces and four temples of the same date have been uncovered around the foot of the tell, yielding a variety of plans and installations, including a room equipped with handmills for corn grinding, and more *sculpture. A storeroom contained pieces of *ivory *furniture inlay finely carved in *Egyptian style, some up to 30 cm high. In one area a group of royal *tombs was located, one retaining its rich contents as a result of an ancient roof fall. Among the items was an Egyptian mace bearing the name of the Thirteenth Dynasty Pharaoh Hetepibre Harnejheryotef, fine *gold *jewellery of styles found in *Babylonia and the *Levant and ivory carving in Egyptian style. The Middle Bronze Age occupation ended in flames about 1600 BC.

Beneath the Ishtar temple in the side of the tell excavators found part of the courtyard and two sides of a brick-built palace of the Early Bronze Age III (Period IIB1, c.2400–2300 BC). At one side of the court was a low dais for the throne, an entry nearby giving access to a staircase, the steps decorated with mosaics in *wooden panels, leading, presumably, to the royal quarters. At right angles to the throne a wider flight of stone steps rose more gently to an upper level. Projecting into the courtyard was a small room in which *archives were stored. The palace was burnt, the fierce fire baking the mudbricks and also the tablets, so preserving them well. Over two thousand documents were recovered. When they were first deciphered, exaggerated claims were made for the scope of Ebla's rule, with references to Sodom and Gomorrah, *Kanesh and *Ashur, but it is now clear that the texts relate to the neighbourhood of Ebla and improving knowledge of the unusual local writing conventions rules out those references. Advancing understanding also removes any grounds for suggesting that personal names occur which might be connected with *biblical names (e.g. Abraham's ancestor Eber), other than their common *Semitic background, and for supposing that the name *Yahweh was current in personal names in the form Ya. The tablets were written by local *scribes trained in a form of the cuneiform tradition at home in northern Babylonia (perhaps *Kish), express-

Mudbrick architecture in restored area of the third-millennium BC Palace G at Ebla. Note the exposed brick where the plaster has peeled off (courtesy of Graham Philip).

ing themselves in an *Akkadian dialect, with many *Sumerian logograms, although they themselves probably spoke a West Semitic *language. To help themselves, they had copies of standard Sumerian *lexical texts with translations into the Akkadian dialect, the earliest examples of the translations known. The archive has not supplied extensive examples of *literature, although there are a few *magic spells and *ritual texts. There are *letters and *treaties, not yet fully understood, and many administrative documents, dealing with deliveries of *taxes in *textiles and *metals and the issue of supplies for the royal family, for officials and visitors and for ritual purposes. They reveal a busy, prosperous kingdom, in which sheep-rearing and textile production had a major role. Many objects found in the palace reflect Babylonian fashions in gold, lapis lazuli, ivory, while *cylinder seals display local variations of Babylonian motifs. Fragments of carved wooden furniture, inlaid with mother-of-pearl or stone, sometimes gold-plated, illustrate material not preserved at Babylonian sites. Remains of an underground vaulted chamber at a lower level than the palace may be a royal tomb. Both the texts and the objects belong to the Early Dynastic III period of Babylonia, raising the problem of the date of the fire which destroyed the palace. The culprit is believed to be either *Sargon of *Akkad, who claims the *god *Dagan 'gave him' *Mari, Ebla and other places, or his grandson *Naram-Sin who claims the god *Nergal gave to him Armanum (=Aleppo?) and Ebla, 'which no king had previously destroyed'. Without a more certain chronology or royal inscriptions, there can be no decision. An Egyptian hieroglyphic inscription on a jar lid naming Pharaoh Pepi I gives only a *terminus post quem*. In the town area around the *tell stood the large Archaic Palace, occupied in two phases, Early Bronze IV and Middle Bronze I (c.2150–1800 BC). Its plan partly determined the shape of a Middle Bronze Age II palace which was built over its ruins. Continuing work and publication will demonstrate the key role of Ebla for understanding *Syrian culture in the period 2400–1600 BC.

Traces of some habitation in the Neo-*Assyrian period were noted, and there was a more substantial building of *Persian date.                                    ARM

A. ARCHI (ed.), *Archivi Reali di Ebla, Testi* (Rome 1981–).

R.D. BIGGS, 'The Ebla Tablets: An Interim Perspective', *Biblical Archaeologist* 43 (1980) 76–87.

——, 'Ebla Texts', *Anchor Bible Dictionary* 2, ed. D.N. Freedman (New York 1992) 263–70.

P. MATTHIAE, *I tesori di Ebla* (Rome 1985).

——, *Ebla, alle origini della civiltà urbana: Trent'anni di scavi in Siria dell'Università di Roma 'La Sapienza'* (Milan 1995).

A.R. MILLARD, 'Ebla and the Bible: What's Left (If Anything)?', *Bible Review* 8/2 (April 1992) 18–31, 60, 62.

## Ecbatana

**Ecbatana** Ecbatana is the ancient Greek name of modern Hamadan (Old Persian *Hagmatana*) in central *Iran. It was the capital city of the *Medes and a royal summer residence of their successors, the *Achaemenids. *Herodotus relates that the *city was founded by *King Deioces and describes the city as being ringed with seven tiers of concentric walls. The battlements of innermost

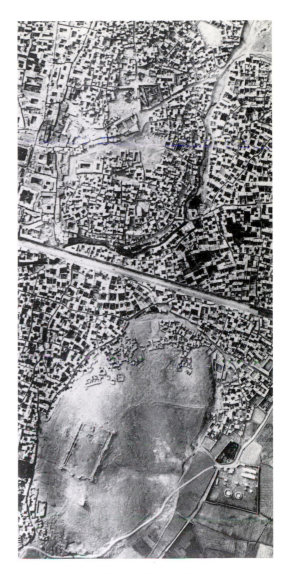

Aerial view of Hamadan, showing some of ancient Ecbatana buried beneath the modern town (from E.F. Schmidt, *Flights over Ancient Cities of Iran* (Chicago 1940) pl. 91).

rings were embellished with *gold and *silver, those of the outer five rings each a different colour (Herodotus I.98). But there are good reasons not to take the description literally. Although the identification is not in doubt, very little archaeological investigation has taken place until recently, largely because the ancient remains were buried beneath the modern town.

Many objects of purportedly Median and Achaemenid date and said to have come from Hamadan have appeared on the international market, but the true origin and even the authenticity of these pieces should be treated with scepticism.

Impressive public structures being currently excavated are apparently post-Achaemenid.                    GDS

K. ABDI, 'Hamadan', *Archaeological Encyclopaedia of Syro-Mesopotamia, Iran and the Iranian Peninsula*, ed. A. Green (forthcoming).

R. BOUCHARLAT, 'À la recherche d'Ecbatana sur Tepe Hegmataneh', *Iranica Antiqua* 33 (1998) 173–86.

O.W. MUSCARELLA, 'Excavated and Unexcavated Achaemenid Art', *Ancient Persia: The Art of an Empire*, ed. D. Schmandt-Besserat (Malibu, CA 1980) 23–42.

M.R. SARRAF, 'Neue architektonische und städtebauliche Funde von Ekbatana-Tepe (Hamadan)', *Archäologische Mitteilungen aus Iran und Turan* 29 (1997) 321–39.

**Economics** The basis of all ancient Near Eastern economies was the production, storage and distribution of *food, based on *agriculture and *animal husbandry. Other resources were also exchanged between individuals, institutions and states. The vast majority of ancient texts from the beginning of *writing are concerned with accounting and recording the organization of resources and the distribution and exchange of goods. Long-distance movement of goods can be traced even in the *prehistoric period, for example the *Neolithic *trade in *obsidian between *Anatolia and other parts of the Near East

Writing developed essentially as an accounting technique to record the economic activities of the huge *temple and *palace estates in *Mesopotamia. Various other procedures, without which any economy could not work effectively, were also standardized, including the *calendar, *weights and measures, and the use of *silver as a unit of accounting. The most detailed information about the functioning of ancient Near Eastern economies comes from the written records of temples, palaces and private *merchants.

A tension between temple and palace estates and economic activities was a characteristic of Mesopotamian history. The temple estates in third-millennium BC Mesopotamia were huge. Temples owned land and *animals, employed workers and artisans and commissioned merchants. Dependent workers were tied to the land and paid in rations. Temples functioned as redistributors of food and other goods. Palace estates and private holdings also existed, however, and the overall administrative role of the palaces gradually increased with time, especially in the highly centralized Ur III bureaucratic system. Within this system, regions were required to send *taxes to the state in the form of animals or other goods. Tens of thousands of texts document these procedures and reflect an almost complete monopoly over economic activities by the Ur III state.

By contrast, in the Old Babylonian period there was a higher level of private enterprise, with private merchants engaged in long-distance trade, though often with capital or loans (and concomitant interest) from the great estates. *Women (especially *nadītu* *priestesses) were able to engage in a variety of business activities, especially the buying, selling and leasing of fields. The existence and organization of a private sector dedicated to making a profit is best illustrated by the colony of Old *Assyrian merchants based in a sector of the Anatolian town of

*Kanesh. Their activities were focused on the acquisition of *gold and silver in exchange for *tin and *textiles brought from Assyria.                                        PB

I.M. DIAKONOFF, 'Main Features of the Economy in the Monarchies of Ancient Western Asia', *Troisième conférence internationale d'histoire économique* (The Hague 1965) 1–32.

E. LIPINSKI (ed.), *State and Temple Economy in the Ancient Near East* (Louvain 1979).

J.N. POSTGATE, *Early Mesopotamia: Society and Economy at the Dawn of History* (London 1992) 155–222.

N. YOFFEE, 'The Economy of Ancient Western Asia', *Civilizations of the Ancient Near East*, ed. J.M. Sasson (New York 1995) 1387–99.

**Edom, Edomites** Edom was the mountainous area of *Transjordan south of the Dead Sea, and an independent kingdom during the first millennium BC. The name 'Edom' comes from a *Semitic word meaning 'red', and perhaps reflects the colour of the sandstone in the area. Occasionally the area was also known as Seir, a word meaning 'hairy'.

The name 'Edom' first appears in *Egyptian texts from the time of the Pharaoh Merneptah about 1206 BC ('Seir' was used in Egyptian texts slightly earlier). According to the *Old Testament, King David conquered Edom and established garrisons in about 1000 BC, initiating a period of 150 years of *Israelite control. In the ninth century BC, Edom revolted during the reign of Jehoram of Judah, and established an independent kingdom.

Edom became a tributary state of *Assyria on its westward expansion under *Adad-nirari III and *Tiglath-pileser III in the eighth century BC. It joined with other states in a coalition against *Sargon II of Assyria, but the rebellion was defeated with the conquest of *Ashdod in 712 BC. Otherwise the Edomites appear to have remained loyal, and later provided troops for *Ashurbanipal's Egyptian campaign. Edom was formally part of the Neo-*Babylonian and *Persian empires, but at some point ceased to exist as an independent state.

Archaeological remains of the Edomite kingdom appear to date no earlier than the eighth century BC, and settlement was probably stimulated by Assyrian interest in the extensive *copper mines of Faynan and by Edom's position on the *trade route for *incense and other luxury goods from *Arabia. Apart from *Busayra, the capital, most of the settlements appear to be open *villages and farms, sometimes located on almost inaccessible mountain tops. The fortified settlement at Tell el-Kheleifeh on

Impression on clay of the seal of 'Qos-Gabr, King of Edom', c.670 BC, found at Umm el-Biyara inside Petra (courtesy of Piotr Bienkowski).

the Gulf of Aqaba may have been connected with the Arabian trade.

Characteristic of Edomite material culture was fine *pottery painted in bands and panels. Edomite script and *language are not well attested, but the script is a local form of the *alphabet and the language appears to be a distinct *Canaanite dialect though closely related to *Hebrew. The few inscriptions discovered on *ostraca, *seals and seal impressions show that the Edomites worshipped a *god called Qos (or Qaus). Similar pottery, and references to Qos, have been found at sites in the *Negev, an area which in *Hellenistic times was called Idumaea, a name probably derived from 'Edom'. PB

J.R. BARTLETT, *Edom and the Edomites* (Sheffield 1989).

P. BIENKOWSKI (ed.), *Early Edom and Moab: The Beginning of the Iron Age in Southern Jordan* (Sheffield 1992).

D.V. EDELMAN (ed.), *You Shall Not Abhor an Edomite for He is Your Brother: Edom and Seir in History and Tradition* (Atlanta, GA 1995).

**Education** Education in the ancient Near East was primarily for the purpose of training *scribes, not only to read and write but also to occupy administrative positions in *palaces and *temples. The evidence for scribal training consists of school exercises and descriptions of school activities, almost entirely from *Babylonia.

School exercises have been found at most sites which yielded tablets, but no actual school has been definitely identified archaeologically. Literary texts describe teaching taking place in a courtyard, with pupils seated on a cloth, sketching their first attempts at *cuneiform signs in the sand. School personnel included the headmaster ('the school father'), assistants ('big brother') and other aides. No text concerning school activities mentions female students, but they must have existed since female scribes, though rare, are attested. It is not known at what age *children started school, or how many years their education lasted. Children were sometimes sent to another *town if a suitable school was not available locally.

Most of the school day consisted of the preparation, writing and reading of tablets. Lunch, brought from home, was eaten at midday. Discipline was strict, pupils being punished for lateness, poor work and misbehaviour, sanctions ranging from corporal punishment to expulsion. Pupils went to school for twenty-four days in each month, with six days off.

The curriculum covered four major areas: language, *literature, *mathematics and *music. The language of instruction was probably *Sumerian, which by the Old Babylonian period was no longer the language of everyday life and so had to be learned specially, although pupils were probably required to provide *Akkadian translations. Teaching was based on rote learning by repeated recitation and writing of sign and word lists. Pupils were taught how to make tablets and hold the stylus. The teacher often wrote the lesson on one side of a round tablet, and the pupil copied it on the reverse. Surviving lists written by or for schoolchildren, and as reference works for scribes, include lists of cuneiform signs and thematic vocabularies, comprising lists of professions, legal terms, *plants, *animals, artefacts, materials, *food and drink, toponyms and stars (see Lexical texts), sometimes bilingual (Sumerian, Akkadian), trilingual (Sumerian, Akkadian, *Hittite, at *Boghazköy), and even quadrilingual (Sumerian, Akkadian, Ugaritic, *Hurrian, at *Ugarit). Advanced students copied Sumerian and, later, Akkadian literary texts, some of which have survived only in school exercises, as well as technical documents such as model *letters, *contracts, legal documents and trial proceedings, and old royal monuments.

Evidence for education in the *Iron Age *Levant is scanty because most *writing was done on perishable materials. Although a case has been advanced for schools in ancient *Israel, the books of the *Bible developing in them, it is not convincing. Instruction was most probably given on the apprentice pattern. A few *Hebrew *ostraca may be scribal exercises in writing numbers, the letters of the *alphabet and standard greetings, and the biblical book of Proverbs (see Wisdom literature) may have served as a lesson-book, as did similar works in Egypt and Mesopotamia. PB

M. CIVIL, 'Education in Mesopotamia', *Anchor Bible Dictionary* 2, ed. D.N. Freedman (New York 1992) 301–5.

G.I. DAVIES, 'Were There Schools in Ancient Israel?', *Wisdom in Ancient Israel*, eds J. Day, R.P. Gordon and H.G.M. Williamson (Cambridge 1995) 199–211.

C.J. GADD, *Teachers and Students in the Oldest Schools* (London 1956).

S.N. KRAMER, 'Schooldays: A Sumerian Composition Relating to the Education of a Scribe', *Journal of the American Oriental Society* 69 (1949) 199–215.

——, *History Begins at Sumer*, 3rd ed. (Philadelphia, PA 1981) 3–13.

A. LEMAIRE, *Les écoles et la formation de la Bible dans l'ancien Israël* (Fribourg 1981).

Å.W. SJÖBERG, 'The Old Babylonian Edubba', *Assyriological Studies* 20 (1975) 159–79.

**Egypt, relations with** In ancient times, Egypt was essentially the cultivated area of the valley of the River Nile, with its southern border at the First Cataract at Aswan, its northern border where the branches of the Nile Delta flow into the Mediterranean Sea. There was almost continual contact between the Near East and Egypt throughout history, but for some periods it is still debated whether the relations were commercial or imperialistic. Egypt was interested in the Near East for its raw materials: *wood, *copper, *tin, *silver, precious *stones, as well as *wine and oil. In return it could offer *gold, *food surpluses (such as the gift of grain to the *Hittites during a famine), linen and papyrus. The artistic tradition of Egypt greatly influenced *art, particularly in the *Levant, and Egyptian motifs are found in most periods in *sculpture, *seals, *jewellery and *ivory carving. Asiatic influence on Egypt is less obvious, but can be traced in *language, *literature and *religion.

Contacts between Egypt and the Near East are attested already in the Predynastic period. *Cylinder seals, decorative motifs, mostly of animals, and mudbrick architecture

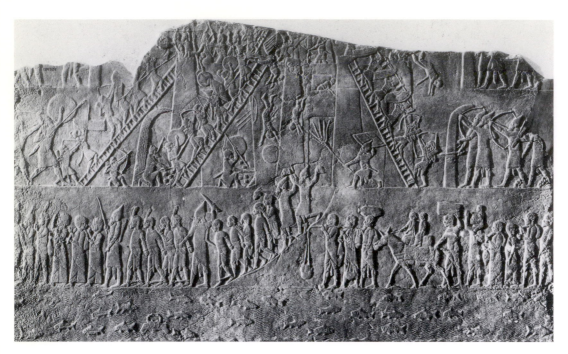

Ashurbanipal's palace at Nineveh included sculptures of his most distant triumph, the capture of major cities in Egypt, as shown here. Egyptian dress and hair style is carefully portrayed. WA 124982.

in recessed panels testify to *Mesopotamian influence in Egypt. Egypt imported lapis lazuli from Afghanistan via *Iran and Mesopotamia, and had close connections with *Byblos, which became the focus of Egyptian *trade. From here came good-quality wood, especially cedar, which the Egyptians used for building and for *coffins, chests and statues. Egyptian *pottery has been found at Early Bronze Age sites in southern *Palestine and *Sinai, and Palestinian pottery in Egyptian tombs. The name of Narmer, possibly to be identified with Menes, the legendary founder of the First Dynasty, has been found at *Arad and Tell Erani, and Egyptian cylinder seal impressions at 'En Besor, leading some scholars to claim Egyptian rule over southern *Canaan.

Egyptian statuary and scarab *seals dating to the Middle Kingdom, contemporary with the Middle Bronze Age, are found in *Canaan, but these are generally not in a good archaeological context and again it is uncertain whether Egypt ruled the area or had only commercial interests (see Execration texts). The *Hyksos Fifteenth Dynasty probably originated in the *Levant, and its expulsion from Egypt coincides with the end of the Middle Bronze Age in Palestine: many scholars argue that destructions at Palestinian sites were the work of the pursuing Egyptian army.

In the Late Bronze Age, Egyptian kings established an empire in Canaan, and their rule and diplomatic contacts with the kings of *Assyria, *Babylonia, *Mitanni and the Hittites are attested in the *Amarna Letters. Egypt's troubled relationship with the Hittites came to a head at the battle of *Kadesh, after which a peace treaty was signed. Egyptian garrisons were stationed at key sites in Canaan, and particular buildings have been identified as possibly the residencies of Egyptian governors (see Provincial administration). During this period, Asiatics appear in Egypt in large numbers as prisoners-of-war, mercenaries and *merchants. *Children of tributary rulers were held hostage in Egypt and educated there, and the worship of Asiatic *gods such as *Astarte was introduced to Egypt.

Egypt defeated the invasion of the *Sea Peoples, among whom were the *Philistines, who later settled on the coast of Canaan. It is not clear how the Egyptian empire in Canaan came to an end, but the period following the end of the New Kingdom in Egypt was one of internal strife. The decline of Egypt's importance is symbolized in the Egyptian story of the official Wenamon, who travels to Byblos to purchase wood and is rudely treated. During a resurgence of Egyptian power in the Twenty-second and Twenty-sixth Dynasties, parts of Palestine were again conquered, but Egypt was itself invaded by *Esarhaddon and *Ashurbanipal and briefly became part of the *Assyrian empire. Ironically, Egypt allied with the remnants of Assyria against *Nebuchadnezzar at the battle of *Carchemish in 605 BC, but was defeated. Later sources record Babylonian invasions of Egypt, but contemporary texts are ambiguous and it is not certain that the Babylonians entered Egypt.     PB

W. HELCK, *Die Beziehungen Ägyptens zu Vorderasien im 3. und 2. Jahrtausend v. Chr.*, 2nd ed. (Wiesbaden 1971).
J.K. HOFFMEIER, 'Egyptians', *Peoples of the Old Testament World*, eds A.J. Hoerth, G.L. Mattingly and E.M. Yamauchi (Grand

Rapids, MI 1994) 251–90.

D.B. REDFORD, *Egypt, Canaan, and Israel in Ancient Times* (Princeton, NJ 1992).

J. WEINSTEIN, 'The Egyptian Empire in Palestine: A Reassessment', *Bulletin of the American Schools of Oriental Research* 241 (1981) 1–28.

**Ekron** Tel Miqne (Arabic Khirbet el-Muqanna'), located c.37 km south-west of *Jerusalem, at a point where the *Philistine coastal plain meets the Judaean hills, is identified with biblical Ekron. J. Naveh made this identification in 1957, and it has been confirmed by excavation and by the recent discovery of an important inscription at the site. Tel Miqne is one of the largest *Iron Age sites in *Israel; it covers some 34 ha, a size which reflects ancient Ekron's apogee during the seventh century BC. It has been excavated by S. Gitin and T. Dothan (1981–96).

Ekron, one of the five principal cities of the Philistines, is mentioned a number of times in the *Old Testament. *Assyrian sources refer to Ekron as *amqar(r)una* and indicate that this *town was important for their control of Philistia and for their advance against *Egypt. A wall relief at *Khorsabad depicts *Sargon II's 712 BC siege of Ekron, and *Sennacherib's *annals describe the defeat of the town and its king, Padi, in 701 BC. *Esarhaddon forced Ekron's *king, Ikausu, to supply building materials for the former's palace in *Nineveh. In 667 BC, Ashurbanipal ordered Ikausu to support the Assyrian campaign against Egypt. The city was taken by *Nebuchadnezzar II in 603 BC. Thereafter, the texts refer to sporadic occupation from *Roman to Islamic times.

Ceramic evidence reflects *Canaanite Ekron's occupation in the fourth and third millennia BC, and Tel Miqne's later occupational history is different on the lower and upper parts of the mound. Generally speaking, the site was occupied in nine major periods from c.1700 to 600 BC. The Late Bronze Age settlement was an unfortified town on the upper part of the *tell; its remains reflect a city with numerous international contacts which ended in a fiery destruction. In the twelfth century BC, however, Ekron was fortified and spread to both upper and lower

parts of the mound. Its material culture indicates the arrival of the Philistines; megaron-type buildings (an oblong room with a central hearth, entered through a porch, common in Mycenaean Greece) and artefacts that display a non-Canaanite background point to the *Aegean origin of this new people. Ekron fell under Assyrian control at the end of the eighth century BC, and citizens in the town's wealthy section owned Assyrian-type and imported Greek vessels and substantial *silver *jewellery. Between c.700 and 625 BC, when Ekron reached its maximum size, it was the largest known producer of olive oil in the Near East.

Along with several industrial areas, some of Ekron's Iron Age cultic installations have been excavated. One of the site's most impressive structures is a possible *temple with a Neo-Assyrian plan, dating to the early seventh century BC. In 1996, a royal dedicatory inscription was found on a limestone block in the destruction debris of this large complex. This five-line text, written in a local form of the *Phoenician *alphabet, names a five-king *dynasty of Ekron – including Achish/Ikausu ('ruler of Ekron') – and says that he built this temple for Ptgyh, an otherwise unknown goddess. GLM

T. DOTHAN, 'Tel Miqne-Ekron: The Aegean Affinities of the Sea Peoples' (Philistines') Settlement in Canaan in Iron Age I', *Recent Excavations in Israel: A View to the West*, ed. S. Gitin (Dubuque 1995) 41–59.

——, 'Tel Miqne-Ekron: An Iron Age I Philistine Settlement in Canaan', *The Archaeology of Israel: Constructing the Past, Interpreting the Present*, eds N. A. Silberman and D. Small (Sheffield 1997) 96–106.

T. DOTHAN and S. GITIN, 'Miqne, Tel', *The Oxford Encyclopedia of Archaeology in the Near East* 4, ed. E.M. Meyers (New York 1997) 30–5.

——, 'Miqne, Tel (Ekron)', *New Encyclopedia of Archaeological Excavations in the Holy Land*, ed. E. Stern (New York 1993) 1051–9.

S. GITIN, 'Tel Miqne-Ekron in the 7th Century B.C.E.: The Impact of Economic Innovation and Foreign Cultural Influences on a Neo-Assyrian Vassal City-state', *Recent Excavations in Israel: A View to the West*, ed. S. Gitin (Dubuque 1995) 61–79.

S. GITIN, T. DOTHAN, and J. NAVEH, 'A Royal Dedicatory Inscription from Ekron', *Israel Exploration Journal* 47 (1997) 1–16.

Royal dedicatory inscription from Ekron, naming a five-king dynasty of Ekron (courtesy Tel Miqne-Ekron Project, photograph by Z. Radovan).

**El** 'El' or 'il(u)' is the common *Semitic noun for *god, and it was also the name of an important deity in parts of the Near East. In *Mesopotamia, the designation 'ilu' was used for deities in general, but no god named Il is known from texts. On the other hand, the term El/el is mentioned over five hundred times in the *Ugaritic texts, with about half the references referring to the specific deity. The noun El appears in the *Bible some 230 times. El was also named in other Semitic languages (e.g. *Phoenician, *Aramaic, Punic) and was known in pre-*Israelite *Canaan.

The Semitic deity El was said to reside with the gods on their sacred mountain, but he was also linked with 'the source of the two rivers, at the confluence of the two deeps'. In the Ugaritic mythology, El was the head of the pantheon, an old, grey-bearded patriarch. He was thought to be the father of the gods and, at Ugarit, was linked with his consort Athirat, though the Bible links Athirat/*Asherah with *Baal. The texts portray El as a wise and benevolent patron of the divine council. The sources present an ambiguous picture concerning Baal's status with regard to El, since the former is clearly the most active deity in the Ugaritic *myths. The latter do not mention a conflict, however, and El is said to have granted permission for the worship of Baal. El was linked with the bull, a clear symbol of strength and honour. As with Baal and other deities, iconographic representations of El are difficult to identify with certainty.

El's name was a common component of *Ammonite personal names, but the god El is not attested in the Ammonite inscriptions. The name El was well known in ancient Israel, as the name for a distinctive Semitic deity and another designation for *Yahweh. As an indication of El's importance, this name appears often in *Hebrew personal names (e.g. Eliezer, Elijah, Eliakim) and in the term 'Israel' itself. Attributes of the Canaanite El were assimilated to Yahweh. For example, the latter was understood as the head of the divine council and was known as the 'Ancient of Days'. Yahweh was known by a number of titles which incorporated the proper name 'El': El-Olam, El-Elyon, El-Shaddai.                                     GLM

W.J. FULCO, 'El', *The Encyclopedia of Religion* 5 (New York 1987) 73–4.

W. HERRMANN, 'El', *Dictionary of Deities and Demons in the Bible*, eds K. van der Toorn, B. Becking and P.W. van der Horst (Leiden 1995) 522–33.

C. L'HEUREUX, *Rank Among the Canaanite Gods: El, Ba'al, and the Rephaim* (Missoula, MO 1979).

U. OLDENBURG, *The Conflict between El and Ba'al in Canaanite Religion* (Leiden 1969).

S.B. PARKER (ed.), *Ugaritic Narrative Poetry* (Atlanta, GA 1997).

M.H. POPE, *El in the Ugaritic Texts* (Leiden 1955).

## Elam, Elamites

From the third to the first millennia BC, Elam, with its principal centres of *Susa and *Anshan, was one of the major powers of the ancient Near East, with close links to *Mesopotamia. The region comprised the south-western part of modern *Iran, a large area including highlands and lowlands which had their own distinctive cultures. The name Elam derives ultimately from Elamite *hatami/haltami*, rendered in *Sumerian as *elam(a)*. The Elamite *language is unrelated to any known ancient language.

The first written documents appear in the Proto-Elamite period (c.3400–2700 BC) at Susa, the largest *city. We are better informed about the Old Elamite period (c.2700–2100 BC), when references to Elam appear in Mesopotamian texts. The kings of *Akkad and later the Third Dynasty of *Ur campaigned against Elam, and Susa came under their rule. The Shimashki *dynasty (c.2100–1900 BC), based in the highlands, ended Ur III rule and looted Ur itself, occupying it for twenty-one years. Under the Sukkalmah ('grand regent') dynasty (c.1900–1600 BC), Elam became one of the largest states

A sculpture from Ashurbanipal's palace at Nineveh shows a new king being introduced to kneeling Elamites (detail of WA 124802).

in the area, with *diplomatic, economic and military concerns in Mesopotamia and *Syria, particularly in the eighteenth century BC when it confronted *Hammurabi of *Babylon.

After several centuries of decline, Elam re-emerged as a major power in the Middle Elamite period (c.1600–1100 BC). A new capital at *Chogha Zanbil was started, but never finished, by Untash-Napirisha. Elamite kings renewed their interest in Mesopotamia: in one *letter, an Elamite king demands the Babylonian throne. Relations with the *Kassites were belligerent, culminating in the Elamite removal of the last Kassite king and the end of the dynasty. During the Neo-Elamite period (c.1100–539 BC), Elam was caught in the conflict between *Assyria and *Babylonia on the one hand, acting as a traditional political refuge for Babylonian opponents of Assyria, and on the other facing increasing pressure from *Medes and *Persians to the north and east. The Assyrian King *Ashurbanipal sacked Susa in 647/6 BC, and Assyrian *palace reliefs provide much detail about Elamite buildings and costumes. By the mid sixth century BC, Elam had ceased to exist as a power and the area fell under *Achaemenid control. Use of the Elamite language continued in administrative documents and in display inscriptions such as the trilingual inscription of Darius I at Bisitun.                                     PB

E. CARTER and M.W. STOLPER, *Elam: Surveys of Political History and Archaeology* (Berkeley, CA 1984).

W. HINZ, *The Lost World of Elam: Re-creation of a Vanished Civilization* (London 1972).

D.T. POTTS, *The Archaeology of Elam* (Cambridge 1999).

E. REINER, 'The Elamite Language', *Altkleinasiatische Sprache, Handbuch der Orientalistik* I, Abt. II, ed. B. Spuler (Leiden 1969) 54-118.

**Ellil:** see Enlil

**Emar** Lying at a major crossing of the Euphrates by the route from *Mesopotamia to the west, Emar was significant in the third and second millennia BC, but its site was located only in 1971 at modern Meskeneh. Excavations were begun there by J.-C. Margueron in 1972 and continue despite Meskeneh's partial flooding by the Tabqa Dam. In the fourteenth century BC a new *town was constructed on a rocky spur overlooking the valley where, it seems, the earlier town lay. The ground was levelled and the slopes terraced to receive *houses, a *palace and *temples. The palace has an early form of the *bīt hilāni plan. Two of the temples each had a porch leading into a main hall with a podium and brick-built *altar. They were dedicated to *Baal and to *Astarte. Another temple contained a diviner's *library of *Akkadian *cuneiform tablets and his *archive (see Omens and divination). Tablets were found in other buildings by the archaeologists and later by local people. They show that the town was the capital of the Ashtata region, ruled by a local *king subject to *Hittite control from *Carchemish. The population bore mainly West *Semitic names and worshipped West Semitic deities, and glosses in various texts indicate that the *scribes spoke a West Semitic *language. Scores of tablets provide details of various *rituals involving both local and *Babylonian traditions, and the same mixture is seen in the legal deeds. The scribes copied standard Babylonian *lexical texts and some *literature (e.g. *Gilgamesh) and many omen compendia, but one '*wisdom' composition is otherwise known only from *Hattusas and *Ugarit. Other texts are written in *Hurrian and Hittite and many legal deeds bear impressions of *seals engraved with Hittite *hieroglyphs. The city fell to enemy attack about 1185 BC. Emar is important for its architectural conception and for the texts which are contemporary with Ugarit's but disclose different aspects of society, notably in the rituals.     ARM

D. ARNAUD, *Emar VI: Textes sumériens et accadiens* 1–4 (Paris 1985–7).
——, *Textes syriens de l'âge du Bronze récent* (Barcelona 1991).
G.M. BECKMAN, *Texts from the Vicinity of Emar in the Collection of Jonathan Rosen* (Rome 1996).
D. BEYER, *Meskéné-Emar: Dix ans de travaux 1972–82* (Paris 1982).
D. FLEMING, 'Rituals from Emar', *The Context of Scripture* 1, eds W.W. Hallo and K.L. Younger (Leiden 1997) 427–43.
J.-C. MARGUERON, 'Quatre campagnes de fouilles à Émar 1972–1974', *Syria* 52 (1975) 53–85.

**Enki:** see Ea


**Enlil**   Enlil (Akkadian Ellil) is one of the more important *gods in the *Mesopotamian pantheon. According to one *Sumerian poem, the other gods could not even look upon his splendour. Sometimes he is said to be the offspring of *An, and brother of the mother goddess Aruru. He is also described as a descendant of Enki and Ninki ('Lord and Lady Earth', not connected with the god Enki). His wife is Ninlil (or Sud). Among the children of Enlil are the goddess *Inana and the gods *Adad, Nanna-Suen, *Nergal, *Ninurta, Pabilsang, Nuska, *Utu, Urash, Zababa and Ennugi. Nuska also serves as Enlil's minister.

The great centre of the cult of Enlil was the *temple E-kur (the 'Mountain House') at *Nippur, at the northern edge of *Sumer, and Enlil is often called the 'Great Mountain' and 'King of the Foreign Lands', which may suggest a connection with the *Zagros mountains. Other images used to describe his *personality are *king, supreme lord, father and creator; 'raging storm' and 'wild bull'; and, unexpectedly, '*merchant'. He is sometimes called by the name Nunamnir. In Mesopotamian *flood *myths, it is Enlil who wishes to destroy humanity.

*Astronomically, Ellil was associated with the constellation Boötes. In Neo-*Assyrian *art Ellil is symbolized by a horned cap.     JAB

H. BEHRENS, *Enlil und Ninlil* (Rome 1978).
M. CIVIL, 'Enlil, the Merchant: Notes to CT 15 10', *Journal of Cuneiform Studies* 28 (1976) 72–81.
——, 'Enlil and Ninlil: The Marriage of Sud', *Journal of the American Oriental Society* 103/1 (1983) 43–66.
D.O. EDZARD, 'Mesopotamien: Die Mythologie der Sumerer und Akkader', *Götter und Mythen im Vorderen Orient*, Vol. 1 of *Wörterbuch der Mythologie*, ed. H.W. Haussig (Stuttgart 1965) 59–61.
G. LEICK, *A Dictionary of Ancient Near Eastern Mythology* (London/New York 1991).


**Enmerkar**   Enmerkar was a legendary *king of the *Sumerian *city of Unug (*Uruk). His principal exploit was the capture of the rich and powerful city of Aratta in highland *Iran, renowned for its *metalworkers and *craftsmen (almost certainly also legendary). In the literary composition 'The Sumerian *King List' Enmerkar is called the builder of the walls of Unug, and a son of Mes-kiag-gasher (an early king of Unug). Other sources (probably confusing two traditions) describe him as son of the sun-god *Utu. The hero Lugalbanda and his seven older brothers served in the army of Enmerkar during the campaign which forms the theme of two Sumerian poems, 'Enmerkar and the Lord of Aratta' and 'Enmerkar and En-suhgir-ana', and the background to two more. In 'Enmerkar and the Lord of Aratta', Enmerkar is depicted as inventing *writing as an aid to memory for a slow-witted messenger. In 'Enmerkar and En-suhgir-ana' he uses *magical means to defeat the ruler of Aratta.     JAB

A. BERLIN, *Enmerkar and Ensuhkešdanna: A Sumerian Narrative Poem* (Philadelphia, PA 1979).
S. COHEN, *Enmerkar and the Lord of Aratta* (University Microfilms International, Philadelphia, PA 1973).
T. JACOBSEN, *The Harps That Once … Sumerian Poetry in Translation* (New Haven, CN 1987) 275–319.
C. WILCKE, 'Lugalbanda', *Reallexikon der Assyriologie* 7 (Berlin/New York 1987) 117–32.


**Epics:** see Stories, myths and epics


**Epipalaeolithic**   This is the period at the end of the Pleistocene and *Palaeolithic dating to c.20,000–10,000 bp (before present, see Radiocarbon dating). The material culture of this period is dominated by chipped stone (*flint) industries characterized by small *tools. These are manufactured from small, elongated flint chips called 'bladelets'. Typical tools are either modified bladelets or segments of bladelets blunted by 'retouch' into distinct shapes, geometric and non-geometric, called microliths. Geometric microliths are more common after c.16,000 bp, at least in the *Levant, where they occur as triangles, trapezes, rectangles and lunates. Since microliths can be very small, as little as 2 by 3 mm, it is clear that they were hafted as part of composite tools. In what were by and large relatively mobile communities, they had the advantage of portability and provided flexibility in the refurbishment or creation of tools. Particular 'designs' of microliths are characteristic of different time periods and areas, perhaps reflecting distinct groups of people.

Epipalaeolithic society consisted of small bands which ethnographic and archaeological evidence combine to suggest would coalesce and disperse to exploit seasonally varying resources and engage in social interaction. Groups would have numbered from a handful of individuals to bands numbering in their tens. This is indicated by Epipalaeolithic sites both in caves and in the open that cover tens of square metres to several hundred square metres. Typically one to seven hearths are found on such sites. Exceptionally sites are larger and show signs of structures. In the early Epipalaeolithic, by Lake Tiberias (the Sea of Galilee), the site of Ohalo II at 19,000 bp has evidence for three oval structures with floors sunk into underlying soil and walls of interlaced branches or reeds. This community exploited a wide range of *plant foods including wild barley, and *fish and water fowl from the lake, as well as large mammals such as deer and gazelle that are the more typical remains of *food at most Epipalaeolithic sites. Plant remains were probably exploited regularly by Epipalaeolithic communities, but are normally under-represented on sites because of archaeological retrieval and preservational problems. An indication of this is provided by the large site of Jilat 6 in the *Jordanian steppe where, alongside the hunting of gazelle and equid, there is evidence for the gathering of a range of steppe grasses, chenopods and tubers. Whilst Epipalaeolithic groups were normally relatively mobile hunter-gatherers, on occasion they took advantage of abundant resources available over a number of seasons to take up longer-term residence and invest in significant site facilities as at Ohalo II. This phenomenon is particularly marked at the end of the Epipalaeolithic at *Natufian sites in the Levant, 12,500 bp–10,000 bp, but at contemporary sites as far away as eastern Turkey, such as Hallan Çemi, the same phenomenon can be noted.　DB

D. HENRY, *From Foraging to Agriculture* (Philadelphia, PA 1989).

## Eponyms

The earliest *Assyrian documents, written in the nineteenth century BC, mostly from *Kanesh, display a dating system by eponym, that is, an official gave his name to the year (like the archons in Greece and the consuls in Rome). The officials were related, in a way not yet understood, to the state *temple of *Ashur. For the system to function, *scribes had to keep lists of the

Part of a cuneiform tablet from Ashurbanipal's library at Nineveh listing eponyms, their titles and an event for each year from 810 to 777 BC. The ruled line marks the accession of Shalmaneser IV. WA K 3403+.

eponyms in order, otherwise they could not calculate how long ago, for example, a loan had been made or a property sold. An early list, from *Mari, covers years before and during the reign of *Shamshi-Adad I (c.1813–1781 BC). That is more than a simple list of the names in order (Eponym List). It reports an event for each year in the form, 'In the eponymate of X, Y took place' and so belongs to the category of Eponym Chronicles. A fragmentary tablet from *Ashur listed eponyms from about 1200 BC, but it is only for the years from 910 to 649 that enough texts survive to give a consecutive list. Documents written between 649 and 612 or later carry eponym dates, but their sequence is not yet assured. Eponym dates before 910 BC can often be placed in particular reigns, but not in order.

Assyrian *kings held the eponymate from at least 1327 BC (Enlil-nerari), at a later period taking the office in the second full year of the reign. Five chief officers of state followed in a fairly regular pattern, then governors of various provinces. Evidently selection took place well in advance, supposedly depending in some way on the casting of dice. After reigning thirty years, the king was eligible for the office a second time, with the officials following as if a new reign had begun, a parallel to the *Egyptian *heb-sed* festival, celebrating the thirtieth anniversary of the accession.

The Eponym Chronicles are an important source of information for Assyrian history, perhaps drawing on a central record, complementing the *annals. The note of a solar eclipse in 763 BC enables the sequence to be pegged to the Julian calendar astronomically, independent of any other ancient sources. When other texts – *Babylonian, Egyptian, *Hebrew – can be correlated with the eponym list, therefore, they can be firmly dated.　ARM

J.-J. GLASSNER, *Chroniques mésopotamiennes* (Paris 1993).

A. MILLARD, *The Eponyms of the Assyrian Empire 910–612 BC* (Winona Lake, IN 1994).

C. SAPORETTI, *Gli eponimi medio-assiri* (Malibu, CA 1979).

R.M. WHITING, 'Tell Leilan/Šubat Enlil: Chronological Problems and Perspectives', *Tall al-Hamadiya 2: Recent Excavations in the Upper Khabur Region*, eds S. Eichler, M. Wäfler and D. Warburton (Freiburg 1990) 167–218.

**Erech:** see Uruk

**Ereshkigal** Ereshkigal, whose name can be translated 'Queen of the Great Below' (a euphemism for the *under-world), is also known in *Akkadian as Allatu. She is the goddess who rules the underworld, mother of the goddess Nungal and, by *Enlil, of the god Namtar, who serves as her messenger and minister. Ereshkigal's first husband was the god Gugal-ana, whose name probably originally meant 'canal inspector of the god *An' and who therefore may have been identical with Ennugi. In the *Sumerian poem '*Inana's Descent to the Underworld', Inana tries to gain entry to the underworld by claiming that she has come to attend the funeral rites of Gugal-ana, the 'husband of my elder sister *Ereshkigal'. A version survives in Akkadian as '*Ishtar's Descent to the Underworld'. The son of Ereshkigal and Gugal-ana was the god Ninazu. In another tradition, Ereshkigal married the god *Nergal, as related in the poem 'Nergal and Ereshkigal', where their passionate lovemaking is described.

Ereshkigal lived in a *palace located at Ganzir, the doorway to the underworld, protected by seven *gates, all of which could be bolted and each of which was guarded by a porter. Although her cult may not have been very important, she plays a prominent role in mythological narratives about the underworld. JAB

B. ALSTER, 'Inanna Repenting: The Conclusion of Inanna's Descent', *Acta Sumerologica* 18 (1996) 1–18.

S.M. DALLEY, *Myths from Mesopotamia* (Oxford 1990) 154–62, 165–81.

G. LEICK, *A Dictionary of Ancient Near Eastern Mythology* (London/New York 1991).

W. SLADEK, *Inanna's Descent to the Netherworld* (University Microfilms International, Philadelphia, PA 1974).

**Eridu** The seven mounds of Eridu, today known as Abu Shahrain, are located in Iraq at the south-western limits of the south *Mesopotamian plain, about 24 km south-west of *Ur. The site is famous for its long series of excavated *temples, spanning at least fifteen hundred years from c.5500 BC or earlier. In *Sumerian *literature Eridu was renowned as one of the most ancient *cities of Mesopotamia and a source of *kingship. Excavations at Eridu were conducted by several early explorers in Mesopotamia before the beginning of scientific investigation by Fuad Safar, Mohammed Ali Mustafa and *Lloyd in the 1940s.

Eighteen successive levels of temple mudbrick architecture were exposed during the 1940s excavations, all

Excavation of Temple XVI at Eridu, looking from the altar across to the door (from F. Safar *et al.*, *Eridu* (Baghdad 1981) fig. 41).

probably dedicated to the worship of the god Enki. The earliest level, Early *Ubaid in date, had a simple plan with recesses and a podium. Through time the plans of the temples grew more complex and elaborate, culminating in large ranges of rooms with decorated façades, all set on monumental platforms. From the floors of the level VII temple came a deposit of fish bones, probably the remains of offerings to the god Enki. The latest levels of the temple survive only as platforms.

Painted *pottery from Eridu provided the basis for a fourfold division of the Ubaid period, making possible better understanding of the development and spread of Ubaid culture, as refined by more recent excavations at Tell el-'Oueili in southern Iraq. An extensive Ubaid-period *cemetery, with bodies deposited in brick-lined *tombs, was also excavated. In general, the temple evidence from Eridu shows remarkable continuity of settlement in this part of southern Mesopotamia.

*Palaces of the Early Dynastic period (early to mid third millennium BC) were excavated on mound 2 at Eridu, and in the *Ur III period, c.2050 BC, a massive *ziggurat was built. There is evidence for later occupation at the site until the fourth century BC. RM

M.W. GREEN, 'The Eridu Lament', *Journal of Cuneiform Studies* 30 (1978) 127–67.

J.L. HUOT (ed.), *Oueili: Travaux de 1978 et 1989* (Paris 1996).

S. LLOYD, 'Abu Shahrein: A Memorandum', *Iraq* 36 (1974) 129–38.

J. OATES, 'Ur and Eridu: The Prehistory', *Iraq* 22 (1960) 32–50.

F. SAFAR, M.A. MUSTAFA and S. LLOYD, *Eridu* (Baghdad 1981).

**Esarhaddon** After *Sennacherib's murder, Esarhaddon (680–669 BC) defeated his brothers, the assassins, who fled to *Urartu, and secured the throne. His reign saw *Assyrian forces facing new foes in the east, *Cimmerians and *Scythians, and long-standing problems elsewhere. Rebels in *Babylon were executed, Sidon was captured, its *king executed and tribute received from twenty-two

Bronze relief showing Esarhaddon with his mother, Naqia (© Pierre et Maurice Chuzeville, Département des Antiquités Orientales, Musée du Louvre AO 20185).

R. BORGER, *Die Inschriften Asarhaddons Königs von Assyrien* (Graz 1956).

J.A. BRINKMAN, 'Babylonia in the Shadow of Assyria (647–626 B.C.)', *Cambridge Ancient History* 3.2, 2nd ed. (Cambridge 1991) 38–47.

A.K. GRAYSON, 'Assyria: Sennacherib and Esarhaddon (704–669 B.C.)', *Cambridge Ancient History* 3.2, 2nd ed. (Cambridge 1991) 122–41.

A.L. OPPENHEIM, in *Ancient Near Eastern Texts*, 3rd ed., ed. J.B. Pritchard (Princeton, NJ 1969) 289–94.

E. REINER, in *Ancient Near Eastern Texts*, 3rd ed., ed. J.B. Pritchard (Princeton, NJ 1969) 534–41 (treaties).

B.N. PORTER, *Images, Power, Politics: Figurative Aspects of Esarhaddon's Babylonian Policy* (Philadelphia, PA 1993).

K. WATANABE and S. PARPOLA, *Neo-Assyrian Treaties and Loyalty Oaths* (Helsinki 1988).

D.J. WISEMAN, 'The Vassal Treaties of Esarhaddon', *Iraq* 20 (1958).

rulers of places in the *Levant and *Cyprus, tribes in northern *Arabia were subjugated and a major *town on the Urartian frontier, Shubria, was captured. The *Babylonian *Chronicle notes these events, with others, while Esarhaddon's inscriptions give some at greater length and with picturesque details, but not in order. One of his most notable activities was in *Babylon. Sennacherib had demolished the city and removed its *gods. The devastation was divinely decreed for seventy years. However, Esarhaddon asserted that *Marduk had reversed the *cuneiform figure, making it eleven (as roman XI reversed becomes IX), and so he could begin restoration work and attempt a rapprochement with the city. He took another step by having his son *Ashurbanipal recognized as heir to the throne of Assyria and another son, Shamash-shum-ukin, as future king of Babylon. Various documents formalised the situation, the most extensive survivors being the 'Vassal *Treaties' which Esarhaddon imposed upon *Median rulers, obliging them to safeguard the succession. His major military goal was *Egypt, probably because it encouraged Assyria's western vassals to revolt. In 678 BC a frontier town, Arza, was taken. He suffered a defeat in Egypt in 673, but in 671 BC Assyrian forces, having endured the privations of the waterless *Sinai desert, captured Memphis, defeating pharaoh Tirhakah. A new campaign mounted in 669 BC was aborted when the king died on the way.

Esarhaddon prepared to build a *palace at *Nimrud, which was not completed. At *Nineveh he built a new palace on the mound now called Nebi Yunus, mostly unexcavated. Besides building inscriptions on prisms, he left inscribed stelae celebrating his power. *Letters and other documents from his reign found at Nineveh reveal him as a superstitious, almost neurotic man, apparently suffering from recurrent, incurable illness. ARM

**Eshnunna** Tell Asmar, ancient Eshnunna, lies 80 km north-east of Baghdad by the Diyala river, a tributary of the Tigris. During the 1930s a major programme of excavations at Tell Asmar, and at nearby Khafaje, Tell Agrab and Ischali, was conducted by Henri Frankfort. The site is important for its architectural remains of the third and early second millennia BC, when Eshnunna was a *town of some significance in eastern *Mesopotamia.

Eshnunna witnessed its first period of growth during the Early Dynastic period, c.3000–2350 BC. The city maintained its importance during the *Akkadian period before expanding to its maximum size in the *Ur III and *Isin–*Larsa periods, c.2100–1800 BC, and was finally abandoned c.1760 BC.

Of great significance is the sequence of *temples possibly dedicated to the god Abu. On the basis of finds from this architectural sequence the Early Dynastic period was first divided into three distinct phases, spanning some five hundred years from c.3000 BC. Overlying remains of late fourth-millennium date, the temples were built in the sequence of: Early Dynastic I (the Archaic Shrine), Early Dynastic II (the Square Temple) and Early Dynastic III (the Single Shrine). While valid for the Diyala region, this threefold division of the Early Dynastic period is less appropriate for the *Sumerian heartland of south Mesopotamia. A hoard of limestone statues, depicting *gods or worshippers, was found beneath the floor of the Square Temple.

The Northern *Palace was built during the Akkadian period, c.2350–2150 BC, and had both domestic and probably craft quarters with drainage facilities. There are indications that *textile production took place in a rebuild of this extensive structure. Below the floor a spectacular hoard of objects of *silver and lapis lazuli was found. Excavations elsewhere in the city revealed many residential *houses of the third millennium BC.

By 2000 BC a temple dedicated to Shu-Sin, king of Ur, had been built, reflecting Eshnunna's domination by Ur. The adjacent Palace of the Rulers, largely of Isin–Larsa date, was an administrative structure, as attested by numerous *cuneiform texts. Hammurabi's conquest of Eshnunna in 1763 BC led to its abandonment. RM

Group of votive statues from the Square Temple of Abu at Tell Asmar (Eshnunna). Early Dynastic I–II, c.3000–2600 BC (courtesy of the Oriental Institute of the University of Chicago).

R.M. ADAMS, *Land Behind Baghdad* (Chicago 1965).

M. CHUBB, *City in the Sand* (New York 1957).

P. DELOUGAZ, H.D. HILL and S. LLOYD, *Private Houses and Graves in the Diyala Region* (Chicago 1967).

P. DELOUGAZ and S. LLOYD, *Pre-Sargonid Temples in the Diyala Region* (Chicago 1942).

H. FRANKFORT, S. LLOYD and T. JACOBSEN, *The Gimilsin Temple and the Palace of the Rulers at Tell Asmar* (Chicago 1940).

S. LLOYD, 'Diyala Region', *The Dictionary of Art* 9, ed. J. Turner (New York/London 1996) 44–6.

**Etana** In the *Sumerian *King List, the twelfth king of the *city-state of *Kish after the time of the *Flood is described as 'a shepherd who ascended to heaven'. The full story is recounted in mythological compositions of the Old *Babylonian, Middle *Assyrian and Neo-Assyrian

Babylonian art rarely illustrates myths and legends, but Etana may be shown on Akkadian-period cylinder seals engraved with a figure sitting on a bird's lap rising upwards while a shepherd leads his flock and a figure churns milk, perhaps to make ring-shaped cheeses. Height 3 cm. c.2300–2200 BC. WA 89767.

periods. Elevated by the gods to the throne of Kish, Etana is still without an heir and prays to the sun-god *Shamash to reveal to him the 'plant of giving birth', which grows only in the heavens. Shamash tells him about an injured eagle languishing in a deep pit (following a conflict with a serpent, recounted at the beginning of the legend). Etana travels to the eagle and stays to feed him until he can fly again and come out of the pit. In return the eagle offers to fly Etana up to heaven to ask the goddess *Ishtar for the birth-giving plan. Etana's fear of heights, however, causes problems and the attempt ends in failure. Nevertheless, back home in Kish Etana has a dream about successfully reaching Ishtar's realm, taken as a sign to make another attempt. This time the eagle secures him well and the pair reach the gate of heaven. Here the extant text breaks off, but it is probable that Etana did obtain the plant of birth, since further fragments and the Sumerian King List mention a son named Balih.

Some *cylinder seals of the *Akkadian period and an impression from one of the Middle Assyrian period show a pastoral scene with a man riding on the back of a large flying bird, thought to relate in some way to the legend of Etana, though the Akkadian seals are two to three hundred years earlier than the oldest texts of the story known.

JAB/AG

R. BERNBECK, 'Siegel, Mythen, Riten: Etana und die Ideologie der Akkad-Zeit', *Baghdader Mitteilungen* 27 (1996) 159–213.

S.M. DALLEY, *Myths from Mesopotamia* (Oxford 1990) 189–202.

W. FARBER, [Review of Kinnier Wilson], *Journal of Near Eastern Studies* 48 (1989) 155.

A.R. GREEN, 'Myths in Mesopotamian Art', *Sumerian Gods and their Representations*, eds I.L. Finkel and M.J. Geller (Groningen 1997) 135–58.

J.V. KINNIER WILSON, *The Legend of Etana: A New Edition* (Warminster 1985).

P. STEINKELLER, 'Early Semitic Literature and Third-millennium Seals with Mythological Motifs', *Literature and Literary Language at Ebla* (Florence 1992) 243–75.

**Eunuchs** Eunuchs played a significant role in society and *administration in the ancient Near East in the second and first millennia BC. The institution may have originated in *Assyria – a classical tradition traces the origin of eunuchs to *Semiramis – but eunuchs were prominent officials also among the *Hittites and in *Urartu, and probably in *Babylonia where the evidence is less clear.

The *Akkadian term *ša rēši* is usually translated as 'eunuch', although its literal meaning is '(One) of the Head', that is, 'Chief', and some scholars think that it referred simply to somebody belonging to the royal entourage. It was a title for an official, attendant, soldier or officer, and it is possible that the specific meaning 'eunuch' developed later. However, it has been proposed that *ša rēši* originally meant 'the one with two heads', a euphemism for 'the one without two heads', where the two heads stood for the two (mutilated) testicles. The *Hebrew word *sarîs* is thought to derive from *ša rēši*, and in the *Bible it can mean either a court official or a eunuch.

People called *ša rēši* are attested in positions from *palace officials to servants in private households, as *scribes and *musicians, and some were *slaves. Eunuchs were high-ranking officers in the Assyrian *army and administration, and it has been calculated that in the ninth and eighth centuries BC more than 10 per cent of the senior officials in Assyria were eunuchs. Special land donations and tax exemptions were reserved for eunuchs. They formed a distinct corps, headed by the 'chief of the eunuchs', who often led the army on campaign. The compound term 'eunuchs and bearded ones' referred to all Assyrian officials at court. In Assyrian reliefs, officials depicted beardless are normally identified as eunuchs, though some could be young boys or even the *king's male relatives. Most Neo-Assyrian seals inscribed for *ša rēši* have depictions of beardless worshippers, suggesting that they were the seals of eunuchs.

The Middle Assyrian palace and *harem edicts have provision for careful examination of royal eunuchs to ensure that they are admissible to the court and harem. Those who passed were admitted to court service after an elaborate ceremony which included receiving a new name referring to the king, since protecting the king was their prime duty. The need for detailed examination may suggest that Assyrian boys were created eunuchs by crushing the testicles. Some eunuchs would have been congenital, and *omens noting babies born without testicles or penises are known. The source of most eunuchs is unknown. In *Media and *Persia eunuchs were often brought from the provinces: *Herodotus records that 500 boys from *Babylonia were sent annually to the Persian court to become eunuchs. It is likely that in Assyria they also came from noble families, who castrated a male child to launch him on a prosperous court career. Castration was also a punishment, and in the Middle Assyrian laws the penalty for an *adulterous or homosexual man was to be turned into a eunuch.

*Cyrus the Younger, the son of the Persian King Darius II, is reported by the Greek historian Xenophon as saying that eunuchs were particularly loyal because they had no other ties or affections. A ruler could presumably rely on a eunuch who had no wife or *children: an Assyrian *omen text reads: 'May your semen dry up like that of a eunuch who cannot beget'. Eunuchs in later cultures could marry and adopt children, but this was probably not the case in the ancient Near East, at least in Assyria, where the king had full authority over a deceased eunuch's estate and was responsible for his burial.     PB

K. DELLER, 'The Assyrian Eunuchs and their Predecessors', *Priests and Officials in the Ancient Near East*, ed. K. Watanabe (Heidelberg 1999) 303–11.

P. GARELLI, 'Remarques sur l'administration de l'empire assyrien', *Revue d'Assyriologie* 68 (1974) 129–40.

A.K. GRAYSON, 'Eunuchs in Power: Their Role in the Assyrian Bureaucracy', *Vom Alten Orient zum Alten Testament*, eds M. Dietrich and O. Loretz (Neukirchen/Vluyn 1995) 85–98.

A.L. OPPENHEIM, 'A Note on *ša rēši*', *Journal of the Ancient Near Eastern Society* 5 (1973) 325–34.

P.O. SCHOLZ, *Der entmannte Eros: Eine Kulturgeschichte der Eunuchen und Kastraten* (Düsseldorf/Zurich 1997).

K. WATANABE, 'Seals of Neo-Assyrian Officials', *Priests and Officials in the Ancient Near East*, ed. K. Watanabe (Heidelberg 1999) 313–66.

**Euphrates–Tigris rescue sites** From the late 1960s onwards the Euphrates and Tigris rivers and their major tributaries have seen and continue to see the construction of huge dams for hydroelectric power and vast irrigation schemes in all the countries through which they flow – Turkey, *Syria and Iraq. The advent of the impressive engineering feats continues to provide opportunities for extensive archaeological investigations, both survey and excavation, mainly in areas where there had been comparatively little previous investigation. The governments of the countries concerned have facilitated an international response to the irrevocable loss of so many vestiges of the past in this vast area of northern *Mesopotamia. This has resulted in a concentration of archaeological research on a scale and intensity not seen before for the ancient Near East.

The response from the archaeological world was

The Assyrian court included many eunuchs. Relief from Sargon II's palace at Khorsabad. WA 11816.

varied, scholars from many countries and institutions becoming involved in what are termed 'rescue' or 'salvage' excavations. Sites of all periods, from the *Palaeolithic to the late medieval, have been investigated, and a vast literature is emerging. Nevertheless, much has inevitably been lost. One aspect of this concentration of work on sites that were to be drowned has been a shift in focus from purely 'research' projects designed to address specific questions or sets of questions to an approach that aimed at the recovery of as much information as possible, often from fairly large multi-period mound sites, before they were lost. Rescue situations remove any concern for the preservation and conservation of excavated buildings and sometimes justify the abandonment of attempts at total recovery of all archaeological evidence that had come to characterize some research excavations in the 1960s.

Generally, the areas concerned have been border and contact zones subject to cultural and political influences, and to the passage of trade and armies, rather than core areas in which distinctive civilizations emerged. The very reasons that make the river valleys suitable for the construction of large dams have inhibited the development of large urban centres (Samsat, ancient Samasata on the Euphrates, is an exception), for the rivers flow in narrow valleys where rich fertile plains, if they exist at all, are restricted in size. Thus the agricultural wealth necessary to support the growth of major urban centres was not usually available in close proximity to the rivers.    GDS

T.L. McCLELLAN, 'Euphrates Dams, Survey of', *The Oxford Encyclopaedia of Archaeology in the Near East* 2, ed. E.M. Meyers (New York 1997) 290–2.

S. MITCHELL, 'The Asvan Project', *Ancient Anatolia*, ed. R. Matthews (London 1998) 85–100.

M. ROAF, 'Eski Mosul Dam Salvage Project', *The Oxford Encyclopaedia of Archaeology in the Near East* 2, ed. E.M. Meyers (New York 1997) 265–8.

——, 'Hamrin Dam Salvage Project', *The Oxford Encyclopaedia of Archaeology in the Near East* 2, ed. E.M. Meyers (New York 1997) 471–4.

J. ZARINS, 'Euphrates', *The Oxford Encyclopaedia of Archaeology in the Near East* 2, ed. E.M. Meyers (New York 1997) 287–90.

## Execration texts

From early pharaonic times in *Egypt, names of hostile Egyptians or foreigners were written on figurines of prisoners or on *pottery vessels. These were ritually broken and buried as part of a *magical rite to curse (execrate) those named. Three series of texts dating to the Middle Kingdom include rulers and places in *Palestine and *Syria: bowls from a fortress at Mirgissa in Nubia (c.1870 BC), bowls now in Berlin (c.1850 BC) and figurines excavated at Saqqara, now in Brussels (c.1800 BC). The basic format of the texts consists of a list of chiefs and places followed by a generalized curse with another list of places. The three groups differ in the number of places mentioned, from five in the Mirgissa series to about sixty in the Brussels series, including *Ashkelon, *Ekron, *Hazor, *Jerusalem and *Byblos. In the Mirgissa and Berlin groups, several chiefs are associated with a single place, while in the Brussels

Execration text written on a pottery figure of a prisoner, from Saqqara, Egypt, c.1800 BC (courtesy of Musées Royaux d'Art et d'Histoire, Brussels, E.7611).

group each place has one chief. The three series have often been compared in an attempt to trace the process of sedentarization in Palestine and Syria in the Middle Bronze Age.    PB

W. HELCK, *Die Beziehungen Ägyptens zu Vorderasien im 3. und 2. Jahrtausend v. Chr.* (Wiesbaden 1962) 49–68.

Y. KOENIG, 'Les textes d'envoûtement de Mirgissa', *Revue d'Égyptologie* 41 (1990) 101–25.

G. POSENER, *Princes et pays d'Asie et de Nubie* (Brussels 1940).

A.F. RAINEY, 'The World of Sinuhe', *Israel Oriental Studies* 2 (1972) 369–408.

D.B. REDFORD, *Egypt, Canaan, and Israel in Ancient Times* (Princeton 1992) 87–93.

K. SETHE, *Die Ächtung feindlicher Fürsten, Völker und Dinge auf altägyptischen Tongefässscherben des mittleren Reiches* (Berlin 1926).

## Exodus

In the *biblical Books of Genesis, Exodus, Leviticus, Numbers and Deuteronomy, ancient *Israelites recalled the migration of Jacob and his family to Egypt where his son Joseph was vizier, a movement which can be placed in the first half of the second millennium BC when there was a flow of *Semites from the *Levant to the Nile Delta, giving rise to the *Hyksos *kings. Many generations later, Jacob's descendants, the twelve tribes of Israel, now numerous, provided a handy labour force for pharaohs building in the Delta. The name of one of the sites, Rameses, points to Ramesses II (c.1290–1224 BC) as the principal oppressor. Appeals by the Israelites' leader, Moses, for some relief met with harsher conditions in the brick-fields, so Israel's God, *Yahweh, demonstrated his power through the Ten Plagues, as Moses warned the Pharaoh. In advance of the final plague, the Israelites were instructed to stay indoors, eating unleavened bread with a roast lamb whose blood had been splashed on their doorways to distinguish them from the Egyptians. That plague, causing the death of all firstborn males in the land, excluding the Israelites, made Pharaoh relent. Jews still celebrate the event at the Passover festival. As the Israelites trekked eastwards, Pharaoh reneged and sent his army in pursuit. The Red, or Reed, Sea, probably one of the Bitter Lakes, seemed a barrier to the fugitives until the waters parted, blown by a 'strong east wind', allowing them through, then flooding back across the Egyptian forces. Marching in stages the Israelites reached Mount *Sinai, fed by quails and daily supplies of manna. Neither the route nor the mountain can be identified with any certainty, although the traditional location at Jebel Musa has a strong claim. There God, *Yahweh, through Moses, gave Israel its constitution in the form of a *covenant, establishing himself as its suzerain. Israel was to acknowledge no other king, to follow Yahweh's ritual and moral requirements, notably the Ten Commandments, and avoid relationships with the people of *Canaan whom God had condemned. For religious ceremonies a portable, prefabricated shrine was made, the Tabernacle, which housed the *Ark containing the tablets incised with the terms of the covenant. The journey from Egypt to Canaan would have been relatively short had the people not failed to follow the divine instructions, so one generation had to die out before Israel could enter its Promised Land. Much of the time was spent with a base camp at Kadesh-Barnea, identified with Ain Kudeirat, and in the plain east of the *Jordan, opposite *Jericho.

The history of religions, literary criticism and other forms of study applied to the *Hebrew books has led to a variety of hypotheses about the story. On one view, a small group escaped from Egypt and joined related tribes in Canaan; or, a separate group (the Kenites), who worshipped Yahweh at Sinai, introduced their *religion to tribes in Canaan and 'converted' them; or, a variety of folk-stories have been woven together, with little or no historical basis; or there was no Exodus and the whole is a pious fiction. Lacking any trace of Joseph, Moses, or Israelites in Egypt, many have concluded they were never there. Yet no pharaoh would boast of the loss of his labour force on a monument, and *administrative records on papyrus, leather or wooden tablets which might have registered such events would perish rapidly in the Delta's damp soil. It is equally unlikely that a camping crowd would leave recognizable remains from a semi-*nomadic life in the Sinai wilderness and in Transjordan. The absence of evidence is not, therefore, evidence of absence! The apparently enormous number of Israelites involved,

Thousands of 'eye idols' were deposited in a temple of the Late Uruk period at Tell Brak. WA 126202 (*left*, *centre*), 126205 (*right*).

over two million, need not be treated literally; 'thousands' may be 'captains' and a mathematical analysis suggests twenty thousand people as a more likely total. The migration of people from one part of the Near East to another is attested in various ages and areas, but none has left so detailed a record nor made the event so basic to its history as Israel.                                              ARM

C. HUMPHRIES, 'The Number of People in the Exodus from Egypt: Decoding Mathematically the Very Large Numbers in Numbers I and XXIV', *Vetus Testamentum* 48 (1998) 196–213.

K.A. KITCHEN, 'Exodus, The', *Anchor Bible Dictionary* 2, ed. D.N. Freedman (New York 1992) 700–8.

**Eye idols**   Stone or clay plaques in the shape of stylized eyes, 2–11 cm high, are found in huge quantities on fourth-millennium BC sites in north *Syria. The figures indicate only the shoulders, neck and eyes, occasionally painted. Individual eyes, pairs, mother-and-child groups or whole *families are found. More than three hundred of these idols and thousands of fragments were discovered in the foundations of the so-called Eye Temple at Tell *Brak, and it is estimated that the total deposited was twenty thousand. They may have been votive gifts associated with a specific *god, or amulets to protect against the evil eye.                                              PB

M.E.L. MALLOWAN, 'Excavations at Brak and Chagar Bazar', *Iraq* 9 (1947) 150–9 and pls. XXV–XXVI.

# *F*

**Faience**   Faience was made from a mixture of silica in the form of sand or powdered quartz and alkaline binders such as natron or plant ash. It is a composite material consisting of a sintered quartz body and a surface glaze. The body is composed of fine quartz grains fused together with small quantities of alkali (lime or soda), and is usually colourless. The glaze is a distinct layer of *glass formed on the surface of a crystalline body (if faience) or ceramic body (if glazed *pottery), and is coloured by the inclusion of metallic salts. These had

Part of a faience drinking cup in the form of a woman's head, from the Ishtar Temple at Ashur. Height 8.5 cm. c.1300 BC. WA 116359.

occurs in both flat and round-based versions. Decoration is often in blue or green glaze with linear or floral designs in matt black. There appears to have been a change in the scale of production in *Syria and Mesopotamia during the Late Bronze Age, and large groups of material are known from *Nuzi and Tell al-*Rimah, while workshop debris has been recovered at *Ugarit and *Emar. The thriving Late Bronze Age faience industry was based in *palace workshops, and it is possible to identify different stylistic groups of artefacts. While faience production continued through the first millennium BC, its role declined as it was gradually superseded by glass.     GP

M. BIMSON and I.C. FREESTONE, *Early Vitreous Materials* (London 1987).
A. KACZMARCZYK and R.E.M. HEDGES, *Ancient Egyptian Faience* (Warminster 1983).
P.R.S. MOOREY, *Ancient Mesopotamian Materials and Industries: The Archaeological Evidence* (Oxford 1994).
P.T. NICHOLSON, *Ancient Egyptian Faience and Glass* (Princes Risborough 1993).

been used as pigments long before their adoption for glazing.

While glass artefacts were formed hot, faience was shaped cold in a mould, for example amulets, pendants and *seals, or by hand; the paste was difficult to throw on a wheel. Afterwards the material was dried, and only then was it fired. Glazed *stone beads could be made easily, provided that the stone upon which the glaze was formed was composed of a rock containing silica, such as steatite, quartz or sandstone. When the bead and the glaze materials are heated together, the silica in the rock reacts with the mix to form a glaze on the surface of the stone.

Firm evidence for faience appears in *Mesopotamia during the *Ubaid period (mid sixth to fifth millennia BC), and at much the same time in *Egypt, in the form of small beads and amulets. During the third millennium BC faience objects were generally small. Few vessels have been reported, although a macehead is known from Tell Chuera in Syria.

Faience production was introduced to the southern *Levant early in the second millennium BC, but drew largely upon Egyptian rather than Mesopotamian manufacturing traditions. A common form in the Levant was the hand-made bottle formed around a core, which

**Family** All ancient Near Eastern cultures regarded the 'family' institution as foundational to society, but none of these peoples operated with a concept equal to the modern Western notion of family. Although there was some variation over time and space, most Near Eastern peoples viewed themselves as part of a patriarchal, patrilineal and patrilocal unit that may be called the 'father's house'. This was an extended family, a number of which formed a 'clan', and the latter were combined into a 'tribe'. The 'family' was a social, economic, legal and religious entity that bound its members in a series of mutual obligations, which could be fulfilled, since members of the 'father's house' usually lived within the same housing complex and worked in the same fields.

A group of nuclear families formed a community

Relief sculptures from a monumental entrance ('The Royal Buttress') at Carchemish. The Hittite hieroglyphic inscriptions explain that the regent Yariris is presenting the young king Kamani and other children, followed by a nurse carrying a baby. Height 1.1 m. Eighth century BC.

whose authority was the patriarch; the primary purpose of this community was the protection and welfare of its members. In the fifteenth and fourteenth centuries BC, the kingdom of Arraphe (east of *Assyria) included family units which engaged in *agriculture and other economic activities. Sons formed their own extended families. The 'household' included various grades of dependency (i.e. *children, the *adopted, partners, indentured workers, debtors and *slaves). The whole structure was held together by common agreement concerning the sacral importance of the *house, *laws of inheritance, a respect for ancestors and household *gods. Even with this strong patriarchal bond, it was possible for the wife in the upper level of Arraphe's society to assume the role of her deceased husband; in effect, she acquired his 'fatherhood' and looked after the welfare of the group.

*Women were normally subordinate to their husbands but also shared in decision-making, household administration, etc. It is clear that the responsibilities of women went beyond their role as mothers. The practice of primogeniture was standard and sons were preferred for economic purposes, but certain laws allowed females to *inherit family property and promote group solidarity. For example, a document from *Emar on the Euphrates speaks about the legal fiction by which some daughters could be treated as sons so they could inherit family property.

The family was protected by numerous laws. In the Code of *Hammurabi the sixty-eight sections concerned with family stability (or lack thereof) regulated behaviour related to *adultery, *marriage, concubinage, desertion, divorce, incest, adoption and inheritance. Throughout the ancient Near East, elderly family members were supposed to receive respect and care. Fathers had the legal right to disinherit delinquent or disobedient sons, but parents had the primary task of caring for and nurturing their children, who were regarded as a sign of divine favour.                                                                    GLM

G. DOSCH, 'Houses and Households in Nuzi: The Inhabitants, the Family, and Those Dependent on It', *Houses and Households in Ancient Mesopotamia*, ed. K.R. Veenhof (Istanbul 1996) 301–8.

L.G. PERDUE *et al.* (eds), *Families in Ancient Israel* (Philadelphia, PA 1997).

A.F. RAINEY, 'Family Relationships in Ugarit', *Orientalia* 34 (1965) 10–22.

I. SIEBERT, *Women in the Ancient Near East* (New York 1974).

L.E. STAGER, 'The Archaeology of the Family in Early Israel', *Bulletin of the American Schools of Oriental Research* 260 (1985) 1–35.

M. STOL, 'Private Life in Ancient Mesopotamia', *Civilizations of the Ancient Near East*, ed. J.M. Sasson (New York 1995) 485–501.

**Fara, (Tell):** see Shuruppak

**Far'ah, (Tell el-)** This name is given to two major *Palestinian sites, one in the north and one in the south. Tell el-Far'ah (North) is located 9.5 km north-east of Nablus (ancient *Shechem), in the hill country of Samaria. The site, covering some 10 ha, stands at the upper end of Wadi Far'ah, which provided a route from the central hill country down to the Jordan Valley. These ruins attracted the attention of many scholars, especially when Tell el-Far'ah was identified as ancient Tirzah; evidence for this equation is circumstantial and reasonable, albeit uncertain. The site's occupational history fits with *biblical references to Tirzah, *Israel's third capital, before Omri moved to *Samaria. There is one possible extra-biblical referenceto Tirzah, which appears in Pharaoh Shishak's campaign records at Karnak.

R. de Vaux excavated Tell el-Far'ah in nine seasons between 1946 and 1960, but his stratigraphic conclusions were faulty. Evidence of occupation at Tell el-Far'ah begins in the *Neolithic period, and it appears that the site was destroyed by the *Assyrians near the end of the eighth century BC and eventually abandoned by c.600 BC. Occupation was sporadic during the *Chalcolithic period and in the *Bronze and *Iron Ages. Tell el-Far'ah's Early Bronze I *cemeteries yielded important materials.

Tell el-Far'ah (South) is located on the west side of Wadi Gaza/Nahal Besor, 29 km south-east of Gaza. *Petrie excavated this 6-ha site in 1928–9 and identified it with biblical Beth-Pelet. In 1929, *Albright identified it with Sharuhen, a *Hyksos and *Egyptian fortress in southern *Canaan. Now, Albright's suggestion has been abandoned, and the ancient name is unknown.

Tell el-Far'ah was *fortified with a wall, glacis, drymoat and gate complex in Middle Bronze II–III, when the site's occupation began. Thereafter occupation was sporadic, but a strong Egyptian presence is indicated by artefacts (found on site and in Middle and Late Bronze Age cemeteries) and architectural remains. The *Philistines settled here in Iron Age I, as indicated by their typical *pottery and anthropoid clay *coffins. *Persian *burials reflect the continuing significance of Tell el-Far'ah's position, but the site's final use came in the *Roman period.                                                                    GLM

Tell el-Far'ah (North):

A.H. JOFFE, 'Far'ah, Tell el-', *The Oxford Encyclopedia of Archaeology in the Near East* 2, ed. E.M. Meyers (New York 1997) 303–4.

R. DE VAUX, 'The Excavations at Tell el-Far'ah and the Site of Ancient Tirzah', *Palestine Exploration Quarterly* 88 (1956) 125–40.

Tell el-Far'ah (South):

E. MACDONALD, J.L. STARKEY and L. HARDING, *Beth-Pelet* 2 (London 1932).

W.M.F. PETRIE, *Beth-Pelet* 1 (London 1930).

D. PRICE-WILLIAMS, *The Tombs of the Middle Bronze Age II Period from the '500' Cemetery at Tell Fara (South)* (London 1977).

**Feasts:** see Banquets and feasts

**Fekheriyeh, (Tell)** Situated south of Ras al-Ain at the sources of the *Khabur, opposite Tell *Halaf, this site was

The life-size statue of Hadad-yithi, ruler of Guzan (Tell Halaf), which he set up in Sikan (Tell Fekheriyeh) about 840 BC. The skirt bears an Assyrian cuneiform inscription on the front and an Aramaic version on the back (Damascus Museum. Photograph by courtesy of Philippe Maillard).

excavated for one season by C. McEwan in 1940. Under *Hellenistic, *Roman and medieval levels an *Aramaean occupation was identified which had a *palace with *bīt hilāni plan (level V). Level VI was the richest, yielding decorative *ivorywork of Syro-*Canaanite style, a handful of *cuneiform tablets dated to the Middle *Assyrian period and *seal impressions, all of the thirteenth century BC. Level VII produced '*Nuzi Ware' and was attributed to the *Mitannian era, while Khabur Ware occurred in the earliest level (VIII). The explorer M. von Oppenheim surveyed the site in 1929 and limited further excavations were made in 1955–6 by A. Moortgat, confirming earlier results. All hoped that the site might prove to be the Mitannian capital, Washshukanni, but nothing was found to make the case.

In 1979 a farmer uncovered a life-size basalt statue of a standing man at the foot of the mound. Inscriptions in *Assyrian and in *Aramaic announced that a ruler of Guzan (=Tell *Halaf) had erected it as a votive monument to honour *Adad of Sikan. The place-name is known in Assyrian royal inscriptions and in a text of the Third Dynasty of *Ur and could be the same as Mitannian Washshukanni, but this is disputed. The statue can be set in the second half of the ninth century BC on stylistic and historical grounds (identifying Shamash-nuri, the father of the man represented, Hadad-yishi, with the *eponym for 866 BC), making it the oldest

lengthy Aramaic text yet known. The Aramaic *alphabet used has unique features, while the *language shows considerable Assyrian influence and displays forms current in the Imperial Aramaic of the *Persian empire. Most of the Aramaic text is translated from the Assyrian and apparently incorporates a *dedication from an earlier piece. A notable feature is the variation of the title of the rulers, '*king' for the Aramaic-speaking local population, 'governor' for the Assyrian overlords.          ARM

A. ABOU ASSAF, P. BORDREUIL and A.R. MILLARD, La statue de Tell Fekherye et son inscription bilingue assyro-araméenne (Paris 1982).
C. McEWAN, Soundings at Tell Fakhariyah (Chicago 1958).

**Fertile Crescent** 'Fertile Crescent' is one of the most widely known geographical designations used by historians and archaeologists, and it refers to one of the world's most important centres of cultural development. The Egyptologist J.H. Breasted coined the term in the original edition of Ancient Times (1916): 'This fertile crescent is approximately a semicircle, with the open side toward the south, having the west end at the south-east corner of the Mediterranean, the centre directly north of Arabia, and the east end at the north end of the Persian Gulf.' Breasted's initial description (pp. 100–7) is accompanied by a full-colour map; this historical-geographical term assumed a high profile in subsequent editions of his – and many other – publications.

By means of this term Breasted expressed an awareness that ancient Near Eastern civilization evolved in a long, crescent-shaped territory, from *Sumer to *Egypt, as a result of its dependence upon a small number of *rivers. The Fertile Crescent was likened to the shores of a great desert-bay, which stretches for some 800 km (from east to west) across the arc's base. Breasted also placed this region in a broader context by discussing the lands and races of western Asia and by using grandiose terms like 'great triangle' and 'Great Northwest Quadrant'. All such terms combined poetic with utilitarian function.

While the designation 'Fertile Crescent' is still used today, though not as often as in previous decades, it can be misleading. It does make a clear distinction between the 'desert and the sown', to use another classic geographical expression. However, although it corresponds more or less to the line of the 200 mm rainfall isohyet below which there is insufficient rainfall to support agriculture without *irrigation (see Climate), this region is 'fertile' only in contrast with the great desert regions to the south of the semicircle. We now know that some of the earliest steps in the domestication of *plants and *animals and sedentary life took place, for example, in the more hospitable piedmont and upland environments north and north-east of Breasted's crescent (e.g. *Çatalhöyük). Extensive *agriculture, especially that based on *irrigation, and the earliest urban civilizations developed in this great, rather inhospitable semicircle because of an abundant *water supply and an organized labour force.          GLM

Y. AHARONI, The Land of the Bible: A Historical Geography, rev. ed. (Philadelphia, PA 1979).

P. BEAUMONT, G.H. BLAKE and J.M. WAGSTAFF, *The Middle East: A Geographical Study*, 2nd ed. (New York 1988).

J.H. BREASTED, *Ancient Times: A History of the Early World* (London 1916).

W.W. HALLO and W.K. SIMPSON, *The Ancient Near East: A History*, 2nd ed. (London 1998).

B.D. SMITH, *The Emergence of Agriculture* (New York 1994).

J.M. WAGSTAFF, *The Evolution of Middle Eastern Landscapes: An Outline to A.D. 1840* (London 1985).

**Fertility** Although the all-embracing 'fertility cult' aspects of ancient Near Eastern *myth and *religion have certainly been exaggerated as a result of the anthropological climate of the 1950s and 1960s, when there was a tendency to see fertility rites in almost every aspect of ancient (and 'primitive' modern) religions, there is no doubt that *agriculture and the productivity of the land were of fundamental importance in much of ancient Near Eastern life, and that this was reinforced by religious belief and *ritual. This is well demonstrated by the importance placed in *Mesopotamia on the cult of *Dumuzi, and pictorially by the place given to *water symbolism with such motifs as the vase with streams and certain agricultural elements such as the winnowing fan of Bau, the barley stalk, the plough and the spade. The abundance of the land was thought to be dependent on the well-being of the *gods and upon the life and health of the ruler. Neo-*Assyrian *prayers and incantations for the life of the *king make clear a belief in a causal connection between the ruler's personal health and the well-being of the state, including the condition of agriculture. The *Sacred Marriage seems to have been a rite related to fertility.

The *Ugaritic Baal myth has been the subject of extensive interpretations which see it as symbolizing the fertility of the land, crucially dependent on rainfall. JAB

J.C. DE MOOR, *An Anthology of Religious Texts from Ugarit* (Leiden 1987).

J.C.L. GIBSON, *Canaanite Myths and Legends*, 2nd ed. (Edinburgh 1978).

H.A. HOFFNER, Jr, *Hittite Myths* (Atlanta, GA 1990).

G. LEICK, *Sex and Eroticism in Mesopotamian Literature* (London/New York 1994).

D. PARDEE, 'The Ba'lu Myth', *The Context of Scripture* 1, eds W.W. Hallo and K.L. Younger (Leiden 1997) 241–74.

**Festivals** Days or periods of public celebration were quite literally essential elements of all ancient Near Eastern *religions. The performance of formal *rituals on these occasions not only marked but was intended to secure the success of, for example, *agricultural activities. Some were tied to *calendrical dates, or specific mythical narratives; some celebrated local patronal deities. A number of important festivals required the presence and even participation of the ruler, especially in *Assyria, where the *king had an important *priestly role. Doubtless such events could also function as impressive displays of pomp and power.

For the *Babylonians, the twelve days of *New Year ceremonies, celebrated in the springtime, were the most important annual festival. Other festivals, such as the *ešeš* (*Akkadian *eššēsu*), were celebrated every month. *Sacred Marriage ceremonies for pairs of local deities were performed regularly at a number of *cities.

Among the *Hittites, the spring *purulli* festival, at which the *myth of the killing of the serpent Illuyanka was recited, was so important that the king had to interrupt a campaign, if necessary, to be present. The myths of 'disappearing deities' were associated with rituals to entice the offended deity to return to his land and people. Many other local rituals were celebrated in which the king had to participate.

At *Ugarit, it has been widely accepted that an important autumn agricultural festival took place at which the *new year was celebrated by the recitation of mythological texts, but explicit evidence for this is lacking. Several annual festivals are prescribed for *Israel in the *Bible, some related to the agricultural cycle, one, the Passover, commemorating the *Exodus (month 1, day 14), and a *sacrifice on the Day of Atonement (month 7, day 10) reconciling the nation with its God. How regularly the festivals were observed in *Iron Age Israel is unknown.

JAB/ARM

M.E. COHEN, *The Cultic Calendars of the Ancient Near East* (Bethesda, MD 1993).

O.R. GURNEY, *Some Aspects of Hittite Religion* (Oxford 1977).

J. RENGER, '*isinnam epēšum*: Überlegungen zur Funktion des Festes in der Gesellschaft', *Actes de la XVIIe Rencontre Assyriologique Internationale, 1969*, ed. A. Finet (Ham-sur-Heure 1970) 75–80.

W. SALLABERGER, *Der kultische Kalender der Ur-III Zeit* (Berlin/New York 1993).

**Figurines** Made from various materials – including clay, *stone and *metal – figurines are found throughout the ancient Near East, and were fashioned from early times. They are generally found in random excavation contexts which cannot easily be interpreted. Their functions have therefore largely been a matter of conjecture: votive, *ritual or *magical images, *children's *toys, decorative arts, or some form of symbolism or substitution. In a very few instances, however, there is written evidence for the use in *Mesopotamia of figurines of various kinds. Some *Kassite figurines of *gods carry *dedications to the goddess Gula, goddess of healing, whose sacred animal (as with Asklepios in Greece) was the dog, and possibly related texts direct the sick to touch a dog for recovery. Neo-*Assyrian *foundation figurines of minor gods and protective spirits, made of various *woods or sun-dried clay, are prescribed in ritual texts to be buried about a *house as a counter to evil *demons and illnesses. Figures of dogs buried to guard buildings are sometimes inscribed 'Don't stop to think! Bite!' Figurines are also prescribed to be used in incantations to restore *sexual potency, and such references have been related to Old *Babylonian model clay beds and clay plaques depicting sexual activity, as well as to Neo-Assyrian models of sexual organs and lead plaques depicting intercourse.

(*above*) Bronze figure of the 'Smiting God', the weather-god, originally holding a weapon, wearing an Egyptian-style crown and kilt. Traces of silver plating remain. Height 11.4 cm. From the Levant, Late Bronze Age. WA 25096.

(*above right*) Terracotta figurine of nude female holding her breasts, from Susa. Middle Elamite, c.1300–1200 BC (© Photo RMN. Louvre Sb 7797).

(*above*) Terracotta figurine of stylised female holding her breasts, from 'Amlash', late second millennium BC(?) (courtesy of the Board of Trustees of the National Museums and Galleries on Merseyside, 66.191).

(*above right*) In the Iron Age Israelites made pottery figurines of heavy-breasted women, perhaps as charms for fertility and childbirth. From a tomb near Bethlehem, seventh century BC. WA 93091.

Other figurines of body parts have been similarly, and plausibly, related to the ailments of the faithful seeking a cure, and it may be that the large numbers of figurines of human forms found in excavations also represent worshippers with illnesses, for which the figures, as substitutes for the people who dedicated them, could remain in constant *prayer. Certain Neo-Assyrian and Neo-Babylonian stone and metal plaques are inscribed with dedications to the evil goddess Lamashtu, who is depicted as expelled and sent back to the *underworld. Sometimes such plaques depict this action as undertaken by the grotesque god Pazuzu, of whom there are also small and large free-standing statuettes and figurines of the god's head. A '*bronze Pazuzu' was prescribed to be worn by a woman during labour as protection for herself and her baby (see Childbirth). Other figurines prescribed in ritual texts would not have survived, for example human figures fashioned in dough or wax to represent the witch in rituals against sorcery, which were to be destroyed during the magical rites. JAB/AG

M.-T. BARRELET, *Figurines et reliefs en terre cuite de la Mésopotamie antique* (Paris 1968).

E.A. BRAUN-HOLZINGER, *Figürliche Bronzen aus Mesopotamien* (Munich 1984).

A. GREEN, *Excavations at Nimrud: The Neo-Assyrian Foundation Figurines* (London, forthcoming).

D. RITTIG, *Assyrisch-babylonische Kleinplastik magischer Bedeutung vom 13.–6. Jh. v. Chr.* (Munich 1977).

E.D. VAN BUREN, 'Figurinen', *Reallexikon der Assyriologie* 3 (Berlin/New York 1957–71) 62–4.

F.A.M. WIGGERMANN, *Mesopotamian Protective Figures* (Groningen 1992).

**Fishing** Remains of fish bones and fishing implements from excavations show that men were fishing from the beginnings of settled life in the ancient Near East and certainly long before. Texts from *Mesopotamia and the *Bible also refer to fishing. The evidence is not so plentiful as in *Egypt, where there are many depictions of fishing in tomb paintings, but the methods were probably similar.

The Mediterranean and Red Seas, lakes, *rivers and canals were all rich in edible fish, and fishing was an important industry. Fishhooks of bone or metal resemble modern examples. Teams of fishermen used large dragnets, while individuals used smaller cast nets, both with *stone or lead sinkers. The earliest nets were made of *plant fibres, and later of linen or cotton. Small pieces

Fishing with hook and line. Relief from Sennacherib's palace at Nineveh. WA 102072.

of netting survive attached to terracotta sinkers from *Khafaje, dated to c.2700 BC. In shallow waters traps were probably used.

Fish were *transported, alive or preserved by drying, salting or pickling, as *trade items and as payments for *tax. Conflicts over fishing waters and concession rights are recorded already in third-millennium BC *Sumer; fishing rights belonged to *temples and local rulers, who leased them to fishermen. Landowners who maintained canals had the right to fish in them as compensation.

The importance of fishing in ancient Near Eastern life is emphasized by its prominence in *mythological texts. The god *Ea owned a fishnet, for example, and *Adapa provided fish for the *gods. Fish offerings were common in Mesopotamia, remnants of them occurring in the *Ubaid-period temples at *Eridu, and later a golden fish thrown into the sea by *Sennacherib for Ea. Because of its association with Ea, the fish came to symbolize wisdom.

PB

M. NUN, 'Fishing', The Oxford Encyclopedia of Archaeology in the Near East 2, ed. E.M. Meyers (New York 1997) 315–17.

A. SALONEN, Die Fischerei im alten Mesopotamien (Helsinki 1970).

**Flint-working** 'Flint' is only one of a number of materials with fracture properties that allow them to be flaked by the application of force to the edge of a block or 'core'. Such materials found in the Near East include most commonly chert, but also basalt, limestones, *obsidian, carnelian and chalcedony. Chipped *stone is therefore a more appropriate term for this category of material, and knapping is the term used to describe the reduction of these materials through the process of chipping.

Throughout *prehistory the bulk of cutting and scraping tools, and projectile points were made from chipped stone. During the *Palaeolithic and *Epipalaeolithic chipped stone tools make up the bulk of the surviving material culture. In the Near East, where *hunting clearly provided an important component of

the diet from the Lower Palaeolithic, butchery, *animal processing *tools, tools associated with the manufacture of hunting *weapons and devices, and projectile tips formed an important part of the chipped stone toolkit. This element undoubtedly remained important to a certain degree through the *Neolithic as well. Chipped stone tools for vegetation harvesting and processing must account for much of the remainder of the tool repertoire and one that became particularly important from the final Epipalaeolithic/*Natufian. Long after the introduction of *metallurgy, that component of chipped stone toolkits survived in the manufacture of sickles (into the *Iron Age) and as threshing sledge inserts even until the modern day in the Near East and *Cyprus.

From the Palaeolithic to the Neolithic highly sophisticated production techniques, often involving a significant level of skill, were developed. These ensured that 'blanks' of predetermined shapes, appropriate for particular tools, were produced. Examples include pointed flakes in the Middle Palaeolithic used for what have been interpreted as projectile points, or elongated flakes with long cutting edges, called 'blades', used for points and cutting tasks and common from the Upper Palaeolithic. These techniques came to include shaping the core in distinctive ways to predetermine the shape of flake produced or applying force using sophisticated tools, for example, vices to hold the core firm, or crutch-like implements or hand-held antler tine pressure flakers to apply slow steady pressure. Such pressure flaking was used to fashion elaborate highly symmetrical tools of significant symbolic as well as utilitarian value, often of exotic flint or obsidian as at *Çatalhöyük.

Interesting technological contrasts in flint production came to characterize different parts of the Near East. In the Pre-Pottery Neolithic B period, pressure production of blades was common in the eastern part of the Near East, in the west a sophisticated core-shaping strategy was

Palaeolithic flint tools from Azraq in Jordan, c.200,000 BC (courtesy of Piotr Bienkowski).

employed to produce long flat blades from boat-shaped or 'naviform' cores. Throughout the region, however, pressure blades were produced from obsidian.

Through the later part of the Neolithic or Pottery Neolithic the sophistication of the general industry declines. This may relate to the more *ad hoc* role of chipped stone in society after the development of full mixed farming and decline of hunting and perhaps some decline in the range of *wood-working after the introduction of *pottery. The more standardized chipped stone tools were now restricted to specific tasks such as woodworking with flint axes and chisels, piercing tools, points for weapons and limited hunting activities, and sickles. This more restricted range of standardized tools may have been produced by more specialized producers certainly active by the Early Bronze Age.

Intriguingly during the *Chalcolithic flint axes and chisels coexist alongside metal counterparts for the best part of a thousand years. This provides insights into the relative rarity of metal or the cost of metal production or acquisition despite its durability. It might also suggest that any utilitarian advantages of metal tools were not enough to outweigh such other factors.          DB

M.L. INIZAN, H. ROCHE and J. TIXIER, *Technology of Knapped Stone* (Meudon 1992).

## Flood and flood stories

Until the construction of modern weirs and dams, *Babylonia was liable to flooding by the Tigris and Euphrates each spring. While canals helped to drain surplus *water, serious inundations were not uncommon, as deposits of water-laid clay or silt at several sites attest. A 3-m-deep layer of clay at *Ur is the result of water standing for a long period, not, as *Woolley asserted, evidence of 'The Flood'.

Babylonian tradition did know of one flood as the most calamitous, marking a break and a new beginning in the *Sumerian *King List, recalled in literary and historical references as a significant event at a remote time. Before the Flood lived the Seven Sages who taught humankind the arts of civilized living. The Sumerian Flood Story, incompletely preserved in a single copy, starts with the beginning of human history, the founding of the first *cities, the *gods' decision to send the flood and the survival of one man who is given immortality, Ziusudra. He is the last *king before the Flood in the Sumerian King List, with which this story has other links. There is common ground with the Babylonian Flood Story, the *Epic of Atrahasis, known from manuscripts copied about 1635 BC, although the epic was probably composed a century or two earlier and circulated over the next thousand years. The Old Babylonian version, copied on three large tablets in 1245 lines, begins with the creation of man (see Creation legends) and his multiplication to the point where human noise prevents *Enlil from sleeping. After unsuccessful attempts at reduction, the gods decree an annihilating flood. *Enki, inventor of mankind, warns his protégé, Atrahasis (=Ziusudra) by a dream to build a *boat and await an ominous sign. He obeys, embarks his *family, *animals wild and domestic,

and seals the door. The storm sweeps over the land, destroying everyone else. The gods lament their action because they have cut off their food supply, the people's offerings, and Nintu, the *mother goddess, mourns for her creatures. A gap deprives us of the immediate sequel, but Atrahasis emerges from the boat to make *sacrifices, attracting the gods like flies. After eating, Nintu blames the gods, then all turn on Enki who claims credit for saving life and argues that each man should pay for his own crimes in future. Nintu is called to produce several classes of people, including various types of *priestess precluded from childbearing, and infant immortality is introduced as means to control human numbers and noise. The poem ends with praise to Enlil. Later versions expand or alter certain parts slightly and a more extensively re-modelled form provides the Flood Story in the *Gilgamesh epic (Tablet XI of the Neo-*Assyrian version). There appears the account of the boat grounding on a mountain in north-eastern *Mesopotamia and the despatch of *birds (dove, swallow, raven) to seek land and vegetation. *Berossus related a Flood story, apparently current in *Sippar, combining elements familiar today from the Sumerian and *Akkadian stories.

Ancient *Israel's story of Noah preserves a similar memory (Genesis 6–9), with the same setting, the boat grounding in Ararat (*Urartu), but in monotheistic terms with a more seaworthy boat (the Babylonian was cuboid), birds in different order (raven, dove) and a

The Babylonian Epic of Atrahasis relates human history from creation by the gods to destruction in the Flood, survival of one family and subsequent re-creation and organization of society. Tablet 1 of three tablets containing 1245 lines in all. Copied c.1635 BC. WA 98741+43.

longer duration of the flood (150 days as opposed to seven). Evidently the *Hebrew and *cuneiform narratives share a common source; the later date of the Hebrew as preserved does not prove it is derived from the Babylonian. There is no trace of a Flood story in *Hittite or *Ugaritic myth, but *scribes in both cultures copied Atrahasis. ARM

S.M. DALLEY, *Myths from Mesopotamia* (Oxford 1989) 1–38.

A.R. GEORGE and F.H.N. AL-RAWI, 'Tablets from the Sippar Library VI: Atrahasis', *Iraq* 58 (1996) 147–90.

W.G. LAMBERT and A.R. MILLARD, *Atra-hasis: The Babylonian Story of the Flood* (Oxford 1969).

D. TSUMURA, 'Genesis and Ancient Near Eastern Stories of Creation and Flood: An Introduction', *I Studied Inscriptions from Before the Flood*, eds R.S. Hess and D.T. Tsumura (Winona Lake, IN 1994) 27–57, especially 44–57.

**Food** Most of the evidence for food comes from *ritual texts listing food and drink offered to *gods, or from *funerary meals surviving in *tombs (see Jericho), and it is uncertain what constituted a typical meal. Archaeological evidence shows contrasts between food remains from sacred places and domestic contexts, so extrapolating from ritual texts may be misleading.

The *Sumerians developed *gardens shaded by tall date palms where they grew peas, beans and lentils, vegetables such as cucumbers, leeks, lettuces and garlic, and fruit including dates, grapes, apples, melons and figs. Later additions were onions, beetroots, turnips, pears, pomegranates, nuts and various herbs. Olives were common in the *Levant and *Anatolia from the *Chalcolithic period on, but less so in *Mesopotamia. Milk, from sheep, goats and cows, may have been drunk fermented, and was used to make butter, cheeses and creams. Bees were domesticated and their honey was used as a sweetener.

Texts from *Mari suggest that two meals were eaten daily. The staples were certainly *bread and *beer, with

In the Assyrian camp open tents reveal cooks preparing food for Sennacherib and his army. Relief from Nineveh. WA 124913–5.

*wine more common in some areas like the *Levant and *Assyria. *Fish were eaten by people of lower status, but meat was largely reserved for the elite. Study of the distribution of bones from sites of different periods all over the Near East suggests that pork was eaten in rural areas and by poorer urban people (though it is rare in *temples, and may have been taboo; see Animal husbandry; Animals), beef was largely redistributed by centralized bureaucracies, and sheep and goat formed the meals of the elite. The rich also ate poultry (after c.1300 BC) and game: ducks, geese, pigeons, partridges and, from *Assyrian times, chickens (see Banquets). There were geographical preferences for delicacies too, with gazelle, mice, hunted hares, crustaceans, turtles, locusts and truffles in *Babylonia, jerboa in Assyria and ostrich eggs at Mari, while *horses were eaten at *Nuzi. Drying, salting and smoking preserved meat and fish in the hot climate. Texts as early as the eighteenth century BC mention the collection and storage in special houses of snow and ice which may have been used for preserving food and were certainly used for sherbets and cool drinks.

A few tablets containing recipes exist from southern *Babylonia, mostly dating to about 1700 BC. Some are lists of ingredients and basic instructions, but others describe in detail the preparation of particular dishes, including the utensils and kitchen installations required. Some texts deal with categories of food in which the dishes were cooked in water enriched with fat, and most of them were a meat or vegetable stew, soup or sauce, with some cooked *birds and meat pastries. They were named after the cut of meat, the animal, the vegetable or occasionally the geographical area, e.g. *Elamite broth. Roasted meat is mentioned in other texts. The most common additions were leeks and garlic, together with salt, herbs and spices, and there is one 'sweet and sour' dish using honey and salted meat. The texts occasionally include advice on presentation ('Cover the assemblage with the crust cover [i.e. a sort of pie] and bring to the table'), and what might best accompany the dish, e.g. garlic, greens and vinegar.

Centralized bureaucracies were responsible for the redistribution of food, most commonly issued as rations to workers in quantities of barley and other products per month, depending on the age and sex of the recipient. They also stockpiled food in case of famine, and imports of food from other countries are attested, for example from *Egypt and *Ugarit to *Hatti.

Food was clearly a major preoccupation of people in the ancient Near East, and much data from excavations and surveys represents activities related to producing, storing or preparing food. Archaeologists working at *Hesban have developed a food systems perspective as a framework for all archaeological data, which has helped to interpret their evidence and highlighted the coexistence of *nomadic and sedentary ways of exploiting land and *animals to produce food. PB

J. BOTTÉRO, 'Küche', *Reallexikon der Assyriologie* 6 (Berlin/New York 1980–3) 277–98.

——, 'The Cuisine of Ancient Mesopotamia', *Biblical Archaeologist* 48/1 (1985) 36–47.

——, *Textes culinaires mésopotamiens/Mesopotamian Culinary Texts* (Winona Lake, IN 1995).

S. DALLEY, *Mari and Karana: Two Old Babylonian Cities* (London 1984) 78–96.

J.J. GLASSNER, A. ÜNAL and P. CALMEYER, 'Mahlzeit', *Reallexikon der Assyriologie* 7 (Berlin/New York 1988) 259–71.

H.A. HOFFNER, Jr, *Alimenta Hethaeorum: Food Production in Hittite Asia Minor* (New Haven, CN 1974).

C. MICHEL, 'À table avec les marchands paléo-assyriens', *Assyrien im Wandel der Zeiten*, eds H. Waetzoldt and H. Hauptmann (Heidelberg 1997) 95–113.

J.M. RENFREW, 'Vegetables in the Ancient Near Eastern Diet', *Civilizations of the Ancient Near East*, ed. J.M. Sasson (New York 1995) 191–202.

**Fortifications** The basic components of ancient fortifications were walls, towers and *gates. The choice of a building site for a *city or fort was the primary consideration in any defensive plan. The top of a hill or the summit of a city's *tell provided an obvious advantage. A moat (fosse) and plastered embankment (glacis) were sometimes added to make the base of a city's ramparts less accessible to attackers. The foundations and lower courses of walls were often built out of *stone and the superstructure out of mudbrick, but walls made entirely of stone, where it was available, were not uncommon. Elaborate battlements at the tops of the walls protected soldiers from enemy fire, and towers projected beyond the city walls so defenders could trap attackers in crossfire. An ideal city plan had to include its inhabitants' *water supply, since some ancient armies (e.g. the *Assyrians) were proficient in siege warfare.

The oldest known large-scale walls are in the Pre-Pottery Neolithic A level at *Jericho, dating to the ninth millennium BC, possibly for defence, with a separate stone tower probably serving as a watchtower. The earliest substantial walls and gates in *Mesopotamia and *Anatolia date to later in the *Neolithic period. In the late fifth to fourth millennia BC, builders at *Mersin protected their gate with projecting towers; this represents an early, more sophisticated approach to defensive architecture.

By the end of the fourth millennium BC, the construction of a defence system was essential for important cities. A mudbrick wall, towers and two gates surrounded *Habuba Kabira. Now defence systems became more sophisticated and extensive. The walls at *Uruk were nearly 9.5 km long. During the second millennium BC, the trend towards massive fortification systems continued at, among other sites, *Qatna, *Hazor and Dan (in *Israel); all of these sites include enormous earthen ramparts. The glacis, a hardened slope that protects the base of city walls, became more common in the Middle Bronze Age. Evidence of Mesopotamia's second-millennium BC defence systems is sparse, but the construction history of *Boghazköy's fortifications is well known. By the thirteenth century BC, the walls of the *Hittite capital enclosed over 162 ha and included a series of large, multi-chambered gate complexes and postern tunnels.

*Iron Age defences at the major Assyrian cities reflect the military might of the empire, and *kings made great efforts to protect their own cities – and to project an image of power. The walls of *Nineveh were 12 km long with stepped crenellations. Major cities all over the Near East tried to ensure their defence systems could face the Assyrian threat. The acropolis of *Zinjirli was protected by a circular system of city walls, and *Lachish by a double system of walls and two gates. At the end of the eighth century BC, Hezekiah cut a water tunnel at *Jerusalem so that his capital could withstand an Assyrian siege. *Babylon's system of defence walls enclosed some 850 ha and spread out on both sides of the Euphrates.

During the Iron Age, 'casemate walls' were built at many sites in *Palestine. Two parallel walls were separated by an open space of c.2 m; the outer walls were joined by short cross walls at regular intervals, creating a series of small rooms. In times of danger, these chambers could be filled with rubble.                                              GLM

K. BITTEL, *Hattusha: The Capital of the Hittites* (Oxford 1970).

Z. HERZOG, *Das Stadttor in Israel und in den Nachbarländern* (Mainz 1986).

——, 'Fortifications (Levant)', *Anchor Bible Dictionary* 2, ed. D.N. Freedman (New York 1992) 844–52.

——, 'Fortifications: Bronze and Iron Ages', *The Oxford Encyclopedia of Archaeology in the Near East* 2, ed. E.M. Meyers (New York 1997) 322–6.

A. KEMPINSKI and R. REICH (eds), *The Architecture of Ancient Israel from the Prehistoric to the Persian Periods* (Jerusalem 1992).

A. MAZAR, 'Fortification of Cities in the Ancient Near East', *Civilizations of the Ancient Near East*, ed. J.M. Sasson (New York 1995) 1523–37.

Y. YADIN, *The Art of Warfare in Biblical Lands in the Light of Archaeological Study* (Jerusalem 1963).

**Foundation deposits** When a public building, especially a *temple, was constructed in ancient *Mesopotamia, there were usually *rituals for its consecration, purification, dedication and spiritual safety. Even private *houses might receive rites of protection against *demons and *disease. Rituals often included the deposition of various items, buried in the foundations or installed at the time of the building's foundation.

*Ubaid infant *burials built into the walls and floors of houses have sometimes been interpreted as human *sacrifices. Some *Uruk-period sites were seemingly purified by fire, and deposits of precious objects and foodstuffs are known. Dating to late Uruk or the beginning of the Early Dynastic period is one case of apparent *animal sacrifice in a temple.

The ubiquitous copper 'peg' figurines are first found in the Early Dynastic II period, becoming common and varied by Early Dynastic III, theoretically pinning a brick to the ground. Together with them, or else alone, inscribed stone and metal conical and oval objects occur as foundation deposits. Offerings of *food and drink and deposits of precious materials are also found.

First known from the time of *Gudea of *Lagash, deposits of 'canephorous' (or basket-carrying) peg figures were heavily promoted by the *kings of the Third Dynasty of *Ur, while earlier local practices, except for the deposition of foods and precious materials, were

A cast copper figure of a bull browsing in the reeds forms an unusual terminal for a foundation peg of Gudea. Height 19.4 cm. From Lagash, twenty-first century BC. WA 135993.

abandoned. From this period we have the first documentary sources for building rites, including those involving the ruler in symbolic manual labour. Inscriptions refer to his carrying a basket of earth and the first brick. Such rites are also depicted in *art, and it has been suggested that the canephorous figurines represent the king in this action. After the fall of Ur, there was some revival of local customs, but also further development. The latest peg figures belong to the *Isin–*Larsa period. They were gradually replaced by more widespread use of commemorative building inscriptions.

From the Old Babylonian period, bronze cylinders of Nur-Adad of Larsa (c.1865–1850 BC) were found at *Ur, re-deposited by an eighth-century king. A few *stone tablets have been found out of context. New to this period are inscribed clay cones and cylinders, the latter continuing in use until *Hellenistic times. Old *Assyrian deposits involve beads and precious *metals, as well as inscribed stone cylinders. *Kassite deposits are scarce, but some stone and clay tablets have been found out of context.

The Assyrian kings made extensive use of building deposits. At first the most common were stone – later also *gold and *silver – tablets, buried in the foundations or built into the walls. Large deposits of beads and *jewellery are common. From the twelfth century BC, inscribed clay prisms and cylinders became increasingly common, as the use of stone tablets declined, becoming rare by the ninth century BC, although some are still known, now deposited in stone boxes. *Magically protective figurines, roughly moulded of sun-dried clay, became common deposits in domestic residences. Their manufacture and burial in boxes beneath the floors, or placement within the rooms, was attended by elaborate ritual. Also known are food and drink offerings, animal sacrifice and the scattering of beads and other small objects in the foundations. Neo-Babylonian foundation deposits were mostly restricted to clay cylinders, although prisms were used in Babylonia by *Esarhaddon. The Neo-Assyrian and Babylonian rites demonstrate a high degree of deliberate archaizing, an aspect of which was the revival of the practice of royal labour.

In imitation of Assyrian practices, the *Achaemenid kings, in Mesopotamia and even *Iran, used as foundation deposits clay cylinders, tablets of stone and clay, and precious metals. Hellenistic monarchs in Mesopotamia adopted the Neo-Babylonian practice, limiting

themselves to clay cylinders. Texts detailing construction rituals were copied, and probably the rites carried out, as late as Seleucid times. Even in the *Parthian period rituals included animal sacrifice and the burial below a temple dais of ancient cylinder seals.

The 'incantation bowls' of the early Christian era carry texts intended to protect houses. These bowls were intended for burial in the foundations, continuing a tradition reaching back to Mesopotamian *prehistory.   AG

R.S. ELLIS, *Foundation Deposits in Ancient Mesopotamia* (New Haven, CN/London 1968).
S.A. RASHID, *Gründungsfiguren und Gründungsbeigaben altmesopotamischer Heiligtümer* (Heidelberg 1965).
——, 'Gründungsbeigaben', *Reallexikon der Assyriologie* 3 (Berlin/New York 1971) 655–61.
——, *Gründungsfiguren im Irak* (Munich 1983).
D. RITTIG, *Assyrisch-babylonische Kleinplastik magischer Bedeutung vom 13.–16. Jh. v. Chr.* (Munich 1977).
E.D. VAN BUREN, *Foundation Figurines and Offerings* (Berlin 1931).
F.A.M. WIGGERMANN, *Mesopotamian Protective Spirits: The Ritual Texts* (Groningen 1992).

**Funerary beliefs:** see Death and funerary beliefs and customs

**Furniture**   The most complete information about early furniture comes from *Egypt, but details about furniture in other parts of the ancient world have been gleaned from a wide variety of sources (e.g. *wall paintings, wall reliefs, statuary, models, *cylinder seals, terracotta plaques, texts, remains or artefacts of actual furniture). These sources reveal a wide range of furniture types (e.g.

The details in Assyrian reliefs help in reconstructing ancient furniture. Here Ashurbanipal's queen uses elaborately decorated couch, chair, footstool and table. WA 124920.

high-backed chairs and thrones, stools, beds and couches, tables and stands, chests and boxes, benches, shelves, mats). There is a shortage of evidence concerning the use of *textiles as furniture (e.g. cushions, pillows, blankets, carpets, rugs).

Most ancient furniture had a framework of *wood, and a great variety of local and imported woods were used. Fragments of furniture recovered from the *Iron Age level at *Hasanlu were made from maple, box, ash, walnut, poplar, almond, peach and elm. Woods imported from the high mountains of *Syria–*Lebanon, *Anatolia, northern *Mesopotamia and other distant regions were also used (e.g. cedar, ebony). Wooden furniture was sometimes made by skilled *craftsmen, who travelled from court to court and disseminated styles and techniques. Other materials used in making furniture included rushes, reeds, palm fronds, leather and cloth for upholstery. *Ivory and shell inlay was widely used. Some elaborate pieces were cast in *metal (e.g. *bronze lion paws on legs of chairs) or had metal parts (e.g. joints, hinges, bolts, nails, tacks). Carpenters used a full kit of tools to prepare wood as furniture parts. Timber was aged before it was joined, and a variety of joints were used.

Some furniture was made so that it could be dismantled for *transport. Glues, varnishes and paints were known in some regions, and sandstone blocks were used to polish wood to a smooth finish.

Most surviving furniture comes from *tombs (e.g. at *Ur, *Jericho, *Gordion), usually *burials of society's upper classes. Furniture was used for dowries and as expensive gifts, and was frequently taken as loot and received as tribute (especially by the *Assyrians).     GLM

H.S. BAKER, *Furniture in the Ancient World: Origins & Evolution 3100–475 B.C.* (London 1966).

P.M.M. DAVIAU, *Houses and Their Furnishings in Bronze Age Palestine* (Sheffield 1993).

E. GUBEL, *Phoenician Furniture: A Typology Based on Iron Age Representations with Reference to the Iconographical Context* (Louvain 1987).

G. HERRMANN (ed.), *The Furniture of Western Asia: Ancient and Traditional* (Mainz 1996).

H.A. LIEBOWITZ, B.A. NAKHAI, and E. STERN, 'Furniture and Furnishings', *The Oxford Encyclopedia of Archaeology in the Near East* 2, ed. E.M. Meyers (New York 1997) 352–8.

E. SIMPSON, 'Furniture in Ancient Western Asia', *Civilizations of the Ancient Near East*, ed. J.M. Sasson (New York 1995) 1647–71.

# G

**Games:** see Toys and games

**Ganj Dareh** Ganj Dareh, in the *Iranian *Zagros in the Kermanshah region, is at a relatively high elevation for an early *Neolithic *village site at 1350 m above sea level. The site covers only about a quarter of a hectare but has deep deposits, standing 8 m above the modern land surface. The site was excavated by P. Smith in the late 1960s and early 1970s.

There are five major phases of occupation, E to A from bottom to top. *Radiocarbon dates from levels D–A fall just before and after 8000 BC, contemporary with the middle Pre-Pottery Neolithic B in the *Levant. A single much earlier date for level E seems unlikely. This earliest level has no evidence of architecture, only shallow oval and circular pits used for roasting. Perhaps the contemporary earliest phase of habitation was quite restricted in extent.

Layer D has very distinctive architecture and consists of a series of closely packed small compartments with mudbrick party walls; many of these 'rooms' are only 1 sq m in area. There are no pathways between groups of compartments or indeed open spaces within the excavated area and therefore it is difficult to distinguish where one building might have started and another ended. Port holes may have given limited access between compartments and were blocked on occasion. However, there are no clear entrances to these complexes. The small size and lack of entrances, and indeed of hearths, suggest that these compartments may have been a basement level to buildings, used partly at least for storage. A range of functions is suggested by the presence of large 'built-in' boulder mortars pointing to *food processing or other grinding activities. In addition one room has a niche with two skulls of caprines affixed to the wall, one above the other. The storage role of many of these compartments is suggested by clay bins and containers and lightly baked clay vessels, a very early form of *ceramics. Some vessels stand up to 80 cm high.

Levels B and C have free-standing rectilinear multi-roomed structures with white plaster floors and hearths suggesting single-storey more conventional Neolithic village structures.

Domestic *plants are attested at the site. It has been suggested for two reasons that the goat remains, whilst belonging to *animals that show no morphological evidence of domestication, may have come from human-controlled herds. One is that an unusual age and sex profile characterizes the goat population as represented in the faunal remains from the site. The cull is dominated by adult females and young. This suggests a managed herd, but wild goats form nursery herds which could present such a demographic profile. However, some of the mudbricks on the site have hoof prints probably from goat and this is suggestive of the proximity of herds. If this identification is accurate this represents one of the earliest clear cases of herding of goat, probably some centuries before it can clearly be attested further west.

DB

J. MELLAART, *The Neolithic of the Near East* (London 1975).

P. SMITH, 'Ganjdareh Tepe', *Iran* 6 (1968) 158–60; 8 (1970) 78–80; 10 (1972) 165–8.

**Gardens** Shade, fragrance, water and privacy: these are the qualities desired for *Mesopotamian gardens. At *Mari and *Ugarit gardens were tended in the internal courtyards of *palaces during the Middle and Late Bronze Ages. *Trees and shrubs were planted, and decorative wild *animals such as small deer were sometimes kept there. These courtyard gardens were used for picnics, courtship and, at Mari, *dynastic *tombs. In sacred courtyards, notably in the *temple of the *New Year festival at *Ashur beyond the city walls, gardens were planted in which, the texts explain, divine courtship took place.

Hunting parks, perhaps outside city walls, were stocked with exotic *plants and animals collected on campaign or through the exchange of diplomatic gifts (see Diplomacy). Organized lion hunts there were a royal prerogative (see Hunting).

*Assyrian *kings took pride in large-scale engineering works which allowed them to imitate natural beauty spots within their cities. *Ashurnasirpal II diverted water from the Upper Zab to help create an artificially landscaped garden at *Nimrud. *Sargon II built artificial hills, a boating lake and pavilions at *Khorsabad, according to the pictorial evidence of a stone *sculpture. *Sennacherib described in detailed inscriptions how he diverted several mountain streams to bring *water on an aqueduct into his garden at *Nineveh, raising it to the top of the garden by means of screws cast in *bronze, and building artificial hills upon *stone vaults. This garden, easily accessible from his 'Palace without a Rival', is shown on a stone

Lions in the park of Ashurbanipal at Nineveh. The artist has shown various flowers and trees. WA 118914.

sculpture of his grandson *Ashurbanipal. It was built for his *Queen Tashmetum-sharrat, declared a wonder for all peoples, and may be the origin of the legend of the Hanging Gardens of *Babylon. Many details in his inscriptions confirm the later classical accounts. Other *Greek sources imply that the Hanging Gardens were not in Babylon.

Neither German excavations nor *Nebuchadnezzar II's own inscriptions support the supposition that the Hanging Gardens were in Babylon proper. However, a text lists plants by groups in the royal garden of Merodach-Baladan II king of Babylon, and foreshadows the neatly arranged physic gardens of later times.

SMD

W. ANDRAE, 'Der kultische Garten', *Welt des Orients* 1 (1952) 485–94.

S. DALLEY, 'Ancient Mesopotamian Gardens', *Garden History* 21 (1993) 1–13.

——, 'Nineveh, Babylon and the Hanging Gardens: Cuneiform and Classical Sources Reconciled', *Iraq* 56 (1994) 45–58.

H. LEACH, 'On the Origins of Kitchen Gardening in the Ancient Near East', *Garden History* 10 (1982) 1–16.

A.L. OPPENHEIM, 'On Royal Gardens in Mesopotamia', *Journal of Near Eastern Studies* 24 (1965) 328–33.

**Garstang, John (1876–1956)** Born in Blackburn, Garstang excavated at several sites in England while studying mathematics at Oxford. From 1899 he worked in Egypt, first with *Petrie and then on his own, principally at Beni Hasan, Hierakonpolis, Esna, Abydos, and then at Meroe in the Sudan. In 1907 Garstang secured a permit to excavate the *Hittite capital of *Boghazköy in Turkey, but moved to *Sakçagözü when the concession was transferred to a German team at the request of the German emperor.

After a period as director of the new British School of Archaeology in Jerusalem and of the Department of Antiquities of Palestine, he excavated at *Jericho (1930–6). He attracted considerable publicity by attributing the destruction of a city wall to the *Israelites, but *Kenyon's later excavations dated the wall much earlier. A more significant result was his reaching of *Mesolithic (*Epipalaeolithic) levels, which took the history of occupation at Jericho back much earlier than suspected.

The Arab uprising of 1936 forced Garstang to move to Turkey, where he excavated at *Mersin. He was largely responsible for the founding of the British Institute of Archaeology at Ankara in 1948, serving as its first director.

Garstang established and taught at the Institute of Archaeology in Liverpool University (1902–41), fundraising tirelessly for it. He was criticized for not publishing his excavations more comprehensively, but believed that his preliminary reports were sufficient.

PB

P. BIENKOWSKI and J. YOUNG, 'John Garstang and his Collection from Meroe', *Meroe in Liverpool Museum and the Lady Lever Art Gallery: Catalogue of Antiquities from the Excavations of John Garstang*, eds P. Scholz and P. Bienkowski (Wiesbaden, forthcoming).

O.R. GURNEY, 'John Garstang', *Dictionary of National Biography 1951–1960* (London 1971) 395–6.

**Gateways and doors** In general terms, there were three types of gateways and doors: those for domestic structures, fortified city gates, and monumental buildings. Doorways in *houses were generally less than 1 m wide and less than 2 m high. They could be closed or blocked with reed matting, other woven material or a *wooden door. When the house was abandoned, its wooden parts (including doors) were removed and taken to the next residence.

Fortified *cities often had small entrances, or posterns, at various places in the *fortification walls so that occupants did not have to travel the distance to one or more larger gates. These postern gates were easily blocked or guarded to guarantee their security. If the city had one – or several – major city gates, security was a problem since the city gate was the weakest point in a city's defences. Engineers strengthened the gate area by constructing a fortified gatehouse attached to the line of walls. These gatehouses – or gate complexes – were built in various sizes and shapes in the ancient Near East. Of primary importance was the defender's ability to block and protect the actual entrance through the wall, i.e. the gate passage. Many gate complexes had towers that projected out from the line of walls; a protective wall surrounded the roof of the gate. The most important feature of the gatehouse was the door itself, the wooden gate that was shut and locked with a *metal or wooden bar. City gates were normally named after gods.

The gate (or door of a house, *palace or *temple) was fixed to a post and held between a *stone threshold (or sill) and a stone or wooden lintel; the latter rested on at least two upright doorjambs, also of stone or wood. Threshold and lintels contained sockets or depressions, in which the doorpost could turn. Sockets were made of basalt or hard limestone, and the gatepost was often capped with metal. Gates and doors usually opened inward, and raised edges on the outside of a threshold and lintel kept the gate from swinging outward. The gate could be locked from within with a bar or bolt, and the wooden gate might be covered or bound with metal so that it would not catch fire during an attack. Remnants of metal sheathing and fittings were found on the gate at *Lachish; this city – and its city gates – fell to *Sennacherib in 701BC. The best examples of metal sheathing from monumental doors are on the *Balawat gates. GLM

R.D. BARNETT, *Assyrian Palace Reliefs in the British Museum* (London 1970).

F. BRAEMER, *L'architecture domestique du Levant a l'Age du Fer* (Paris 1982).

M.S.B. DAMERJI, *The Development of the Architecture of Doors and Gates in Ancient Mesopotamia* (Tokyo 1987).

Z. HERZOG, *Das Stadttor in Israel und in den Nachbarländern* (Mainz am Rhein 1986).

——, 'Fortifications (Levant)', *Anchor Bible Dictionary* 2, ed. D.N. Freedman (New York 1992) 844–52.

A. KEMPINSKI and R. REICH (eds), *The Architecture of Ancient Israel from the Prehistoric to the Persian Periods* (Jerusalem 1992).

S.H. PAUL and W.G. DEVER (eds), *Biblical Archaeology* (New York 1974).

**Gawra, (Tepe)** Tepe Gawra is an important *prehistoric site in the rolling hills of northern *Mesopotamia, 24 km north-east of the modern city of Mosul on the Tigris river. The site, a high but small mound, was occupied more or less continuously from the *Halaf period into the Middle Bronze Age, c.6000–1800 BC. Excavations were conducted by Ephraim Speiser in the 1930s.

Halaf remains at Gawra include circular buildings (called *tholoi*) and Late Halaf painted *pottery in level XX. These levels are succeeded by a long sequence of *Ubaid-period occupation, comprising substantial *religious buildings and evidence for administrative sophistication. The first Ubaid *temple appears at Gawra in level XIX, and there is evidence for increasing social and economic complexity throughout the Ubaid period, culminating in the construction of three impressive buttressed temples in level XIII. Considerable quantities of lapis lazuli, imported from Afghanistan, and clay sealings with *stamp seal impressions indicate the exercise of control over the movement of goods.

Level XII sees the start of the *Uruk period at Gawra, c.4000 BC, dominated by the White Room building complex and more evidence of seal use in *administration. The regional importance of the site throughout the Uruk period is borne out by its material remains, including temples, storehouses, kilns and private *houses. During the latest Uruk occupation, level VIII, the settlement featured a temple, craft areas and storage facilities.

In subsequent times Gawra gradually declined in significance, its high mound hosting a succession of modest agricultural villages, way stations and storehouses through the third and into the second millennia BC. The major importance of the site is in the light it sheds on the evolution of social and economic complexity within the context of north Mesopotamian cultural development in the millennia before the evolution and spread of true urbanism. RM

M.S. ROTHMAN, 'Tepe Gawra', *The Oxford Encyclopedia of Archaeology in the Near East* 5, ed. E.M. Meyers (New York 1997) 183–6.

E.A. SPEISER, *Excavations at Tepe Gawra* 1 (Philadelphia, PA 1935).

Tepe Gawra looking north-west, April 1938 (A. Tobler, *Excavations at Tepe Gawra* 2 [1950] fig. XXVIII:a. University of Pennsylvania Museum neg. S5-45051).

A. TOBLER, *Excavations at Tepe Gawra* 2 (Philadelphia, PA 1950).

**Gelidonya** Located at the western side of the Bay of Antalya, Cape Gelidonya represents the southernmost point of the *Anatolian peninsula. At least four *ships sank in this vicinity, but the oldest of them – dated to c.1200 BC – holds special interest. The wreck was discovered in 1954 and excavated by George Bass in 1960. This was the first *shipwreck excavation carried to completion on the seabed, the first directed by a diving archaeologist and the first conducted following the standards of terrestrial excavation. If Bass's work at Cape Gelidonya was pioneering in the methodological sense, the results of the project were also important.

There is dispute over the date, 'nationality' and purpose of the ship, but the origin of the cargo has been determined with reasonable certainty. It is most likely that this private *merchant vessel sank between 1250 and 1150 BC, after its hull – made with mortise-and-tenon joints – was ripped open by a rock that was below the water. A date of 1200 BC was reached through the study of firmly dated *pottery vessels and a radiocarbon date. On the basis of literary and artistic evidence and a careful study of the cargo, Bass concluded that the ship was

Return visits to Cape Gelidonya in the late 1980s located two well preserved Mycenaean stirrup jars about 50 m from the main area of wreckage (courtesy of the Institute of Nautical Archaeology).

*Phoenician or *Canaanite. It is possible that the Gelidonya wreck was Cypriot (see Cyprus) and that its crew came from a variety of places. At any rate, it is clear that the Mycenaean *Greeks did not hold any monopoly on sea *trade in the Late Bronze Age Mediterranean.

The ship's cargo was strewn across a rocky bottom at a depth of 26–8 m. Its crew had loaded a ton of *metal on this vessel, which was 8–9 m long, during a recent stop at Cyprus. Most of its cargo was *copper 'oxhide' ingots but also included copper 'bun' ingots and badly corroded *tin, probably shipped in bars. The goods also included broken *tools that were destined to be recycled (perhaps with *metalworking tools carried on the ship) and a variety of smaller artefacts from all over the eastern Mediterranean.                                    GLM

G.F. BASS, 'Cape Gelidonya', *The Oxford Encyclopedia of Archaeology in the Near East* 1, ed. E.M. Meyers (New York 1997) 414–16.

——, *Cape Gelidonya: A Bronze Age Shipwreck* (Philadelphia, PA 1967).

——, 'Cape Gelidonya and Bronze Age Maritime Trade', *Orient and Occident: Essays Presented to Cyrus Gordon*, ed. H.A. Hoffner, Jr (Kevelaer 1973) 29–37.

——, 'Nautical Archaeology and Biblical Archaeology', *Biblical Archaeologist* 53 (1990) 4–12.

E.H. CLINE, *Sailing the Wine-dark Sea: International Trade and the Late Bronze Age Aegean* (Oxford 1994).

A.J. PARKER, *Ancient Shipwrecks of the Mediterranean and the Roman Provinces* (Oxford 1992).

**Gender:** see Women/gender

**Gezer** Tell Jezer (or Tell el-Jazari) is identified with ancient Gezer, mentioned in the *Bible and in *Egyptian and *Assyrian texts. The equation was made in 1874 after C. Clermont-Ganneau recognized the similarity in names and found a *Hebrew inscription near the site which read 'boundary of Gezer'. Gezer is located c.8 km south-east of modern Ramla, along the line where the Judaean hill country meets the northern Shephelah; the site offered Gezer's occupants access to *water sources and control of an important crossroads, where the road from *Jerusalem runs down to the main coastal highway.

The site has been excavated by R.A.S. Macalister (1902–9) and G.E. Wright, W.G. Dever and J.D. Seger (1964–74). Gezer's twenty-six strata span the period between the *Chalcolithic and *Roman periods. The Early Bronze Age occupation of Gezer began c.3200 BC, but there appears to be a gap between 2400 and 2000 BC. During the Early Bronze Age, the site was not *fortified, and people lived in *houses and caves.

The *Canaanite settlement reached its zenith c.1800–1500 BC. It was fortified c.1650 BC (stratum XIX) with walls, towers and a glacis. The erection of a line of ten large standing stones (Macalister's 'High Place') dates to this same period; the line of monoliths must have served some kind of ceremonial function, perhaps in relation to a covenant. A number of rich *tombs come from Middle Bronze Age Gezer, which was destroyed, probably by

Pharaoh Tuthmosis III (c.1482 BC) who mentions his capture of the *city in an inscription from Karnak.

By Late Bronze II (stratum XVI) the city was refortified and excavation has recovered numerous Egyptian imports. Gezer is mentioned in ten of the *Amarna Letters, and a fragment of a similar tablet was found on the site. At the end of the Late Bronze Age, Gezer declined, and this may be linked to Pharaoh Merneptah's conquest of the city; his name appears on a sundial recovered by Macalister.

*Philistine *pottery comes from Strata XIII–XI, and a discernible shift – associated with the Solomonic period – occurs with stratum VIII. A fine six-chamber *gate, dating to the mid tenth century BC, connected to a casemate defence wall, is almost identical to the 'Solomonic' city gates excavated at *Megiddo and *Hazor. The 'Gezer Calendar', a limestone tablet with a Hebrew inscription, dates to c.925 BC and lists a cycle of *agricultural tasks that kept the city's farmers busy throughout the year. Late in the tenth century BC, Gezer was destroyed, perhaps by Pharaoh Shishak.

During Iron Age II, the six-chamber gate was rebuilt as a four-chamber structure, and a water system, similar to those at Megiddo and Hazor, was constructed. The stratum VI city was destroyed by *Tiglath-pileser III (c.734 BC), an event depicted on a palace relief at *Nimrud. Macalister found two Neo-*Assyrian *cuneiform tablets at Gezer; they are *contracts dealing with land ownership made when this region was under Assyrian control. The stratum V city was probably destroyed during the *Babylonian invasion of *Judah (586 BC), after which Gezer passed into *Persian hands (stratum IV).

GLM

W.G. DEVER, 'Gezer', Anchor Bible Dictionary 2, ed. D.N. Freedman (New York 1992) 998–1003.

——, 'Gezer', The Oxford Encyclopedia of Archaeology in the Near East 2, ed. E.M. Meyers (New York 1997) 396–400.

H.D. LANCE, 'Gezer in the Land and in History', Biblical Archaeologist 30 (1967) 34–47.

R.A.S. MACALISTER, The Excavation of Gezer, 1902–1905 and 1907–1909, 3 vols (London 1912).

J.F. ROSS, 'Gezer in the Tell el-Amarna Letters', Biblical Archaeologist 30 (1967) 62–70.

## Ghassul, (Teleilat)

Ghassul consists of a complex of low mounds ('*tells'), hence the term Teleilat, located at the southern end of the Jordan Valley north-east of the Dead Sea. The site dates to the Late *Neolithic and *Chalcolithic and, reaching 20 ha in the latter part of the period of its occupation, is one of the largest sites of the Chalcolithic. It has given its name to a manifestation of the later Chalcolithic in the southern *Levant, the Ghassulian.

The site has been excavated by the Pontifical Biblical Institute (1929–38), R. North (1960), J.B. Hennessy (1967 and 1975–7) and S. Bourke (1994–). The sequence at the site is now clear, with an early phase of Pottery Neolithic represented by semi-subterranean circular structures.

The middle phases at the site see the introduction of the traditions that typify the Ghassulian, including

One of the Chalcolithic wall paintings from Teleilat Ghassul, showing three masked figures in procession (courtesy of J.B. Hennessy).

distinctive *ceramic types e.g. fenestrated stands, ceramic 'churns' and cornets (long thin vessels with pointed bases probably for drinking). Elaborate *wall painting techniques characterize the distinctive rectilinear architecture. The site covers about 10 ha in this middle phase which may be broadly dated to the earlier Chalcolithic. In late phases at the site – the Late Chalcolithic, c.4500–3600 BC – the settlement expanded to cover 20–5 ha and may have had distinct zoning.

In the middle and late phases most buildings are relatively similar except for the presence in some of wall paintings. Whilst some paintings have essentially decorative elements, the contents of others are clearly pictorial and symbolic. One such painting appears to depict a procession of human-like figures, at least one of whom bears a *tool, *weapon or symbol of authority. Another component of a larger composition depicts a large star. Whether these 'decorated' buildings, often not otherwise distinct from their contemporaries, had a special role or were elaborately and symbolically decorated domestic dwellings is difficult to discern given the state of current evidence.

There is in the late phase, however, a building complex distinct from its contemporaries, as part of the broader functional zoning of the site that appears to accompany its expansion. Hennessy identified a sanctuary complex in the south-west area of the site. This is separated from the rest of the site by boundary walls enclosing *stone-built rectangular structures. A path leads from the entrance of one of these to a demarcated area. Within this area a concentration of crushed ceramic vessels suggests *ritual activity.

Recent work by Bourke's project on the nature of *plant and *animal exploitation provides important new evidence. From the middle phases, that is earlier Chalcolithic, it is suggested, from the ages at which sheep and cattle were killed, that exploitation of wool, milk and traction may have been an important feature of *animal husbandry. Alongside wheat cultivation that of olive, flax and date become significant, and this may be related to the production of oils and linen as well as the direct consumption of the fruits.

In the Late Chalcolithic there is evidence for inter-regional exchange attested by the presence of *copper tools, *faience beads, alabaster maceheads, imported ceramics and fine basalt vessels. DB

S. BOURKE, 'The Urbanisation Process in the South Jordan Valley: Renewed Excavations at Teleilat Ghassul 1994/5', *Studies in the History and Archaeology of Jordan* 6 (1997) 249–59.

J.B. HENNESSY, 'Teleilat Ghassul and its Place in the Archaeology of Jordan', *Studies in the History and Archaeology of Jordan* 1 (1982) 55–8.

R. KOEPPAL, A. MALLON and R. NEUVILLE, *Teleilat Ghassul 2* (Rome 1940).

A. MALLON, R. KOEPPAL and R. NEUVILLE, *Teleilat Ghassul 1* (Rome 1934).

## Ghirshman, Roman (1895–1979)

A leading authority on the *archaeology of *Iran, Ghirshman was born in Karkhov, Russia, but left during the revolution and settled in France in 1923. He started working in Iran in 1931, excavating at Tepe *Giyan and Tepe *Sialk. After the Second World War he became director of the French archaeological delegation in Iran, excavating at *Susa, at *Chogha Zanbil and at Kharg Island in the Persian Gulf, continuing fieldwork until the age of seventy-seven. Ghirshman was meticulous in publishing the results of his excavations, but also wrote general books on the *art and archaeology of Iran which brought the subject to a wider audience. PB

A. SPYCKET, 'Ghirshman, Roman', *The Oxford Encyclopedia of Archaeology in the Near East* 2, ed. E.M. Meyers (New York 1997) 401–2.

## Gilgamesh

The *Sumerian *King List names Gilgamesh as fifth *king of the First *Dynasty of *Uruk, the second after the *Flood, giving him a reign of 127 years. By current reckoning that would place him in the Early Dynastic III period, about 2600 BC. None of the rare documents from that time mentions him, but both he and Lugalbanda, often called his father, have divine status in tablets from *Shuruppak written a century or two later. By the end of the Third Dynasty of *Ur he was receiving offerings as an established *underworld deity, and was called 'brother' by the kings of Ur. In the nineteenth century BC a king of Uruk claimed he had reconstructed the *city wall which Gilgamesh had built. Stretches of Uruk's wall uncovered are built of the typical Early Dynastic plano-convex bricks. One Sumerian poem tells of a war between Agga of *Kish and Gilgamesh. Agga was the son of Enmebaragesi, a king known from an apparently contemporary vase fragment engraved with his name and title. Thus, while no inscription of Gilgamesh has been found, this belongs to the time in which his story is set.

Gilgamesh was the hero of five separate Sumerian

The hero fighting a bull on this terracotta is often identified as Gilgamesh. Ur III period, c.2100–2000 BC (© Musées Royaux d'Art et d'Histoire, Brussels, photo ACL, 0.1054).

poems: (1) 'Gilgamesh, Huwawa and the Cedar Forest'; (2) 'Gilgamesh and the Bull of Heaven'; (3) 'Gilgamesh, Enkidu and the Netherworld'; (4) 'Gilgamesh and Agga'; (5) 'The Death of Gilgamesh'. Nos 1–3 were drawn upon for the *Akkadian *Epic (see below). No. 4 tells how Gilgamesh refused to obey Agga, who, as he laid siege to Uruk, was captured, then freed. No. 5 explains how the *gods only are immortal, man cannot gain that status, the theme of the epic. These poems may have been composed in connection with the cult of Gilgamesh during the Third Dynasty of Ur, incorporating older traditions. (A narrative about Lugalbanda was found among Early Dynastic III tablets at Abu Salabikh.)

The Akkadian Epic has immortalized Gilgamesh, the recovery of the tablets in the nineteenth century restoring to knowledge a lost literary masterpiece. A poet composed the single lengthy work shortly after 2000 BC, using the exploits of Gilgamesh to illustrate his message that life is transient, man cannot expect immortality, the only way to ensure that his memory survives is through fame. Parts of Old *Babylonian versions survive, and extensive sections of the 'Standard Version' come from first-millennium BC *libraries, at *Nineveh, *Ashur, Sultantepe, *Babylon and Uruk. Other fragments are known from the Late Bronze Age from *Babylonia and from *Emar, *Ugarit, *Megiddo and *Hattusas, where there were copies in Akkadian, *Hittite and *Hurrian. The Standard Version was created at that time, perhaps by a Babylonian *scribe, Sin-leqe-unninni, who is named in later colophons (see Libraries). It is usually cited from an edition copied on twelve tablets. There is considerable differences between the Old Babylonian and later versions; the overall story remains the same, but episodes are altered and attitudes changed. The Standard Version adds the twelfth tablet and may have incorporated the *Flood story from the Epic of Atrahasis; at present it is not clear if the Flood featured in the Old Babylonian version. Both versions present major characters uttering important reflections on life and display high levels of poetic skill.

Gilgamesh is introduced as a superman, two-thirds divine, who tyrannizes Uruk. The gods create a savage, Enkidu, to rival him. After being tracked by a hunter and tamed by a harlot, Enkidu is brought to meet Gilgamesh and wrestles him to the ground. They become friends and, against advice and after extensive preparations, march to the Cedar Forest, kill its ferocious guardian Huwawa (Humbaba) and return to Uruk with valuable timbers. The goddess *Ishtar, attracted by Gilgamesh, invites him to become her lover. He rejects her, reciting the fates of earlier lovers. Furious, she asks *Anu, her father, to send the bull of heaven to kill Gilgamesh. Notwithstanding its terrifying impact, Gilgamesh and Enkidu kill the bull, offer its heart to *Shamash, the sungod, and Enkidu throws its shoulder at Ishtar. The gods cannot brook the killing of Huwawa and the bull, so they decree Enkidu's death. He curses the harlot who humanized him and, with Gilgamesh, laments his fate. He dies, deeply mourned by Gilgamesh, who erects a statue in his memory. At a loss to understand death, Gilgamesh sets out to find the only immortal man, Utnapishtim, the Babylonian 'Noah'. The long trail leads him to the fearsome scorpion-men, then through darkness to Shamash, the rising sun, who warns him he will not find the life he seeks, to the jewel-laden garden of the gods and to Siduri, their 'bar-maid'. She fails to dissuade him from his quest, in the Old Babylonian version advising him to 'live and enjoy today' rather than endure more hardship, yet points him to the ferryman who can take him across the 'waters of death' to Utnapishtim. Gilgamesh, expecting a vigorous figure, is surprised to meet an extremely old man, for eternal youth was not his, only immortality. That was granted after he survived the great *Flood, as he explains. Gilgamesh cannot have that experience. If he can stay awake six days and seven nights he might be successful; protesting he can, he sleeps through the week! Utnapishtim offers a last opportunity: Gilgamesh could pick a plant from the sea bed that had rejuvenating powers. Like a pearl-fisher, Gilgamesh dives and plucks the plant. Rather than eat it himself, he resolves to test it on an old man in Uruk. As he bathes in a pool on his way, a snake eats the plant, sloughing its skin as it leaves. Recognizing his failure, Gilgamesh returns to Uruk and points to its splendour, his monument. The twelfth tablet is an Akkadian version of the last half of the Sumerian poem 'Gilgamesh, Enkidu and the Netherworld' in which Enkidu is sent to reclaim something Gilgamesh had let fall into the underworld. Failing to take proper precautions, Enkidu is detained there, his spirit returning to tell Gilgamesh of the state of the dead.

Attempts to identify Gilgamesh in *art convince in only a few cases. Scenes of two figures killing a *monster probably show Gilgamesh, Enkidu and Huwawa. The hero wrestling with a bull antedates the time of Gilgamesh, although later ages may have equated him with Gilgamesh. ARM

S. DALLEY, *Myths from Mesopotamia* (Oxford 1989) 39–153.
A. GEORGE, *The Epic of Gilgamesh: The Babylonian Epic Poem and Other Texts in Akkadian and Sumerian* (Harmondsworth 1999).
A. HEIDEL, *The Gilgamesh Epic and Old Testament Parallels* (Chicago 1949).
J.H. TIGAY, *The Evolution of the Gilgamesh Epic* (Philadelphia, PA 1982).
R.-J. TOURNAY and A. SHAFFER, *L'épopée de Gilgamesh* (Paris 1994).

**Giyan, (Tepe)** A site in the north-west *Luristan area of *Iran, Tepe Giyan was important for establishing the stratigraphy of western Iran in the *prehistoric and early historic periods and linking it with *Mesopotamian sequences. It was excavated by G. Contenau and *Ghirshman (1931–2). The mound is 19 m high, and its original length was c.350 m. Four trenches were excavated. Five main levels date from the *Ubaid period to c.700 BC, with some gaps. Level V, the earliest, had four subdivisions covering the early Ubaid to *Uruk periods, and included traces of a mudbrick building. The top layer contained 119 *tombs apparently dating to the first millennium BC. There is some evidence for a Neo-Assyrian building, with characteristic Assyrian architectural details. PB

G. CONTENAU and R. GHIRSHMAN, *Fouilles du Tépé-Giyan près de Néhavend 1931 et 1932* (Paris 1935).
W. NAGEL, 'Giyan, Tepe', *Reallexikon der Assyriologie* 3 (Berlin/ New York 1971) 405–7.

**Glass** Glass blowing was unknown prior to the final centuries BC and was not used by ancient Near Eastern glass-makers. The evidence for glass prior to the middle of the second millennium BC consists mainly of occasional beads, although glass fragments, including a piece of blue-white raw glass, have recently been found in late third-millennium BC levels at Tell *Brak, along with a glass rod from Tell Asmar and a lump of raw blue glass from *Eridu.

There appears to have been a major change in glass production around 1600 BC, when new techniques and colours appear and fragments from glass vessels are first identified, for example at *Alalakh. The major technique used for vessel production during the second millennium BC was core-forming. A core made of straw-tempered mud or a clay-dung mixture was formed around a *metal rod and molten glass applied around the core by dipping it in liquid glass, or by trailing a thread of molten glass over it. The object was then rolled while the glass was soft. Vessels were frequently polychrome, most often blue, with decoration in yellow and white, often in the form of coloured blobs and threads. When the glass cooled, the

(*above left*) Glass bottle formed around a sand core. Blue glass threads wound around the outside were combed to make a chevron pattern. Height 11.8 cm. From Ur, probably thirteenth century BC. WA 120659.

(*above right*) Glass vase cast in a mould, then cut and polished and inscribed for Sargon II of Assyria (721–705 BC). From Nimrud, height 8.8 cm. WA 90952.

core was scraped out. The technique was best suited to the production of small vessels such as perfume containers, and glass was very much a luxury, high-status material.

Although a good collection of Late Bronze Age glass was recovered from *Nuzi, it is debatable whether the supposed association of glass with the *Hurrians is valid. Glass was not always used where it was made, and could be transported in ingot form. Examples in blue glass have been recovered from a fourteenth-century BC *palace at Tell *Brak, and from the *Ulu Burun *shipwreck. Glass was also employed for the production of amulets, pendants, *figurines, and beads imitating precious *stones. Clear glass, produced in imitation of rock crystal, appeared in the ancient Near East by 700 BC. Another innovation around this time was the production of thin-walled vessels using moulds, probably by the lost-wax method. Polychrome core-formed vessels appear to have been reintroduced to *Mesopotamia during the Neo-*Assyrian period, after a gap of several centuries. Baby-lonian and Hittite *scribes wrote instructions for making coloured glass from the mid second millennium BC onwards.                                                                                                  GP

D. BARAG, *A Catalogue of Glass in the Department of Western Asiatic Antiquities in the British Museum I: Ur III–AD 200* (London 1985).

P.R.S. MOOREY, *Ancient Mesopotamian Materials and Industries: The Archaeological Evidence* (Oxford 1994).

P.T. NICHOLSON, *Ancient Egyptian Faience and Glass* (Princes Risborough 1993).

A.L. OPPENHEIM et al., *Glass and Glassmaking in Ancient Mesopotamia* (New York 1970).

**Glueck, Nelson (1900–71)** As a student of *Albright's *pottery typology and methods of surface reconnaissance, Glueck made his major contribution in large-scale surveys of *Transjordan, the Jordan Valley and the *Negev. He was, in many respects, similar to his good friend and fellow advocate of 'biblical archaeology', Albright, although less versatile. He became a professor

at Hebrew Union College, Cincinnati, his hometown, in 1928, and president in 1947 (it later combined with the Jewish Institute of Religion). Under his administration, HUC opened a school for biblical and archaeological studies in Jerusalem, renamed after Glueck in 1972. In 1964, the Glueck School of Biblical Archaeology launched the *Gezer project, which has had a significant impact on the practice of *archaeology in the Near East today. Glueck carried out extensive archaeological research, especially surface survey, in *Palestine, the Israeli Negev, and Transjordan. During the Second World War, he served with the United States Office of Strategic Services, the predecessor of the CIA, commissioned to map water sources in the desert which could support a retreat from El Alamein.

Glueck came to *Jerusalem in 1927 and emulated Albright by undertaking a lifetime of excavation and surface exploration; he learned how to 'read' *pottery from Albright at Tell *Beit Mirsim in 1930 and 1932. In 1937 Glueck excavated at Khirbet et-Tannur, a *Nabataean *temple in central Jordan, work which has stood the test of time and helped to seal Glueck's lifelong fascination with the Nabataean Arabs; his book *Deities and Dolphins* is most important in this regard. Glueck's research at Tell el-Kheleifeh, just north of Aqaba, has not endured as well. He originally identified this site as *biblical Ezion-Geber and linked it with Solomon's smelting activity, but most of his conclusions have been rejected – even abandoned by Glueck himself.

Glueck's outstanding achievement was his long-term, monumental survey of Transjordan (1932–47) and the Negev (1952–64). In four technical volumes, *Explorations in Eastern Palestine* (1934–51), he described his study of more than a thousand sites in *Ammon, *Moab and *Edom, summarizing his results in *The Other Side of the Jordan* (1940; rev. ed. 1970). Glueck reported his survey of more than five hundred sites in the Israeli Negev in the popular *Rivers in the Desert* (1959). On the basis of this surface exploration, Glueck attempted to reconstruct the occupational history of Transjordan and the Negev. This historical reconstruction has been challenged – or rejected outright – at several points, especially the postu-lated long gap in sedentary occupation in southern Transjordan for most of the Middle and Late Bronze Ages. The latter has a direct bearing on the nature and date of the Hebrew migration through Transjordan and the rise of the *Iron Age kingdoms of Moab and Edom. This gap has been filled in, at least in part, by more recent surveys. Glueck's reconstruction of the *Bronze Age settlement history in the Negev relates to the historicity of the Hebrew *patriarchal narratives. Considering the con-ditions under which he worked and the time that these surveys required, it is amazing that Glueck accomplished so much and that his work continues to stimulate modern research.                                                                          GLM

S. GITIN, 'Glueck, Nelson', *The Oxford Encyclopedia of Archaeology in the Near East* 2, ed. E.M. Meyers (New York 1997) 415–16.

P.R.S. MOOREY, *A Century of Biblical Archaeology* (Cambridge 1991).

J.A. SAUER, 'Transjordan in the Bronze and Iron Ages: A Critique of Glueck's Synthesis', *Bulletin of the American Schools of Oriental Research* 263 (1986) 1–26.

E.N. STERN, *Dreamer in the Desert: A Profile of Nelson Glueck* (New York 1980).

**Glyptic:** see Seals

**Godin Tepe**  A large mound in the Kangavar Valley in west-central *Iran, Godin Tepe controlled the most important east–west route through the *Zagros mountains between Baghdad and Hamadan. Excavations were conducted by T.C. Young Jr between 1965 and 1973 at Godin Tepe itself and the nearby site of Seh Gabi.

Seh Gabi is a collection of small mounds where four phases (Godin periods XI–VI) belonging to the ceramic *Neolithic (c.7000–5500 BC) were recorded.

Godin itself, c.15 ha, comprises three elements: outer *town, citadel and, rising from one corner, an upper citadel. The total height is some 30 m above the plain. Excavated levels are divided into eleven periods, I–XI, I being recent Islamic. Periods XI–VI belong to the ceramic Neolithic, and are better known from Seh Gabi.

Period V, late fourth millennium BC, has a 'Proto-*Elamite' colony with three major buildings, a *gatehouse and a magazine within an oval defensive wall on the citadel with a local Late *Chalcolithic settlement around it on the lower mound. Southern *Mesopotamian elements appear, notably bevelled rim bowls and clay tablets bearing numerical impressions and a single Proto-Elamite sign. Some would see this as part of an extensive trading system, either south Mesopotamian (*Uruk IV) or Proto-Elamite (Susan Acropole 17).

Period IV represents a brief incursion from the north of the Early Trans-*Caucasian culture, typified by handmade red and black burnished *pottery with incised and excised decoration. In Period III, spanning the later third and the first half of the second millennium BC, Godin reached urban proportions. A complicated sequence of building levels (termed 'spiral stratigraphy' by the excavator) and an inhumation *cemetery yielded, like other sites in western Iran, much painted pottery with geometric and *bird motifs in a distinctive local style.

Period II is *Median, founded in the eighth century BC and perhaps extending into the early *Achaemenid period. Occupation was restricted to the high citadel. The original fortified manor *house comprised a square columned hall with 5 by 6 rows of *stone bases for *wooden columns and a raised mudbrick podium, and a rectangular hall with 2 by 8 rows of column bases. To this were gradually added a third hall with 2 by 4 rows, a large magazine and other features. Characteristic are hollow rectangular towers, and recessed and buttressed façades pierced by arrow-shaped windows. These structures appear to represent the fortified residence of a powerful local chief.                                                  GDS

R.C. HENRICKSON, 'Godin III and Chronology of Central Western Iran circa 2600–1400 B.C.', *The Archaeology of Western Iran*, ed. F. Hole (Washington, D.C. 1987) 205–27.

T.C. YOUNG, Jr, *Excavations at Godin Tepe: First Progress Report* (Toronto 1969).

T.C. YOUNG, JR and L.D. LEVINE, *Excavations at Godin Tepe: Second Progress Report* (Toronto 1974).

H. WEISS and T.C. YOUNG, JR, 'The Merchants of Susa: Godin V and Plateau–Lowland Relations in the Late Fourth Millennium B.C.', *Iran* 13 (1975) 1–17.

**Gods, goddesses**  The gods of the ancient Near Eastern peoples, in historical times, were almost without exception anthropomorphic, male or female. They were imagined as of gigantic size and exuded a terrifying splendour, with superhuman powers, although the power of all the gods was by no means equal: some were relatively minor or of restricted influence. They shared the emotions and foibles of humankind. Generally speaking they were immortal, although there were certain gods about whom *myths are recounted which involve their deaths, or visits to the *underworld. Although they lived in heaven or the underworld, an extension of their personality also inhabited the various cult statues erected to them by humankind: when a statue was first dedicated, the *Babylonians performed the 'Washing the mouth' and 'Opening the mouth' *rituals for it in order to enable it to become imbued with the divine presence.

The largest group of gods are the deities of the various *city pantheons. Local deities were particularly important in the heterogeneous *Hittite *religion. There were also gods and goddesses representing natural forces, birth-goddesses (see Childbirth), groups of anonymous gods, and minister deities who attend more important gods and goddesses. The personal gods of individuals ('a man's god') are not usually named. Some human rulers were also deified (see Deification).

More than three thousand names of deities have been recovered from *Mesopotamia alone. These were organized by the Mesopotamians into groups resembling households, extended *families or states. The divine patrons of the various cities participate, in myths, in a consultative assembly of the gods, which may reflect a human phenomenon of the Third Dynasty of *Ur. A god worshipped under the same name in two different places might have two quite different cults. In due course the overall number of deities was reduced by equating or regarding as forms of each other deities whose character was similar. At its most extreme this led to the so-called monotheistic tendencies of the cult of *Marduk.

In *art, Mesopotamian gods are generally shown wearing the horned cap with up to seven superimposed sets of bull's horns, described as a mark of their divinity. They can also be identified by their distinctive symbols and attributes (see Divine symbols). When not represented together with a god, these motifs nevertheless symbolize their associated deities.

The *Ebla texts reveal a local *Syrian pantheon c.2300 BC, worship of a few of the deities continuing later. In the *Levant during the Middle and Late Bronze Ages the principal deities represented natural forces (*Anat, *Asherah, *Astarte, *Baal, *Reshep), with *El, 'god', at their head. *Seals and *sculptures depict them in various

Spears, one with a gold head, one with a silver head, shafts decorated with gold bands. 92.5 and 1.47 m long. From the Royal Cemetery at Ur, c.2500 BC. WA 121410–1.

ways, often without distinctive attributes to assure their identity. Worship of some was sustained in the *Iron Age, when several states had specific national gods (e.g. Chemosh in *Moab), *Yahweh of *Israel being unique in having no official consort. *Phoenician *towns continued to have individual patron deities, such as *Melqart at *Tyre. The *Aramaeans incorporated several Mesopotamian gods into their pantheon (e.g. *Nabû, Sîn), beside *Canaanite ones and their own.                     AG/JAB/ARM

J.A. BLACK and A.R. GREEN, *Gods, Demons and Symbols of Ancient Mesopotamia: An Illustrated Dictionary*, 2nd ed. (London 1998).

D.O. EDZARD, 'Mesopotamien: Die Mythologie der Sumerer und Akkader', *Götter und Mythen im Vorderen Orient*, Vol. 1 of *Wörterbuch der Mythologie*, ed. H.W. Haussig (Stuttgart 1965) 17–139.

I.L. FINKEL and M.J. GELLER (eds), *Sumerian Gods and their Representations* (Groningen 1997).

P.W. HAIDER, M. HUTTER and S. KREUZER (eds), *Religionsgeschichte Syriens: Von der Frühzeit bis zur Gegenwart* (Stuttgart 1986).

W.G. LAMBERT, 'The Historical Development of the Mesopotamian Pantheon: A Study in Sophisticated Polytheism', *Unity and Diversity*, eds H. Goedicke and J.J.M. Roberts (Baltimore/London 1975) 191–200.

G. LEICK, *A Dictionary of Ancient Near Eastern Mythology* (London/New York 1991).

D. PARDEE, 'An Evaluation of the Proper Names from Ebla from a West Semitic Perspective: Pantheon Distribution According to Genre', *Eblaite Personal Names and Semitic Name-giving*, ed. A. Archi (Rome 1988) 119–51.

F. POMPONIO and P. XELLA, *Les dieux d'Ebla: Étude analytique des divinités éblaïtes à l'époque des archives royales du IIIe millénaire* (Münster 1997).

H. RINGGREN, *Religions of the Ancient Near East* (London 1973).

E. VON SCHULER, 'Kleinasien: Die Mythologie der Hethiter und Hurriter', *Götter und Mythen im Vorderen Orient*, Vol. 1 of *Wörterbuch der Mythologie*, ed. H.W. Haussig (Stuttgart 1965) 141–215.

G. SELZ, *Untersuchungen zur Götterwelt des altsumerischen Stadtstaates von Lagaš* (Philadelphia, PA 1995).

K. VAN DER TOORN, B. BECKING and P.W. VAN DER HORST (eds), *Dictionary of Deities and Demons in the Bible* (Leiden 1995, 2nd ed. 1999).

**Gold** Scarcity, malleability and beauty made gold a desirable medium for the execution of valuable objects, and for use as *money and *coinage. Typical goldwork included *jewellery, dress pins, decorative *weapons and vessels. Cult statues could be made from gold, although many were made from other materials and simply given an outer layer of gold foil. In *Mesopotamia, goldsmiths

were distinguished from other categories of *metalworker.

The earliest gold objects currently known are a group of large gold rings dating to the late fifth millennium BC found in a cave at Nahal Qana in *Palestine. While occasional gold objects occur in fourth-millennium BC contexts in Mesopotamia, including a finely made wolf's head from Tepe *Gawra, there appears to be have been a big expansion in production just before the middle of the third millennium BC, when large collections of gold artefacts are documented from rich *graves at *Ur and *Alaca Hüyük, and in 'hoards' from *Troy.

The rings from Nahal Qana contained up to 30 per cent *silver. This and similar instances make it clear that much of the gold occurring in the ancient Near East was electrum, a naturally occurring alloy of gold and silver. Gold was most probably acquired from sources in eastern *Anatolia, although there are textual references to gold being obtained via the Persian Gulf. The role of Egyptian gold resources remains unclear until the Late Bronze Age when the *Amarna Letters contain requests from Near Eastern rulers for gold from the pharaoh. These letters makes it clear that gold played an important role in international *diplomacy as tribute from lesser to greater rulers, and as a 'greeting gift'.

The recycling of precious metals had a major impact on the range of goldwork surviving today. Textual evidence from ancient *Syria suggests that notions of 'artistic value' were of little importance when it came to valuing artefacts, which were quite literally worth their weight in gold.                     GP

P.T. CRADDOCK, *Early Metal Mining and Production* (Edinburgh 1995).

K.R. MAXWELL-HYSLOP, *Western Asiatic Jewellery c. 3000–612 B.C.* (London 1971).

P.R.S. MOOREY, *Ancient Mesopotamian Materials and Industries: The Archaeological Evidence* (Oxford 1994).

B. MUSCHE, *Vorderasiatischer Schmuck von den Anfangen bis zur Zeit der Achaemeniden (ca. 10,000–330 v. Chr.)* (Leiden 1982).

J. OGDEN, *Ancient Jewellery* (London 1992).

**Göllü Dağ** Göllü Dağ is an extinct volcano, 2000 m above sea level and containing a crater lake, in the central *Anatolian Melendiz range 60 km to the north of modern Nighde. It is the site of a Neo-*Hittite *city and *palace but occupation must have been seasonal since snow can fall as early as September and occasionally as late as May. Research has been carried out by O.R. Arik (1935),

Aerial view of the Neo-Hittite site of Göllü Dağ on the edge of an extinct volcano, taken from a hot-air balloon (from W. Schirmer, 'Die Bauanlagen auf dem Göllüdağ in Kappadokien', *Architectura* (1993) 121–32).

B. Tezcan (1968–9) and W. Schirmer (1993–).

Presumably constructed in the late eighth century BC by Warpalawas, the greatest king of the Neo-*Hittite state of Tuwana whose capital was at Tyana (modern Kemerhisar), the buildings and much of the *sculpture appear to have been finished at the time of abandonment. Although the site is unique in its setting and state of preservation it presumably represents elements of Neo-Hittite urban design and architecture from the Anatolian plateau that have not otherwise been brought to light.

GDS

W. SCHIRMER, 'Die Bauanlagen auf dem Göllüdağ in Kappadokien', *Architectura* (1993) 121–32.

**Gordion** The capital of the kingdom of *Phrygia, Gordion lies on a major ancient east–west route in an area of springs and arable land on the Sakarya river about 100 km south-west of modern Ankara in Turkey. It consists of a 17.5-ha mound, Yassıhöyük, lower and outer *towns, and an outlying *cemetery area. It was discovered and identified as Gordion by Alfred Körte in 1893, and excavated by the Körte brothers (1900), Rodney Young (1950–73) and Mary Voigt (1988–). The name Gordion comes from Gordius, the father of *Midas, best known from the *Roman writer Arrian's story of the *chariot he dedicated at Gordion, binding the yoke to the pole with the Gordian knot, later cut by Alexander the Great.

The citadel has occupation from the Early Bronze Age to the Roman period. Particularly significant is the stratified sequence of Phrygian citadels with their *fortifications, dating mostly to the ninth and eighth centuries BC. The Phrygian citadel was subdivided into an upper north-east enclosure and a lower south-west area. The buildings within the inner enclosure were of so-called megaron plan, rectangular structures with a roofed front porch and doorways set axially, some paved with multi-coloured pebbles. One, Megaron 3, may have been the eighth-century BC *palace, perhaps even of Midas, and

contained *bronze vessels, *ivory-inlaid *furniture and *textiles. A large terrace supported two buildings for the provision and preparation of *food, supplies and *clothing.

A cemetery to the north-east has about one hundred tumuli dating from the eighth century BC to the *Hellenistic period, including the burials of Phrygian royalty and nobility. Most are individual *burials in flat-roofed wooden chambers, covered with rock piles and earth mounds. The largest tumulus, often attributed to Midas, contained the body of a man in his mid-sixties laid on a bier with elaborate *textile covers, *wooden *furniture with intricate designs and inlay, *bronze vessels, fibulae, studded leather belts and *pottery.

The destruction of Gordion about 700 BC is usually attributed to the *Cimmerians. The citadel was reconstructed, either immediately by the Phrygians or possibly later by the *Lydians.

PB

A. GUNTER, *The Bronze Age: The Gordion Excavations Final Reports* 3 (Philadelphia, PA 1991).

G. and A. KÖRTE (eds), *Gordion: Ergebnisse der Ausgrabungen im Jahre 1900* (Berlin 1904).

M. MELLINK, 'The Native Kingdoms of Anatolia', *Cambridge Ancient History* 3.2, 2nd ed. (Cambridge 1991) 622–43.

M. VOIGT, 'Gordion', *The Oxford Encyclopedia of Archaeology in the Near East* 2, ed. E.M. Meyers (New York 1997) 426–31.

R.S. YOUNG et al., *Three Great Early Tumuli: The Gordion Excavations Final Reports* 1 (Philadelphia, PA 1981).

**Graves:** see Tombs

**Greeks** In ancient Near Eastern sources, the Greeks were known as Ionians, after the inhabitants of eastern Greece. In *Akkadian, this was written as *Yaman*, in the *Old Testament as *Yawan*.

During the Late Bronze Age, there had been close contact and *trade between Mycenaean Greece and the *Levant, but after the destruction of the Mycenaean kingdoms this ceased. Imported Greek *pottery reappeared certainly in the ninth century BC, possibly in the tenth century BC at *Tyre. *Phoenician trade goods appeared in Greece from the ninth century BC on, probably brought by Phoenicians, not only by returning Greeks.

The permanent presence of Greek merchants in the Levant is assumed almost entirely from the presence of Greek pottery at Levantine sites; there are no fully Greek sites in the Levant at this period, and the scale of actual Greek presence is uncertain. Al Mina on the north *Syrian coast is usually identified as the first truly Greek settlement in the Levant, dated to c.825 BC. Greek imports here increased steadily, with some disruptions, until Al Mina was replaced as a trading emporium by Seleucia in 301 BC. The excavated buildings at Al Mina have been identified as warehouses; other Greek settlements in the Levant have been tentatively identified, particularly Tell Sukas in *Lebanon where there was a sanctuary possibly of Greek design. Greek *merchants were presumably interested in trading in the sorts of goods that the *Assyrians recorded as booty or tribute from the Phoenician and north Syrian states: *textiles, *silver, *gold, worked and unworked *metals. Among metalwork, *bronze cauldrons with cast animal-head attachments made principally in *Urartu were imported into many parts of the Greek world in the eighth and seventh centuries BC.

In return, the Greeks may have been supplying *slaves. The earliest Assyrian reference to Greeks is a report to *Tiglath-pileser III in c.738 BC concerning an attack by Greeks ('Ionians') on a coastal Phoenician city, apparently in search of slaves, foiled by the Assyrian governor. Later, *Sargon II recorded catching 'like fishes, the Ionians who live amid the Sea of the Setting Sun'. *Sennacherib used captive Greek sailors in his war against *Elam, and *Esarhaddon received the submission and tribute of Greece (*Yaman*).

Greek mercenaries were used by the *Egyptians against the *Babylonians between 616 and 605 BC. Such mercenaries were probably stationed in the fort at Mesad Hashavyahu in *Palestine, where late seventh-century BC Greek pottery has been found associated with a workshop for making *iron implements. References to 'Kittim' in *Hebrew *ostraca from the fortress at *Arad may also refer to Greek mercenaries fighting for *Judah. *Cuneiform tablets recording rations distributed to deportees in *Babylon include 'Ionian' *craftsmen, but this may refer to *Anatolians rather than Greeks.

Greece was also influenced by the Near East: by the flow of finished goods resulting in an 'orientalizing' art between the eighth and sixth centuries BC, by the Greek adoption of the Phoenician *alphabet, probably in the ninth century BC, and by the use of words in Greek borrowed from Near Eastern *languages.                    PB

J. BOARDMAN, *The Greeks Overseas: Their Early Colonies and Trade* (London 1980).

T.F.R.G. BRAUN, 'The Greeks in the Near East', *Cambridge Ancient History* 3.3, 2nd ed. (Cambridge 1982) 1–31.

S. DALLEY and A.T. REYES, 'Mesopotamian Contact and Influence on the Greek World 1: To the Persian Conquest', *The Legacy of Mesopotamia*, ed. S. Dalley (Oxford 1998) 85–106.

P.J. RIIS, 'Griechen in Phönizien', *Phönizier im Westen*, ed. H.G. Niemeyer (Mainz am Rhein 1982) 237–60.

J.C. WALDBAUM, 'Greeks *in* the East or Greeks *and* the East? Problems in the Definition and Recognition of Presence', *Bulletin of the American Schools of Oriental Research* 305 (1997) 1–17.

## Gudea

Gudea, 'the called', son of Ur-Bawa, ruled *Lagash in the twenty-first century BC. Gudea is famous for the two dozen or so statues and heads carved in diorite and other *stones found at Girsu (now Tello), some life-size, some smaller. (The authenticity of some is disputed and there are undoubted forgeries.) The figures show the ruler standing, or sitting, twice holding a drawing board and plan of a *temple precinct on his lap. They continue the technical mastery of the *Akkad period, although they are static, votive *sculptures. The *craftsmen also produced vases and other carvings and cast *foundation figures in *copper. Some of the statues carry inscriptions

Torso and head of Gudea of Lagash c.2100 BC. Height 76.6 cm. WA 122810.

telling of Gudea's piety and an expedition to the west for cedar timbers to use in the temple he built. One reports a raid on *Elam with booty captured. Two large clay cylinders preserve poetic accounts of Gudea's devotion. His patron *god, Ningirsu, appeared in a *dream to instruct him about the building work, but he did not understand, so had to go to a goddess for an explanation. He then made every provision for the divine household. These compositions are hailed as the most extensive examples of classic *Sumerian. Gudea ruled only the area around Lagash and shortly after his death it was taken by *Ur-Nammu of *Ur.                    ARM

D.O. EDZARD, *Gudea and His Dynasty. Royal Inscriptions of Mesopotamia, Early Periods* 3.1 (Toronto 1997).

F. JOHANSEN, *Statues of Gudea, Ancient and Modern* (Copenhagen 1978).

## Guran, (Tepe)

A site in the hilly *Luristan area of *Iran, south-west of Tepe *Giyan, Tepe Guran is an oval mound measuring 110 by 80 m, with 8 m of deposit containing eighteen building levels excavated by Jørgen Meldgaard in 1963. It was occupied between c.7500 and 6500 BC, though the dating has been uncertain owing to unreliable radiocarbon dates. Its stratigraphic sequence is important for the *Neolithic of Iran, since it includes an aceramic phase followed by sequences of distinctive painted *pottery. The building sequence suggests that *wooden huts were succeeded by mudbrick *houses, and there may have been a transformation from a semi-permanent winter camp to a permanent *village. PB

F. HOLE, 'Chronologies in the Iranian Neolithic', *Chronologies in the Near East*, eds O. Aurenche, J. Evin and F. Hours (Oxford 1987) 364–6.

J. MELDGAARD, P. MORTENSEN and H. THRANE, 'Excavations at Tepe Guran, Luristan', *Acta Archaeologica* 34 (1963) 97–133.

**Guti** Very little is known about the Guti (or Gutians), who appear to have been barbarian raiders from the *Zagros who brought to an end the *dynasty of *Akkad and destroyed its capital c.2200 BC. Gutium, a mountainous area in south-west *Iran, was a troublesome part of the Akkadian empire, and the year names of the last kings of Akkad record campaigns against the region. The only contemporary description of the fall of Akkad is in a poetic *letter which tells how the *gods became angry and sent the Guti and famine against *Sumer and promised the destruction and ruin of Akkad and all its people. Later texts recalled this momentous event, although inaccurately. One concerns the last proper king of Akkad, Shar-kali-sharri, whose omen is 'the ruin of Akkad, the enemy will fall on your peace'. The 'Kuthean Legend' tells how the fearsome warriors attacked *Naram-Sin, while a chronicle states that *Marduk twice raised up against Naram-Sin the Guti, who received his kingdom.

The *King List records twenty or twenty-one Gutian kings ruling Sumer and Akkad, totalling 125 years, although it is uncertain whether at the time of the invasion they had a king or were still barbarian hordes. The Guti left very few traces of their rule, except for a few monuments and dedications inscribed with their names. They adopted *Mesopotamian culture and traditions and Akkadian personal names. Although there is little evidence, it is likely that their rule was only partial and that other dynasties ruled parts of the land at the same time, including two further obscure kings of the dynasty of Akkad.

The Guti were finally expelled by Utuhegal, king of *Uruk, c.2100 BC. A copy of Utuhegal's own account of his victory denounces the Guti as 'the stinging serpent of the hills, who was the enemy of the gods, who had carried off the kingship of Sumer to the mountains and filled Sumer with evil', robbing wives and *children and committing all wickedness in the land. Utuhegal marched out of Uruk and fought the Guti, led by a king called Tirigan who had been on the throne for only forty days, at a place called Ennigi. Tirigan was defeated and fled but was captured and returned to Utuhegal. This victory was remembered in later omen texts. PB

C.J. GADD, 'The Dynasty of Agade and the Gutian Invasion', *Cambridge Ancient History* 1.2, 2nd ed. (Cambridge 1971) 454–63.

W.W. HALLO, 'Gutium', *Reallexikon der Assyriologie* 3 (Berlin/New York 1957–71) 708–20.

**Guzan:** see Halaf, (Tell)

# H

**Habiru** The *habiru* are mentioned in texts from all over the Near East throughout the second millennium BC. They generally comprise refugees, fugitives or brigands living on the margins of settled life outside the control of the *city-states, and occasionally raiding settlements. The expression sometimes denotes those of low social standing who are employed by the state as unskilled labourers or mercenaries: a prism of a mid-second-millennium BC north *Syrian *king lists 438 workers with *Hurrian and *Semitic names, all identified as *habiru*. In the *Amarna Letters, 'habiru' may also be used as a derogatory term, sometimes referring to a king of a city-state who is considered by a neighbouring king to be a public enemy. That the *habiru* were considered to be a serious problem is confirmed by passages in international *treaties in which both signatories promise to extradite citizens who have sought refuge among the *habiru*.

The word *habiru* (or *hapiru*) is *Akkadian, although it was probably in origin West Semitic (*'abiru* or *'apiru*); in *Sumerian it is written SA.GAZ or SAG.GAZ. *Habiru* is probably to be translated as 'fugitive' or 'refugee'. Although it was once considered to be the Akkadian equivalent of 'Hebrew', this is unlikely since *habiru* is a social designation, not an ethnic one, and it is known over such a wide area. PB

J. BOTTÉRO, *Le problème des Habiru à la 4ᵉ rencontre assyriologique internationale* (Paris 1954).

——, 'Habiru', *Reallexikon der Assyriologie* 4 (Berlin/New York 1972–5) 14–27.

——, 'Entre nomades et sédentaires: Les Habiru', *Dialogues d'histoire ancienne* 6 (1980) 201–13.

M. GREENBERG, *The Hab/piru* (New Haven 1955).

M. SALVINI, *The Habiru Prism of King Tunip-Teššup of Tikunani* (Rome 1996).

**Habuba Kabira** The ancient settlement of Habuba Kabira lies on the west bank of the Euphrates river in northern *Syria, and is closely related to the nearby religious and administrative centre of Jebel Aruda. Habuba Kabira is best known for the important information it has yielded on the subject of the northwards expansion of

View of a Late Uruk house with its contents at Habuba Kabira South (courtesy of Eva Strommenger/Deutsche Orient-Gesellschaft Berlin, photograph by Wolfgang Bitterle).

early *Mesopotamian civilization from its south Mesopotamian homeland during the last centuries of the fourth millennium BC, the Late *Uruk period. Excavations at various parts of Habuba Kabira were conducted by Ernst Heinrich, Eva Strommenger and André Finet prior to construction of the Tabqa Dam and the flooding of the area (1969–75).

The settlement comprises several elements. To the north is the high mound of Tell Habuba Kabira (mainly of third-millennium BC date), while several hundred metres downstream lies the main walled city, Habuba Kabira South, with its acropolis at Tell Qannas. Much of the *city was occupied for only a short time during the late fourth millennium BC. The importance of the site in the Late Uruk period stemmed from its control of north–south *trade routes, overseeing the movement of raw materials from the *Anatolian highlands down the Euphrates and on to the Mesopotamian plains, at the time of the evolution of the world's first urban, proto-literate civilization.

Extensive excavation in Habuba Kabira South has revealed large numbers of Late Uruk residential buildings, not known from elsewhere in the Uruk world. The city may have reached twenty or more hectares at its most populous, and was carefully planned in terms of the layout of buildings and streets. The religious and administrative core of the city was located at Tell Qannas, where monumental mudbrick buildings were excavated. A 3-m-wide city wall enclosed the settlement on its north and west sides at least.

The immediate precursors of *writing were found at Habuba Kabira South, including bullae (clay tags) with tokens and impressed marks, as well as clay tablets with numerical signs. But the absence of true writing at the site suggests that the city was abandoned some time before the invention of writing around 3200 BC in south Mesopotamia.                                           RM

G. ALGAZE, The Uruk World System (Chicago 1993).

E. STROMMENGER, Habuba Kabira: Eine Stadt vor 5000 Jahren (Mainz 1980).

R. VALLET, 'Habuba Kebira (Syrie) ou la naissance de l'urbanisme', Paléorient 22 (1996) 45–76.

**Hacilar** The site of Hacilar was excavated by James Mellaart (1957–60). It is located in the lakes region of south-western *Anatolia.

Hacilar is a small site of only a few hectares. Several phases of occupation were documented. The earliest levels may be aceramic *Neolithic although this is disputed. The earliest major exposures revealed a late Neolithic *village dating to about 6500 BC, just a little later than the excavated portions of *Çatalhöyük east. In the late Neolithic levels a few dwelling units were exposed. They abutted each other, and a repetitive pattern of living rooms with attached kitchens can be noted. These levels had a distinctive range of clay female *figurines portraying portly, perhaps matronly figures, and younger lither figures.

The best preserved levels belong to the Early *Chalcolithic dating between 6000 and 5000 BC. These phases on the site are characterized by distinctive, elaborately, carefully and skilfully painted *pottery. In level II virtually a whole village plan was exposed. The settlement was surrounded by a wall 1.5–3 m thick that may have served for defensive purposes and to help contain the village livestock. There are clearly two main zones within the settlement. In the west, grouped around a large courtyard area entered directly from one of the *gates, were eight structures repeating more or less the same plan – that is a rectangular room with rectangular antechamber. Whilst Mellaart suggested that one of these might have been a granary and one a shrine, the repetitiveness of the basic fixtures suggests that these are all ordinary dwellings. In the centre of the settlement, to the east of this courtyard, were three rooms of different plan clearly associated with pottery production. Along the eastern edge of the settlement was a large complex of interconnected rooms; in one was a large well. Some of these rooms had domestic fixtures, but the northernmost of these also had a limited number of *burials. Clearly something distinguished those living in the eastern block of the village from the western.

These features give much insight into the nature of an Early Chalcolithic community. A significant component of what must have been a relatively small community – no more than sixteen co-resident units (*families?) – was

Early Chalcolithic painted pottery from Hacilar, c.6000–5000 BC. The painting is in red on a white slip (courtesy of the Board of Trustees of the National Museums and Galleries on Merseyside, 1967.213).

apparently involved in pottery production, perhaps for exchange outside the settlement, and there was a major distinction between one part of the community and another.                                                                DB

J. MELLAART, *Excavations at Hacilar* (Edinburgh 1970).

**Hadad:** see Adad

**Hair dressing**  Women and men in antiquity spent just as long arranging their hair as their modern counterparts, according to the elaborate styles and changing fashions depicted in monumental *sculpture and *seals. Of course, just as in the modern Near East, head coverings, such as close-fitting caps, turbans, headdresses or veils were common, so hair was often hidden. *Assyrian *women are rarely shown in sculpture, but we know from texts that married women wore veils outside their homes, while prostitutes had to be bareheaded by *law to denote their status. One type of Assyrian *temple prostitute

Stone wig for a statue of the goddess Lama, dedicated by a priest for the life of Shulgi, king of Ur, c.2050 BC. WA 91075.

was characterized by curly hair. Particular categories of people traditionally had the same sorts of hairstyles in all periods and regions, although there are exceptions: Babylonian *priests were usually clean-shaven and had shaved heads or a tonsure (in the Old *Babylonian period perhaps just with a forelock left unshaved), but this was forbidden to Israel's priests; *kings were generally bearded. In the Old Babylonian period, *slaves had a distinctive hairstyle, and manumission of slaves was formally known as 'clearing the forehead', performed by barbers who held official posts in *palaces, *temples and law courts.

There was a tremendous variety of men's and women's hairstyles, and as far as we can tell the hair that is depicted on sculptures is natural, not wigs as was often the case in *Egypt. Men could have their heads shaved, or have short or shoulder-length hair, be bearded or beardless. In Assyria, beardless individuals depicted in reliefs were either *eunuchs or youths. The hair and beards of Assyrian men were long, thick and elaborately curled. Men often wore a headband to keep long hair in place, and this is known from the *Uruk until the Neo-Assyrian period, when a headband might also be fixed over a turban.

Women's hairstyles varied from simple, shoulder or

waist-length curled hair, sometimes braided in plaits, to the elaborate styles of the Early Dynastic period when hair was plaited and piled on top of the head or confined by a net or scarf, covered by a headdress. On one Early Dynastic figure a woman wears a hat with a hole in the top through which her hair hangs down. Even the earliest hairstyles of the *Neolithic period are fairly elaborate. A female *figurine from *Hacilar has her hair drawn back in a thick plait that hangs down her back, while contemporary figurines from other sites have their hair piled on their heads in a topknot. Seals of the late Uruk period depicting women engaged in everyday activities show their hair worn in a pigtail. Women, like men, sometimes wore headbands or ribbons to secure their hair. Headbands could be decorated or plain, with or without streamers.

*Children are rarely depicted, but in Egyptian tomb paintings of the mid second millennium BC illustrating *Syrians, they have shaved heads, except for plaited locks.

In antiquity, just like today, the appearance of grey hairs was a worrying sign, and Assyrian physicians and *magicians were readily on hand to prescribe lotions and incantations to restore hair colour.                                    PB

D. COLLON, 'Clothing and Grooming in Ancient Western Asia', *Civilizations of the Ancient Near East*, ed. J.M. Sasson (New York 1995) 503–15.
A. SPYCKET, 'La coiffure féminine en Mésopotamie', *Revue d'Assyriologie* 48 (1954) 113–29, 169–77, 49 (1955) 113–28.

**Halaf, (Tell)**  Located at the headwaters of the *Khabur river in northern *Syria near the border with Turkey, Tell Halaf was excavated by Max von Oppenheim between 1899 and 1929. Two main periods were investigated, the first belonging to the sixth to fifth millennia BC, the second to the *Iron Age.

The *prehistoric Halaf period, c.6000–5000/4500 BC, is named after the discoveries at Tell Halaf. Distinctive painted *pottery, well fired and beautifully decorated with designs of *animals, humans, *birds and geometric patterns, has since been found at many sites over much of the Near East, including eastern Turkey, Syria and northern Iraq, and is the first widespread cultural horizon of prehistoric *Mesopotamia. At Tell Halaf itself there are traces of a pre-Halaf level followed by occupation of Early to Late Halaf. Other artefacts include *figurines, *stamp seals, sling bullets and small pieces of

The ninth-century BC palace at Tell Halaf was decorated with stone slabs carved in low relief displaying mythological, religious, military and domestic scenes. Height 59 cm. WA 117102.

*copper, all typical elements of a Halaf assemblage. No convincing architecture of this period was recovered at Tell Halaf, but at other sites the Halaf period is characterized by the use of circular structures, or *tholoi*, as well as by rectangular buildings.

During the Iron Age Tell Halaf was known as Guzan, as attested in *Assyrian sources from the site and elsewhere. Inscriptions survive from the time of the *Aramaean ruler Kapara, tenth to ninth centuries BC, who resided in the large north-western *palace at Tell Halaf. The palace was adorned with carved orthostats depicting soldiers, animals and mythological *ritual scenes. Particularly impressive human, lion, sphinx, griffin and bull figures, all free-standing, guarded the gateways in imposing fashion. Many other luxury artefacts were recovered from the ruins of the palace, including glazed bricks and items of *gold, *silver and *ivory, all attesting the great wealth of Guzan during this period.

The *city was under the control of the Assyrian empire during the ninth to seventh centuries BC (see Tell Fekheriyeh), and part of the governor's residence of this period has been excavated. Little is known of the later, classical and Islamic occupation of Tell Halaf. RM

C. BRENIQUET, *La disparition de la culture d'Halaf: Les origines de la culture d'Obeid dans le nord de la Mésopotamie* (Paris 1996).

S. CAMPBELL, 'The Halaf Period in Iraq: Old Sites and New', *Biblical Archaeology* 55 (1992) 182–7.

R.H. DORNEMANN, 'Halaf, Tell', *The Oxford Encyclopedia of Archaeology in the Near East* 2, ed. E.M. Meyers (New York 1997) 460–62.

I. HIJJARA, *The Halaf Period in Northern Mesopotamia* (London 1997).

M.F. VON OPPENHEIM, *Tell Halaf: A New Culture in Oldest Mesopotamia* (London 1933).

**Hama (Hamath)** An important *city, especially in the *Iron Age, Hama is situated in central *Syria 209 km north of *Damascus on the Orontes river, which runs through the modern town. The ancient *tell measures 400 by 300 m, with *cemetery areas to the south and west. Hama was excavated by a Danish team (1931–8), revealing a long series of phases labelled from M (*Neolithic) to A (medieval), which for many years was the main reference point for archaeological sequences in Syria.

The early phases were exposed only in limited areas, but from the *Bronze Age (phases J, H, G) were found *houses in narrow streets, the earliest contemporary with the mention of Hama ('Amatu') in texts from *Ebla. During the Middle Bronze Age large cylindrical grain silos were constructed in the centre of the town. The Iron Age city (phases F, E), with monumental buildings, a *gateway and a *cremation cemetery, corresponds to the kingdom of Hamath known from *Assyrian records and the *Old Testament. The entrances to several buildings were flanked by lion *sculptures. The excavators identified two buildings as a *temple and a *palace, the latter with a battered façade, entrance court, numerous storerooms, and an upper storey possibly for the royal residence.

The *king of Hamath took part in the coalition against *Shalmaneser III in 853 BC at the battle of Qarqar, which lay within the city's territory; the same king, Urahilina (or Irhuleni), is known from three Luwian *hieroglyphic inscriptions found at Hama in the nineteenth century which refer to the temple of the *goddess Baalat. A later king of Hamath, Zakkur of the eighth century BC, is known from an *Aramaic victory stela found at Tell Afis 110 km north of Hama, erected following success against an enemy coalition which included *Aram. The last known king of Hamath, a usurper named Iaubi'di, was defeated and killed by *Sargon II in 720 BC. Hamath was incorporated as a province of the Assyrian empire (see Provincial administration) and some of its inhabitants were *deported. The Iron Age phase E levels on the *tell appear to have been destroyed by fire in the late eighth century BC, perhaps to be attributed to Sargon's attack. A few remains date to the seventh and sixth centuries BC (phase E/D), but the site was not properly resettled until the *Hellenistic period, when it was renamed Epiphaneia. PB

M.-L. BUHL, 'Hamath', *Anchor Bible Dictionary* 3, ed. D.N. Freedman (New York 1992) 33–6.

E. FUGMANN, *Hama 2.1: L'architecture des périodes préhellénistiques* (Copenhagen 1958).

J.D. HAWKINS, 'Hamath', *Reallexikon der Assyriologie* 4 (Berlin/New York 1972–5) 67–70.

——, 'Irhuleni', *Reallexikon der Assyriologie* 5 (Berlin/New York 1976–80) 162.

P.J. RIIS, *Hama 2.3: Les cimetières à crémation* (Copenhagen 1948).

P.J. RIIS and M.-L. BUHL, *Hama 2.2: Les objets de la période dite Syro-Hittite (Âge du Fer)* (Copenhagen 1987).

I. THUESEN, *Hama 1: The Pre- and Protohistoric Periods* (Copenhagen 1988).

**Hamadan:** see Ecbatana

**Hammurabi** Hammurabi, c.1792–1750 BC, raised *Babylon, a hitherto unimportant *town, to a pre-eminence in *Mesopotamia which it enjoyed for over a millennium. Sixth *king of the *Amorite *dynasty in Babylon, which had ruled little more than the surrounding area, including the town of *Sippar, Hammurabi took advantage of circumstances to enlarge his realm and dominate Mesopotamia. Early in his reign he captured *Isin and *Uruk from the king of *Larsa in the south and was involved in other local wars. Then, for almost twenty years, he improved the *irrigation and defensive systems of his kingdom, making alliances with some of his neighbours, notably *Zimri-Lim of *Mari, after the death of *Shamshi-Adad of *Assyria, who may have been Hammurabi's overlord. Zimri-Lim helped Hammurabi to campaign against the forces of *Eshnunna and *Elam. One Mari *letter lists four leading kings, setting Hammurabi on a par with the kings of Larsa, Eshnunna and *Qatna, each having ten to fifteen kings in support, with *Yamhad (Aleppo) having twenty. At that time Hammurabi titled himself 'king of *Sumer and *Akkad' and

Detail of a stone slab dedicated with a prayer for the life of Hammurabi of Babylon, who is probably the figure standing in an attitude of worship. WA 22454.

'king of all the Amorite land'. Eventually he changed the situation. Year 29 (1764 BC) is named for his defeat of an alliance of Elamites, *Guti and others in the east, year 32 (1761 BC) for the annexation of the kingdom of Larsa, bringing all *Babylonia under his rule, and year 33 (1760 BC) for the conquest of Mari and other northerly towns. The wall of Mari was destroyed two years later. Years 37 (1756 BC) and 39 (1754 BC) were named for more campaigns in the north and year 38 (1755 BC) for the final conquest of Eshnunna, by diverting *water across it. His last four year names record building activities, as do many for his early years.

Letters from Mari and other centres, notably Larsa, illuminate Hammurabi's reign with glimpses of *court life, *diplomacy and intrigue. The king was irritated by complaints about his generosity, concerned about cases of injustice among his staff, attentive to administrative problems. His great monument is his *law code, known from the *stone stela found at *Susa, one of at least three which had been taken thither as booty from Babylonian towns. The stelae had been erected for consultation (see Literacy), and the laws, written in *Akkadian, circulated on clay tablets also, continuing to be copied for over one thousand years apparently as examples of *language and royal justice. The laws served as a model (no evidence exists for their imposition), the king enacting them as part of his royal role 'to protect the orphan and widow', and to regulate society, ensuring equity. Hammurabi's reign was followed by a decline in power, but his era saw the emergence of a fully fledged Akkadian *literature which lasted until the rise of Hellenism.          ARM

D.R. FRAYNE, Old Babylonian Period (2005–1595 BC). Royal Inscriptions of Mesopotamia, Early Periods 4 (Toronto 1990).

C.J. GADD, 'Hammurabi and the End of his Dynasty', Cambridge Ancient History 2.1, 2nd ed. (Cambridge 1973) 176–227.

M. ROTH, Law Collections from Mesopotamia and Asia Minor (Atlanta, GA 1995).

J.M. SASSON, 'King Hammurabi of Babylon', Civilizations of the Ancient Near East, ed. J.M. Sasson (New York 1995) 901–15.

**Hanging Gardens of Babylon:** see Gardens

**Hapiru:** see Habiru

**Harem**  The existence and regulations of the harem – the name both for an organized system of royal concubines and for the part of the *palace reserved for them – are best known from the Middle *Assyrian Palace and Harem Edicts dating between the fourteenth and twelfth centuries BC. The edicts comprise eight fragmentary texts compiled in the reign of *Tiglath-pileser I (c.1115–1077 BC) containing rules for behaviour in the palace and harem. Twenty-three regulations date to three periods, the oldest attributed to Ashur-uballit I (c.1365–1330 BC), and the last four to Tiglath-pileser I himself. Some concern the *king and members of the royal court, but others refer specifically to the harem.

The harem was the residence of the *queen mother, the king's wives, concubines and servants. It was a closed, segregated world with strict regulations where misconduct was severely reprimanded. *Eunuchs were the only men allowed access into the harem and even they could not approach within seven paces of a *woman, who had to be properly dressed. It was forbidden to have illicit contact with a harem woman, the penalty for both parties being death. The women were not allowed to give presents of *gold, *silver or precious *stones to *slaves. The edicts refer to the women fighting and arguing. However, if a man overheard the women quarrelling, he could be beaten or have an ear cut off. A harem woman was permitted to give her maid thirty strokes of the rod, but not to kill her. Many of the concubines gave birth to princes and princesses, who also lived in the palace, but the *children of the 'official' wife normally had priority in terms of succession. The edicts make it clear that members of the harem accompanied the king on journeys outside his *city.

There are some similarities between these edicts and certain *Hittite regulations, and certainly the harem as an institution continued into the Neo-Assyrian period. However, it is still debated whether the harem originated in the Middle Assyrian period or earlier. From the Old *Babylonian period there is no definite evidence for an organized harem, for eunuchs or for a system of segregating palace women, although the existence of a harem is sometimes assumed. It was once thought that harem women at *Mari were taken on without change by a usurping *dynasty, but it now seems that the women concerned were singers, although some scholars still think they may also have been royal concubines. A relief from *Ashurbanipal's North Palace at *Nineveh shows the king and queen feasting in the harem *gardens.    PB

G. CARDASCIA, 'Gesetze', *Reallexikon der Assyriologie* 3 (Berlin/New York 1957–71) 286–7.

S. DALLEY, *Mari and Karana: Two Old Babylonian Cities* (London 1984) 99–101.

J.-M. DURAND, 'Trois études sur Mari', *Mari: annales de recherches interdisciplinaires* 3 (1984) 127–80.

——, 'Les dames du palais de Mari à l'époque de Haute Mésopotamie', *Mari: Annales de Recherches Interdisciplinaires* 4 (1985) 385–436.

A.K. GRAYSON, *Assyrian Royal Inscriptions* 1 (Wiesbaden 1972) 46–7.

E.F. WEIDNER, 'Hof- und Harem-Erlasse assyrischer Könige aus dem 2. Jahrtausend v. Chr.', *Archiv für Orientforschung* 17 (1956) 257–93.

N. ZIEGLER, *Le harem de Zimri-Lim* (Paris 1999).

The Hasanlu Gold Bowl, c.800 BC, now in Tehran Museum. Width 28 cm. (University of Pennsylvania Museum, neg. S35-78114:25).

## Harran

Harran, 44 km south-east of Urfa in south-eastern Turkey, is one of the largest mounds on the north *Syrian plain. It is best known for its supposed links with the *Patriarch Abraham when, the *Mari texts attest, it was an important centre, already dedicated to the cult of *Sîn, the moon-god. In the seventh century BC, Ashurbanipal restored the temple and, according to *cuneiform texts, the mother of *Nabonidus was chief *priestess. Inscribed stelae re-used in the great mosque, recovered by T. Storm Rice, together with inscribed bricks and a tablet fragment discovered by N. Yardýmcý, suggest that the *temple lies below the mosque. Harran was taken over after 610 BC by the *Medes who, according to Nabonidus, allowed the temples to fall into disrepair.

Archaeologically very little is known about the pre-medieval levels at Harran itself, more being known from *Lloyd's excavations at nearby Sultantepe and new work at Kazane Höyük by P. Wattenmaker. Extensive excavations within the medieval city and intensive survey of the Harran plain have been carried out by Yardýmcý since 1983.    GDS

P.-A. BEAULIEU, *The Reign of Nabonidus King of Babylon* (New Haven, CN 1989).

O.R. GURNEY, 'Sultan Tepe and Harran', *Ancient Anatolia*, ed. R. Matthews (London 1998) 163–76.

S. LLOYD and W. BRICE, 'Harran', *Anatolian Studies* 1 (1951) 77–111.

J.N. POSTGATE, 'Harran', *Reallexikon der Assyriologie* 4 (Berlin/New York 1975) 122–5.

K. PRAG, 'The 1959 Deep Sounding at Harran', *Levant* 2 (1970) 63–94.

## Hasanlu

Hasanlu is the largest and most important mound site in the Solduz-Ushnu valley, close to the south-west corner of Lake Urmia, north-western *Iran. Soundings were first made by *Stein in 1936, followed by the Iranian archaeologists A. Hakemi and M. Rad. From 1956 to 1977 Robert H. Dyson Jr directed the Hasanlu Project which included examination of the settlement history over the entire valley from the *Neolithic to the

conquest by Alexander the Great. Other sites of note are Hajji Firuz Tepe and Dinkha Tepe. The most important level, Hasanlu IV, is *Iron Age and was violently destroyed around 800 BC. Amongst the burnt ruins were found skeletons of people and *horses, victims of the attack. Three men, two of whom were armed, apparently died while fleeing a burning building with the Hasanlu *Gold Bowl. Neither the ancient name of the *city nor the identity of the attackers has been determined.

Hasanlu itself comprises a High Mound, some 200 m in diameter and 25 m in height, and a Lower Mound, sometimes termed Citadel and Outer Town. The earliest level reached, Hasanlu VI, dates back to the mid second millennium BC. Hasanlu V, c.1450–1250 BC, is assigned to the period termed Iron I in western Iran. Level IV with three sub-phases, C–A, each destroyed by fire, spans Iron II, c.1250–750 BC. IIIB, equated with Iron III, ends around 600 BC, around the same time as the demise of *Urartu. Level IIIA extends through the *Median and *Achaemenid periods.

Hasanlu IVB provided a rich corpus of arms and armour, horse trappings, wheeled vehicles, *seals, personal ornaments and high-status objects. Architectural remains were well preserved, individual structures being termed Burned Buildings (BB). The principal form is the two-storeyed columned hall that develops from having a single portico and rooms along one side in Period IVC to more elaborate and symmetrical forms in VIB. No Period VIB defences were found, the 'Triple Road System' in fact being stables.

The *fortification wall, now properly assigned to Period III, represents Urartian domination under King Menua.    GDS

R.H. DYSON, JR. and M.M. VOIGT (eds), 'East of Assyria: The Highland Settlement of Hasanlu', *Expedition* 31/2–3 (1989).

S. KROLL, 'Ein "Triple Road System" oder "Stallbauten" in Hasanlu IV B?', *Archäologische Mitteilungen aus Iran* 25 (1992) 65–72.

O.W. MUSCARELLA, *The Catalogue of Ivories from Hasanlu, Iran*
  (Philadelphia, PA 1980).
I.J. WINTER, *A Decorated Breastplate from Hasanlu, Iran*
  (Philadelphia, PA 1980).

**Hassuna**   Hassuna is both a *Neolithic site and the type
site for one of the major *prehistoric cultures of northern
*Mesopotamia. It was excavated by *Lloyd and Fuad Safar
(1943–4).

The site is located in north Iraq just west of the Tigris
river, about 35 km south-west of *Nineveh. It is, therefore, in the rolling steppe of the dry farming zone of
north Mesopotamia. The mound covers approximately
3 ha and excavations revealed seven main phases of occupation.

The architecture consists mainly of rectangular buildings constructed of tauf (i.e. packed mud not mudbrick).
The buildings have adjacent courtyards and a main room
often with a series of very small rooms attached, these last
likely to be for storage.

Three main phases were distinguished at Hassuna.
An early phase, sometimes also characterized as Proto-
Hassuna, has similarities with perhaps somewhat earlier
*ceramics, best typified at Umm Dabaghiyah. In the
Archaic Hassuna, from Hassuna levels Ib–II, burnished
red painted ware vessels are more common; in later standard Hassuna neatly and elaborately incised ware is more
common. This sequence also established the contempo-
raneity of at least the later periods of the Hassuna with
the *Samarran culture to the south on the central Tigris
and Euphrates. Imported elaborately decorated Samarran pottery is present from Hassuna levels III–VI.

The common architecture, ceramics and other features of Hassuna culture, as defined at the type site, are
distributed across north Mesopotamia and can be dated
between 7000 and 6000 BC, preceding the development of
*Halaf material culture features out of the Hassuna.

The period is characterized by the proliferation of
sites on the open steppe of north Mesopotamia where few
preceding aceramic Neolithic sites are known. This may
be attributed to the successful adaptation to the moist
steppe plains of the relatively new mixed farming regime,
combining sheep and goat herding, *hunting of steppe
*animals, and wheat and barley cultivation.

In some ways these and other developments prefigure
the Halaf, although the evidence for specialization and
hierarchy is less clear. Exchange is represented at least
by imported Samarran pottery and *obsidian from
*Anatolia albeit in lower quantities than in the Halaf. Fine
stone vessels were manufactured and could be exchanged
(see Jarmo and Tell es-Sawwan). Small stone objects with
incised decoration might be *seals and point to very early
and limited *administrative practices.          DB

S. LLOYD and F. SAFAR, 'Tell Hassuna', *Journal of Near Eastern
  Studies* 4 (1945) 255–89.

**Hatti:** see Hittites

**Hattusas:** see Boghazköy

**Hattusilis**   Three *kings appear in the *Hittite records
with this name, meaning 'man of *Hattusas'. Only the first
and last are well known.

Hattusilis I (c.1650–1620 BC) made *Hattusas the
capital. His predecessors may have ruled at an unidenti-
fied place called Kussara. His '*annals' provide a detailed
account of his campaigns aimed to the north of Hattusas
and into north *Syria, which considerably extended
Hittite territory. Another important text known as the
'political testament of Hattusilis I' describes a plot by
his nephew whom the king had already designated as his
successor. The nephew was banished and Mursilis I,
Hattusilis' grandson, is presented as the new successor.

Hattusilis II (c.1410–1400 BC): his genealogy is uncertain but he appears to be one of the energetic rulers of
the early Empire period. There are a few inscriptions,
including *seal impressions, which can be dated securely
to his reign.

Hattusilis III (c.1275–1245 BC) describes his rise to the
throne in a long text known as the 'Apology'. He had
gained power and prestige through his appointment to a
province in the north by his brother, King Muwatalis. His
campaigns against various groups led to the recapture of
the capital city, Hattusas. When his nephew Urhi-Teshub
ascended the throne with the name Mursilis III, the new
king attempted to reduce his uncle's territory. Hattusilis
acted quickly and deposed and exiled Mursilis. He signed
a peace *treaty with the Egyptian King Ramesses II in
1259 BC of which both the Hittite and Egyptian versions
survive. *Diplomatic *marriages also took place between
the two powers, probably motivated by the increasing
threat of *Assyria.          PTC

O. GURNEY, *The Hittites*, rev. ed. (Harmondsworth 1990).
——, 'The Annals of Hattusilis III', *Anatolian Studies* 47 (1997)
  127–39.
P. HOUWINK TEN CATE, *The Records of the Early Hittite Empire
  (c. 1430–1370 BC)* (Leiden 1970).
J.G. MACQUEEN, *The Hittites* (London 1986).
H. OTTEN, *Die Apologie Hattusilis III: Das Bild der Überlieferung*
  (Wiesbaden 1981).
TH. P.J. VAN DEN HORST, 'The Apology of Hattusili I', *The
  Context of Scripture* 1, eds W.W. Hallo and K.L. Younger
  (Leiden 1997) 199–204.

**Hazor**   Tell el-Qedah, a site in *Palestine 14 km north of
the Sea of Galilee, was identified by J.L. Porter in 1875
with *biblical Hazor. Hazor is first mentioned in the
*Execration texts and in documents from *Mari which
show that it was involved in the *tin *trade with *Babylonia. It appears in *Egyptian lists of conquered *cities in
the Late Bronze Age, and in the *Amarna Letters, where
its *king is accused of joining the *habiru. In the *Old
Testament, Hazor is an important *Canaanite city
destroyed by the invading *Israelites; it was later rebuilt
by Solomon and conquered by *Tiglath-pileser III.

Hazor, excavated by *Garstang (1928), Yigael Yadin
(1955–8, 1968–9) and Amnon Ben-Tor (1990–), consists

Reconstruction of a Late Bronze Age shrine at Hazor. Several small stelae are guarded by a lion in relief (© The Israel Museum, Jerusalem).

of an upper city on the 12-ha mound occupied from the Early Bronze Age to the *Hellenistic period, and a large lower city of 70 ha occupied only in the Middle and Late Bronze Ages. The lower city was once regarded as an enclosure or camp for infantry and *chariotry, but it is now certain that it was a fortified built-up area.

Hazor was the largest city in Canaan in the Middle and Late Bronze Ages, with a population estimated at twenty thousand. The massive *defences, erected in the Middle Bronze Age and perhaps re-used, enclosed a *palace, domestic structures, *temples and *tombs; several *cuneiform tablets, one noting the arrival at Mari of livestock from Hazor, and an inscribed liver model reflect Hazor's Babylonian connection. The Late Bronze Age city suffered a massive destruction, with statues deliberately smashed. Several *Iron Age strata show the development of the fortified *Israelite city, with its citadel including a 'Solomonic' six-chamber gateway, residential quarters, workshops and stores. A *water system consisted of a shaft cut through rock leading to an underground spring. After a destruction attributed to *Tiglath-pileser III (734 BC), a series of citadels was constructed until the Hellenistic period, after which the site was abandoned. PB

A. BEN-TOR, Hazor 5 (Jerusalem 1997).
Y. YADIN, Hazor: The Head of All Those Kingdoms (London 1972).
——, Hazor: The Rediscovery of a Great Citadel of the Bible (London 1975).
Y. YADIN et al., Hazor 1–4 (Jerusalem 1958, 1960, 1961, 1989).
Y. YADIN and A. BEN-TOR, 'Hazor', The New Encyclopedia of Archaeological Excavations in the Holy Land, ed. E. Stern (Jerusalem 1993) 594–606.

**Hebrew**  The *language of *Israel and Judah is known from brief letters and accounts on *ostraca from the eighth to sixth centuries BC, from other short inscriptions and from the *Bible. The oldest biblical manuscripts are the Dead Sea Scrolls, copied between 200 BC and AD 67, but the earliest complete copies are only about a thousand years old, although they preserve many centuries of scribal tradition (the Massoretic Text) and show remarkably accurate copying over many centuries. Hebrew was written in a form of the *Canaanite *alphabet and so for centuries scribes marked only a few long vowels by using 'weak' letters (h, w, y), the system being extended in the *Hellenistic period and special signs to mark vowels of all values ('points') being created in the early Middle Ages. Many books within the Bible are written in Standard Biblical Hebrew, which probably represents the literary language of the kingdom of Judah. They contrast with books from the *Persian period (Ezra, Nehemiah, Esther, Chronicles) which display marked differences in grammar and syntax with noticeable *Aramaic influence which continues in the Dead Sea Scrolls and other documents of Hellenistic and *Roman times.

Hebrew belongs to the North-West *Semitic language group, being a form of Canaanite close to *Phoenician. Nouns have lost their case-endings, there is a prefixed definite article (ha-) and a relative pronoun 'ašer, in certain circumstances še. The suffixed verbal form marks the simple past (qātal), the prefixed form the imperfective (yiqtōl), but in narrative older uses survive, so that, when preceded by w, 'and', these forms appear to assume opposite roles ('waw conversive'). Subtle shifts of meaning are conveyed by varying use of verbal forms, particles and circumstantial clauses. Biblical Hebrew vocabulary reflects its Canaanite roots with grafts from many others, especially Aramaic from the north, for the country was never isolated, was open to invaders, *trade and migration. There are also Egyptian, *Assyrian and Persian loan words, the last being absent from books written in the Monarchy. ARM

E.Y. KUTSCHER, A History of the Hebrew Language (Leiden 1982).
R.C. STEINER, 'Ancient Hebrew', Semitic Languages, ed. R. Hetzron (London 1998) 145–73.
B.K. WALTKE and M. O'CONNOR, An Introduction to Biblical Hebrew Syntax (Winona Lake, IN 1990).
I. YOUNG, Diversity in Pre-exilic Hebrew (Tübingen 1993).

**Hellenistic period**  By 330 BC, Alexander the Great had defeated the *Achaemenid empire and conquered all its territories and even beyond. After his death in 323 BC the empire was divided among his army commanders, who reigned as governors and later as independent *kings. This is known as the Hellenistic period.

Initially, Seleucus ruled in *Babylon, Lysimachus in western *Anatolia, Antigonus Monophthalmus ('the One-Eyed') in the *Levant, northern *Mesopotamia and parts of Anatolia, and Ptolemy in Egypt. Antigonus was defeated at the battle of Ipsus in 301 BC, and his kingdom divided between Seleucus and Ptolemy; the Ptolemies ruled southern *Syria and *Palestine, known as Coele ('Hollow') Syria, until their defeat by the Seleucids at Paneion in 200 BC.

Seleucus defeated Lysimachus in 281 BC, acquiring western Anatolia, and extended his kingdom to the frontiers of *India. His successors, the Seleucid *dynasty, were more or less confined to the area of modern Syria through defeats by the *Romans and *Parthians and the reassertion of local dynasties. The kings of the Seleucid dynasty were all called Seleucus (I–IV) or Antiochus (I–XIII); they founded several *cities named after them Seleucia or Antioch. The Seleucid kingdom was annexed by Pompey in 64 BC to form the Roman province of Syria.

These dynasties made *Greek the normal *language of *administration and introduced Greek culture and *religion throughout their realms.                              PB

F.E. PETERS, *The Harvest of Hellenism: A History of the Near East from Alexander the Great to the Triumph of Christianity* (London 1972).

C. PRÉAUX, *Le monde hellénistique* (Paris 1978).

S. SHERWIN-WHITE and A. KUHRT, *From Samarkhand to Sardis: A New Approach to the Seleucid Empire* (Berkeley, CA 1993).

E. WILL, *Histoire politique du monde hellénistique (323–30 avant J.-C.)* (Nancy 1979).

## Herodotus (c.484–420 BC)

A Greek traveller and historian born at Halicarnassus in Asia Minor, Herodotus was called 'the father of history' by Cicero. Exiled for political reasons, Herodotus moved to Samos, then Athens, and finally to the Athenian colony of Thurii in southern Italy, where he died. Between 430 and 425 BC, he wrote nine books of *Histories* which are essentially a narrative account of the wars between the *Greeks and *Persians. He integrated into this account descriptions of events in different parts of the world that led up to the wars. To demonstrate the comparatively recent arrival of the Persians, he traced the background of all the peoples the Persians eventually absorbed, thus considering *Babylonia and *Assyria (and occasionally confusing them), Egypt, the *Levant and the *Anatolian states. His description includes history, anthropology and geography, written in a lively, dramatic style with elements of tragedy.

It is often difficult to correlate Herodotus' account specifically with historical evidence: his order of events is sometimes confused and some of his stories are obvious fiction. His sources were not necessarily reliable, and it is disputed how much of his information was derived from personal observation during travels and how much from informants. Some parts have been shown to be essentially accurate, for example his description of the layout of *Babylon, but others, especially descriptions of customs, seem to be influenced by how far other cultures deviate from the civilized norm of Greek social behaviour.

Herodotus' account of eastern history was superseded by that of Ctesias, a Greek doctor at the Persian court at the end of the fifth and beginning of the fourth century BC, who produced a twenty-three-volume work on Persian history, including three books on the Assyrian empire. Ctesias' version became the standard account by the third century BC and was followed by later compilers of universal histories, such as Diodorus Siculus, though his information was much less reliable than that of Herodotus.                                                      PB

J.A.S. EVANS, *Herodotus* (Boston, MA 1982).

F. JACOBY, *Griechische Historiker* (Stuttgart 1956) 7–164.

A. KUHRT, 'Ancient Mesopotamia in Classical Greek and Hellenistic Thought', *Civilizations of the Ancient Near East*, ed. J.M. Sasson (New York 1995) 57–60.

O.E. RAVN, *Herodotus' Account of Babylon* (Copenhagen 1932).

## Hesban

Tell Hesban is one of the most important and impressive archaeological sites in the *Transjordanian highlands. It is located near the north-eastern corner of the *Moabite tableland, c.55 km east of *Jerusalem and c.20 km south-west of Amman. The mound, which covers c.6 ha, occupies an excellent location in terms of *trade and *travel, *water resources, farmland and pasturage. Literary references and archaeological evidence reflect long-term occupation by a number of people groups, with only occasional gaps.

The tell was excavated by S.H. Horn and L.T. Geraty (1968–76), and a new phase of research was opened in 1996, under the direction of Ø.S. LaBianca. Excavations have recovered remains from nineteen strata, which stretch from c.1200 BC until c.AD 1500. On the basis of geographic and linguistic factors, Hesban is usually identified as ancient Heshbon, a name which appears thirty-eight times in the *Bible. Hesban's archaeological remains, like other well known sites (e.g. *Jericho, *Ai), do not seem to 'fit' the chronological constraints presented by biblical accounts. Specifically, the remains of an unfortified *village from c.1200 BC, the earliest on the site, do not correspond with what might be expected for the capital of the *Amorite *King Sihon of Heshbon (cf. Numbers 21). Various explanations are offered, including the possibility that Tell Hesban was not the location of Heshbon at the end of the Late Bronze Age.

The four *Iron Age strata, covering c.1200 to 500 BC, were damaged by later buildings. For most of its Iron Age history, the people at Tell Hesban lived in an unfortified village sustained by a mixed *agricultural and pastoral economy. A large plastered reservoir belongs to stratum 17 (ninth to eighth centuries BC); some have dated this pool to an earlier period and have linked it to a reference in the biblical Song of Songs 7: 4. Stratum 16 includes well preserved material from the seventh to sixth centuries BC; *ostraca and *pottery from this level point to *Ammonite occupation. According to biblical texts, control of Hesban passed between Amorites, *Israelites, Moabites and Ammonites.

After a long occupational gap through most of the *Persian and *Hellenistic periods, the site was settled in Late Hellenistic times. Tell Hesban was an important town in the Hellenistic and *Roman periods, when it became known as Esbus. Occupation continued through the Byzantine and Early and Middle Islamic periods, until the site was abandoned c.AD 1500. During the nineteenth century, settlement resumed around the base of the *tell, and this village continues today.                              GLM

L.T. GERATY, 'Hesban', *The Oxford Encyclopedia of Archaeology in the Near East* 3, ed. E.M. Meyers (New York 1997) 19–22.

——, 'Heshbon', *New Encyclopedia of Archaeological Excavations in the Holy Land*, ed. E. Stern (New York 1993) 626–30.

L.G. HERR, 'The Search for Biblical Heshbon', *Biblical Archaeology Review* 19 (1993) 36–7, 68.

A. LEMAIRE, 'Heshbôn=Hisbân', *Eretz-Israel* 23 (1992) 64–70.
D. MERLING and L.T. GERATY (eds), *Hesban after 25 Years* (Berrien Springs, MI 1994).

## Hesi, (Tell el-)

Tell el-Hesi is an imposing site located in the transitional zone where the northern *Negev, coastal plain and the Shephelah meet. It lies c.26 km north-east of Gaza, c.23 km from the Mediterranean Sea. Today, the site consists of a 10-ha terrace between tributaries of Wadi Hesi, and a higher mound that covers some 1.5 ha. Much of the latter was cut away in the excavations of 1891–2. The oldest known reference to 'Hesi' dates to the Crusades. Its ancient name is unknown, although scholars of previous generations identified it as *Lachish or Eglon. The most recent excavations indicate that this site was occupied almost continuously from the *Chalcolithic to the *Hellenistic periods; *Roman sherds and *Palaeolithic remains have been found in the immediate vicinity.

The first period of excavation ran from 1890 to 1892, when 'Hesy' was dug by *Petrie and F.J. Bliss. Petrie established here the foundation of the methodology used in Syro-Palestinian *archaeology to this day. He explored a 'section' of the mound exposed by erosion and established the principles of ceramic typology and stratigraphic excavation. The Joint Archaeological Expedition completed the second phase of excavation in eight seasons (1970–83).

Chalcolithic remains are not numerous here, but Early Bronze Age occupation covered the entire site. Hesi was apparently abandoned during Early Bronze III, and no structures from the Middle Bronze Age were found, although some Middle Bronze Age sherds have turned up. The Late Bronze Age settlement was substantial, and Bliss recovered a *cuneiform tablet from the *Amarna period in his 'City III'. Evidence from Iron I was minimal, but in the ninth century BC the entire 'acropolis' (or upper *tell)

Tell el-Hesi looking north-west in 1973. Petrie's pioneering work in 1890 was on the sheer face on the right.
The modern excavations of the Joint Expedition can be seen on the left (courtesy of J.A. Blakely, photograph by W. Nassau).

was surrounded by an impressive wall. Hesi's Iron II occupation came to an end in the sixth century BC, perhaps at the hands of the *Babylonians. The site continued to play a military role in the *Persian and Hellenistic periods.                                    GLM

F.J. BLISS, *A Mound of Many Cities, or, Tell el Hesy Excavated* (London 1894).
B.T. DAHLBERG and K.G. O'CONNELL (eds), *Tell el-Hesi: The Site and the Expedition* 4 (Winona Lake, IN 1989).
V. M. FARGO, 'Hesi, Tell el-', *New Encyclopedia of Archaeological Excavations in the Holy Land*, ed. E. Stern (Jerusalem 1993) 630–4.
W.M.F. PETRIE, *Tell el Hesy (Lachish)* (London 1891).
L.E. TOOMBS, 'The Joint Archaeological Expedition to Tell el-Hesi and the Results of the Earlier Excavations', *Palestine Exploration Quarterly* 122 (1990) 101–13.

## Hieroglyphic scripts

The *Greek term 'priestly signs' was applied to ancient Egyptian writing as it was supposedly used only for religious purposes. It is now extended to any script of pictorial signs. The basic idea of drawing a picture to represent each object or concept inevitably produces large numbers of signs (as in Chinese). Discovery of the rebus principle (see Writing) helped to overcome the problem in *Babylonian (see Cuneiform) and to a great extent in Egyptian, but there the pictorial shapes were retained and could have the value of their representations until the end of the script's life. Several scripts used a restricted number of hieroglyphs as shorthand signs for common words ('king', 'woman' etc.).

On Crete from about 1750 BC *seals and clay tablets bear signs called 'Cretan Hieroglyphs', although they may be syllabic. They are unread. The 'Linear A' and 'Linear B' scripts of the following centuries may be derived from them. Linear B retained a number of such hieroglyphs or ideograms.

In *Anatolia the *Hittites used a hieroglyphic script about the middle of the second millennium BC which was probably invented for the Luwian *language in the west of the country under the influence of Egyptian. There are about 150 signs for frequent words (some never written syllabically, so their Luwian forms are unknown and they are represented in Latin by Hittitologists) and sixty syllabic signs, mostly for a consonant plus a vowel, which were used to spell out words. Inscriptions of the Hittite empire period (c.1400–1200 BC) are found on seals and a few monuments. From the Neo-Hittite states of southern Anatolia and northern *Syria in the period 1100–700 BC there are many more monuments and some documents engraved on lead strips. In the eighth century BC the script was used occasionally for writing *Urartian.

At *Byblos about 1500 BC some *scribes invented a script of 114 signs (called 'pseudo-hieroglyphic') which have some similarities with Egyptian and which are probably a syllabary, although the handful of inscriptions has not been convincingly deciphered.                        ARM

J.D. HAWKINS, 'Writing in Anatolia: Imported and Indigenous Systems', *World Archaeology* 17/3 (1986) 363–75.

Drawing of a Hittite Hieroglyphic inscription of Uratamis, son of Urhilina, king of Hamath, mid ninth century BC. The hand and arm at the top right mean 'I am' with a sign for the phonetic complement -mi, part of the Hittite word, below (drawing by courtesy of David Hawkins).

J.J. KLEIN, 'Urartian Hieroglyphic Inscriptions from Altintepe', *Anatolian Studies* 24 (1974) 77–94.

J.P. OLIVIER, 'Cretan Writing in the Second Millennium B.C.', *World Archaeology* 17/3 (1986) 377–89.

## Hilprecht, Hermann Vollrat (1859–1925)

Although born in Germany, Hermann Hilprecht became one of the foremost American Assyriologists of the nineteenth century, but his arrogance involved him in bitter controversies which harmed his reputation and eventually caused his resignation.

Hilprecht excavated at *Nippur (1888–1900), and established his name with the publication of the Old *Babylonian inscriptions in 1893: the beauty and accuracy of his copies and his skill as a translator were recognized immediately, setting high standards for the future. The so-called Peters–Hilprecht controversy (1905–8) was started by J.P. Peters' allegation that Hilprecht had exaggerated his claims of finding a *temple *library at Nippur and had deliberately falsified the provenance of tablets. The 'library' had actually been unearthed by John Henry Haynes, field director of the Nippur excavations, who was left broken in health and spirit by Hilprecht's attempts to discredit him. Hilprecht was also accused of keeping for himself tablets and artefacts donated by the Ottoman Sultan to the University of Pennsylvania Museum. Although a committee exonerated Hilprecht, another dispute concerning his publication of a tablet that he claimed confirmed the *biblical *Flood story forced him to resign from the university in 1911.　　　　PB

H.V. HILPRECHT, *Old Babylonian Inscriptions Chiefly from Nippur* (Philadelphia, PA 1893).

——, *The So-called Peters-Hilprecht Controversy* (Philadelphia, PA 1908).

——, *The Earliest Version of the Babylonian Deluge Story and the Temple Library of Nippur* (Philadelphia, PA 1910).

B. KUKLICK, *Puritans in Babylon: The Ancient Near East and American Intellectual Life, 1880–1930* (Princeton, NJ 1996).

R.L. ZETTLER, 'Hilprecht, Hermann Vollrat', *The Oxford Encyclopedia of Archaeology in the Near East 3*, ed. E.M. Meyers (New York 1997) 26–7.

## Hissar, (Tepe)

Located on the rich and fertile delta of the Damgahan *river as it debouches from the Elburz mountains into the desert of central *Iran, Tepe Hissar is one of the most significant late *Chalcolithic and Early Bronze Age urban sites in north-central Iran. Hissar's importance lies in its location on the *prehistoric east–west *trade route that later became known as the Great Khorasan Road, and is underscored by an adjacent *Sasanian *palace and a later fortress or caravanserai. Large-scale and productive excavations were undertaken by Erich Schmidt for the University of Pennsylvania in 1931–2. Several brief studies of surface remains were followed, in 1976, by re-examination of the site by a joint expedition from the University of Pennsylvania, Turin University and the Iranian Center for Archaeological Research.

Originally substantially larger, today the mound covers only some 400 by 400 m, c.12 ha. It has been greatly denuded by wind and water. Above the earliest level examined, Hissar I extending from the late fifth millennium BC to c.3600 BC, Schmidt recognized two major phases of settlement, IIA–B and IIIA–C. Re-study has brought some refinement and greater complexity to Schmidt's fundamentally correct assessment. Of particular importance is the evidence for *copperworking, probably including production of *tin *bronzes, and for the manufacture of *stone *jewellery. Some of the latter was of semi-precious lapis lazuli, a soft blue mineral all of which appears to have come to the ancient Near East from the mountains of Afghanistan, much presumably passing through Tepe Hissar where a certain amount was retained for local workshops. It might be suggested that tin from Turkmenistan came into northern *Mesopotamia via the same route.

Tepe Hissar is crucial to the debate concerning the date of arrival of *Indo-European tribes into Iran and the direction from which they came. Introduction of monochrome black and grey burnished *pottery in a range of new forms in Hissar IIA has been linked to the later appearance of grey ware in western Iran and thus with the Indo-European migration. At Hissar, however, the new grey ware styles go hand in hand with the older painted tradition. Whether the new pottery can be seen to represent the infiltration of a new ethnic element is uncertain.　　　　GDS

R.H. DYSON, JR and S.M. HOWARD (eds), *Tappeh Hesar: Reports of the Restudy Project 1976* (Florence 1989).

E.F. SCHMIDT, 'Tepe Hissar Excavations 1931', *The Museum Journal* 23/4 (1933) 324–483.
——, *Excavations at Tepe Hissar, Danghan* (Philadelphia, PA 1937).

**Historiography** Arranging and correlating accounts of past events with some explanation of cause and effect is commonly held to be a Greek achievement, descending from *Herodotus, 'the father of history'. However, a variety of ancient Near Eastern texts indicate there were some who had the same aim much earlier. *Assyrian *annals are primarily *autobiographical and report episodes within individual reigns, rarely referring to what happened earlier: they justify the *kings' actions because vassals rebel, by breaking a *treaty, or enemies attack, although their responses may be specified as the results of divine commissions. Some Assyrian texts list kings of Assyria and *Babylonia synchronically, adding the names of their viziers, for unknown purposes. The *Eponym Chronicle, a form known as early as the eighteenth century BC, is also a factual list of officials and events. Another Assyrian text, the Synchronistic History, reporting clashes between Assyria and Babylonia and consequent frontier changes, has been taken as a form of history writing, but is better understood as a collection of notices from the *boundary stelae. Closer to modern concepts of history writing is the 'Weidner Chronicle', an account in the form of a *letter to an Old Babylonian king explaining how a long series of rulers from Agga of *Kish (see Gilgamesh) onwards had met with disaster, sometimes at the hands of foreigners (notably *Naram-Sin and the *Guti) because they neglected the cult of *Marduk at *Babylon. The propagandist purpose of this text is obvious. A sequence of factual reports, sometimes of events in other countries, characterizes the Babylonian *Chronicle, highly valued by modern historians, although its ancient purpose is unknown. In fact, many Babylonian 'historical' records may have been preserved for use in compiling lists of *omens. Although mention of ominous signs is very rare in the Chronicle texts, historical notices are appended to observations of movements of heavenly bodies from the sixth century BC onwards, suggesting the link.

Relating past events to explain the present frequently formed the introduction to *Hittite treaties, giving the reasons for their conclusion, often at some length and with representation of the thoughts and speech of the parties concerned. This practice is even more pronounced in the 'Apologies' in which Hittite kings (Telepinu, *Hattusilis III) defend their assumption of the crown.

Israelite writers composed consecutive histories of their people unique in the ancient Near East, aware of the continuity of events in a way other nations were not. The rise and fall of *Israel and Judah are chronicled in a style basically similar to Assyrian and *Aramaean royal inscriptions, but impersonally, like the Babylonian Chronicle. The organizing scheme of the 'Deuteronomic' history (seen in the Books of Deuteronomy, Joshua, Judges, Samuel, Kings) is the covenant between God and his chosen nation, a concept not far removed from the view of Assyria as the nation of *Ashur with its king the intermediary responsible to the god. Criteria of judgement for the ancient writers were loyalty to the divine rule and performance of the divine commands. Where *Hebrew writers differed from their contemporaries was in the concept of a single god in control of events, who had a purpose in view and revealed his will to his people, whereas the gods of other nations acted to maintain a current situation or to change it at their individual whims, people suffering because of divine quarrels.

Ancient Near Eastern historiography accepts divine intervention in human affairs as normal. Today's historians do not, but that does not mean that ancient narratives involving supernatural occurrences should be dismissed as unhistorical, for the records still report things that happened, even if the writers could, or did, not explain them in modern terms. Ancient history writing usually had propagandist aims, but, when that is recognized, the narratives themselves are basic historical sources which, where independent witnesses are available, almost always show themselves to reflect events, rather than to be literary or theological inventions. The temptation to judge ancient texts by current fashions has to be resisted.                                                        ARM

B. ALBREKTSON, *History and the Gods* (Uppsala 1967).
G.A. BECKMAN, *Hittite Diplomatic Texts* (Atlanta, GA 1996).
A.K. GRAYSON, 'Assyria and Babylonia', *Orientalia* 49 (1980) 140–94.
H.A. HOFFNER, JR, 'Histories and Historians of the Ancient Near East: The Hittites', *Orientalia* 49 (1980) 283–332.
W.G. LAMBERT, 'Destiny and Divine Intervention in Babylon and Israel', *Oudtestamentische Studiën* 17 (1972) 65–72.
V.P. LONG, *The Art of Biblical History* (Grand Rapids, MI 1994).
A.R. MILLARD, J.K. HOFFMEIER and D.W. BAKER (eds), *Faith, Tradition and History* (Winona Lake, IN 1994).
H. TADMOR and M. WEINFELD (eds), *History, Historiography and Interpretation: Studies in Biblical and Cuneiform Literatures* (Jerusalem 1983).

**Hittites** A people of *Indo-European origin, the Hittites entered *Anatolia probably c.2300 BC and in the centuries that followed became one of the greatest powers of the ancient Near East. The first definite evidence of their presence is Hittite names in texts from Old *Assyrian colonies in Anatolia dating to c.1920–1740 BC. Our name 'Hittite' derives from their own geographical name for central Anatolia, *hatti*, derived from their predecessors, the Hattians. Most information about Hittite society and history comes from thousands of clay tablets excavated from their capital, *Hattusas. Three distinct *languages, written in *cuneiform and *hieroglyphic scripts, were used by Hittite populations – Hittite (which they called Neshite), Luwian and Palaic – although many words were borrowed from the pre-existing local population and from surrounding peoples.

Hittite history begins with the establishment of the Old Kingdom (c.1700–1400 BC) first at a *city named Kussara, then at Hattusas. Two of its kings, *Hattusilis I and Mursilis I, campaigned to the south and east, the

Pendant figure of a god wearing typical Hittite conical hat, short coat and upturned shoes. From the Boghazköy area. Gold, height 2.5 cm. 1400–1200 BC. WA 126389.

latter sacking *Babylon c.1595 BC and ending its first *dynasty. After his death there was a period of internal weakness, ending with a new line of kings from c.1400 BC, referred to as the Hittite New Kingdom or Hittite Empire period. Its kings, notably *Suppiluliumas I and Hattusilis III, campaigned extensively in *Syria, conquering *Mitanni and fighting against the *Egyptians. Hatti became one of the great powers, in *diplomatic and *trade contact with other great kings. After the battle of *Kadesh, Hattusilis III signed a *treaty with Ramesses II and gave him a Hittite princess in a diplomatic *marriage.

The empire fell when Hattusas was destroyed c.1200 BC; it is unknown who was responsible, although the *Sea Peoples are sometimes proposed. Parts of the royal family survived in provincial centres, especially *Carchemish, and founded local Neo-Hittite dynasties based on individual city-states. These, together with neighbouring *Aramaean states with whom they were often in conflict, were eventually absorbed into the Neo-*Assyrian empire.

PB

T. BRYCE, *The Kingdom of the Hittites* (Oxford 1998).

O.R. GURNEY, *The Hittites*, rev. ed. (London 1990).

H.A. HOFFNER, JR, 'Hittites', *Peoples of the Old Testament World*, eds A.J. Hoerth, G.L. Mattingly and E.M. Yamauchi (Grand Rapids, MI 1994) 127–55.

J.G. MACQUEEN, *The Hittites and their Contemporaries in Asia Minor*, rev. ed. (London 1986).

**Horse** Wild equids are known from *Palaeolithic sites in the ancient Near East, and the domestic horse reached the area from the Eurasian steppe in the third millennium BC. However, bones of horses, donkeys and onagers from archaeological excavations cannot always be distinguished, and they are often identified generally as equids.

The *Sumerian term for horse means 'donkey of the mountains', but horses were never used much for *agriculture or *transport. Their main use was for drawing *chariots, though mounted cavalry was developed in the first millennium BC. Proper saddles, stirrups and horseshoes were unknown, though saddle blankets were used. Depictions from *Mesopotamia suggest that the first horse riders sat towards the back, as on a donkey. Horses were originally controlled by a nose-ring attached to a single cord, as for cattle, but true bits appeared around the sixteenth century BC, made of *bronze and later *iron.

At first, mounted cavalry were used only as scouts or messengers, and they appear lightly armed in representations. Earlier *Assyrian cavalry rode in pairs, with one soldier controlling both horses, leaving the other free to use his bow. Later, new types of bridles meant that a rider could let go of the reins and use his *weapon, and henceforth cavalry became a proper fighting unit. Reliefs show that most Assyrian horses wore ornaments on their heads and necks, and occasionally breastplates or coats of mail. The Assyrians required large numbers of horses, and often listed them as part of war booty. An *archive from *Nineveh records the receipt of horses from all around the empire. Large horses used for chariots came from Egypt and Nubia, and a small breed ideal for cavalry from the north and north-east, particularly *Urartu.

Ancient texts record interest in the breeding, health and handling of horses. From *Nuzi come horse genealogies; a *Kassite archive from *Nippur concerns the registration and use of horses; a *Hittite text and Middle Assyrian ones contain instructions for the handling of horses; a text from *Ugarit discusses the treatment of *diseases in horses, giving prescriptions echoed later in a *Roman handbook. Horses and other equids were *ritually *buried throughout the ancient Near East, in Mesopotamia and the *Caucasus with humans and wheeled vehicles, and in the *Levant occasionally accompanying human burials, especially in the Middle Bronze Age.

PB

M.A. LITTAUER and J.H. CROUWEL, *Wheeled Vehicles and Ridden Animals in the Ancient Near East* (Leiden/Cologne 1979).

R.H. MEADOW and H.-P. UERPMANN (eds), *Equids in the Ancient World*, 2 vols (Wiesbaden 1986, 1991).

D. PARDEE, *Les textes hippiatriques* (Paris 1985).

The value Assyrians placed on horses is indicated by the attention to their grooming given in this relief from Ashurnasirpal II's palace at Nimrud. c.865 BC. WA 124548.

**Houses** The earliest houses so far discovered in the Near East date to the eighth millennium BC in *Mesopotamia and the *Levant, and are round or oval single-room structures built of mud and stone. Caves or rock shelters were also used as houses throughout antiquity, although often little evidence remains inside them. There is a great variety of house plans, from round to rectangular, single to multi-room, with some subterranean, but in the fourth millennium BC in Mesopotamia the courtyard house was introduced. This has an open central courtyard with rooms on one, two, three or four sides. Buildings with courtyards soon became the basis for most ancient Near Eastern architecture, including houses, *temples and *palaces. Later they formed the basis for Islamic architecture and are still used in the Near East today.

The enclosed courtyard provided light, air and a shady place during the long hot summers. Larger houses had more than one court. Many houses probably had an upper storey, which does not often survive archaeologically and so its plan is unknown. Stairs of *wood or brick led to the upper storey or the roof, where occasionally *rituals were performed. There is evidence that often the ground floor was used for *shops, workshops, storage and livestock, with the upper storey for dining, sleeping and entertaining. Kitchens can be identified by ovens, and in Mesopotamia and occasionally elsewhere the houses of the rich had bathrooms and toilets, sometimes with pottery drains. One room occasionally served as a sanctuary, and *tombs are found under the floors of houses at *Ugarit, *Ur, *Mari and throughout Mesopotamia. Inventories in *inheritance and dowry documents give information about *furniture; in the Old *Babylonian period, for example, one table and four chairs were standard. Artificial light was provided by *pottery lamps using oil and flax wicks. Window openings do not often survive, but are depicted on *ivory plaques and on terracotta models of houses. Windows were of course unglazed, but might have grilles of wood or baked clay.

Most houses were built of sun-dried mudbrick on two or three layers of *stone foundations; in stone-rich areas, like southern *Transjordan, houses were often entirely of stone (see Building materials). A typical floor was trodden earth, occasionally plastered or paved with stone. Walls were often plastered. The ceiling and flat roof were made of wooden beams and reeds packed together with earth and straw. The Ugaritic poem about *Aqhat recounts that it was the job of the sons of the *family to plaster the roof with mud to prevent seepage of *water during the rainy season. House-building was a craft profession (see Craftsmen), but people often also did their own construction work.

In Mesopotamian *cities, houses were built in solid blocks with neighbouring houses sharing party walls. Texts record disputes about property rights to the shared wall (see Property ownership and inheritance), and house-sale *contracts provide for this eventuality. Beams and doors made of date-palm wood were considered precious parts of the house, and often specific doors are listed in sale or inheritance texts. To protect the inhabitants *magically, small statues were often buried beneath the outer door or inside, in the toilet and bedroom.    PB

O. AURENCHE, *La maison orientale: L'architecture du Proche Orient ancien des origines au milieu du quatrième millénaire* (Paris 1981).

P.M.M. DAVIAU, *Houses and their Furnishings in Bronze Age Palestine: Domestic Activity Areas and Artefact Distribution in the Middle and Late Bronze Ages* (Sheffield 1993).

J.S. HOLLADAY, 'Syro-Palestinian Houses', *The Oxford Encyclopedia of Archaeology in the Near East* 3, ed. E.M. Meyers (New York 1997) 94–114.

A. KEMPINSKI and R. REICH (eds), *The Architecture of Ancient Israel* (Jerusalem 1992).

E.C. STONE, 'Mesopotamian Houses', *The Oxford Encyclopedia of Archaeology in the Near East* 3, ed. E.M. Meyers (New York 1997) 90–4.

K.R. VEENHOF (ed.), *Houses and Households in Ancient Mesopotamia* (Istanbul/Leiden 1996).

Reconstruction of typical Old Babylonian house at Ur, c.1800 BC.

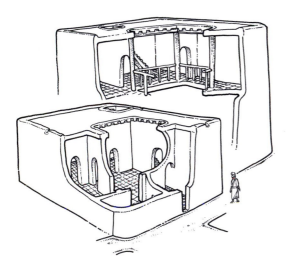

**Humour and wit** A full range of humour and wit survives from the ancient Near East, largely from *Mesopotamian texts. *Letters, *stories, *myths and *school texts often contain jokes or humorous passages. The range and type of humour is characteristic of all human societies.

Laughter can be provoked by referring to basic bodily functions such as excretion, flatulence and urination: a *Sumerian expression alludes to a girl breaking wind in her marital bed, an example of humour breaking taboos. An *Akkadian parody refers to a meal of hot bread and donkey anus stuffed with dog turds and fly dirt. There are many stories where an apparently more dignified person is outwitted by someone less important. This is a form of social satire, providing humour through the usual pleasure of seeing someone's comeuppance and the triumph of the underdog. An ostensibly learned man asks directions to a house, is answered by a *woman in Sumerian, the *language of learning and scholarship, but fails to recognize it; the moral is that this ignoramus should be run out of town.

*Sex of course was a favourite subject, but becomes meaningful only in a context of the usual privacy and prudery; wedding songs and 'love lyrics' are uninhibited and ribald, the latter sometimes mocking. One lover puts a watchbird in his girlfriend's vulva, telling it not to peck at the fungus and to avoid the stench of her armpits. Some humour verges on slapstick, for example contradictory statements in a buffoon's routine, such as 'Stealing is an abomination to me, whatever I see does not stay where it was'.

*Animal caricatures, in which animals are satirically represented carrying out human activities, are well known in Mesopotamia and Egypt. These might be linked with animal stories and debates, like the *Babylonian debate between a dog and a fox in which the dog praises its own importance to humans. Some types of jokes appear to have survived virtually unchanged into modern times, particularly the ethnic joke, made at the expense of a misunderstood minority. Sumerians joked about the barbarous *Amorites who knew none of the benefits of civilization, and the *Old Testament is full of satirical *Hebrew *wordplays concerning the ancestry of their neighbours.

A profession called *aluzinnu* seems to refer to jesters or clowns, whose *songs and routines, known from texts, appear very similar to those of modern stand-up comedians.

Modern books on the ancient Near East occasionally state that its peoples were fatalistic and religious and lacked humour, but this is quite wrong. No society has ever been without humour, although it can sometimes be difficult to interpret exactly what was intended to be humorous in antiquity. It is occasionally unclear whether a passage is meant to be humorous or should be read at face value.                                                         PB

B.R. FOSTER, 'Humor and Cuneiform Literature', *Journal of the Ancient Near Eastern Society of Columbia University* 6 (1974) 69–85.
——, 'Humor and Wit – Mesopotamia', *Anchor Bible Dictionary* 3, ed. D.N. Freedman (New York 1992) 328–30.
——, 'Humor and Wit in the Ancient Near East', *Civilizations of the Ancient Near East*, ed. J.M. Sasson (New York 1995) 2459–69.

## Hunting

**Hunting** For the earliest hunter-gatherers in the ancient Near East, hunting was a necessity in order to acquire *food. Little evidence survives of *prehistoric hunting, except for flint arrow- and spearheads that were originally attached to *wooden shafts; *wall paintings at *Çatalhöyük depict various species of *birds and *animals, including a large red bull, associated with many human figures dressed in spotted loincloths, who may be hunters.

Later, hunting, especially of lions, became a symbolic activity of *kings, to promote a royal image of bravery and victory against fierce beasts. Already in the late fourth

Ashurbanipal's palace at Nineveh included several lion-hunt scenes. This 'dying lion' belonged to a series of small-scale reliefs in an upper storey. Height 16.6 cm. WA 1992.4-4.1.

Hunting scenes occur on Uruk-period seals. The upper seal is engraved with a design of dogs attacking lions. Height 2.9 cm. WA 89356.

The lower seal shows an archer hunting ibex, two crossed lions and two hunting dogs. From Nineveh (Kuyunjik), height 3.6 cm. WA 123348.

millennium BC, a stela from *Uruk depicts two scenes of a king killing a lion with a spear and with a bow and arrow, and similar scenes appear on *cylinder seals. The *Mari *letters record the capture of wild lions intended for the royal hunt. *Tiglath-pileser I claimed that during one hunt he killed four wild bulls, ten elephants and 920 lions, 800 from his *chariot and 120 on foot.

The royal hunt became a standard scene on Neo-*Assyrian *palace reliefs, especially those of *Ashurbanipal from *Nineveh. The king was portrayed hunting lions and bulls with spear and bow from a chariot or on horseback, or killing them at close range with a sword. The reliefs show various stages in the hunt: lions are released from cages, leap at the king, and are killed. Sometimes large numbers of lions, wild asses and gazelles are driven into nets or towards a pit where the king is hiding. Some of the most vivid and poignant Assyrian reliefs depict hunted lions in the throes of death. The purpose was not only to show the king's prowess but to demonstrate his protective powers and to make an offering to the *gods, and the king is depicted pouring libations over dead lions. Inscriptions accompanying these reliefs describe the terror of tributary kings who were forced to take part in the hunt. The hunt took place in a large park where onlookers, including *women, could watch from the top of a mound while eating their picnics. The tradition of the royal hunt continued under the *Achaemenid kings, depicted in carvings at *Persepolis and on *cylinder seals. Scenes of non-royal people hunting a variety of animals appear in most periods on cylinder seals.                                                                                                PB

J.K. ANDERSON, *Hunting in the Ancient World* (Berkeley, CA 1985).

——, 'Hunting', *The Oxford Encyclopedia of Archaeology in the Near East* 3, ed. E.M. Meyers (New York 1997) 122–4.

R.D. BARNETT, *Sculptures from the North Palace of Ashurbanipal at Nineveh, 668–627 B.C.* (London 1976).

D. COLLON, *First Impressions: Cylinder Seals in the Ancient Near East* (London 1987) 154–7.

——, *Ancient Near Eastern Art* (London 1995) 152–6.

A. SALONEN, *Jagd und Jagdtiere im alten Mesopotamien* (Helsinki 1976).

E. WEISSERT, 'Royal Hunt and Royal Triumph in a Prism Fragment of Ashurbanipal (82-5-22,2)', *Assyria 1995*, eds S. Parpola and R.M. Whiting (Helsinki 1997) 339–58.

**Hurrians** The Hurrians were an ethnic group present in the ancient Near East from the third to the first millennia BC, whose kingdom of *Mitanni became one of the great powers rivalling *Egypt and *Hatti. Their material culture is difficult to characterize, apart from *Nuzi Ware and Mitannian *seals, and they are best attested through their *language, which is known from Hurrian tablets and personal names from many second-millennium BC sites.

Hurrian was mostly written in *cuneiform except for a few texts in the *Ugaritic *alphabetic script. The longest Hurrian text, and the key to the language, is one of the *Amarna Letters written by Tushratta of Mitanni to Amenophis III of Egypt. Hurrian is non-*Indo-Euro-

'Nuzi Ware', first discovered in quantity at Nuzi, is found from the Zagros to the Mediterranean on sites of the mid second millennium BC, and is often associated with the Hurrians. These examples were found at Alalakh. Height of beaker 21.5 cm. WA 125993–4.

pean, and the only other language to which it might be related is *Urartian.

The earliest Hurrian names appear on tablets dating to the *Akkadian period, which testify to Hurrian rule of small states in north and north-east *Mesopotamia, such as Urkesh. *Kings of the *Ur III *dynasty campaigned against them, and Hurrian names were borne by high officials in conquered areas or by prisoners of war. Over the following centuries they expanded south and into the *Levant, appearing in texts from *Mari, *Emar, *Alalakh, *Ugarit and elsewhere. The Hurrian kingdom (or confederation of kingdoms) of Mitanni became one of the great powers of the region in the fifteenth century BC. After the decline of Mitanni, the Hurrians came under Hittite and *Assyrian rule. Hurrian rulers are still attested in north-east *Mesopotamia in the twelfth century BC, and Hurrian names are known there as late as the mid first millennium BC.

Hurrian social, economic and religious practices are best attested in the archives from *Nuzi, which had a predominantly Hurrian population. It appears that the Hurrians were ruled by an Indo-European military aristocracy skilled in the use of *chariots. This elite was known as *maryannu*, which probably comes from the Indo-European word *marya*, 'young man or warrior'. Much of the Hurrian *religion was taken over by the Hittites, including their chief deity, the weather god *Teshup. Other Hurrian *gods were adopted from the Mesopotamian pantheon. An important part of their religious practices were *magical *rituals accompanied by incantations.                                                                       PB

G. WILHELM, *The Hurrians* (Warminster 1989).

**Hyksos** 'Hyksos' is the *Greek form of the Egyptian phrase *heqa khasut*, meaning 'rulers of foreign lands'. Manetho, who wrote a history of *Egypt in the third century BC, used 'Hyksos' to describe the rulers of the Fifteenth Dynasty (c.1650–1550 BC).

The Hyksos Fifteenth Dynasty ruled the eastern Delta of Egypt and at least part of Upper Egypt from their capital at Avaris, identified with Tell ed-Dab'a. The material culture at this and other Delta sites is a mixture of *Levantine and Egyptian features, with *temples, *metalwork and *pottery similar but not identical to *Canaanite types, and donkey sacrifices outside *tombs as at some sites in *Palestine. Scarab *seals of typically 'Hyksos' type and other Egyptian objects found on many Palestinian sites demonstrate connections between the Fifteenth Dynasty and the Middle Bronze Age *city-states of the Levant. *Wall paintings at Tell ed-Dab'a show links with Minoan Crete, like similar examples from *Alalakh.

The Hyksos were expelled from Egypt by the kings of the Seventeenth and Eighteenth Dynasties, who pursued them as far as Sharuhen, probably to be identified with Tell el-'Ajjul on the coast of southern Palestine. 'Ajjul may have been a Hyksos stronghold and *trading centre. The destruction and abandonment of many other Palestinian towns at the end of the Middle Bronze Age is often attributed to the Egyptian army's pursuit of the Hyksos, but this is difficult to prove.

Although contemporary texts from Egypt refer to *heqa khasut*, often the Fifteenth-Dynasty kings were called specifically 'Asiatics'. Hyksos names appear to be West *Semitic, not Egyptian. Archaeological and documentary evidence suggests that the ethnic origins of the Hyksos lie in the Middle Bronze Age Levant.     PB

M. BIETAK, *Avaris: The Capital of the Hyksos* (London 1995).

W.V. DAVIES and L. SCHOFIELD (eds), *Egypt, the Aegean and the Levant: Interconnections in the Second Millennium* BC (London 1995).

B.J. KEMP, 'Old Kingdom, Middle Kingdom and Second Intermediate Period *c.* 2686–1552 BC', *Ancient Egypt: A Social History*, eds B.G. Trigger *et al.* (Cambridge 1983) 149–74.

E. OREN (ed.), *The Hyksos: New Historical and Archaeological Perspectives* (Philadelphia, PA 1997).

D.B. REDFORD, *Egypt, Canaan, and Israel in Ancient Times* (Princeton, NJ 1992) 98–129.

C.A. REDMOUNT, 'Pots and Peoples in the Egyptian Delta: Tell El-Maskhuta and the Hyksos', *Journal of Mediterranean Archaeology* 8/2 (1995) 61–89.

J. VAN SETERS, *The Hyksos: A New Investigation* (New Haven, CN 1966).

## Hymns and prayers

**Hymns and prayers** Elaborate hymns and formal (rather than impromptu) prayers were an important feature of *temple cult in ancient *Mesopotamian *religion. Hymns addressed to deities form a considerable part of the surviving *Sumerian *literature. In addition there are so-called 'royal hymns', in which praise of a deity is incorporated with a prayer to the deity for the health and well-being of a named deified *king. These were performed in the lifetime of the kings and copied after their deaths. From an early date, hymns are also addressed to temples, praising them as centres of worship and as beautiful and sacred buildings. Numerous Sumerian *šu-ila* and *er-ša-hunga* prayers were recorded, the latter intended 'to calm the heart' of the deities addressed. In *Akkadian, similar genres are attested, extensive collections of *šuillakku*, prayers 'of the raising of the hand(s)' (a gesture which accompanied the act of prayer).

*Magical and *medical *rituals also often contain prayers which must be performed either by the magician or by the patient, to ensure functioning of the magic.

Because of the *Hittite king's important position in the cults of various deities, some of the hymns and prayers which are preserved are specifically worded for the king himself to perform.

In the west *Ugarit has yielded one brief prayer embodied in a short ritual and the *Keret *epic describes prayer. From the first millennium BC comes the extensive collection of 150 hymns and prayers in the *Hebrew *Bible's Psalms which can be categorized basically as hymns of praise and personal thanksgiving, *lamentations, blessings and cursings, and royal and *wisdom compositions. The Bible and inscriptions such as the *Aramaic stela of Zakkur of *Hama report prayers and divine answers.     JAB/ARM

A. FALKENSTEIN and W. VON SODEN, *Sumerische und akkadische Hymnen und Gebete* (Zurich/Stuttgart 1953).

H. GUNKEL, *The Psalms: A Form-critical Introduction* (Philadelphia, PA 1967).

O.R. GURNEY, 'Hittite Prayers of Mursili II', *Liverpool Annals of Archaeology and Anthropology* 27 (1940) 3–163.

A. LIVINGSTONE, *Court Poetry and Literary Miscellanea*, State Archives of Assyria 3 (Helsinki 1989) 3–27.

M.-C. LUDWIG, *Untersuchungen zu den Hymnen des Išme-Dagan von Isin* (Wiesbaden 1990).

D. PARDEE, 'Ugaritic Prayer for a City Under Siege (RS 24.266)', *The Context of Scripture* 1, eds W.W. Hallo and K.L. Younger (Leiden 1997) 283-5.

W.H.P. RÖMER, *Sumerische 'Königshymnen' der Isin-Zeit* (Leiden 1965).

Å. SJÖBERG, *The Collection of the Sumerian Temple Hymns* (Locust Valley, NY 1969).

# I

## Igigi

**Igigi** Igigu or Igigi is a term of unknown origin first encountered in the Old *Babylonian period as a name for the (ten) 'great gods'. While it sometimes kept that sense in later periods, from Middle Babylonian times on it is generally used to refer to the *gods of heaven collectively, just as the term *Anunnakku was later used to refer to the gods of the *underworld. In the *Epic of *Creation, it is said that there are 300 Igigu of heaven.     JAB

B. KIENAST, 'Igigu und Anunnakku nach den akkadischen Quellen', *Studies in Honor of Benno Landsberger*, ed. H.G. Güterbock (Chicago 1965) 141–58.

——, 'Igigu', *Reallexikon der Assyriologie* 5 (Berlin/New York 1976) 40–4.

W. VON SODEN, 'Die Igigu-Götter in altbabylonischen Zeit', *Iraq* 28 (1966) 140–5.

## Illuyanka

**Illuyanka** The serpent Illuyanka was a *Hittite *monster whose *myth formed the introduction to a Hittite seasonal *festival celebrated at Nerik, the cult centre of the storm-god Zaliyanu. Two versions of the myth are preserved on one tablet, both dictated by a *priest called Kella. Both versions involve a human ally for the storm-god. In one, the god is first defeated by Illuyanka, but then kills him with the help of a human enlisted by a goddess in return for *sexual favours. In the second story, Illuyanka has weakened the storm-god by taking his heart and eyes. The storm-god then has a son by the human daughter of a poor man; their son, in turn marries Illuyanka's daughter and returns his father's heart and eyes. The storm-god goes into battle again, and kills Illuyanka and his own son. It has been suggested that these myths reflect a real historical conflict between the Hittites (the storm-god) and their traditional enemies, the Kashkaeans (Illuyanka).                              PB

G. BECKMAN, 'The Anatolian Myth of Illuyanka', *Journal of the Ancient Near Eastern Society of Columbia University* 14 (1982) 11–25.

H. GONNET, 'Institution d'un culte chez les Hittites', *Anatolica* 14 (1987) 88–100.

H.A. HOFFNER, JR, *Hittite Myths* (Atlanta, GA 1990) 10–14.

**Ilu:** see El

**Imdugud:** see Anzû

**Inana:** see Ishtar

**Incense and spices** Gums and spices from many *plants were burned as incense in the ancient Near East to produce a sweet smell, or were ingredients in *medicine and *cosmetics. The most valued and expensive were frankincense and myrrh, which grew in south *Arabia and east Africa. These became important *trade products along the so-called 'incense route' between south Arabia and the *Levant. The bark of the *trees was incised and the 'tears' of resin collected when dry, and in this form they were easily *transported. Ancient texts often do not specify the exact type of incense, so it is not always certain that 'incense' means frankincense from south Arabia. Other trees which produced incense grew in *Anatolia, the Levant and *Mesopotamia. *Egyptian inscriptions record tribute of incense sent from *Syria, and two of the *Amarna Letters list oil of myrrh as gifts from Tushratta of *Mitanni to the Egyptian *king.

Between the hawk and the winged ibex on this Achaemenid cylinder seal stands an elaborate incense burner, its tall lid secured by a chain. Height 2.7 cm. Fifth century BC. WA 128865.

Offerings of incense were part of the daily cult in Mesopotamian *temples, and were used at *festivals, like the *New Year festival at *Babylon. A text associated with a golden incense *altar in the temple of *Marduk at Babylon specifies that its purpose was to purify and to ask the *god for forgiveness. *Ashurbanipal's *prayer to *Shamash states that the gods inhaled incense. Mesopotamian medical texts refer to the use of incense, and it was also part of *magic *rituals, apparently to please the gods. *Omens were read from the movement of incense smoke. Other resins, particularly pine resins, were used as sealants for the insides of *wine jars. Spices extracted from plants are mentioned in Mesopotamian culinary texts as *food flavourings.

Incense used in ritual contexts was burned on charcoal on special altars, and sprinkled using censers and shovels. Cuboid incense burners inscribed with names of incense materials are known from south Arabia, and many similar objects have come from sites in the Levant, dating between the eighth and fifth centuries BC, although the type is much older. Tall incense burners, probably of *metal, appear on *seals and reliefs from the second half of the second millennium BC onwards.                     PB

N. GROOM, *Frankincense and Myrrh: A Study of the Arabian Incense Trade* (London 1981).

A.B. KNAPP, 'Spice, Drugs, Grain and Grog: Organic Goods in Bronze Age East Mediterranean Trade', *Bronze Age Trade in the Mediterranean*, ed. N.H. Gale (Jonsered 1991) 21–68.

K. NIELSEN, 'Incense', *Anchor Bible Dictionary* 3, ed. D.N. Freedman (New York 1992) 404–9.

W. ZWICKEL, *Räucherkult und Räuchergeräte* (Göttingen 1990).

**India** Prior to the *Persian period, ancient Near Eastern contacts with India are best attested in the third and early second millennia BC. A country called Meluhha, now normally identified as the Harappan civilization of the Indus Valley, appears in texts together with *Dilmun and *Magan as a wondrous country alongside the 'Lower Sea' south of *Babylonia. Its name was still used as part of his title by *Esarhaddon in the seventh century BC. In *myths, Meluhha was regarded as a source of *silver and *gold. In economic texts it was certainly one of the most easterly countries trading with Babylonia. It was a source of *wood, gold, *ivory and carnelian, although some goods probably originated elsewhere but came via Meluhha. It was accessible by sea, since *Sargon of *Akkad boasts that *ships from Meluhha docked at Akkad.

Archaeologically, contact with Meluhha is reflected by characteristic Harappan inscribed square *stamp seals found in *Mesopotamia at *Babylon, *Kish, *Ur, Tell Asmar and *Nippur and in *Iran at *Susa, and Harappan cuboid *weights and *pottery are known from Susa and *Oman. The Indus Valley script on these seals was probably stimulated by Mesopotamian and *Elamite *writing.

There is no doubt that the contact was direct, involving at least the presence of Meluhhans in the Near East. A toponym dating to the Ur III period refers to a 'Meluhha village' in the territory of *Lagash which may represent a settlement of people from the Indus Valley. A

Characters of the 'Indus Valley' script, still undeciphered, on a seal from Harappa, c.2000 BC. OA 1912.6-29.1.

*cylinder seal of a 'Meluhha translator' indicates that the *language of Meluhha was unintelligible to Babylonians. However, there is little evidence of Babylonian presence in the Indus Valley, although locally made cylinder seals and some Mesopotamian motifs are attested.

Urban society in the Indus Valley declined after c.1900 BC, and it appears that close contacts with the Near East were re-established only during the expansion of the *Persian empire and the campaigns of Alexander the Great.　　　　　　　　　　　　　　　　　　　　　PB

W. HEIMPEL, 'Meluhha', Reallexikon der Assyriologie 8 (Berlin/New York 1993) 53–5.
D.T. POTTS, 'Distant Shores: Ancient Near Eastern Trade with South Asia and Northeast Africa', Civilizations of the Ancient Near East, ed. J.M. Sasson (New York 1995) 1451–63.
S. RATNAGAR, Encounters: The Westerly Trade of the Harappan Civilization (Delhi/Oxford 1981).
J.E. READE (ed.), The Indian Ocean in Antiquity (London 1996).

**Indo-European** The Indo-European *languages form the largest linguistic family in the world, including most modern European languages but also ancient languages such as Greek, Latin, the *Anatolian group (*Hittite, Luwian, *Lydian, *Lycian) and Indo-Iranian or Aryan languages (e.g. Sanskrit, *Persian). All these languages have close grammatical similarities in the structure of nouns and verbs, and many similar words: for example, 'daughter', Tochter (German), thugatéra (Greek), dokhtar (Persian), is first documented as duatra in thirteenth-century BC Anatolia.

The earliest attested Indo-European elements are found in Hittite, dating to c.2000 BC. In recent years there has been much scholarly debate concerning the original homeland of Indo-European, based on the assumption that it was once a single language whose origin can be traced by projecting backwards from its later dialects. The current consensus is that this single language, so-called 'common Indo-European', may have originated in the Black Sea area ('Pontic–Caspian region') in the Late *Neolithic period, c.5500–4500 BC, and may have started to diverge into several languages by 2500 BC. This consensus is based on the observation that all Indo-European languages or dialects share words reflecting the 'Neolithic revolution', especially *agriculture and domestication of *animals.

Attempts have been made to correlate the pattern of the spread of Indo-European with *archaeology, for example the spread of many distinctive cultural features from the Pontic–Caspian region into Europe and Asia. However, scholars now agree that linguistics and archaeology work with different types of data and that archaeological evidence such as *pottery styles cannot be used to reconstruct language patterns. The archaeological evidence does not completely support the linguistic hypothesis of a spread of Indo-European from the Pontic–Caspian region, but that may be because language change and cultural change are not synchronous.　　PB

D.W. ANTHONY, 'The Archaeology of Indo-European Origins', Journal of Indo-European Studies 19 (1991) 193–222.
T.V. GAMKRELIDZE and V.V. IVANOV, Indo-European and the Indo-Europeans: A Reconstruction and Historical Analysis of a Proto-language and a Proto-culture, ed. W. Winter (Berlin 1995).
J. MALLORY, In Search of the Indo-Europeans (London 1989).
G. WINDFUHR, 'Indo-European Languages', The Oxford Encyclopedia of Archaeology in the Near East 3, ed. E.M. Meyers (New York 1997) 149–58.
N. YOFFEE, 'Before Babel: A Review Article', Proceedings of the Prehistoric Society 56 (1990) 299–313.

**Indus Valley:** see India

**Inheritance:** see Property ownership and inheritance

**Iran** Modern Iran lies between the Caspian Sea and the Persian Gulf. Its central plateau is surrounded by mountains, the *Zagros in the west, the Elburz and Kopet in the north, and a barren region of peaks and desert in the east. The central and eastern parts of the central plateau are two huge salt deserts where settlement is almost impossible. The densest ancient settlement was always in western Iran, which had close contacts with *Mesopotamia. Important *prehistoric sites include *Ali Kosh, *Ganj Dareh, Tepe *Giyan, Tepe *Guran, Tepe *Hissar, *Susa and Tepe *Yahya. From the third millennium BC, south-west Iran was called *Elam, until the arrival of the *Medes and *Persians in the first millennium BC, and later the *Parthians and *Sasanians.

There is often confusion between use of the terms 'Iran' and 'Persia' to refer to the country. Until 1935 the official name was Persia, although strictly speaking this should be used only for the modern province of Fars (ancient Parsa). The name was changed to Iran as a politi-

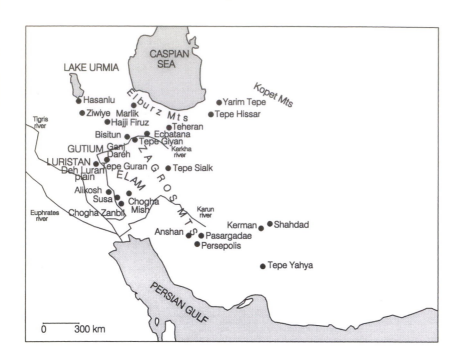

Map of Iran, showing principal ancient sites.

cal decision by the founder of the Pahlavi dynasty to identify his country ethnically as Aryan, as part of a policy of modernization. The name 'Iran' comes from Old Iranian *aryanam khshathram*, meaning 'land of the Aryans', which became Modern Persian *Iranshahr*, shortened to *Iran*. The Aryans were an *Indo-European people. 'Aryan' derives from the term *arya*, which might mean 'noble', and was used by the *Achaemenid King Darius I, in the Zoroastrian books and in the Vedas, Indian religious writings; eventually it referred specifically to the western Aryans, that is, the Iranians.                                    PB

R.N. FRYE, *The History of Ancient Iran* (Munich 1984).

**Iron**  Although iron (*Akkadian *parzillu*) became common only during the first millennium BC, it is mentioned in second-millennium BC texts from *Mari, *Nuzi and *Bogazköy and even earlier in the Third Dynasty of *Ur. Knowledge of iron ores probably originated through their use as pigments, for example red ochre. Although early iron objects were once thought to be made of meteoric iron, it appears more likely that iron was first produced as a by-product of *copper smelting, through the use of iron oxides as fluxing agents. Iron objects are recorded from contexts as early as the fourth millennium BC at *Uruk and Jebel Aruda, and occur as 'exotica' in high status *Bronze Age *graves including *Alaca Hüyük and the tomb of Tutankhamun.

The techniques employed in the production of iron artefacts were different from those required to work copper. The high melting point of iron (1534°C) rendered casting impossible, and iron objects had to be individually shaped by hot forging. Wrought iron is not obviously superior to *bronze in terms of hardness or cutting edge. However, it can be hardened by quenching the hot object in cold water, followed by tempering, reheating to at least 150°C to avoid brittleness, and by carburization. The latter is the process whereby hot iron in contact with charcoal absorbs carbon to produce steel. Although carburized iron was superior to bronze, it is not clear to what extent early smiths could control the process. In a *letter to *Adad-nirari I of *Assyria, the *Hittite *King *Hattusilis III comments that 'it is a bad time for making iron'. A collection of tenth-century BC artefacts from Taanach in *Palestine includes both carburized and uncarburized examples of otherwise similar artefacts.

Iron sources are more numerous and accessible than those of copper, and its adoption may have owed as much to matters of cost and availability as to technical factors. In the *Levant and *Cyprus, the emergence of iron as a utilitarian metal took place between the twelfth and tenth centuries BC. The evidence from *Mesopotamia is less

By the eighth and seventh centuries BC iron was extensively used for armour. This iron helmet decorated with bronze bands was found at Nimrud. Height 30.8 cm. WA 22496.

clear, and there is little archaeological iron from *Assyria predating the late eighth century BC, although its frequency within the lists of tribute taken by Neo-Assyrian rulers attests to its importance. There has been little scientific work on iron sources in the ancient Near East, although ores occur in north-west *Iran, in *Anatolia and near Ajlun in *Jordan. The replacement of bronze by iron as a utilitarian material was a gradual process, but, once established, iron was preferred for *weapons, tools and construction work, while bronze was retained for certain categories of object. GP

P.T. CRADDOCK, *Early Metal Mining and Production* (Edinburgh 1995).

P.R.S. MOOREY, *Ancient Mesopotamian Materials and Industries: The Archaeological Evidence* (Oxford 1994).

J.D. MUHLY, 'Mining and Metalworking in Ancient Western Asia', *Civilizations of the Ancient Near East*, ed. J.M. Sasson (New York 1995) 1501–21.

O.W. MUSCARELLA, *Bronze and Iron: Ancient Near Eastern Artifacts in the Metropolitan Museum of Art* (New York 1988).

T.A. WERTIME and J.D. MUHLY, *The Coming of the Age of Iron* (New Haven, CN 1980).

The scenery on one of Sennacherib's reliefs from Nineveh includes men lifting water from one channel to another with water-sweeps. WA 124820.

**Iron Age** The Iron Age is the third age of the 'three age system' of Stone, Bronze and Iron Ages (see Bronze Age). In the ancient Near East, the term 'Iron Age' is applied systematically only in *Anatolia, *Iran and the *Levant, where it dates c.1200–500 BC and is further subdivided. In the Levant it includes the period of the kingdoms of *Israel, Judah, *Ammon, *Moab, *Edom, *Aram and the *Phoenician states, in Anatolia the Neo-*Hittite kingdoms and the kingdoms of *Urartu, *Phrygia, *Lycia, *Lydia and *Caria, and in Iran the Neo-*Elamite period. It is contemporary with the Neo-*Assyrian and Neo-*Babylonian periods in *Mesopotamia. The term 'Iron Age' is now largely an abstract chronological concept, since it is clear that *iron was already being made before the start of the Iron Age proper, and that use of *bronze for *tools and weapons continued. PB

**Irrigation** The earliest farming communities were in areas of natural rainfall, in northern *Mesopotamia and the *Levant, where little control of the *water supply was required. Large-scale artificial irrigation first developed in the late fourth millennium BC in *Sumer, where complex canal systems fed by the Tigris and Euphrates *rivers, supplemented by natural rainfall, were associated with the growth of the state.

Sumerian irrigation essentially consisted of two elements: strong dikes to protect the fields against the wild spring river floods, and long canals exploiting gravitational flow to run water on to the land. Water was not usually lifted up to fields, although the water-sweep or *shaduf*, a device for raising water, is attested in Mesopotamia from early times. The major canal systems drew water from the Euphrates and flowed east to the Tigris.

The best written documentation on irrigation is a *school text from the *Ur III period, a farmer's almanac in which a ploughman instructs his son about grain farming practice through the year. Fallow fields were irrigated in summer in preparation for weeding and ploughing, followed by four irrigations after sowing in the autumn. There was a network of larger and smaller canals, each watercourse bordered by thin strip fields.

Canals were essential for food production and transport and so were state-controlled. The building and maintenance of canals was a regular boast of Mesopotamian *kings throughout history. The *Mari *archives too include correspondence of governors concerned with canals, water control and irrigation. Stipulations in *law codes show that canals were also the legal responsibility of landowners and cultivators. Old *Babylonian *mathematical texts calculate the volumes of water from different sources necessary to irrigate fields to a certain depth. The Sumerian irrigation system depended on regular maintenance of canals and dikes. Salinization of soils due to intensive irrigation was certainly a problem, and is often cited as the main factor in the decline of the system, although political instability was perhaps as important a cause.

In other areas, water control depended on collecting run-off rain water, for example at Jawa in *Transjordan in the Early Bronze Age with a system of catchment basins, dams and gravity canals, and in the *Negev in the first millennium BC where run-off water was collected in cisterns. In *Iran from *prehistoric times the *qanat* was used, a horizontal tunnel carrying water from the mountains, a system eventually introduced into *Egypt by the *Persians and into *Arabia at some unspecified date, perhaps as early as the beginning of the first millennium BC. PB

R.Mc. ADAMS, *Heartland of Cities: Surveys of Ancient Settlement and Land Use on the Central Floodplain of the Euphrates* (Chicago 1981).

C.J. EYRE, 'The Agricultural Cycle, Farming, and Water Management in the Ancient Near East', *Civilizations of the Ancient Near East*, ed. J.M. Sasson (New York 1995) 175–89.

T. JACOBSEN, *Salinity and Irrigation Agriculture in Antiquity* (Malibu, CA 1982).

J.-R. KUPPER, 'L'irrigation à Mari', *Bulletin on Sumerian Agriculture* 4 (1988) 93–104.

M.A. POWELL, 'Evidence for Agriculture and Waterworks in Babylonian Mathematical Texts', *Bulletin on Sumerian Agriculture* 4 (1988) 161–71.

J. RENGER, 'Rivers, Water Courses, and Irrigation Ditches and Other Matters Concerning Irrigation Based on Old Babylonian Sources, 2000–1600 B.C.', *Bulletin on Sumerian Agriculture* 5 (1990) 31–46.

**Ishtar** The *goddess named in *Sumerian Inana or Innin and in *Akkadian Eshtar or, later, Ishtar, goddess of *sex and *war, was the most important female deity in ancient *Mesopotamia in all periods. Her Sumerian name is thought to derive from an earlier conjectured form Nin-ana 'Lady of Heaven'. The sign for the name occurs in the earliest written texts. The Akkadian name is probably connected with that of the South *Arabian god Athtar or Ashtar and the *Syrian goddess Ashtart, *Astarte or Athtart, *biblical Ashtoreth, with whom Ishtar was certainly connected. The name is first found as an element in (male and female) personal names of the *Sargonic period. The goddess at this time was already equated with Sumerian Inana, who may originally have been a separate deity. Probably several separate local deities – including the Inanas of the cities of *Uruk, Zabala, *Akkad and *Kish, as well as the *Assyrian Ishtars of *Nineveh and Arbela (Erbil) – by syncretism formed the goddess's personality. Originally the term Ishtar may have designated the planet Venus; as the morning star, this planet was a male god, and, as the evening star, a goddess. In Assyria and *Babylonia the two deities were combined into a single deity – female, but retaining 'masculine' traits, especially as goddess of war. Beyond this, elaborate explanations have been offered for Ishtar's seemingly irreconcilable aspects as deity of love and war – yet her province was physical love and war, and if we substitute the words 'sex' and 'violence' the apparent contradiction disappears, even to our own cultural modes of thought. No tradition ascribes to her a permanent spouse, nor, with the possible exception of the god Shara, any children. *Dumuzi (biblical Tammuz) is often described as Ishtar's 'lover', but has an ambiguous relationship with her; she is finally responsible for his death.

In *art, Inana is usually shown as a warrior goddess, often winged, sometimes also betraying by her evocative posture and state of dress her role as goddess of sex and prostitutes. In Neo-Assyrian and Neo-Babylonian art a female, shown full frontal and nude or nude from the waist down, wearing a horned cap indicating divinity is probably Ishtar in more clearly sexual aspect. The goddess's sacred *animal was a lion, her *divine symbol a star or star-disk, sometimes perhaps a rosette.          JAB/AG

H. BALZ-COLCHOIS, *Inana: Wesenbild und Kult einer unmütterlichen Göttin* (Gütersloh 1992).

The goddess Ishtar, dressed for war, stands on her animal, the lion, on a finely engraved Neo-Assyrian cylinder seal. A worshipper stands before her, with two goats and a palm tree behind, and an earring above. Height 4.3 cm. WA 89769.

G. COLBOW, *Die kriegerische Ištar: Zu den Erscheinungsformen bewaffneter Gottheiten zwischen der Mitte des 3. und der Mitte des 2. Jahrtausends* (Munich/Vienna 1991).

B.R.M. GRONEBERG, 'Die sumerisch-akkadische Inanna/Ištar: Hermaphroditos?', *Welt des Orients* 17 (1986) 25–46.

——, *Lob der Ištar: Gebet und Ritual an die altbabylonische Venusgöttin* (Groningen 1997).

H.L.J. VANSTIPHOUT, 'Inanna/Ištar as a figure of controversy', *Struggles of Gods*, eds H.G. Kippenberg et al. (Berlin 1984) 225–38.

C. WILCKE, 'Inanna/Ištar', *Reallexikon der Assyriologie* 5 (Berlin/New York 1976–80) 74–87.

**Isin** The *city of Isin in southern *Mesopotamia first came to prominence when Ishbi-Erra, an official of the Third Dynasty of *Ur, founded the First Dynasty of Isin c.2017 BC and came to control most of what had been the core of Ur's empire. For the next two hundred years the *dynasty attempted to retain its territory against rival city-states, principally *Larsa and *Babylon. Isin's conquest by Larsa c.1794 BC was commemorated by a number of *lamentations in which the divine Lady of Isin (Nin-Isina) mourns the fate of the city. The legacy of the First Dynasty of Isin includes the *law code of Lipit-Ishtar, the fifth ruler, and the oldest example of the use of a substitute *king. According to the *Babylonian *Chronicle, the ninth ruler, Erra-imitti, died in his *palace 'when he sipped a hot broth'. He was replaced by the subsitute he had appointed, a gardener, Enlil-bani, who retained the throne and eventually had himself deified.

The Second Dynasty of Isin was not founded until the twelfth century BC, coming to power after the *Elamites defeated the *Kassites and seized the cult statue of *Marduk from *Babylon. Ruling principally from Babylon, the most famous king of the dynasty, *Nebuchadnezzar I, invaded Elam, sacked *Susa and retrieved the statue.

Isin was identified with modern Ishan al-Bahriyat, 20 km south of *Nippur, by K. Stevenson in 1923, and excavated by A.T. Clay and S. Langdon (1924) and B. Hrouda (1973–89). The ruins cover about 1.5 sq km in a marshy area that was surrounded by water until the beginning of the twentieth century (the modern name means 'high point of the lakes'). Traces of occupation go back to the *Ubaid period. A *temple to Gula, the goddess of healing, and her husband *Ninurta, is on the highest part of the *tell, with a staircase of nineteen steps leading to the main entrance. It was probably founded in Early Dynastic times (c.2700 BC), used primarily in the Kassite period and last restored by Nebuchadnezzar II. It is surrounded by a wall founded by Ishme-Dagan of Isin in the nineteenth century BC and rebuilt in the Kassite period. The excavations uncovered a possible administrative or palatial building and an *archive of about eighty *cuneiform tablets, among them notes of deliveries to the lucky substitute king, Enlil-bani.          PB

B. HROUDA (ed.), *Isin-Išan Bahriyat* 1-4 (Munich 1977–92).

## Israel and Judah

The early *Iron Age saw various tribal groups in lands of the *Levant which had been divided between the many Late Bronze Age *city-states. Israel and Judah occupied much of the former *Egyptian province of *Canaan, developing into the kingdom of Israel in the eleventh century BC. Under the second *king, David, Israel's power reached its peak, while the 'great powers' of *Assyria and Egypt were in decline, controlling territories east of the Jordan down to Aqaba and the tract from *Damascus to the Euphrates, with *Hamath and *Tyre in peaceful alliance. Solomon, his son, built magnificently in *Jerusalem, but gradually lost the foreign subjects, the kingdom dividing after his death into Israel and Judah. Israel extended from the foot of Mount Hermon to Bethel, just north of Jerusalem, along the coast from Mount Carmel to Joppa and into *Transjordan south of Galilee to the north of the Dead Sea. Judah was much smaller, its eastern border being the Dead Sea, its western the *Philistine cities, the *Negev forming its southern territory. Both kingdoms suffered Pharaoh Shishak's invasion c.926 BC, which reached as far north as *Megiddo.

Israel never enjoyed long periods of peace or stability. Of its twenty kings, none was succeeded by more than four generations, *palace revolts and conspiracies breaking the lines. Significant kings were Jeroboam I (c.931–910 BC), who broke away from David's line, setting up cult centres at Dan and Bethel to replace Jerusalem, and Omri, who made *Samaria the capital, giving his name to the ruling house, and married his son Ahab to the Tyrian princess Jezebel. Ahab joined *Aram-Damascus against *Shalmaneser III, but the kings of Damascus from Ben-Hadad II to Rezin were Israel's major foe, trying to reduce it to a province. Assyria's expansion from 875 BC onwards brought it into contact with Israel, Assyrian inscriptions naming the ancestor of the dynasty Omri, Ahab, Jehu, Jehoash, Menahem and Hoshea in the order and at the chronological points which correlate with their appearance in the *Hebrew histories in the *Bible. Jeroboam II (c.782–753 BC) extended Israel's rule to the frontier with Hamath after a period of weakness, but Assyria's advancing power incorporated Samaria into its provincial system in 720 BC.

In the southern highlands and foothills, Judah was poor and less liable to attack, although Israel was frequently hostile and wars occurred. Ahaz (c.732–716 BC) is the earliest king named in Assyrian texts, paying tribute to persuade *Tiglath-pileser III to attack his enemies (2 Kings 16: 5–9; 2 Chronicles 31: 16–21), Damascus and Samaria. His son Hezekiah (c.716–687 BC) broke the agreement, precipitating *Sennacherib's attack in 701 BC, an event reported in his *annals, depicted in his reliefs at *Nineveh, related in the Bible (2 Kings 18: 13–19: 26; 2 Chronicles 32: 1–21) and attested in excavations (e.g. at *Lachish). Hezekiah submitted to Sennacherib, Judah paying tribute for several decades (his son Manasseh (c.687–642 BC) is named in records of *Esarhaddon and *Ashurbanipal) until Josiah (c.640–609 BC) asserted independence as Assyria weakened, only to be killed opposing Pharaoh Necho. In Judah's last three decades, its kings vacillated between loyalty to Egypt and to *Babylon, suffering from each, especially *Nebuchadnezzar II, who ended its kingdom in 586 BC.

The history of Israel and Judah is known in greater detail than that of any other Iron Age kingdom in the Levant because the selective accounts in the Books of Samuel, Kings and Chronicles became part of the Bible. Their obvious religious interests are like much ancient Near Eastern reporting and do not diminish their values as sources for the historian seeking to reconstruct ancient events. The narratives depict the careers of two small kingdoms which can be seen to exemplify the fates of most contemporary states in the Levant, eventually falling under the yoke of Assyria or Babylon.

The material culture implied by the texts and revealed by excavation belongs to a largely rural community, with a capital (Samaria, Jerusalem), a few major towns (*Hazor, Hebron, Megiddo) and numerous *villages and hamlets. At various times there were frontier fortresses, best known in the Negev. Building was done with field *stones and mudbrick, the stones sometimes roughly squared for doorways, corners and pillars, and carefully worked as ashlar masonry for official buildings. *Houses commonly followed the 'four room' or 'Israelite' plan, but most work was done outside. Walled towns had one or more *gates and, wherever possible, a *water supply inside; at Gibeon, Hazor and Megiddo large shafts were cut with steps leading to underground sources, and Jerusalem was supplied by 'Hezekiah's tunnel'. *Pottery vessels were well formed, usually plain, black, buff or red-

Handle of a storage jar from Lachish. Such jars were often stamped with seals bearing a four-winged scarab or a two-winged device (as here). Above is the Hebrew word 'royal' (*lmlk*) and below the name of one of four places, here Socoh (*šwkh*). The production of these jars is associated with the administration of Judah under King Hezekiah at the end of the eighth century BC. Width of seal 3.5 cm. WA 160142.

brown; they might be burnished, but decoration was rare. *Bronze vessels and, presumably, *silver and *gold graced the dwellings of the rich. Little trace of real wealth is found, apart from the *ivory *furniture decorations in the palace at Samaria. Small quantities of silver *jewellery – finger rings, earrings, bangles – and a very few gold pieces have come from *burials. *Seals and *ostraca illustrate the use of *writing and *administration. Terracotta *figurines of *women and *animals may be relics of popular religious practices, but the national cult of *Yahweh has left no indisputable material remains.  ARM

J. BRIGHT, *A History of Israel* (London 1972).

J.H. HAYES and J.M. MILLER (eds), *Israelite and Judaean History* (London 1977).

B.S.J. ISSERLIN, *The Israelites* (London 1998).

T.C. MITCHELL, 'Israel and Judah until the Revolt of Jehu (931–841 B.C.)', *Cambridge Ancient History* 3.1, 2nd ed. (Cambridge 1982) 442–87.

——, 'Israel and Judah from Jehu until the Period of Assyrian Domination (841– c.750 B.C.)', *Cambridge Ancient History* 3.1, 2nd ed. (Cambridge 1982) 488–510.

——, 'Israel and Judah from the Coming of Assyrian Domination until the Fall of Samaria and the Struggle for Independence in Judah (c. 750–700 B.C.)', *Cambridge Ancient History* 3.2, 2nd ed. (Cambridge 1991) 322–70.

——, 'Judah until the Fall of Jerusalem (c. 700–586 B.C.)', *Cambridge Ancient History* 3.2, 2nd ed. (Cambridge 1991) 371–409.

**Ivory carving**  Ivory was used throughout the Near East for small-scale carvings and *furniture decoration. Until the end of the second millennium BC, most ivory came from hippopotami, which were common in the *Levant, elephant ivory being restricted to prestige objects. In the first millennium BC, elephant ivory was used almost exclusively, although sources of the material are uncertain because it is difficult to differentiate between the ivory of African, Indian (Asian) or local '*Syrian' elephants after centuries of burial (see Animals). *Egyptian and *Assyrian kings hunted elephants in north Syria, but they were extinct by the mid first millennium BC. *Cuneiform texts from *Ur dating to about 2000 BC mention ivory obtained from Meluhha (the Indus Valley: see India).

The Levant was always the main area of ivory production, beginning in the *Chalcolithic period with stylized, elongated standing human *figurines from the *Beer Sheba area. *Anatolia also had a long tradition of ivory carving. From Açem Höyük and *Kültepe, dating to the nineteenth and eighteenth centuries BC, come ivory figurines, decorated boxes and furniture fittings, some overlaid with *gold leaf, with a mixture of Egyptian, *Hittite and *Mesopotamian influences. Few ivories have been discovered from the period of the Hittite empire, although inventories on cuneiform tablets mention ivory furniture, images, combs and hair clasps.

Mixing motifs characterized ivory carving in the Late Bronze Age, known particularly from *Ugarit, *Megiddo and *Lachish. Common are furniture plaques, depicting *feasts and triumph scenes, *cosmetic bowls, boxes, and fragments used for the flesh parts of composite statues,

In the first half of the first millennium BC wooden furniture was extensively decorated with carved ivory work. This plaque from Nimrud was carved by a Phoenician craftsman after an Egyptian model; the hieroglyphs are meaningless. The hollows were originally inlaid with coloured stones or glass, and much of the surface covered with gold foil. Height 7.6 cm. WA 118120.

including an impressive male head from Ugarit. *Queen Ahat-milku of Ugarit is recorded as owning three beds with such ivory plaques. Ivory was also used at Ugarit to make inscribed model livers for guidance in divination. Some ivories were imported from *Cyprus, Egypt and Anatolia.

*Nimrud has yielded thousands of ivories from the ninth and eighth centuries BC. Although ivories have been discovered at other sites, notably *Samaria, those from Nimrud probably came as booty and tribute taken by *Assyrian kings. Most of the ivories were plaques decorating furniture, but there were also small portable objects such as fly-whisks, mirrors, cosmetic bowls and boxes, *horse ornaments and parts of figurines. Many were originally overlaid with gold, inlaid or coloured. The three main decorative styles are: Syrian, using earlier motifs such as animal contests and processions; *Phoenician, using Egyptian motifs; and Assyrian, employing narrative scenes and animal friezes. In *Urartu and *Phrygia furniture combined ivories with *metal.

Few workshops have been identified. The best example, at Chalcolithic Bir es-Safadi near Beer Sheba, contained a work bench, an elephant tusk, three awls with bone handles and probably a bow-drill. At Nimrud, the backs and tenons of ivory plaques had fitters' marks, mostly letters of the West *Semitic *alphabet, as a guide to the cabinet-maker who assembled them on the wooden furniture.  PB

R.D. BARNETT, *Ancient Ivories in the Middle East* (Jerusalem 1982).

A. CAUBET and F. POPLIN, 'Matières dures animales: étude du matériaux', *Ras Shamra Ougarit* III, ed. M. Yon (Paris 1987) 273–306.

——, 'Le travail de l'os, de l'ivoire et de la coquille en Terre Sainte du 7e au 1er millénaires av. J.C.', *Studies in the History and Archaeology of Jordan* 5 (1995) 489–95.

G. HERRMANN, *Ivories from Nimrud IV, 1: Ivories from Room SW 37 Fort Shalmaneser* (London 1986).

——, *Ivories from Nimrud V: The Small Collections from Fort Shalmaneser* (London 1992).

P.R.S. MOOREY, *Ancient Mesopotamian Materials and Industries: The Archaeological Evidence* (Oxford 1994) 115–27.

# J

**Jarmo** The site of Qalat Jarmo lies in the hills east of the Tigris in north-east Iraq at 800 m above sea level in the oak woodland belt where the wild ancestors of cereals would have been common and where rainfall is moderately plentiful. For this reason it formed the focus of the first interdisciplinary investigation into the origins of *agriculture by Robert Braidwood between 1948 and 1955.

The site covers about 1.5 ha and has approximately 7 m of deposit with twelve main building phases identified. It was occupied over the transition from aceramic to pottery *Neolithic (c.7500–6500 BC) and is contemporary with late Pre-Pottery Neolithic B and with the *Hassuna cultures. The pottery Neolithic phases were the most extensively exposed. Ironically for Braidwood's investigations, most of the site, as excavated, dates to the period after the transition to a fully fledged mixed farming economy.

The site has many similarities with contemporary Hassuna settlements not far to the west. Architecture is packed mud or tauf rather than mudbrick. Typical *houses appear to consist of a number of rooms, an average of seven, many so small that they were probably for storage. These buildings cover a total of 30 sq m of which only half was probably available for living and sleeping. In this use of space they are very similar to contemporary Hassuna settlements, although specific details differ.

As in the Hassuna, fine *stone vessels are common and were probably manufactured on site by turning against distinctive *obsidian *tools, also found at Hassuna and in aceramic Neolithic eastern *Anatolia at sites like *Çayönü, hence their name Çayönü tools. Obsidian was not uncommon, and blades were trimmed by the distinctive side blow blade flake method where small flakes were taken off the ends of blades by pressure (see Flint-working) on the upper surfaces of the blades, a technique found also in the Hassuna.

A large number of clay *animal and human *figurines and small clay geometric shapes called 'tokens' were found. Some believe that these 'tokens' were part of a simple accounting system (see Writing).

Sheep and goat were herded, wheat, barley, pea and lentil cultivated. A significant range and quantity of species were hunted. These represent a very diverse set of economic strategies very similar to the Hassuna despite the moister setting.                                                    DB

L. BRAIDWOOD *et al.*, *Prehistoric Archeology along the Zagros Flanks* (Chicago 1983).
F. HOLE, *The Archaeology of Western Iran* (Washington, D.C./London 1987).

**Jemdet Nasr** Jemdet Nasr is located in modern Iraq to the south of Baghdad. The ancient name of the settlement may be represented by a five-pointed star. On the smaller of the two mounds are remains of *Ubaid, Early Dynastic and *Parthian date, including a baked-brick building on the summit. Most of the excavations have taken place on the larger mound, which covers 7.5 ha and has occupation dating to c.3400–2800 BC.

Excavations by Stephen Langdon in the 1920s, and again by Roger Matthews in the 1980s, uncovered a mudbrick building, measuring 92 by 48 m. The building comprised ranges of long rooms built upon a solid brick platform, and may have functioned as a *palace or an *administrative centre. A notable assemblage of objects was recovered, including *pottery with designs in black and dark red paint and *cylinder seals with stylized

Proto-cuneiform text from Jemdet Nasr (photograph by Roger Matthews, by courtesy of the Visitors of the Ashmolean Museum, Oxford).

designs of human and *animal figures. The distinctive nature of these objects led to the naming of a Jemdet Nasr period, lasting for a few centuries around 3000 BC, although some scholars have doubted the validity of this period definition. More recent work suggests that the Jemdet Nasr period is a valid term only for a restricted region of southern *Mesopotamia.

Most significantly, an *archive of 240 clay tablets with very early *writing was recovered from the building. These tablets date to around 3000 BC, shortly after the first appearance of proto-*cuneiform writing in south Mesopotamia. The Jemdet Nasr tablets are concerned with the administration of land, animals, crops and people, apparently under the control of a large institution, perhaps a *temple.

Many of the tablets have impressions on their surfaces made by cylinder seals. Of particular importance is the occurrence on thirteen tablets of a seal impression which lists the names of several early Mesopotamian *cities, including *Ur, *Larsa, *Nippur, *Uruk, *Kish, Zabala and Urum. The existence of this seal seems to indicate the communal co-operation, across several hundred kilometres, of many of the major cities of ancient Mesopotamia, and thus gives us a unique insight into political and social realities at the very dawn of urban civilization.

RM

Pre-Pottery Neolithic tower at Jericho (courtesy of Piotr Bienkowski).

Pre-Pottery Neolithic plastered skull from Jericho. WA 127414.

A desiccated human brain, one of the organic items which survived in the Middle Bronze Age tombs at Jericho (courtesy of Piotr Bienkowski).

R.K. ENGLUND and J.P. GRÉGOIRE, *The Proto-cuneiform Texts from Jemdet Nasr* (Berlin 1991).

U. FINKBEINER and W. RÖLLIG (eds), *Gamdat Nasr: Period or Regional Style?* (Wiesbaden 1986).

R.J. MATTHEWS, 'Jemdet Nasr: The Site and the Period', *Biblical Archaeologist* 55 (1992) 196–203.

**Jericho** The 4-ha mound of Tell es-Sultan in the Jordan Valley, 11 km north-west of the Dead Sea, is generally identified with Jericho of the *Bible. Several springs *irrigate the area, and in ancient times Jericho was famous for its *plant life, orchards and *gardens.

In the Bible Jericho was the first *town conquered by the *Israelites on their entry into *Canaan. From the fourth century AD, Christian pilgrims left records of their travels to Jericho, searching for details related to biblical accounts. The first archaeological work was undertaken by Charles Warren in 1868, then more extensively by Ernst Sellin and Carl Watzinger (1907–9, 1911), *Garstang (1930–6) and *Kenyon (1952–8).

The archaeological importance of Jericho is its nearly continuous occupation from the *Mesolithic (or *Epipalaeolithic) to the *Iron Age (c.10,000–600 BC). The earliest Mesolithic occupation consisted of a possible shrine, followed by flimsy clay huts in the Proto-*Neolithic. The town expanded in the Pre-Pottery Neolithic, with an estimated population of 3500, and was *fortified by a stone town wall with a circular tower. Human skulls buried beneath house floors were moulded with plaster to resemble living heads (see Ain Ghazal).

After periods of abandonment and resettlement, the town walls of the Early Bronze Age show seventeen successive phases of rebuilding; collapses due to earthquakes were localized by deliberate intervals in the course of the walls. The dead were buried outside the mound in rock-cut *tombs used for multiple successive *burials, which became the norm in later periods.

After a period of 'camp-site' occupation associated with 346 excavated tombs, the town of the Middle Bronze Age was extended and fortified with a huge three-stage rampart faced with plaster. The streets were well built, with wide cobbled steps and drains beneath. The ground floor of *houses was used for storage and livestock, while the living rooms were on the first floor. Organic material survived in the tombs, making it possible to identify wooden *furniture, clothes, fruit and meat, and even human skin and hair.

Following a destruction by fire, Jericho was abandoned, and only scanty structures and some tombs remain from the Late Bronze Age. No town wall or destruction can be associated with the Israelite conquest (see Exodus). The mound was abandoned, and re-occupied fairly extensively in the Iron Age with houses terraced into the slope. In the seventh century BC Jericho was probably under the administration of the kingdom of *Judah.                                                    PB

J.R. BARTLETT, *Jericho* (Guildford 1982).

P. BIENKOWSKI, *Jericho in the Late Bronze Age* (Warminster 1986).

T.A. HOLLAND and E. NETZER, 'Jericho', *Anchor Bible Dictionary* 3, ed. D.N. Freedman (New York 1992) 723–40.

K.M. KENYON, *Excavations at Jericho* 1–3 (London 1960, 1965, 1981).

K.M. KENYON and T.A. HOLLAND, *Excavations at Jericho* 4–5 (London 1982, 1983).

H. and M. WEIPPERT, 'Jericho in der Eisenzeit', *Zeitschrift der Deutschen Palästina-Vereins* 92 (1976) 105–48.

Aerial view of Jerusalem from the south-west, showing the temple area, and the city's setting in the hill country of Judah (photograph courtesy of Sonia Halliday Photographs).

**Jerusalem** Jerusalem is located c.56 km east of the Mediterranean coast and c.24 km west of the northern end of the Dead Sea. *Bronze and *Iron Age Jerusalem was shaped differently from today's walled 'Old City', whose ramparts date to the sixteenth century AD. The earliest occupation was on the Ophel Ridge, located immediately south of the Old City's eastern side. At the northern end of the Ophel Ridge, just inside the Old City walls, is the so-called 'Temple Mount', about 740 m above sea level, overlooking the Kidron Valley to the east which separates Jerusalem's main plateau from the higher Mount of Olives. To the south, the Ophel Ridge descends into the Hinnom Valley. A shallower valley separated Ophel from the rest of the Jerusalem plateau to the west.

This small *city played an important role in *Canaanite history, and it was capital of ancient *Israel and later Judah until it was destroyed by the *Babylonians in 586 BC. Early work was carried out by C. Wilson (1864), C. Warren (1867–70), and F.J. Bliss and A.C. Dickie (1894–7). Excavations have been conducted by R. Weill (1913–14, 1923–4), R.A.S. Macalister and J.G. Duncan (1923–5), J.W. Crowfoot and G.M. FitzGerald (1927–9), *Kenyon (1961–7), and Y. Shiloh (1978–85). Among other Israeli scholars, D. Ussishkin surveyed the Iron Age cemetery of Silwan, on the lower slope of the Mount of Olives, east of Ophel.

Jerusalem's name might be related to the name of a Canaanite deity, 'Salem', known from the *Ugaritic tablets. The city is mentioned in the *Execration texts and *Amarna Letters. Its relatively defensible topography and the springs near the floor of the Kidron Valley were critical in the choice to settle and later fortify the Ophel hill. The earliest remains on Ophel date to the *Chalcolithic, and Early Bronze I is represented in *tombs and *pottery. Early Bronze II–III are not found at Jerusalem, but Early Bronze IV use is reflected in tombs. During Middle Bronze II, the Canaanites fortified Ophel with a city wall and towers; the Amarna texts and archaeological evidence suggest that Jerusalem prospered in the Late Bronze Age.

Evidence antedating David's takeover at Jerusalem is meagre. According to the *Bible, David's soldiers took the city from the 'Jebusites'. No Iron I material can be attributed to the Davidic period with certainty, but some of Ophel's substantial architectural remains, including retaining walls (*millo* of 2 Samuel 5: 9?), may date to this early Israelite occupation. It is also possible that the Canaanite *water system relates to the means by which David's troops reportedly gained entry into Jerusalem. The dating of this early water system is uncertain, but there are no grounds for disputing the identity of an Iron II water system as the work of Hezekiah, probably in preparation for *Sennacherib's attack. Walls, houses and a large number of tombs from Iron II have been excavated. The Bible remains the most important literary source for the city's history, although Neo-Babylonian records provide helpful information on Jerusalem's fall at the beginning of the sixth century BC. A renewal of Hebrew activity in Jerusalem is dated by the Bible to the end of the 'Babylonian Exile', when *Cyrus II allowed captured populations to return to their homelands and rebuild their national identities.

The best known structure in Jerusalem was the Solomonic *temple (1 Kings 6–7), which has not been found. A small *ivory pomegranate from Jerusalem is probably the only artefact which can be linked to this building; a mid-eighth-century BC palaeo-*Hebrew inscription on the ivory identifies it as coming from 'the temple of [*Yahweh]'.

GLM

K.J. ASALI (ed.), *Jerusalem in History: From 3,000 B.C. to the Present Day* (London 1997).

G. AULD *et al.*, *Jerusalem: From the Bronze Age to the Maccabees* (Macon, GA 1996).

H. GEVA (ed.), *Ancient Jerusalem Revealed* (Jerusalem 1994).

K. KENYON, *Digging Up Jerusalem* (London 1974).

H. SHANKS, *Jerusalem: An Archaeological Biography* (New York 1995).

Y. YADIN (ed.), *Jerusalem Revealed: Archaeology in the Holy City 1968–1974* (Jerusalem 1975).

**Jewellery** Jewellery has been worn by men, *women and children since earliest times for three main reasons: for self-adornment, as a prestige item to proclaim the wearer's wealth and social status, and for amuletic purposes as protection against evil forces.

Among the most common objects found on excavations of Near Eastern sites are beads, used as jewellery and for sewing on to *clothes. Colourful or unusual materials were popular, for example *obsidian from Turkey, already used in a necklace from *Arpachiyah dated to c.5000 BC. *Gold and *silver of course became pre-eminent for jewellery; *burials at Tepe *Gawra dating to 3500–3000 BC included gold rosettes originally sewn on to clothing. The most spectacular early jewellery comes from the Royal Tombs at *Ur, dating to c.2500 BC. Here, the earliest recorded use of filigree and granulation produced flower-shaped hair ornaments in sheet gold, crescent-shaped earrings, rings and necklaces of gold, carnelian, lapis lazuli and agate. Similar techniques were used for the jewellery from *Troy, dating to c.2500–2300 BC.

The finest jewellery of the second millennium BC comes from the *Levant, from the *tombs at *Ebla and in particular from hoards and graves at Tell el-Ajjul on the coast of *Palestine: sheet-gold pendants and earrings, neck ornaments or belts, many showing *Egyptian influence, especially scarabs mounted in gold and silver. This Levantine tradition continued into the *Iron Age, seen

Gold earring decorated with minute gold granules, from Tell el-'Ajjul. 4.5 cm wide. Late Bronze I, c.1550–1400 BC. WA 130762.

in the extremely intricate jewellery from *Phoenicia. Egyptian motifs were popular, sometimes transformed into meaningless shapes. *Assyrian influence was strong from the eighth century BC, for example bracelets with central rosette ornaments. From Assyria itself, the most spectacular jewellery comes from rich eighth-century BC graves of high-ranking women discovered between 1988 and 1990 in subterranean chambers under the floors of the North-West Palace at *Nimrud. There were huge numbers of gold earrings, necklaces, anklets, bracelets, fibulae, clothing plaques, a headband with a tasselled fringe, and an intricate *crown or headdress, which have revolutionized understanding of Assyrian craftsmanship.

Ancient texts provide information on jewellery and workshops and reveal that jewellery was plundered during military campaigns, exchanged as gifts between rulers and lovers, given as wedding gifts and *inheritances, and formed parts of dowries. Texts also explain the amuletic properties of jewellery: different materials possessed *magical powers, so women in labour, for instance, could wear an image of the *demon Pazuzu as protection for the child. Statues of *gods were regularly adorned with jewellery. Representations of people, gods and supernatural creatures in *art, particularly Assyrian *sculpture, also depict how jewellery was worn in different periods. A jeweller's hoard from *Larsa, of the Old Babylonian period, shows the tools of a professional jeweller, including tweezers, a miniature anvil, *weights, and fragments of jewellery for melting down and reworking. PB

Z. BAHRANI, 'Jewelry and Personal Arts in Ancient Western Asia', *Civilizations of the Ancient Near East*, ed. J.M. Sasson (New York 1995) 1635–45.

K.R. MAXWELL-HYSLOP, *Western Asiatic Jewellery c. 3000–612 B.C.* (London 1971).

B. MUSCHE, *Vorderasiatische Schmuck von den Anfängen bis zur Zeit der Achämeniden (ca. 10,000–330 v. Chr.)* (Leiden 1992).

J. OGDEN, *Jewellery of the Ancient World* (London 1982).

B. SASS, 'Jewelry', *The Oxford Encyclopedia of Archaeology in the Near East* 3, ed. E.M. Meyers (New York 1997) 238–46.

**Jordan:** see Transjordan

**Judah:** see Israel and Judah

# K

**Kadesh** Kadesh (Qidshu), the Kinza of Late Bronze Age *cuneiform texts, is identified as Tell Nebi Mend on the Orontes, south of Homs in *Syria. Excavations by M. Pézard (1921–2) and P.J. Parr (1975–96) revealed early Pottery *Neolithic, Early, Middle and Late *Bronze Age, *Iron Age, *Hellenistic, *Roman and Byzantine levels and a middle Neolithic occupation with *Halaf traits at nearby Arjune. The length of occupation promises a major sequence of stratified *pottery for this region. In the Middle Bronze Age there was a *city wall. Among the

A view of Tell Nebi Mend, ancient Kadesh on the Orontes (courtesy of Alan Millard).

few Late Bronze Age cuneiform tablets are two *letters in *Akkadian to *King Niqmad (see below), and a fragment of a storage jar was inscribed before firing with a notice in a shorter form of the cuneiform *alphabet.

The king of Kadesh opposed Tuthmosis III at the battle of *Megiddo (c.1479 BC) then fell under *Egyptian control. In the *Amarna Letters, Aitakama of Kadesh appears to play off the Egyptians against the *Hittites. His son Niqmad murdered him and was forced to submit to the Hittites. Thereafter the Egyptians claimed control again under Horemheb and Seti I (who erected a stela there), but when Ramesses II led his forces to the battle of Kadesh, Kadesh was on the Hittite side. After the battle (1275 BC), the Hittites took control. The city probably fell to the *Sea Peoples about 1200 BC. There was considerable Iron Age occupation, and the place is mentioned in *Assyrian administrative texts.                    ARM

K.A. KITCHEN, *Ramesside Inscriptions, Translations 2* (Oxford 1996) paras. 5–46, *Notes and Comments II* (Oxford 1999) 3–54.

H. KLENGEL, *Syria, 3000 to 300 B.C.: A Handbook of Political History* (Berlin 1992) 157–60.

L. MARFOE, L. COPELAND and P.J. PARR, 'Arjoune', *Levant* 13 (1981) 1–27.

V.T. MATHIAS and P.J. PARR, 'The Early Phases at Tell Nebi Mend', *Levant* 21 (1989) 13–32.

A.R. MILLARD, 'A Text in the Shorter Cuneiform Alphabet from Tell Nebi Mend', *Ugarit-Forschungen* 8 (1976) 459–60.

——, 'Qadesh et Ugarit', *Les Annales Archéologiques Arabes Syriennes* 29–30 (1979–80) 201–5.

P.J. PARR, 'The Tell Nebi Mend Project', *Les annales archéologiques arabes syriennes* 33 (1983) 99–117.

M. PÉZARD, *Qadesh* (Paris 1931).

## Kamid el-Loz

Ancient Kumidi, known from *Egyptian texts of the second millennium BC as an important *city-state and part of the Egyptian empire, was identified as modern Kamid el-Loz by A. Guthe in 1897, a suggestion confirmed by the discovery of four *cuneiform tablets in 1969. At 300 by 240 m in area and 26 m high, it is one of the largest *tells in the Beqa' Valley in *Lebanon, close to two major ancient *roads and two springs. Kamid el-Loz was excavated by Arnolf Kuschke and then Rolf Hachmann between 1963 and 1981, but the site has since been largely destroyed by treasure hunters.

The excavations concentrated on the *fortified Late Bronze Age city, but *Neolithic, Early Bronze Age (out of context) and extensive fortified Middle Bronze Age remains were also found. The Late Bronze Age double-court *temple and the *palace, separated from each other by an esplanade which opened on to a street leading outside the city, were both destroyed and rebuilt several times. East of the palace was a building with three rich *burials beneath it, perhaps the tombs of Kumidi's rulers.

After a period of abandonment, there were eight levels of unfortified Iron I villages with small *houses built of *wood. No Iron II settlement was found, and the tell was later used as a *cemetery in the *Persian, *Hellenistic and *Roman periods.                    PB

L. BADRE, 'Kamid el-Loz', *The Oxford Encyclopedia of Archaeology in the Near East* 3, ed. E.M. Meyers (New York 1997) 265–6.

R. HACHMANN (ed.), *Kamid el-Loz, 1977–1981* (Bonn 1986).

——, *Kamid el-Loz, 1963–1981: German Excavations in Lebanon (Part 1). Berytus* 37 (Beirut 1989).

## Kanesh

Kültepe, ancient Nesha, lies 21 km north-east of modern Kayseri at the centre of *Roman Cappadocia in *Anatolia. The site lies at the crossroads of east–west and north–south routes on the Anatolian plateau, and it was an independent Anatolian *city state and the centre of the network of Old *Assyrian trading colonies in the Middle Bronze Age.

*Cuneiform tablets which appeared on the European market, without provenance, in 1871, were suspected of having originated at Kültepe. Excavations were conducted by E. Chantre (1893–4) and H. Winckler (1906). In 1925 B. Hrozny established that the tablets came from extensive digging by villagers. Excavations have been conducted by T. Özgüç since 1948.

The site comprises the high city mound on a natural hill and a lower city, Kanesh, known by the Assyrian term *kārum*, meaning trading colony or commercial centre. Of the eighteen levels on the city mound, 18–14 are late Early Bronze I–II. Levels 13–11 are Early Bronze III, by which time extensive connections had been established with north *Syria, evidenced by *cylinder seals, *metal objects and *pottery.

In the Middle Bronze Age the strongly fortified city mound, some 550 m in diameter and 20 m above the plain, contained *palaces and *temples of the ruling elite and the lower town or *kārum* was established. By Karum II (c.1920–1850 BC), when the first tablets appear, all written in *Akkadian, the lower town was surrounded by a wall some 2.5–3 km in diameter enclosing well appointed *houses and paved streets. Resident in the lower town were Assyrian *merchants from *Ashur, and their agents. Tablets attest highly organized and extensive *trade, in *textiles and raw *tin, which is largely unattested by either objects or architecture. Donkey caravans took up to three months to make the trip by established and protected routes along which taxes were levied. There was also considerable manufacturing

Cuneiform tablet and envelope with seal impressions from Kanesh. WA 113572.

industry within the *kārum* itself. Assyrian merchants had a degree of autonomy, applying their own *laws and *administration and sometimes taking local wives. Karum II was destroyed by fire.

Fewer tablets were found in Karum Ib, also destroyed by fire along with City Mound level 7 around 1740 BC; from this level came a *bronze spearhead inscribed 'Palace of Anitta the King' with important implications for early *Hittite history. Relevant here is the identification of Kanesh as the *kārum* of Nesha; the Hittite *language was called Neshite by the Hittites.

In the Neo-Hittite period, levels 5–4 on the city mound represent a town in the land of Tabal.

Dates are tentative as dendrochronology (tree-ring *dating) at Kültepe may resolve the long-standing controversy concerning absolute dating of the second millennium BC.                                                    GDS

P. GARELLI, *Les Assyriens en Cappadoce* (Paris 1963).
M.T. LARSEN, *Old Assyrian Caravan Procedures* (Istanbul 1967).
L.L. ORLIN, *Assyrian Colonies in Cappadocia* (The Hague 1970).
T. ÖZGÜÇ, *Kültepe-Kaniš: New Researches at the Centre of the Assyrian Trade Colonies* (Ankara 1959).
——, *Kültepe and its Vicinity in the Iron Age* (Ankara 1971).
——, *Kültepe-Kaniš II: New Researches at the Centre of the Assyrian Trade Colonies of the Ancient Near East* (Ankara 1986).
K.R. VEENHOF, *Aspects of Old Assyrian Trade and its Terminology* (Leiden 1972).

**Karana:** see Rimah, (Tell al-)

**Karatepe and Domuztepe** Karatepe and its twin Domuztepe are located either side of the Ceyhan *river (now a lake owing to the construction of a dam) near Kadirli, c.100 km north-east of Adana in the mountains to the east of the upper Adana Plain in *Anatolia. The sites were discovered in 1946 by H. Bossert who, with B. Alkim and H. Çambel, conducted the first investigations. Since then both sites have been diligently investigated and restored by Çambel. They control the route through the mountains from the Adana Plain which, according to an inscription, Karatepe was constructed to protect. Both sites are forested, so that excavation has

been largely restricted to the *defences.

Karatepe measures c.200 by 400 m. It is the site of the eighth-century BC walled *city of Azatiwadas, named after its founder, one Azatiwada, a vassal of Urikki *king of the Danunians, famous for its two monumental sculpted stone *gates with a long inscription in *hieroglyphic Luwian (*Hittite) paraphrased in *Phoenician. Attempts, however, to read the name Mopsus, the legendary founder of Mopsuestia in Cilicia, and the considerable implications of such a reconstruction, may be dismissed. The inscription is on basalt orthostats (standing stone slabs) carved with lively scenes which have been fundamental in the stylistic analysis of Neo-Hittite *art and in the decipherment of hieroglyphic Luwian. Stylistic division of the sculptures into two distinctive groups has led to the plausible suggestion that Domuztepe was the earlier of the two towns and that perhaps some earlier reliefs were transferred to Karatepe where they were re-used. The later sculptural style and the Phoenician inscription attest growing Phoenician influence in Cilicia and beyond, which has been recently reinforced by the discovery of further bilingual inscriptions, most notably at Ivriz. The sculptures themselves are somewhat idiosyncratic, including a *banqueting scene in which the king has a monkey beneath his table and is entertained by dancing bears, musicians and a parade of soldiers.                                          GDS

E. AKURGAL, *The Art of the Hittites* (London 1962).
R.D. BARNETT, 'Karatepe, the Key to Hittite Hieroglyphs', *Anatolian Studies* 3 (1953) 53–95.
H.T. BOSSERT and U.B. ALKIM, *Die Ausgrabungen auf dem Karatepe* (Ankara 1950).
H. ÇAMBEL, *Karatepe-Aslantas: The Inscriptions, facsimile edition*. Corpus of Hieroglyphic Luwian Inscriptions 2 (Berlin 1999).
W. ORTHMANN, *Untersuchungen zur späthethitischen Kunst* (Bonn 1971).
I. WINTER, 'On the Problems of Karatepe: The Reliefs and their Context', *Anatolian Studies* 29 (1979) 115–51.

**Kassites** The Kassites were the longest ruling *dynasty in *Babylonian history, but their tribal origins are obscure. They may have emigrated from *Iran, over the *Zagros into Babylonia. They are first mentioned in texts of the eighteenth century BC, particularly from *Sippar, as individuals or tribal groups, hiring themselves out for *agricultural or *military work. Relations with the sedentary Babylonians were not always peaceful, and Old Babylonian year names refer to confrontations with Kassite troops. Within two hundred years they had spread over a wide area of the Near East, and, when the *Hittite *King Mursilis I raided *Babylon in c.1595 BC bringing to an end the dynasty of *Hammurabi, the Kassites were able to assume power.

The Babylonian *King List records thirty-six kings of the Kassite dynasty, but of the first two hundred years the sources reveal very little. In c.1475 BC King Ulam-Buriash defeated the Sealand dynasty in the south and unified Babylonia, initiating more than three hundred years of stability and prosperity. Babylonia became a major power, in *diplomatic and *trade contact with the other great powers, as revealed in the *Amarna Letters. The Kassite Kings Kadashman-Enlil I and Burnaburiash II exchanged ambassadors and gifts and arranged diplomatic *marriages with *Egypt, Hatti and *Assyria. Major building and restoration works were undertaken in the principal *cities, and Kurigalzu I founded a new capital named after himself at Dur-Kurigalzu (*Aqar Quf).

The most characteristic aspect of Kassite material culture are *kudurrus, or boundary stones. Kassite kings rewarded favoured subjects with grants of royal land, and kudurrus commemorated this gift and designated its *boundaries. Other innovations were the systematic breeding of *horses and new developments in *chariot technology. Kassite kings promoted the collection and composition of *literature, and many of the standard literary works found in the later Neo-Assyrian *libraries are copies of Kassite originals and compilations. Under the Kassites, *Akkadian became the common diplomatic *language of the Near East, as used in the Amarna Letters. Of the original Kassite language we know little and it cannot be related to any other language: no Kassite text has survived, and the main sources are two Kassite–Akkadian dictionaries which list divine and personal names and some basic vocabulary. Our word 'Kassite' comes from the Akkadian kaššu, but they called themselves galzu. In *religion they worshipped Babylonian *gods, although coronations took place in a special shrine in the *palace at Babylon consecrated to two Kassite mountain gods, Shuqamuna and Shimaliya.

The Kassite dynasty was ended by an *Elamite invasion in c.1155 BC, but Kassites continued to live in *Mesopotamia and even to hold important official posts at least until the ninth century BC. Thereafter they are attested as a warlike tribal people in the hills of eastern Iraq and Iran, and perhaps supplied troops for the *Achaemenid *army against Alexander the Great, who had to campaign against Kassite groups in the mountains. One classical account states that the Kassites were expert bowmen, lived in caves and ate acorns, mushrooms and the smoked flesh of wild *animals.                    PB

K. BALKAN, Kassitenstudien I: Die Sprache der Kassiten (New Haven, CN 1954).

J.A. BRINKMAN, 'The Monarchy in the Time of the Kassite Dynasty', Le palais et la royauté: archéologie et civilisation, ed. P. Garelli (Paris 1974) 395–408.

——, Materials and Studies for Kassite History I: A Catalogue of Cuneiform Sources Pertaining to Specific Monarchs of the Kassite Dynasty (Chicago 1976).

——, 'Kassiten', Reallexikon der Assyriologie 5 (Berlin/New York 1980) 464–73.

W. SOMMERFELD, 'The Kassites of Ancient Mesopotamia: Origins, Politics, and Culture', Civilizations of the Ancient Near East, ed. J.M. Sasson (New York 1995) 917–30.

## Kenyon, Kathleen Mary (1906–78)

Born in London, the elder daughter of Sir Frederic Kenyon (later Director and Principal Librarian of the British Museum), Kathleen Kenyon studied at Oxford and gained experience of archaeological work at the ruins of Great Zimbabwe and, with Mortimer and Tessa Wheeler, at Verulamium (St Albans) in England. Here the Wheelers were pioneering new, systematic methods of stratigraphic excavation and recording, which Kenyon began implementing in *Palestine when she joined the excavations at *Samaria in 1931.

Kenyon's methods of excavation at *Jericho (1952–8) literally revolutionized Palestinian *archaeology. They were based essentially on the cutting of trenches, the meticulous observation of stratigraphy and the drawing of sections to decipher the history of occupation. She showed that the 'Late Bronze Age' destruction, which *Garstang had attributed to Joshua, was in fact Early Bronze Age, about a thousand years earlier. Her excavations took the history of Jericho back to the tenth millennium BC, and produced a well stratified sequence of material from a site with a long continuous occupation.

*Jerusalem, a stone-built site and a living city, posed greater technical problems than Jericho. Nevertheless, Kenyon's excavations (1961–7) established and dated the lines of the defensive walls at various periods, although some of her results have been modified by more recent work.

Although she did not live to complete the final publication of her excavations, Kenyon did produce books aimed at both the scholar and the general reader. The most influential of these was Archaeology in the Holy Land (1st ed. 1960), which still remains a basic text. As well as excavating and writing, Kenyon was involved in various administrative posts. She taught at the Institute of Archaeology in London from its foundation in 1935 before becoming Honorary Director of the British School of Archaeology in Jerusalem in 1951. She became Principal of St Hugh's College, Oxford, in 1962, and a Dame of the British Empire in 1973.                    PB

P.R.S. MOOREY, A Century of Biblical Archaeology (Cambridge 1991) 94–9, 122–6.

——, 'British Women in Near Eastern Archaeology: Kathleen Kenyon and the Pioneers', Palestine Exploration Quarterly 124 (1992) 91–100.

K. PRAG, 'Kathleen Kenyon and Archaeology in the Holy Land', Palestine Exploration Quarterly 124 (1992) 109–23.

A.D. TUSHINGHAM, 'Kathleen Mary Kenyon 1906–1978', Proceedings of the British Academy 71 (1985) 555–82.

## Keret (Kirta)

A series of three clay tablets unearthed at *Ugarit carry the poem about this ancient *king in the local *language and *alphabetic *cuneiform script. They were copied by the prominent *scribe Ilu-milku, probably in the thirteenth century BC. Although the tablets are damaged and at least one more is missing at the end of the story, its content is clear. The king, whose name is written with consonants only, KRT (perhaps Kirta, or Kurita, rather than Keret), lost his brothers and seven wives and had no heir. Praying for a son, he was advised in a *dream by the chief *god, *El, to *sacrifice to *Baal, then march with his *army to Udmu to ask for its king's daughter Hurriya as wife. On the way he vowed to give 'twice her weight in *silver, thrice in *gold' to the goddess Athirat (*Asherah) of *Tyre if he were successful. Rejecting the king of Udmu's attempt to buy him off, Keret won the girl and took her home, where El blessed the couple with the promise of numerous *children. Apparently Keret did not fulfil his vow to Athirat, who struck him with a mortal illness. He, his wife and his son lamented his fate, then, in sympathy, earth's *fertility ceased. El took steps to heal Keret, creating a female spirit who cured him so that he sat on his throne again. The tale ends with an account of one son who proposed that Keret should give place to him, complaining of the chaos that had resulted during his illness, but he received Keret's curse for his impudence. Whether Keret was perceived as an ancestor of the kings of Ugarit, or as the ruler of another *city in the *Levant, is uncertain. The *story is set in that region, although, apart from Tyre and *Sidon, no other places can be identified.                                    ARM

J.C.L. GIBSON, *Canaanite Myths and Epics* (Edinburgh 1978) 82–102.
D. PARDEE, 'The Kirta Epic', *The Context of Scripture* 1, eds W.W. Hallo and K.L. Younger (Leiden 1997) 333–43.

## Kerkenes Daǧ

A middle *Iron Age *city located on a low mountain-top close to the centre of Turkey, Kerkenes is the largest pre-*Hellenistic site on the *Anatolian plateau. *Stone *defences, 7 km long with seven *gates, enclose 2.5 sq km. It was first visited by J.J.G. Anderson in 1899, surveyed by H.H. von der Osten and F.H. Blackburn in 1927 and dated through test excavations by E.F. Schmidt in 1928. Since 1993 G.D. and M.E.F. Summers have been conducting an innovative survey using remote-sensing techniques that include balloon photography and photo rectification, geophysical survey of sub-surface features and Geographical Information Systems (GIS) analysis of the urban infrastructure. Test excavations in 1996 and 1998 by M. Özcan and G.D. Summers confirmed the validity of the geophysical survey and recovered a number of high status objects.

The site is of a single period with a restricted span of occupation. Total and intense burning provides evidence that the city was put to the torch. Urban zoning is apparent within the city walls, the high southern end comprising a large area of public buildings that display the characteristics of centralized planning. The *kale* (castle) has later defences and may have functioned as a citadel within the Iron Age city. Much of the city was divided into walled urban blocks at the time of foundation. Some of these blocks contained elite residential complexes with columned halls that apparently display *Iranian influence.

A substantial extramural building, probably a *temple, is located at Karabas to the north of the city.

A variety of circumstantial evidence supports the idea, first suggested by Przeworski in 1928, that the city was ancient Pteria (*Herodotus I.74, 76). If this is correct, the city would have been founded by the *Medes in the early sixth century BC and destroyed by *Croesus, king of *Lydia, traditionally in 547 BC.

A unique *ivory plaque embellished with amber, *gold leaf and perhaps *silver was recovered in 1987.

Kusaklý Höyük (Yozgat), a mound site to the north of the city, has been identified with the *Hittite city of Zipallanda and Kerkenes Daǧ with the sacred Hittite mountain Daha.                                    GDS

O.R. GURNEY, 'The Hittite Names of Kerkenes Dağ and Kuşakli Höyük', *Anatolian Studies* 45 (1995) 69–71.
G.D. SUMMERS, 'The Identification of the Iron Age City on the Kerkenes Dağ in Central Anatolia', *Journal of Near Eastern Studies* 56/2 (1997) 81–94.
G.D. SUMMERS *et al.*, 'The Kerkenes Dağ Survey: An Interim Report', *Anatolian Studies* 46 (1996) 201–34.

Website: Http://www.metu.edu.tr/home/wwwkerk/index.html

## Khabur

A tributary of the Euphrates, the Khabur *river has its source in the mountainous region of south-east Turkey. With its own tributaries and the *Balikh it waters the region known as the Jazira, a vast level expanse of grassland and semi-desert in north *Syria. It has one of the richest concentrations of archaeological sites in Syria, including Tell *Brak, *Chagar Bazar, Tell *Fekheriyeh, Tell *Halaf, Tell *Leilan, Tell *Mozan and Tell *Sheikh Hamad. It can be divided into the Upper Khabur (or Khabur triangle) and the Lower Khabur, ranging from a fertile, agricultural region with adequate rainfall in the north to very dry areas further south. Excavations intensified from the 1970s prior to flooding due to barrage construction.

The earliest occupation so far discovered in the Khabur is at Tell Feyda, dating to the Pre-Pottery *Neolithic B. Settlement reached a peak in the late third and early second millennia BC, both in number of sites and in population, but thereafter was relatively sparse until the present. The *Assyrians resettled deportees from *Samaria along the Khabur, which is already attested by that name in Assyrian and *biblical sources.                                    PB

T.L. McCLELLAN, 'Khabur', *The Oxford Encyclopedia of Archaeology in the Near East* 3, ed. E.M. Meyers (New York 1997) 286–8.
D.A. WARBURTON, 'Previous Archaeological Work in the Habur Region', *Tall al-Hamidiya* 1, eds S. Eichler *et al.* (Göttingen 1985) 13–30.

Aerial photograph of Kerkenes Daǧ taken from a hot-air balloon, showing the 7 km of city wall (courtesy of G.D. Summers).

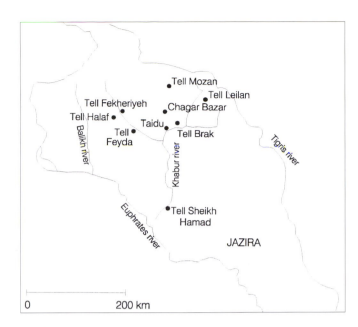

Map of the Khabur region showing main archaeological sites.

A kilted figure (goddess?) grasping a snake in each hand stands between two lions in relief carving around a chlorite vase found at Khafaje. The vase also shows a bull being killed by a lion and a figure with streams of water flowing from his hands. The vase was probably made in Elam about 2700 BC. Height 11.4 cm. WA 128887.

Aerial view of the Temple Oval at Khafaje in 1933 (courtesy of the Oriental Institute of the University of Chicago).

**Khafaje** Like the ancient *city of *Eshnunna, Khafaje is located to the north of the confluence of the Diyala and Tigris *rivers, about 80 km north-east of Baghdad. For at least part of its history, Khafaje's ancient name was Tutub. During the 1930s, a major programme of excavations at Khafaje, and at nearby Eshnunna and Tell Agrab, was conducted by Henri Frankfort.

In total, the four mounds of Khafaje were occupied from the Late *Uruk period, c.3300 BC, until the middle of the second millennium BC. Excavations mainly took place on mound A, the largest area of settlement, where occupation began in the Late Uruk period. Of great importance for *Mesopotamian *archaeology and *chronology was the excavation of the so-called *Sin *Temple, a long sequence of religious buildings originally thought to have been dedicated to the moon-god Sin. The Sin Temple underwent many rebuilds, spanning the *Jemdet Nasr and Early Dynastic I–III periods, c.3000–2350 BC. Nearby, a long sequence of early third-millennium domestic *houses was also investigated. *Pottery from these stratified building levels, along with evidence from the Abu Temple sequence at nearby Eshnunna (Tell Asmar), provided the means by which Mesopotamian third-millennium chronology was provisionally established.

The major structure on mound A at Khafaje, however, was the Temple Oval, of Early Dynastic date. Constructed on a deliberate deposit of clean sand and adjacent to the town wall, the Temple Oval comprised a temple built upon a substantial raised platform, with outer courtyard and ranges of rooms located within a double oval wall, all of mudbrick. Between the two enclosure walls lay a large building, House D, perhaps the residence of the chief *priest. Mound A was abandoned during the *Akkadian period, c.2300 BC.

During the Old Babylonian period, mound B became the site of a large fortress built by Samsuiluna, successor to *Hammurabi of *Babylon, in c.1726 BC. At this time,

Khafaje was known as Dur-Samsuiluna. Excavations on mound D uncovered part of a *fortification wall, a temple, domestic houses and an *archive of *cuneiform tablets, all dating to the early second millennium BC.

RM

P. DELOUGAZ, *The Temple Oval at Khafajah* (Chicago 1940).
——, *Pottery from the Diyala Region* (Chicago 1952).
D.P. HANSEN, 'Khafajeh', *The Oxford Encyclopedia of Archaeology in the Near East* 3, ed. E.M. Meyers (New York 1997) 288–90.

**Khirbet Kerak** This site is also known as Beth Yerah. It is located in *Palestine at the southern end of the Sea of Galilee (Lake Tiberias) where the Jordan *river exits from the lake, and was therefore well situated to exploit river and lake resources. It currently sits on the west bank of the river but it is not impossible that in the earlier periods of its occupation a branch of the river flowed to the site's west. It may have been situated on an island.

The site is principally known for its Early Bronze Age occupation. In the Early Bronze I period the site seems to have grown rapidly to an impressive size. By about 3300 BC it appears to have covered c.20–5 ha. This rapid and large growth should certainly be attributed to the development of the site as an urban centre. By early in the succeeding Early Bronze II period, c.3000 BC, the site had acquired a *fortification wall 8 m thick possibly pointing to the intensification and increasing scale of conflict related to the appearance of urbanism in the region.

A major public building helps illustrate these developments in the Early Bronze III period dating to c.2500 BC. Constructed out of large basalt boulders, this building consists of four huge platforms each almost 10 m wide surrounding a courtyard area c.100 sq m in area containing a structure. The structure as a whole covers 30 by 40 m. Sitting on these platforms are the bases of circular installations each over 7 m in diameter, each with the foundations of four narrow radial walls. It has been suggested that these are the foundations for massive dome-shaped granaries. If so, the scale of storage would be massive, and would point to the surplus at the disposal of central authority. Alternatively this building might represent a religious structure. It is clearly a monumental structure representing the marshalling of considerable public resources.

The site gives its name to a distinctive category of *pottery – Khirbet Kerak Ware – from the Early Bronze III period with highly burnished red and black surfaces. Fine open vessels often have relief decoration perhaps in imitation of more valuable *metal vessels. This pottery is virtually identical with similar ceramics which occur sporadically further north in the *Levant, at sites like *Ras Shamra and clearly derives its inspiration from Early Bronze Age pottery in eastern Turkey, itself initially intrusive to this region of *Anatolia. The appearance of this pottery type in the southern Levant has suggested to researchers the appearance of newcomers from the north. Perhaps, however, its production merely accompanies the circulation of more valuable metal vessels, which would clearly have been exchange items. Recent petrographic work (i.e. microscopic study of the clay minerals and inclusions in pottery) at sites like *Beth Shan indicates that Khirbet Kerak Ware is largely a local product, despite its exotic inspiration. Its sporadic occurrence throughout the Levant remains distinctive and is not satisfactorily explained. Perhaps it relates to the potentially rather random spread of itinerant specialist potters and the also potentially random transference of their skills to other potters. DB

B. MAZAR, M. STEKELIS and M. AVI-YONAH, 'The Excavations at Beth Yerah (Khirbet el-Kerak)', *Israel Exploration Journal* 2 (1952) 165–73, 229–48.

**Khorsabad** Khorsabad is the modern name for the site of Dur-Sharrukin ('Sargonsburg'), 12 km north-east of Mosul in northern Iraq, built from 713 BC as the capital of *Sargon II of *Assyria, which status it adopted in 707 BC. Though unfinished at the king's death, and giving way as capital to *Nineveh, it may have remained a provincial centre until the fall of Assyria in 612 BC.

The site saw the first large-scale excavations in the Near East, beginning with *Botta in 1843–5. *Layard worked there in 1849. French excavations were renewed under *Place in 1852–5, when photography was employed for the first time in Near Eastern *archaeology. In 1927–35 the site was excavated by the University of Chicago. There were Iraqi excavations in 1957.

The 7-km perimeter wall, with seven *gates, enclosed

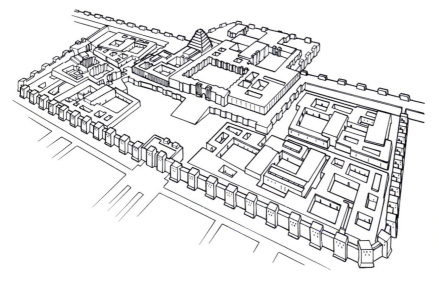

Conjectural reconstruction of the citadel at Khorsabad, showing Sargon's palace with a ziggurat and other palaces beside it.

a 275-ha square, roughly the same size and shape as the City of London. In the north-west, a wall with two gates enclosed the 23-ha government quarter. Lacking pre-Assyrian settlement, there was no 'citadel', but the Royal *Palace and *Temple of *Nabû were built on artificial terraces, the palace standing higher than the temple. The palace consisted of about 240 rooms, many lined with carved bas-reliefs, and organized into administrative, ceremonial and domestic wings. There were six internal temples. Built into the construction was a painted *ziggurat. According to Sargon's own record, his palace contained a *bīt hilāni in the *Syrian style, a feature not clearly identified on the ground.

The Temple of *Nabû comprised some forty-five rooms. Of the other four buildings in this government area, extensively decorated with mural *paintings, the largest was the residence of Sargon's brother.

Against the *city wall in the south-west was a smaller walled-off compound, enclosing a large building also raised on a platform. It has been only partly excavated, but may have been the city's armoury.

In the lower town there have been only small excavations, in the Temple of the Sebittu south of the main compound; in a large residence to the east; and in a building near the centre of the city. No ordinary domestic housing has yet been located. AG

P. ALBENDA, The Palace of Sargon, King of Assyria (Paris 1986).

P.-É. BOTTA, with E.N. Flandin, Monuments de Ninive, 5 vols (Paris 1849–50).

G. LOUD and C.B. ALTMAN, Khorsabad, Parts 1–2 (Chicago 1936–8).

V. PLACE, with F. Thomas, Ninive et l'Assyrie, 3 vols (Paris 1867–70).

F. SAFAR, 'The Temple of the Sebitti at Khorsabad', Sumer 13 (1957) 219–21.

## King Lists

**King Lists** About 1800 BC a *Babylonian scholar compiled a list of *kings who had ruled the land from the institution of kingship by the *gods until his own day. Over twenty copies of the *Sumerian King List or parts of it are known, most from the same period, but it was read in *Ashurbanipal's *library over a millennium later. The most extensive copy begins with eight kings who ruled from five *towns, 'then came the *Flood'. This antediluvian section was a separate composition, affixed to the main list. It is absent from some copies and existed separately in at least one copy. The towns in this section were never seats of kingship in later times. The List proper begins with twenty-three kings who ruled at *Kish, then names eighteen other *dynasties, the last being the First Dynasty of *Isin, when the text was put into its present form. Although they are presented as a sequence, other sources show many dynasties overlapped or were entirely contemporary with each other. One tablet lists kings of *Lagash, not included in the main King List. The lengths of reign are in hundreds of years for the First Dynasty of Kish, but reduce in later dynasties, *Gilgamesh in the First Dynasty of *Uruk being given 126. How the high figures, higher before the Flood (e.g. 43,200 years), may be explained is debatable; a convincing

solution is awaited, and dismissing them as worthless is no solution. Babylonian *scribes prepared other lists of kings, of one or two dynasties perhaps for computational purposes, of longer spans for other reasons. The badly damaged Babylonian King List A sets out rulers by dynasty with lengths of reign from the First Dynasty of *Babylon to the rise of Nabopolassar. The tradition continued into Seleucid times (see Hellenistic period), one list covering rulers between 330 and 125 BC.

A document from the late seventeenth century BC, now called 'The Genealogy of the *Hammurabi Dynasty', lists those kings by name alone, the final lines revealing that it was part of a *ritual in which the names of the dead were read out to ensure their rest in the *underworld. That was also the purpose of lists of *Hittite kings, of *Ugarit's kings and of one from *Ebla (also of some Egyptian king lists).

In *Assyria scribes drew up the Assyrian King List, also starting as early as they could, with 'seventeen kings who lived in tents' who can be placed slightly before 2000 BC. The compilers aimed for completeness and included kings whose names they apparently found only on inscribed bricks and others whose lengths of reign were unknown. The arrangement of the opening sections is inconsistent, revealing different and incomplete sources, one tracing ancestors of *Shamshi-Adad I in reverse order, perhaps deriving from a *funerary ritual like the 'Genealogy of the Hammurabi Dynasty' with which it shares some names (see above). Thereafter each king is named, with his relationship to his predecessor and the length of his reign. The extant copies of this king list belong to Neo-Assyrian times and were probably designed to establish the ongoing line as well as aiding computations and, possibly, serving in commemorative rites. For other purposes, the scribes made lists of Assyrian kings with their Babylonian contemporaries and their chief ministers, the 'Synchronistic King Lists'.

Ancient *Israel preserved lists of names and ages of a line of '*Patriarchs' before the Flood, including Methuselah, who reached 969 years, and of the line from Noah to Abraham, which have some similarities with the Sumerian King List, although no kingly claims are made (Genesis 5; 11: 10–32). Later genealogies trace the line of King David (Ruth 4: 18–22; Matthew 1: 1–17), but do not list his successors in King List style.

Hellenistic and later writers such as *Berossus and Ptolemy had access to some ancient king lists or similar sources, preserving the information with varying degrees of accuracy, sometimes being the only source, as Josephus is for *Tyre. ARM

Sumerian:

D.O. EDZARD, 'Königslisten', Reallexikon der Assyriologie 6 (Berlin/New York 1980–3) 77–86.

T. JACOBSEN, The Sumerian King List (Chicago 1939).

A.L. OPPENHEIM, in Ancient Near Eastern Texts, 3rd ed., ed. J.B. Pritchard (Princeton, NJ 1969) 265–6.

C.-A. VINCENTE, 'The Tall Leilan Recension of the Sumerian King List', Zeitschrift für Assyriologie 85 (1995) 234–70.

Babylonian and Assyrian:

A.K. GRAYSON, 'Königslisten', Reallexikon der Assyriologie 6

(Berlin/New York 1980–3) 86–135.

A.R. MILLARD, 'Babylonian King Lists', *The Context of Scripture* 1, eds W.W. Hallo and K.L. Younger (Leiden 1997) 461–5.

A.L. OPPENHEIM, in *Ancient Near Eastern Texts*, 3rd ed., ed. J.B. Pritchard (Princeton, NJ 1969) 564–7.

Ugarit:

K.A. KITCHEN, 'The King List of Ugarit', *Ugarit-Forschungen* 9 (1977) 131–42.

D. PARDEE, *Les textes para-mythologiques de la 24e campagne, Ras Shamra-Ougarit* 4 (Paris 1988) 165–78.

K.L. YOUNGER, 'Ugaritic King List', *The Context of Scripture* 1, eds W.W. Hallo and K.L. Younger (Leiden 1997) 356–7.

Ebla:

A. ARCHI, 'Die ersten zehn Könige von Ebla', *Zeitschrift für Assyriologie* 76 (1986) 213–17.

## Kings and kingship

In all areas of the ancient Near East for which there are written records, the basic form of government was monarchy, normally by kings (exceptionally *queens), and normally hereditary, passing from father to eldest son. Of course the hereditary line was sometimes broken by early death, conquest or usurpers, and new *dynasties arose, but being able to claim descent from a line of kings was regarded as a form of legitimacy, and proudly proclaimed in royal inscriptions, even when it was patently untrue.

In theory, the king's power was absolute in every aspect of state life, although, particularly in *Babylonia, *religion was largely the province of the high *priest, sometimes a member of the royal *family, but *Sumerian rulers often also held priestly offices. During the Babylonian *New Year Festival, the high priest slapped the king's face and pulled his ears to remind him that he was a humble servant of the *gods. At certain times and places kings were regarded as divine (the first being *Naram-Sin of *Akkad) – and occasionally there is evidence for the worship of statues of kings – but more usually they regarded themselves as the representatives on earth of the state's supreme god. In Babylonian *mythology, kingship was handed down to mankind by the gods, and indeed kings stressed that they had been divinely selected. From Early Dynastic times there appears to have been a formal coronation, kings being invested with their symbols of office in *temples (see Crowns and royal regalia).

A king's responsibility was to nourish the gods by building and maintaining temples, to look after (literally 'shepherd') his people, and to administer justice (see Law). He participated in *rituals to ensure the prosperity of his land, some, like the *Sacred Marriage ritual in Babylonia, involving *sexual intercourse with a goddess, perhaps represented by a priestess. The images of themselves favoured by kings varied: the ideal Babylonian king was a pious legislator and administrator, while *Assyrian kings portrayed themselves as mighty warriors. There may have been a real difference in their manner of rule, Babylonian kings traditionally being available for direct appeals from private citizens, Assyrian kings being largely inaccessible even to courtiers, outsiders having to be brought before the king blindfolded. Kings lived in what we call '*palaces', although in Mesopotamia the *Akka-

From very early times the lion was associated with kingship as the most powerful of beasts. Kings were called 'lion' or shown overcoming lions, as Ashurbanipal (668–?627 BC) is on several reliefs from his palace at Nineveh. WA 124875.

Impression of the cylinder seal of Sin-Ishmeanni, showing him standing before his enthroned master, Sumu-Yamutbal, who holds a cup. A dwarf stands between them and a goddess behind. c.1850 BC. WA 134757.

dian term *ekallu* meant 'big *house' and included not only the king's residence but also the centre of government.

*Letters, especially from *Mari and *Nimrud, written by officials to kings show that they were concerned with matters of detail relating to the running of their territory or empire. Certain Assyrian kings, particularly *Esarhaddon, were highly superstitious and did not do anything unless there were favourable *astrological *omens. As protection against evil omens, sometimes the king fasted, wore the *clothes of a nanny or sat for a week in a reed hut and was treated as if he were ill. In the case of a particularly bad omen, a substitute king would be placed on the throne, the first recorded substitute being a gardener during the First Dynasty of *Isin in the nineteenth century BC who remained on the throne when the real king died. In Neo-Assyrian times this might happen several times in one reign, and from the reigns of Esarhaddon and *Ashurbanipal alone there are thirty letters dealing with the substitute king. The substitute married and reigned for one hundred days, taking on whatever evil had been foretold for the king. At the end of the period, the substitute and his 'queen' were put to *death and buried with great ceremony. It is assumed that during this period the real king kept a low profile, not carrying out any of his ceremonial duties but discreetly running the state in the background.                                    PB

G. BECKMAN, 'Royal Ideology and State Administration in Hittite Anatolia', *Civilizations of the Ancient Near East*, ed. J.M. Sasson (New York 1995) 529–43.

J. BOTTÉRO, *Mesopotamia: Writing, Reasoning, and the Gods* (Chicago 1992) 138–55.

D.O. EDZARD and M.-J. SEUX, 'Königtum', *Reallexikon der Assyriologie* 6 (Berlin/New York 1980–3) 140–73.

H. FRANKFORT, *Kingship and the Gods: A Study of Ancient Near Eastern Religion as the Integration of Society and Nature* (Chicago 1948).

J.N. POSTGATE, *Early Mesopotamia: Society and Economy at the Dawn of History* (London 1992) 260–74.

**Kirta:** see Keret

**Kish**  The extensive mounds of the *Sumerian *city of Kish lie in central Iraq, 15 km east of *Babylon. Kish was occupied from the *Ubaid period, c.5000 BC, through the *Jemdet Nasr, Early Dynastic, Old *Babylonian and Neo-Babylonian periods, and into the *Achaemenid, *Parthian and *Sasanian ages before an abandonment around the sixth century AD. Kish was of unique importance to the Sumerians in the third millennium BC, the title '*king of Kish' indicating political hegemony, in name at least, over ancient Sumer. Major excavations at Kish were conducted by Henri de Genouillac (1912) and Stephen Langdon (1923–33).

Kish comprises the mounds of Ingharra (ancient Hursagkalama) and Uhaimir with other areas of settlement. Some of the earliest evidence comes from the Y sounding in Ingharra where Jemdet Nasr *pottery and Early Dynastic *houses and *graves were excavated. Several graves are *chariot burials comparable in many respects to the graves of the Royal Cemetery of *Ur. Two immense brick platforms, or *ziggurats, were built at Ingharra during the Early Dynastic period, probably c.2500 BC, and are characteristic of Sumerian religious architecture. To the south of Ingharra, on mound A, an Early Dynastic *palace was uncovered. At least 150 graves dating to c.2400–2300 BC were dug into the ruins of this Sumerian palace. To the north-west of Ingharra, in area P, lay an extensive storage and administrative building, called the Plano-Convex Building because of the shape of its bricks, also Early Dynastic in date.

The main features of the Uhaimir area of Kish are important Old Babylonian remains, c.2000–1595 BC, including a ziggurat-*temple complex of the *god Zababa and a *cuneiform scribal *school. In mound W, west of Ingharra, a *library of Neo-*Assyrian tablets of the seventh century BC was recovered. Neo-Babylonian remains at Kish include a large temple complex at Ingharra. The eastern extremities of the settlement formed the important Sasanian city at Kish, adorned with stucco-decorated buildings.

In sum, the material remains of Kish, taken in conjunction with scattered historical references in cuneiform literature, indicate the unique importance of the site, in particular through the third millennium BC when the city was viewed by the Sumerians as the prime source of kingship.                                                          RM

M. GIBSON, *The City and Area of Kish* (Miami 1972).

D.P. HANSEN, 'Kish', *The Oxford Encyclopedia of Archaeology in the Near East* 3, ed. E.M. Meyers (New York 1997) 298–300.

P.R.S. MOOREY, *Kish Excavations 1923–1933* (Oxford 1978).

**Koldewey, Robert (1855–1925)**  While uncovering the glories of *Nebuchadnezzar's *Babylon, Robert Koldewey pioneered systematic methods of excavation which revolutionized *Mesopotamian *archaeology. Born in Blankenberg, Germany, he studied architecture, archaeology and history of art and acquired wide experience of excavation in Mesopotamia, *Syria, Greece, Italy and Sicily. At Babylon (1899–1917) he found spectacular remains and *cuneiform tablets particularly of the Neo-*Babylonian period, including the imposing Processional Way and the *Ishtar Gate, and excavated the foundations of the *ziggurat, the legendary '*Tower of Babel'. Koldewey identified a vaulted building as the substructure of the famous Hanging Gardens of Babylon, a claim accepted for many years (see Gardens). In fact it was probably an *archive storeroom, which included tablets recording issues of rations to captives, notably Jehoiachin of *Judah, known from the *Bible.

Koldewey developed new methods, now universal, of tracing mudbrick walls and distinguishing them from fills and foundation trenches. He was much admired and described as patient, methodical and austere, although he was lively and unstuffy and fond of writing amusing letters and rhymes.                                              PB

C.W. CERAM, *Gods Graves and Scholars* (London 1954) 192–204.

B. FAGAN, 'Koldewey, Robert', *The Oxford Encyclopedia of Archaeology in the Near East* 3, ed. E.M. Meyers (New York 1997) 303.

R. KOLDEWEY, *The Excavations at Babylon* (London 1914).

——, *Heitere und ernste Briefe* (Berlin 1925).

***Kudurru***  Owning land was a major form of security and wealth in *Babylonia, so written deeds transferring or proving ownership were created from almost the beginning of writing and sometimes given permanent form by inscription on *stone.

The term *kudurru* has been applied to those third-millennium documents, but it primarily refers to deeds produced between the fourteenth and seventh centuries BC. *Kassite *kings granted large tracts of land to faithful servants, gifts recorded on stone boulders or blocks and also on clay, the *kudurru*. These monuments were kept in *temples, perhaps occasionally in shrines on the property, to publicize the donation; legally valid sealed tablets were preserved in *archives. Some were carved with symbols of the *gods in relief, rarely with captions to aid identification (see Divine symbols), and, from the

Black stone *kudurru*, 36 cm high, carved with divine emblems and an inscription recording a gift of land. Curses in the text and the gods invoked were intended to prevent counter-claims or attempts to alter the boundary. c.1155 BC. WA 102485.

The figure of a god, c.1.35 m high, carved on the rock wall of the Hittite royal sanctuary at Yazýlýkaya, outside Boghazköy. The ear of corn marks him as Kumarbi (courtesy of David Hawkins).

eleventh century BC onwards, some had a picture of the Babylonian king concerned. The pictures illustrated the *cuneiform texts. These gave details of the property, occasionally with a plan, the reason for the presentation, notices of special conditions, such as *tax exemption, lists of witnesses and curses in the names of the gods on anyone who should feloniously change the situation. In a few cases *kudurru*s relate disputes over ownership, giving the history. After the Kassite period, *kudurru*s may take tablet shape and record private transactions.     ARM

J.A. BRINKMAN and U. SEIDL, 'Kudurru', *Reallexikon der Assyriologie* 6 (Berlin/New York 1980–3) 267–77.

I.J. GELB, P. STEINKELLER and R.M. WHITING, *Earliest Land Tenure Systems in the Near East: Ancient Kudurrus* (Chicago 1991).

L.W. KING, *Babylonian Boundary Stones and Memorial Texts in the British Museum* (London 1912).

U. SEIDL, 'Die babylonische Kudurru-Reliefs', *Baghdader Mitteilungen* 4 (1968) 7–220.

**Kültepe:** see Kanesh

**Kumarbi** Kumarbi was the *Hurrian grain-*god, known from *mythological texts from *Boghazköy, cultic texts from *Mari, *Nuzi and *Ugarit, and a first-millennium BC Luwian *hieroglyphic stela from Tell Ahmar. An obscure myth concerning *silver links him with *Urkesh, which might have been one of his cult centres. At Boghazköy he was identified with *Enlil, and at Ugarit with both *El and *Dagan. The grain god depicted in the *Hittite pantheon at *Yazýlýkaya is probably to be identified as Kumarbi. 'Kumarbi' was the form of the name used in the late second millennium BC, while 'Kuparma', known from Hurrian contexts of the first millennium BC, was probably a later version.

Several Hittite versions of Hurrian myths starring Kumarbi exist, particularly concerned with quarrels between gods for the *kingship of heaven. Kumarbi is often described as 'king of the gods' in the texts. In one myth, Kumarbi attacks *Anu, who is deposing Alalu. Kumarbi bites off Anu's genitals, and eventually it seems that he gives birth to the *weather-god, probably *Teshup, who in turn defeats him. In 'The Song of Ullikummi', Kumarbi attempts unsuccessfully to overcome Teshup by creating a stone monster called Ullikummi. The main theme of these myths appears to be the changing of the kingship of the gods between the generations, Alalu–Anu–Kumarbi–Teshup, a theme echoed in later classical mythology (e.g. Uranus–Kronos–Zeus).     PB

H. GÜTERBOCK, *Kumarbi: Mythen vom churritischen Kronos* (Zurich 1946).

——, 'Kumarbi', *Reallexikon der Assyriologie* 6 (Berlin/New York 1980–3) 324–30.

H.A. HOFFNER, JR, *Hittite Myths* (Atlanta, GA 1990) 38–61.

R. LEBRUN, 'From Hittite Mythology: The Kumarbi Cycle', *Civilizations of the Ancient Near East*, ed. J.M. Sasson (New York 1995) 1971–80.

H. OTTEN, *Mythen vom Gotte Kummarbi: Neue Fragmente* (Berlin 1950).

**Kurgan** A kurgan was a distinctive *burial mound characteristic of the *Bronze Age in the *Caucasus, which gave its name to the Kurgan or Pit-Grave Culture. Kurgans first appeared towards the end of the third millennium BC, but continued to be used by the *Scythians in the first millennium BC. A kurgan consisted of a single burial with the body lying on its back with its legs contracted and knees up, with a barrow of stones and earth heaped over it. Often kurgans contained *gold and *silver *jewellery, elaborate *tools and weapons, and *horse and *chariot burials. A particularly grand kurgan was found at *Maikop.     PB

C. BURNEY and D.M. LANG, *The Peoples of the Hills: Ancient Ararat and Caucasus* (London 1971) 79–85.

# L

**Lachish** Ancient Lachish is identified with the 12-ha mound of Tell ed-Duweir, located in the Judaean hill country c.38.5 km south-east of *Jerusalem. This identification was first proposed by *Albright. The position of Lachish was strategic and offered its population *water and good farmland; these factors allowed the *city to flourish over a long period of time, especially between the Early Bronze Age and the *Persian period.

Lachish has been excavated by J.L. Starkey (1932–8), ending with his murder by robbers, Y. Aharoni (1966–8) and D. Ussishkin (1973–8). It was already a sizeable settlement in the Early Bronze Age, and in the Middle and Late Bronze Ages was protected by a glacis (or ramp) and a fosse (or rock-cut moat). Middle Bronze Lachish, including its huge *palace at the top of the site, was destroyed by fire c.1550 BC. Three successive *temples were built in the fosse during the Late Bronze Age, the period when Lachish is referred to in the *Amarna Letters. The final phase of *Canaanite Lachish (stratum VI) was totally destroyed by fire towards the end of the twelfth century BC, perhaps by the *Sea Peoples or by the Hebrews.

At the end of the tenth century BC, Lachish IV emerged as a fortified city, second only to Jerusalem in regional importance. During the period of Israel's Divided Monarchy, two city walls protected Lachish, one half-way down the slope of the mound and one around its summit. A large *gate bastion allowed entrance through the lower wall, and the inner *fortifications were entered through a six-chambered gate. In the upper city stood a large palace, which was almost certainly the residence of the local governor.

Much of the *Iron Age fortification system was rebuilt during stratum III, but this period ended when *Sennacherib invaded *Judah and destroyed Lachish in 701 BC. Accounts of the *Assyrian invasion are found in the *Bible and in Sennacherib's *annals. Assyrian artists carved the siege of Lachish in relief to decorate Sennacherib's palace at *Nineveh. Excavations have uncovered

remains and artefacts portrayed in these Assyrian reliefs (e.g. walls and gatehouse, siege ramp, Assyrian armour, arrowheads, slingstones). Excavations have recovered almost 440 Israelite *seal impressions bearing the typical, royal four-winged symbol. These seals are mostly from Iron II storage jars and point to a system of local *trade or *administration in the reign of Hezekiah, just before the 701 BC destruction.

After a period of abandonment, the settlement was refortified in the seventh century BC (stratum II). Rooms in the smaller gate complex yielded a collection of *Hebrew *ostraca known as the 'Lachish Letters' written shortly before Lachish was captured and destroyed by the *Babylonians in 587/6 BC. Several are reports sent to a Judaean commander in Lachish (Yaosh/Yaush) by one of his subordinates who was in a position to see the signal fires of Lachish and nearby Azekah.

Lachish stratum I includes remains from the Babylonian, Persian and early *Hellenistic periods. During the Persian period, Lachish was partially rebuilt to serve a local administrative function.                         GLM

Y. AHARONI, *Investigations at Lachish: The Sanctuary and the Residency (Lachish V)* (Tel Aviv 1975).

H. TORCZYNER et al., *Lachish I: The Lachish Letters* (London 1938).

O. TUFNELL, *Lachish III: The Iron Age* (London 1953).

O. TUFNELL, C.H. INGE and G.L. HARDING, *Lachish II: The Fosse Temple* (London 1940).

O. TUFNELL et al., *Lachish IV: The Bronze Age* (London 1958).

D. USSISHKIN, *The Conquest of Lachish by Sennacherib* (Tel Aviv 1982).

**Lagash** The important *Sumerian *city-state of Lagash comprised three urban centres: Lagash itself (modern Al-Hiba), Girsu (modern Tello) and Nina-Sirara (modern Zurghul). These extensive urban sites are located in southern Iraq. Excavations were conducted at Lagash by *Koldewey and Donald Hansen, at Girsu by Ernest de Sarzec, Henri de Genouillac and André Parrot, and at Zurghul by Koldewey. Girsu (Tello) was the first Sumerian city extensively excavated (from 1877 onwards), and the display of finds from Girsu in Paris in the 1880s caused a sensation.

Lagash (Al-Hiba) is one of the largest archaeological sites in the Near East, covering some 600 ha in all. The city was at its peak during the Early Dynastic I period, c.3000–2700 BC, when much of the site was occupied by large *temple precincts. Again in the Early Dynastic III period, c.2600–2350 BC, extensive temple complexes dominated the city, including the Bagara of Ningirsu and the Ibgal of Inana. There was also a large *administrative building with *cuneiform tablets mentioning the *kings Eannatum and Enanatum I. Lagash (Al-Hiba) was mainly abandoned around 2500 BC, although there is

A central room in Sennacherib's palace at Nineveh was adorned with sculptures showing the attack on Lachish. Layard made drawings of the sculptures *in situ*. Or. Dr. I,59.

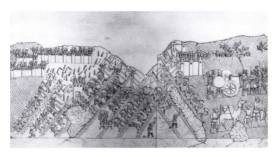

Many carvings of men who ruled Lagash were uncovered, set up in temples to remind the gods and later generations of royal piety. This fragment shows Enanatum II, c.2370 BC. Height 19 cm. WA 130828.

some evidence of renewed occupation in the early second millennium BC.

Girsu lies 25 km to the north-west, a separate but connected city belonging to the Lagash state. There is evidence for *Ubaid occupation, but the main period of settlement is Early Dynastic III, when Girsu was capital of the Lagash state. Although few buildings were identified, great quantities of cuneiform tablets were recovered from Girsu, and they provide some basis for reconstructing early Sumerian history. Masterpieces of Sumerian *art from Girsu include the Stela of the Vultures, showing scenes of battle and *myth, and, from the Neo-Sumerian period (c.2100–2000 BC), beautifully carved statues of *Gudea, king of Lagash, but thereafter the city went into a long decline.

The site of Zurghul, 10 km south-east of Lagash (Al-Hiba), also dates principally to the Early Dynastic and Neo-Sumerian periods, but little work has been carried out there.                                                                RM

V.E. CRAWFORD, 'Excavations in the Swamps of Sumer', *Expedition* 14/2 (1972) 12–20.

D.P. HANSEN, 'Royal Building Activity at Sumerian Lagash in the Early Dynastic Period', *Biblical Archaeologist* 55 (1992) 206–11.

R.J. MATTHEWS, 'Girsu and Lagash', *The Oxford Encyclopedia of Archaeology in the Near East* 2, ed. E.M. Meyers (New York 1997) 406–9.

**Lamentations**  As a literary genre, lamentations are an important feature of *Sumerian *literature. Upwards of fifty major laments are known, composed in the Emesal ('*women's language') dialect, and written sources indicate that, although many have traditional origins in the third millennium BC, they were still being performed at *Babylon in the first century BC by choirs of *priests accompanied by drums. Typically they deplore the destruction of *temples; the responsibility is often laid mysteriously at the door of the *gods themselves. They abound in references to desolate goddesses, abandoned ruin mounds, scattered populations and interrupted cults. Closely related to these is a group of six lamentations over the destruction of Sumerian *cities including *Ur, *Uruk and *Eridu. These may be related to historical events at the turn of the third millennium BC (when waves of hostile *nomadic peoples entered southern *Mesopotamia), but in some cases the lamentations were actually composed to *celebrate* the restoration by later *kings of the cities concerned.

Similar themes are echoed in *Akkadian *literature, and it is easy to find striking parallels in other religious works of the ancient Near East, such as the *Bible. There the Book of Lamentations bewails the destruction of *Jerusalem in 586 BC, interpreting it as divine punishment for the people's apostasy from *Yahweh. The Book of Psalms includes both communal and personal laments.                                                         JAB/ARM

J.A. BLACK, 'Eme-sal Cult Songs and Prayers', *Velles paraules*, eds P. Michalowski *et al.* (=*Aula Orientalis* 9 (1991) 23–36).

M.E. COHEN, *The Canonical Lamentations of Ancient Mesopotamia* (Potomac 1988).

P.W. FERRIS, *The Genre of the Communal Lament in the Bible and the Ancient Near East* (Atlanta, GA 1992).

M.R. GREEN, 'The Eridu Lament', *Journal of Cuneiform Studies* 30 (1978) 127–67.

——, 'The Uruk Lament', *Journal of the American Oriental Society* 104 (1984) 253–79.

W.W. HALLO, *Origins: The Ancient Near Eastern Background of Some Modern Institutions* (Leiden 1996) 223-42.

P. MICHALOWSKI, *The Lamentation Over the Destruction of Sumer and Ur* (Winona Lake, IN 1989).

S.J. TINNEY, *The Nippur Lament* (Philadelphia, PA 1996).

**Languages**  The ancient Near East was host to representatives of several of the world's major language families (*Semitic, Caucasian, Indo-Aryan, *Indo-European) and to languages which are not assigned to any of them (*Sumerian, *Elamite, Hattic, *Hurrian and *Urartian). Travellers in the Near East quickly become aware of the variety of languages current now. In ancient times the variety was even greater; Semitic languages were widespread from the third millennium BC, but none dominated in the way Arabic does today. Although there can be no certainty without written records, we may surmise that the people of *Samarra and *Ubaid communities spoke a different language to those of the *Halaf. Shortly after the appearance of *writing, Sumerian is attested and the Sumerian *King List has both Sumerian and Semitic *Akkadian names for *kings in the first dynasty after the *Flood, at *Kish, implying that speakers of both languages were then living in *Babylonia. By 2500 BC *scribes with Akkadian names were copying Sumerian texts, and a little later Sumerian texts were translated into a form of Akkadian at *Ebla. Over the next two millennia Elamite, Hurrian, Urartian, Luwian and its close Indo-

Bilingual word lists appeared early in the history of writing as scribes faced several foreign languages. The Kassite rule over Babylonia led to the compilation of this list of Kassite words (left) with Akkadian equivalents (right). WA 93005.

European relatives are known from *cuneiform texts. The long written history of Akkadian, in particular, with its many well dated texts, offers linguists an important opportunity to trace the changes and developments which occurred in the language. In other cases, the evidence comes from a short period only (as at *Ugarit), or is fragmentary (as is *Aramaic) or from largely standardized sources (as with *Hebrew). Sumerian is the oldest known written language, but it contains words (e.g. *pahar*, 'potter') and place names which are thought to belong to an earlier people living in *Mesopotamia who spoke a language now called 'Ubaidian' or 'Proto-Euphratean'.

Although the majority of people would need only one language in most societies, travellers of all sorts (*merchants, pedlars, *diplomats and messengers) would need and have to learn others. In the third millennium BC, scribes at Ebla who translated texts (see above) probably spoke a West Semitic language. A *seal from the *dynasty of *Akkad proclaims its owner 'interpreter of *Meluhha', and that role had continuing importance. Without such help, language could be a barrier, as *Ashurbanipal implies when he records that a messenger arrived from *Lydia whom no one could understand, or as the *Bible characterizes *Jerusalem's enemies as 'a people whose language you do not know' (Jeremiah 5: 15).

It is essential to distinguish language from writing. Language can exist without writing. A writing system may record one or more languages, some of them being very different from that for which the script was devised, as cuneiform was probably invented for Sumerian, then used for Semitic Akkadian and Indo-European *Hittite, and as the *alphabet demonstrates above all other scripts.

A single language may be written in more than one script (as Hittite was written both in *hieroglyphic and cuneiform scripts).

A Sumerian *epic and the Bible (see Tower of Babel) look back to an age when everyone spoke the same language, but modern attempts to reconstruct a single, primal language are unconvincing. ARM

B. LANDSBERGER, *Three Essays on the Sumerians* (Los Angeles 1974).

**Larsa** The capital of an important kingdom of the early second millennium BC, Larsa (modern Tell Senkereh) lies c.20 km south-east of *Uruk in southern *Mesopotamia. It has been excavated by W.K. Loftus (1853–4), *Andrae (1903), André Parrot (1933, 1967), Jean-Claude Margueron (1969–70) and Jean-Louis Huot (1976–91). The ruins stretch for nearly 2 km north–south and east–west, and are dominated by a religious complex dedicated to *Shamash and the *ziggurat, which have been the focus of excavation.

Although no remains earlier than the third millennium BC have been found, there is evidence that Larsa was occupied from the *Ubaid to the *Parthian periods. The major remains date to the early second millennium BC. At that time, Larsa alternated with *Isin in controlling southern Mesopotamia, until its conquest and annexation by *Hammurabi in c.1763 BC. *Letters from *Mari describe Hammurabi's six-month assault of Larsa with ramps, battering rams and towers. Its king, Rim-Sin, who had been on the throne for sixty years, was captured alive.

The religious complex at Larsa, built after Hammurabi's conquest, consists of a series of buildings and courtyards decorated with semi-engaged spiral columns, and lined with chapels and workshops. The palace of King Nur-Adad (c.1865–1850 BC) was never completed or occupied, and consists of the typical arrangement of throne room and administrative areas. PB

J.-C. MARGUERON and J.-L. HUOT, 'Larsa', *Reallexikon der Assyriologie* 6 (Berlin/New York 1984) 500–6.

**Law** One of the main responsibilities of ancient Near Eastern *kings was to uphold justice on behalf of the *gods they represented. In theory, the king was always the supreme judge. In *Mesopotamia, the god of justice was *Shamash.

Several law 'codes' are known, which together with court records and *contracts give a picture of the legal structure of ancient Near Eastern states. In *Sumerian there are the codes of Urukagina (c.2350 BC), *Ur-Nammu (c.2100 BC) and Lipit-Ishtar (c.1930 BC); in *Akkadian those of *Eshnunna (c.1900 BC), *Hammurabi (early eighteenth century BC), the Middle *Assyrian laws (twelfth century BC), and fragments of Neo-*Babylonian laws. The *Hittite laws were drawn up early in the Old Kingdom, and refer to changes made to even earlier laws; a Hittite New Kingdom version introduced more changes. The *Hebrew laws recorded in the *Bible,

Law Code of Hammurabi, on a diorite stela found at Susa, where it formed part of the booty brought back from Mesopotamia by the Elamites (© Photo RMN – H. Lewandowski. Louvre Sb 8).

hired the ox may take an oath by the life of a god and be released'. In the Hittite laws, acts of sorcery and *magic directed against other Hittites were considered illegal, but such crimes do not appear in the Mesopotamian law collections.

On a local level, justice was administered by the town assembly or elders, sometimes bringing in royal or *temple officials. Three to six judges chosen from among the leading members of the community heard cases. Parties in a dispute represented themselves. These local courts dealt with most property disputes. Commercial disputes were handled by the *merchants' organization (Akkadian *kārum*). More serious criminal offences were referred to royal judges and officials. Hearings were often held in city temples. Oaths were sworn by claimants, defendants and witnesses, and included touching or moving sacred emblems or weapons of a god.

Judicial verdicts were regarded as final, and anyone contesting them was liable to punishment ranging from a fine to the death penalty. If Babylonian judges could not reach a verdict, they resorted to the *river ordeal. Court cases were recorded on a tablet, or in the first millennium BC in *Aramaic on a leather scroll.                    PB

G.R. DRIVER and J.C. MILES, *The Assyrian Laws* (Oxford 1935).
——, *The Babylonian Laws* (Oxford 1952–5).
J. FRIEDRICH, *Die hethitischen Gesetze* (Leiden 1959).
S. GREENGUS, 'Legal and Social Institutions of Ancient Mesopotamia', *Civilizations of the Ancient Near East*, ed. J.M. Sasson (New York 1995) 469–84.
H.A. HOFFNER, Jr, 'Legal and Social Institutions of Hittite Anatolia', *Civilizations of the Ancient Near East*, ed. J.M. Sasson (New York 1995) 555–69.
S. LAFONT, *Femmes, droit et justice dans l'Antiquité orientale: contribution à l'étude du droit pénal au Proche-Orient ancien* (Fribourg 1999).
M.T. ROTH, *Law Collections from Mesopotamia and Asia Minor* (Atlanta, GA 1997).

especially those in the book of *Exodus, are often treated as part of this group of codes, although they were edited in their final form many centuries after their first formulation. All these codes share similarities in structure and content.

Although traditionally called 'codes', these were not comprehensive collections of laws used as reference works in legal disputes; indeed there is no evidence from contracts and court records that they were referred to at all. Each code is inconsistent and omits many legal situations. The Mesopotamian codes at least are collections of numerous social and economic reforms which kings had originally issued as decrees, dressed up as royal inscriptions with the addition of a prologue and epilogue. Hammurabi's laws, for example, were inscribed on stone stelae set up in at least two major cities, *Sippar and *Babylon, and additional copies were written on clay tablets. His code was recopied and preserved for centuries as a scribal textbook.

The laws contained in the codes covered all manner of *crime, *property rights, *family and inheritance law, prohibitions on certain *sexual relations, debt regulations, ill-treatment of *slaves, loans and hire, and regulation of prices for commodities and wages for workers. They were normally presented in the form of cases, like this example from Hammurabi's code: 'If a man has hired an ox and a god struck it down and it died, the man who

## Layard, (Sir) Austen Henry (or Henry Austen) (1817–94)

British traveller, archaeologist, cuneiformist, art historian, draughtsman, collector, writer, politician and career diplomat, Layard (pronounced '*laird*', not '*lay-ard*') is famous for his pioneering excavations at *Nimrud. Though of less than ten years' duration, his fieldwork in northern *Mesopotamia (Iraq) strongly promoted Assyriology.

Born in Paris, brought up in Florence, he learned drawing and studied Italian art, continuing after his family's return to Britain in 1829. In 1833–9 he worked as solicitor's clerk for his uncle in London, before departing overland for Ceylon (Sri Lanka), to practise law. Lingering in the Near East, he drew ancient rock reliefs and copied *cuneiform inscriptions. At Mosul in 1840 he met *Botta and visited *Nineveh and *Nimrud. From 1842 the British Ambassador at Istanbul employed Layard on unofficial missions, before sponsoring him to excavate.

Layard worked at Nimrud 1845–7 and 1849–51, from late 1846 funded by the British Museum. He soon discovered two *Assyrian royal *palaces, many of whose rooms contained carved stone wall reliefs, statues, carved

Layard exploring Assyrian rock sculptures at Bavian.
Or. Dr.I, 1.

*ivories and cuneiform tablets. By 1847 Layard had found no fewer than eight palaces and *temples.

At Nineveh in 1849–51 Layard unearthed the palace of *Sennacherib, and tablets from the Assyrian state *archive, which assisted the decipherment of cuneiform and provided much knowledge about Assyro-*Babylonian history and culture. Layard also made soundings at *Ashur, *Khorsabad, *Babylon, *Nippur and other sites. In 1851, however, he left Mesopotamia for good.

Layard's discoveries caused a sensation in Britain and Europe, and were successfully popularized in his *Nineveh and its Remains* (1849) and *Discoveries in the Ruins of Nineveh and Babylon* (1853). The antiquities sent to London formed the core of the Mesopotamian collections of the British Museum. These discoveries stimulated the 'Assyrian Revival' movement in European art, especially after their display at the Great Exhibition of 1851, and were used by both sides in debate over *biblical truth.

After completing his basic reports (1853), Layard drew on his fame in *archaeology to launch himself in politics. As a (Liberal) MP, he held a couple of junior government posts, before his appointments as Minister in Madrid (1869–77) and Ambassador at Istanbul (1877–80). In 1869, aged fifty-two, he married Enid Guest, then twenty-five. In 1882 he retired to Venice, where he installed his collection of Italian Renaissance paintings in Ca' Cappello, now the Oriental Institute of Venice University. He died in London.          AG

J. ANDERSON, 'Layard, Sir Austen Henry', *The Dictionary of Art* 18, ed. J. Turner (New York/London 1996) 896–7.
R.D. BARNETT, 'Lady Layard's Jewelry', *Archaeology in the Levant: Essays for Kathleen Kenyon*, eds R. Moorey and P. Parr (Warminster 1978) 172–9.
F.N. BOHRER, 'The Printed Orient: The Production of A.H. Layard's Earliest Works', *Culture and History* 11 (1992) 85–105.
F.M. FALES and B.J. HICKEY (eds), *Austen Henry Layard: Tra l'Oriente e Venezia: Venezia, 1983* (Rome 1987).
H.W.F. SAGGS, 'Introduction' to Layard's *Nineveh and its Remains* (New York 1970) 1–64.
G. WATERFIELD, *Layard of Nineveh* (London 1963).

**Lebanon** The name for the modern Republic of Lebanon, a tiny nation at the eastern end of the Mediterranean, derives from a *Semitic term (meaning 'white') given to the high mountains which rise from this coast. While the nation itself was created between the world wars, the name given to the mountains ('white') is very ancient and easy to explain. These mountains receive much rain, and their peaks are snow-covered for much of the year. It is not surprising that various ancient peoples believed that *gods lived in these mountains, which are linked with legend and *mythology.

The Mediterranean coastal plain is between 3 and 32 km wide; this was home to the sea-oriented *Phoenicians and famous *city-states like *Tyre and *Sidon in antiquity. The Lebanon range, sometimes called Mount Lebanon, runs parallel to the seaboard and extends for c.160 km, from the Amanus mountains of *Syria to Upper Galilee. In some places, the almost bare peaks rise to c.3050 m; these slopes were heavily forested in antiquity. In the centre of modern Lebanon, east of the coastal range, is the well watered Beqa' Valley, which has an elevation of over 1000 m. Out of this valley flow the Orontes and Litani *rivers, to the north and south respec-

Map of Lebanon showing main archaeological sites.

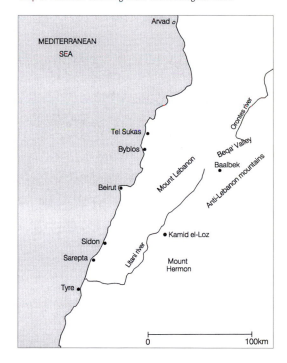

tively. In classical times, the Beqa' was known as Coele Syria (Latin for 'Hollow Syria'), and the region was famous because of the great *temple at Heliopolis (Baalbek). East of this valley – and running along the modern border with Syria – is the Anti-Lebanon ('behind the Lebanon') range. With an elevation of over 2800 m, Mount Hermon (ancient Sirion/Senir) sits at the southern end of this chain; its melting snows feed the tributaries that merge into the Jordan river in northern *Israel. With such rugged terrain, the route between Beirut and *Damascus was tortuous.

Because the western (coastal) slopes of Mount Lebanon receive up to 1520 mm of rain each year, they were covered with forests of pine, cypress and cedar *trees. The Lebanon range is mentioned almost seventy times in the *Bible, where the mountains are noted for their cedar trees and *fertility. In Old *Babylonian times, the cedar forest of the *Gilgamesh *epic was located in Lebanon. Beginning in the third millennium BC, the *Egyptians shipped large quantities of *wood from the Lebanese coast to the Nile Valley. From the twelfth century BC, the *Assyrians began to exploit these same forests. According to the *Old Testament, Hiram of *Tyre supplied Solomon with cedars to build his *palace and the temple in *Jerusalem; cedars of Lebanon were used to rebuild the temple in the *Persian period.

Much archaeological research remains to be done in Lebanon; sites from *Palaeolithic to Ottoman times are already well known. During the *Bronze and *Iron Ages, the region of Lebanon was occupied by the *Canaanites, *Amorites, *Aramaeans and Phoenicians. Important ancient cities included *Byblos, Beirut, *Arvad, Tyre and Sidon.

GLM

J.P. BROWN, *The Lebanon and Phoenicia* 1 (Beirut 1969).

P.K. HITTI, *Lebanon in History* (London 1957).

W. RÖLLIG, 'Lebanon', *Dictionary of Deities and Demons in the Bible*, eds K. van der Toorn, B. Becking and P.W. van der Horst (Leiden 1995) 945–8.

R.H. SMITH, 'Lebanon', *Anchor Bible Dictionary* 4, ed. D.N. Freedman (New York 1992) 269–70.

W.A. WARD, 'Archaeology in Lebanon in the Twentieth Century', *Biblical Archaeologist* 57 (1994) 66–85.

M. WEIPPERT, 'Libanon', *Reallexikon der Assyriologie* 6 (Berlin/New York 1980–3) 641–50.

**Legacy** The ancient Near East has left a rich legacy to the modern world, and many of the things we take for granted today had their origin in that area. Here were invented *agriculture, *writing, the *alphabet (including the order and names of the letters in our ABC), the first *cities, *administration, *coins, and the basic principles of *mathematics and *astronomy, including the sexagesimal system by which we still divide the circle into 360 degrees and the hour into sixty minutes and 3600 seconds. The division of the day into twenty-four hours is a result of the crossing of *Egyptian and *Babylonian

Full-size reconstruction of Babylon in the late sixth century BC, built on a vacant lot near the intersection of Sunset and Hollywood Boulevards in Hollywood, for the silent film *Intolerance* (1916) directed by D.W. Griffith (Wark Producing Company, courtesy of The Kobal Collection).

influence. A basic principle of modern mathematics, place value notation (whereby the place of the numeral denotes its value, e.g. 56 = (5 × 10) + 6), was the basis of the Babylonian numerical system, transmitted into early Indian astronomy, and later in the first millennium AD into Islamic civilization and into the western world as the so-called arabic numerals.

Ancient Near Eastern *myths and *literature have become part of our modern heritage through the *Bible and Greek and Roman literature. The biblical accounts of the *creation and the *Flood closely parallel other Near Eastern myths, and Babylonian *wisdom literature influenced certain books of the Bible. The stories about Herakles/Hercules in Greek and Roman literature owe much to the *Epic of *Gilgamesh, and there are parallels in other myths. There are many similarities between Mesopotamian epic literature, especially Gilgamesh, and the *Iliad* and *Odyssey*. Themes from Gilgamesh were incorporated into the Alexander Romance, a romantic legend that grew up around the heroic figure of Alexander the Great and became one of the most widely known pieces of fiction in late antiquity and the Middle Ages, written in many versions and languages from *Iran to western Europe.

Modern *music theory has its roots in ancient Mesopotamia. The standard modern major scale was already used in the Old Babylonian period c.1800 BC. Knowledge of music theory and practice spread to the *Levant and Greece by the first millennium BC. Pythagoras, the sixth-century BC Greek philosopher and mathematician best known to modern schoolboys for his theorem, stated that he learned his mathematics and music in the Near East. In architecture, the Ionic column, best known from classical Greece and revived in western neo-classical architecture, originated in the early reed structures of southern Mesopotamia, later copied in *stone. Some early Islamic minarets, for example at *Samarra in Iraq, are thought to have been based on the *ziggurat. Many ancient Near Eastern symbols have survived to the present day – the crescent, *swastika, Maltese cross, the 'tree of life' represented often in oriental rugs and in Christian art; the rod with intertwined serpents, today symbolizing the healing professions, especially pharmacy, was in Mesopotamia the distinguishing mark of Ningishzida, son of the healing god Ninazu (see Adapa). Common words which have been transmitted into English from the *languages of the ancient Near East include alcohol, gypsum, cane, abyss, jasper, sack and sparrow.

Until the rediscovery of Mesopotamia in the nineteenth century, western art and literature used stereotyped images of the ancient Near East, normally episodes familiar from the Bible and classical authors: the *Tower of Babel, Belshazzar's Feast, the burning of *Babylon. These tended to display a hostile attitude to Mesopotamian civilization, which was regarded as decadent; Babylon itself was used in art and literature as a metaphor for any large, corrupt commercial city. The decipherment of ancient Near Eastern scripts and research into ancient languages provided a fresh perspective, but also occasion-ally stimulated religious and racial controversy and anti-Semitism, most notoriously with a lecture in Berlin in 1902 by Friedrich Delitzsch entitled 'Babel und Bibel', in which he attempted to show that Babylon was the origin of many Old Testament stories and practices and indeed of much current religious thinking. Later he denied that the Old Testament was a divinely inspired book and his views became progressively more extreme, paralleling the rise of Nazism in Germany.

The rediscovery of Mesopotamia, especially *Layard's books, inspired *Assyrianizing designs and themes in architecture, decorative arts, jewellery and theatrical design, although most art historians rejected Mesopotamian *art as worthy of serious study compared with Greek. Later, ancient Near Eastern themes and designs were used in the cinema, most famously in the silent film *Intolerance* (1916) by D.W. Griffith, one of whose four stories is set in Babylon at the time of its fall to *Cyrus II; Griffith used the most up-to-date information on Babylonian and *Persian culture for his sets and costumes, even winning the praise of Assyriologists. The film later inspired Mesopotamian fashions in dress, particularly in the USA.                                                                PB

S. DALLEY (ed.), *The Legacy of Mesopotamia* (Oxford 1998).

W.W. HALLO, *Origins: The Ancient Near Eastern Background of Some Modern Western Institutions* (Leiden 1996).

H.W.F. SAGGS, *The Greatness that Was Babylon* (London 1962) 483–504.

J.M. SASSON (ed.), *Civilizations of the Ancient Near East* (New York 1995) 33–120.

G. SIEVERNICH and H. BUDDE (eds), *Europa und der Orient* (Berlin 1989).

**Leilan, (Tell)** An important regional centre in the *Khabur in the third and second millennia BC, this 90-ha site was known first as Shekhna and later as Shubat Enlil, the capital of *Shamshi-Adad I. Excavations since 1979 by Harvey Weiss have uncovered six main strata numbered from VI (oldest, *Ubaid period) to I (Old *Assyrian period).

Leilan expanded in the mid third millennium BC and eventually became a regional centre of the *Akkadian empire. To this period belong a public ritual quarter on the acropolis, with a mudbrick altar with burnt plaster surfaces, possibly sacrificial, and close by a room with an ash-filled pit containing human bones. This cult quarter was surrounded by a defensive wall early on, with the lower town walled only in the Akkadian period, perhaps to protect the imperial administration.

Leilan was abandoned between c.2200 and 1900 BC, in common with many settlements in northern *Mesopotamia following the collapse of the Akkadian empire. It was resettled by the *Amorites and became a regional administrative centre/capital of Shamshi-Adad I and his successors, inscriptions of whose officials have been found at the site. On the acropolis were discovered three levels of a long-room *temple with spiral mudbrick columns, perhaps reflecting a tradition of building columns from palm trunks: a *letter from Shamshi-Adad I in the *Mari archives reports *transport of palms,

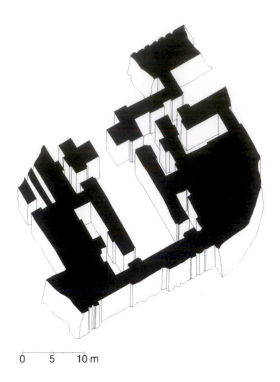

Isometric plan of Old Babylonian temple on the acropolis at Tell Leilan (after H. Weiss (ed.), *Ebla to Damascus: Art and Archaeology of Ancient Syria* (Washington, D.C. 1985) 209).

cypresses and myrtles to Shubat Enlil and other *cities. The lower town included *palace buildings, among the most extensive of the period in Mesopotamia, containing hundreds of *cuneiform tablets, some with royal *seals, and an *archive concerned with royal *beer supplies and distribution.

The city was destroyed by Samsuiluna of *Babylon in c.1728 BC, and not reoccupied until the early twentieth century AD.                                                             PB

H. WEISS, 'Tell Leilan on the Habur Plains of Syria', *Biblical Archaeologist* 48 (1985) 5–34.

——, 'Leilan, Tell', *The Oxford Encyclopedia of Archaeology in the Near East* 3, ed. E.M. Meyers (New York 1997) 341–7.

**Letters**   The *Sumerian *epic '*Enmerkar and the Lord of Aratta' tells how Enmerkar was the first to send a letter written on a clay tablet because the message was too complex for the messenger to memorize. Whether that is true or not, *writing changed the nature of messages entirely: what was previously committed to memory could now be conveyed by a messenger unaware of its contents. Sumerian letters surviving from the second half of the third millennium BC are mainly brief, official orders and notes, but a few longer ones, such as those between the last *king of *Ur and his lieutenant Ishbi-Erra, served as *scribal exercises in the Old *Babylonian period and so copies are preserved (otherwise the royal

*archive of Ur has disappeared). The early second millennium BC saw a great growth in letter writing, according to the available evidence. The thousands of letters of the *Assyrian *merchants at *Kanesh, the voluminous archives of *Mari and the correspondence between *Hammurabi and his subordinates show that, at the official level, the hundreds of letters which passed between other officials, businessmen, merchants and citizens made demands on scribes for writing letters in urban life. Merchants travelling far from home may even have written their own letters. Among the *Amarna Letters of the fourteenth century BC, the outstanding collection of *diplomatic correspondence from the ancient Near East, there are two letters with requests to the pharaoh's secretary to present their content to his master in the appropriate courtly style (Abdi-hepa of *Jerusalem). The archives of *Nineveh yielded a large number of letters addressed to the later kings of Assyria, dealing with diplomatic and military matters, domestic affairs and the observations of ominous phenomena and their significance. Letters continued to be written in *cuneiform into the Seleucid period. People wrote letters to give and receive instructions, to seek advice or help, to accuse or defend, to protest loyalty. Most writers were men; some letters were sent by royal ladies and *priestesses. One girl wrote a pathetic letter to beg her master to visit her as the baby she was carrying had died and she knew she would die shortly (Oppenheim, no. 17). Letters written on

Letters written on clay tablets were enclosed in clay envelopes which the recipients cracked open. This rare survivor bears the name of the addressee and the sender's seal impression. Old Babylonian, c.1700 BC. WA 82199.

cuneiform tablets were usually enclosed in a clay envelope, which would bear the name of the addressee and possibly of the sender. These envelopes rarely survive because the recipients broke them to read the letters.

A person of equal status would address his correspondent by name, perhaps as 'brother' and ask the *gods to bless him, a junior writing to a senior would address him as 'my lord', sometimes with other flattering titles and a lengthy blessing. In the Late Bronze Age and after, the superior's letter usually begins 'Thus says *X* to *Y*', while the inferior would write 'To *X*, my lord, thus says *Y*, your servant'.

*Akkadian was the *lingua franca* in the second millennium BC, but interpreters or bilingual scribes were needed in some places. Kings of *Egypt and of the *Hittites probably wrote to each other in their own languages; Tushratta of *Mitanni sent at least one letter to Egypt in *Hurrian and from *Ugarit there are letters in Akkadian and the local language.

The *Bible and *Hebrew *ostraca preserve some short letters from *Israel and Judah, showing the same basic style as those in cuneiform.

Ancient letters open a window on to the ancient societies in a more vivid and personal way than any other documents, revealing the matters that were of most concern; they sometimes preserve traces of the colloquial speech of their time. ARM

F.R. KRAUS (ed.), *Altbabylonische Briefe* I– (Leiden 1964–).

J.M. LINDENBERGER, *Ancient Hebrew and Aramaic Letters* (Atlanta, GA 1994).

P. MICHALOWSKI, *Letters from Early Mesopotamia* (Atlanta, GA 1993).

A.L. OPPENHEIM, *Letters from Mesopotamia* (Chicago 1967).

S. PARPOLA et al., *The Correspondence of Sargon* 2 (Helsinki 1987, 1990).

——, *Letters from Assyrian and Babylonian Scholars* (Helsinki 1993).

**Levant** An overall term for the regions bordering the east coast of the Mediterranean Sea, comprising *Palestine, *Syria and *Lebanon. *Transjordan, although inland, is also normally regarded as part of the Levant. The name comes from a French word (originally from Latin) meaning 'rising', as in the rising sun, or the East. PB

W.G. DEVER, 'Levant', *The Oxford Encyclopedia of Archaeology in the Near East* 3, ed. E.M. Meyers (New York 1997) 350–1.

**Lexical texts** Among the earliest examples of *writing are lists of words in categories – *animals, *fish, *wooden objects – and such lists remained basic to the *education of *scribes in *cuneiform for three millennia. At *Ebla c.2300 BC, some *Sumerian lists current in *Babylonia were provided with *Semitic translations, a process attested in Babylonia in the Old Babylonian period when *Akkadian-speaking scribes had to understand Sumerian. The scribes produced large numbers of copies of a wide variety of lists, ranging from simple syllables (tu, ta, ti, nu, na, ni) to compendia of legal formulae and grammatical tables. Some listed Sumerian logograms with their pronunciations and Akkadian meanings (*a*: *ea*: *naqu*, growing to over fourteen thousand entries), others were lists of Sumerian words with Akkadian equivalents, arranged by category (*ur₅.ra*: *hubullu*, with about ten thousand entries) and an entirely Akkadian compilation of synonyms (*malku*: *šarru*). The *Kassite invasion stimulated production of lists of Kassite names and words with Babylonian renderings, in *Hattusas scribes listed *Hittite words and their Akkadian meanings, in *Ugarit they set out Sumerian, Akkadian, *Hurrian and Ugaritic equivalents in parallel columns, in *Canaan (at Aphek) local words were listed beside Sumerian and Akkadian, and the *Amarna *archive includes a fragment of an Egyptian–Akkadian glossary. In the late period some lexical extracts were written in Greek script as exercises on clay tablets.

The lexical texts reveal systematization of knowledge, and the Sumero–Akkadian grammatical texts show notable linguistic perception. These compilations helped scribes to produce bilingual texts from the early second millennium BC onwards, both royal inscriptions and literary works. Some Sumerian literary texts have occasional words translated into Akkadian, some have whole lines and a few were eventually copied in completely bilingual form (e.g. *myths about *Ninurta). Outside *Mesopotamia some Sumerian or Akkadian works were translated into Hittite and Hurrian and there are a few brief examples of Ugaritic versions of Akkadian writings. The final contribution of these scribal encyclopaedias is crucially to aid modern understanding of Akkadian and especially of Sumerian. ARM

J. BLACK, *Sumerian Grammar in Babylonian Theory* (Rome 1991).

A. CAVAIGNEAUX, 'Lexikalische Listen', *Reallexikon der Assyriologie* 6 (Berlin/New York 1980–3) 609–41.

M. CIVIL, 'Lexicography', *Sumerological Studies in Honor of Thorkild Jacobsen*, ed. S.J. Lieberman (Chicago 1976) 123–36.

——, 'Ancient Mesopotamian Lexicography', *Civilizations of the Ancient Near East*, ed. J.M. Sasson (New York 1995) 2305–14.

B. LANDSBERGER et al., *Materials for the Sumerian Lexicon: A Reconstruction of Sumerian Lexical Lists* (Rome 1937–).

**Libraries** Specific collections of *books for reading or reference are found as relics of *scribal training (see Education) which required their copying and, perhaps, learning, and, in later periods, exegesis, as the holdings of *temples, *palaces and private persons.

Most famous and representative is the 'Library of Ashurbanipal' found in the palaces at *Nineveh. The *king tried to collect copies of all known *cuneiform *literature, having the *towns of *Babylonia searched, and one agent reported with joy his discovery of a tablet from the time of *Hammurabi, over one thousand years old. Although Ashurbanipal boasted of reading ancient tablets 'written before the Flood', old tablets were copied and the originals returned to their homes or discarded; it was the contents, not the manuscripts, that mattered. At the end of the tablet a colophon, acting like a title-page,

Ashurbanipal's ownership notice is written at the end of this tablet. WA K3353+.

might state that the copy had been made from an original of *Babylon or some other town, often with a further notice that the tablet belonged to the king, with a curse on anyone who stole it! The library held between one thousand and fifteen hundred titles, many works existing in multiple copies. They comprise multitudes of *omen texts, *rituals and spells, *lexical texts which aided the scribes in their understanding, *hymns and prayers and the *epic poems and *wisdom literature which have most appeal today. Lists of books, some with their supposed authors, exemplify a simple cataloguing system by subject in boxes or baskets, or on shelves. Ashurbanipal's library incorporated the library of a scholar from *Nimrud, Nabu-zuqup-kena, one of many exorcists, *priests, diviners, singers and scribes who kept smaller collections in their own *houses. These might be separated from the household archives, or mixed with them. This situation is known from the middle of the third millennium BC (at Abu Salabikh) onwards and beyond *Babylonia, at *Ugarit, for example. The collections of the Old Babylonian period are particularly valuable because they contain most of the known *Sumerian *literature, much of which was forgotten thereafter. Temples had their own libraries; one uncovered at *Sippar still had the tablets in brick compartments built in the wall. Scribes sometimes copied texts to present to temple libraries as acts of piety. Where papyrus or leather was the writing material, libraries are unlikely to survive, but the analogies from cuneiform-using areas and from Egypt indicate that works of literature would not be confined to palaces and temples in *Israel and Judah, or in the *Aramaean or *Phoenician cities.                                    ARM

A.L. OPPENHEIM, *Ancient Mesopotamia: Portrait of a Dead Civilization*, 2nd ed. (Chicago 1977) 15–21.

O. PEDERSÉN, *Archives and Libraries in the Ancient Near East 1500–300 B.C.* (Bethesda, MD 1998).

K.R. VEENHOF (ed.), *Cuneiform Archives and Libraries* (Leiden 1986).

**Literacy**  The numerous signs of the *cuneiform script and the complications of their use restricted reading and *writing where that script was current to a small class of people who had passed through a system of *education, most of whom became professional *scribes, some becoming specialists in *priestly and state roles. A few female scribes are known. The thousands of cuneiform tablets extant imply very frequent use of writing for *administration at certain periods, such as the Third Dynasty of *Ur, Neo-*Assyrian *Nineveh, and for individuals' activities in others, such as the legal deeds from *Nuzi. In the Old *Babylonian period the number of *letters from one person to another, dealing with official, business and personal matters, may indicate a wider spread of writing in society; travelling *merchants may have written their own letters when far from home.

With very limited literacy, we have to suppose writing was mysterious to the majority of the population, whether on a royal monument or a memorandum, unless a scribe was to hand. However, a good number who had no need to read or write in their daily lives themselves would have been aware that the scribes' actions as they surveyed fields or listed personnel could affect them when *taxes were due or the summons to corvée duties came. The epilogue to *Hammurabi's *Laws instructs anyone with a grievance to 'have my inscribed monument read and listen to my precious words' (col. xli 11). The *Akkadian term rendered 'to read' means primarily to 'call out', suggesting that reading was done aloud (the same is true in *Hebrew), although the verb 'to see' was also used to express 'when you have read my letter', which could imply silent reading. *Ritual texts include passages to be read or recited, *hymns and prayers were, presumably, chanted and at the *New Year and certain other *festivals the Babylonian *Creation poem was recited. The tablets served as memory aids for these occasions. The function of Babylonian *myths and epics is not clear; some pieces may have been exercises in scribal training, others may have been recited in public.

There is nothing to suggest any wider literacy in the *Hittite realm, despite the simpler form of the script, nor in *Ugarit where the cuneiform *alphabet flourished beside Babylonian cuneiform.

When the *alphabet had taken root, the possibility of literacy increased as only twenty-two characters had to be learned, although the system had its difficulties. Numerous *ostraca and hundreds of *seals and seal impressions from ancient *Israel in particular imply a higher percentage of literates or a greater use of writing than in the *Mesopotamian cultures, but it is unlikely the number was above ten per cent for, as in Mesopotamia, most people would have no need to read or write. The *Hebrew *Bible takes writing for granted as a part of life, mentioning letters and *contracts as well as laws and reports. The ostraca of the eighth and seventh centuries BC support this, supplying examples of clerical activity in ephemeral receipts, accounts and letters, some found at small military outposts; more substantial texts, written on papyrus, leather or *wood are lost through decay. Evidence from *Ammon and *Moab points to a fairly ready use of writing, but there is much less from *Phoenician and *Syrian sites, despite the survival of a greater number of royal monuments.                    ARM

J. BAINES and A.R. MILLARD, 'Literacy', *Anchor Bible Dictionary* 4, ed. D.N. Freedman (New York 1992) 333–40.

**Literature** *Writing was invented as a memory-aid and it was not long before *scribes used it to record *magic spells and then narratives about *gods and heroes. The earliest literary texts in *cuneiform are *Sumerian ones from the Early Dynastic II period, but are hardly intelligible. There are many more from Early Dynastic III and sense can be made of many of them. The principal discoveries have been made at Fara (ancient *Shuruppak), *Lagash and Abu Salabikh. Scribes wrote out *hymns and prayers, *wisdom texts and *stories about past *kings often in several copies, probably as exercises in writing and accurate copying. Some of these compositions continued to be copied over the next eight or ten centuries, enabling developments in language and writing as well as literary form to be traced. From the Akkadian and Ur III periods there are relatively few literary texts, *Gudea's cylinders being notable exceptions, but the Old Babylonian period supplies the largest number. Tablets from *Ur, *Larsa, *Nippur, *Sippar and other sites show that the same corpus of Sumerian texts was copied throughout *Babylonia, some works being known in fifty or more manuscripts. These were mostly training exercises, sometimes signed by the pupil-scribe. They include the famous stories of *Gilgamesh and major *myths as well as debates between opposites (e.g. Summer and Winter) and descriptions of a student's life which may have been model compositions. This period saw the growth of literature in *Akkadian, some works imitating Sumerian (e.g. royal hymns), a few being translations, others developing in different ways, like the Epic of *Gilgamesh. Many texts created then continued to be copied and developed until the end of the cuneiform tradition in *Parthian times, being found in most '*libraries' in a sort of standard collection. Beside the myths and epics which appeal today, numerous hymns, prayers, *rituals and magical texts survive. It is known that the Babylonian *Creation poem was recited at the *New Year and at other *festivals, but the purpose of other narrative texts is unknown, whether they had magical properties (for instance, to make the reciter victorious like the hero), were intended to educate (e.g. in past history, as the stories of *Sargon of *Akkad), or were simply for amusement; we assume all were read aloud. A story like the 'Tale of the Poor Man of Nippur' appears to be simply humorous (see Humour and wit). The amount of written literature surviving has to be reckoned as only a part of what was told or sung. A few pieces seem to represent the sort of folk-literature which was not usually written, introducing medical remedies, for example. Most of these texts are *poetry, but some royal inscriptions in prose deserve to be classed as literature, notably *Sargon II's letter to *Ashur.

Some Sumerian and much Akkadian literature spread across the *Fertile Crescent in the second millennium BC, examples being found at *Emar, *Ugarit, *Hattusas and in the *Amarna archive. Changes occurred in transmission, the local scribes not always understanding their exemplars.

The *Hittites wrote their own literature, myths and legends, magical and ritual texts and historical narratives and translated some works from Akkadian (e.g. a hymn to the sun-god) and from *Hurrian. Hurrian literature, preserved especially at Hattusas and also at Ugarit, covered the same ground and, again, included translations from Akkadian of *omen texts, Gilgamesh and many other works.

The tablets from Ugarit reveal a local West Semitic tradition of poetic narratives about gods and heroes (*Baal, *Aqhat, *Keret), each composition known from a single copy, and there are a few magic spells and prayers.

West Semitic literature of the *Iron Age is almost non-existent, apart from the *Bible. The inscribed plaster from Tell *Deir Alla shows there were scribes composing poetic literature in an *Aramaic dialect about 800 BC, but that is a lone survivor. The royal inscriptions of *Moab and *Aramaean states hint at continuous prose composition.

The *Hebrew Bible has survived because of its religious importance and because of its literary merit. The love lyrics of the Song of Songs, the impassioned poetry of the prophets, the deeply personal psalms, the bewildered speeches of Job, the sparing prose of the story of Joseph and the colourful account of King David find some parallels in other ancient Near Eastern literature, but no true equals. Preserved only in copies made long after their composition, the literary history of these texts cannot be traced. Hypotheses about that have little value unless they accord with the facts attested in neighbouring cultures.
ARM

B.R. FOSTER, *Before the Muses* (Bethesda, MD 1996).

O.R. GURNEY, *The Hittites*, rev. ed. (Harmondsworth 1990).

W.W. HALLO and K.L. YOUNGER (eds), *The Context of Scripture 1: Canonical Compositions from the Biblical World* (Leiden 1997).

S.B. PARKER and M.S. SMITH, *Ugaritic Narrative Poetry* (Atlanta, GA 1997).

E. REINER, *Your thwarts in pieces, Your mooring rope cut: Poetry from Babylonia and Assyria* (Ann Arbor, MI 1985).

## Lloyd, Seton (Howard Frederick) (1902–96)

British archaeologist, architect, writer and teacher, who excavated extensively in Iraq and Turkey, Lloyd was born in Edgbaston, Birmingham. After qualifying in architecture in 1926, he worked in an architectural practice until attracted to archaeology while architect to Henri Frankfort at Tell el-Amarna, 1928–30. Until 1937 he assisted Frankfort in Iraq, at *Assyrian *Khorsabad and Jerwan and at sites near the Diyala river (Asmar, *Khafaje). He improved methods of excavating mudbrick and introduced kite photography. In 1937–9, Lloyd worked with *Garstang at *Mersin, and conducted a survey of the Sinjar region in northern Iraq.

As Technical Adviser to the Iraq Directorate-General of Antiquities, 1939–49, Lloyd excavated at *Hassuna, Tell *Uqair, Tell Harmal and *Eridu. Appointed Director of the newly founded British Institute of Archaeology at Ankara, 1949–61, in Turkey he conducted several excavations (Polatli, *Beycesultan, Sultantepe) and a couple of architectural surveys (Islamic *Harran, Seljuk Alanya).

In 1962–9 Lloyd succeeded *Mallowan as Professor of Western Asiatic Archaeology in London. In 1965 he excavated the *Urartian site of Kayalýdere in eastern Turkey. He was President of the British School of Archaeology in Iraq (1978–83), retiring through ill health. He died in Oxford.

Lloyd's record of publication was prolific and wideranging. His archaeological site reports are illustrated by his informative architectural plans and skilful drawings by his wife 'Hydie' (Margery Ulrica *née* Fitzwilliams Hyde, m. 1944, d. 1987), an artist and sculptress. Preliminary reports were promptly produced – though his final co-authored reports were sometimes delayed by political considerations. As an innovative excavator and scholar, he is often compared favourably with his backward-looking contemporary Mallowan, and he successfully brought Near Eastern archaeology to a wider readership.                                              AG

D. COLLON, 'Lloyd, Seton (Howard Frederick)', *The Dictionary of Art* 19, ed. J. Turner (New York/London 1996) 519–20.

J.D. HAWKINS, 'Seton Howard Frederick Lloyd, 1902–1996', *Proceedings of the British Academy* 97 (1998) 359–77.

S. LLOYD, *The Interval: A Life in Near Eastern Archaeology* (Faringdon 1986).

——, 'Seton Lloyd', *The Pastmasters: Eleven Modern Pioneers of Archaeology*, eds G.E. Daniel and C. Chippindale (London, not dated) 61–88.

'Seton Lloyd: A Bibliography', *Iraq* 44 (1982) 221–4 (supplemented in S. Lloyd, *The Interval*, p. 179).

G.R.H. WRIGHT, 'Seton Lloyd: His Work in Middle Eastern Archaeology', *Bibliotheca Orientalis* 53 (1996) cols 318-24.

## Love poems: see Poetry

## Lugalbanda

The hero Lugalbanda was a deified *king of the *Sumerian *city of Unug (*Uruk). His wife was the *goddess Ninsun. In most literary traditions they were regarded as the parents of *Gilgamesh. Lugalbanda is mentioned together with Ninsun in a list of gods as early as the Early Dynastic period, and a short fragment of a literary composition about him dates from the same period. All the kings of the Third Dynasty of *Ur sacrificed to the divine Lugalbanda at *Nippur, and in the praise *poetry addressed to these kings it is common to find Lugalbanda and Ninsun described as the king's divine 'parents' (which made Gilgamesh the king's brother). Lugalbanda was also worshipped at Kuara near Uruk and at Umma.

In two heroic narrative poems, Lugalbanda is presented as the eighth 'little brother' of seven mighty heroes, and succeeds in crossing dangerous mountains on his own, despite a near-fatal illness. He clearly has a special connection with *Inana. The Sumerian *King List, based on a different legendary tradition, describes him as a shepherd who ruled Uruk for 1200 years. At least one of the stories was known in *Ashurbanipal's *library.     JAB

J.A. BLACK, *Reading Sumerian Poetry* (London 1998).

C. WILCKE, *Das Lugalbandaepos* (Wiesbaden 1969).

——, 'Lugalbanda', *Reallexikon der Assyriologie* 7 (Berlin/New York 1987) 117–32.

Bronze cheek-piece and bit from Luristan, formed as a fantastic animal and rider. Width 10 cm. WA 1920.5-11.1.

## Luristan bronzes

Luristan in west central *Iran is an area of mountains and well watered plains. In the late 1920s *bronze objects said to be from Luristan started appearing on the antiquities market (with forgeries following from the 1930s). The vast majority were dug up by local tribesmen and practically nothing is known still about their context or who produced them. The bronzes consist of weapons and *tools, especially axes ending in animal heads; whetstone handles; *horse cheekpieces and harness trappings; finials or standards, often with a so-called 'master-of-animals', a double-headed human figure grappling with two beasts; decorated tubes; pins, including elaborate examples with large disk-shaped heads; personal ornaments; vessels; and sheet-metal objects such as belts and quiver plaques. Nearly all have cast-bronze decoration consisting mostly of animals, imaginary beasts and fantasized humans.

Virtually all the bronzes come from plundered *cemeteries of stone-built cist or gallery *graves. A few have come from excavations of cemeteries, and of settlement sites at Baba Jan and Surkh Dum, the latter including a sanctuary. The sparse chronological evidence available suggests that the classic Luristan bronzes were manufactured from c.1200 to 800 BC. Other bronzes from the same area date earlier, but the term 'Luristan bronzes' is normally restricted to the distinctive first-millennium BC bronzes from Luristan itself.

Although it is generally accepted that the prevalence of horse trappings and portable objects indicates a *nomadic lifestyle, it is also argued that only a sedentary population could produce such varied bronzework. In fact, sedentary and nomadic lifestyles probably coexisted, but there is so little reliable evidence that this must remain speculation.                                         PB

P. CALMEYER, *Datierbare Bronzen aus Luristan und Kirmanshah* (Berlin 1969).

——, 'Luristan-Bronzen', *Reallexikon der Assyriologie* 7 (Berlin/New York 1988) 174–9.

A. GODARD, *Les bronzes du Luristan* (Paris 1931).

P.R.S. MOOREY, *Catalogue of the Ancient Persian Bronzes in the Ashmolean Museum* (Oxford 1971).

——, *Ancient Bronzes from Luristan* (London 1974).

O.W. MUSCARELLA, *Bronze and Iron: Ancient Near Eastern Artifacts in The Metropolitan Museum of Art* (New York 1988) 112–206.

——, 'The Background to the Luristan Bronzes', *Bronzeworking Centres of Western Asia, c.1000–539 B.C.*, ed. J.E. Curtis (London 1988) 33–44.

**Lycia** Lycia is a mountainous district on the south-west coast of *Anatolia. There are few sources of information about it prior to its conquest by *Persia in c.546 BC. People known as Lycians had settled in the area by the early first millennium BC, and it is usually assumed that they were related to the Lukka, known from Late Bronze Age sources. The first possible reference to the Lukka is in the mid fifteenth century BC when they joined an alliance against the *Hittite King *Tudhaliyas I. No *kings of the Lukka are known and they were probably subject to Hittite authority. They are mentioned in texts from *Ugarit and *Egypt as connected with the coast and were described as aggressive by the king of *Alashiya in one of the *Amarna Letters. However, the location of the Lukka is disputed, some placing them in north-west Anatolia, others in the south-west in the area of later Lycia.

According to Homer, the Lycians were allied with *Troy during the Trojan War. There are indications in *Greek literary sources of Rhodian settlement on the Lycian coast from the early seventh century BC on. The earliest population centres developed around the Xanthos Valley in western Lycia, centred on the city of Xanthos, which appears to date from the eighth century BC. This was probably the area identified as Lycia at the time of the Persian conquest.

The Lycian script is *alphabetic, and the majority of letters correspond closely to Greek prototypes. The *language is closely connected with Luwian, an *Indo-European language, but is still only partly deciphered,

despite the existence of a small number of Lycian–Greek bilingual texts. PB

T.R. BRYCE, *The Lycians in Literary and Epigraphic Sources* (Copenhagen 1986).

A.G. KEEN, *Dynastic Lycia: A Political History of the Lycians and their Relations with Foreign Powers c. 545–362 B.C.* (Leiden 1998).

O. MASSON, 'The Lycian Language', *Cambridge Ancient History* 3.2, 2nd ed. (Cambridge 1991) 671–4.

M. MELLINK, 'Lycia', *Cambridge Ancient History* 3.2, 2nd ed. (Cambridge 1991) 655–62.

**Lydia** The *Iron Age kingdom of Lydia in western *Anatolia, west of *Phrygia, is known mainly from *Greek writers, particularly *Herodotus, who recounts the story of its *kings in great detail. No Lydian historical *chronicles survive. Lydian power peaked in the seventh and sixth centuries BC after the collapse of *Phrygia, when the Lydian kings of the Mermnad dynasty extended their rule to include the Phrygian plateau and campaigned against the Greek cities on the Mediterranean coast.

Gyges, the founder of the Mermnad dynasty, is also the first Lydian king known from *Assyrian records (as Guggu of Ludu), when he requested help from *Ashurbanipal against the *Cimmerians, some time between 668 and 665 BC. Ashurbanipal's texts relate that Gyges was inspired by a dream to seek Assyrian aid, but, when the Lydian messenger arrived at *Nineveh, his *language was not understood. Gyges later supported *Egypt's rebellion against Ashurbanipal.

The Cimmerians invaded Lydia several times, killing Gyges and partially destroying the capital, *Sardis, but the kingdom survived. One of Gyges' successors, Alyattes, finally drove the Cimmerians from Lydia. He also fought a long war against the *Medes, signing a treaty with them in 585 BC. It may have been during Alyattes' reign that *coins, made of electrum, were first introduced, though Greek tradition ascribed this to his son, *Croesus. He was buried in a large mound, next to that attributed to Gyges,

Map showing location of Lycia.

Lydian necropolis north of Sardis: the large tumulus is attributed to King Gyges (courtesy of Sonia Halliday Photographs).

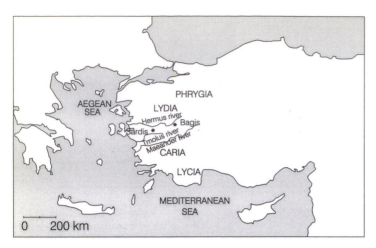

Map of Lydia showing principal sites and rivers.

with a marble *burial chamber north of Sardis, investigated and excavated by several nineteenth-century European travellers, one of whom claimed that it took him ten minutes to ride around it. It is in fact the largest tumulus in Anatolia. The Lydians appear to have borrowed and adapted the Phrygian tradition of tumulus burial. Sixth-century BC tombs at Bagis contained vessels and *jewellery of *silver, *gold and electrum, evidence of Lydian wealth which was proverbial in Greek tradition. According to Herodotus, Lydian kings made lavish gifts to Greek sanctuaries.

Alyattes was succeeded by his son Croesus, the last Lydian king, under whom the empire reached its greatest extent. He was defeated by *Cyrus II in 547 BC, and Lydia became part of the *Persian empire, with Sardis the residence of a satrap.

The Lydians appear to have been native to Anatolia. Their language was *Indo-European, written in a modified Greek and Phrygian *alphabet, which continued in use long after the demise of the independent Lydian kingdom.

PB

M. COGAN and H. TADMOR, 'Gyges and Ashurbanipal: A Study in Literary Transmission', *Orientalia* 46 (1977) 65–85.

C.H. GREENEWALT, 'Croesus of Sardis and the Lydian Kingdom of Anatolia', *Civilizations of the Ancient Near East*, ed. J.M. Sasson (New York 1995) 1173–83.

O. MASSON, 'The Lydian Language', *Cambridge Ancient History* 3.2, 2nd ed. (Cambridge 1991) 669–71.

M. MELLINK, 'The Native Kingdoms of Anatolia', *Cambridge Ancient History* 3.2, 2nd ed. (Cambridge 1991) 643–55.

# M

**Magan:** see Oman

**Magic** Magic was not a disapproved activity in the ancient Near East, and it was normal to use white magical means, among others, to bring comfort and, possibly, healing. However, sorcery (deliberately harmful black magic) was regarded as evil because of its social effects, but very probably its methods were the same as those used in standard magical practice. Magic was used to insure against, to drive away or to overcome *demons; to undo the bad effects of certain 'sinful' actions (usually social misdemeanours); to counteract the potential effects of certain portended effects; to increase *sexual potency; to secure the favours of a loved one; to quieten squalling infants; and, among many other functions, to frustrate the activity of hostile sorcerers.

Clearly the practice of magic is very close to both *medicine and *divination, and sometimes difficult to separate from them. Magic was often used in addition to decoctions, poultices, ointments, enemas etc. In *Babylonia it was carried out by the same person, the *āšipu*, who might be attached to a *temple as part of its clergy. Another specialist, the *asû*, was more specifically a physician (see Medicine).

The forms in which *Babylonian magic survives to us are incantations or spells in *Sumerian, *Akkadian and sometimes other *languages such as *Elamite or *Hurrian, sometimes garbled but rarely complete mumbo-jumbo; '*rituals', that is, systematic descriptions (addressed to the magician) of the actions to be followed, including a list of the incantations to be used at certain points, said either by the magician or by the 'patient'; amulets, usually inscribed with excerpts from well known

The head of the demon Pazuzu was worn on necklaces and hung on houses to ward off his evil attentions. c.700 BC. WA 93089.

BC, contemporary with the later of the rich burials at *Alaca Hüyük in central *Anatolia. The Maikop barrow has been identified as a royal burial. It was prepared by building a circle of undressed limestone slabs inside which a trench was dug (1.42 m deep, 5.33 by 3.73 m in area) to form the burial chamber. This was lined with *wood and paved with pebbles. In the main chamber were seventeen vessels of *gold, *silver and *stone, including two engraved silver jars, as well as *copper and *pottery vessels, *tools and weapons. Two smaller compartments contained a single skeleton each, one male and one female. The bodies were painted with red ochre. Over the whole burial pit was erected a wooden roof, covered with a thin layer of earth and supported by four wooden corner posts. Above this was built a second roof, and over this a great mound of earth and stone, containing a single ochre burial accompanied by copper spearheads and silver spiral rings. The barrow rose to a height of 10.65 m.

PB

C. BURNEY and D.M. LANG, *The Peoples of the Hills: Ancient Ararat and Caucasus* (London 1971) 80–3.

F. HANCAR, *Urgeschichte Kaukasiens* (Leipzig 1937) 247–52.

**Malatya:** see Arslantepe (Malatya)

### Mallowan, (Sir) Max (Edgar Lucien) (1904–78)

British archaeologist, excavator, teacher, author and administrator, Mallowan was most notable for his excavations at *Nimrud. Of Austrian–French parentage, born in London, on graduating Mallowan (pronounced '*mál-owan*') became for six successive seasons *Woolley's assistant at *Ur (1925–31). In *Mesopotamia he met the mystery writer Agatha Christie; they married in 1930. The Ur sounding prepared Mallowan for supervising the sounding at *Nineveh, 1931–2, the foundation for the study of north Mesopotamian *prehistory. In 1933 Mallowan conducted the first extensive work on a *Halaf period site, *Arpachiyah.

When Iraq stopped sharing finds, foreign excavators transferred to north-east *Syria. Mallowan worked in the *Khabur basin at *Chagar Bazar (1935–7) and Tell *Brak (1937–8) and at sites in the *Balikh Valley (1938). At Chagar Bazar he found a long Halaf sequence and an early second-millennium BC occupation with *Khabur Ware and tablets of *Shamshi-Adad I, while Brak showed a succession of Late *Uruk temples containing numerous large-eyed *figurines, and a major public building, probably of *Naram-Sin.

During the Second World War Mallowan worked in Air Force intelligence. Afterwards he was appointed to the new Chair of Western Asiatic Archaeology in London, 1947–62. This he held concurrently with the Baghdad Directorship of the British School of Archaeology in Iraq, working at Nimrud 1949–57. He was, as he wrote, 'an unashamed supporter of the bygone days of digging' and derided those who 'miss nothing, and tend to find nothing'. His standards of excavation were no improvement, after thirty years, on those of Woolley, his recording

incantations and worn around the neck, or occasionally hung on the wall of a *house; and apotropaic *figurines.

Some aspects of *Hittite magical incantations and rituals were borrowed from *Mesopotamian or Hurrian culture; others derived from simple popular beliefs of indigenous Hattic origin.

The very earliest incantations which survive date from the Early Dynastic period, about 2400 BC. One of the best-preserved Babylonian magical collections is that called *Šurpu* ('burning'). Quite different in nature are the incantation rituals called in Akkadian *namburbû*, which are intended to undo or avert the effect of future evil detected in advance by portents. Some aspects of these rites recur in the long nocturnal ritual known as *Maqlû* (also meaning 'burning'), performed when the patient is convinced he has been bewitched.

Collections (so-called 'series') of incantations are organized into, and accompanied by directions for, complex rituals in which the sequence of actions and incantations is crucially important. The incantations have been gathered from various sources and woven into a ritual sequence in the belief that proliferation of the magic would make it more effective. The orthodox monotheism of ancient *Israel forbade the practice of magic, but there is adequate archaeological evidence for popular superstition.

JAB

R.D. BIGGS, *ŠÀ.ZI.GA: Ancient Mesopotamian Potency Incantations* (Locust Valley, NY 1967).

G. CUNNINGHAM, '*Deliver Me from Evil': Mesopotamian Incantations 2500–1200 BC* (Rome 1997).

W. FARBER, 'Witchcraft, Magic and Divination in Ancient Mesopotamia', *Civilizations of the Ancient Near East*, ed. J.M. Sasson (New York 1995) 1895–909.

G. FRANTZ-SZABO, 'Hittite Witchcraft, Magic and Divination', *Civilizations of the Ancient Near East*, ed. J.M. Sasson (New York 1995) 2007–19.

M.J. GELLER, *Forerunners to Udug-hul: Sumerian Exorcistic Incantations* (Stuttgart 1985).

**Maikop** The finest barrow *burial in the *Caucasus, Maikop lies in the Kuba Valley and dates to c.2300–2200 inferior and the level of publication a marked regression – in part because of a curious and conscious desire to emulate *Layard. His large-scale operations, however, were successful in providing extensive, if oversimplified, information.

After 1958 Mallowan was heavily involved in the administration and promotion of Near Eastern archaeology in Britain, and was an effective fund-raiser. He remained Director of the Iraq school until 1961, was editor of the journal *Iraq* 1949–71, and the School's Chairman (1966–70) and President (1970–8). As Vice-President of the British Academy, 1961–2, he helped found institutes in Tehran and Kabul, of the former of which he was first President (1961–78).

Mallowan retired in 1961, taking up a research fellowship at Oxford (1962–71). In 1968 he was knighted, but also suffered a debilitating stroke. Agatha died in 1976, and the following year Mallowan married his former London colleague and Nimrud assistant, Barbara Parker (d. 1993). He died in Greenway, Devon.　　　AG

J. CURTIS (ed.), *Fifty Years of Mesopotamian Discovery* (London 1982).

H.R.F. KEATING, 'Mallowan, Sir Max Edgar Lucien', *The Dictionary of National Biography 1971–1980* (Oxford/New York 1986) 540–1.

M.E.L. MALLOWAN, *Nimrud and its Remains*, 3 vols (London 1966).

——, *Mallowan's Memoirs* (London 1977).

D. OATES, 'Max Edgar Lucien Mallowan 1904–1978', *Proceedings of the British Academy* 76 (1990) 499–511.

**Malyan, (Tall-i):** see Anshan

**Maps and plans** *Babylonian *scribes drew plans of properties and buildings on clay tablets for over two thousand years, from 2300 BC or before. The need to delimit estates, calculate areas to be developed and guide builders lay behind these plans. Carefully drawn plans of buildings may mark dimensions of rooms in cubits, and are sometimes drawn on a grid. One *temple plan outlines the individual bricks and may indicate that a scale of 1:66.66 was in use. Best known of the building plans is one on the lap of a *Gudea statue, an enclosure wall with six *gateways and many towers, with a graduated ruler beside it. (As the statue is not life-size, calculating the actual units of length is difficult.) Several tablets, or fragments, present plans of *towns. Most extensive is one from *Nippur of c.1500 BC, possibly drawn to scale, marking and naming city gates, two canals, the Euphrates and the temple of *Enlil, and giving dimensions for certain structures. A map of a larger area of Nippur demarcates properties belonging to royal and religious estates lying around the hairpin bend of a watercourse, separated by *irrigation channels. Still larger areas are covered in a few maps. One shows settlements with canals and a linking *road, another part of *Babylonia with the city of *Sippar, the Euphrates and canals. Oldest is a tablet from *Nuzi of Old Akkadian date. Two ranges of hills, indicated by scale-like marks, bound an area bisected by a

The Babylonian 'Map of the World' marking various known places, including Babylon (the rectangle) bisected by the Euphrates river. Distant regions protrude beyond an encircling ocean. Sixth century BC. WA 92687.

Fragment of a map of Sippar (the square) and its surroundings, the Euphrates above and canals below. 8 by 9 cm. Mid first millennium BC. WA 50644.

river or canal, with plots of land and places, one known from other sources to be near Nuzi. Noteworthy are the annotations on three sides, 'west', 'east', 'north', with 'north' at the left (although if the script were still read in vertical columns, 'north' would be at the top; see Cuneiform). The 'Babylonian World Map' is a diagram to relate various distant regions known from *omen and literary texts to Babylonia. They are triangles rising beyond the salty ocean which encircles the main area. Two parallel lines are obviously the Euphrates, which runs to the southern marshes. *Babylon lies on the river, small circles mark *Assyria, *Urartu and other places, without much attention to geography. The use of scale plans and orientation is a significant step in understanding map-making. The Babylonians may have created larger maps on perishable materials, such as wax tablets, for use on military expeditions. Surviving itineraries might be derived from maps or provide the basic information for them.　　ARM

E. HEINRICH and U. SEIDL, 'Grundrisszeichnungen aus dem alten Orient', *Mitteilungen der Deutschen Orient-Gesellschaft zu Berlin* 98 (1967) 24–45.

W. HOROWITZ, 'The Babylonian Map of the World', *Iraq* 50 (1988) 147–65.

A.R. MILLARD, 'Cartography in the Ancient Near East', *The History of Cartography*, eds J.B. Harley and D. Woodward (Chicago 1987) 107–16.

W. RÖLLIG, 'Landkarten', *Reallexikon der Assyriologie* 6 (Berlin/New York 1980–3) 464–7.

**Marduk** The *god Marduk was a patron god of the *city of *Babylon from early times, and his worship is attested as early as the Early Dynastic period, although nothing further is known of his origin. Later on he was often known simply by the common Semitic term Bel (Lord).

Marduk seems to have absorbed the personality of a local deity of the *Eridu region, Asarluhi, who was regarded as a son of Enki; consequently Marduk became the son of Enki/*Ea. Marduk's great shrine was the *temple called Esagil at Babylon, where he was worshipped together with his wife Zarpanitu.

The rise of the cult of Marduk is closely connected with the political rise of Babylon from city-state to the capital of an empire. From the Old Babylonian period, Marduk became more and more important until it was possible for the author of the *Babylonian *Epic of *Creation to maintain that not only was Marduk king of all gods but that many of the latter were no more than aspects of his persona – hence the hymn of the Fifty Names of Marduk incorporated into the epic, to which a contemporary list of gods adds sixty-six more.

Marduk was also a popular god in *Assyria, from about the fourteenth century BC. He was associated with *magic and *wisdom (derived from his connection with Asarluhi), *water and vegetation (connected with his father Ea) and judgement (suggesting a connection with the sun-god *Shamash/Utu). In the reign of *Sennacherib (704–681 BC), some aspects of Marduk's cult, *mythology and *rituals were attributed to the Assyrian state god *Ashur.

The worship of Marduk in its most extreme form has been compared with monotheism, but it never led to a denial of the existence of other gods, or to the exclusion of female deities.

Marduk's symbol of a triangular-headed spade or hoe, the *marru*, may possibly reflect an origin of the god as a local agricultural deity. The snake-dragon (*mušhuššu*) as animal of Marduk and *Nabû was taken over from

Tishpak, local god of *Eshnunna, possibly soon after the conquest of that city by *Hammurabi of Babylon.    JAB

J. BOTTÉRO, 'Les noms de Marduk, l'écriture et la "logique" en Mésopotamie ancienne', *Essays on the Ancient Near East in Memory of Jacob Joel Finkelstein,* ed. M. de Jong Ellis (Hamden 1977) 5–28.

W.G. LAMBERT, 'Studies in Marduk', *Bulletin of the School of Oriental and African Studies* 47 (1984) 1–9.

D. RITTIG, 'Marduk. B. Archäologisch', *Reallexikon der Assyriologie* 7 (Berlin/New York 1987–90) 372–4.

W. SOMMERFELD, *Der Aufstieg Marduks: Die Stellung Marduks in der babylonischen Religion des zweiten Jahrtausends v. Chr.* (Neukirchen/Vluyn 1982).

——, 'Marduk. A. Philologisch. I. In Mesopotamien', *Reallexikon der Assyriologie* 7 (Berlin/New York 1987–90) 360–70.

**Mari** In August 1933, Syrian peasants digging a grave into a hill called Tell Hariri on the Euphrates *river found a *stone statue. Within months French archaeologists had begun excavations and identified the site as ancient Mari, known from the *Sumerian *king list and later in the Old *Babylonian period as the centre of a kingdom controlling *trade and river traffic between *Babylonia and *Syria. Excavations have continued to the present, initially directed by André Parrot and since 1979 by Jean-Claude Margueron.

Mari appears to have been a circular *city, half of which has been washed away by the Euphrates, founded in the early third millennium BC. Remains of the Early Dynastic and *Akkadian periods include *palaces, *temples and *houses, surrounded by a dike as protection against floods, and some very fine Early Dynastic *sculpture. Its importance is largely due to the Ur III and Old

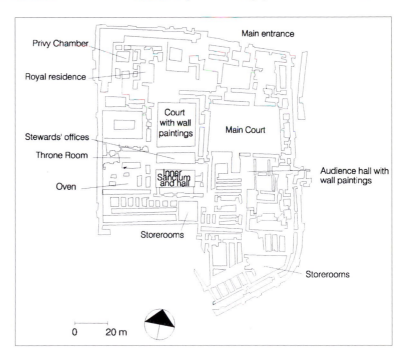

Plan of the great palace at Mari in its final stage c.1780 BC.

0    20 m

Babylonian palace, built over an earlier Early Dynastic palace, whose entire plan was uncovered and which is the richest and best-preserved palace of the entire *Bronze Age in the Near East. Completed by the *Amorite *King *Zimri-Lim, the palace covered more than 2.5 ha and had over 260 rooms, courtyards and passages at ground level alone; walls survive to a height of 4 or 5 m. Built over a period of more than two hundred years in the shape of a trapezium and with a second storey over much of the building, the palace plan is essentially a multiplication of a typical Babylonian house, with a number of rooms grouped around open courts, together with reception rooms and religious shrines. Areas included the *king's residence, with reception rooms, storerooms, kitchen and administrative quarters; the residential area for the court *women (possibly to be identified as a *harem); a temple area; the main storerooms and a palace *market. Several rooms, including the throne room and audience chamber, and especially the main courtyard, were decorated with *wall paintings, the largest composition showing the 'investiture' of the king before the *gods. At least one of the courtyards was planted with palm *trees.

The palace included workshops, especially for *textile production. More than twenty thousand *cuneiform tablets were found in various rooms, including royal *letters, *administrative and *omen texts. Accounts record the arrival of luxury products and foodstuffs sent by neighbouring kings, testifying to the city's importance; its contacts were far-flung, including *Hazor in *Palestine. Mari was conquered, destroyed and pillaged c.1760 BC by *Hammurabi of *Babylon. It continued to be occupied into the first millennium BC, a Middle *Assyrian cemetery in the ruins of the palace revealing a certain affluence, but the city never again achieved a position of importance. PB

S. DALLEY, *Mari and Karana: Two Old Babylonian Cities* (London 1984).

M.-H. GATES et al., 'The Legacy of Mari', *Biblical Archaeologist* 47 (1984).

J.-C. MARGUERON, *Recherches sur les palais mésopotamiens de l'âge du Bronze* (Paris 1982).

A. PARROT, *Mission archéologique de Mari* 1-4 (Paris 1956–68).

G.D. YOUNG (ed.), *Mari in Retrospect: Fifty Years of Mari and Mari Studies* (Winona Lake, IN 1992).

**Markets:** see Shops and markets

**Marlik** Marlik lies in the northern Elburz mountains in north-central *Iran in the province of Gilan. The site itself is a natural hill on the bank of the Gohar Rud (Crystal *river), a tributary of the Sefyd Rud (White river). Today the area is covered with terraced rice paddies and olive groves. In the 1950s and 1960s many antiquities attributed to the region of Amlash were appearing on the art market. Ezat Negahban and a small devoted team braved physical dangers from the dealers and their associates and their professional positions. Excavation lasted for a continuous fourteen months, uncovering fifty-three

Stylized pottery bull from Marlik, late second to early first millennium BC (courtesy of the Board of Trustees of the National Museums and Galleries on Merseyside, 1968.187).

unplundered stone-and-clay *tombs cut into a high rocky spur, until a combination of intrigue and corruption led to its close.

The hill was used as an elite inhumation *burial ground in the late second and early first millennia BC, and produced such an astonishing wealth of precious objects that the excavator dubbed it a 'royal *cemetery'. A number of other sites in the vicinity were also examined, none of which was of such high status. No associated settlement was found and nothing is known of the inhabitants. The graves were constructed of rough *stone walls between rock outcrops, a varying proportion of the stone in each grave being brought in from some 12 km away. In some of the graves, warriors were laid to rest on parallel rows of *weapons laid tip to tip. Burials were accompanied by vessels, many in *gold with elaborate repoussé and engraved embellishment, *jewellery and other ornaments; also by *pottery vessels that include striking representations of naked men and *women and highly accomplished humped bulls. *Military equipment was mostly of *bronze, although there were a few *iron blades.

Most of the objects seem to have been of inspired local manufacture while a few items, such as the frit *cylinder seals, were probably of foreign origin. The particular importance of the site, apart from its sheer wealth, is that it provides a secure archaeological context for groups of burial gifts that are otherwise known only from the art market. 'Amlash' seems also to be used by dealers to cover unprovenanced antiquities from other areas. GDS

P. CALMEYER, 'Marlik, Tepe', *Reallexikon der Assyriologie* 7 (Berlin/New York 1989) 426–9.

E.O. NEGAHBAN, *Marlik: The Complete Excavation Report* (Philadelphia, PA 1996).

——, 'Marlik', *The Oxford Encyclopedia of Archaeology in the Near East* 3, ed. E.M. Meyers (New York 1997) 421–4.

**Marriage** Marriage was the normal formal partnership arrangement between men and *women throughout the ancient Near East. Marriage was arranged by fathers, or in their absence by other relatives. Girls married as teenagers, men were about ten years older. Monogamy was the norm, but a man was allowed to take a second wife if the first did not bear children.

The process of getting married went through several phases, from first agreement to wedding, and involved parties and paying of a bride price, although there are some differences geographically and over time. Most of the relevant documents are *contracts or legal stipulations, indicating that marriage was a link between *families or larger groups as much as between individuals. A marriage contract was essential and is stipulated by the *law codes, but could be an oral agreement. The texts deal mainly with the bride price, paid by the groom to the bride's father; the dowry given to the bride by her father; divorce; and remarriage. Bride price seems to have been heavily dependent on whether the bride was a virgin and potentially fertile, the difference between bride price for first and second marriages being significant. If a man outlived his wife, her dowry belonged to her *children, unless she was childless, in which case in certain circumstances he was entitled to a portion. The bride price and the value of the dowry appear to have been equivalent, and could be paid in instalments until the first child was born, at which point the marriage became final.

The actual wedding lasted from five to seven days, although little is known of the ceremonies. At its culmination, the groom removed the veil which covered the bride. A group of the bride's friends seem to have been responsible for her chastity, and after the wedding night showed the evidence of her virginity.

The texts, particularly those from *Nuzi, show a great concern with *fertility and stress that the main purpose of marriage was procreation. Many legal texts dealing with marriage contain clauses referring to the possibility of childlessness. A clause in *Hammurabi's Code states that a wife could provide her husband with a female *slave as a surrogate for herself. Texts refer to two types of living arrangements: the wife and husband living in her father's *house, or in the husband's house. Documents from Nuzi show that if a woman was living in her father's house and her husband died, and she was childless, her father-in-law could marry her to the son of his choice. This may have been a means of keeping the estate within the family. A similar arrangement occurred at *Ugarit with *King Arhalba, who willed that his wife should marry his brother and no one else.

There is some evidence, in the *Hittite laws, for men and women living together without being married. After a certain period elapsed, between two and four years, their union became legally recognized, and as with formally married people the woman assumed the man's social status, even if he was not free. Legal texts also cover divorce, normally covering issues such as division of the estate and arrangements for the children, although women were treated unequally in the event of divorce. (See also Sacred Marriage.)　PB

S. GREENGUS, 'Old Babylonian Marriage Ceremonies and Rites', *Journal of Cuneiform Studies* 20 (1966) 55–72.

——, 'The Old Babylonian Marriage Contract', *Journal of the American Oriental Society* 89 (1969) 503–32.

K. GROSZ, 'Dowry and Bride Price in Nuzi', *Studies on the Civilization and Culture of Nuzu and the Hurrians*, eds M. Morrison and D. Owen (Winona Lake, IN 1981) 161–82.

M.T. ROTH, *Babylonian Marriage Agreements 7th–3rd Centuries BC* (Kevelaer 1989).

M. STOL, 'Private Life in Ancient Mesopotamia', *Civilizations of the Ancient Near East*, ed. J.M. Sasson (New York 1995) 485–501.

R. WESTBROOK, *Old Babylonian Marriage Law* (Horn 1988).

**Mathematics** What we know of mathematics in the ancient Near East is essentially *Babylonian mathematics, and the vast majority of texts date from the Old Babylonian period. Mathematics developed by c.3000 BC from a system of arithmetical recording or accounting based on small clay tokens, which had been in use over much of the Near East for several millennia and which probably also inspired the development of *writing. The earliest *Sumerian mathematics was probably created for the purposes of practical *administration, and *scribes were taught mathematics in *school so that they could calculate areas of fields or the quantity of work a labourer could produce in one day. Until the Third Dynasty of *Ur all mathematical texts were written in Sumerian, even in *Ebla, but from the Old Babylonian period they were in *Akkadian.

In the first half of the second millennium BC Babylonian pupils were set geometrical problems calculating the areas of various shapes, as shown on this tablet. WA 15285.

The surviving mathematical texts can be divided into tables and compilations of problems. Tables included multiplication, squares, square and cube roots, reciprocals, key numbers or constants, powers and exponents for selected numbers. Problems, many theoretical rather than practical, included quadratic and cubic equations, arithmetic progressions, and various geometric problems, such as areas of plane geometric shapes (rectangles, triangles, circles etc.) and solid geometric objects (cubes, cylinders etc., which were never presented as abstract shapes but as 'bricks', 'containers' etc.). Applied problems included canal, dike and siege ramp construction, and computation of market rates and prices and interest rates.

Babylonian geometry determined rectilinear objects by the lengths of their sides, not by their angles which became a central concept only in *Greek geometry. The 'Pythagorean theorem' was known at least by the Old Babylonian period. A characteristic feature of Babylonian mathematics was a system of positional notation and calculation using the number 60 as a base, known as the sexagesimal system, probably invented towards the end of the fourth millennium BC. In this system, large numbers were calculated as multiples of 60, rather than hundreds as in our modern decimal system. Babylonian mathematics also used a form of algebra, though not founded on symbols, with one or several unknown values.

Babylonian mathematics remained essentially elementary, and among the elements missing are trigonometry (a result of the absence of any concept of angle) and the geometry of cones, pyramids and spheres. Although Babylonian mathematics was capable of a high level of numerical precision, occasionally it settled for gross approximations, especially using the value 3 for *pi* (the ratio of the circumference of a circle to its diameter, actually 3.142).

From the late third millennium BC 'sacred numbers' were associated with the *gods, and in the first millennium BC numbers could be used cryptographically in *astrological *omen texts, or as a code, *Sargon II claiming that the 'number of his name' was 16,283. Signs on royal sculptures, once thought to be royal names written as numerical ciphers, have now been interpreted as a form of picture writing or hieroglyph.                    PB

I. FINKEL and J.E. READE, 'Assyrian Hieroglyphs', *Zeitschrift für Assyriologie* 86 (1996) 244–64.

J. FRIBERG, 'Mathematik', *Reallexikon der Assyriologie* 7 (Berlin/New York 1990) 531–85.

J. HOYRUP, *Measure, Number, and Weight* (New York 1994).

H.J. NISSEN, P. DAMEROW and R.K. ENGLUND, *Archaic Bookkeeping: Writing and Techniques of Economic Administration in the Ancient Near East* (Chicago/London 1993).

M.A. POWELL, 'Metrology and Mathematics in Ancient Mesopotamia', *Civilizations of the Ancient Near East*, ed. J.M. Sasson (New York 1995) 1941–57.

D. SCHMANDT-BESSERAT, *How Writing Came About* (Austin, TX 1996).

**Media, Medes**  The Medes, a shadowy federation of *Indo-European tribes often thought to have migrated into *Iran from the north in the early *Iron Age, coalesced into a kingdom in the central *Zagros mountains, with a capital at Hamadan, ancient *Ecbatana, in the eighth century BC. In 614 BC the Medes sacked *Ashur and in 612 BC, together with the *Babylonians, took the Neo-*Assyrian capital of *Nineveh, leading to the creation of a Median empire which reached westwards to the Halys river (modern Kýzýlýrmak). A five-year war between the Medes and *Lydia ended at the 'Battle of the Eclipse', 28 May 585 BC, followed by an international peace *treaty that fixed the border between Media and Lydia along the river and was sealed by a royal *marriage. The extent of Median power in the east is unknown but may have been extensive. The Medes, under Astyages, brother-in-law of *Croesus, were treacherously betrayed by their own general Harpagus and overthrown by *Cyrus II c.550 BC; thereafter they formed an extremely important element in the *Achaemenid empire, contributing key words about administration. Their influence was so strong that the Greeks long spoke of the Persians as Medes.

Written sources for Media are extremely poor, and Median *writing, if it existed, has not yet been discovered. The lack of both written sources and archaeological evidence have led some to downplay the role of the Medes. The major source is *Herodotus, whose account it is fashionable, but not necessarily correct, to largely dismiss because of evident inconsistency, incorrect equation of personal names and chronological difficulties. There are scanty references in Assyrian texts from the second half of the ninth century BC and even fewer clues in *Babylonian texts, all of which are difficult to interpret, although the construction of the 'Median Wall' in Babylonia surely suggests that the Medes and their allies posed a serious threat by the mid sixth century BC.

Archaeologically few sites are known, Ecbatana lying within the modern city of Hamadan, but largely unexcavated. Tepe *Nush-i Jan and *Godin Tepe are important Median sites in west-central Iran. Whether or not Baba Jan was also Median remains moot. To the west, Tell Gubba in Iraq, Tille Höyük, on the Euphrates near Adýyaman, and *Kerkenes Dağ, in north-central *Anatolia, may be Median.

Very little is known of Median *religion, although the *temples at Nush-i Jan might indicate an early origin for Zoroastrian fire worship. Equally, very little is known of Median *art. Much 'Median' *metalwork has appeared on the art market but none has been securely authenticated and not a single example has been scientifically excavated.
                                                                GDS

I.M. DIAKONOFF, 'Media', *Cambridge Ancient History of Iran* 2 (Cambridge 1985) 36–148.

M. ROAF, 'Media and Mesopotamia: History and Architecture', *Later Mesopotamia and Iran*, ed. J. Curtis (London 1995) 54–66.

T.C. YOUNG, JR, 'Medes', *The Oxford Encyclopaedia of Archaeology in the Near East* 3, ed. E.M. Meyers (New York 1997) 448–50.

——, 'The Early History of the Medes and the Persians and the Achaemenid Empire to the Death of Cambyses', *Cambridge Ancient History* 4, 2nd ed. (Cambridge 1988) 1–52.

Cylinder seal impression of demons being driven out of a sick man lying on his bed. Neo-Assyrian, ninth–eighth centuries BC (by courtesy of the Visitors of the Ashmolean Museum, Oxford, Stevenson Loan 1).

This bronze plaque shows a similar scene with a sick man in bed (third register) and the demon Lamashtu expelled by boat to the underworld by the demon Pazuzu. c.700 BC? WA 108979.

## Medicine

The *cuneiform records of *Mesopotamia include a great deal of information about medical practices. Learned manuals, *letters and other texts speak of the threat posed by dirty *water, urban epidemics and famine. There are references to taboos against contacting people with certain skin diseases, and among the most frequent problems were eye ailments, impotence and digestive complaints. The two main professional healers were the *āšipu* and the *asû*. The *āšipu* was an expert in magic spells and rituals designed to drive out the invading *demons believed to cause illness. The *asû* used the direct application of herbs and bandages. It is not clear whether both acted against demonic attack or whether different conditions were believed to have different causes. Spells and prayers designed to cure or relieve the illness were often addressed to the deities *Marduk, *Ea and *Ishtar. At the *city of *Isin the *goddess Gula was particularly important for healing. The consultants

practised at court but there were also private practices. Some *laws (such as those of *Hammurabi) mention medical services and malpractice.

Many of the best known *Hittite medical texts are translations or adaptations of Mesopotamian models. Illnesses mentioned include disorders of the eyes, mouth, throat and intestines. The causes of illness were numerous and included the sins of past generations which could be washed away. Specialist healers are known from the Hittite Old Kingdom (c.1700–1400 BC) and some later letters also mention professionals from *Egypt and Mesopotamia.

Much of the information relates to the urban and literate society; however, the majority of patients would have lived outside cities and probably relied on a range of folk healers.                                               PTC

H.I. AVALOS, *Illness and Health Care in the Ancient Near East: The Role of the Temple in Greece, Mesopotamia and Israel* (Atlanta, GA 1995).

R.D. BIGGS, 'Medizin', *Reallexikon der Assyriologie* 7 (Berlin/New York 1987–90) 623–9.

E.K. RITTER, 'Magical Expert (=Āšipu) and Physician (= Asû): Notes on Two Complementary Professions in Babylonian Medicine', *Studies in Honor of Benno Landsberger on his Seventy-fifth Birthday, April 21, 1965*, eds H.G. Güterbock and T. Jacobsen (Chicago 1965) 299–321.

H.E. SIGERIST, *A History of Medicine* (New York 1961).

## Megiddo

The ruins of ancient Megiddo survive as Tell el-Mutesellim, at the western end of the Jezreel Valley in *Palestine. Megiddo commanded a strategic position where the road to Galilee, the Jordan Valley and points beyond passed through Wadi Ara/Nahal Iron to link with the important route that ran along Palestine's Mediterranean coast. Rich farmland and *water enhanced the significance of this crossroads. Occupation produced a mound that rises nearly 30 m above the surrounding plain and whose summit covers c.5 ha. Some biblical interpreters link Megiddo with Armageddon, which Revelation 16: 16 identifies as the scene of a great apocalyptic conflict at the end of time.

Megiddo has been excavated by G. Schumacher (1903–5), C.S. Fisher, P.L.O. Guy, R.S. Lamon and G. Loud (1925–39), Y. Yadin (1960–72), I. Dunayevsky and A. Kempinski (1965), A. Eitan (1974) and I. Finkelstein, D. Ussishkin and B. Halpern (1992–). Twenty major archaeological strata have been identified, with occupation stretching from Pre-Pottery *Neolithic B. Significant religious structures survive from the site's *Chalcolithic and Early Bronze Age phases. The Middle Bronze Age *city was heavily fortified with a glacis, city *gate, and walls with stone foundations and mudbrick superstructure. Megiddo was captured by Tuthmosis III c.1479 BC, and it is mentioned in eight *Amarna Letters. A fragment of the *Gilgamesh *epic and an enormous collection of *ivories that reflect various regional styles demonstrate this city's cosmopolitan culture during the Late Bronze Age. The latter were sealed by destruction debris from c.1130 BC, when Egyptian control of *Canaan ended.

A view through the Late Bronze Age gateway of Megiddo (photograph by Paul Shrago, by courtesy of Baruch Halpern and the Megiddo Expedition).

Early *Israelite Megiddo is linked with stratum VB, c.1000 BC, and Solomon's building activities (1 Kings 9: 15) are associated with stratum VA–IVB. The identification of any remains with Solomon (e.g. *palaces, stables, casemate walls, six-chamber gate) is problematic, and many scholars have attempted to resolve the stratigraphic and ceramic controversies. 1 Kings 9: 15 is especially significant, since virtually identical six-chamber gates have been excavated at Hazor, Gezer and Megiddo; all three are often attributed to Solomon, but this association is not certain.

Stratum IVA is associated with the period of Israel's Divided Monarchy. Important finds from this era include Megiddo's 'Northern Stables' (or warehouses) and an impressive water system (with rock-hewn shaft and tunnel), both of which are dated to the reign of King Ahab (874–853 BC). In 732 BC, *Tiglath-pileser III added northern Israel to the *Assyrian provincial system, and Megiddo served as an administrative centre; *pottery and other artefacts from Strata III–II point to the Assyrian presence. In 609 BC, King Josiah was killed by Pharaoh Necho at Megiddo; the former attempted to stop the Egyptians from helping Assyria in their war with the *Babylonians. Megiddo was abandoned in the latter part of the fourth century BC.                                         GLM

G.I. DAVIES, *Megiddo* (Cambridge 1986).

A. KEMPINSKI, *Megiddo: A City-state and Royal Centre in North Israel* (Munich 1989).

K.M. KENYON, *Royal Cities of the Old Testament* (London 1971).

A. MAZAR, *Archaeology of the Land of the Bible 10,000–586 B.C.E.* (New York 1990).

D. USSISHKIN, 'Megiddo', *Anchor Bible Dictionary* 4, ed. D.N. Freedman (New York 1992) 666–79.

——, 'Megiddo', *The Oxford Encyclopedia of Archaeology in the Near East* 3, ed. E.M. Meyers (New York 1997) 460–9.

**Melid:** see Arslantepe (Malatya)

**Melqart** Melqart was the *city *god of *Tyre, one of the wealthy trading cities along the *Lebanese coast. His name is understood as an appellative: 'King of the City'. He is mentioned as one of the city deities invoked to seal a *treaty between the *Assyrian *King *Esarhaddon and the king of Tyre.

A stela found near Aleppo, set up by a Bar-Hadad of *Aram in honour of Melqart, bears a relief figure of the god bearing an axe.

In the *Hellenistic period he was identified with Hercules. This connection, as well as that with *Reshep, the fire-god, suggests that he had solar characteristics. He seems to have also been regarded as a dying and resurrecting deity. He was known as a protector of seafarers.

GL

C. BONNET, *Melqart: Cultes et mythes de l'Héraclès Tyrien en Méditerranée* (Leuven/Namur 1988).

M. HUTTER, 'Syro-phönizische Religion des 1.Jahrtausends', *Religionsgeschichte Syriens*, eds P.W. Haider, M. Hutter and S. Kreuzer (Stuttgart 1996) 131–2.

**Meluhha:** see India

**Merchants** Although it is possible to trace *trade in the archaeological record, the exchange of goods does not require the existence of specialized merchants. The earliest merchants appear to have acted for the *palace or *temple, and royal inscriptions make it clear that a *king's duty included the maintenance of *roads for ease of *transport. The first extensive evidence for merchants comes from the trading centre at *Kanesh in *Anatolia between c.1900 and 1800 BC. *Assyrian merchants came to dominate the colony and the network of trade routes which linked it with the rest of Anatolia. Thousands of *cuneiform texts from the site detail the activity of these merchants. Assyrian *families, often in partnership to increase capital and extend credit, sent *textiles manufactured or traded through *Ashur along with *tin on

Overland trade was often carried by donkeys, as depicted on this Egyptian tomb painting from Beni Hasan in Egypt, nineteenth century BC, which shows a group of Asiatics coming to Egypt (from P.E. Newberry, *Beni Hasan* 1 (London 1893) pl. XXXI).

donkey caravans to Anatolia. Here *taxes were paid to the local authorities and the goods exchanged for *gold and *silver. The merchants took the financial risks and managed the venture. Actual transport was given over to agents and professional caravaneers. The Ashur partnerships supplied funds to the carriers for *food and lodgings as an interest-free loan while the transporters were free to purchase and take along additional merchandise for resale.

During the Old *Babylonian period, private merchants are attested under the supervision of royal officials. Investors lent capital and were guaranteed a return. Many of the *laws of *Hammurabi are concerned with the activities of merchants, and in a decree by King Ammisaduqa of *Babylon (1647–1626 BC) debts incurred to form trading ventures were not cancellable. Texts make it clear that trade relations between the *Hittite capital *Hattusas and the *towns such as *Ugarit and *Alalakh as well as *Mesopotamia were intense but the importance of individual merchants within this network is unclear. A Hittite text mentions merchants killed en route. By the first millennium BC the caravan routes seem to have been handled by *Aramaean and *Arab tribes but there are few textual references detailing the traders involved. The *Old Testament, however, speaks of contempt for Babylon's and *Nineveh's overland merchants (e.g. Nahum 3: 16).

PTC

M.C. ASTOUR, 'The Merchant Class of Ugarit', *Gesellschaftsklassen im alten Zweistromland und in den angrenzenden Gebieten*, ed. D.O. Edzard (Munich 1972) 11–26.

D. CHARPIN, 'Marchands du palais et marchands du temple à fin de la 1re dynastie de Babylone', *Journal Asiatique* 270 (1982) 25–65.

A.L. OPPENHEIM, *Ancient Mesopotamia: Portrait of a Dead Civilization*, 2nd ed. (Chicago 1977).

M.T. LARSEN, *The Old Assyrian City-state and Its Colonies* (Copenhagen 1976).

W.F. LEEMANS, *Foreign Trade in the Old Babylonian Period as Revealed by Texts from Southern Babylonia* (Leiden 1960).

C. ZACCAGNINI, 'The Merchant at Nuzi', *Iraq* 39 (1977) 171–89.

**Mersin** Yümük Tepe, in the north-western part of the modern city of Mersin in Turkey, is located in the Cilician plain, immediately south of the Taurus mountains where the plain starts to narrow to form an extremely confined coastal strip. First excavated by *Garstang between 1938 and 1946, it is now the object of continuing work by Isabella Caneva. The site has a diameter of c.250 m.

The site provides an important *prehistoric sequence for the area. First occupied in the early Pottery *Neolithic c.7000 BC, contemporary with *Çatalhöyük, the material culture hints at strong coastal connections with sites as far away as *Byblos. At the same time contact with the *Anatolian plateau over the Taurus barrier is clearly indicated by significant quantities of *obsidian from central Anatolian sources.

Within the prehistoric sequence important evidence of the *Chalcolithic period exists. Indications of exchange are plentiful, including imported *Halaf *pottery and quantities of obsidian and *copper. In level XVI copper *tools are particularly common, especially axes or adzes. The Late Chalcolithic levels (XVI) have an impressive *fortification system with a major *gate with two projecting towers approached by a ramp and regular *houses built along the inside of the 2-m-wide wall. This points to a significant scale of *warfare and considerable organization relating to settlement planning and the construction of defensive works hinting at a notable degree of social hierarchy.

Later periods are well represented. Fortifications of the Late Bronze Age are in a distinctive style found at *Hittite sites, although this architectural style may have been a general Anatolian development. These fortifications have casemate walls and square towers projecting at regular intervals. There is also a street running along the inside of the wall allowing rapid access to the fortifications as at *Hattusas and Alishar. During the Late Bronze Age this may have been a fortified town guarding coastal routeways.

In the *Iron Age *Greek imports are well represented, showing the high degree of maritime contact between Cilicia and the *Aegean.

DB

J. GARSTANG, *Prehistoric Mersin* (Oxford 1953).

**Mesolithic** The term 'Mesolithic' ('Middle Stone Age', see Chronology) is not in general use in the Near East. The only archaeologist to use it regularly was Dorothy Garrod referring to *Natufian sites. The period between the *Palaeolithic and the *Neolithic is now known as the *Epipalaeolithic.

DB

**Mesopotamia** The Greek term for the land 'between the *rivers' Tigris and Euphrates is usually extended to include the lands watered by them and their tributaries. The area is a funnel shape, its mouth where the rivers issue from the Turkish foothills, its constriction just north of Baghdad in modern Iraq, the rivers then flowing to the Gulf, today joining before they reach the sea. Much of this area lies outside the 200 mm isohyet and so the southern part depends on the rivers for *irrigation, canals being drawn from the slower running Euphrates and also supplying a means of communication, either by *water or along their banks. Further north there are large regions of dry steppe, except close to the rivers, part of the Euphrates' course running in a narrow valley, but the northernmost section of Upper Mesopotamia falls within the rain shadow, allowing extensive settlement, aided by the many streams which flowed into the *Khabur and *Balikh rivers in *Syria, although slight fluctuations in climate could have very damaging effects.

In the fifth to third millennia BC (*Ubaid, *Uruk, Early Dynastic and Akkadian periods) there were many *towns in Upper Mesopotamia, some quite large (e.g. Tell *Brak), supported by extensive barley farming and sheep raising, trading in all directions. Colonists from southern Mesopotamia took control in the Uruk period, probably in

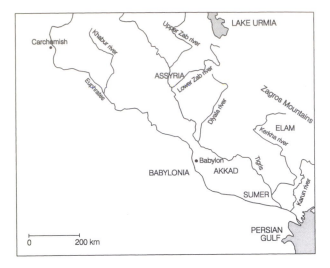

Map of Mesopotamia, showing principal ancient areas.

importance of metals and ores had become universal in the Near East by the fourth and especially the third millennium BC. Most of the better sources for metal ores are in *Anatolia, upper *Mesopotamia and northern *Iran, but the development of urban cultures in the *Fertile Crescent increased demands for the importation of metals and metalworking skills. It is assumed that finished metal products, ores and metalworking technology spread by means of the well established *trade routes. Information about ancient metallurgy comes from ancient texts, artefacts and artistic representations of metal objects and metalworking.

Metals were adopted for the production of – among other items – *tools (including ploughshares), weapons, *jewellery, kitchen utensils, sheathing for *furniture, *coins, *chariot parts, and religious *figurines. The primary metals used in the ancient Near East were *copper, *tin (alloyed with copper to produce *bronze), *gold, *silver, lead, *iron, and steel (an alloy of iron and carbon, developed in the late second millennium BC). Metals of lesser importance were electrum (a natural and artificial alloy of gold and silver), antimony and brass (an alloy of copper and zinc, developed in the early first millennium BC). In regions like Mesopotamia, which was poor in metal ore, the acquisition of metals (along with timber, building *stone, etc.) was a major factor in ancient political-military policies. Questions remain about how much of the early Mesopotamian metallurgy industry

their quest for *metals, but thereafter contact with the south diminished and the Ninevite V culture took hold in the north. Southern influence crept up the Euphrates in Early Dynastic II and III, the area then being known as Subir or Subartu, until the kings of *Akkad conquered the whole of Mesopotamia. Towards the end of the third millennium BC occupation declined, almost certainly as a result of drought and consequent famine. At the start of the second millennium BC *Amorite tribes spread here, developments in well-digging techniques enabling them to open new routes and graze land previously unusable. *Shamshi-Adad I set his capital at Shubat Enlil (Tell *Leilan) whence he was able to control his empire to the south-east and the south-west. At this time the caravans travelling from *Ashur to *Kanesh and other centres passed through the area.

In the mid second millennium BC, the *Hurrians, who had long been active in Upper Mesopotamia, set up the state of *Mitanni with its capital at Washshukanni (see Tell *Fekheriyeh), developing their *horse-training in the steppe. Political events eventually led to *Assyria ruling most of the area from about 1350 BC, with major centres, such as *Dur-Katlimmu until the *Aramaean tribes ousted them about 1100 BC, perhaps in another period of drought. In turn, the Aramaean tribal states (*Guzan, Bit-Adini) fell to the Neo-Assyrian kings who placed their garrisons across the region.                                    ARM

M. LEBEAU (ed.), About Subartu: Studies Devoted to Upper Mesopotamia (Turnhout 1998).
H. WEISS (ed.), The Origins of Cities in Dry-farming Syria and Mesopotamia in the Third Millennium B.C. (Guildford, CN 1986).

**Metalworking** Archaeological evidence for the use of metals comes from before the seventh millennium BC, much earlier than previously thought. The economic

An archaeologist working on a row of copper oxhide ingots from the Ulu Burun shipwreck off the coast of Turkey; 354 ingots were found in the wreck (courtesy of the Institute of Nautical Archaeology).

was state-dominated and how much was in private hands and market-driven.

The development of the major utilitarian metals – copper, bronze and iron – forms a technological framework for understanding Near Eastern metallurgy, and these three metals were originally the basis for the chronological periods named after them: *Chalcolithic, *Bronze Age and *Iron Age. Copper was used extensively by the fourth millennium BC. Bronze was developed in the third millennium BC and became widely available in the second millennium BC, continuing in use after the widespread introduction of iron in the first millennium BC.

The extraction of metals from their ores usually began at the *mining sites. High temperatures were needed to smelt copper and iron ore; this was achieved by burning *wood, reeds and charcoal, and bellows helped the technicians reach the desired temperature. The technology of smelting was used already in the early seventh millennium BC to produce a lead bracelet found at *Yarim Tepe. Metals were cast in open and closed moulds and by means of the lost-wax process. Distinctive 'oxhide' copper ingots were cast in a practical shape so they could be handled more easily for export. Various techniques (e.g. hammering, annealing and burnishing) were used to bring the metal to its final state. GLM

J.E. CURTIS (ed.), *Bronzeworking Centres of Western Asia, c. 1000–539 B.C.* (London 1988).

P.R.S. MOOREY, *Ancient Mesopotamian Materials and Industries: The Archaeological Evidence* (Oxford 1994) 216-301.

J.D. MUHLY, *Copper and Tin: The Distribution of Mineral Resources and the Nature of the Metals Trade in the Bronze Age* (New Haven, CN 1973).

——, *Supplement to Copper and Tin: The Distribution of Mineral Resources and the Nature of the Metal Trade in the Bronze Age* (New Haven, CN 1976).

V.C. PIGGOT, 'Near Eastern Archaeometallurgy: Modern Research and Future Directions', *The Ancient Near East in the Twenty-first Century: The William Foxwell Albright Centennial Conference*, eds J.S. Cooper and G.W. Schwartz (Winona Lake, IN 1996) 139–76.

J.C. WALDBAUM, *From Bronze to Iron: The Transition from the Bronze Age to the Iron Age in the Eastern Mediterranean* (Göteborg 1978).

T.A. WERTIME and J.D. MUHLY (eds), *The Coming of the Age of Iron* (New Haven, CN 1980).

## Midas

According to *Greek and Roman authors, Midas of *Phrygia was a legendary figure who acquired the ability to turn to *gold everything he touched. Midas was a historical ruler who appears in *Assyrian *annals and in one *letter from *Nimrud as Mita of Mushki. In coalition with the king of *Carchemish, Mita revolted unsuccessfully against *Sargon II in 717 BC, later capturing *towns in the Taurus mountains, and is last mentioned in 709 BC offering tribute to Sargon.

Some classical authors preserve historical information about Midas which fits in well with his Assyrian dates. According to Eusebius (fourth century AD), Midas came to the throne in 738 BC and committed suicide by drinking bull's blood in 696/5 BC. Strabo (first century BC/AD)

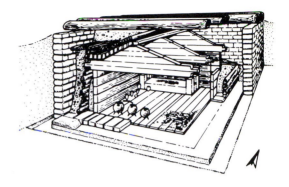

Reconstruction of the Midas Mound at Gordion, c.700 BC (after S. Lloyd, *Ancient Turkey* (London 1989) fig. 24).

relates that Midas' end was linked with the *Cimmerian invasion of Phrygia.

Midas' father was Gordius, after whom the Phrygian capital, *Gordion, was named. The largest and richest of the *burial tumuli at Gordion is known as the Midas Mound, containing the burial of an elderly man. It is impossible to say whether the *tomb really is that of Midas or perhaps of another member of Phrygian royalty, but the date of c.700 BC would fit, though some scholars think that it was Midas who built the tomb but that he was not buried in it. Midas was remembered as a heroic ruler by his people: at *Midas City in the Phrygian highlands is a rock-cut relief probably dating to the sixth century BC, dedicated to Midas and describing him as 'king and leader of the people'. PB

S. EITREM, 'Midas', *Paulys Real-Encyclopaedia* 15 (1932) 1526–40.

J.D. HAWKINS, 'Mita', *Reallexikon der Assyriologie* 8 (Berlin/New York 1994) 271–3.

M. MELLINK, 'Mita, Mushki and Phrygians', *Anadolu Arastirmalari* 2 (1965) 317–25.

——, 'The Native Kingdoms of Anatolia', *Cambridge Ancient History* 3.2, 2nd ed. (Cambridge 1991) 622–43.

O.W. MUSCARELLA, 'King Midas of Phrygia and the Greeks', *Anatolia and the Ancient Near East*, eds K. Emre *et al.* (Ankara 1989) 333–44.

G.K. SAMS, 'Midas of Gordion and the Anatolian Kingdom of Phrygia', *Civilizations of the Ancient Near East*, ed. J.M. Sasson (New York 1995) 1147–59.

## Midas City

Located in the highlands of *Phrygia on the western *Anatolian plateau, the ancient name remains unknown. The name Midas City, Turkish Midas Sehir, comes from the name *Midas that can be read on the Phrygian rock inscription on the so-called Midas Monument.

The city itself, like lesser Phrygian sites in the region, stands on an elevated table-topped hill. The approach was by way of a wide rock-cut ramp to one side of which is a group of carvings of uncertain date and function. The buildings are poorly preserved, the double 'throne' and lesser rock-cut elements being the most noteworthy extant monuments. The poor preservation is the result of erosion, later occupation and a building tradition of *timber and mudbrick.

Dominating the approach to the site is the Midas Monument or Yazýlýkaya. The rock-cut façades, besides being great examples of Phrygian monumental *art and design, provide evidence for gabled roofs with *acroteria* (finials) and ornamented wall surfaces. The wall decoration surely imitated terracotta tile façades. Neither the Midas Monument nor the other middle *Iron Age rock-cut architectural façades can be dated with certainty, but a sixth-century BC date would be compatible with elements in the decoration, especially on the Küçük Yazýlýkaya, with the inscriptions and with the imitation tile work. It is possible that the inscriptions were carved at different times after the elaborate geometric designs. The function of the façades is also unclear, although there is general agreement that the Midas Monument itself was a shrine and that the niche contained a cult image, quite possibly of Cybele. Of the other architectural façades, some are evidently *tombs while others appear to be associated with rock-cut shafts behind them. Close by is another rock-cut façade known as the Arezastis Monument from a name that can clearly be made out in the long and undeciphered inscription. Both the Arezastis and the Küçük Yazýlýkaya appear to be unfinished.  GDS

E. AKURGAL, *Phrygische Kunst* (Ankara 1955).

G. DE FRANCOVICH, *Santuarie e tombe rupestri dell'antica Frigia* (Rome 1990).

A. GABRIEL, *Phrygie* 2 (Paris 1952).

——, *Phrygie* 4 (Paris 1965).

C.H.E. HASPELS, *The Highlands of Phrygia* (Princeton, NJ 1971).

——, *Phrygie* 3 (Paris 1951).

**Midian, Midianites**  The Midianites are known only from the *Old Testament (and the Quran) as a people living in southern *Transjordan and north-west *Arabia.

Painted juglet in Midianite ware (photograph by David Harris, by courtesy of E. Borowski. E. Borowski Collection, Jerusalem, Israel).

No contemporary inscriptions mentioning the Midianites have come to light, although most of the biblical Midianite names occur in pre-Islamic Arabic inscriptions.

The term 'Midianite Ware' (also known as Qurayya Painted Ware) is often applied to a distinctive painted *pottery with bichrome or polychrome decoration and geometric, animal or human motifs. This pottery is found at sites in north-west Arabia and southern Transjordan and at *Timna. The date of this pottery is still debated. It was certainly used at Timna in the thirteenth and twelfth centuries BC, but it has been suggested that it is linked to painted wares from north-west Arabia dating to the sixth century BC. The dating of the sites in Arabia where it is found is consequently uncertain. These include Qurayya, where much of this pottery was manufactured, whose vast ruins include substantial defences, the walled oasis city of *Tayma where *Nabonidus spent his exile, and Mugha'ir Shu'ayb, probably the oasis known to classical and Arab writers as Madian or Midyan, names which derive from biblical Midian. The debate on the chronology of these sites concerns whether there was an uninterrupted continuation of 'oasis urbanism' from the thirteenth to the sixth centuries BC, or a non-urban phase between the eleventh and seventh centuries BC.

The makers of 'Midianite Ware' are often referred to as Midianites, and this should be understood as quite separate from Old Testament references. There have been recent suggestions that these Midianites were an early group of *Sea People settled in north-west Arabia by the Egyptians, but lack of systematic excavation of sites in north-west Arabia means that their early history and development cannot yet be traced.  PB

G. BAWDEN and C. EDENS, 'Tayma Painted Ware and the Hejaz Iron Age Ceramic Tradition', *Levant* 20 (1988) 197–213.

E.A. KNAUF, *Midian: Untersuchungen zur Geschichte Palästinas und Nordarabiens am Ende des 2. Jahrtausends v. Chr.* (Wiesbaden 1988).

——, *Ismael: Untersuchungen zur Geschichte Palästinas und Nordarabiens im 1. Jahrtausend v. Chr.* (Wiesbaden 1989).

P.J. PARR, 'Further Reflections on Late Second Millennium Settlement in North West Arabia', *Retrieving the Past*, ed. J.D. Seger (Winona Lake, IN 1996) 213–18.

P.J. PARR, G.L. HARDING and J.E. DAYTON, 'Preliminary Survey in N.W. Arabia, 1968', *Bulletin of the Institute of Archaeology, University of London* 8–9 (1970) 219–41.

B. ROTHENBERG and J. GLASS, 'The Midianite Pottery', *Midian, Moab and Edom: The History and Archaeology of Late Bronze and Iron Age Jordan and North-West Arabia*, eds J.F.A. Sawyer and D.J.A. Clines (Sheffield 1983) 65–124.

**Military organization**  Evidence for the organization of armies and the military hierarchy comes primarily from *Mesopotamian and *Hittite documents. The *king was in practice the supreme commander of the army, and often led it into battle. The elite *Assyrian royal corps was headed by the 'Chief *Eunuch', who might lead the army in place of the king. Other Assyrian military officers were known by their court functions, such as 'Chief Cupbearer'. The king's bodyguard was a *chariotry corps.

Infantry on the 'Royal Standard' from Ur. c.2500 BC.
WA 121201.

Among the Hittites, the hierarchy immediately below the king was normally formed from his immediate *family, the royal princes being high-ranking officers commanding brigades of one thousand men with titles such as 'Chief of the Chariot Warriors of the Right'. The *Mitannian courts included a chariot-owning aristocracy called *maryannu* based in the *palace.

Armed forces were typically divided into infantry, chariotry, cavalry and, in some instances, navy. There was usually a standing army, but campaigning was a seasonal activity (see Warfare). Armies were mustered after the harvest in April. Many workers were allowed to grow their own crops on palace land in return for military and other service. Foreign ethnic groups were drafted into armies, often as discrete corps, for example *Amorites, Khanaeans (used for political activities) and *Kassites (specialist horsemen) in the Old *Babylonian period, and *Elamites, Nubians and *Samarians in Assyrian times.

Numbers of fighting men in Old Babylonian times are occasionally recorded in texts, and vary from sixty thousand men taken by *Shamshi-Adad I to besiege a *city to the more usual ten thousand or so mentioned in *letters from *Mari and elsewhere. By the time of the latest Neo-Assyrian inscriptions, the size of forces is recorded as around two hundred thousand men. By contrast, Late Bronze Age *Canaanite rulers asked the pharaoh for archers to support them in groups of tens. For the huge late Assyrian army, a new type of building was created, the *ekal mašarti* (Review Palace). The best example, Fort Shalmaneser at *Nimrud, consists of large internal courtyards for marshalling troops, storage rooms and residential units. PB

R.H. BEAL, *The Organisation of the Hittite Military* (Heidelberg 1992).

——, 'Hittite Military Organization', *Civilizations of the Ancient Near East*, ed. J.M. Sasson (New York 1995) 545–54.

S. DALLEY, 'Ancient Mesopotamian Military Organization', *Civilizations of the Ancient Near East*, ed. J.M. Sasson (New York 1995) 413–22.

F. MALBRAN-LABAT, *L'armée et l'organisation militaire de l'Assyrie* (Paris/Geneva 1982).

J.-P. VITA, *El ejército de Ugarit* (Madrid 1995).

**Mines and mining** *Metal ores, like the green *copper ore malachite, were first employed as coloured stones. It is likely that ancient prospecting relied upon the recognition of outcrops of distinctive ores. Systematic studies of ancient mining are few, and the best documented mining complexes are those in *Oman, *Timna in *Palestine and Faynan in *Jordan. Mining evidence in *Cyprus and *Anatolia has not yet been systematically studied, and the best indication of copperworking is often the presence of large quantities of smelting slag and crucible fragments at sites located near to the copper deposits; the Late Bronze Age site of Apliki Karamallos in Cyprus is a good example.

Mining is the extraction of metal ores from host rocks. Ancient miners simply followed veins of ore along exposed surfaces, or where necessary dug into the host rock. Typical evidence for ancient mining includes *stone hammers, often with a groove around the centre, which were used to pound and crack rock, and the presence of soot and charcoal within ancient galleries, indicative of firesetting in order to shatter rock. Marks made by metal *tools such as chisels may also be seen on the walls of ancient workings. However, as many sources were worked and reworked over a long period, it can be hard to establish precise dates for particular features. Other typical mining tools would have included *wooden wedges to split rock, shovels, perhaps of wood, and baskets for transporting ore for pounding and crushing outside the mines. From the first millennium BC, *iron tools became increasingly important.

At Timna, thirteenth- to twelfth-century BC workings reached up to 35 m in depth, and horizontal galleries were ventilated by vertical shafts. Although the earliest stage of copper exploitation at Faynan is believed to have involved the use of high-grade secondary ores, a process which produces very little slag, Iron Age II operations at nearby Khirbet en-Nahas produced a few large slag heaps which were associated with the smelting of more complex sulphide ores, and which indicate the concentration of smelting activities at a few specific locations.

The control of mining was a matter of interest to political authorities. *Assyrian interest in *Urartu may have been partly to gain access to the east Anatolian mines. The evidence from Cyprus suggests that the growth of settlements on the south coast featuring substantial public architecture, such as Maroni and Kalavassos, reflects their growing wealth resulting from their role in the *transportation of copper from mining areas towards the coast. There is little evidence for rich communities within the mining areas themselves. (See Gold; Silver; Tin.) GP

P.T. CRADDOCK, *Early Metal Mining and Production* (Edinburgh 1995).

A. HAUPTMANN, E. PERNICKA and G. WAGNER (eds), *Old World Archaeometallurgy* (Bochum 1989).

P.R.S. MOOREY, *Ancient Mesopotamian Materials and Industries: The Archaeological Evidence* (Oxford 1994).

J.D. MUHLY, 'Mining and Metalworking in Ancient Western Asia', *Civilizations of the Ancient Near East*, ed. J.M. Sasson (New York 1995) 1501–21.

**Mitanni** A powerful *Hurrian state in north *Mesopotamia and *Syria, Mitanni is first mentioned in an *Egyptian tomb inscription dating to the early fifteenth century BC, and last attested at the time of the *Assyrian *King *Tiglath-pileser I (c.1115–1077 BC). The name 'Mitanni' comes from a personal name, 'Maitta', known from *Nuzi, changed into a geographical name, 'Maittani' and later 'Mittani' or 'Mittanne'. The spelling 'Mitanni' is conventionally used by scholars but is technically incorrect. The state was also known by other names: 'Hurri' in Hurrian, 'Khanigalbat' in Assyrian and some other texts, 'Khabigalbat' in *Babylonian, and 'Naharina' or 'Nahrima' in Egyptian.

The core of Mitanni was the *Khabur Valley, and its capital, Washshukanni, must be located somewhere there, although it has not yet been positively identified. Its identification with Tell *Fekheriyeh is disputed. The sources for the history of Mitanni are primarily Egyptian, *Hittite and Mesopotamian texts. Its *chronology and history are still problematic, and correlations with the histories of neighbouring states, especially the *Hittites, still differ from scholar to scholar.

By the mid fifteenth century BC, Mitanni had conquered the kingdoms of Aleppo, Assyria, Nuzi, *Alalakh and Kizzuwatna, and stretched to the Mediterranean Sea. Its kings campaigned against Egypt and Hatti and eventually signed peace *treaties with them. The treaty with Egypt was confirmed by a series of *diplomatic *marriages, and Tushratta of Mitanni twice sent the statue of *Ishtar of *Nineveh to Egypt to help heal the pharaoh. When *Suppiluliumas I conquered *Carchemish in c.1340 BC and the Assyrians raided Washshukanni, Tushratta was murdered by one of his sons. Although Mitanni survived for a while it was eventually annexed by the Assyrian king *Shalmaneser I (c.1274–1244 BC).

Mitannian culture shows a blend of influences from its neighbours and there seems to be little that is characteristic. It has been argued that the expansion of *glass production in the fifteenth or fourteenth century BC should be attributed to Mitanni, and the best early glass comes from Nuzi, but the correlation of glass innovation with the Hurrians has not been proved.          PB

A. HARRAK, *Assyria and Hanigalbat: A Historical Reconstruction of Bilateral Relations from the Middle of the Fourteenth to the End of the Twelfth Centuries B.C.* (Hildesheim 1987).

P.R.S. MOOREY, 'The Hurrians, the Mittani and Technological Innovation', *Archaeologia Iranica et Orientalis: Miscellanea in Honorem Louis Vanden Berghe*, eds L. De Meyer and E. Haerinck (Ghent 1989) 273–86.

G. WILHELM, *The Hurrians* (Warminster 1989).

——, 'The Kingdom of Mitanni in Second-millennium Upper Mesopotamia', *Civilizations of the Ancient Near East*, ed. J.M. Sasson (New York 1995) 1243–54.

**Moab, Moabites** Moab was one of the small *Iron Age kingdoms in *Transjordan, bordering *Ammon to the north and *Edom to the south. At the height of its power, Moab included an area measuring c.100 km from north to south and c.32 km from west to east. Located on the plateau immediately east of the Dead Sea, it comprised gently rolling tableland, cut into small segments by extensive wadi systems that drained the region. In certain periods, the Moabites controlled only their undisputed heartland between the Wadi Mujib (the biblical Arnon river) and the Wadi Hasa (the biblical Zered river). The Jordan Valley, which separated Moab from ancient *Judah, was an effective boundary on the west, and the *Syrian desert established the limit of sedentary occupation on Moab's eastern fringe. The climate was Mediterranean, but the Moabites' eastern frontier was an arid zone. With this topographic isolation and relatively dry environment, the Moabites managed to make a living through dry farming, *pastoralism and exchanging *trade goods with their neighbours.

According to the *Bible, the eponymous ancestor of the Moabites was the son of Lot, but evidence of human occupation in this region dates back to the *Palaeolithic. Hundreds of archaeological sites reflect a relatively continuous settlement history down to the present, although the intensity of sedentary occupation fluctuated dramatically from period to period. The third millennium BC is

The Moabite Stone, recording the achievements of Mesha, king of Moab c.853–830 BC, from Dhiban (© RMN. Louvre AO 2142-5060-5066).

well represented in the archaeological record, but there was a decline in settled life during much of the Middle and Late Bronze Ages. There is no clear explanation for this pattern, but the number of permanent sites increased steadily from the very end of the Late Bronze Age until the end of the Iron Age.

The Bible records extensive contacts between Moab and the Israelites. Most of these contacts were hostile, from the days of the Hebrew migration through to the reigns of Saul, David and the Omride dynasty. Solomon was said to have had Moabite *women in his *harem and to have built a shrine for their chief deity, Kemosh. The famous Mesha inscription – or Moabite Stone – dates to c.830 BC and reports on *King Mesha's victory over Moab's Israelite oppressors; this basalt monument was discovered at Dhiban (ancient Dibon) in 1868. Another fragmentary memorial stela, found at Karak in 1958, mentions the name of Mesha's father, Kemoshyat, who also ruled at Dibon. During the eighth and seventh centuries BC Moab was a vassal state of *Assyria. Neo-Assyrian texts name four more kings, but no precise chronology can be constructed. The Hebrew prophets frequently denounced the Moabites, who eventually fell to the *Babylonians early in the sixth century BC. The Moabite state disappeared for good and was later absorbed into the broad sweep of history during the *Persian, classical and Islamic periods.

The archaeological evidence from Moab reflects a people whose material culture shared many features with surrounding regions. Some *pottery forms and decorative techniques are distinctive, but Moabite architecture includes widely distributed elements (e.g. multi-chambered *gates, proto-Ionic capitals). Two important basalt *sculptures have been found, the 'Balu' stela' and the 'Shihan Warrior stela', dating to c.1200 and the eighth century BC respectively. The Moabites spoke a *Semitic dialect that was similar to *Hebrew, Ammonite and Edomite. Their *religion was polytheistic, but the *god Kemosh was almost certainly viewed as a national god.

GLM

'The Archaeology of Moab', special thematic issue of *Biblical Archaeologist* 60 (1997).

P. BIENKOWSKI (ed.), *Early Edom and Moab: The Beginning of the Iron Age in Southern Jordan* (Sheffield 1992).

J.A. DEARMAN (ed.), *Studies in the Mesha Inscription and Moab* (Atlanta, GA 1989).

G.L. MATTINGLY, 'Moabites', *Peoples of the Old Testament World*, eds A.J. Hoerth, G.L. Mattingly and E.M. Yamauchi (Grand Rapids, MI 1994) 317–33.

J.M. MILLER (ed.), *Archaeological Survey of the Kerak Plateau* (Atlanta, GA 1991).

S. TIMM, *Moab zwischen den Mächten: Studien zu historischen Denkmälern und Texten* (Wiesbaden 1989).

**Money**  Until the *Persian period, *trade was by barter or exchange, and *coinage did not exist. *Silver was commonly a measure of value from the third millennium BC onwards, usually expressed in the shekel *weight (about 8 g), although day-to-day transactions would not necessarily involve silver; prices, like *taxes, were often paid in kind. However, there is evidence of silver as a form of currency in frequent mention of silver rings used as payment from the Akkadian to Old Babylonian periods (*Sumerian *har*, *Akkadian *šewerum*). Silver rings and coils found at Akkadian and later sites in *Babylonia and elsewhere illustrate those texts. The weights vary, but the five-shekel size dominates. All payments in *metal were made by weighing (see Genesis 23: 16), so snippets of silver were added to the rings or coils, or cut from them to reach the amount required. Hoards of scrap silver from *Iron Age *Megiddo, *Ekron and other places include chopped silver rings, parts of ingots and small pieces of vessels, *jewellery and melted lumps, any of which could be weighed for exchange. *Copper, *tin and, in the *Kassite-*Amarna age, *gold were also media of exchange.

During the second millennium BC, *kings issued tariffs for staple goods and wages, either setting extremes or ideals, *Hammurabi fixing some wages and rates of hire in his *laws. Prices of basic commodities fluctuated, rising before harvest and falling afterwards, unless the harvest was poor. Inflation can be traced in a general way through the rise in the average price of *slaves.     ARM

J.D. HAWKINS, 'Royal Statements of Ideal Prices: Assyrian, Babylonian and Hittite', *Ancient Anatolia: Aspects of Change and Cultural Development*, eds J.V. Canby et al. (Madison 1986) 93–102.

J.N. POSTGATE, *Early Mesopotamia: Society and Economy at the Dawn of History* (London 1992) 202–5.

**Monsters:** see Demons and monsters

**Moon-gods**  It seems that in all the cultures of the ancient Near East the moon was imagined as a male deity (contrast the *Greek goddess Selene or Roman Diana). In *Anatolia, the *Hurrian moon-*god was Kushuh, corresponding to earlier Hattic Kashku, and Luwian Arna. The name was usually written with the name of the *Mesopotamian moon-god *Sin or the numeral 30 (representing the thirty days in a lunar month). A myth tells how Kashku fell from the sky during a storm. The goddess of healing and magic, Kamrusepa, used her *magic to help him resist the raging of the *weather-god and to return to his place in the heavens.

In *Ugarit, the moon-god was Yarih. The goddess Nikkal (corresponding to Mesopotamian *Ningal) is married to him by her father Harhab, 'king of the summer fruit'. The Kotharat deities are summoned to bless her and give her a son.     JAB

J.C.L. GIBSON, *Canaanite Myths and Legends*, 2nd ed. (Edinburgh 1978).

W. HERRMANN, *Yarih und Nikkal und der Preis der Kutarat-Göttinnen: Ein kultisch-magischer Text aus Ras Schamra* (Berlin 1968).

H.A. HOFFNER, Jr, *Hittite Myths* (Atlanta, GA 1990).

A. KAMMENHUBER, 'Die protohattische Bilingue vom Mond der vom Himmel gefallen ist', *Zeitschrift für Assyriologie* 51 (1955) 102–23.

E. LAROCHE, 'Hattic Deities and their Epithets', *Journal of Cuneiform Studies* 1 (1947) 187–216.

**Mot** The *Semitic word Mot means 'death'. Philo of Byblos in the first century AD mentions that the *Phoenicians had a *god called Muth whom they identified with the Roman underworld-deity Pluto. Little is known of a cult associated with Mot, and he is mainly attested in *myths from *Ugarit. In the *Baal cycle he is Baal's great adversary and counterpart with whom he is locked in a perpetual sequence of mutual triumph and defeat. Mot as the 'son of *El' is part of the cosmic order but his realm is the depth of the *underworld, an inhospitable land, the 'charnel-house of the earth'. Mot's most salient characteristic is his enormous appetite, he is forever hungry for 'all (living beings) that die'. With his huge jaws he devours the living and swallows Baal 'like an olive'. Having eaten Baal, whose disappearance causes the rains to stop and the vegetation to wither, Mot is challenged by *Anat, who descends to the underworld to do battle with him. The treatment she metes out to Mot refers to *agricultural practices but also has connotations with destructive *magical acts: she cuts him to pieces, burns, grinds and winnows his remains which she scatters over the fields for the birds to eat. This procedure brings about the rebirth of Baal. Mot also revives 'after seven years' and he sends a message to Baal seeking redress for the wrongs done to him by Anat and asks for one of Baal's brothers to be delivered to him. Baal sends him 'sons of Mot' (also sons of El, perhaps boars, traditionally used as sacrificial animals for death rituals). When Mot discovers the trickery he comes to Baal to fight him again, though neither can prevail over the other. Their struggle is eventually terminated by the sun-goddess Shapash, who threatens to take away Mot's kingship over the underworld if he does not stop, to which Mot acquiesces.

Interpretations of this myth have tended to highlight the seasonal and *ritual aspects of a society dependent on rain-fed agriculture in a climate where hot and dry summers alternate with wet and cold winters. It also reaffirms that *death is dependent on the forces of vitality to produce life and that the balance between life and death, though precarious at times, is ultimately maintained.
GL

B. MARGALIT, *A Matter of Life and Death: A Study of the Baal – Mot Epic* (Neukirchen/Vluyn 1980).

J.H. MARKS and R.M. GOOD, *Love and Death in the Ancient Near East* (Guildford, CN 1987).

D. PARDEE, 'The Ba'lu Myth', *The Context of Scripture* 1, eds W.W. Hallo and K.L. Younger (Leiden 1997) 241–74.

M.S. SMITH, *The Ugaritic Baal Cycle: Vol. 1 – KTU 1.1 –1.2* (Leiden 1994).

P. WATSON, *Mot, the God of Death at Ugarit and in the Old Testament* (Neukirchen/Vluyn 1970).

**Mother goddesses** For the historical periods of ancient *Mesopotamia and *Anatolia we have fairly definite information about mother *goddesses and birth-goddesses. In one sense any goddess could become a 'mother goddess' – a goddess who is a mother – but usually motherhood of most of the early gods was ascribed to one particular goddess who by the second millennium BC appears under a variety of interchangeable names, some of which are really titles, but who may in origin have been several different deities. In Mesopotamia these are: Aruru; Mami or Mama (clearly 'mother'); Dingirmah ('exalted deity'); Ninmah ('exalted lady'); Nintud ('lady of birth'); Ninmena ('lady of the crown'); Belet-ili ('lady of the gods' in *Akkadian); and Namma.

Damgalnuna seems earlier to be a mother goddess but later to be more particularly the wife of Enki (so mother of *Marduk). Ninmah's name was changed by her son *Ninurta to *Ninhursanga ('lady of the mountains') commemorating his creation of the mountains. Namma is usually creatrix of *An and Ki, and of the early gods, including Enki, but she also creates mankind in one poem.

The making of a *figurine of clay which is then brought to life is another image for creation. Usually it is a goddess (under one of the above names) who pinches off and moulds the clay, especially in connection with the creation of mankind (although occasionally Enki is responsible). An additional goddess sometimes acts as 'midwife' in both these types of creation, and these divine midwives can conveniently be termed birth-goddesses. In the complex account of the creation of the first seven men and seven women in the *Epic of Atrahasis (see Creation legends and cosmogonies), the mother goddess is assisted by fourteen *šassūrātu* (literally 'wombs'), each of whom oversees the 'shaping' or 'preparing' of one of the clay figurines during a period of ten (lunar) months.

In the Atrahasis *story, Enki assists Mami as she mixes the clay and blood; and in the poem 'Enki and Ninmah', the creatures called *sig-en-sig-du* nip off the clay into lumps for Namma to mould after she has first kneaded it, while Ninmah acts as midwife.

In *Hittite *mythology, the ancient Hattic goddess Hannahanna (meaning 'Grandma') is a mother goddess.
JAB

W. HELCK, *Betrachtungen zur grössen Göttin und den ihr verbundenen Gottheiten* (Munich/Vienna 1971).

H.A. HOFFNER, Jr, *Hittite Myths* (Atlanta, GA 1990).

B. KIENAST, 'Überlegungen zum "Pantheon Babylonicum"', *Orientalia* 54 (1985) 106–16.

W.G. LAMBERT, 'Goddesses in the Pantheon', *Comptes rendus de Rencontre Assyriologique Internationale 33, 1986* (Paris 1987) 125–30.

T. URBIN-CHOFFRAY, 'Déesse-mère', *Dictionnaire des religions* (Paris 1983) 380–1.

**Mozan, (Tell)** Located on the *Khabur plains in *Syria, Tell Mozan has in recent years been positively identified with ancient Urkesh, a *city prominent in *Hurrian *mythology as the residence of the *god *Kumarbi. Surveyed and excavated by *Mallowan (1934) and since 1984 by Giorgio Buccellati and Marilyn Kelly-Buccellati, it consists of a main mound of 18 ha and an outer city of 135 ha used for *burials and *housing. Occupation began in the *Halaf period c.6000 BC, continuing to the mid second millennium BC characterized by private houses.

The major occupation dates to the late third millennium BC. A *temple with a monumental entrance reached by a long stone ramp is similar in plan and dimensions to

Seal impressions from Mozan, about 2300 BC, have designs unusually related to their owners' functions. The upper one belonged to the royal nurse, the lower to the royal cook, who is about to butcher an animal (drawings by Cecily Hildsdale, by courtesy of Giorgio Buccellati and the International Institute for Mesopotamian Area Studies).

**Music** Music was an important part of cultic, official and daily life in the ancient Near East. Music and some instruments are listed among the essentials of civilization in *Babylonian texts. Most of the evidence comes from *Sumerian, *Akkadian and *Hittite *cuneiform tablets, representations on *cylinder seals and other carvings, and occasionally surviving instruments from excavations.

Instruments included strings, wind and percussion, many preserved in the Royal Tombs at *Ur. Lyres could be large or small, the wooden sound box at first bovine-shaped, and after about 2000 BC rectangular or trape-zoidal. The *Hittite vase from Inandik depicts six such lyres. Harps had curved soundboxes, later angular. The long-necked lute, normally two-stringed, appeared about 2300 BC, depicted on *Akkadian *seals; *Shulgi of the Third Dynasty of Ur boasted that he could play the lute the first time he tried. Psalteries (like a zither) appear on an *Assyrian *ivory pot being played by dancing *women. Stringed instruments could be played with or without a plectrum. Flutes are known made of *silver, *bone and *pottery; the earliest rim-blown flute appears on a cylinder seal dating to c.2200 BC. Double pipes and panpipes are also known. Trumpets and horns were used for directing work gangs and making public announcements. Drums, with skin heads, of various shapes and sizes are often depicted, small ones frequently played by nude women, others accompanying processions, concerts, boxing practice and ritual events. Sistra, cymbals, rattles, clappers and bells are known from the Early Dynastic period onwards.

Music was part of the *school curriculum in *Mesopotamia from about 1800 BC. Some *temples may have had music schools, and musicians are listed as palace staff receiving rations. Professional orchestras and performers are well attested; the Hittite archives especially indicate a hierarchy of musical personnel, e.g. 'the superintendent

one at *Ebla. A large storehouse consists of a reception suite, a large hall with a vault, and probably a courtyard and an interior storage space. This may have been a royal storehouse where goods were stored in boxes, baskets and jars. In the vault were discovered over six hundred *seal impressions dating to the early *Akkadian period, some inscribed with the names of the *king and *queen of Urkesh which confirmed the ancient name of the city. The majority of the seals belonged to the queen, and the western wing of the structure may have been assigned for storage of her goods. Also in the vault were over one hundred human and animal *figurines. *Administrative *cuneiform tablets, some with Hurrian personal names, were found in the storehouse and in a private house.   PB

G. BUCCELLATI and M. KELLY-BUCCELLATI, 'Mozan, Tell', *The Oxford Encyclopedia of Archaeology in the Near East* 4, ed. E.M. Meyers (New York 1997) 60–3.
——, 'Urkesh: The First Hurrian Capital', *Biblical Archaeologist* 60 (1997) 77–96.

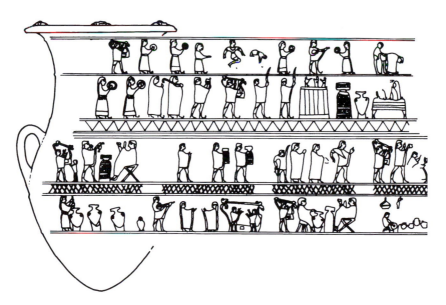

Hittite vase from Inandik, mid–late second millennium BC (original in the Archaeological Museum, Ankara). The upper register shows an orchestra with instrumentalists playing the lute, lyre and tambourines or cymbals, followed by two dancers. The same instruments appear on the lower registers, with a harp on the bottom.

Reconstruction of a lyre from the grave of Pu-abi in the Royal Cemetery at Ur, c.2500 BC. Whether the strings were fibre, gut or wire is unknown, so the sounds cannot be reproduced. WA 121198a.

of performers'. Assyrian administrative documents mention singers from other countries. *Biblical texts also refer to a range of musical instruments, players and singers in *Israel's cult and society.

Music and *song were used in *magical rites, royal ceremonies, weddings, cult *festivals, and in taverns. One commonly depicted scene was a *feast accompanied by a small orchestra consisting of a harp or lyre player, a piper and a percussionist. Cylinder seals attest to platforms on which musicians performed. Individual instruments had their specific positions within the orchestra. Lutenists and small-drum players were not part of orchestras until the first millennium BC; their performances, often in the nude, were occasionally accompanied by *sexual activity, *dancing and acrobatic performances. Occasionally, *priests and other officials are noted as playing instruments, some of which had apparent magical qualities. Hittite texts particularly attest to the use of music in religious ceremonies, accompanying *ritual actions and processions, combined with *dances and songs.

In Mesopotamia, two musical systems coexisted, the Sumerian and Akkadian. The Sumerian system used fixed tunings and prescribed patterns; the Akkadian system used seven musical scales and nine musical strings. Musical notation has survived on *cuneiform tablets from Mesopotamia and *Ugarit. Hittite tablets suggest the existence of folk music characteristic of different *cities.                                                    PB

J. BRAUN, 'Musical Instruments', The Oxford Encyclopedia of Archaeology in the Near East 4, ed. E.M. Meyers (New York 1997) 70–9.

A.D. KILMER, 'Music and Dance in Ancient Western Asia', Civilizations of the Ancient Near East, ed. J.M. Sasson (New York 1995) 2601–13.

A.D. KILMER et al., 'Musik', Reallexikon der Assyriologie 8 (Berlin/New York 1995–7) 463–91.

S. DE MARTINO, 'Music, Dance, and Processions in Hittite Anatolia', Civilizations of the Ancient Near East, ed. J.M. Sasson (New York 1995) 2661–9.

J. RIMMER, Ancient Musical Instruments of Western Asia in the British Museum (London 1969).

**Myths:** see Stories, myths and epics

# N

**Nabataeans** The kingdom of the Nabataeans, with its capital at Petra in *Transjordan, flourished in the late *Hellenistic and early *Roman periods. Although their origins are still obscure, they were originally *nomadic herdsmen and *merchants from *Arabia who came to control the major *trade routes between Arabia and *Syria. It is still debated whether they are to be identified with the Nabaiati *Arabs who appear in *Assyrian inscriptions. The Nabataeans dealt mostly in *incense and spices, but also in *animals, *metals, fabrics, sugar and *ivory, trading with the Far East, *Egypt, Greece and Rome. They were also great *water engineers, *irrigating their land with ingenious systems of dams and canals.

They manufactured a distinctive eggshell-thin painted red *pottery, probably the finest pottery ever produced in the ancient world. Although Arabic-speaking, they used *Aramaic *language and script which developed into the classical Arabic *alphabet. The Nabataean kingdom was annexed by Rome in AD 106.                             PB

G.W. BOWERSOCK, Roman Arabia (Cambridge, MA 1983).

P. HAMMOND, The Nabataeans: Their History, Culture and Archaeology (Gothenburg 1973).

J. STARCKY, 'Pétra et la Nabatène', Supplément au Dictionnaire de la Bible 7 (1966) 886–1017.

R. WENNING, Die Nabatäer (Göttingen 1987).

Rock-cut façade at Petra, probably first century BC/AD, with battlements or crenellations with stepped sides, used on Nabataean tombs; this decoration is often called Assyrian crowsteps because it was used centuries earlier in Assyria, but no direct influence has been established (courtesy of Piotr Bienkowski).

**Nabonidus** *Nebuchadnezzar's son was killed by Neriglissar, and his son, Labashi-Marduk, was killed in a conspiracy which put Nabonidus (Nabû-na'id, 'Nabu is praised') on the throne of *Babylon in 556 BC. He was a prominent citizen, perhaps the Labynetus whom *Herodotus (I.74) says the *king of Babylon sent to mediate between the *Medes and *Lydia in 585 BC. His early years saw campaigns to maintain control in Cilicia and *Syria, reaching *Edom. Nabonidus then moved on into *Arabia where he settled for ten years, fortifying Tayma and building a *palace there, sending his forces further south to capture Yathrib (Medina). Why Nabonidus left Babylon for so long is debated. Control of lucrative *trade in *incense and *gold, or imperialist ambition are possibilities, as are need to escape plague and famine. The strongest reason seems to be religious. Nabonidus was particularly devoted to *Sîn, installing his daughter as *priestess at *Ur, in accordance with ancient tradition, and rebuilding the Sîn *temple at *Harran ruined in 609 BC when Babylonians and Medes crushed the last *Assyrian king. His mother was also a devotee of Sîn, commemorated in an autobiographical stela at Harran. Nabonidus' own inscriptions emphasize his concern for correct *ritual – he restored temples of various *gods in many places – and he speaks of opposition from people and priests in the old Babylonian *cities, so it may be that he upset long-standing positions and interests and felt it better to remove himself. That is certainly the claim of the fiercely hostile *Persian Verse Account, written after Nabonidus was deposed, asserting that he introduced an improper statue of Sîn, changed the form of worship, built a new shrine and tried to replace *Marduk with Sîn. However exaggerated, that may well explain the root of the problem, irreconcilable religious convictions. By the time Nabonidus was back in Babylon, before 543 BC, the international scene had become threatening. The Medes had fallen under *Cyrus II of Persia in 550 BC who conquered Lydia in 547 BC and loomed in the east. In 539 BC Nabonidus gathered gods of several towns into Babylon, but Cyrus advanced to Opis, then, on 13 October, his forces entered Babylon by diverting a watercourse, according to Herodotus. Nabonidus, *Greek tradition reports, was sent to govern Carmania (Kirman) in southern *Iran. His son, Belshazzar, to whom he had 'entrusted the kingship' while he was in Arabia, was killed, as related in the *biblical book of Daniel.          ARM

P.-A. BEAULIEU, *The Reign of Nabonidus, King of Babylon, 556–539 B.C.* (New Haven, CN 1989).

———, 'King Nabonidus and the Neo-Babylonian Empire', *Civilizations of the Ancient Near East*, ed. J.M. Sasson (New York 1995) 969–79.

A.L. OPPENHEIM, in *Ancient Near Eastern Texts*, 3rd ed., ed. J.B. Pritchard (Princeton, NJ 1969) 305–7, 308–15, 560–3.

D.J. WISEMAN, 'Babylonia 605–539 B.C.', *Cambridge Ancient History* 3.2, 2nd ed. (Cambridge 1991) 243–51.

Upper part of a stone stela showing Nabonidus holding a long staff topped with the moon crescent, standing before symbols of the moon-god, the sun and Ishtar (Venus). Height 58 cm. WA 90837.

**Nabopolassar** Nabopolassar, '*Nabû guard the son', first *king of the Neo-*Babylonian or '*Chaldaean' line, took the throne in 626 BC, following unrest after the death of Kandalanu (see Ashurbanipal). The *Assyrians tried to repress him and held *Nippur for another ten years, fighting him for control of *Uruk and other places. In 616 BC Nabopolassar campaigned up the Euphrates and also in southern Assyria, attacking *Ashur the next year, without success. Then the *Medes advanced from *Iran and took Ashur, Cyaxares, their king, making a *treaty with Nabopolassar after the battle. The crown prince *Nebuchadnezzar married the Mede's daughter. Although an Assyrian counterattack pushed Babylonian troops back, in 612 BC they and the Medes laid siege to *Nineveh and captured it. The allies moved on to *Harran and ousted the last Assyrians in 610 BC. Egyptian contingents arrived under Necho II to support the Assyrian remnant and, after several battles, were utterly defeated at *Carchemish in 605 BC, by Nebuchadnezzar, just before his father's death. Meanwhile Nabopolassar marched into south-west *Urartu to subdue unruly tribesmen (609–607 BC).

Clearly he was an able king who took the opportunity to exploit Assyria's weakness and establish his own throne. He was not a member of a royal family, but made an advantageous alliance and ultimately removed the major rival from the scene.

In *Babylon he began to restore many of the major buildings. *Foundation inscriptions record his pious works, and the Babylonian *Chronicle gives most of the historical information for his reign. ARM

J. OATES, 'The Fall of Assyria (635–609 B.C.)', *Cambridge Ancient History* 3.2, 2nd ed. (Cambridge 1991) 172–84.
D.J. WISEMAN, *Chronicles of Chaldaean Kings* (London 1961).
S. ZAWADZKI, *The Fall of Assyria and Median–Babylonian Relations in the Light of the Nabopolassar Chronicle* (Poznan 1988).

**Nabû** Nabû is the *Mesopotamian *scribe-*god, the divine scribe of the destinies, a scribes' god and patron of *writing. He later joined *Ea (Enki) and *Marduk as a god of *wisdom, and in some traditions he absorbed attributes of *Ninurta and was therefore associated with *agriculture. His spouse was the goddess Tashmetu. He may have been identified with the planet Mercury.

The worship of Nabû may have reached *Babylonia from *Syria with the *nomadic *Amorites in the early second millennium BC. His cult centre became *Borsippa and he was absorbed into the circle of the god Marduk, first as Marduk's minister and later (from the *Kassite period) as his son. Later Nisaba was regarded as his wife. At the *New Year ceremonies, Nabû was brought from Borsippa to 'visit' his father Marduk at Babylon. In time Nabû became supreme god of Babylonia alongside Marduk. In Neo-Assyrian times his worship was accepted in *Assyria too and he almost became an 'Assyrian' god in the reigns of *Esarhaddon and *Ashurbanipal.

A symbol of Nabû is a single wedge, vertical or horizontal, possibly a writing stylus, sometimes resting on a clay tablet. Occasionally this, or the god himself, is shown riding on the back of the snake-dragon.

The worship of Nabû was long-lived and spread outside Mesopotamia among expatriate communities of *Aramaic-speakers in *Egypt and *Anatolia during the fourth century BC. By the time of Augustus a Meso-potamian pantheon of gods including Nabû was being worshipped in central and northern Syria at Palmyra and Dura Europos, and survived until at least the second century AD. In post-Babylonian Mesopotamia, Nabû's cult continued, and he was identified by the Greeks with Apollo. AG/JAB

F. POMPONIO, *Nabû: il culto e la figura di un dio del Pantheon babilonese ed assiro* (Rome 1978).
F. POMPONIO and U. SEIDL, 'Nabû', *Reallexikon der Assyriologie* 9 (Berlin/New York 1998) 16–29.

**Nanna:** see Sin

**Naram-Sin** Naram-Sin of *Akkad (c.2260–2223 BC) campaigned far and wide, like his grandfather *Sargon, but faced serious revolt at home and a major attack from the east. Contemporary inscriptions, later copies of his monuments, epic poems and *omen and *chronicle traditions give information about his reign. His notable innovation was his self-deification part way through his rule, perhaps after he crushed the coalition of *Babylonian *cities raised against him in nine battles in one year, so giving him a higher status than any rival. His forces were victorious in *Iran, where he made a *treaty with the *king, partially preserved in an *Elamite version. In the Gulf he reached *Magan, whence booty was taken, including *stone bowls duly inscribed, recovered in modern times. In the north he went to the 'sources' of the Tigris and Euphrates and erected a stela near Diyarbekir. Like Sargon, he marched up the Euphrates where he fought the *Amorites in Jebel Bishri and proceeded to Armanum (probably Aleppo), *Ebla and the Cedar Mountains of the Amanus (the last noted in a year name) and up to the area of Gaziantep, north-west of *Carchemish.

The *epics about Naram-Sin have more fantastic elements than those about Sargon. Known from Old Babylonian times onwards, with one small fragment from the Akkadian era, they deal with the 'Great Revolt', a western campaign and the great invasion (the 'Cuthean Legend'). The last tells of irruptions by barbarians who killed 360,000 of Naram-Sin's men and overwhelmed the land when Naram-Sin ignored divine indications and tried to repel them. Driven to despair, he was allowed some respite by the *gods, teaching him that they were in charge. The epic is built upon the invasion of the *Guti tribes from the east who eventually ended the Akkadian dynasty. Naram-Sin is depicted as unlucky in other traditions, accused in one of angering *Marduk by his activities in *Babylon.

A stela from *Susa showing the king triumphing over mountain tribes is the principal work of art surviving been concentrated in the southern Levant, but they are found as far afield as the Euphrates Valley in *Syria at Abu Hureyra and Mureybet, although some dispute the application of the term Natufian to these sites.

Natufian sites share a number of features. One of the most abundant and characteristic elements of the material culture is the microlithic *flint tools (see Epipalaeolithic) made with a crescent-shaped back, which would have been inserted into hafts and shafts, and therefore termed lunates. These would have formed components of projectiles and other tools. An Early and Late Natufian can be distinguished on the basis of the lengths and retouch of these lunates. Earlier Natufian lunates are longer and have a distinctive retouch, known as 'Helwan'.

A number of features of Natufian sites suggest major changes in human behaviour in the Natufian compared with the earlier phases of the Epipalaeolithic. These include changes in site sizes, site architecture and facilities, *burial evidence, artwork and ornamentation, and subsistence practices. There are a number of large Natufian sites reaching 2000 sq m in area, far exceeding the size of all but an exceptional few earlier Epipalaeolithic sites. In addition circular stone-built structures, sunk into the ground, are a common feature of most Natufian sites. Such architecture is exceptional in earlier sites. Early Natufian buildings are larger than Late Natufian structures: the former have diameters between 7 and 9 m, the latter 3–7 m. The size of these structures suggests that most were dwellings. Other built features on sites include lined and unlined pits, some likely to be for storage. In addition large ground stone tools and bedrock mortars were permanent fixtures on such sites. This, along with evidence of *hunting and gathering activities at a number of seasons at the same sites, suggests that these sites were occupied on average by larger groups for longer periods of time on a more repetitive basis than earlier sites. This pattern may have approached and embraced, in some instances, permanent year-round occupation over a considerable number of years, although these issues are a matter of ongoing debate.

Stela of Naram-Sin, found at Susa, celebrating his victory over the Lullubi. Sandstone (© Photo RMN – H. Lewandowski. Louvre Sb 4).

from his reign. Most provinces were put under the king's men, with a regular communication system to the capital. A fortress built at Tell *Brak in the Khabur region was probably one of many, serving as garrison and store-post, some of its bricks stamped with his name.                    ARM

D.R. FRAYNE, *Sargonic and Gutian Periods (2334–2113 BC)* (Toronto 1993) 84–181.

C.J. GADD, 'The Dynasty of Agade and the Gutian Invasion', *Cambridge Ancient History* 1.2, 2nd ed. (Cambridge 1971) 440–5.

J. GOODNICK WESTENHOLZ, *Legends of the Kings of Akkade* (Winona Lake, IN 1997) 173–368.

**Natufian** The Natufian period belongs to the final part of the *Epipalaeolithic in the *Levant between c.11,500 and 9500 BC. Excavation of Natufian sites has

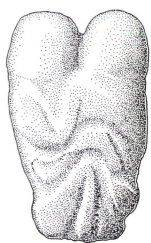

Stone figurine of a couple apparently in coitus, from Ain Sakhri in Palestine, usually dated to the Natufian. Height 10 cm. PRB 1958.10-7.1, drawing courtesy of Jill Cook.

Such developments may be attributed to the more widespread occurrence of cereals and legumes at the end of the last glaciation and increased reliance on these high-yield and eminently storable foods. Hunting, in particular of gazelle, remained important (hence partly the importance of microliths). Suggestions of the incipient domestication of *plants and *animals in the Natufian tend to be viewed sceptically. However if we see plant domestication in the following Pre-Pottery *Neolithic A (see Agriculture) we cannot rule out a shift towards behaviour associated with plant cultivation during the Natufian.

Burials are common on Natufian sites, pointing not just to prolonged site occupancy but also to other new behaviours. In the Early Natufian group burials are important, many, such as those at El Wad (see Carmel caves), featuring a single individual in the group, usually a young or mature female, spectacularly adorned with sea shell or animal tooth headdress or other ornamentation. To have such an individual singled out at death within a small and presumably related group suggests specific roles for such females in society (see Women/gender). The suggestion that it indicates the development of a social hierarchy is a matter of considerable debate.

Evidence of ornamentation and production of *art work and decoration, whether of utilitarian items like *stone bowls and *bone sickle hafts or of purely representational objects, is much more common in the Natufian than in earlier periods. It attests to the increased intensity of social interactions within and between communities, as a result of increasing sedentism and group size.                                    DB

O. BAR-YOSEF, 'The Natufian in the Southern Levant', *The Hilly Flanks and Beyond*, eds T. Young, P. Smith and P. Mortensen (Chicago 1983) 11–42.

O. BAR-YOSEF and F. VALLA, *The Natufian Culture in the Levant* (Ann Arbor, MI 1991).

B. BYRD, 'The Natufian: Settlement Variability and Economic Adaptations at the End of the Pleistocene', *Journal of World Prehistory* 3/2 (1989) 159–97.

B. BYRD and C. MONAHAN, 'Death, Mortuary Ritual, and Natufian Social Structure', *Journal of Anthropological Archaeology* 14 (1995) 251–87.

D. HENRY, *From Foraging to Agriculture: The Levant at the End of the Ice Age* (Philadelphia, PA 1989).

**Navigation**  Ancient Near Eastern sailors have left no texts explaining how they set and kept course for their destinations without compasses or charts. There is only indirect evidence suggesting that they navigated using the stars and sun. For example, Homer describes Odysseus steering by the stars, and this is likely to have been the normal method in the first millennium BC and earlier. *Phoenician sailors were regarded as extremely able, and pilots from *Sidon as the most skilled, knowing which constellations best to steer by. When the *Persian *King Darius I planned an expedition against Greece, he hired Sidonians, and *Herodotus records how they sailed along the shore making careful notes. It is usually assumed that

prior to the mid or late first millennium BC seagoing *ships followed the coast rather than sailing the open sea. Odysseus' sea journey home after the Trojan War was essentially island-hopping rather than long-distance sailing. Written sailing directions have survived from the fourth century BC onwards, for example the *Periplus* of Scylax of Caryada, an account of the harbours and landmarks of the Mediterranean.

Herodotus mentions the use of a lead and line as a navigating instrument to judge the distance and character of the approaching shore, by measuring the depth of the water and bringing up a specimen of the sea-floor mud or silt. *Birds were probably used as aids in navigation. The *Epic of *Gilgamesh and the *biblical *Flood story both mention the releasing of birds (dove, swallow, pigeon or raven) to find land. The birds indicated the height of the water but also by their flight the direction of dry land. Fifth-century BC *Indian sources, and the later classical historian Pliny, mention sailors using birds to locate land when their *ship was lost.                          PB

J. HORNELL, 'The Role of Birds in Early Navigation', *Antiquity* 20 (1946) 142–9.

P. POMEY, *Navigation dans l'antiquité* (Paris 1997).

E.R.G. TAYLOR, *The Haven-finding Art: A History of Navigation from Odysseus to Captain Cook* (London 1956).

**Nebuchadnezzar**  Nebuchadnezzar, 'Nabû protect the heir', was the name of two *kings of *Babylon.

Nebuchadnezzar I, c.1126–1105 BC, was the principal king of the Second Dynasty of *Isin, celebrated for recovering the statue of *Marduk taken from Babylon by the *Elamites. Inscriptions known from later incomplete copies contain Nebuchadnezzar's prayers to Marduk and an account of the *god relenting from his anger against the *city, resulting in the triumph over Elam. A *kudurru* gives a vivid description of the battle. The restoration of Marduk's statue may have stimulated the composition of the *Babylonian *creation poem, *Enuma eliš*, written to laud the god. Nebuchadnezzar reconstructed shrines in Babylon and *Nippur and honoured *Sin at *Ur, possibly installing his daughter as *priestess. He twice attacked *Assyria, unsuccessfully.

Nebuchadnezzar II inherited the throne from *Nabopolassar in 605 BC and reigned until 562 BC. He was married to the daughter of his father's ally, the *Median king. Entries for his first ten years survive in the Babylonian *Chronicle; thereafter there is little historical information. After defeating the Egyptians at *Carchemish just before his accession, he imposed his rule throughout the *Levant over the next eight years, securing *Damascus, containing *Egypt behind her frontier, subduing *Jerusalem and *Arab tribes. Jerusalem's king rebelled, hoping for Egypt's help, so the city was taken in 597 BC, but the king whom Nebuchadnezzar imposed also rebelled, so the city was finally reduced in 586 BC, many citizens being *deported on both occasions. During that period, *Greek sources report a thirteen-year siege of *Tyre, and the *Bible (Jeremiah 43: 8–13) and Greek writers imply an invasion of Egypt; a *cuneiform text of

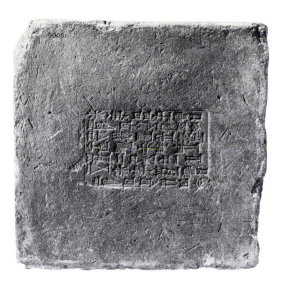

Nebuchadnezzar II had his name stamped on many bricks in Babylon and other cities to record his restoration of the temples of Marduk and Nabû. Length c.32 cm. WA 90081.

Nebuchadnezzar I:

J.A. BRINKMAN, *A Political History of Post-Kassite Babylonia* (Rome 1968) 41–2, 104–16.

B.R. FOSTER, *Before the Muses I* (Bethesda, MD 1993) 290–303.

G. FRAME, *Rulers of Babylonia from the Second Dynasty of Isin to the End of Assyrian Domination (1157–612 BC)* (Toronto 1995) 11–35.

D.J. WISEMAN, 'Assyria and Babylonia c.1200–1000 B.C.', *Cambridge Ancient History* 2.2, 2nd ed. (Cambridge 1975) 454–7.

Nebuchadnezzar II:

D.J. WISEMAN, 'Babylonia 605–539 B.C.', *Cambridge Ancient History* 3.2, 2nd ed. (Cambridge 1991) 229–51.

——, *Nebuchadnezzar and Babylon* (Oxford 1985).

uncertain interpretation may also mention it. In 595 BC there was action against the Elamite region and suppression of a revolt in Babylonia itself. Various documents show that the kingdom embraced almost all of the former Assyrian empire, except the territories in Iran.

Nebuchadnezzar's reputation rests upon his deportation of the Jews from Jerusalem and his building works at Babylon. He excelled all previous beautifiers of the city. Double walls and a moat surrounded it and a bridge crossed the Euphrates to the new city on the west side. The *ziggurat at the centre, Etemenanki, was largely rebuilt and also the *temple of *Marduk, Esagila, beside it. At the north end was the largest *palace in the citadel, with royal quarters facing west on terraces by the river, the famous 'Hanging *Gardens' perhaps being planted there. The palace flanked the Processional Way on the east, after it passed through the *Ishtar Gate, which, like parts of the palace, was covered with glazed bricks. Nebuchadnezzar proclaimed his responsibility for his constructions in Babylon and other towns by stamping his names and titles on bricks and engraving them on paving slabs, as well as having longer descriptions of his work written on clay cylinders. One text depicts him in traditional style, concerned with justice, giving examples of his practice.

Beside references to his military actions, the Bible tells of his pride in Babylon and subsequent madness in the Book of Daniel. No Babylonian record of that exists – the king would hardly report it himself – yet it is unwise to dismiss it out of hand when events of his later years are unknown.

Amel-Marduk, his son, succeeded Nebuchadnezzar, to be assassinated within two years by his sister's husband, Neriglissar, who ruled until 556 BC.                               ARM

**Negev** The *Hebrew word 'Negev' (or Negeb) means 'dry' or 'south' and refers to the area of *Palestine west of the Wadi Arabah, south of the hill country of *Judah, and north-east of *Sinai. The environment changes from north to south, and this is reflected in the different types of human occupation in the region. The north is semi-arid and suitable for dry farming, and throughout history had urban settlements and *villages. The climate becomes progressively drier through the central highlands to the desert of the south, with occupation usually by *pastoral nomads, but with *copper-mining sites at *Timna. The term 'Negev' in the *Bible probably referred mostly to the northern region.

The north had a similar occupational history to the rest of Palestine, with *Chalcolithic settlement best known from *Beer Sheba and *Shiqmim, the Early Bronze Age at *Arad, abandonment and non-urban occupation in Early Bronze IV, and re-urbanization in the Middle and Late Bronze Ages, for example at Tell el-*Far'ah (South). In the *Iron Age, *fortified towns were built, as at Beer Sheba and Arad, and forts, as at Tel Ira and Horvat 'Uzza, probably as part of a southern defence line of *Israel and later Judah. It is possible that *Edomite *pottery found at sites such as Horvat Qitmit and 'En Haseva may be evidence of Edomite presence in the Negev in the seventh century BC; this is often cited as evidence for an Edomite invasion of the Negev, but Qitmit has been alternatively explained as an isolated wayside shrine serving a variety of groups, among them Edomites.

In the central Negev highlands, the only two periods of settled occupation were Early Bronze IV, with large villages of up to two hundred structures, and an early *Iron Age network of citadels, forts and agricultural structures. It is still debated whether these were official Israelite forts or settlements of indigenous desert inhabitants, and whether they date to the eleventh or tenth century BC.                               PB

I. FINKELSTEIN, *Living on the Fringe: The Archaeology and History of the Negev, Sinai and Neighbouring Regions in the Bronze and Iron Ages* (Sheffield 1995).

N. GORING-MORRIS *et al.*, 'Negev', *The New Encyclopedia of Archaeological Excavations in the Holy Land*, ed. E. Stern (Jerusalem 1993) 1119–45.

**Neolithic** In the Near East this period runs from c.9000 BC until 5000 BC. The term has been applied to particular cultural units, defined by regionally distinctive material culture in terms of ceramics, lithics (flint) and architecture, and 'the Neolithic' therefore begins and ends at slightly different dates in different areas. Inevitably as applied it has a rather arbitrary significance.

The earlier part of the Neolithic is aceramic (pottery was not used). This aceramic Neolithic dates from c.9000 to 7000 BC almost everywhere in the Near East. In the *Levant and to some degree in Turkey, it is divided into an earlier aceramic, Pre-Pottery Neolithic A (PPNA), c.9300–8500 BC, and later aceramic Pre-Pottery Neolithic B (PPNB). Full mixed farming with grain crop cultivation and herded sheep and goat does not commonly appear until the end of this period, c.7500 BC (late PPNB). However, villages are witnessed from the beginning of this time period in the PPNA of the Levant between c.9300 and 8500 BC. Cereal and legume cultivation may

have started during the PPNA in the southern Levant, e.g. *Jericho, but this could be disputed. Cultivation is not claimed elsewhere in the Near East during this period. Cultivation is, however, widespread by the period 8500–8000 BC.

Some PPNA sites are much larger than their *Natufian predecessors. Jericho may cover 1–3.5 ha at this period. By 8000 BC a number of sites in the Near East are as large as 5 ha and by 7500 BC sites like *Ain Ghazal, Basta, Abu Hureyra and *Çatalhöyük as large as 10–20 ha emerge. These probably had populations in the thousands. The result of the adoption of cultivation seems to have been considerable population growth and the potential for considerable population aggregation.

There is much evidence for social complexity. 'Public' or community buildings are attested, by their large size (e.g. *Beidha), their arrangement around large public spaces (e.g. *Çayönü), their distinctive plans and contents (e.g. skulls at Çayönü), or at the site of Göbekli massive

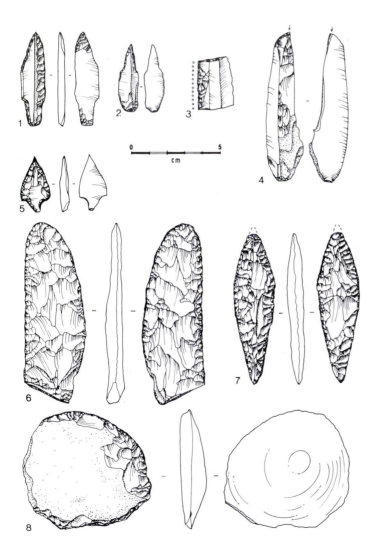

Neolithic flint tools from Dhuweila, Jordan. 1–4 are Pre-Pottery Neolithic B, 5–8 are Pottery or Late Neolithic (courtesy of Alison Betts).

stone orthostats or totems carved in the shapes of fantastic crocodile-like beasts, snakes and lions. On this basis one wonders whether wooden totems that do not now survive were common. Evidence for exchange is also common (see Obsidian). Differentiation in domestic dwellings is attested (Çayönü), and mortuary practices point to different grades in society. Metal is cold and hot worked at sites like Çayönü, and evidence for melted and smelted *copper comes from slightly later Çatalhöyük and *Hassuna sites.

Neolithic society was far more complex and diverse than was realized in the 1970s. DB

E.B. BANNING, 'The Neolithic Period: Triumphs of Architecture, Agriculture, and Art', Near Eastern Archaeology 61 (1998) 188–237.

B. BENDER, Farming in Prehistory (London 1975).

P. CRABTREE, D. CAMPANA and K. RYAN (eds), Early Animal Domestication and its Cultural Context (Philadelphia 1989).

J. MELLAART, The Neolithic of the Near East (London 1975).

C. REDMAN, The Rise of Civilization (San Francisco 1978).

**Nergal** *Babylonian *god of the *underworld. The possibly foreign original of the name is unknown, but the Babylonians seemingly created a false etymology meaning 'lord of the underworld'. It has been suggested that down to the *Akkadian period Nergal should be regarded not as the name of a specific deity but as a title for any underworld-god. The cult of a particular god Nergal, with his cult centre at Kutû, however, received the patronage of the *Sargonic *kings, and by the Old Babylonian period this god had apparently been assimilated with several other *Sumerian underworld deities. Another cult centre was Mashkan-shapir (Tell Abu Dhawari). A number of *temples were dedicated to him in various Babylonian *cities, his name was a frequent element in personal names, and he was often addressed in prayers and *hymns intended to avert the dangers associated with him. In *Assyria he was particularly worshipped during the time of the *Sargonid *dynasty.

Mesopotamian literary compositions describe Nergal as a 'fallen' sky-god. According to the Babylonian *myth 'Nergal and *Ereshkigal', he was sent for a visit to the underworld by the gods of heaven as divine punishment for his misdeeds, being condemned to stay permanently after having *sex with Ereshkigal, queen of the infernal realm. A text of the *Kassite period associates a 160-day stay by Nergal in the underworld with the winter season. However, he is also described as a god of light, and associated with the planet Mars. Hymns characterize Nergal as a warrior, a god of pestilence, *disease and forest fires, but also of *fertility and vegetation.

Erra, also worshipped at Kutû, was in origin a different deity, but eventually became closely identified with Nergal. The Babylonian poem 'Ishum and Erra' relates how Erra obtains for a time control of the world and ravages Babylonia; the myth may reflect invasions of the country between the twelfth and ninth centuries BC by *nomadic peoples such as the *Aramaeans or 'Suteans'.

In *Mesopotamian *art, especially of the Old Baby-lonian period, Nergal is represented as of human appearance, often holding a scimitar and/or his *divine symbol of a double lion-headed standard, often trampling the diminutive body of a man, or riding his *chariot. Many clay *figurines of the same period show him as a dead god wrapped in a *burial shroud and lying in his sarcophagus.

In the *Parthian period Nergal was identified with the Greek Herakles. JAB/AG

W.G. LAMBERT, [Review of von Weiher], Bibliotheca Orientalis 30 (1973) 355–63.

E. PORADA, 'Nergal in the Old Babylonian Period', Sumer 7 (1951) 66–8.

P. STEINKELLER, 'The Name of Nergal', Zeitschrift für Assyriologie 77 (1987) 151–68.

E. STONE, 'Mashkan-shapir', The Oxford Encyclopedia of Archaeology in the Ancient Near East 3, ed. E.M. Meyers (New York 1997) 430–2.

F. VON WEIHER, Der babylonische Gott Nergal (Neukirchen/Vluyn 1971).

**New Year ceremonies** The twelve days of New Year ceremonies were celebrated at *Babylon at the beginning of Nisannu, the first month of the year, approximately at the time of the spring equinox. The ceremonies at Babylon were centred on the cult of *Marduk, but related ceremonies were performed at other *cities for other deities, and had been performed for a very long time. The akītū festival performed at *Ur under the Third Dynasty, for the god Nanna, took its name from the *Akkadian akītū, one of the New Year ceremonies.

The *Babylonian ceremonies consisted of a sequence of rites which were concerned with celebrating or marking the spring barley harvest; with a patronal festival of the city god, Marduk, including his enthronement (known as 'taking Bel by the hand'), incorporating symbolic representation of certain episodes in the Babylonian *Epic of *Creation; with marking the calendrical aspect of the New Year; with the affirmation of the *king as bearer of the sacred duties of kingship; and with the reception and enthronement of the *god *Nabû. A very late copy of a set of *ritual instructions for the *priests gives precise details of the ceremonies of the second to fifth days, but the sequence of events on the other days is far less clear. It certainly included a procession and journey out to the bīt akīti ('akītū building'), a ritual humiliation of the king and an 'offering' (most probably a reading), on the fourth day, of the Epic of Creation, in addition to a whole series of *magical and cultic rites of various significance.

The last known occasion when the akītū of Marduk was celebrated at Babylon was when Cambyses, king of *Persia, 'took Bel by the hand' in 538 BC. However, akītū ceremonies were still celebrated for the deities *Anu and *Ishtar at *Uruk during the second century BC. JAB

J.A. BLACK, 'The New Year Ceremonies in Ancient Babylon: "Taking Bel by the Hand" and a Cultic Picnic', Religion 11 (1981) 39–59.

A. KUHRT, 'Usurpation, Conquest and Ceremonial: From Babylon to Persia', Rituals of Royalty, eds D. Cannadine and S. Price (Cambridge 1987) 20–55.

**Nimrud** Nimrud is the present-day name of Kalhu (biblical Calah) on the east bank of the Tigris *river, c.35 km south-east of Mosul, northern Iraq. The site was occupied from *prehistoric times, but is mostly known as the royal capital of the *Assyrian empire in the ninth to eighth centuries BC.

Little is known about the early phases, as there has never been a deep sounding. There was apparently an early third-millennium BC settlement, of unknown size and nature. Ninevite 5 surface *pottery is said to have been found, and a cist *grave has been dated to c.1750 BC.

Kalhu was founded probably in c.1280 BC. Thirteenth-century BC texts suggest it was already of importance. Middle Assyrian levels are believed to have been reached in some areas, but effort has been concentrated on the Neo-Assyrian *city.

Around 878 BC, *Ashurnasirpal II made Kalhu the royal capital, initiating the large-scale building pro-gramme that was to continue sporadically under his successors. He constructed a new city wall, a royal *palace, and, he says, nine *temples, of which three have been certainly identified. The city wall, c.7.5 km long, originally mudbrick, encloses a roughly square area of c.360 ha, some 20 ha occupied by the citadel mound, surrounded by its own *fortification wall. Kalhu was the capital until succeeded by *Khorsabad in 707 BC. There-after, it remained an important city. Extensive renova-tions were undertaken by *Esarhaddon. The *Medes and *Babylonians may have sacked Kalhu in 614–612 BC. Some occupation may have continued, although it is uncertain whether Nimrud is the ruined Median city Larissa mentioned by Xenophon. There was a village settlement in *Hellenistic times.

The first known modern excavations at Nimrud were in c.1815 and minor digging was conducted by British and Russian visitors in 1844. The first large-scale British excavations were carried out by *Layard (1845–51). Thereafter there has been further archaeological work by expeditions from Britain (1853–5, 1873, 1877–9,

1949–63, 1989), Poland (1974–6), Italy (1987–9) and Iraq (1956, 1959–60 and since 1969).

Several palaces and temples have been incompletely excavated on the citadel. Most imposing is the 'North-West Palace', more than 200 by 120 m, built by Ashur-nasirpal II and renovated by *Shalmaneser III and probably later kings until the reign of *Sargon II. Four vaulted tombs beneath the palace were excavated by the Iraqis in 1987–90. Inscriptions in one of the tombs suggest they are the graves of several Assyrian *queens, and they contained precious *metal vessels and large quantities and varieties of *gold *jewellery.

The most important religious building, founded by Queen Sammu-ramat (*Semiramis), was Ezida, or the Temple of *Nabû. The temple *archive housed *religious and *magical texts and several '*treaties', including the so-called 'vassal treaties' of *Esarhaddon, his last will and testament. In the outer town the most important complex was the Royal Armoury, dubbed by the excavators 'Fort Shalmaneser'. Founded by Shalmaneser III and refur-bished by Esarhaddon, it occupied some 5 ha. This and buildings on the citadel have yielded some thousands of exquisitely carved *ivories.                                    AG

J. CURTIS, 'Nimrud', *The Oxford Encyclopedia of Archaeology in the Ancient Near East* 4, ed. E.M. Meyers (New York 1997) 141–4.

S. DALLEY, 'Nineveh after 612 BC', *Altorientalische Forschungen* 20 (1993) 134–47.

M.S.B. DAMERJI, 'Gräber assyrischer Königinnen aus Nimrud', *Jahrbuch des Römisch-Germanischen Zentralmuseums* (Mainz) 45 (1998).

A. GREEN, *Excavations at Nimrud 1845–1989: Neo-Assyrian Foundation Figurines* (London, in press).

M.E.L. MALLOWAN, *Nimrud and its Remains*, 3 vols (London 1966).

J. MEUSZYNSKI, S. PALEY and R. SOBOLEWSKI, *Die Rekon-struktion der Reliefdarstellungen und ihrer Anordnung im Nordwestpalast Kalhu (Nimrud) / The Reconstruction of the Relief Representations and their Positions in the North West Palace at Kalhu (Nimrud)* 1–3 (Mainz am Rhein 1981–92).

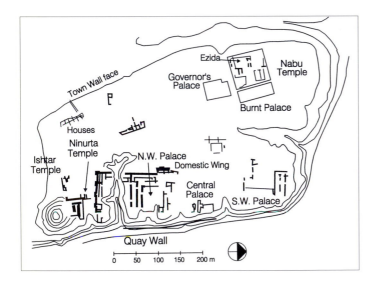

Overall plan of the citadel at Nimrud in the Neo-Assyrian period.

J.N. POSTGATE and J.E. READE, 'Kalhu', *Reallexikon der Assyriologie* 5 (Berlin/New York 1977–80) 303–23.

J.B. STEARNS, *Reliefs from the Palace of Ashurnasirpal* 2 (Graz 1961).

**Nineveh**  Nineveh is the English biblical form of the name of the city of ancient Ninua, on the east bank of the Tigris *river, opposite medieval and within present-day Mosul, northern Iraq. The site includes the high mounds of Kuyunjik and Nebi Yunus. As the site of an important Islamic shrine, the latter has been little investigated. Kuyunjik, however, was almost continuously occupied from the seventh millennium BC until the early Middle Ages. In the seventh century BC Nineveh was the royal capital of the *Assyrian empire, until sacked by the *Babylonians and *Medes in 612 BC.

The site has received much investigation, although its size and the rather patchy nature of exploration make an overview still difficult. French excavations by *Botta (1842) found little. British expeditions were led by *Layard (1846–51), *Rassam (1852–4), W.K. Loftus (1854), George Smith (1873–4), L.W. King (1903–4) and finally R. Campbell Thompson (1927–32), who made a 30-m-deep sounding into the *prehistoric levels of Kuyunjik. This latter operation, supervised by *Mallowan, provided the first early *pottery sequence for northern *Mesopotamia. There were Iraqi excavations in 1967–9, and David Stronach worked there in 1987–90.

The earliest phases are little known, but the site was influenced by the *Uruk culture centred on southern Mesopotamia and also had a sizeable settlement in the subsequent Ninevite 5 period. The city is mostly known for the building programmes of the Assyrian kings. From the time of *Shalmaneser I, several monarchs built *palaces on the heights of Kuyunjik, and on the ground to the north an extensive lower *town developed. The main expansion, to some 750 ha, took place under *Sennacherib, who moved the capital from *Khorsabad to Nineveh, constructing his Royal Palace ('South-West Palace') on Kuyunjik, a Royal Armoury (still unexcavated) at Nebi Yunus, and around the city an imposing double defensive wall, some 12 km long with fifteen *gates. At the north-west of the lower town a new industrial area and an affluent residential quarter then developed.

Esarhaddon and Ashurbanipal carried out some limited building works on Nebi Yunus, and the latter built a Royal Palace ('North Palace') on Kuyunjik, adorned with superb wall reliefs (see Sculpture). One of these showing a royal park watered by a tall aqueduct gives a good picture of the urban landscape, which we know was provided with parks and botanical and zoological *gardens, all facilitated by technical advances in dam and aqueduct construction. It has even been suggested that the famed Hanging Gardens may have been sited not at *Babylon but in Assyrian Nineveh.

The approximately twenty-four thousand *cuneiform tablets unearthed from Ashurbanipal's state *archive are an important source of information about Assyrian and Babylonian history and culture.

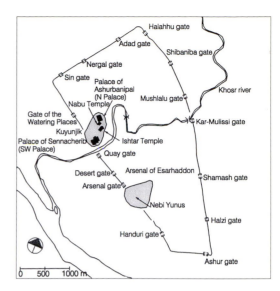

Outline plan of Nineveh in the time of Sennacherib (after M. Roaf, *Cultural Atlas of Ancient Mesopotamia* (Oxford 1990) 186).

After the fall of the city in 612 BC, there was some further limited occupation in *Hellenistic, *Parthian and *Roman times.                                                        AG

R.D. BARNETT, E. BLEIBTREU and G. TURNER, *Sculptures from the Southwest Palace of Sennacherib at Nineveh* (London 1998).

S. DALLEY, 'Nineveh after 612 BC', *Altorientalische Forschungen* 20 (1993) 134–47.

J.M. RUSSELL, 'Nineveh', *The Dictionary of Art* 25, ed. J. Turner (New York/London 1996) 152–5.

D. STRONACH, 'Notes on the Fall of Nineveh', *Assyria 1995*, eds S. Parpola and R.M. Whiting (Helsinki 1997) 307–24.

D. STRONACH and K. CODELLA, 'Nineveh', *The Oxford Encyclopedia of Archaeology in the Ancient Near East* 4, ed. E.M. Meyers (New York 1997) 144–8.

**Ningal**  The *goddess Ningal was the wife of the *moon-god Nanna/*Sîn and the mother of the sun-god Utu/*Shamash. She was worshipped together with Sîn at *Ur, and also at Sîn's sanctuary at *Harran in northern *Syria. Her cult developed independently in Syria as early as the second millennium BC, where her name was altered to Nikkal, a form which is sometimes used in *Babylonia. The cult of Nikkal seems to have lasted in Syria well into the first millennium AD.                                      JAB

D.O. EDZARD, 'Mesopotamien: Die Mythologie der Sumerer und Akkader', *Götter und Mythen im Vorderen Orient*, Vol. 1 of *Wörterbuch der Mythologie*, ed. H.W. Haussig (Stuttgart 1965) 111.

G. LEICK, *A Dictionary of Ancient Near Eastern Mythology* (London/New York 1991).

**Ningirsu:** see Ninurta

**Ninhursanga** Ninhursanga was the *Sumerian name of one of the *mother goddesses. She was known as the 'mother of the gods' and was considered to have been responsible for the birth of many of the *gods and goddesses. Many human rulers liked to name her as their 'mother' also.

In the Sumerian *myth 'Enki and Ninhursanga', Ninhursanga (who is also called Nintur, Damgalnuna and Ninsikila in the poem) is inseminated by Enki, who then rapes the daughter of their union in the first of a series of incestuous rapes. Eventually they have intercourse again and Ninhursanga gives birth to eight divinities favourable to man. In another poem, *Lugale*, a myth explains the origin of Ninhursanga's name: the god Ninurta, having defeated the *demon Asag and his army of stone warriors, builds the mountains out of the stones, and decides to rename his mother Ninmah with the new name Ninhursanga ('lady of the mountains').

Being virtually identical with the goddess Ninmah, Ninhursanga was worshipped at the *temple of E-mah in the city of Adab. However, it appears that she was also connected with the city of Kesh (*not* *Kish), since she is sometimes known as the 'Belet-ili of Kesh' or as 'she of Kesh'. JAB

P. ATTINGER, 'Enki et Ninhursaga', *Zeitschrift für Assyriologie* 74 (1984) 1–52.

T. JACOBSEN, 'Notes on Nintur', *Orientalia* 42 (1973) 274–98.

J.J.A. VAN DIJK, *Lugal ud me-lám-bi nir-gál: Le récit épique et didactique des Travaux de Ninurta, du Déluge et de la Nouvelle Création* (Leiden 1983).

**Ninurta** The worship of the warlike *god Ninurta was very ancient in *Sumer. As a son of *Enlil, his principal cult centre was the *temple E-shu-me-sha at *Nippur. His wife was regarded as either Gula or, because of his close association with the god Ningirsu, Bau. The personalities of the two gods Ninurta and Ningirsu are closely intertwined and, although his origin may have been independent, in historical times Ningirsu was a local form of Ninurta.

Several *myths relate his martial exploits, mainly directed against the enemies of Sumer and in particular against the so-called 'rebel lands' or 'hostile lands' (the regions in the mountains to the east of *Mesopotamia). Ninurta (or Ningirsu) is the gods' champion against the *Anzû bird when its steals the tablet of destinies from Enlil, thereby endangering the stability of civilization. Ninurta (or Ningirsu) kills the Slain Warriors in a myth several times alluded to but nowhere preserved in full.

A contrasting aspect, also to be found with Ningirsu, is Ninurta's role as a farmer god. In the Sumerian 'Farmer's instructions', Ninurta gives detailed advice on the farmer's activities throughout the year. The plough is captioned as a symbol of Ningirsu on *Kassite *kudurru*s, and so perhaps represented Ninurta in Neo-*Assyrian *art. Another symbol of Ninurta in the Neo-Assyrian period was a perched *bird.

The two aspects, warrior and farmer, are combined in the Sumerian poem *Lugale*, in which Ninurta succeeds in defeating the terrible demon Asag and his army of stone allies, and then proceeds to organize the world, making the Tigris and Euphrates useful for *irrigation and facilitating *agriculture. He returns to Nippur with his battle trophies in the poem *Angim*.

The Assyrian *kings were devoted to the cult of Ninurta, as a warlike god who would help them against their enemies. At his new capital Kalhu (modern *Nimrud), *Ashurnasirpal II built a temple to Ninurta adjacent to the *ziggurat (which may also have been dedicated to Ninurta). The scene carved on *stone relief slabs at either side of the main doorway of the temple may represent, uniquely in Neo-Assyrian monumental art, a mythological scene: Ninurta's defeat of the Asakku (Asag) or else of the Anzû bird. AG/JAB

J.A. BLACK, 'The Slain Heroes: Some Monsters of Ancient Mesopotamia', *Bulletin of the Canadian Society for Mesopotamian Studies* 15 (May 1988) 19–25.

——, 'Some Structural Features of Sumerian Narrative Poetry', *Mesopotamian Epic Literature: Oral or Aural?*, eds M.E. Vogelzang and H.L.J. Vanstiphout (Lewiston/Queenston/Lampeter 1992) 71–101.

M. CIVIL, *The Farmer's Instructions* (Barcelona 1994).

J.S. COOPER, *The Return of Ninurta to Nippur* (Rome 1978).

T. JACOBSEN, *The Harps that Once … Sumerian Poetry in Translation* (New Haven, CN 1987) 233–72.

J.J.A. VAN DIJK, *Lugal ud me-lám-bi nir-gál: Le récit épique et didactique des Travaux de Ninurta, du Déluge et de la Nouvelle Création* (Leiden 1983).

**Nippur** The site of the *temple of *Enlil, one of the most important *Mesopotamian *gods, Nippur was a major religious centre which benefited from construction projects and donations from *kings who wished to demonstrate their piety. Its ruins lie c.180 km south-west of Baghdad, measuring 1.5 km across and 20 m high. It was excavated by *Layard (1851), the University of Pennsylvania (1888–1900), and intermittently between 1948 and 1990 under various directors by the Oriental Institute, Chicago (until 1952 jointly with Pennsylvania).

Nippur was occupied from the sixth millennium BC until AD 800, with a gap in the mid second millennium BC before revitalization under the *Kassites. The *Inana temple has the longest archaeological sequence for Mesopotamia, consisting of twenty-two building levels from the *Uruk to the *Parthian periods. There are sequences of temples in other areas covering the Early Dynastic to *Achaemenid periods, a *ziggurat, private *houses of most periods, and a Kassite *palace. Tens of thousands of *cuneiform tablets came mostly from private houses, and include almost all important *Sumerian *literary works as well as economic and lexical texts from Old Babylonian, Kassite and later periods. PB

M.D. ELLIS (ed.), *Nippur at the Centennial* (Philadelphia, PA 1992).

R.L. ZETTLER, 'Nippur', *The Oxford Encyclopedia of Archaeology in the Near East* 4, ed. E.M. Meyers (New York 1997) 148–52.

**Nomads** Nomads in the ancient Near East were almost invariably pastoral nomads, moving seasonally with their herds to seek the best grazing grounds. The earliest sheep and goat pastoralists can be traced in the *Zagros and the *Levant in the seventh millennium BC, although they were not common until the *Chalcolithic period. *Camel nomadism was not important until the first millennium BC. Camels survive on less *water than sheep or goats, so camel pastoralists were able to travel across wide expanses of desert, especially the *trade route in *incense and spices from southern *Arabia (see Transport and travel).

Pastoral nomads do not wander randomly but normally follow carefully planned and annually repeated migratory routes. They do not leave behind their own written texts or much physical evidence of their presence, but are occasionally mentioned in the records of states through which they passed, particularly the *Guti, *Amorites and *Aramaeans. They have traditionally been regarded as hostile to sedentary peoples; ancient texts show how urban *scribes despised nomads and their lack of civilization. Nomads used to be blamed for most cultural change in the ancient Near East, in outdated reconstructions which described waves of nomads destroying and then replacing sedentary civilizations. In fact, the process seems to have been a gradual one of semi-sedentary and then sedentary occupation such as continues to this day.

There is now considerable evidence that pastoralists had close relations with sedentary communities, by exchanging goods, hiring themselves out as shepherds, or grazing on fallow fields. There was probably continual movement and overlap between the two modes of life. It is likely that pastoralism developed as an offshoot of sedentary *agricultural life and the domestication of *animals (see Animal husbandry).                    PB

P. BRIAND, *État et pasteurs au Moyen-Orient ancien* (Cambridge/Paris 1982).

R. CRIBB, *Nomads in Archaeology* (Cambridge 1991).

S.H. LEES and D.G. BATES, 'The Origins of Specialised Nomadic Pastoralism: A Systemic Model', *American Antiquity* 39 (1974) 187–93.

T.E. LEVY, 'The Emergence of Specialised Pastoralism in the Levant', *World Archaeology* 15 (1983) 15–36.

M. ROWTON, 'Enclosed Nomadism', *Journal of the Economic and Social History of the Orient* 17 (1974) 1–30.

G.M. SCHWARTZ, 'Pastoral Nomadism in Ancient Western Asia', *Civilizations of the Ancient Near East*, ed. J.M. Sasson (New York 1995) 249–58.

**Nush-i Jan** A small, fortified *Median site that was evidently a religious complex of considerable importance, Nush-i Jan was probably founded in the eighth century BC, on a small, prominent hill in the Malayer-Jowkar plain 70 km south-east of *Hamadan in western *Iran. No associated settlement was discovered on the plain below. Excavated by David Stronach in the 1960s and 1970s, the site measures some 100 by 40 m and was surrounded by a defensive wall. The earliest building appears to have been the central *temple, followed by a second, similar temple called 'The Old Western Building'. Added to these were the so-called fort followed by the columned hall.

General view of the excavations at Nush-i Jan (courtesy of J.E. Curtis).

Silver rings (see Money), part of a hoard of silver objects found in a bronze bowl at Nush-i Jan. The hoard was probably buried in the sixth century BC, but some of the objects are much older. WA 135072–85.

The distinctive architecture was remarkably preserved, to a height of 8 m, because the central temple had been deliberately filled with shale and encased in mudbrick. The temples have unusual stepped plans, internal stairs and *altars to one side of the sanctuaries. The preserved mudbrick altar in the central temple had clear traces of burning in the centre, perhaps indicative of fire worship foreshadowing later Zoroastrian practice.

Architectural characteristics include recessed and buttressed façades pierced by long arrow-shaped windows, internal ramps to upper floors, internal stepped niches with pendent dentils and the use of mudbrick struts for arches and vaults. The ground floor of the 'fort', all that was preserved, was a magazine. The columned hall, with wooden columns standing on *stone bases, belongs to an Iranian tradition, exemplified at *Hasanlu, and is thought to be a precursor of later Achaemenid columned halls. A large and apparently unfinished tunnel of obscure purpose was dug down at an angle of 30° from the centre of the columned hall.

A hoard of *silver from this site contained many objects apparently of pre-Median date.

Some Median squatter occupation followed abandonment in the sixth century BC and, after a long hiatus, there were levels representing a short-lived village of *Parthian date.                                                                 GDS

J. CURTIS, *Nush-i Jan 3: The Small Finds* (London 1984).

P.R.S. MOOREY, 'Nush-i Jan', *Cambridge Ancient History* 4, 2nd ed., Plates (Cambridge 1988) 7–8.

D. STRONACH, 'Tepe Nush-i Jan: The Median Settlement', *Cambridge Ancient History of Iran* 2 (Cambridge 1985) 832–7.

D. STRONACH and M. ROAF, *Nush-i Jan 1: The Median Settlement* (forthcoming).

**Nuzi** Thousands of *cuneiform tablets discovered in private, public, *administrative and *religious areas at Yorgan Tepe (third-millennium BC Gasur, second-millennium BC Nuzi) in north-eastern Iraq give a unique broad insight into a provincial *town of the ancient Near East. The site was excavated by Edward Chiera (1925–8), Robert H. Pfeiffer (1928–9) and Richard F.S. Starr (1929–31). It consists of a main mound measuring c.200 by 200 m and several smaller mounds, of which only three were investigated. The main mound was occupied from the *Ubaid to the *Mitannian/Middle *Assyrian periods, with some occupation in the Neo-Assyrian, *Parthian and *Sasanian periods.

The most significant finds from Nuzi came from the mid second millennium BC, when it was a town of the kingdom of Arrapha, a province of Mitanni. The population was mainly *Hurrian, and the *archives illuminate Hurrian social, economic, legal and religious institutions, although many of the customs were Babylonian in origin. The archives are currently dated between 1445/1425 and 1350/1330 BC. Levels of this period, often called the Nuzi period, were completely excavated on the main mound. The *palace and *temple area was surrounded by public buildings and *houses in several distinct neighbourhoods. Outside the walls of the settlement were five houses whose owners can be identified from their archives as wealthy landowners and senior officials. The palace, of tripartite plan with over one hundred rooms and courts, had a drainage system, bathrooms and toilets, marble paving, and *wall paintings influenced by *Egyptian and *Aegean designs. Since no *king of Nuzi is known, and the chief local official was a 'mayor', some scholars refer to the 'palace' as a 'government house'.

The characteristic fine *pottery, termed Nuzi Ware, has a white pattern, often geometric, painted on a dark background, and is found as far as the *Amuq plain in *Syria and in *Babylonia. The cuneiform tablets from Nuzi came from public and private archives, and consist of ration and personnel lists, *contracts, legal texts and *letters. The *seals on the tablets belonged to people from all walks of life, the principals involved and witnesses. The tablets document declining socio-economic conditions over several generations and increasing military activity. The destruction and looting of the site are normally attributed to the Assyrians.                          PB

M.P. MAIDMAN, 'Nuzi: Portrait of an Ancient Mesopotamian Provincial Town', *Civilizations of the Ancient Near East*, ed. J.M. Sasson (New York 1995) 931–47.

R.F.S. STARR, *Nuzi: Report on the Excavation at Yorgan Tepa near Kirkuk, Iraq* (Cambridge, MA 1937, 1939).

D.L. STEIN, 'Nuzi', *The Oxford Encyclopedia of Archaeology in the Near East* 4, ed. E.M. Meyers (New York 1997) 171–5.

# O

**Oaths and curses** Oaths and curses derive their efficacy through their appeal to deities who are thought to ensure by divine sanction that the conditions set out in the oath or curse are fulfilled. Hence, while the breaking of an agreement can be a matter for legal restitution through the court, the punishment for perjury is meted out by agencies controlled by the *gods. The phraseology of an oath invokes the consequences that should befall the person swearing the oath, in a form of self-imprecation. Such solemn oaths were not used for mundane purposes but reserved for serious issues which were ultimately beyond the retribution of authorities, as for instance in *treaties between independent states or the acceptance of some form of obligation from one ruler to another, or a group of persons towards the ruler. The gods appealed to in such cases are those of one's own country (for instance in the 'state treaties' concluded between the *Hittites and *Mitanni, the *Egyptians and the Hittites in the second millennium BC, or the 'vassal treaties' of *Esarhaddon).

In *Mesopotamia the oath was also a legal recourse in cases where tangible evidence for a person's guilt or innocence was lacking. Again this was generally reserved for serious allegations and crimes although the *law code of *Eshnunna also allows *property disputes to be settled by one party agreeing to 'swear an oath at the gate of Tishpak'. The accused could be ordered to swear an oath or be given the choice between accepting a charge or swearing an oath, which according to many legal documents often had the desired effect. Obviously the fear of divine punishment outweighed the material loss incurred. This practice was widespread in all areas of the ancient Near East, in Mesopotamia from the third millennium BC, in *Anatolia among the Hittites, and in *Syria and *Palestine as documented in *Ugaritic, *Aramaic and *Old Testament sources.

The curse and especially the curse formula differ from the oath in so far as the curse is always directed against another person who acts in a way that is detrimental to the intention of the one uttering the curse. Again, divine authority is appealed to and this sets up an automatic, irreversible mechanism that activates or triggers the curse as soon as certain carefully stipulated circumstances arise. Curse formulae also usually protect objects which embody the wish of a donor to be remembered. For instance, *stone monuments, *sculptures, stelae and *foundation deposits in Mesopotamia were thus supernaturally 'insured' against theft, breakage, vandalism, and usurpation. The merit of commissioning such a monument should forever remain linked to the original donor; if someone else were to delete the name of this person and write his own instead, the usurper should be punished by the gods. In Mesopotamia and elsewhere in the ancient Near East, the most potent and most frequently uttered curse was that the offender should be without issue and die without leaving a name. In the *Kassite period *kudurrus* recording land and property donations had lengthy curses which not only protected the actual monument but also guaranteed the legal substance of the inscription. GL

D.O. EDZARD, 'Zum sumerischen Eid', *Sumerological Studies in Honor of Thorkild Jacobsen*, ed. S.J. Lieberman (Chicago 1975) 63–98.

J.R. KUPPER, 'Les formules de malédiction dans les inscriptions royales de l'époque paléo-babylonienne', *Revue d'Assyriologie* 84 (1990) 157–63.

S. LAFONT (ed.), *Jurer et maudire: pratiques politiques et usages juridiques du serment dans le Proche-Orient ancien* (L'Harmattan 1996).

N. OETTINGER, *Die militärischen Eide der Hethiter* (Berlin 1976).

W. SOMMERFELD, 'Flüche und Fluchformeln als Quelle für die altorientalische Kulturgeschichte', *Mesopotamica – Ugaritica – Biblica: Festschrift für Kurt Bergerhof zur Vollendung seines 70. Lebensjahres am 7. Mai 1992*, eds M. Dietrich and O. Loretz (Neukirchen/Vluyn 1993) 447–64.

K. WATANABE, 'Die literarische Überlieferung eines babylonisch-assyrischen Fluchthemas mit Anrufung des Mondgottes Sin', *Acta Sumerologica* 6 (1984) 99–119.

**Obsidian** Obsidian is a volcanic glass, usually black and semi-translucent, but also clear, mottled, brown and red. The main sources in the Near East are in central and eastern Turkey. In *prehistory obsidian was used for making chipped stone *tools (see Flint-working), vessels, mirrors and *jewellery, and from the *Chalcolithic to the *Bronze Age for valuable vessels, *seals and figurative *art.

Obsidian's distinctive flaking properties made it easy to knapp with precision. The converse of this distinctive quality was that, as a material, it was not as hard as the flints and cherts used in much flint knapping. Often, then, there are clearly functional differences in the tools made from obsidian and flint, especially in assemblages where both materials are relatively common. Piercing and drilling tools are thus often made in flint rather than obsidian. Obsidian pressure flakes precisely and easily, so pressure techniques were commonly used on obsidian to produce long regular blades useful for composite tools and elaborately flaked tools like some projectile points. These utilitarian qualities, its rareness, aesthetic qualities, and the fact that it had to travel considerable distances to reach many areas where it was used, may have all given obsidian a particular value in prehistory.

Its extensive distribution indicates the degree of early exchange contacts. A small amount of obsidian is found at *Natufian sites such as Eynan/Mallaha, over 1000 km from source, as early as the tenth millennium BC. The amount being transported increases in the *Neolithic. In the *Halaf period in north *Mesopotamia, over 200 km from sources, more than half of the chipped stone in assemblages is obsidian. It is in this period and area that we first see significant use of obsidian for jewellery and fine vessels (see Arpachiyah). In other areas, *Anatolia especially, it can be much more common, not only because of proximity to source but also because at sites like *Çatalhöyük obsidian is one of the closest available chippable raw materials and it was also polished for mirrors.

More of the mechanisms of exploitation and distribution are now understood and they are clearly complex. Near the central Anatolian sources specialized workshops produced distinctive, standardized blanks for specific sorts of tools, using different methods at the same workshop. Only the desired blanks left the workshops. In other cases prepared blocks left workshop sites and travelled, for example, to a limited number of Halaf production centres for further reduction in north Mesopotamia or to similar production centres as far afield as Hagoshrim in northern Israel.

By the second millennium BC obsidian vessels were being produced for high status gift exchange and possibly other sorts of transactions. Some were produced at sites like the *Assyrian and other foreign traders' colony at *Kanesh. The value of these objects is indicated by the fact that, embellished by *gold fittings, such vessels were considered suitable presents from the pharaohs of *Egypt to the royal house of *Byblos in the Middle Bronze Age.

DB

M.-C. CAUVIN, 'Rapport sur les recherches sur l'obsidienne en Cappadoce, 1993–1995', Anatolia Antiqua 4 (1996) 249–71.

C. RENFREW, J. DIXON and J. CANN, 'Obsidian and Early Cultural Contacts in the Near East', Proceedings of the Prehistoric Society 32 (1966) 30–72.

## Old Testament: see Bible

## Oman

**Oman** Located in the south-eastern part of the Arabian Peninsula, the modern Sultanate of Oman has a long coastline extending for 1600 km along the Indian Ocean. Oman provided *Mesopotamia with *copper ore and objects from the late fourth millennium BC on, and later the *Indus Valley too. Oman has been identified with ancient Magan, which first appears in texts under *Sargon of *Akkad when *ships of Magan were reported to have docked at Akkad. Relations became more belligerent under later Akkadian kings, but trade continued to be recorded in the *Ur III period, including *trade in goods which came through Magan but originated further east, for example *ivory. Magan is described as one of the lands alongside the 'Lower Sea' south of *Babylonia. In literary texts it is treated as a virtual paradise, although its appearance in economic texts proves that it was a real place.

Occupation in Oman contemporary with the Magan references appears to be an oasis economy with settlement characterized by mudbrick towers, either residences

of local rulers or storage buildings, and *stone-built *graves, sometimes with hundreds of skeletons, with grave goods including imports from Mesopotamia. Evidence from *mining sites shows that copper crushing and smelting and *tool production were often carried out on the spot, and copper was exported to Mesopotamia at various stages of the metallurgical process.

There appears to have been a decline in Oman between c.1800 and 1000 BC, numerous mass graves perhaps reflecting a shift to a *nomadic lifestyle, but a revival of *towns and villages in the *Iron Age is still largely unexplained. It may have been connected with the development of the falaj/qanat *irrigation system in which *water from an aquifer is brought downstream underground to fields and villages. Contacts with Mesopotamia are illustrated by *King Pade of Qade who brought tribute to *Ashurbanipal: he lived in Izkie, possibly modern Izki in Oman, known locally as the oldest town in Oman. Oman was now called Qade in *Akkadian, although *Esarhaddon still used the ancient name in his grandiose title 'king of the kings of *Dilmun, Magan and *Meluhha'.

PB

R. BOUCHARLAT, 'Archaeology and Artifacts of the Arabian Peninsula', Civilizations of the Ancient Near East, ed. J.M. Sasson (New York 1995) 1335–52.

S. CLEUZIOU and M. TOSI, 'The Southeastern Frontier of the Ancient Near East', South Asian Archaeology 1985, eds K. Frifelt and P. Sorensen (London 1989) 15–48.

W. HEIMPEL, 'Magan', Reallexikon der Assyriologie 7 (Berlin/New York 1988) 195–9.

D.T. POTTS, The Arabian Gulf in Antiquity (Oxford 1990).

## Omens and divination

**Omens and divination** Divination was widely used in *Mesopotamia. It is based on the idea that to some extent the future is predetermined; but that the *gods, especially *Shamash (Utu) and *Adad (Ishkur), have made available to humankind certain indications of the future (omens or portents) in the world about us, which can be interpreted (divined) by those with specialist knowledge.

Some forms of divination required special solicited *rituals. Particularly important from *Sumerian times was extispicy, in which the liver, lungs or colon spiral of a specially slaughtered young ram were inspected for peculiarities during a nocturnal rite. By the Old *Babylonian period, extispicy was highly developed and had a complex technical vocabulary. Also used were lecanomancy (in which the behaviour of oil on water was observed) and libanomancy (the behaviour of smoke from *incense). Necromancy (calling up the spirits of the dead) was used only rarely and considered to be dangerous.

Other forms of divination involved the observation of unsolicited natural occurrences, and these forms gradually became more widespread. The study of celestial omens (*astrological and meteorological) came to surpass even extispicy in popularity and survived until after the end of Mesopotamian civilization. Also important were teratological omens (from monstrous births among *animals), terrestrial omens (from a whole range of everyday occurrences), hemerological and menological

Babylonian diviners made models in clay of sheep's livers and wrote on them the ominous significance of unusual features. Old Babylonian period. WA 92668.

omens (based on the idea of favourable and unfavourable days), prognostic omens (predicting the course and outcome of *diseases), physiognomic omens (from the appearance and behaviour of individual people), augury (the observation of *birds) and oneiromancy (the interpretation of *dreams), a branch of the subject with its own specialized practitioners.

Divination could be used to control the behaviour of *kings and important persons. Private correspondence shows that extispicy was resorted to by many people of lesser rank to investigate the future (often in connection with specific questions). Before or during *military campaigns, before building a *temple, when appointing civil servants, in weather forecasting, to ensure the king's well-being and safety – and also on a much more homely level as a form of personal fortune-telling – divination played an important part in decision-making.

The *Hittites used extispicy and augury extensively, as well as another native *Anatolian form of divination, possibly a form of lottery, which was the special preserve of female diviners called the 'Old Women'.

Babylonian divinatory practices spread to the west in the second millennium BC, as texts from *Emar, *Ugarit and *Hazor show, and eventually reached the Etruscans. These ways of discerning the future were forbidden to *Israel in the *Bible. (See Magic.) JAB

A. JEFFERS, *Magic and Divination in Ancient Palestine and Syria* (Leiden 1996).

U. JEYES, 'The Act of Extispicy in Ancient Mesopotamia: An Outline', *Assyriological Miscellanies* 1 (Copenhagen 1980) 13–32.

A.L. OPPENHEIM, *The Interpretation of Dreams in the Ancient Near East, with a Translation of an Assyrian Dream-book* (Philadelphia, PA 1956).

——, *Ancient Mesopotamia: Portrait of a Dead Civilization*, rev. ed. completed by E. Reiner (Chicago 1977) 206–27.

S. PARPOLA, *Letters from Assyrian and Babylonian Scholars to the Kings Esarhaddon and Assurbanipal* (Kevelaer 1970, 1983).

I. STARR, *Rituals of the Diviner* (Malibu, CA 1983).

**Oracles:** see Prophecies and oracles

**Ostraca** Potsherds used as writing material are termed *ostraca*, singular *ostracon*, the *Greek word for potsherd. They are distinguished from names or notes of content scratched on whole vessels, which may be termed graffiti. With the rise of the *alphabet, written with ink, the *Egyptian habit of using potsherds for brief notes and messages spread through the *Levant. One Late Bronze Age example is known from Beth Shemesh, scores in *Hebrew from *Iron Age sites in *Palestine, notably *Arad, *Lachish, *Samaria, and a very few in *Aramaic from *Nimrud. Ostraca continued to be written through *Persian and *Roman times into the Middle Ages. Sherds were free, whereas sheets of leather or papyrus had to be manufactured and paid for. They were the scrap-paper of antiquity and it is ironic that they can survive, unless careless excavators scrub away the ink, where the more important and valuable papyrus and leather documents and *books have perished through damp and decay. Their use in Egypt for *scribal training suggests they may have had the same purpose in *Semitic circles, and one from Arad (no. 88) may be part of a historical report copied in a writing lesson. ARM

G.I. DAVIES, *Ancient Hebrew Inscriptions: Corpus and Concordance* (Cambridge 1991).

J.C.L. GIBSON, *Textbook of Syrian Semitic Inscriptions*, 1: *Hebrew*, 2: *Aramaic* (London 1971, 1975).

A.R. MILLARD, 'An Assessment of the Evidence for Writing in Ancient Israel', *Biblical Archaeology Today* (Jerusalem 1985) 301–12.

J. RENZ and W. RÖLLIG, *Handbuch der althebräischen Epigraphik* (Darmstadt 1995).

Potsherd from Lachish used as writing material for a brief message in Hebrew from a garrison captain to his superior officer, thanking him for an earlier communication and wishing him well. 10 by 9 cm. c.590 BC. WA 125702.

# P

**Painting:** see Wall painting

**Palaces** The word for 'palace' throughout most of the ancient Near East derived from the *Sumerian term meaning 'big house'. Like a *house, a palace served a variety of functions: it was the residence of the *king, his *family, and their personal servants; a place of storage for the royal household's needs and for the royal treasure; a workshop for domestic activities as well as weaving and perhaps other *crafts; a place for state ceremonies; and a centre of government and *administration. It is often difficult to distinguish true palaces from the residencies of governors (who in the eyes of the local population were in practice kings: see Provincial administration), and any monumental building which appears to have served both residential and administrative functions tends to be identified as a palace.

The characteristic features of most Near Eastern palaces developed in *Mesopotamia. Although there are earlier monumental buildings which were clearly centres of power, such as third-millennium BC structures at *Kish and *Eridu, the essential features of most later Mesopotamian palaces first appeared c.2000 BC at *Ur and *Eshnunna. These features were a division between an

This furniture decoration in ivory from Nimrud reproduces the form of a recessed palace window with balustrade. Height 8.2 cm. Eighth century BC. WA 118159.

Palaces at Eridu, Sennacherib's South-West Palace at Nineveh, and Alalakh.

outer courtyard, where public affairs were conducted and which included administrative offices, service quarters and storerooms, and an inner courtyard used for more private functions. Connecting the two courtyards was the throne room, used by the ruler as an audience hall. This was the room of greatest ostentation, and already in Early Dynastic times, at Kish and *Ebla, throne rooms were decorated with propaganda scenes, eventually culminating in *stone slabs carved with *religious, ceremonial, *hunting or military scenes in the *Assyrian palaces (see Sculpture). Palaces were also usually demarcated from the rest of the town by a solid defensive wall.

This arrangement is the classic layout of later Mesopotamian palaces, even if they are more extensive complexes built over several centuries, such as *Mari and later the Southern Citadel at *Babylon with its series of five courtyards. The palace of *Ugarit in *Syria had more in common with these than with the smaller *Levantine *Bronze Age palaces which tended to have a single courtyard surrounded by small rooms, and extended for two or three storeys. The *Hittite palace at *Boghazköy did not follow the same pattern, being an extensive complex formed from the association of separate buildings.

The Assyrian palaces at *Nimrud, *Khorsabad and *Nineveh are the culmination of the Mesopotamian type, sometimes with the addition of a portico (*bīt hilāni) borrowed from north Syrian palaces. Assyrian and north Syrian palaces were situated on citadels at the edges of the cities, together with the main *temples. Most *Iron Age palaces in the Levant are fairly small in comparison and seem to follow the basic courtyard plan, though some may have been the residencies of Assyrian governors. The *Achaemenid palaces at *Pasargadae and *Persepolis inaugurated a different design, characterized by the use of numerous columns for halls and porticoes.                PB

H. FRANKFORT, *The Art and Architecture of the Ancient Orient* (Harmondsworth 1969).

E. HEINRICH, *Die Paläste im alten Mesopotamien* (Berlin 1984).

A. KEMPINSKI and R. REICH (eds), *The Architecture of Ancient Israel from the Prehistoric to the Persian Periods* (Jerusalem 1992) 105–20, 202–22.

J.N. POSTGATE, *Early Mesopotamia: Society and Economy at the Dawn of History* (London 1992) 137–54.

**Palaeolithic** The Palaeolithic is divided into four periods, the Lower Palaeolithic, in the Near East between 1.5 million and 150,000 bp, the Middle Palaeolithic between c.150,000 and 45,000 bp, the Upper Palaeolithic between c.45,000 and 20,000 bp and the *Epipalaeolithic, 20,000–10,000 bp ('bp' stands for 'before present' and is the typical way in which dates are published when referring to the Palaeolithic; see Radiocarbon dating).

In general the Palaeolithic period embraces several significant developments, notably the evolution of the human species, their colonization of most of the earth's surface, fundamental technological developments like use of *tools and fire, and the development of our own species *Homo sapiens* and, by the Upper Palaeolithic, of certain 'modern' human behaviour patterns.

The Near East has a particular importance in the study of certain of these issues. In particular the Near East forms a land bridge for the spread of human species which evolved in Africa, across the rest of the world, including into Europe. These include some of the earliest hominids and, also, almost certainly of hominid *Homo sapiens*.

The earliest well preserved Lower Palaeolithic site so far excavated in the Near East is found in Israel on the edge of the *Levantine rift (a northwards extension of the African rift valley) at Ubeidiya. This site probably dates to between 1.5 million and 800,000 bp. It represents a range of deposits which accumulated on the edge of and in lake environments. The hominids using the site manufactured a typical early Lower Palaeolithic stone tool industry consisting of large bifacial core tools (see Flint-working) as well as a series of flake tools. Sixty-six different *bird and fifty-six different mammal species are represented on the site. Although not all are there because of human *hunting and scavenging, a significant proportion are likely to be present because of such activity and point to the range of hunting and gathering at this period. Burnt flint attests the use of fire.

In the Middle Palaeolithic the Near East is noted for the presence of the Neanderthal species from the Levant to the *Zagros (see Carmel caves and Shanidar). However, in the southern Levant at least, ancestors of our own species are identified also at the sites of Skhul (Carmel caves) and Qafzeh dated to c.92,000 bp. The presence of both species has prompted much controversy, but this early move of our species out of Africa is intriguing. The southerly distribution of these early *sapiens* may be related to climate change and helps confirm the fact our ancestors were probably hominids adapted to a warm climate. Whilst we cannot be sure that Neanderthals and *sapiens* shared the same geographical area at the same time, given the tool assemblages present in the caves where the relevant individuals were buried, it seems clear that they both used the same sort of stone tool manufacturing technology and toolkits and indeed both practised similar *burial. This suggests that culturally they may not have been very far apart in this region.

Such evidence brings to the fore questions about the transition to the Upper Palaeolithic when stone tool technologies change markedly and other new features appear coincident with the disappearance of Neanderthals. The Levant is important too because here there appears to be *in situ* development of the new blade industries (see Flint-working) out of pre-existing Middle Palaeolithic flake industries. Upper Palaeolithic sites are not common in the Near East and are mostly small with limited material culture. It may be that climatic conditions were not favourable either to the aggregation of large groups or to the preservation of Upper Palaeolithic sites.                DB

T.E. LEVY (ed.), *The Archaeology of Society in the Holy Land* (London 1995).

R. SOLECKI, *Shanidar: The First Flower People* (New York 1971).

C. STRINGER and C. GAMBLE, *In Search of the Neanderthals* (London 1993).

E. TRINKHAUS, *The Shanidar Neanderthals* (New York 1983).

**Palestine** Few geographical designations boast such a long – and chequered – history as the name 'Palestine'. In antiquity, Palestine referred sometimes to a geographical region and sometimes to a political entity; a degree of ambiguity persists in the modern use of this term. Broadly speaking, Palestine is part of the *Levant, the narrow strip of land that extends from *Lebanon to the *Sinai and represents the south-western arm of the *Fertile Crescent.

The word 'Palestine' derives from the word *peleset* found in the *Old Testament, referring to the land of the *Philistines. Technically, the region of 'Philistia' included only a small area in the south-western part of *Israel. It was in this area, which included what is now called the Gaza Strip, that the Philistines settled in the twelfth century BC. *Herodotus first used the term *Palaistine* as an adjective with reference to 'Philistine Syria', the coastline known by the *Greeks. This awkward term was abbreviated, the proper noun *Palestine* was born. Philo used it as a synonym for biblical *Canaan, while Josephus used it to refer to the ancient land of Philistia.

After AD 135, the *Roman Emperor Hadrian eliminated the name *Provincia Judaea* and replaced it with *Provincia Syria Palaestina*, which was eventually shortened to *Palaestina*. The Arabs used the name *Filastin* for territory on the west side of the Jordan river, but nineteenth-century Europeans spoke about Western Palestine and Eastern Palestine, which were separated by the Jordan. Under the British Mandate, the term Palestine was used for territory west of the river, as opposed to Transjordan. The United Nations' 1948 partition of Western Palestine was supposed to create Israel and a modern Arab state of Palestine.

Archaeologists normally use the term 'Palestine' as a general geographical-cultural label, not a political designation, as in the terms 'Palestinian *pottery' or

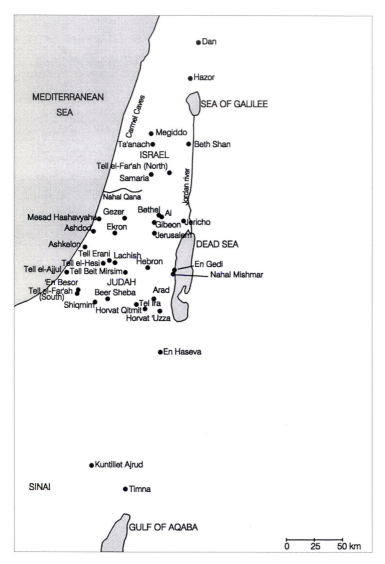

Map of Palestine showing main archaeological sites.

'Syro-Palestinian *archaeology'. Because of its varied topography, and its position between sea and desert, Palestine exhibits a wide range of environmental zones. The Palestinian landscape is, nevertheless, dotted with thousands of archaeological sites, which date from *Palaeolithic to Ottoman times. Though it is relatively small and poor in natural resources, Palestine has served as a strategic crossroads for *trade, *travel and conquest throughout history. Abundant contacts with *Egypt, *Mesopotamia, the *Aegean and points beyond are reflected in this region's archaeological record.        GLM

F.-M. ABEL, *Géographie de la Palestine* 1 (Paris 1933).

Y. AHARONI, *The Land of the Bible: A Historical Geography*, rev. ed. (London 1979).

A.J. BRAWER, 'Palestine', *Encyclopaedia Judaica* 13 (Jerusalem 1971) 29–30.

D.M. JACOBSON, 'Palestine and Israel', *Bulletin of the American Schools of Oriental Research* 313 (1999) 65–74.

P.J. KING, 'Palestine', *HarperCollins Bible Dictionary*, rev. ed. (San Francisco 1996) 796–802.

C.N. RAPHAEL, 'Geography and the Bible (Palestine)', *Anchor Bible Dictionary* 2, ed. D.N. Freedman (New York 1992) 964–77.

G.A. SMITH, *The Historical Geography of the Holy Land*, 25th ed. (London 1931).

## Parrot, André (1901–80)

Parrot was a French archaeologist who worked at Neirab in *Syria (1926) with E. Dhorme, his teacher at the École Biblique in Jerusalem. In 1930 he joined excavations at Tello (see Lagash), directing them 1931–3, and at *Larsa (1933, 1967–8). In 1933 he was invited to investigate the site of Tell Hariri in eastern Syria, soon identified as *Mari, and conducted twenty-one seasons there until 1974. He was employed in the Department of Near Eastern Antiquities at the Louvre, 1937–68, becoming Director of the Louvre 1968–72, and taught in the École du Louvre where he had first studied. He was General Secretary of the Committee on Excavations at the Quai d'Orsay 1959–73, giving much advice and encouragement to French archaeologists working abroad. He was elected to the French Academy in 1963. Parrot contributed regular reports of his excavations and of the Louvre's acquisitions to the journal *Syria*, of which he was an editor from 1942. He set the publication of the Mari archives on course and produced six volumes of reports on the site and its finds. Parrot was concerned to inform his students and the wider public. His *Archéologie mésopotamienne* (vol. 1 1949, vol. 2 1953) is still useful for its surveys of earlier excavations and research, although the sections on techniques are now dated. In association with André Malraux, he inaugurated the series *Univers des Formes*, writing *Sumer* (1960) and *Assur* (1961) for it. He created a series of small books describing discoveries which relate to the *Bible, a particular interest linked to his role as a Lutheran pastor; many of these were translated into English (e.g. *The Flood and Noah's Ark* 1953, *Babylon and the Old Testament* 1958).        ARM

P. AMIET, 'André Parrot', *Archiv für Orientforschung* 28 (1981–2) 281–2.

P. DEMARGUE, 'Allocution a l'occasion du décès de M. André Parrot', *Comptes rendus de l'Académie des Inscriptions et Belles Lettres* (1980) 511–15.

J.-C. MARGUERON, 'Parrot, André', *The Oxford Encyclopedia of Archaeology in the Near East* 4, ed. E.M. Meyers (New York 1997) 248–9.

A. PARROT, *L'aventure archéologique* (Paris 1979).

## Parthians

The period between c.238 BC and AD 224 in *Iran and *Mesopotamia is termed the Parthian period. Parthia, a region south-east of the Caspian Sea, was part of the *Achaemenid empire. The Parthians were originally *nomads from Central Asia, and in 238 BC, under their leader Arsaces, they revolted against the Seleucids (see Hellenistic period), eventually extending their Parthian (or Arsacid) empire from the *Indus to the Euphrates. The Euphrates became their frontier with Rome, and for nearly three centuries the Parthians and *Romans fought for control of *Syria and Mesopotamia.

Parthian wealth was based on control of the Silk Route, benefiting from *trade between China and Rome. The Parthians had several capitals, originally probably at Nysa, and the last a winter capital founded at Ctesiphon on the Tigris. Ctesiphon's capture by the Emperor Trajan in AD 116 ended their threat to Rome, and thereafter Parthian power declined. The last Parthian king was overthrown in AD 224 by the *Sasanians.        PB

M.A.R. COLLEDGE, *The Parthians* (London 1967).

——, *Parthian Art* (London 1977).

R.N. FRYE, *The Heritage of Persia*, 2nd ed. (London 1976) 199–235.

R. GHIRSHMAN, *Iran: Parthians and Sasanians* (London 1962).

E. YARSHATER (ed.), *The Seleucid, Parthian and Sasanian Periods*, Cambridge History of Iran 3 (Cambridge 1983).

## Pasargadae

Pasargadae was the first royal seat of the *Achaemenids, founded by *Cyrus the Great after his usurpation of power in 559 BC, on the ancient *road between Isfahan and Shiraz, in the Dast-i Morghab plain

Parthian bronze belt buckle designed as an embracing couple. Height 4.8 cm. Second to third century AD. WA 135126.

in the province of Fars, ancient Parsa, in *Iran. It is a sprawling, unwalled conglomeration of *palaces, pavilions, free-standing *gates, formal *gardens with stone-lined water channels, the citadel-like Tall-i Takht, a sacred precinct, the enigmatic tower called the Zendan-i Sulaiman (Prison of Solomon) and the Tomb of Cyrus. Despite its importance as the formal seat of Achaemenid power, Pasargadae was not in any sense an urban centre. Excavations were conducted by David Stronach (1961–3).

The *sculpture displays something of the mixture of influences from different satrapies (provinces) of the Achaemenid empire, particularly *Assyria, *Babylonia and *Egyptianizing elements from *Phoenicia, besides elements of dress that that have more local, *Elamite, antecedents. This tendency to display iconography from various parts of the empire publicly reached its apogee at *Persepolis, and is echoed by the trilingual inscriptions at Pasargadae, in Old Persian, Elamite and *Akkadian, which are now thought to be no earlier than the reign of Darius I.

The Tall-i Takht comprises a huge stone platform on which stood, it is reasonably assumed, the palace of Cyrus. The workmanship of dressed ashlar masonry, with metal clamps and masons' marks, is closely paralleled at *Lydian *Sardis, in south-western Turkey, indicative of Lydian and Ionian workmanship. The construction of the Takht cannot, therefore, have begun before the fall of Lydia to Cyrus in, traditionally, 547 BC.

A royal park, or paradise, formally laid out with broad walkways and carefully engineered stone channels, contained two Palaces, S and P, and two Pavilions, A and B. The whole complex was constructed over a considerable period of time and some evolution may be observed in both the architecture and the sculpture.

The Zendan is a free-standing square tower (c.7 by 7 m) with buttressed corners, standing on a low podium and capped by a low pyramidal pitched roof. An external staircase leads to a single chamber half-way up. The function is uncertain but there is a close parallel in the Achaemenid period Ka'bah-i Zardusht (Cube of Zoroaster) at Naqsh-i Rustum near Persepolis. The structure displays clear *Urartian influence in its plan and in the use of blind windows in black stone.

The free-standing Tomb of Cyrus, which still contained a *gold sarcophagus and the body of Cyrus when visited by Alexander the Great, is conspicuously different to later Achaemenid royal *tombs that had façades cut into cliff faces. The form, a single chamber with a pitched roof standing on a stepped podium, is often thought to be east *Greek, perhaps specifically Lydian, in inspiration.

The open-air Sacred Precinct contains two stone fire *altars of the type depicted on the tomb of Darius I. A stone-paved terrace appears to have been an addition of unknown date.                                              GDS

C. NYLANDER, *Ionians in Pasargadae* (Uppsala 1970).

D. STRONACH, *Pasargadae* (Oxford 1978).

——, 'Pasargadae', *Cambridge History of Iran* 2 (Cambridge 1985) 338–55.

**Pastoral nomadism:** see Nomads

**Patriarchs** The *Hebrew *Bible traces the origins of Israel back to Abraham, his son Isaac and Isaac's son Jacob, also called *Israel, the Patriarchs. Their biographies are given in the Book of Genesis. Briefly, Abraham's father took him from *Ur of the Chaldees to *Harran, then he migrated to *Canaan, at God's command, where he lived a semi-*nomadic life, camping for long periods in one place, never living in *towns. During a famine he made a calamitous visit to *Egypt; he also led a force of retainers to retrieve his nephew from a raiding party of eastern *kings. Without an heir, despite God's promise, he had Ishmael by his wife's maid Hagar, then his wife Sarah bore Isaac and Hagar and Ishmael were eventually sent away. At divine command, Abraham offered Isaac in *sacrifice, being stopped from slaughtering him only at the last moment when a ram was provided instead. This was a test of the faith he had already displayed. At Sarah's death, he bought land near Hebron and buried her there in a cave which became the family tomb and is marked today by the enclosure wall King Herod built around it late in the first century BC. When Isaac needed a wife, Rebekah was fetched from the family left in Harran, rather than his taking a local Canaanite. Their son Isaac maintained the same life-style, confronting men of Gerar over water rights at *Beer Sheba, as his father had done. The younger of his twin sons, Jacob, became prominent, spending years as a herdsman with the Harran family, then returning to Canaan and acquiring land near Shechem. Jacob's favourite son Joseph was sold by his brothers as a slave and rose to power in Egypt, where he invited his family to settle during a famine. Their descendants lived there until the *Exodus.

The Patriarchs worshipped a single God, under the name *Yahweh, or as El ('God') with various titles, making sacrifices on *stone *altars and, in Jacob's case, erecting memorial stelae. Some of their practices do not conform to the Laws of Moses.

Biblical scholarship has tended to treat these narratives as anything but historical accounts. They have been interpreted as retrojections from much later ages, as astral or totemic myths and as folk-stories. Literary analysis has discerned separate sources of different dates, using distinctive words and expressions and separate names for God, the combination of these source producing 'duplicate' episodes, such as the conflicts at Beer Sheba. The 1980s and 1990s have seen these views reach extreme forms in the work of some authors.

When the Patriarchal narratives are read in the context of the early second millennium BC, which the biblical chronology seems to presuppose, their content can be seen to be largely consistent with it, although the style of *Hebrew shows that their present form is later. Biographical reports offer parallel forms (especially the Egyptian Sinuhe), while *Babylonian and *Ugaritic *epics about ancient kings (*Gilgamesh, *Sargon, *Keret) exemplify a stage beyond the Genesis text when the recollections were reformulated as *poetry. The debatable question is how far the narratives reflect the lives of actual individuals. No extra-biblical reference to Abraham, Isaac or Jacob is known, not unexpectedly, as they were not great kings, nor lived in cities where documents might survive. No written reports of their contacts with rulers in Canaan or Egypt are available. The Patriarchs are best placed in this context in several respects, among them their personal names, their lifestyle, the political situations in Canaan and Egypt. The presence of *camels, *Philistines and *Aramaeans is often signalled as evidence for dates after 1200 BC when these become well known from other sources. Yet camels are not unknown earlier, 'Philistine' may have replaced an older name for migrants from the *Aegean, and the early history of the Aramaeans is too obscure to rule them out. It would be strange for Israelites in the Monarchy to claim descent from Aramaeans, their major enemy at that time. Israel had special need to know her early history because of its claim that the land of Canaan was Israel's by gift of God to Abraham. His biography was a form of title-deed, the events of his life evidence of God acting on his behalf, and so might be carefully preserved; the more sceptical view would argue that it was composed for the same reason long after his supposed lifetime.　　　　ARM

A.R. MILLARD, 'Abraham', *Anchor Bible Dictionary* 1, ed. D.N. Freedman (New York 1992) 35–41.

A.R. MILLARD and D.J. WISEMAN (eds), *Essays on the Patriarchal Narratives* (Leicester 1980).

G.J. WENHAM, *Genesis* (Waco, TX 1987, 1994).

C. WESTERMANN, *Genesis* (London 1984, 1986).

**Persepolis** Persepolis lies on the eastern edge of the Marv Dasht plain, Fars province, south-west *Iran. It was chosen by the *Achaemenid *King Darius I as a new royal capital, replacing *Pasargadae. The site comprises a rocky hill with a defensive circuit wall and, on the plain in front, a great stone terrace, some 300 by 400 m, on which was erected a series of monumental royal buildings embellished with *sculptures. Lesser buildings exist on the plain, but there is no trace of an urban residential area. Darius and three of his successors had monumental *tomb façades carved into the face of a cliff 6 km to the north at Naqsh-i Rustum. The site was burned by Alexander the Great, whether in revenge or drunken exuberance being disputed.

The site was cleared by E. Hertzfield (1931–4) and E.F. Schmidt (1935–9), the latter producing a masterful series of publications. More recent studies, especially those by Nylander, Roaf, Root and Tilia, have greatly enhanced understanding of this magnificent site.

Persepolis is thought to symbolize the Achaemenid empire. It contained architectural elements and *building materials from the major parts of the empire, and doubtless many foreign masons, sculptors and *craftsmen contributed besides those known from written evidence to have come from *Lydia and the east *Greek world. Both the concept of the monumental complex itself, and the subject matter of the famous reliefs of tribute bearers from all corners of the empire on the grand staircase, would seem to reflect an idealized concept of the empire as envisioned by Darius, rather than simply a represen-

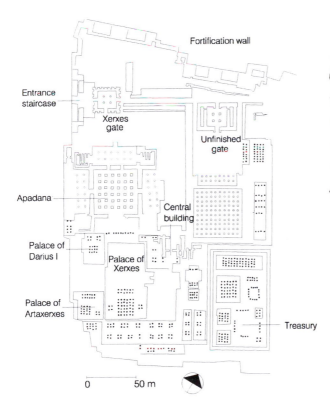

Plan of the Achaemenid palace at Persepolis in its final state c.340 BC.

Assyrian motifs are echoed in this carving from Persepolis of a winged human-headed lion. Height 75 cm. Early fifth century BC. WA 129381.

tation of the *New Year festival. The whole scheme appears to have reflected secular power, no shrine or *temple having been recognized.

Monumental structures on the platform include the *apadana* (a ceremonial hall), two monumental *gates, a series of *palaces constructed by different kings and the so-called treasury. These were approached via the monumental, sculpted, double stairway. Beyond this Xerxes added a great gate. Characteristic is the prolific use of columns, both *stone and *timber, the individual architectural elements, the sculpted stone entrances and, not least, a scale that reflected the might and power of the empire. Walls were of mudbrick and flat roofs supported by massive timber constructions. Stone column capitals were surmounted by animal protome capitals. What survives today are the stone foundations, stone gate and door jambs, stone columns with their bases and capitals, and stone bases for wooden columns.                    GDS

M. ROAF, 'Sculptures and Sculptors at Persepolis', *Iran* 21 (1983).
M.C. ROOT, *The King and Kingship in Achaemenid Art* (Leiden 1979).
E.F. SCHMIDT, *Persepolis I: Structures, Reliefs, Inscriptions* (Chicago 1953).
——, *Persepolis II: Contents of the Treasury and Other Discoveries* (Chicago 1957).
——, *Persepolis III: The Royal Tombs and Other Monuments* (Chicago 1957).
A.B. TILLA, *Studies and Restorations at Persepolis and Other Sites in Fārs* (Rome 1972, 1978).

**Persia** The name Persia comes from the Old Persian *Parsa*, the modern province of Fars. *Iron Age geography in *Iran, including the precise location of Parsa at any particular time, is complex and poorly understood. Persia, synonymous with modern Iran, comprises a desert plateau surrounded by high mountains. The vast country can be divided into regions, each of which gave rise to its own cultures. Modern political boundaries often divide these geo-cultural regions. The picture is one of diversity rather than unity, of passage rather than permanence. Different peoples have crossed and re-crossed the regions, sometimes as traders, sometimes settling, sometimes in a path of destruction. In the past, as today, there is a complex mix of peoples, *languages and cultures existing side by side in various degrees of harmony. Unlike other areas of the ancient Near East, written records are few, being restricted, with a few exceptions, to ancient *Elam until the *Achaemenid period.

Archaeological research was largely in its infancy when interrupted by the Iranian revolution in 1979. Human occupation is attested from the *Palaeolithic period onwards. The precise role played by communities in the mountains of Persia in the transition towards *agriculture, the domestication of *animals and the rise of settled *village life remains enigmatic despite the existence of aceramic *Neolithic villages. Nor is the role of transhumance and *nomadism in the development of early *prehistoric cultures in Iran understood. There appears to have been a long period of settled village life

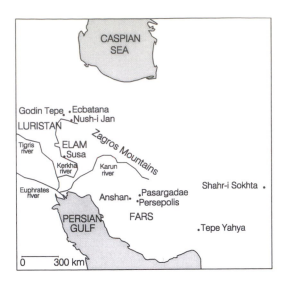

Map of Persia showing main archaeological sites.

throughout the later Neolithic and most of the *Chalcolithic periods, but in the late Chalcolithic, or *Uruk, period at least the Susiana plain witnessed the rise of urbanism and the development of literate *administration. The extent to which these developments were the direct result of an expansion of south *Mesopotamian power is disputed. Only with the rise of *Persian or Achaemenid power from the seventh century BC onwards does Persia have any semblance of political unity in the face of diversity.

One great and ongoing debate in the archaeology of Iran is the identification and origins of the earliest *Indo-Europeans, usually thought to have entered Iran from the north-east some time in the second millennium BC. Persian languages, modern Farsi and its predecessors, Middle and Old Persian, belong to the eastern branch of the Indo-European family.

Iran has been and continues to be subject to plunder of its ancient art and cultural remains to a far greater extent than any other area of the Near East, at least until the 1990s when looting in Iraq and Afghanistan attained equally high levels. Many of the objects in museums and private collections attributed to regions or even specific sites have in fact come from the art market, and have thus been removed from any cultural context that they might once have had.                    GDS

L. VAN DEN BERGHE, *Bibliographie analytique de l'archéologie de l'Iran ancien* (Leiden 1979).
L. VAN DEN BERGHE and E. HAERINCK, *Bibliographie analytique de l'archéologie de l'Iran ancien: Supplément 1, 1978–1980* (Leiden 1979).
——, *Bibliographie analytique de l'archéologie de l'Iran ancien: Supplément 2, 1981–1985* (Leuven 1985).
E. HAERINCK and K.G. STEVENS, *Bibliographie analytique de l'archéologie de l'Iran ancien: Supplément, 1986–1996* (Leuven 1996).

W.B. FISCHER (ed.), *Cambridge History of Iran I: The Land of Iran* (Cambridge 1968).

F. HOLE (ed.), *The Archaeology of Western Iran* (Washington, DC 1987).

M.M. VOIGT and R.H. DYSON, JR, 'The Chronology of Iran ca. 8000–2000 B.C.', *Chronologies in Old World Archaeology* 1, 3rd ed., ed. R.W. Ehrich (Chicago 1992) 122–5.

M.A. DANDAMAEV and V.G. LUKONIN, *The Cultural and Social Institutions of Ancient Iran* (Cambridge 1989).

R.N. FRYE, *The History of Ancient Iran* (Munich 1984).

I. GERSHEVITCH (ed.), *Cambridge Ancient History of Iran* 2 (Cambridge 1985).

T.C. YOUNG, JR, 'Persians', *The Oxford Encyclopedia of Archaeology in the Near East* 4, ed. E.M. Meyers (New York 1997) 295–300.

**Persians** Persians or Iranians are speakers of *languages from the eastern branch of the *Indo-European family of languages. In the past these languages included Old and Middle Persian and others that have not left recognizable trace. Modern Persian languages include Farsi and Kurdish. The Persian languages, and presumably peoples, are usually thought to have arrived on to the Iranian plateau from north-east of the Caspian Sea in the second millennium BC. By the mid ninth century BC some of these tribes had reached the region of the central *Zagros mountains in western *Iran where they are known to us from *Assyrian written sources. Some of these tribes coalesced to form a Median state with a capital at *Ecbatana (modern Hamadan). The extent and nature of the early Median empire is controversial, but it is clear that by the early sixth century BC it covered considerable parts of eastern Iran and stretched westwards to the Halys river in central Turkey. Median rule gave way to Persian following the usurpation of power by *Cyrus the Great. Persian genealogy and the true claims to the *Achaemenid line are as hotly and ingeniously contested. The empire rapidly became the largest that had existed, generally known as Persian or Achaemenid.                                         GDS

A gold plaque from the Oxus Treasure is embossed with the figure of a man wearing the short Persian sword and a hood and carrying a bundle of sticks, perhaps the barsom used in Zoroastrian sacrifices. Height 15 cm. Fifth century BC. WA 123949.

## Petrie, William Matthew Flinders (1853–1942)

Flinders Petrie holds an esteemed position in the history of Egyptology, Syro-Palestinian *archaeology and archaeology in general. Because he was a sickly child, Petrie was educated by his mother, who instilled in him strong antiquarian interests, and his father, who taught him the art of surveying. Endowed with these skills, Petrie represents a turning point in archaeological method, since he introduced 'scientific' (i.e. systematic) excavation procedures and advocated the prompt publication of finds.

In 1880, Petrie went to Egypt to prove Piazzi Smythe's theories about the Great Pyramid and biblical prophecy. His careful measurements convinced him to discard these bizarre views, although it must be said that Petrie's career was always marked by a measure of eccentricity. While working at Giza, he developed an intense interest in ancient Egypt and was shocked by the destructive nature of excavation techniques. Although Petrie did not live up to the high standards of General Pitt Rivers, he advanced far beyond the organized pillage practised by most of his contemporaries, some of them famous Egyptologists. Petrie brought curiosity and energy to his fieldwork and publishing, but he is best known for his awareness that 'unconsidered trifles', like undecorated *pottery, hold a wealth of information and should be collected and examined. During the lengthy Egyptian phase of his career, Petrie worked under the auspices of the Egypt Exploration Fund/Society and his own British School of Archaeology in Egypt (digging at such sites as Abydos, Coptos, Naqada, Tell el-Amarna and Thebes – where he discovered the Merneptah Stela in 1896). He also worked in the *Sinai and had two periods of fieldwork in 'Egypt over the border', working for the Palestine Exploration Fund. Wherever he worked, a Petrie dig was marked by an infamous frugality, yet he still managed to hold the interest of young archaeologists who learned much by associating with their mentor (e.g. Starkey, Tufnell, Harding, Bliss).

During his first period of work in *Palestine, for an interval of six weeks in 1890, Petrie earned the title 'father of systematic excavation in Palestine'. Through his excavation at Tell el-*Hesi, he spelled out two major principles which remain fundamental to modern excavation methodology – stratigraphy and typology. Although *Schliemann had developed a basic approach to the excavation of a 'tell' at Hissarlik (*Troy), it was Petrie who realized that Palestinian sites are composed of superimposed layers of debris resulting from multiple periods of occupation. Through survey, drawing, photography, etc., he emphasized architecture and removed soil by arbitrary levels and did not follow a genuine stratigraphic approach. Because the east side of Tell el-Hesi had been

*Expedition*, eds B.T. Dahlberg and K.G. O'Connell (Winona Lake, IN 1989) 37–67.

N.A. SILBERMAN, 'Petrie, William Matthew Flinders', *The Oxford Encyclopedia of Archaeology in the Near East* 4, ed. E.M. Meyers (New York 1997) 308–9.

E.P. UPHILL, 'A Bibliography of Sir William Matthew Flinders Petrie (1853–1942)', *Journal of Near Eastern Studies* 31 (1972) 356–79.

Sir William Matthew Flinders Petrie, by Philip de Laszlo, 1934. Petrie is holding a Predynastic pottery jar from Egypt (by courtesy of the National Portrait Gallery, London, 4007).

eroded away, Petrie also saw that the pottery exposed in this 'section' changed styles through time. His experience in Egypt allowed him to work out a system of sequence dating and to make links between Palestinian artefacts and well dated Egyptian materials. Between 1926 and 1938, Petrie also undertook major excavations at Tell Jemmeh, Tell el-*Far'ah (South), and Tell el-'Ajjul.

Petrie excavated at more than sixty important sites in Egypt and Palestine and published his fieldwork and viewpoints in over a hundred books and almost 950 articles and reviews. Beginning in 1892, he served as professor of Egyptology at the University of London and was knighted for his contributions to scholarship in 1923. Petrie retired from fieldwork in 1938 and moved to the American School of Oriental Research, in Jerusalem, where he died in 1942.                    GLM

J.A. CALLAWAY, 'Sir Flinders Petrie: Father of Palestinian Archaeology', *Biblical Archaeology Review* 6 (1980) 44–55.

M.S. DROWER, *Flinders Petrie: A Life in Archaeology* (London 1985).

V. FARGO, '*BA* Portrait: Sir Flinders Petrie', *Biblical Archaeologist* 47 (1984) 220–3.

J.M. MATTHERS, 'Excavations by the Palestine Exploration Fund at Tell el-Hesy 1890–1892', *Tell el-Hesi: The Site and the*

**Philistia, Philistines** The territorial designation 'Philistia' refers to the south-western coast of *Palestine. The modern term 'Palestine' is derived from the name recorded for this region in the *Bible, *peleset*. The Philistines themselves were a non-Semitic people who migrated to the south-eastern Mediterranean by sea from somewhere in the *Aegean basin at the beginning of the twelfth century BC, one of a number of migrating groups known collectively as '*Sea Peoples'.

A defining event in the history of the Philistines occurred in 1180 BC, when Ramesses III waged a fierce naval battle with the Sea Peoples. The *Egyptian victory forced the Philistines to settle in the region now known as Philistia, the territory between modern Tel Aviv and the 'Brook of Egypt', south of Gaza. Excavation has shown that Philistine settlement at some sites follows the destruction of a Late Bronze *Canaanite stratum, while the Philistines sometimes established their residence at previously unoccupied locations.

The so-called 'Philistine Pentapolis', a group of five *city-states, was the centre of Philistine culture in south-western Palestine: these cities were Gaza, *Ashkelon, *Ashdod, Gath (Tell es-Safi?) and *Ekron (Tel Miqne). Philistine territorial boundaries are defined in the *Old Testament; this area conforms fairly well to what is known about the concentration of sites where the Philistines' telltale painted *pottery is found. This distinctive pottery, derived from the Late Mycenaean IIIC style, seems to have developed only about fifty years after they had settled. The region had good *agricultural potential, and artefacts reflect a far-ranging commercial network. The Philistine cities prospered in this setting, and the *Bible describes the unfriendly – and sometimes warlike – conditions that existed between *Israel and the Philistines during the *Iron Age. The only Philistine *temple to have been completely excavated is at Tell Qasile, which developed in several phases from a one-room structure to a complex consisting of a main temple and an adjacent shrine.

Although the Philistines intermarried with the local population and their distinctive pottery motifs had largely disappeared after c.1000 BC, a Philistine identity was still noted as late as the *Persian period. The *Assyrians captured Philistine cities in the latter part of the eighth century BC, and *Esarhaddon and *Ashurbanipal used Philistia as a staging area for their invasion of Egypt during the first half of the seventh century BC. When the *Babylonians deported Philistia's rulers c.600 BC, the region lost its independence.                    GLM

J.F. BRUG, *A Literary and Archaeological Study of the Philistines* (Oxford 1985).

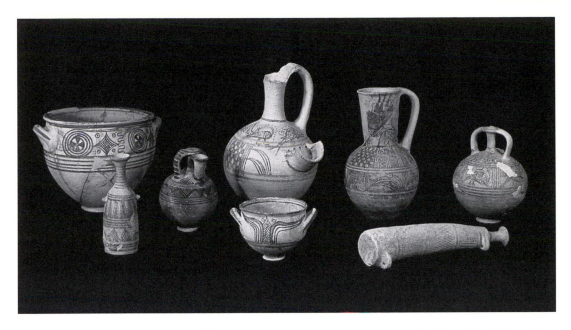

Philistine Bichrome pottery from a number of Philistine sites (courtesy of S. Gitin, photograph by Z. Radovan).

S. BUNIMOVITZ, 'Problems in the "Ethnic" Identification of the Philistine Material Culture', *Tel Aviv* 17 (1990) 210–22.

T. DOTHAN, *The Philistines and Their Material Culture* (Jerusalem 1982).

T. DOTHAN and M. DOTHAN, *People of the Sea: The Search for the Philistines* (New York 1992).

C.S. EHRLICH, *Philistia in Transition: A History of the Philistines from ca. 1000–730 B.C.E.* (Leiden 1996).

B.J. STONE, 'The Philistines and Acculturation: Culture Change and Ethnic Continuity in the Iron Age', *Bulletin of the American Schools of Oriental Research* 298 (1995) 7–32.

Map of Philistia showing main archaeological sites.

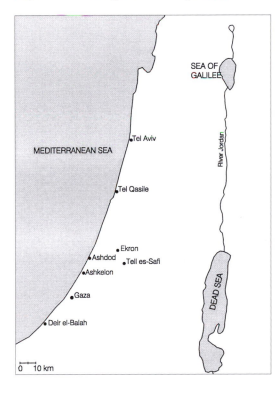

**Phoenicia, Phoenicians** During the *Bronze Age, the occupants of the *Lebanese coast were essentially *Canaanites, but the term 'Phoenician' usually refers to inhabitants of this region in the *Iron Age. This name (from Greek *phoinix*, derived from the word for 'red', perhaps signifying the colour purple) was applied to them by the *Greeks, who maintained constant relations with the Phoenician coast. The Phoenicians excelled in the arts and industries – including *ivories, *glass, *furniture, purple dye (from murex snails), and elaborate *textiles. Their coastal location at an important crossroads between the sea and the interior of western Asia enabled them to absorb and disseminate wide-ranging cultural elements (e.g. *Aegean, *Egyptian, Neo-*Hittite, *Assyrian).

After the Late Bronze Age civilization came to a sudden end, Phoenicia built its maritime hegemony on the collapse of Mycenaean international *trade. Although little is known concerning the first two centuries of Phoenicia's Iron Age history, it appears that the coastal *cities flourished in this period. The fundamental features of Phoenician culture had already developed by the tenth century BC. The Phoenicians traded in *metals, timber and manufactured goods. According to the *Bible,

One of numerous bronze bowls found by Layard at Nimrud illustrates Phoenician skill in using foreign motifs for decoration, here Egyptian figures with an un-Egyptian central pattern. Diameter c.21 cm. Eighth century BC. WA 115505.

Many aspects of the Phoenicians' *religion were derived from Canaanite antecedents, but the beliefs and practices of the Iron Age differed considerably from those of the Late Bronze Age. No pantheon can be identified as specifically Phoenician, since different religious practices evolved in the city-states. *Baal was known by different epithets at *Byblos, and the goddess *Astarte held a prominent position in Sidon. *Melqart played a leading role in the city of Tyre. The Phoenician princess Jezebel, wife of the ninth-century BC King Ahab, was criticized because she introduced Phoenician religious practices into Israel. The Phoenicians were associated with child *sacrifice in many ancient texts, but the evidence related to Tanit and the tophets at Carthage and Tyre remains controversial.                                              GLM

M.E. AUBET, *The Phoenicians and the West: Politics, Colonies and Trade* (Cambridge 1993).
*Bulletin of the American Schools of Oriental Research* 279 (1990), special thematic issue on the Phoenicians.
E. LIPINSKI (ed.), *Phoenicia and the East Mediterranean in the First Millennium B.C.* (Louvain 1987).
——, 'Phoenicians', *Civilizations of the Ancient Near East*, ed. J.M. Sasson (New York 1995) 1321–33.
S. MOSCATI (ed.), *The Phoenicians* (New York 1988).
W.A. WARD, 'Phoenicia', *The Oxford Encyclopedia of Archaeology in the Near East* 4, ed. E.M. Meyers (New York 1997) 313–17.

Hiram of Tyre established a trading partnership with David and Solomon of *Israel and supplied them with timber, skilled *craftsmen and sailors.

The foreign policy of the Neo-Assyrian empire allowed Phoenicia to continue its vital role as middlemen in the lucrative Mediterranean trade, although Assyrian officials monitored political and economic activities. Beginning in the ninth century BC, the Assyrians exacted tribute from the Phoenician commercial centres. Phoenicia's commercial and colonial activities increased between the ninth and sixth centuries. Regular contacts were established between the Lebanese coast and southern Spain – and at many other points in the Mediterranean basin; one of the most significant steps in Phoenicia's expansion was the founding of Carthage c.800 BC. By the time of *Sennacherib and his immediate successors, however, the Phoenician cities of *Tyre and Sidon refused to pay tribute and were dealt with harshly. When *Nebuchadnezzar II took control of the greater part of the *Levant, Phoenicia paid tribute to *Babylon, and the latter allowed the coastal city states to operate as they had in the past. Phoenician commercial life thrived under *Persian control.

The Phoenician *language is a late form of Canaanite, and most surviving examples are brief *funerary or monumental inscriptions. Most Phoenician history is known from secondary accounts written by non-Phoenicians. Its script was closely related to that used in neighbouring kingdoms (e.g. *Aram, Israel, *Ammon, *Moab). Since Phoenician *merchants and sailors were in regular contact with the Aegean world, they are credited with the transmission of their consonantal *alphabet to the Greeks.

**Phrygia**  The *Iron Age kingdom of Phrygia in west-central *Anatolia is known from classical sources, including *Herodotus. For classical authors its most famous king was *Midas, who appears in *Assyrian records as Mita of Mushki. The Mushki were a tribe from eastern Anatolia first mentioned in Assyrian texts in the twelfth century BC. There is still debate about whether Phrygia and Mushki should be equated, since the name Phrygia itself is not attested in Near Eastern sources. It is possible that Mita simply ruled over the Mushki but that the core of his kingdom of Phrygia was to the west.

The Phrygians were originally from south-east Europe and migrated to Anatolia after the collapse of the *Hittite empire. The history of Phrygia is largely unknown except for classical references to Midas, and study of the Phrygian kingdom is based on linguistic analysis and archaeological exploration. Their language was *Indo-European, their script an adaptation of the *Greek *alphabet, well known particularly from rock-cut inscriptions.

It is still uncertain when the Phrygian state was formed, but it certainly flourished in the eighth century BC. The most recognizable cultural characteristics are *burial in tumuli, best attested at the capital, *Gordion, but also found elsewhere, and rock-cut architectural façades with geometric patterns and lion *sculptures in the highlands (see Midas City). Distinctive Phrygian use of geometric and animal designs is found on their painted *pottery and remarkably preserved *wooden *furniture from Gordion. At the centre of Phrygian *religion was a *goddess referred to as 'Mother' and 'Kubileya', probably the origin of the classical Kybele.

The independent kingdom of Phrygia may have been

Map of Phrygia showing principal sites.

Late Phrygian painted jug showing an archer, probably a goddess, hunting. Late seventh century BC (courtesy, Museum of Fine Arts, Boston: Edward J. and Mary S. Holmes Fund).

ended by the *Cimmerian invasion in c.700 BC, although recent evidence suggests that the political system survived. The area was later dominated by *Lydia and then the *Persians.                                               PB

E. AKURGAL, *Phrygische Kunst* (Ankara 1955).

R.D. BARNETT, 'Phrygia and the Peoples of Anatolia in the Iron Age', *Cambridge Ancient History* 2.2, 2nd ed. (Cambridge 1975) 417–42.

M. MELLINK, 'The Native Kingdoms of Anatolia', *Cambridge Ancient History* 3.2, 2nd ed. (Cambridge 1991) 622–43.

O.W. MUSCARELLA, 'The Iron Age Background to the Formation of the Phrygian State', *Bulletin of the American Schools of Oriental Research* 299/300 (1995) 91–101.

G.K. SAMS, 'Midas of Gordion and the Anatolian Kingdom of Phrygia', *Civilizations of the Ancient Near East*, ed. J.M. Sasson (New York 1995) 1147–59.

## Place, Victor (1818–75)

Victor Place began a diplomatic career at Santo Domingo from 1847 to 1851 before his appointment as French consul at Mosul. Excavation was an expected part of a diplomat's work at this time and when he arrived in *Mesopotamia in 1852 Place brought with him the novelty of a photographer rather than an artist to record the digs. He reached an agreement with *Rawlinson on dividing the excavations of the Kuyunjik mound at *Nineveh between the French and British and took on the responsibilities for the excavations at *Khorsabad which had been left unfinished by *Botta. The demanding work of consul meant excavation came second place but over the next two years he revealed the palace of *Sargon II of *Assyria at Khorsabad. In 1855, 235 cases of Khorsabad material, as well as objects from

Kuyunjik and elsewhere, were loaded on to rafts and floated down the Tigris towards Basra. At Qurnah, where the Tigris and Euphrates join to form the Shatt al-Arab, the flotilla was attacked by brigands and most of the material was lost in the river, including all of Place's notes and plans. Eventually twenty-six cases reached the Louvre in 1856. The Khorsabad excavation report finally appeared between 1867 and 1870 as the three volumes of *Nineve et l'Assyrie*. The draughtsmanship was excellent but the placing of the buildings was made from memory so is less reliable.

Place was subsequently appointed to consular posts in Turkey and Calcutta and finally in 1870 as Consular-General in New York. Here he was accused of accepting a bribe over an arms contract. Found guilty and sentenced to two years' imprisonment, he was immediately pardoned. In 1872 he left France for Romania, where he died in 1875.                                               PTC

M.T. LARSEN, *The Conquest of Assyria: Excavations in an Antique Land 1840–1860* (London/New York 1996).

M. PILLET, *Un pionier de l'assyriologie: Victor Place, consul de France à Mossoul, explorateur du palais de Sargon II (722–705 av. J.-C.) à Khorsabad* (Paris 1962).

## Plants and flowers

From the end of the fourth millennium BC there are numerous representations in *Mesopotamian *art of plants and flowers, many of them highly stylized. A common motif was a rosette with eight petals made of coloured stones set into the walls of temples. Multi-petalled rosettes of materials like shell were inlaid into objects or were shaped from *gold and *silver into *jewellery such as the decorative floral combs found in the Royal Graves of *Ur or sewn on to *clothing. Occasionally actual plants such as flax, reeds and a variety of *trees may be identified on *stone reliefs. Plants and flowers are mentioned throughout the *Old Testament and a great variety of plants are also mentioned in the *cuneiform texts, especially those concerned with *medicine. The precise identification of these is, however, very difficult but some are proposed on the basis of more

An early example of floral decoration, a rosette of white and black stone from Tell Brak. The centre is the head of a peg to hold it to the wall. Diameter 15 cm. c.3000 BC. WA 126397A.

recent use of plants in local folk medicine or studies of the modern environment. Increasingly it is the examination of ancient carbonized seeds and ancient pollen that is helping to identify the plants that actually grew in the past.                                                                 PTC

E. BLEIBTREU, *Die Flora der neuassyrischen Reliefs* (Vienna 1980).
*Bulletin on Sumerian Agriculture* 2, 3 (Cambridge 1985, 1987).
G. DIMBLEBY, *Plants and Archaeology* (London 1978).
F.N. HEPPER, *Encyclopedia of Bible Plants* (Leicester 1993).
R.C. THOMPSON, *A Dictionary of Assyrian Botany* (London 1949).

**Poetry**  A wide range of genres survives in both *Sumerian and *Akkadian literatures, from short *song-like poems to complex and extended narratives, *hymns and praise songs. Sumerian poems rarely exceed 750 lines, but Akkadian has both short songs and extended *epics such as *Gilgamesh (over three thousand lines) or the Epic of *Creation (c.926 lines).

Almost all literary compositions in Sumerian and Akkadian are written in verse. The lines are laid out on the clay tablet in *cuneiform writing exactly as modern poetry: left-justified, with the continuation of an exceptionally long line indented to show that it is not a new line. *Mesopotamian poetry was not based on rhyme or metre, although comparable effects were sometimes exploited. A line of Akkadian verse is typically divided into two by a caesura (often indicated graphically by a gap), with up to two stressed syllables in each half; but sometimes other analyses seem to fit better. Apart from the medial caesura, no system of stress or quantity seems to fit Sumerian. In both *languages, lines can often be grouped in twos, threes or fours on the basis of linguistic or structural parallelism; refrains sometimes occur.

Owing to the restricted literacy of Mesopotamian society, poetry was transmitted orally, and often performed *musically, sometimes by solo singers with the accompaniment of the lyre or harp. Praise poetry and some cultic poetry was sung by one or more singers accompanied by drums.

Poetry in West Semitic is well represented in the Late Bronze Age at *Ugarit and in the *Iron Age in the *Hebrew *Bible. Ugaritic poetry is almost entirely narrative, epics and myths (see Aqhat, Baal, Keret), whereas Hebrew poetry is used for hymns, prayers and laments (Psalms), victory poems (Exodus 15; Judges 5), love songs (Song of Songs), wisdom literature (Proverbs, Job, Ecclesiastes) and prophecy. Both share the basic features seen in Akkadian poetry, parallelism being basic. The simple form ('My son, listen to your father's instruction, do not forsake your mother's teaching') can be expanded in numerous ways to produce attractive variations and emphases. This device also has sets of words which often appear in the same order in the two halves of the line (e.g. 'earth: dust', 'to eat: to drink'). Rhyme is rare, stress patterns define the lines, 2+2 or 3+3 being common, 3+4, 4+4, 5+5 also occurring, while 3+2 is found especially, but not exclusively, in laments (see Lamentations). The skill of the poets in manipulating these forms gives rise to continuing analysis; although they are frozen on paper for modern readers, like the Sumerian and Akkadian, they were almost all originally written for lively recitation or singing.                                            JAB/ARM

J.A. BLACK, *Reading Sumerian Poetry* (London 1998).
D.O. EDZARD and G. WILHELM, 'Metrik', *Reallexikon der Assyriologie* 8 (Berlin/New York 1993) 148–50.
W.G.E. WATSON, *Classical Hebrew Poetry* (Sheffield 1995).
M.L. WEST, 'Akkadian Poetry: Metre and Performance', *Iraq* 59 (1997) 175–87.

**Pottery**  The term 'pottery' normally refers to vessels made from fired clay, i.e. ceramic. Other fired-clay objects, such as *figurines, are generally termed 'terracottas'. Fragments of broken pottery, called sherds, are virtually indestructible and are found scattered in huge quantities over most ancient sites in the Near East. As a result, pottery is probably the most useful artefact for the archaeologist and a great deal of information can be derived from it. Changing vessel forms, decoration, techniques of manufacture and fabrics allow different pottery types to be readily distinguished and are usually the archaeologist's prime evidence for *dating; pottery can also be a useful guide to *trade, and economic, technological and sometimes ethnic change. Recognition of the usefulness of pottery for *archaeology was pioneered at Tell el-*Hesi in 1890 by *Petrie, who first suggested sequences of pottery types through time and the division of pottery into typological groups.

The world's earliest known pottery, from Japan, dates to the eleventh millennium BC. Pottery seems to have been independently invented in the Near East by about 7000 BC. The earliest fired vessels come from *Ganj Dareh, made by hand using slab construction and lightly fired. Some unfired vessels, perhaps earlier, come from Chogha Mish in *Iran. It is possible that the idea of firing pottery developed from the practice of firing limestone paste to make vessels and burnished floors. The main technological advances in pottery manufacture were the building of efficient kilns, the potter's wheel and the invention of glazes. However, throughout history 'primitive' and 'sophisticated' methods of pottery manufacture coexisted, and there is no evidence of unilateral progression.

The first kilns would have been simple fires with the pottery covered with brush, straw or other fuel. The earliest known built kiln, at *Yarim Tepe, dates to about 6000 BC and has a separate combustion chamber sunk into the ground. The so-called 'slow' potter's wheel, essentially a turntable rotated by hand, was in use in *Mesopotamia probably by 4000 BC, and may have been connected with craft specialization and mass-production for a market rather than for domestic consumption. The 'fast' potter's wheel, which uses centrifugal force to 'throw' pottery – and requires preparation of quite different, plastic clay – was in use well before 2000 BC in

Bowl of 'Ninevite 5' painted ware, from Nineveh, c.3000 BC. WA 1932-12-12, 25.

Pottery vessel with incised decoration of 'Ninevite 5' type found across northern Mesopotamia in the first half of the third millennium BC. From Nineveh. WA 1932-12-12, 38.

Mesopotamia and from about 2000 BC in the *Levant. The first glazes on pottery appear at *Alalakh level VI, probably dating about 1600 BC, and may have spread from there to Mesopotamia, known particularly from *Nuzi.

Pottery was decorated with incised lines, applied clay, burnish, slip or paint from earliest times. There is a remarkable sequence of distinctive painted wares in Mesopotamia in the *Hassuna, *Samarra, *Halaf and *Ubaid periods, followed by largely undecorated and standardized mass-produced forms in the later historic periods. The earliest painted pottery was monochrome, but by the Halaf period at least three colours could be produced. The most common paint in all regions was formed from a combination of iron oxide with other minerals.

Textual evidence from Mesopotamia indicates that potters' quarters were situated away from *towns, and there is reference to 'villages' of potters (see Craftsmen). The *Ur III archives mention groups of between two and ten potters working under a supervisor. The best example of an excavated potters' quarter is from Sarepta in *Lebanon, dating to the Late Bronze and Iron Ages, and consisting of a main work area, a drying area and the kilns. It is possible that a roof or awning protected each potter. Although evidence is inconclusive, it is generally supposed that hand-made pottery was made by *women, while wheel-made pottery, more suitable for mass-production, was made by men.

Pottery occasionally appears allegorically in Mesopotamian texts. In some *creation myths, a deity moulds man by hand from a lump of clay, perhaps mixed with the blood of a slain *god. Similarly, 'to return to the original clay' was a euphemism for *death. Broken pots and sherds were used as literary images of shattering and abandonment.                                                                     PB

R. AMIRAN, *Ancient Pottery of the Holy Land* (New Brunswick 1970).

G.A. LONDON *et al.*, 'Ceramics', *The Oxford Encyclopedia of Archaeology in the Near East* 1, ed. E.M. Meyers (New York 1997) 450–79.

F.R. MATSON, 'Potters and Pottery in the Ancient Near East', *Civilizations of the Ancient Near East*, ed. J.M. Sasson (New York 1995) 1553–65.

P.R.S. MOOREY, *Ancient Mesopotamian Materials and Industries: The Archaeological Evidence* (Oxford 1994) 141–63.

**Prayers:** see Hymns and prayers

**Prehistory** This term describes that period of the human past before the appearance of *writing and texts. In the Near East this embraces the Lower *Palaeolithic to the Late *Chalcolithic, c.1.5 million years bp ('before present') to c.3400 BC. The term 'proto-history' is sometimes applied to the Early Bronze Age during the third millennium BC, because the earliest texts are limited in scope and geographical distribution, particularly in areas like the *Levant or *Anatolia which receive only passing and occasional mention in *Mesopotamian and *Egyptian texts, or where texts are restricted to few sites, like *Ebla, late in the period. Prehistory is not, therefore, abruptly and clearly demarcated from 'historical' periods.

The human past has to be studied by *archaeology alone in the absence of written records. Material culture and environmental evidence of past human behaviour and changing climate frequently do not relate to aspects of human behaviour recorded in texts and, therefore, he study of human behaviour in prehistory is far from simply the study of human history without texts.

Prehistory has been divided up into broad blocks of time mainly by reference to dominant technologies and economic practices. Thus in the Palaeolithic subsistence was derived from *hunting and gathering, and *stone *tools represent the main surviving form of material culture. In the *Neolithic *farming develops and *pottery is introduced. In the Chalcolithic *copper use becomes common, but the terms are applied only loosely. Partly because of this a more regional/geographical classification scheme has been employed so that sites with similar material culture, stone tools, pottery, architecture and decorative items are grouped together as 'cultures' with distinct spatial and chronological dimensions e.g. *Hassuna, *Halaf and *Samarra in Mesopotamia, *Natufian and *Ghassulian in the Levant. The significance of the existence, and sometimes even the existence itself, of such units of shared material culture is a major matter of debate in prehistoric studies. DB

**Priest, priestess** In almost the earliest written documents from *Mesopotamia are found lists of the titles of officials, including various classes of priest. Some of these are *administrative functionaries of the *temple bureaucracy and others are *religious specialists dealing with particular areas of the cult. Later records make it clear that a complex hierarchy of clergy was attached to temples, ranging from 'high priests' or 'high priestesses' down to courtyard sweepers. It is not clear whether there were fixed distinctions between sacerdotal clergy and administrative clergy: one particular type of priest is called 'anointed'; others are 'enterers of the temple', suggesting that certain areas of the shrines had restricted access. Generally speaking, female clergy were more common in the service of female deities, but a notable exception was the *en* (*Akkadian *entu*), the chaste high priestess in the temples of some gods in the *Sumerian and Old *Babylonian periods, notably that of the moon-god Nanna-Suen at *Ur – where the office was revived by *Nabonidus in Neo-Babylonian times. Sometimes the office was held, for partly political reasons, by a daughter of the *king.

Among other priestesses were some who lived secluded lives in a residence within the temple (although they could own property and engage in business), such as the *nadītu* priestesses of the sun god *Shamash at *Sippar and, by contrast, others who may have been involved in *ritual *prostitution. The priestly classes included *magicians specializing in *medical and magical rites to

An Assyrian cylinder seal has a priest dressed in a fish-skin cloak, and a worshipper by an altar, with the stylized tree and winged disk between them. Eighth century BC. WA 104499.

ensure protection from *demons, disease and sorcery; diviners specializing in extispicy (see Omens and divination); priests expert in purification rituals; *dream interpreters; and singers and instrumental musicians (see Songs; Music), cooks, slaughterers and brewers, as well as several categories of administrators.

Priests and priestesses may have entered the clergy through dedication. They were probably distinguished by their priestly dress, especially by their hats, or (in some cases) by being shaven-headed, or shaven apart from a forelock, or by their nudity. The titles and functions of the priests varied, of course, from one period to another and in different places.

Little is known of the hierarchy and duties of priests and priestesses in the *Levant, but they will have paralleled the Mesopotamian in many ways. At *Emar there was a lengthy rite for installing a high priestess and at *Ugarit a priestly official copied some of the mythological texts.

Elaborate instructions for the consecration and conduct of *Israelite priests, all drawn from the tribe of Levi, are given in Exodus to Deuteronomy in the *Bible. Their age is disputed, but they are comparable in many ways with those from other texts of the Late Bronze Age (e.g. Emar), perhaps stricter and without priestesses. The *king had no priestly role, the high priest taking the lead. Priests, alone, officiated in the Temple, but as Israel was, in theory, 'the people of *Yahweh', their duties covered many other aspects of life, such as determining guilt in cases of *adultery and certifying recovery from disease. Priestly families had designated properties as well as income from offerings. JAB/ARM

D. CHARPIN, *Le clergé d'Ur au siècle d'Hammurabi* (Paris 1986).
A. CODY, *A History of the Old Testament Priesthood* (Rome 1969).
D. FLEMING, 'Installation Ritual for a High Priestess', *The Context of Scripture* 1, eds W.W. Hallo and K.L. Younger (Leiden 1997) 427-31.
G.J.P. McEWAN, *Priest and Temple in Hellenistic Babylonia* (Wiesbaden 1981).

J. RENGER, 'Untersuchungen zum Priestertum der altbabylonischen Zeit', *Zeitschrift für Assyriologie* 58 (1967) 110–88 and 59 (1969) 104–230.

**Property ownership and inheritance** Defensive walls around early settlements (e.g. *Jericho, Tell es-*Sawwan) defined their *boundaries and prevented free entry to the property. Delineating and protecting land or securing goods became essential concerns wherever groups of people mixed, resulting in the use of *seals and, early in the history of *writing, of formal documents. In *Babylonia *temples owned much land in the fourth and third millennia BC, and the *kings of *Akkad granted land in return for service. *Shulgi put the temples under local governors so that their surpluses reverted to the crown, but there were other landowners, too, and some land was bought and sold. Deeds carefully list all the parties who had an interest in the property, to avoid disputes later. In the second millennium BC more land was privately owned and there are numerous cases of property transfer between individuals, by sale, by exchange or by bequest. There was a widespread concept of *family land which should not be alienated, although it is uncertain how extensively the rule held. At *Nuzi and other places, creditors had themselves *adopted by their debtors so that they could be repaid by inheriting some of the estate, precisely specified in the adoption deeds. Wills show the patrimony being divided, perhaps by lot, the eldest son receiving a double share, sometimes with the paternal *gods. After a property had been divided in this way, legatees might make exchanges or sales between themselves to produce viable holdings. A childless man might adopt an orphan or a *slave to be his heir, to continue his line and to perform the regular rites for his spirit. In ancient *Israel family land could not be sold (cf. the case of Naboth, 1 Kings 21) and when a man died childless, his brother was required to marry his widow, the first son born becoming the dead man's heir ('Levirate marriage'). In *Mesopotamian society many people did not have land of their own, working as tenants for the wealthy or, more often, for the king in return for payment or for some form of feudal service, in the army or corvée work. Some were tied to the land and sold with it. Lawgivers claimed to protect such people from oppression, and *Hammurabi's *letters show him ensuring that tenants wrongly evicted were restored. Such tenancies could be bequeathed to successive generations.　　　　ARM

R. WESTBROOK, *Property and the Family in Biblical Law* (Sheffield 1991).

**Prophecies and oracles** The *gods might reveal their will through any phenomena, so unusual or abnormal speech might convey a divine message. Oracles given through *dreams or *omens are reported in the third millennium BC (e.g. *Gudea), but it is early in the second millennium BC that prophetic speech is first recorded and some have suspected that it was introduced by the *Amorites. The *Mari *archives contain numerous accounts of people speaking or hearing oracles, usually in shrines. Oracular speech might be induced or uttered extempore, sometimes in a trance. When they seemed to concern state affairs, oracles would be reported in *writing to the *king, sometimes with the dispatch of a piece of the speaker's *clothing to serve as a guarantee of, or be subject to a test for, authenticity. The trustworthiness of an oracle was a basic question which only time could answer, and keeping written records was the best means of checking. The shrine of *Ishtar at Arbela was a major source of oracles for the kings of *Assyria. Groups of oracles were collected on large tablets for preservation, the individual ones being sent on small tablets. They vary from one or two to thirty or more lines, all concerning the king's welfare and reassuring him. Beside impromptu oracles, the gods, principally *Shamash and *Adad, were often asked to answer questions on royal policy or personal conduct; a long series survives, put by *Esarhaddon and *Ashurbanipal, many involving military strategy. *Rituals to encourage the gods to respond are known from Old Babylonian and later times.

The *Hittite 'Plague Prayers' of Mursilis II refer to inspired speakers, and the Egyptian 'Story of Wenamon' notes that his mission to *Byblos was approved by ecstatic utterance there. In the *Levant two *Iron Age inscriptions relate to this subject. At Tell *Deir Alla a text written on a plastered wall late in the ninth century BC recounts visions of future catastrophes which the gods gave to the seer Balaam son of Beor, and the Aramaic stela of Zakkur of *Hamath, about 800 BC, refers to guidance the god Baal-Shamayn gave to him through seers, assuring him of victory. Oracles and prophecies were the main ways of learning the divine will in *Israel and Judah according to the *Bible. A seer could be asked for help in finding a lost donkey or to advise on whether or not a king should go to war, as in other cultures. Israel's prophets differ from their contemporaries in the length and ethical content of their messages, their independence of, and frequent opposition to, the kings and their constant denunciation of anyone failing to keep the *covenant made at *Sinai. The prophetic books of the Bible, many containing magnificent *poetry, are subject to continuous study and interpretation.　　　　ARM

M. DE J. ELLIS, 'Observations on Mesopotamian Oracles and Prophetic Texts: Literary and Historiographic Considerations', *Journal of Cuneiform Studies* 41 (1989) 127–86.

H.B. HUFFMON, 'Prophecy: Ancient Near Eastern Prophecy', *Anchor Bible Dictionary* 5, ed. D.N. Freedman (New York 1992) 477–82.

A. MALAMAT, *Mari and the Early Israelite Experience* (Oxford 1984) 70–121.

S. PARPOLA, *Assyrian Prophecies* (Helsinki 1997).

I. STARR, *Queries to the Sungod* (Helsinki 1990).

C. WESTERMANN, *Basic Forms of Prophetic Speech* (London 1967).

**Prostitution and ritual sex** Prostitution certainly existed in ancient *Mesopotamia, and is often referred to. The prostitute Shamhat first seduces Enkidu in the *Epic of *Gilgamesh. On his deathbed, Enkidu curses her in a passage which implies that the normal places for prostitutes would be in the tavern, by the *city walls, at the crossroads and in the desert. Prostitutes are mentioned together with various groups of *women engaged in more or less *religious activities. *Inana/Ishtar was a protective *goddess of prostitutes. Possibly prostitution was organized like other female activities (such as midwifery or wet nursing) and manipulated through the *temple organization.

Numerous objects from Mesopotamia ranging in date from *prehistoric to Middle *Assyrian times depict scenes of *sexual intercourse. A distinctive type of bed with animal legs, the presence of other figures besides the lovers and, occasionally, banquets suggest that a definite *ritual, and not private intercourse, is involved. In the early second millennium BC, numerous baked clay plaques show a scene of sexual intercourse with the man entering the woman from behind while she is bending over, drinking from a vessel through a long straw.

Middle Assyrian lead *figurines depict ritual intercourse (always with the man standing and the woman resting on an *altar). Together with models of male and female human sexual organs, they were found in the temple of Ishtar at *Ashur and are associated with her cult as the goddess of physical love and prostitution. They doubtless had some amuletic property. *Babylonian incantations to help overcome sexual impotence prescribe, as part of the accompanying procedures: 'You make a figurine', to be placed at the head of the bed during intercourse. Old Babylonian period clay plaques with scenes of a sexual nature may have served such a function.

*Herodotus, writing about *Babylon in the fifth century BC, states that every woman once in her life had to go to the temple of 'Aphrodite', i.e. Ishtar, and sit there waiting until a stranger cast a coin in her lap as the price of her favours. Then she was obliged to go with him outside the temple and have intercourse, to render her duty to the goddess. The story is probably highly imaginative. The second-century AD writer Lucian describes, apparently from personal knowledge, a very similar custom in the temple of 'Aphrodite' (probably *Astarte) at *Byblos in *Lebanon.                    AG/JAB

R.D. BIGGS, ŠÀ.ZI.GA: Ancient Mesopotamian Potency Incantations (Locust Valley, NY 1967).

T. FRYMER-KENSKY, In the Wake of the Goddesses: Women, Culture and the Biblical Transformation of Pagan Myth (New York/Oxford 1992).

W.G. LAMBERT, 'Prostitution', Aussenseiter und Randgruppen: Beiträge zu einer Sozialgeschichte des Alten Orients, ed. V. Haas (Konstanz 1992) 127–57.

G. LEICK, Sex and Eroticism in Ancient Mesopotamia (London 1994).

S. MAUL, 'kurgarrû und assinnu und ihr Stand in der babylonischen Gesellschaft', Aussenseiter und Randgruppen: Beiträge zu einer Sozialgeschichte des Alten Orients, ed. V. Haas (Konstanz 1992) 159–71.

**Provincial administration** As *city-states expanded into empires, their rulers had to decide how to administer the newly conquered territories. All available options were attempted in the ancient Near East – leaving local rulers in place, replacing them with puppet *kings, or with provincial governors – and occasionally, as in the *Assyrian empire, all were in use simultaneously.

In the earliest records, *Sumerian conquerors appear to have had only nominal overlordship over local kings. *Sargon of *Akkad for the first time introduced the concept of separate administration of conquered territories, by appointing Akkadian governors supported by military garrisons in the defeated Sumerian cities. This system was refined by the Third Dynasty of *Ur into a massive centralized bureaucracy. The state was divided into over twenty core provinces which supplied *agricultural and industrial products mainly to the state *temples (the so-called bala institution), with autonomous provinces in the peripheral conquered territories, which contributed *taxes paid in livestock by the *military personnel living there. The core provinces, at least, had a dual administrative hierarchy, with a civilian governor dealing with legal (see Law) and *religious affairs, and an independent military governor. *Shulgi, the third king, introduced a system of messengers and road stations, elements in the infrastructure necessary to support an empire.

The *Hittites and *Mitannians employed quite a different three-tier structure. *Suppiluliumas I appointed his own sons as kings of Aleppo and *Carchemish, tied to him by formal *treaties. These kings in their turn had vassal kings separately subservient to them. In the same period, best documented in the *Amarna Letters, the *Egyptian empire in *Canaan left native rulers on their thrones, but imposed *oaths of allegiance and carried off hostages to Egypt (often to return them later as 'loyal' rulers), as well as deporting rebels to Nubia. Canaan was divided into three administrative districts, each under an Egyptian governor directly responsible to the pharaoh, supplemented by an array of officials. Certain areas were considered as Egyptian crown property and their harvest was stored in royal granaries to supply Egyptian military garrisons, although strictly speaking Canaan remained a distinct land and not a province of Egypt.

Probably the best organized and best documented provincial system was that of the Assyrians, who eventually opted for a hybrid package of administrative approaches. In the eighth century BC, an expanded Assyria was divided into provinces administered by governors. Peripheral tributary states remained independent, though local rulers were sometimes replaced, and occasionally Assyrian agents were posted to local courts. Assyrian provincial governors were autonomous, supplied with a *palace, court and army in a provincial capital, and the regular appointment of *eunuchs as governors was perhaps a way of ensuring the loyalty of the provinces; loyalty of subject populations was enhanced by forced *deportations to other parts of the empire. *Taxes were paid both to the king and to provincial governors. Communications were vital to the smooth running of the empire, and the governors were responsible for the maintenance of a royal *road with garrisoned way stations and a regular messenger service, and there was frequent exchange of *letters between the king and the governors. This Assyrian provincial system appears to have been taken over largely intact by the Neo-*Babylonians and *Persians.                                    PB

A.K. GRAYSON, 'Assyrian Rule of Conquered Territory in Ancient Western Asia', *Civilizations of the Ancient Near East*, ed. J.M. Sasson (New York 1995) 959–68.

M. LIVERANI (ed.), *Neo-Assyrian Geography* (Rome 1995).

J.N. POSTGATE, 'The Land of Assur and the Yoke of Assur', *World Archaeology* 23/3 (1992) 247–63.

——, 'Royal Ideology and State Administration in Sumer and Akkad', *Civilizations of the Ancient Near East*, ed. J.M. Sasson (New York 1995) 395–411.

D.B. REDFORD, *Egypt, Canaan, and Israel in Ancient Times* (Princeton 1992) 198–213.

P. STEINKELLER, 'The Administrative and Economic Organization of the Ur III State: The Core and the Periphery', *The Organization of Power: Aspects of Bureaucracy in the Ancient Near East*, eds M. Gibson and R.D. Biggs (Chicago 1987) 19–41.

**Punishment:** see Crime and punishment

# Q

**Qatna** *Cuneiform tablets found at Mishrifeh, south of *Hama near the Orontes *river in central *Syria, identify it as ancient Qatna, known from the *Mari, *Amarna and *Egyptian *hieroglyphic texts. Qatna appears to have been founded in the third millennium BC, and in the early second millennium BC formed one of the main *Amorite kingdoms in Syria. Later it was under *Mitannian control, and was destroyed in the fourteenth century BC, possibly by the *Hittites. It was resettled by *Aramaeans in the first millennium BC, becoming an important *trading centre in the Neo-*Babylonian period.

Qatna has been excavated by Robert du Mesnil du Buisson (1924–9) and from 1994 by the Syrian Department of Antiquities following clearance of the modern village from the *tell. Measuring 100 ha, the site is surrounded by walls, some standing 20 m high, incorporating a Middle Bronze Age glacis *fortification and four triple-chambered town *gates. Also dating to the second millennium BC are the *palace and the *temple of Ninegal, the goddess of Qatna whose name was originally *Sumerian. A fifteenth-century BC cuneiform *archive found in the temple is often referred to as a temple inventory; it lists items, accounts, administrative arrangements, and names of *kings and private persons, mostly *Canaanite and *Hurrian, although there were also a few economic and other texts.                          PB

J. BOTTÉRO, 'Les inventaires de Qatna', *Revue d'Assyriologie* 43 (1949) 1–41, 137–216.

——, 'Autres textes de Qatna', *Revue d'Assyriologie* 44 (1950) 105–22.

R. DU MESNIL DU BUISSON, *Le site archéologique de Michrifé-Qatna* (Paris 1935).

**Queens** The usual form of rule in the ancient Near East was monarchy, normally by men. Only rarely did *women rule in their own right as queens. The first known ruling queen is Ku-Bau (or Ku-Baba), recorded by the *Sumerian *King List as reigning one hundred years as the sole ruler of the Third Dynasty of *Kish, in the Early Dynastic period. The King List also mentions that she was a former tavern keeper. In *Anatolia, Old *Assyrian tablets from *Kanesh refer to princesses, and later *Hittite tradition records a legendary queen of Kanesh. Neo-Assyrian royal inscriptions record *Arab queens as rulers who paid tribute to Assyria, and the *Old Testament records the queen of *Sheba as ruling in her own right. Daughters of kings made *dynastic *marriages to secure alliance or loyalty in other states.

More often, queens were wives or mothers of kings and did not rule in their own right, but nevertheless could be prominent. The wife of *Zimri-Lim of *Mari was very active in the *palace and dealt with many administrative details, especially concerning *food supplies and personnel. Her counterpart at Tell al-*Rimah ran

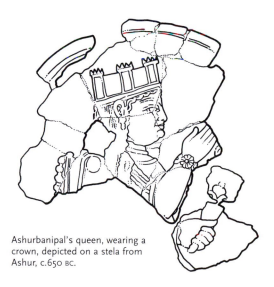

Ashurbanipal's queen, wearing a crown, depicted on a stela from Ashur, c.650 BC.

the palace *textile industry. Hittite queens may have corresponded with foreign *courts and had administrative responsibilities for *temples. Sammu-ramat (*Semiramis), the wife of *Shamshi-Adad V and mother of *Adad-nirari III, set up inscriptions and is named beside the king, her son. Naqia-Zakutu, wife of *Sennacherib, may have been instrumental in ensuring the succession of her son *Esarhaddon. She presented votive inscriptions on behalf of herself and her son, but probably exercised only the traditional prerogatives of a queen mother. Her activities may have been one of the sources for the many stories about Semiramis in Greek legend. The considerable prestige and status of mothers, wives and daughters of kings is demonstrated by the lavish burials of Assyrian queens, wives of kings, discovered at *Nimrud in 1989.

PB

J. ARZT, 'Near Eastern Royal Women', *Yale Graduate Journal of Anthropology* 5 (1995) 45–56.

L. BAYUN, 'The Legend about the Queen of Kaniš: A Historical Source?', *Journal of Ancient Civilizations* 9 (1994) 1–13.

S. DALLEY, *Mari and Karana: Two Old Babylonian Cities* (London 1984) 97–110.

A.K. GRAYSON, 'Assyria: Ashur-Dan II to Ashur-nirari V (934–745 B.C.), *Cambridge Ancient History* 3.1, 2nd ed. (Cambridge 1982) 274–5.

W.W. HALLO, *Origins: The Ancient Near Eastern Background of Some Modern Western Institutions* (Leiden 1996) 252–61.

P. MICHALOWSKI, 'Royal Women of the Ur III Period', *Journal of Cuneiform Studies* 28 (1976) 169–72, 31 (1979) 171–6, *Acta Sumerologica (Japan)* 4 (1982) 129–42.

M.-J. SEUX, 'Königtum', *Reallexikon der Assyriologie* 6 (Berlin/New York 1980–83) 159–62.

# R

## Radiocarbon dating

Radiocarbon dating is based on the fact that all organic material (i.e. from living organisms, such as *wood or *ivory) contains a radioactive isotope, Carbon 14, which after death decays at a known rate so that half of it will have disappeared after 5730 years. Measuring the proportion of Carbon 14 left in the material enables its age (i.e. the year of its death, so for a *tree the year it was cut down) to be calculated. There are two problems. One is that the dates provided by analysis have a level of uncertainty, so that the date provided is within a band of plus or minus a certain number of years, the older the sample the greater the uncertainty. For the first millennium BC in the Near East, for example, when historical dates can be related to precise reigns of *Assyrian *kings, a Carbon 14 date of plus or minus fifty years gives a band of one hundred years within which the object can be dated, which might not be very helpful for an overall chronology. The second problem is that the level of Carbon 14 in the earth's atmosphere has fluctuated over time, and it is only recently that these fluctuations have been charted in detail by comparison with tree-ring data. Raw Carbon 14 dates provided by a laboratory must be calibrated against a chart of this fluctuation to provide a date in 'real time' as opposed to an uncalibrated radiocarbon date. To distinguish between these types of dates, some archaeologists use the convention of 'BC' (capital letters) after calibrated, real-time dates, and 'bc' (small letters) after uncalibrated raw radiocarbon dates. A similar convention is used for *Palaeolithic and earlier dates, with 'BP' ('before present', calibrated) and 'bp' (uncalibrated); conventionally, a date 'before present' is the number of years which separates the tested object from AD 1950.

PB

S. BOWMAN, *Radiocarbon Dating* (London 1990).

C. RENFREW and P. BAHN, *Archaeology: Theories, Method and Practice* (London 1991) 101–48.

## Ras Shamra: see Ugarit

## Rassam, Hormuzd (1826–1910)

Born into a *Chaldaean Christian family in Mosul, Iraq, then part of the Ottoman empire, Rassam was taken on in 1846 as *Layard's assistant at *Nimrud and later *Nineveh. In 1852, after Layard's departure, the British Museum appointed him to continue excavations in *Assyria. Suspecting the remains of another *palace at Nineveh in an area allocated to the French, Rassam dug clandestinely at night and discovered the north palace of *Ashurbanipal with its lion hunt reliefs and part of the royal *library.

He was posted by the British government to southern Arabia, and later to Abyssinia to free British Jewish missionaries. He was imprisoned by King Theodore for two years until released by a British military expedition. He returned to look for *cuneiform tablets and record buildings in Assyria from 1878–82, again on behalf of the British Museum. He worked at *Babylon, *Borsippa, *Sippar, Tello, Nineveh, Nimrud, *Sheikh Hamad, *Toprakkale and *Balawat, where he discovered the *gates of *Ashurnasirpal II and *Shalmaneser III.

Rassam was fascinated by the English and their culture, and essentially turned himself into an Englishman, directing most of his work in the heat wearing a coat, waistcoat and top hat (although he was often absent and the excavations were directed by trusted overseers). He was never fully accepted into society as an authentic Englishman, though, which may partially account for the belittling of his achievements – *Rawlinson was for long credited with the discovery of the Nineveh palace – and the sustained attacks on his reputation which he was forced to defend with a libel suit. As a result, he lived the rest of his life in Brighton, England, in obscurity and published very little of his discoveries.

PB

Hormuzd Rassam, a native of Mosul, began his career as Layard's assistant and developed a great love for England. Portraits in native costume and in English dress, probably by F.C. Cooper, about 1851.

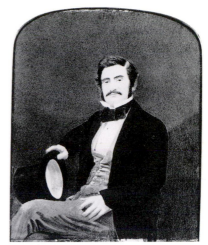

S. LLOYD, *Foundations in the Dust: The Story of Mesopotamian Exploration*, rev. ed. (London 1980) 144–57.

T.G. PINCHES, 'Rassam, Hormuzd', *Dictionary of National Biography 1901–1911* (London 1927) 158–61.

H. RASSAM, *Asshur and the Land of Nimrod* (New York 1897).

J. READE, 'Hormuzd Rassam and his Discoveries', *Iraq* 55 (1993) 39–62.

Sir Henry Creswicke Rawlinson, by Sir Leslie Ward ('Spy'), 1873 (by courtesy of the National Portrait Gallery, London, 4737).

**Rawlinson, Henry Creswicke (1810–95)** One of the decipherers of *cuneiform, Rawlinson was born in Oxfordshire, England. He joined the East India Company, learned Oriental languages and was posted to Kurdistan where he attempted to decipher Darius I's trilingual cuneiform inscription on the Great Rock of Bisitun. He copied the inscription from 1835 to 1837, at first unaided, but later with ropes and ladders to read the remoter panels. He acquired a squeeze (an impression of the engraved signs on large sheets of damp paper) of the *Babylonian inscription only in 1847 with the help of a 'wild' Kurdish boy; fifty years later this squeeze was partly eaten by mice in the British Museum.

The clue to Rawlinson's decipherment of the *Persian version were the Persian royal names 'Darius' and 'Xerxes' and their titles, which gave him enough phonetic values to identify other proper names. He gave papers on his translation to the Royal Asiatic Society in 1837 and 1839, which are his claim to be the 'father of cuneiform', although today it is recognized that Edward Hincks also contributed substantially to the decipherment.

Later, while British Consul in Baghdad from 1843, he worked on the cuneiform tablets from *Layard's excavations at *Nimrud and *Nineveh, particularly pointing out the importance of *Ashurbanipal's *library from Nineveh. In 1853 he excavated the *ziggurat of *Borsippa and discovered commemorative cylinders of *Nebuchadnezzar II.                    PB

M.T. LARSEN, *The Conquest of Assyria: Excavations in an Antique Land 1840–1860* (London 1994).

S. LLOYD, *Foundations in the Dust: The Story of Mesopotamian Exploration*, 2nd ed. (London 1980).

G. RAWLINSON, *Memoir of Major-General Sir Henry Creswicke Rawlinson* (London 1898).

H.C. RAWLINSON, *The Persian Cuneiform Inscription at Behistun Decyphered and Translated* (London 1846).

The impression of a chalcedony cylinder seal depicts a worshipper in a shrine before an armed god standing on a bull. Two scorpion-men stand guard. Height 3.3 cm. Asssyrian, eighth to seventh century BC. WA 89364.

**Reisner, George Andrew (1867–1942)** Born in Indianapolis, George Reisner studied *Semitic history and *languages before becoming drawn to ancient Egypt. For most of his life he excavated in Egypt and the Sudan, particularly at Giza, setting new standards in excavation and recording, being one of the first to use photographs and section drawings systematically.

It was this attention to detail that Reisner brought to *Samaria, which he excavated 1908–10, discovering the important Samaria *ostraca. He had a clear understanding of the structure of a *tell, realizing the importance of careful recognition and separation of layers of debris in order to date structures and associated objects correctly, although it is unclear how far he actually put this theory into practice at the complex tell of Samaria. Nevertheless, his publication is widely regarded as a watershed in the development of field *archaeology in Palestine, anticipating the methods of *Kenyon. Unfortunately, Reisner did not remain to develop his methodology, but returned to Egypt, and most of his contemporaries in *Palestine continued to use more archaic methods.     PB

P.R.S. MOOREY, *A Century of Biblical Archaeology* (Cambridge 1991) 35–6.

P.V. PODZORSKI, 'Reisner, George Andrew', *The Oxford Encyclopedia of Archaeology in the Near East* 4, ed. E.M. Meyers (New York 1997) 421.

G.A. REISNER, *Israelite Ostraca from Samaria* (Boston, undated).

G.A. REISNER, C.S. FISHER and D.G. LYON, *Harvard Excavations at Samaria, 1908–1910* (Cambridge, MA 1924).

**Religion** The term 'religion' has a very broad range of meaning, centring on the belief in one or more superhuman controlling powers, especially *gods entitled to obedience and worship. But *ritual practice in many cases may be more ancient and enduring than consciously articulated beliefs. Archaeological finds from the earliest times provide evidence of behaviour and artefacts which it is difficult to explain as purely pragmatic or exclusively decorative, and which are generally taken as proof of religious practice, itself implying religious belief. The organized forms of religion develop as societies themselves become more populous and need administrative control; the earliest evidence for it is probably to be found in *temple architecture, and in similar practices repeated at discrete locations.

With the advent of *writing, a vast amount of explicit and detailed information is available for the reconstruction of religious practices and beliefs, both indirectly and from descriptions of ritual procedures. Written 'rituals' are amply documented both from *Mesopotamia, where they were prepared for *priestly practitioners, and from the *Hittite empire, whose rulers personally participated in numerous local rituals of the heterogeneous peoples under their rule. By contrast, *Ugaritic religion is known mainly from *myths, which it is hypothesized were performed as part of rituals. Israelite religion is extensively documented in the *Bible, which gives extensive prescriptions for orthodox worship of one God (*Yahweh). Personal and collective piety is exemplified in the Psalms. Israel's *prophets denounced the people for the sort of superstition and syncretism which was common throughout the ancient Near East and is represented by female *figurines in pottery ubiquitous on Late Bronze and *Iron Age sites.

Throughout its history, religion in Mesopotamia is characterized by two opposing trends: the proliferation of many local cults and deities at a level at least as small as the *village and possibly in some cases individual to particular people; and the syncretism of these to form urban and, later, national pantheons, *festivals and cult practices (see Magic). Scholarly dispute over the dating of the books of the Bible results in widely differing views about the development of Israel's religion. The texts as they stand present a pristine monotheism associated with the Late Bronze Age leader Moses then declining as Israel mixed with the *Canaanites, the prophets urging reformation. Commonly today it is supposed that the Israelites were polytheistic, with Yahweh as their national God, the monotheistic faith developing from the eighth century BC onwards, worship of other deities being suppressed in Judah by Hezekiah about 700 BC and Josiah about 620 BC.     JAB/ARM

J.A. BLACK and A.R. GREEN, *Gods, Demons and Symbols of Ancient Mesopotamia: An Illustrated Dictionary*, 2nd ed. (London 1998).

E. DHORME, *Les religions de Babylonie et d'Assyrie* (Paris 1948).

O.R. GURNEY, *Some Aspects of Hittite Religion* (Oxford 1977).

W. HEIMPEL, 'Mythologie', *Reallexikon der Assyriologie* 8 (Berlin/New York 1997) 537–64.

W.G. LAMBERT, 'Ancient Mesopotamian Gods: Superstition, Philosophy, Theology', *Revue de l'Histoire des Religions* 207 (1990) 115–30.

**Rephaim** The word in this form occurs in the *Bible; its likely *Ugaritic counterpart is usually vocalized as Rapi'uma. The etymology is not clear but contexts suggest that it denotes supernatural beings connected with *death. They are the subject of several fragmentary compositions and incantations from Ugarit. The term may refer to shades and in some texts more specifically to the spirits of dead *kings whom the new king addresses in order to obtain their blessing for his new *administration.

In the *Old Testament the verb *rp'* refers to healing and the renewal of *fertility. Rephaim are sometimes referred to as having a *bird shape, an image also current in *Mesopotamia.                                              GL

M. DIJKSTRA, 'The Legend of Danel and the Rephaim', *Ugarit-Forschungen* 20 (1988) 35–51.

J.N. FORD, 'The Living Rephaim of Ugarit: Quick or Defunct?', *Ugarit-Forschungen* 24 (1992) 73–101.

T.J. LEWIS, 'Towards a Literary Translation of the Rapiuma Texts', *Ugarit, Religion and Culture*, eds W.G.E. Wyatt and J.B. Lloyd (Münster 1996) 115–49.

W.T. PITARD, 'A New Edition of the Rapi'uma Texts KTU 1.20–22', *Bulletin of the American Schools of Oriental Research* 285 (1992) 33–77.

K. SPRONK, *Beatific Afterlife* (Neukirchen/Vluyn 1986).

**Reshep** The etymology of this name reveals a connection with fire. He was associated with the sun and, like other solar deities, the *underworld. He was worshipped in *Syria from the third millennium BC. In *Ugarit he received regular offerings and often featured in personal names although he is not prominent in the *myths, where *Mot plays a much more important role. He remained a much invoked deity in the *Aramaic states of the first millennium BC and was also popular with *Phoenicians. In *Mesopotamia he was identified with *Nergal.

Reshep is an underworld deity and is made responsible for epidemics and fevers. As such he also protects from contagious *diseases and various forms of evil. In the *Old Testament he does not appear as a divine figure but the word stands metaphorically as a result of *Yahweh's destructive powers in parallel to hunger and pestilence.                                              GL

D. CONRAD, 'Der Gott Reshef', *Zeitschrift für alttestamentliche Wissenschaft* 83 (1971) 157–83.

W.J. FULCO, 'The Canaanite God Reshep', *American Oriental Society Essays* 8 (1976) 1–32.

P. XELLA, 'D'Ugarit à la Phénicie: sur les traces des Rashap, Horon, Eshmun', *Welt des Orients* 19 (1988) 45–65.

**Rich, Claudius James (1787–1820)** Rich was a British business agent, traveller, writer and amateur historian and archaeologist. Born in Dijon, he was brought up in Bristol. From an early age demonstrating an uncommon capacity for Oriental *languages, in 1803 he joined the East India Company, taking up a post in Bombay in 1807. The following year he married the eldest daughter of the Bombay governor, and at the age of twenty-one was appointed Baghdad Resident of the East

Oil painting of Claudius James Rich by Thomas Phillips, RA. WA 188197.

India Company. In this post, which he held until shortly before his death, he showed a flair for administration and promoting British interests. While in Baghdad, he played host to several British explorers, and used much of his leisure time assembling historical materials and visiting the sites of ancient *Mesopotamian *cities, sketching, drawing site plans and collecting. His collections of antiquities and manuscripts were after his death purchased by the British Museum and became the foundation not only of its Mesopotamian collections but of Mesopotamian studies in Britain. Most of his researches were originally published in the Viennese journal *Mines d'Orient*, including his famous accounts of the remains of *Babylon. During periods of prolonged ill-health, he was given leave to undertake extended travel, which he did in 1813–14 and 1820. On the latter occasion he travelled through northern Mesopotamia and Kurdistan, afterwards writing a stimulating travelogue which is also the first nineteenth-century geographical and archaeological account of the region. While visiting Shiraz, he died of cholera, aged thirty-three.                                              AG

S. LANE-POOLE, 'Rich, Claudius James', *The Dictionary of National Biography* 16 (Oxford/London, not dated (reprinted 1921–2)) 996–7.

C.J. RICH, *Memoir on the Ruins of Babylon* (London 1815).

——, *Second Memoir on Babylon* (London 1818).

——, *Narrative of a Residence in Koordistan, and on the Site of Nineveh* (London 1836).

——, *Narrative of a Journey to the Site of Babylon in 1811* (London 1839).

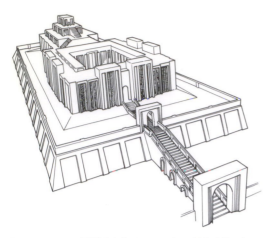

Reconstruction of Old Babylonian temple at Tell al-Rimah (after S. Dalley, *Mari and Karana: Two Old Babylonian Cities* (London 1984) fig. 36).

**Rimah, (Tell al-)**  Located in northern Iraq, 65 km west of *Nineveh, this was a small *trading *city which flourished in the late third and second millennia BC, also known from the *Mari texts. Its name in the Old *Babylonian period is generally thought to have been Karana, but it is possible that it was Qattara, the other major city of its kingdom. The site was described by *Layard (1850), surveyed by *Lloyd (1938) and excavated by David Oates (1964–71).

Though occupied already in *prehistoric times, those levels were not excavated, and the most impressive remains are of the walled city of the second millennium BC, particularly the *temple and the *palace dating to the Old Babylonian period. The temple, in the central and highest part of the city, was built on two terraces and approached through a courtyard via a monumental stairway. On its western side was a *ziggurat. The exterior was decorated with mudbrick columns imitating palm *tree trunks. The temple was perhaps dedicated to *Adad or to the goddess Geshtinanna, and built by *Shamshi-Adad I.

Only a small part of the contemporary palace was excavated, including a throne room with a dais. That building was demolished and replaced with a new one, which included *cuneiform tablets contemporary with *Zimri-Lim of Mari, and a group of two hundred *letters and *administrative records concerning *Queen Iltani, wife of the ruler Aqba-hammu, probably a vassal of *Hammurabi of *Babylon; part of a royal *wine *archive was also found.

The site continued to be occupied throughout the rest of the second millennium BC, with temples, administrative buildings and *houses excavated, and business records of the Middle *Assyrian period relating to *tin and barley. It was then completely abandoned, partly resettled in the Neo-Assyrian period, renamed Zamahe, repopulated probably with deportees (see Deportation), and a new temple erected to Adad. Inside the temple was

a stela of *Adad-nirari III recording a campaign against *Syria, *Phoenicia and *Israel and receipt of tribute.   PB

S. DALLEY, 'Karana', *Reallexikon der Assyriologie* 5 (Berlin/New York 1980) 125–46.

——, *Mari and Karana: Two Old Babylonian Cities* (London 1984).

——, 'Rimah, Tell er', *The Oxford Encyclopedia of Archaeology in the Near East* 4, ed. E.M. Meyers (New York 1997) 428–30.

S. DALLEY, C.B.F. WALKER and J.D. HAWKINS, *The Old Babylonian Tablets from Tell al Rimah* (London 1976).

C. POSTGATE, D. OATES and J. OATES, *The Excavation at Tell al Rimah: The Pottery* (Warminster 1998).

**Ritual**  Prescribed orders of performing religious or solemn observance or acts are an element of all *religions. In the ancient Near East, such details were often written down, whether to record practice for historical purposes or for training practitioners. *Mesopotamian religious rituals may involve the performance of religious *songs or *music, the reciting of *prayers or poems, and a great variety of symbolic acts whose significance is sometimes difficult to elucidate but which was doubtless validated by long practice. Numerous *magical rituals are described in detail, some in the context of *medical practices. Typically, magical rituals involve the reciting of incantations, sometimes in a fixed sequence, and the performance of sympathetic magical actions, for example melting an image of the witch or sorcerer, peeling an onion or unravelling matting into a fire (to 'undo' sins). So-called *namburbû* rituals are intended to undo or avert in advance the effect of evil detected by *divination, and may consist of enclosure rites (where the location of the ritual is separated off from the world outside), purification rites (for the patient or beneficiary), offerings to the *gods and the deified River (which will carry away

A priest introduces King Nabû-apla-iddina of Babylon (c.870 BC) to the sun-god Shamash whose emblem stands on a table before him. The scene heads a stone tablet recording the restoration of the god's statue and the endowment of his temple in Sippar. Width 17.75 cm. WA 91000.

the waste matter), apotropaic rites (involving symbolic or sympathetic destruction or driving away of the evil) and final rites (to restore the patient to the everyday world).

*Hittite rituals exhibit great variety, many of them being local to particular parts of the country and of great antiquity. *Cuneiform tablets from *Emar of the thirteenth century BC include descriptive rituals detailed in somewhat the same way as *Israelite rituals in the *Bible. At *Ugarit, more than eighty tablets contain brief rituals, mostly concerning the *king and listing *sacrifices. All these texts aimed to ensure that human beings could be acceptable to the various deities, often through ceremonial purification and sacrifices. *Cylinder and *stamp seals depict various scenes of worship and ritual.          JAB/ARM

G. BECKMAN, *Hittite Birth Rituals* (Wiesbaden 1983).
J. BOTTÉRO, *Mythes et rites de Babylone* (Paris 1985).
D. FLEMING, 'Rituals, *The Context of Scripture* 1, eds W.W. Hallo and K.L. Younger (Leiden 1997) 431-43.
B. MENZEL, *Assyrische Tempel* (Rome 1981).
J. QUAEGEBEUR (ed.), *Ritual and Sacrifice in the Ancient Near East* (Leuven 1993).
E. REINER, *Šurpu* (Graz 1958).
J.-M. de TARRAGON, 'Les rituels', *Textes Ougaritiques 2: Textes religieux, rituels, correspondance* (Paris 1989) 127-238.

**River ordeal**  In *Mesopotamia from the Old *Babylonian period on, if the sworn testimony by the parties involved in a legal dispute conflicted (see Law), or if for some reason the case was not solvable by rational means, it was usual to refer the decision to the river-*god: in other words to decide by means of a river ordeal. This solemn expedient was in effect a form of *divination, and the judgement would then be declared in the name of Id (the 'Divine River'), or Shazi (son of the 'Divine River'), or *Ea (Enki).

It seems likely that only one of the litigants, selected by lot, underwent the ordeal. He had to submerge himself in the river at a special location in the presence of the authorities, and possibly to swim a certain distance. If he came out safe, he was cleared. If he was overcome by the current and sank, he was guilty and had to return to court for sentencing (fine or execution). It was not intended that he should drown.

The usual name for the river ordeal was *huršan* (*Sumerian *id lu rugu*). Sometimes the river of the ordeal was identified with a specific (deified) river, such as the Daban or Diyala (both lying north-east of *Babylonia) or Hubur (possibly identical with the Habur, an affluent of the upper Euphrates). All these rivers lie outside Babylonia, and it is possible that the river of the ordeal in these cases is connected with the river of the *underworld, perhaps thought to lie at a distant extremity of the known world. Otherwise the river is called the (deified) River; as such it also features in *magical incantations.          JAB

T. FRYMER-KENSKY, *The Judicial Ordeal in the Ancient Near East* (University Microfilms International, Philadelphia, PA 1977).
O.R. GURNEY, *The Middle Babylonian Legal and Economic Texts from Ur* (London 1983) 10–12.

**Rivers**  It would be difficult to exaggerate the importance of rivers in the historical-cultural development of the ancient Near East. The people who lived in the arid or semi-arid regions of the Near East learned how to maximize available resources, including *water; this is evident in the variety of installations that were built to collect, conserve and transport water to where it was needed. Rivers provided an almost endless supply of water, and some of the first steps in the development of urban culture were made at sites along the courses of the Nile and the Tigris and Euphrates, and some tributaries of the latter.

In the northern reaches of the Euphrates, farmers could harvest crops watered by rainfall alone. Further south, where rainfall was significantly less, the alluvial plain that separated the Tigris and Euphrates was occupied, irrigated and brought under cultivation during the fifth and fourth millennia BC. With their centralized governments and large-scale work forces, the *city-states of *Mesopotamia built networks of *irrigation canals and raised wheat and barley where it would not have grown otherwise. During their early summer floods, the Tigris and Euphrates flowed with such volume that tender crops planted near the banks had to be protected with dikes that forced excess water into reservoirs for summertime irrigation.

The twin rivers of Mesopotamia shifted their courses through the centuries, and settlement patterns reflect this movement. Irrigation was practised so successfully that the farmers eventually had to face the problems caused by soil salinization. Remote sensing has enabled scholars to trace the amazing web of water channels. The construction and maintenance of these canals is well documented in *Sumerian texts and the *Mari tablets.

The Tigris and Euphrates flow from the mountains of eastern *Anatolia, which receive a large amount of annual rainfall and snow. These great rivers follow circuitous – and sometimes parallel – beds until they merge and empty into the Persian Gulf. In antiquity, the Gulf extended further north and these rivers entered the sea separately. In addition to providing an abundance of water for irrigation, the Tigris and Euphrates were important avenues of *travel. River craft hauled supplies of *food, *timber, building *stone, and other products and were especially useful for the southerly route. The land route was taken for the return north, or *boats could be pulled by men or oxen along the bank. Sometimes rivers needed to be crossed, and *Assyrian reliefs show soldiers swimming across with the help of inflated animal skins.

Major tributaries of the Euphrates were the *Balikh and the *Khabur, and important tributaries of the Tigris were the Upper Zab, Lower Zab, Adhain and Diyala. The Kerkha and Karun rivers merge and flow into the Persian Gulf from the *Zagros mountains. The Halys river drained the highlands of the *Hittite kingdom, and the Orontes and Litani drain much of western *Syria and *Lebanon, respectively. The ancient rivers of *Damascus, the Abana (modern Barada) and Pharpar, rise in the Anti-Lebanon range; the Jordan river's tributaries also flow from the melting snows of the southern Anti-Lebanon. As it makes its way southward, the Jordan is joined by four major tributaries on the east – Yarmuk, Jabbok (Zarqa), Arnon (Mujib) and Zered (Hasa). All of these rivers are linked with major cities, city-states or empires, and some served as *boundaries between ancient kingdoms.    GLM

C.J. EYRE, 'Agricultural Cycle, Farming, and Water Management in the Ancient Near East', *Civilizations of the Ancient Near East*, ed. J.M. Sasson (New York 1995) 175–89.

D. HILLEL, *Rivers of Eden: The Struggle for Water and the Quest for Peace in the Middle East* (New York 1994).

M.G. IONIDES, *The Regime of the Rivers Euphrates and Tigris* (London 1937).

M.B. ROWTON, *The Role of Watercourses in the Growth of Mesopotamian Civilization* (Neukirchen/Vluyn 1969).

F. STOLZ, 'River', *Dictionary of Deities and Demons in the Bible*, eds K. van der Toorn, B. Becking and P.W. van der Horst (Leiden 1995) 1333–8.

J.M. WAGSTAFF, *The Evolution of Middle Eastern Landscapes: An Outline to A.D. 1840* (London 1985).

**Roads**   In the ancient Near East, people *travelled and transported goods by *water or overland routes. Land travel and transport was accomplished on foot, on the backs of *animals (donkeys, *horses, mules and *camels) or by means of wheeled vehicles. Wheeled transportation was in common use by the third millennium BC, and this created a greater demand for road construction and maintenance. Travel on roads across open stretches of countryside was tiring and often dangerous, because of bandits. Hard-packed surfaces were easy to maintain and allowed for rapid movement, until the rainy season. Most work on such early roads was simply a matter of levelling out beds and keeping them clear of obstacles. Roads

through mountains were more difficult to build and maintain. Ancient travellers and road builders typically followed the 'path of least resistance' (i.e. they avoided topographic barriers), but some routes necessarily crossed rivers. Bridges were built, perhaps as early as the second millennium BC, and travellers learned where fords and ferryboats were located. Once these ancient roads had been built and tested through time, the same itineraries were followed over the centuries, with many such routes continuing into modern times. This fact, along with written documents and locations of archaeological sites, enables scholars to discern the routes used in antiquity.

International travel was surprisingly routine in ancient times; people travelled long distances for commercial, political, *diplomatic, *military or *religious reasons. Improved roadways that facilitated such long trips were already common in the third millennium BC, in *Anatolia, *Mesopotamia and the *Levant. Because the east Mediterranean lands connected *Egypt and Anatolia and Mesopotamia, the great trunk road that ran up the Levantine coast and split into three branches at *Megiddo was a very important route. Towns that were situated at strategic crossroads became quite famous (e.g. *Hazor, *Damascus, Aleppo, *Mari, *Babylon). In fact, roads were usually named according to their major destinations (e.g. 'road to *Kish', '*Uruk road', 'road to Horonaim', 'way to the land of the *Philistines'). An important Old *Babylonian account describes an arduous round-trip from *Larsa, in Lower Mesopotamia, to *Emar, in north *Syria. Unfortunately, the purpose of this six-and-a-half-month journey on the famous 'road to Emar' is not disclosed.

The reasons for long-distance travel in antiquity were

(*below left*) Cobbled stepped street in Middle Bronze Age Jericho (courtesy of Piotr Bienkowski). (*below right*) Iron Age II road approaching Tell Jalul in Jordan (courtesy of Randall Younker/Institute of Archaeology, Andrews University).

normally spelled out in no uncertain terms. For example, *Sumerian demand for lapis lazuli had opened routes into western *Iran by the late fourth millennium BC. From the nineteenth century BC, Old *Assyrian texts offer a glimpse into private *trade (in *tin, *textiles and *copper) between *Ashur and *Kanesh, in Cappadocia; these tablets provide details on the 1200-km route followed by the donkey caravans. Because of international trade in *timber, precious *metals, *spices and a host of other products, many texts identify ancient overland routes.

Paved roads were rare, especially outside urban centres. Streets were sometimes cobbled, and processional roads in places like *Babylon, *Khorsabad and *Nineveh were laid down in ways that rivalled the later work of *Roman engineers. Even in open country, roads were maintained and recognized sufficiently to serve as *property *boundaries. Winter rains necessitated the repair of roadways. In the Mesha Inscription, this *Moabite *king claimed that he repaired a highway that crossed the Arnon; the modern road through the Wadi Mujib still requires repair after damage caused by winter rains. Road maintenance was often left to the local population, but highways that were important to affairs of state were posted with guard stations and kept in repair by the central government. This probably included roads referred to in *cuneiform texts as 'royal road' (i.e. the main or public road); this meaning may be applicable to the 'King's Highway', which is mentioned in the *Bible.

In the days before the *Persian and Roman road networks, the Assyrians excelled in road construction and maintenance. Their *provincial system was built on good communication, and good roads enabled the Assyrian high command to send infantry and cavalry over long distances to promote stability or conquer new territories. Several Assyrian kings left accounts of their own road-building activities while leading campaigns, including the building of bridges of boats over *rivers.          GLM

Y. AHARONI, *The Land of the Bible: A Historical Geography*, rev. ed. (Philadelphia, PA 1979).

M.C. ASTOUR, 'Overland Trade Routes in Ancient Western Asia', *Civilizations of the Ancient Near East*, ed. J. M. Sasson (New York 1995) 1401–20.

B.J. BEITZEL, 'Roads and Highways (Pre-Roman)', *Anchor Bible Dictionary* 5, ed. D.N. Freedman (New York 1992) 776–82.

L. CASSON, *Travel in the Ancient World* (London 1974).

D.A. DORSEY, *The Roads and Highways of Ancient Israel* (London 1991).

——, 'Roads', *The Oxford Encyclopedia of Archaeology in the Near East* 4, ed. E.M. Meyers (New York 1997) 431–4.

**Roman period** Although the Romans were active on the borders of the Near East from the late third century BC, their later conquests of different areas came at different times and so the dates of the Roman period vary from region to region.

The first eastern Roman province, and eventually the richest, was Asia, based on the kingdom of Pergamum in *Anatolia, which its last *king left to Rome on his death in 133 BC. The province of Asia gradually expanded but was

eventually split up into smaller provinces by Diocletian in AD 207. *Mesopotamia was fought over by *Parthia and Rome until it was conquered by Trajan and made into a province in AD 114–17, although the control became effective only under Septimius Severus in AD 194 with proper frontier defences. *Syria was made into a province by the Roman general Pompey in 64/3 BC. Neighbouring client kingdoms were gradually annexed: Judaea became a separate province in AD 70 and was added to Syria in AD 132–4, while the *Nabataean kingdom was annexed as part of the new province of Arabia in AD 106. The Roman period proper ends in AD 324 when Constantine I founded Constantinople (modern Istanbul) as the eastern counterpart to Rome, inaugurating the Byzantine empire.          PB

S.E. ALCOCK (ed.), *The Early Roman Empire in the East* (Oxford 1997).

B. ISAAC, *The Limits of Empire: The Roman Army in the East*, rev. ed. (Oxford 1992).

A.H.M. JONES, *Cities of the Eastern Roman Provinces*, 2nd ed. (Oxford 1971).

F. MILLAR, *The Roman Near East 31 BC–AD 337* (London 1993).

M. SARTRE, *L'Orient romain* (Paris 1991).

**Royal court** Surrounding all ancient Near Eastern *kings, and supporting them in their arduous work of conquest and rule, was an entourage of relatives, high officials, concubines and servants. Many of the members of the royal court probably lived in the *palace as well as

Glazed brick from Nimrud, depicting the Assyrian king with attendants. Probably from the reign of Ashurnasirpal II (883–859 BC). Height 41 cm. WA 90859.

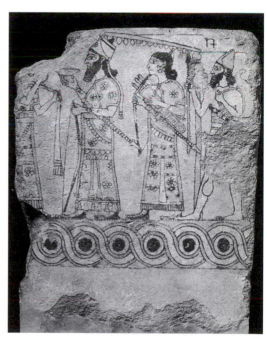

working there, since the palace was not only the principal residence of the king but also the head office for craft industries, agricultural estates and commercial ventures.

Closest to the king were the highest officials, responsible for state *administration, the *military, and court protocol and etiquette. In the Neo-*Assyrian period, for example, these were the vice-chancellor, the field marshal and the major-domo, the latter the only person with direct access to the king. The next rank of officials was apparently responsible for running the palace, and included the chief cupbearer, the steward and the palace herald. However, by Neo-Assyrian times these were not simply palace servants but senior army officers and *provincial governors. Their titles reflect ancient tradition and derive from domestic functions, a process echoed by *Hittite titles such as 'chief of the *wine'.

The *queen, concubines and royal *children all lived in the palace and were part of the royal court, although the *harem may not have been systematically organized and segregated until the late second millennium BC. Sometimes the king would leave his palace and visit parts of his kingdom, or even other kingdoms, and on those occasions part at least of the royal court travelled with him, including the harem.

Some texts mention a royal bodyguard, and the king would have been protected both inside and outside the palace. A *Hittite text contains instructions for royal bodyguards, describing how they should take their places in a palace courtyard in the morning, giving rules for the opening of various *doors, describing where they all go during processions with the king, and even mentioning the *food they receive from the kitchen (a roasted limb and a pitcher of sweet milk). The text includes detailed regulations for going to the toilet while on duty. The guard had to say 'I shall go to the pot', and this request was passed on through the ranks to the chief-of-guards who was expected to say 'Let him go'. But if the king noticed a guard who obviously needed to go, this became a royal matter.　　　　　　　　　　　　　　　　PB

H.G. GÜTERBOCK and T.P.J. VAN DEN HOUT, *The Hittite Instruction for the Royal Bodyguard* (Chicago 1991).

J.N. POSTGATE, *Early Mesopotamia: Society and Economy at the Dawn of History* (London 1992) 144–53.

——, 'Royal Ideology and State Administration in Sumer and Akkad', *Civilizations of the Ancient Near East*, ed. J.M. Sasson (New York 1995) 395–411.

**Rusahinili:** see Toprakkale

# S

## Sacred animals

**Sacred animals** Many Near Eastern deities had their distinctive natural or hybrid *animals, which may be counted among their *divine symbols. They are often depicted together with them in *art. Generally, natural animals were associated with *goddesses, such as the lion with *Ishtar, while hybrid creatures were associated with gods, such as the dragon with *Marduk, *Nabû or *Ashur.

However, in the first millennium BC the sun-god *Shamash was associated with a natural *horse, and the distinction between 'real' and 'unreal' animals was not always clearly defined, so that it is unclear to what extent hybrids were imagined as actually existing, perhaps in distant lands.　　　　　　　　　　　　　　JAB/AG

A. GREEN, 'Mesopotamian Religious Iconography', *Civilizations of the Ancient Near East*, ed. J.M. Sasson (New York 1995) 1837–55.

U. SEIDL, 'Göttersymbole und -attribute', *Reallexikon der Assyriologie* 3 (Berlin/New York 1957–71) 483–90.

——, *Die Babylonischen Kudurru-Reliefs: Symbole*

An Assyrian king, probably Sennacherib (704–681 BC), flanks a procession of seven gods on their sacred animals on a rock relief at Maltai in northern Iraq (from F. Thureau-Dangin, *Revue d'Assyriologie* 21 (1924) 187).

*Mesopotamischer Gottheiten* (reprint, with added appendix and table, of *Baghdader Mitteilungen* 4 (1968) 7–220) (Fribourg/Göttingen 1989).

F.A.M. WIGGERMANN and A. GREEN, 'Mischwesen', *Reallexikon der Assyriologie* 8 (Berlin/New York 1993–7) 222–64.

**Sacred Marriage** Sacred Marriage is a term borrowed from the history of Greek religion (*hieros gamos*) to describe at least two different sorts of *ritual in ancient *Mesopotamia. In a ritual of which records date mostly from the Neo-*Assyrian and Neo-*Babylonian periods or later, a *marriage between two deities was enacted in a symbolic ceremony (called *hašadu*) in which their cult statues were brought together. A ceremonial bed was required so that the statues could 'marry'. Such symbolic ceremonies are known for *Marduk and Zarpanitu (forming a part of the *New Year ceremonies); *Nabû and Tashmetu (or Nanaya), *Shamash and Aya; and *Anu and Antu. These 'marriages' do not appear to have been directly related to particular *myths.

Quite different from this, and known only from earlier periods, is a ritual lovemaking apparently between a deified human *king and the *goddess *Inana, seen as a symbolic counterpart to the mythical union of the god *Dumuzi with Inana. The exclusively literary evidence for this 'marriage' dates from the period of the Third Dynasty of *Ur and the *Isin period. The beautiful *songs and poems in *Sumerian belonging to the Inana–Dumuzi cult suggest that the *fertility of vegetation, *animals and humans was believed in some way to depend on the union of Inana and Ama-ushumgal-ana (an aspect of Dumuzi); but as no exact description of a ritual survives (in the way that descriptions are preserved for the New Year ceremonies), it is still uncertain whether (as has been suggested on the basis of comparisons with other cultures) a real (temporary) 'marriage' between the king and a human *priestess representing Inana actually took place, or whether the whole ritual was purely symbolic. A 'marriage' between an *entu* priestess and a local storm-god, probably *Adad or Wer, is known from the *Syrian town of *Emar in the fourteenth century BC. Possibly here too a ruler impersonated the god.

It is not known what the immediate source of information was for the story recounted by *Herodotus (who may have visited *Babylon in the fifth century BC) according to which a *woman spent the night in a shrine on top of the *ziggurat of Babylon, waiting to be visited by Bel himself, although it is clearly reminiscent of what is known from earlier periods in *Mesopotamia.    AG/JAB

B. ALSTER, 'Sumerian Love Songs', *Revue d'Assyriologie* 79 (1985) 127–59.

S.N. KRAMER, *The Sacred Marriage Rite* (Bloomington, IN 1969) chapters 3–5.

W.G. LAMBERT, 'Divine Love Lyrics from Babylon', *Journal of Semitic Studies* 4 (1959) 1–15.

——, 'Divine Love Lyrics from the Reign of Abi-Ešuh', *Mitteilungen des Instituts für Orientforschung* 12 (1966) 41–56.

E. MATSUSHIMA, 'Le lit de Šamaš et le rituel de mariage à l'Ebabbar', *Acta Sumerologica* 7 (1985) 129–37.

J. RENGER and J.S. COOPER, 'Heilige Hochzeit', *Reallexikon der Assyriologie* 3 (Berlin/New York 1975) 251–69.

**Sacred tree:** see Stylized tree

**Sacrifice and offering** The widespread *Mesopotamian idea of humans having been created to act as the servants of the *gods meant that it was considered necessary to feed and clothe the gods constantly and to make them presents. The term sacrifice refers especially to the killing and offering of an *animal. Exactly the same *foods and drinks were offered to the gods as were consumed by humans, with perhaps more emphasis on the luxury items, including the burning of *incense and aromatic woods. 'Regular' offerings were offered at meal times daily throughout the year; and special, occasional offerings were made at *festivals which might be monthly or annual. *Clothing was also offered. The offerings were redistributed to the *temple staff (according to strict hierarchical regulations, from high *priests down to courtyard sweepers) after being presented to the gods. In

Men bring animals for sacrifice during Shalmaneser III's visit to the source of the River Tigris. Detail from the Balawat gates, c.845 BC. WA 124656.

A priest is portrayed offering a fish and other sacrifices before divine emblems on this seventh-century BC cylinder seal. WA 89470.

addition to the organized offerings, individuals might make personal offerings as they chose.

Offerings made as presents fall into three categories. Firstly, those which were 'useful' to the gods – beds, chairs, *boats, cups and vessels, *weapons dedicated from war booty, and *jewellery – were all absorbed into the temple treasury as part of the 'property' of the god. Secondly, statues of the offerers might be placed before the gods to represent them in constant *prayer before the deity. These and other thank-offerings often carry inscriptions stating that they were offered 'for the life of' the offerer, or on behalf of some other person. Finally, offerings might be made as a form of request. Models of human limbs (to procure recovery), of beds, of pregnant women (to aid fertility) and *figurines of animals may have been of this type.

Offerings of food and drink were also made to the dead on a regular basis.

In the earliest periods in southern Mesopotamia certain places outside the temple proper were specifically demarcated for sacrifice. Offerings exclusively of *fish were made at *Eridu and *Lagash. Burnt offerings of various sorts were made in round structures and in specially constructed pans and trenches in the ground. These were apparently the scene of continual and repeated sacrifice, and sometimes the deposit of ash became so deep that the walls had to be raised to accommodate it.                                    AG/JAB

M. SIGRIST, *Les sattukku dans l'Ešumeša durant la période d'Isin et Larsa* (Malibu, CA 1984).

A. TSUKIMOTO, *Untersuchungen zur Totenpflege (kispum) im alten Mesopotamien* (Neukirchen/Vluyn 1985).

E. D. VAN BUREN, 'Places of Sacrifice ("*Opferstätten*")', *Iraq* 14 (1952) 76–92.

## Sa'idiyeh, (Tell es-)

Tell es-Sa'idiyeh is a large mound in the central Jordan Valley, located c.2 km east of the Jordan *river. The site consists of two parts, a higher eastern mound which rises about 40 m above the surrounding plain and a western bench-like mound whose surface is only half as high. Together, the mounds cover c.13 ha. Sa'idiyeh occupies a prominent position on a large alluvial fan, which gave it control of rich agricultural land. *Albright identified Sa'idiyeh as biblical Zaphon, while *Glueck thought it was Zarethan; neither identification is certain.

The site has been excavated by J.B. Pritchard (1964–7) and J.N. Tubb (1985–96). A number of *burials were excavated on the low, western mound, mostly dating to the twelfth century BC; these *graves cut into Early Bronze Age occupational debris. Some tombs were rich in artefacts and some skeletons had been wrapped in cloth and covered in bitumen. On the high mound, an impressive and unique staircase was uncovered; originally, 140 steps gave the town's twelfth-century BC occupants camouflaged access to a major *water source and the stone-lined pool to which it led. *Egyptian influence is apparent in certain burials and in the design of some building complexes on the upper tell, and Sa'idiyeh may have played an important role in Egyptian administrative and/or economic activity in *Canaan in the twelfth century BC.

The *town was destroyed by fire in the middle of the twelfth century BC, and Tell es-Sa'idiyeh witnessed alternating sporadic and intensive occupation between the eleventh century BC and the *Roman period. During the ninth to early eighth centuries BC, the town was *fortified and consisted of closely built *houses, industrial installations and streets. *Textile manufacturing was important during much of the site's *Iron Age history, as demonstrated by the large number of loom weights recovered here. There was a large residence from the *Persian period on the higher mound.                              GLM

Bronze bowl, to which fragments of textile are adhering, with an ivory cosmetic box in the shape of a fish. The bowl was found in a grave at Tell es-Sa'idiyeh, covering the genitals of the deceased, who had the skeletons of three fishes placed on the back of the skull. Late Bronze Age, c.1200–1150 BC. WA Z87T232.1–2.

J.B. PRITCHARD, *The Cemetery at Tell es-Sa'idiyeh, Jordan* (Philadelphia, PA 1980).

——, *Tell es-Sa'idiyeh: Excavations on the Tell, 1964–1966* (Philadelphia, PA 1985).

J.N. TUBB, 'Sa'idiyeh, Tell es-', *The New Encyclopedia of Archaeological Excavations in the Holy Land* 4, ed. E. Stern (New York 1993) 1295–300.

——, 'Sa'idiyeh, Tell es-', *The Oxford Encyclopedia of Archaeology in the Near East* 4, ed. E.M. Meyers (New York 1997) 452–5.

——, *Canaanites* (London 1998).

## Sakçagözü

Sakçagözü is the name of the modern *village in the territory of which lies the mound today known as Coba Höyük. In recent literature Sakçagözü is usually used in discussion of the Neo-*Hittite relief *sculptures whereas either name might be used with reference to the *prehistoric levels. The Sakçegözü Plain lies east of Gaziantep in south-eastern Turkey, forming a well watered and fertile part of the *Levantine Rift Valley. Much evidence for *Palaeolithic exploitation has been recorded along the valley sides.

The mound of Coba Höyük, originally transliterated Jobba, one of the smallest in the region, is distinguished by the copious spring that flows from its base. Carved orthostats (standing stone slabs) brought the site to the attention of scholars in the late nineteenth century and led *Garstang to conduct excavations in 1908 and 1911, continued by Veronica Seton-Williams and John Waecher in 1949.

The earliest levels, probably of late *Neolithic date (c.7000–6000 BC), are characterized by dark burnished *pottery with pattern-burnished and incised decoration. From a horizon transitional from the *Ubaid to the *Uruk periods (middle to late *Chalcolithic, c.4500–3500 BC) come 'Coba' or 'Flint Scraped' bowls, important for their distinctive technique of manufacture and wide distribution.

Perched on the top of the small conical mound is a Neo-Hittite enclosure, some 50 by 70 m, protected by a buttressed wall with a single monumental *gate embellished with sculpted reliefs depicting a lion *hunt. Across the courtyard from the gate, in the east corner of the enclosure, was a structure with a sculpted portico of the type often termed a *bīt hilāni. There is a column base in the form of a pair of double human-headed sphinxes. The entrance is flanked by lions. These orthostats are relatively small for the period. Lesser structures filled the north-eastern side of the enclosure.

Although the function of the Neo-Hittite structure, called a *palace by Garstang, is unknown it is surely reasonable to associate it with the spring. The site most probably fell within the territory of Sam'al (*Zinjirli).

GDS

A. GARRARD, 'Palaeolithic and Neolithic Survey at a South-eastern "Gateway" to Turkey', *Ancient Anatolia*, ed. R. Matthews (London 1989) 7–16.

J. GARSTANG, 'Excavations at Sakje-Geuzi in North Syria: Preliminary Report for 1908', *Liverpool Annals of Archaeology and Anthropology* 1 (1908) 97–117.

——, 'Second Interim Report on the Excavations at Sakje-Geuzi in North Syria', *Liverpool Annals of Archaeology and Anthropology* 5 (1913) 63–72.

J. GARSTANG, W.J. PHYTHIAN-ADAMS and M.V. SETON-WILLIAMS, 'Third Report on the Excavations at Sakje-Geuzi 1908–22', *Liverpool Annals of Archaeology and Anthropology* 24 (1937) 119–40.

J. DU PLAT TAYLOR, M.V. SETON-WILLIAMS and J. WAECHER, 'The Excavations at Sakçe Gözü', *Iraq* 12 (1950) 53–138.

D. USSISHKIN, 'The Date of the Neo-Hittite Enclosure at Sakçagözü', *Bulletin of the American Schools of Oriental Research* 181 (1966) 193–201.

J. WAECHER, S. GOGUS and M.V. SETON-WILLIAMS, 'The Sakça Gözü Cave Site 1949', *Belleten* 15 (1951) 193–201.

## Samaria

In c.870 BC, Samaria was established as capital of the northern kingdom of *Israel by King Omri; it is located c.56 km north of *Jerusalem. The site is now known by the Arabic name Sebastiyeh, which derives from Sebaste, the name given to Samaria by Herod the Great. The ancient *city covered the summit and slopes of a high hill and had a commanding view of the region's *roads and fertile valleys; the royal citadel of Omri and his successors was built on this terraced pinnacle and included a *palace, public buildings, *fortifications and

Iron Age inner wall at Samaria from Crowfoot's excavations (1933), showing typical 'Israelite' masonry including the core of the wall (by permission of the Palestine Exploration Fund).

storerooms. Samaria was an important city from the *Iron Age until the Byzantine period.

Samaria has been excavated by G. Schumacher (1908), G.A. Reisner and C. Fisher (1909–10) and J.W. Crowfoot, E.L. Sukenik and *Kenyon (1932–5). Kenyon's conclusions regarding Samaria's building and ceramic phases are controversial and must be adjusted to take pre-Omride occupation into account. According to the *Bible, Omri shifted his capital from Tirzah to Samaria, after purchasing the latter from Shemer. Samaria became synonymous with greed and corruption, and special reference was made to the use of *ivory decorations by Samaria's upper class; an impressive collection of *Phoenician-style ivories was found at Samaria.

The Omride *dynasty ended with a coup by Jehu c.841 BC, but over a century later the *Assyrians continued to call the region around Samaria the 'House of Omri'. During the reign of Jeroboam II (c.782–754 BC), the region of Samaria enjoyed a period of prosperity; the luxurious lifestyle in this era was condemned by the prophet Amos. Sixty-three *Hebrew *ostraca called the 'Samaria Ostraca' record the shipments of *wine and oil to the city from the surrounding district.

Samaria's rebellion against Assyria led to the city's destruction in 722 or 721 BC by *Shalmaneser V or *Sargon II. Much of Samaria's population was *deported, and the region was resettled with peoples from various parts of the Assyrian empire. Little has been recovered from the days of Assyrian, *Babylonian and *Persian rule in Samaria, but it is known that the city was an *administrative centre. When Herod renamed Samaria as Sebaste (the Greek equivalent of Augustus), he acknowledged his great benefactor and rebuilt the city in grand fashion, a reflection of its monumental status in the days of Omri.

GLM

B. BECKING, *The Fall of Samaria: An Historical and Archaeological Study* (Leiden 1992).

K.M. KENYON, *Royal Cities of the Old Testament* (London 1971).

J.D. PURVIS, 'Samaria (City)', *Anchor Bible Dictionary* 5, ed. D.N. Freedman (New York 1992) 914–21.

R.E. TAPPY, *The Archaeology of Israelite Samaria, Volume I: Early Iron Age through the Ninth Century B.C.* (Atlanta, GA 1992).

——, 'Samaria', *The Oxford Encyclopedia of Archaeology in the Ancient Near East* 4, ed. E.M. Meyers (New York 1997) 463–7.

Ostraca:

I.T. KAUFMAN, 'Samaria (Ostraca)', *Anchor Bible Dictionary* 5, ed. D.N. Freedman (New York 1992) 921–6.

A. LEMAIRE, *Inscriptions hébraïques: les ostraca* (Paris 1978) 23–81.

J. RENZ and W. RÖLLIG, *Handbuch der althebräischen Epigraphik* 1 (Darmstadt 1995) 79–109.

**Samarra** This site is located on the middle Tigris *river in central Iraq in an area that receives too little rainfall for reliable dry farming. The setting for a major *city of the Islamic period, it also became the type site for a *prehistoric culture, the Samarran, dated to the seventh millennium BC.

The site was excavated by Ernst Herzfeld (1904–5),

and the most notable feature of the excavations is its *cemetery. The most extensively excavated Samarran site is Tell es-*Sawwan close by. The culture extends across central *Mesopotamia between the Tigris and Euphrates and as far east as the foothills of the *Zagros, from Baghouz on the Middle Euphrates to Chogha Mami at the foot of the Zagros. The architecture is well represented at Tell es-Sawwan, and that at Chogha Mami is clearly related, with relatively large multi-room mudbrick rectangular structures, between 36 and 63 sq m in area and with between eight and twelve rooms.

The most characteristic feature of the Samarran is its distinctive painted *pottery. The exteriors of the vessels are often decorated in horizontal bands with fine, tightly meshed geometric designs carefully and precisely executed. On the interior of large bowls naturalistic designs are found arranged repetitively in a circle around the centre, including representations of human figures, some *dancing, and figures holding hands; *animal designs are also common with *birds, *fish, deer, goats, crabs, spiders and scorpions represented. Some distinctive jars have faces painted at their rims. The dynamism of some of the naturalistic scenes makes them attractive to the modern eye and also potentially in the past.

The effort involved in the manufacture of some of these vessels and their potential aesthetic qualities may have made some of this pottery relatively highly valued and explain its export. Samarran ceramics are found on *Hassuna and Hassuna-period sites in north Mesopotamia, often in some quantity. Ceramics may have been part of inter-regional *trade but so were exotic stones, sea shells and *copper for beads, and *obsidian for chipped *stone *tools. Given the evidence for the manufacture of fine stone vessels, the existence of intra-regional trade should not surprise us.

At Chogha Mami there is evidence for a similar range of crops, including advanced wheat, six-row barley and flax, as at Tell es-Sawwan, suggesting the importance of *irrigation agriculture in this low rainfall area.

The Samarran culture seems to represent an early stage in the transference of mixed farming to the arid region of central Mesopotamia that probably resulted in specific adaptations, including the development of systematic irrigation agriculture with distinct social attributes. Aspects of the economy and society that developed in the Samarran may well have persisted for a long time in this region, possibly even into historic periods.

DB

E. HERZFELD, *Die Vorgeschichtlichen Töpfereien von Samarra* (Berlin 1930).

J. MELLAART, *The Neolithic of the Near East* (London 1975).

**Sardis** Sardis, modern Sart, capital of ancient *Lydia, lies in the valley of the Hermus (modern Gediz Çay) at its confluence with the Pactolus stream and at the foot of Mount Tmolus (modern Boz Dağ), c.100 km east of Izmir. The naturally defensible spur on which the citadel was constructed, control of an important route from the *Aegean to the *Anatolian plateau, the fertility of the

The acropolis at Sardis, seen across the modern vineyards (photograph by Jane Taylor, courtesy of Sonia Halliday Photographs).

valley and the alluvial *gold for which the Pactolus was famous contributed to the importance of the *city.

European antiquarians reported on the site from the seventeenth century onwards and the first excavations at Bin Tepe (see below) date from the mid nineteenth century. Sustained American excavations began under H.C. Butler (1910–4, 1922), were resumed by G.M.A. Hanfmann in 1959 and continue under C.H. Greenewalt, Jr.

The Lydian Mermnad dynasty was founded by Gyges in the early eighth century BC and came, under Alyattes and Croesus, to rule an empire that stretched from the Aegean to the Halys (modern Kýzýlýrmak) *river. In, traditionally, 547 BC Sardis was captured by *Cyrus the Great and made the seat of the satrap of Sparda. The importance of Sardis at this time is underscored by its choice as the western terminus of the Persian Royal Road, which linked the different parts of the empire. Remains of the Lydian and *Persian periods are largely obscured by the later *Hellenistic to Byzantine city.

The Lydian city comprised a high and waterless acropolis and a lower city surrounded by massive *defences, some 20 m thick at the base, with a mudbrick wall on *stone foundations and a large *gate and complexity of buttresses and recesses, known as the 'Colossal Lydian Structure'. The total area within the walls was around 115 ha. Lydian *houses roofed with decorated terracotta tiles and a goldworking area have been excavated. Dramatic evidence for the burning of the city by Cyrus has come to light, including the body of a victim, a unique helmet, *weapons and vehicle elements. The destruction level is also yielding important caches of local and imported ceramics. In the Persian period the defences were remodelled and massive monuments of ashlar

masonry were constructed on the citadel and one of its spurs.

To the north of the city, on a low ridge overlooking the Gygaean lake, is Bin Tepe (Thousand Hills), so named after the many tumuli. Two of these burial *mounds, attributed to Gyges and Alyattes, have diameters greater than 350 m.                                                          GDS

H.C. BUTLER, *Sardis: The Excavations, 1914–22* (Leiden 1922).
C.H. GREENEWALT, JR, 'When a Mighty Empire was Destroyed: The Common Man and the Fall of Sardis', *Proceedings of the American Philosophical Society* 136 (1992) 247–72.
——, 'Arms and Weapons at Sardis in the mid Sixth Century B.C.', *Arkeolji ve Sanat* 79 (1997) 2–20.
G.M.A. HANFMANN, *Sardis from Prehistoric to Roman Times* (Cambridge, MA 1983).
J.G. PEDLEY, *Ancient Literary Sources on Sardis* (Cambridge, MA 1972).

## Sargon

**Sargon**  Sargon, 'the king is true, legitimate', was the name of two famous *kings and one other.

Sargon of *Akkad, c.2340–2284 BC, the founder of the *dynasty of Akkad, is known from one badly damaged contemporary inscription, a few year names and documents of his *family and retainers. Most information about his reign comes from accurate copies of inscriptions on monuments he erected in the *temple of *Enlil at *Nippur, made by *scribes about five hundred years later. At that time *epic poems about Sargon were also current, and spread to the *Hittites, and traditions about him were included in *omen and *chronicle texts, many still being copied in the first millennium BC. Tablets of that time alone tell of his birth. How much of this information has factual basis is disputed.

The 'Birth Legend' explains that his mother was a *priestess who had to conceal his birth, so put him in a basket in the Euphrates. A gardener rescued and raised him, then the goddess *Ishtar 'loved' him and he rose to *kingship. The *Sumerian *King List reports that he replaced Ur-Zababa of *Kish. Sargon established his seat at Akkad then conquered Lugal-zaggesi of *Uruk and his allies, so gaining control of southern *Mesopotamia. In the east he subdued *Elam and Simurrum to its north and he claims that *ships from the Gulf moored at Akkad. His most famous actions were to the west. A year name records his conquest of *Mari and names the more distant *Ebla, the Cedar Forest and the Silver Mountains, the last lying in southern *Anatolia. The Epic 'King of Battle', found among the *Amarna Letters and in later copies, carries him further, to Purushhanda (now Açem Hüyük?) in central Anatolia to relieve his *merchants from a local oppressor. At *Ur he installed his daughter Enheduanna as priestess of the *moon-god. She composed Sumerian *hymns which have survived.

Sargon's sons Rimush and Manishtusu, ruling for at most fifteen years each, also campaigned in southern Mesopotamia, *Iran and the Gulf, and his grandson *Naram-Sin more widely. Their actions may be seen as sequels to Sargon's, although earlier Sumerian kings may have ventured as far west and east (see Gilgamesh). Sargon's achievement was to lay the basis for a pan-Mesopotamian kingdom, former kings becoming vassals or governors; this was developed under his grandson, Naram-Sin. References to 5400 men eating daily with

A life-size relief of Sargon II of Assyria (left) with a courtier. WA 118822.

Sargon may indicate the institution of a standing *army. Sargon's impact reverberated throughout Babylonian history, as the life of the traditions testifies, and his statues received offerings as late as the sixth century BC. He was a *Semite, and his unifying force is seen in the use of *Akkadian beside Sumerian in royal inscriptions and in daily business documents, a use which came to dominate.

Sargon I of *Assyria, c.1850 BC, is known only from the Assyrian King List and *seal impressions from *Kanesh. Later texts tell that he built the wall at *Ashur.

Sargon II of Assyria ascended the throne in 721 BC, immediately after the *death of *Shalmaneser V, although his relationship to him is unclear. Sargon proved himself an able strategist; *letters from *Nineveh and *Nimrud attest his attention to political and administrative affairs. At his accession revolts broke out in *Hamath and *Samaria which were quickly suppressed. The *Chaldaean Merodach-Baladan seized *Babylon and troubled Sargon throughout his reign. A battle at Der was inconclusive, both sides claiming victory and the Babylonian *Chronicle giving it to the Elamites. Not until 709 BC did Sargon gain control of Babylon, when he proclaimed himself king, removing huge booty and *deporting thousands of people.

Sargon gave most attention to the north-east and north-west. *Treaties with Mannaean tribes east of the *Zagros involved Assyrian troops marching to protect them when other tribes attacked at *Urartu's instigation in 716 BC. In 714 BC Sargon moved against Urartu. His 'Letter to the God Ashur' gives a graphic description of the campaign, setting out its legal basis and making colourful observations on local features and customs. New peoples and kingdoms were arising in Anatolia. The Mushki (*Phrygians) led by *Midas and the Urartian king supported Tabal, so Sargon campaigned against Tabal (718, 713 BC) and reduced it to a province. Further unrest drew Sargon there again in 705 BC and he was killed in battle.

Sargon built at *Nimrud and in 717 BC founded a new capital at Dur-Sharrukin (now *Khorsabad). More splendid than earlier foundations, it was occupied in 707/6 BC, then abandoned after Sargon's death. Its extensive wall *sculptures were uncovered by *Botta and some brought to the Louvre. They continue the style of *Tiglath-pileser III on a larger scale. At least one copy of the Assyrian King List was made for the new *palace.

ARM

Sargon of Akkad:
D.R. FRAYNE, Sargonic and Gutian Periods (2334–2113 BC) (Toronto 1993) 7–39.
C.J. GADD, 'The Dynasty of Agade and the Gutian Invasion', Cambridge Ancient History 1.2, 2nd ed. (Cambridge 1971) 417–40.
J. GOODNICK WESTENHOLZ, Legends of the Kings of Akkade (Winona Lake, IN 1997) 33–169.

Sargon I:
A.K. GRAYSON, Assyrian Rulers of the Third and Second Millennia BC (to 1115 BC) (Toronto 1987) 45–46.

Sargon II:
P. ALBENDA, The Palace of Sargon King of Assyria (Paris 1986).

A. FUCHS, *Die Inschriften Sargons II. aus Khorsabad* (Göttingen 1994).

A.K. GRAYSON, 'Assyria: Tiglath-pileser III to Sargon II (744–705 B.C.)', *Cambridge Ancient History* 3.2, 2nd ed. (Cambridge 1991) 86–102.

D.D. LUCKENBILL, *Assyrian Royal Inscriptions* 2 (Chicago 1927) 1–114 (Letters 78–99).

**Sasanians** The Sasanian *dynasty ruled in *Iran from AD 224 until the Islamic conquest in AD 651. Its first *king, Ardashir, overthrew the *Parthians, and the dynasty was named after an ancestor, Sasan, who according to one tradition was descended from the *Achaemenids. The Sasanians deliberately associated themselves with the glories of the Achaemenid empire, and their ambition to restore Iran's greatness brought them into conflict with *Rome and later Byzantium. At its greatest extent the Sasanian empire stretched from the Euphrates to the *Indus and included large parts of central Asia. Their best known monuments are rock reliefs carved by many kings, in conscious imitation of the Achaemenids. Intricately decorated Sasanian *silver vessels have survived in large quantities, but forgeries are common. PB

R.N. FRYE, *The Heritage of Persia*, 2nd ed. (London 1976) 236–67.

R. GHIRSHMAN, *Iran: Parthians and Sasanians* (London 1962).

P.O. HARPER, *The Royal Hunter: Art of the Sasanian Empire* (New York 1978).

G. HERRMANN, *The Iranian Revival* (Oxford 1977).

E. YARSHATER (ed.), *The Seleucid, Parthian and Sasanian Periods*. Cambridge History of Iran 3 (Cambridge 1983).

Fine silver dishes, embossed and engraved, characterize the Sasanian period. King Bahram V (AD 421–39) continues the ancient royal tradition of hunting lions, while holding a lion cub as a decoy. Diameter 27 cm. WA 124092.

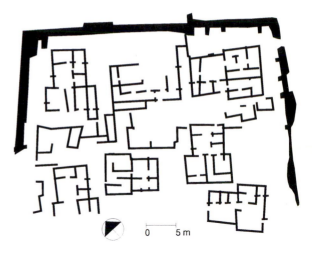

Partial plan of the level III Neolithic settlement at Tell es-Sawwan, which comprised several buildings of T-shaped plan, surrounded by a defensive wall.

**Sawwan, (Tell es-)** Tell es-Sawwan is located on the east bank of the middle Tigris *river. It sits on a bluff overlooking the floodplain and covers over 2 ha. Excavated by B. Abu Es-Soof in the 1960s, the site belongs to the *Samarran culture and should be dated to the seventh millennium BC, contemporary with the *Hassuna to the north. The upper levels III and IV have classic Samarran *pottery, but the earliest have plain, cruder ceramics, some incised, reminiscent of Hassuna pottery.

The earliest settlement at Sawwan was surrounded by a rectangular ditch. In level III there is evidence for a rectangular buttressed wall, 1–2 m thick, along the course of the earlier ditch. It may well be considered a *fortification wall.

Architecture in all phases consists of large mudbrick buildings, usually over 60 sq m in area, with many rooms, a tradition that persists in central and southern Mesopotamia over a long period. Typically buildings at Sawwan had over ten 'rooms', in earlier levels often twelve to fourteen. In later levels III and IV, a T-shaped building is standard, with one wing broader than the other. The patterned variation in size and shape of these rooms suggests different dedicated purposes for different rooms. The number of rooms and size of buildings suggest relatively large co-resident groups, perhaps 'extended' *families.

Beneath building 1 in level I were found 130 *graves, mainly *children, but also adults, a feature also seen in the later *Ubaid site of Abada. It seems such buildings, and those associated with them, may have had a special role in society. The *burials were accompanied by a range of items of personal adornment, often made of beads of imported sea shells and exotic stones. In addition, many *stone female *figurines and phalli were found in the *cemetery and a large range of elaborate finely manufactured *stone vessels.

Sheep and goat were herded and *agriculture was almost certainly practised with the aid of *irrigation, given the low rainfall and presence of crops such as six-row naked barley, advanced forms of wheat, and flax.

Sawwan has features similar to those of the Hassuna culture, but it is also a good example of the developments associated with the transfer of early village farming practices to central and southern *Mesopotamia. There, adaptations to low rainfall were required, and settings were good for irrigation or were naturally 'moist' owing to high water tables and flooding.    DB

B. ABU ES SOOF, 'Tell es Sawwan: Excavations of the Fourth Season', *Sumer* 24 (1968) 3–16.

H. HELBAEK, 'Early Hassunan Vegetable Food at Tell es Sawwan near Samarra', *Sumer* 20 (1964) 45–8.

W. YASIN, 'Excavations at Tell es Sawwan Sixth Season', *Sumer* 26 (1970) 3–11.

## Schaeffer, Claude Frédéric-Armand (1898–1982)

Schaeffer was an Alsatian excavator who began his career with several important publications on the Bronze Age in Europe, becoming curator of the Strasbourg Museum in 1924. He contributed largely to the exposure of the Glozel forgeries. His interests in the eastern origins of the European Bronze Age marked him as the one to be seconded to explore the *Syrian site of Minet el-Beidha after a rich *tomb was found there in 1928. Thus in 1929 he began excavations which quickly moved to the adjacent *tell of Ras Shamra, which inscriptions soon proved to be ancient *Ugarit. He conducted thirty-two seasons there over forty-one years (with a break 1940–7). In 1933 he was appointed Assistant Keeper at the Museum of National Antiquities, St Germain-en-Laye. The same year saw him excavate Bellapais-Vounos in *Cyprus and the next year he discovered the important Late Bronze Age town of Enkomi on the east coast of Cyprus. During the Second World War Schaeffer worked in cryptography for the Free French in London, then as a historical adviser. His breadth of interest was demonstrated in *Stratigraphie comparée et chronologie de l'Asie occidentale* (London 1948). In 1946 he returned to Enkomi, working there until 1971 and in 1947–51 he dug at *Arslantepe near Malatya in southern Turkey. In 1946–9 he served on the Committee on Excavations at the Quai d'Orsay as General Secretary, then as Vice-President. He was employed by the Centre d'Études et de Recherches Scientifiques (CNRS) 1951–4, then held a specially created chair at the Collège de France, 1954–69. In 1953 he was elected to the French Academy. Schaeffer published preliminary reports promptly and volumes of essays by himself and others dealing with particular aspects of the sites he explored. His successors continue his major work at Ugarit, reassessing and refining his results.    ARM

J.-C. COURTOIS, 'Claude Schaeffer', *Syria* 60 (1983) 343–5.

R. MARICHAL, 'Allocution a l'occasion du décès de M. Claude Schaeffer', *Comptes rendus de l'Académie des Inscriptions et Belles Lettres* (1982) 508–11.

J.M. ROBINSON, 'Claude Frédéric-Armand Schaeffer-Forrer (1898–1982): An Appreciation', *Biblical Archaeology Review*

9/5 (Sept.–Oct. 1983) 56–61.

S. SWINY, 'Schaeffer, Claude', *The Oxford Encyclopedia of Archaeology in the Near East* 4, ed. E.M. Meyers (New York 1997) 496–7.

## Schliemann, Heinrich (1822–90)

Best known as the excavator of *Troy, Heinrich Schliemann was born in Germany and at first held a variety of jobs from grocer's apprentice to clerk. When he had made his fortune as a commodities dealer, he travelled extensively and eventually decided to engage in *archaeology. A lifelong fascination led him to excavate Hissarlik in north-west Turkey, identified as Homer's Troy, between 1870 and 1890, and later Mycenae, Orchomenos and Tiryns in Greece.

At Troy, Schliemann uncovered nine successive settlements, including one which he identified as the Troy of Homer, now dated much earlier to c.2500 BC. His enthusiasm led him to be uncritically convinced that a collection of *gold and *silver *jewellery was 'Priam's Treasure' (as later at Mycenae he found 'the mask of Agamemnon') and to identify structures as those described by Homer. Nevertheless, Schliemann was one of the first archaeologists to recognize archaeological stratigraphy and the importance of *pottery, helped from 1822 by his assistant Wilhelm Dörpfeld, who introduced systematic architectural recording.

Schliemann believed he had proved the historicity of the Trojan war, a claim still disputed and debated, but the excitement generated by his finds created a new audience eager for archaeology. His popular accounts of his excavations were bestsellers, and research on the *Aegean and north-west *Anatolian *Bronze Ages is still influenced by the materials he excavated. He is known occasionally to have acted fraudulently, and his own accounts of his life and excavations contain many lies and inconsistencies. As a result, there have been attempts to prove him a liar and fraud in much of his archaeological work, but these remain unproved.    PB

W.M. CALDER and J. COBET (eds), *Heinrich Schliemann nach hundert Jahren* (Frankfurt 1990).

D.F. EASTON, 'Schliemann, Heinrich', *The Oxford Encyclopedia of Archaeology in the Near East* 4, ed. E.M. Meyers (New York 1997) 497–8.

J. HERRMANN (ed.), *Heinrich Schliemann: Grundlagen und ergebnisse moderner Archäologie 100 Jahre nach Schliemanns Tod* (Berlin 1992).

E. LUDWIG, *Schliemann: The Story of a Gold Seeker* (Boston 1931).

H. SCHLIEMANN, *Troy and its Remains* (London 1875).

## Science and technology

Evidence for science in the ancient Near East is limited to *Mesopotamia, and the written evidence for Mesopotamian science is limited to *mathematics, *astronomy and *medicine. There is virtually no evidence for physics and chemistry, apart from a few recipes for *glass, perfume (see Cosmetics) and *beer. There are no texts concerning the technical aspects of *metalworking, architecture, *irrigation or crafts, although the technical achievements in these fields were outstanding. It is generally thought that these were never written down, and that knowledge of such 'practical' sciences was transmitted orally, in contrast to the elite, 'clean' sciences of mathematics and astronomy. Many scholars attribute this to a sort of intellectual snobbery of Mesopotamian *scribes, who were interested in recording only those sciences associated in some way with higher social status. This is perhaps more likely than an older view that such technical knowledge was kept deliberately secret.

More generally, the systematic formulation of knowledge represented by the lists of words in various categories is evidence of a scientific approach. Likewise, it has been pointed out that some *omen series include observations that could not possibly have occurred, and these can be explained as a form of 'scientific' inference, taking existing observations to their logical conclusion to cover all possible (and impossible) eventualities.

For many crafts, particularly *pottery and metalworking, it is possible to reconstruct the technical processes involved by analysis of the surviving artefacts. There have been attempts to relate archaeological finds to Mesopotamian chemistry, and certain objects have been identified as crucibles, filtering, distillation and extraction apparatus, and drip bottles. Mesopotamian chemists must have been familiar with acids, sodas and silicates, and lime in order to tan leather, dye wool and produce soap, glazes, frits and glass. Different types of furnace provided sources of heat. In the first millennium BC, fire was produced by striking flint against metal to light tinder, and a number of *ritual texts refer to the use of sulphur in producing flame.                                        PB

R. LABAT, 'Les sciences en Mésopotamie', *Revue de la Mediterranée* 17 (1957) 123–58.

M. LEVEY, *Chemistry and Chemical Technology in Ancient Mesopotamia* (London/New York 1959).

O. NEUGEBAUER, *The Exact Sciences in Antiquity*, 2nd ed. (Providence 1957).

M.A. POWELL, 'Metrology and Mathematics in Ancient Mesopotamia', *Civilizations of the Ancient Near East*, ed. J.M. Sasson (New York 1995) 1941–57.

R.C. THOMPSON, *A Dictionary of Assyrian Chemistry and Geology* (Oxford 1936).

**Schools:** see Education; Scribes

**Scribes**  The advent of *writing generated a new profession, the scribe. *Sumerian and *Babylonian scribes had a lengthy training, their *education including accurate copying of both Sumerian and *Akkadian *languages from about 2000 BC onwards and sufficient *mathematics for accountancy and surveying, as well as basic reading and writing skills. In other areas using *cuneiform scripts, competence in more languages might be required, as multilingual vocabularies demonstrate (at *Ugarit in Sumerian, Akkadian, *Hurrian and Ugaritic, at Amarna in Egyptian and Akkadian). The ordinary scribes probably earned their living writing letters and legal deeds for *merchants and landowners, either haphazardly as

In the eighth century BC Assyrian scribes wrote in cuneiform on clay tablets (left-hand figure) and in Aramaic on leather or papyrus (right-hand figure). Relief from the palace of Tiglath-pileser III at Nimrud, c.730 BC. WA 118882.

required or serving one employer, an individual or an institution. Scribes may have had their pitches at the *town *gate, a place where business was often done. One had his name inscribed on a block in a gate at *Hattusas. The *king, the *administration and the *temples had scribes in their service, some being specialists in composing reports of royal achievements for public display or for posterity, others preparing religious works or compiling and consulting *omens, *medical and other scientific compendia (see Science and technology), with the majority occupied in the daily work of running property, livestock and workshops.

Accuracy was essential in writing legal deeds (see Law), so scribes might append their names to them both as witnesses to the transaction and as accepting responsibility for recording them. In that and other situations, the scribe had considerable power. That is well illustrated by requests King Abdi-Heba of *Jerusalem made at the end of *letters to the pharaoh, asking the Egyptian secretary to help him win favour: 'I am your servant; present acceptable words to my lord the king (on my behalf)' (*Amarna Letters (EA) 286, 287, 289). In celestial realms, *Nabû, the Babylonian scribe of the *gods, kept a ledger in which he recorded people's fate, death or life, as God

Assyrian sculptors mastered the art of low relief carving (bas relief), using it to present the tumult of the battle at Til Tuba in Elam. From the North Palace of Ashurbanipal (668–627 BC) at Nineveh. WA 124801.

did in *Israelite thought (e.g. Exodus 32: 32, 33; Psalm 69: 28).

Although the rise of the *alphabet permitted wider *literacy, scribes retained their importance as the professional writers and readers. From the eighth and seventh centuries BC, a relief from *Zinjirli shows an *Aramaean scribe standing before the king, and *Assyrian *sculptures and a *wall painting show pairs of scribes, one writing in cuneiform on a clay tablet or waxed boards, the other writing on papyrus, presumably in *Aramaic. Later in Jewish society the scribe became more specifically the interpreter of Scripture by virtue of his close relationship with the text.                                   ARM

**Sculpture**  The first sculptures in the ancient Near East were small clay *figurines of humans and *animals found on *Neolithic sites, as well as larger plaster statues of humans (at *Ain Ghazal) and over-life-size stone sculpture from Nevali Çori in *Anatolia, alabaster statuettes of nude *women (at Tell es-*Sawwan), and gypsum reliefs mostly of bulls' heads (at *Çatalhöyük). Larger scale *stone statuary appeared in *Mesopotamia only at the end of the fourth millennium BC. Popularity of sculpture was always dependent on the availability of good quality stone. In northern Mesopotamia (*Assyria) and *Anatolia, stone was plentiful, while in the south (*Babylonia) it had to be imported, hence the generally small scale of the statues; similarly, sculpture in the round was rare in the *Levant because of the absence of stone suitable for carving, basalt being too hard and limestone too soft.

Sculpture in the round and in relief, like all ancient Near Eastern *art, was not made for its own sake but was functional and symbolic. Statues were never portraits, but communicated a message, although when discovered out of context their function is not always clear. Sculptural conventions seen already in the Hunt Stela from *Uruk of the late fourth millennium BC, depicting a *king *hunting a lion in two registers, remained essentially the same until the *Hellenistic period. In relief sculpture, head, pelvis, legs and feet were shown in profile, chest normally frontally, face in profile but eye frontally. Sculptors used registers to separate the action, starting from the bottom, though already on a stela showing *Naram-Sin ascending a mountain at the head of his army, found at *Susa where it had been taken as booty, registers give way to a single scene. More important persons were depicted larger than the others, and *gods larger than kings.

Statues of humans were often placed in *temples as dedications, like the numerous votive figures from the Abu temple at Early Dynastic Tell Asmar (c.3000–2600 BC), or the later statues of *Gudea standing or seated. Life-size cult statues of kings were worshipped in Mesopotamia, but with some exceptions these represented deceased rulers. Of Assyrian kings, only statues of *Ashurnasirpal II and *Shalmaneser III are known. These were not portraits but idealized symbols of Assyrian might, meant to inspire fear and respect. A *letter to an Assyrian king asks him to choose between alternative images of himself, presented as drawings on papyrus or clay.

Statues of divinities survive from the beginning of the second millennium BC, with characteristic headdresses decorated with horns. An eleventh-century BC limestone statue of a nude woman from *Nineveh lacks anatomical detail and may have been a statue of a goddess dressed

One of a pair of winged 'bull' figures which guarded an entrance in the palace of Sargon II (721–705 BC) at Khorsabad. The sculptors were unable to carve the legs free, so showed the figure with two at the front and four at the side to be as realistic as possible. Height 4.42 m. WA 118809.

during temple ceremonies, although the inscription states that it was set up 'for the enjoyment of the people'.

Animals most frequently represented by statues were bulls, lions and sphinxes in stone, *copper or *bronze, or occasionally in clay baked in sections, often guarding *gates to *cities or *palaces in Assyria, Anatolia and the Levant. Porches of *bīt hilāni buildings were sometimes supported by caryatid statues representing gods mounted on their animal attributes. In Assyria, guardian winged genies were a mixture of sculpture in the round and high relief, with the body of a lion or bull and the head of a bearded human. Reliefs from the palace of *Sennacherib at Nineveh show how such sculptures were *transported: the figure was roughed out in the quarry, placed on a large sledge on wooden rollers, pulled to the *river and floated downstream to its destination.

Large-scale reliefs in Assyria, north *Syria and Anatolia also lined gates or processional ways to palaces, depicting *military campaigns, *court life and *religious scenes. Assyrian kings lined interior rooms and façades of their palaces with reliefs, no doubt to send a propagandistic message of power and prestige to their courtiers

and visiting dignitaries. Assyrian and *Hittite kings also carved rock reliefs commemorating their victories in places of strategic importance, for purposes of propaganda. Rock reliefs were characteristic of Hittite open sanctuaries, the most impressive being at *Yazýlýkaya, showing a pantheon of gods and goddesses.     PB

P. AMIET, Art of the Ancient Near East (London 1980).
H. FRANKFORT, Art of the Ancient Near East, rev. ed. (Harmondsworth 1977).
K. KOHLMEYER, 'Anatolian Architectural Decorations, Statuary, and Stelae', Civilizations of the Ancient Near East, ed. J.M. Sasson (New York 1995) 2639–60.
A. SPYCKET, La statuaire du Proche-Orient ancien (Leiden 1981).
——, 'Reliefs, Statuary, and Monumental Paintings in Ancient Mesopotamia', Civilizations of the Ancient Near East, ed. J.M. Sasson (New York 1995) 2583–600.
I.J. WINTER, 'Art in Empire: The Royal Image and the Visual Dimensions of Assyrian Ideology', Assyria 1995, eds S. Parpola and R.M. Whiting (Helsinki 1997) 359–81.

**Scythians** In the Late Bronze Age *horse-riding *nomads dominated the steppe lands stretching from central Asia into south-eastern Europe and were all related through *language and culture. Our knowledge of these people comes from *Assyrian and later *Greek texts, particularly the history of *Herodotus, as well as the more recent *archaeology of their homelands. They are known by the general name of Saka (Sacae) or Scythians and are described as highly skilled in archery and horse-riding. Associated with other tribal groupings known as the *Cimmerians, during the first millennium BC Scythian tribal confederations pushed in against the Assyrian empire, especially threatening Assyrian vassals in Cilicia. A number of *military campaigns were launched against them by Assyrian *kings; eventually *Esarhaddon made an alliance and concluded a *marriage with the daughter of Bartatua, one of the most powerful Scythian rulers. Herodotus emphasizes the initial power of the Scythians over *Iran but he

Scythian bronze openwork plaque of an elk's head, found in a group of five tumuli of the fourth century BC at Kerch in the Crimea (courtesy of the Visitors of the Ashmolean Museum, Oxford, 1885.466).

says that they were eventually driven across the *Caucasus by the *Medes. Under the *Persian empire inscriptions of Darius I tell of a victorious campaign against the Scythians in his third year (519 BC) but it is unclear quite where this took place and Herodotus suggests that the Persian king barely saved his armies from destruction.

The most important archaeological remains of the Scythians are the *burial monuments called *kurgans. Some of the richest kurgans discovered are around the Aral Sea and contained rich *jewellery, *weapons and horse equipment. The favourite artistic motifs included representations, often highly stylized, of wild *animals and *birds and especially horses.                      PTC

V.N. BASILOV (ed.), *Nomads of Eurasia* (Los Angeles 1989).
R.N. FRYE, *The History of Ancient Iran* (Munich 1984).
P.L. KOHL, *Central Asia: Paleolithic Beginnings to the Iron Age* (Paris 1984).

**Sea Peoples**  The term 'Sea Peoples' was first used by the nineteenth-century Egyptologist Gaston Maspero to refer to a variety of peoples who emigrated across the Mediterranean in the late thirteenth and early twelfth centuries BC. The ancient sources never referred to these groups with a single label but knew them by separate and specific names: Denyen, Shardana (Sherden), Lukka, Meshwesh, Teresh (Tursha), Ekwesh, Shekelesh, Peleset (*Philistines), Tjeker and Weshesh. Linguistic clues indicate that they came from different regions (e.g. *Anatolia, Greece, and the Mediterranean islands).

The Sea Peoples are connected in some way to the demise of Late Bronze Age culture, when the *Hittite empire and Mycenaean civilization collapsed and *Troy, *Ugarit and other *cities were destroyed. Scholars do not know what caused this widespread upheaval, but various suggestions have been made – e.g. famine, natural disaster, political decay. Some suggest that the appearance of better *weapons and new tactics enabled invaders to defeat great armies that relied too heavily on *chariot forces. The solution is perhaps found in a combination of factors. It is not even known if the Sea Peoples caused this cultural disruption or if they were refugees escaping from it. Some scholars claim that the Sea Peoples were a warrior class who, like Vikings or pirates, brought destruction to the places where they landed. Other evidence indicates that they were accompanied by *women and *children, which makes them look more like refugees looking for a safe haven. Some should be classified as mercenaries. For example, the Shardana had sided with the *Egyptians and fought against the Hittites at the battle of *Kadesh in 1275 BC. During the reign of Merneptah, however, the Shardana fought alongside the Libyans – and other 'foreigners from the sea' – against Egypt.

Ramesses III recorded his victory over the Sea Peoples who fought Egyptian forces near the mouth of the Nile in 1191 BC on the walls of his mortuary *temple at Medinet Habu; his account traces the movement of the Sea Peoples from Anatolia to their aborted invasion of Egypt. At least five groups of Sea Peoples, including the Philistines, are depicted; they wear distinctive garb, are armed with a variety of weapons, and are attacking in *ships that bear recognizable Aegean features. Another Egyptian text says that Ramesses settled the Philistines, Tjeker and Sherden in the coastal plain of *Canaan; the text notes that the *cities of *Ashkelon, *Ashdod and Gaza fell within Philistine territory. These Philistines might have been under nominal Egyptian control, but they established themselves in the Philistine plain for six centuries and fought with Canaanites, *Israelites, *Assyrians and *Babylonians. Excavators at Philistine sites often recover distinctive Mycenaean IIIC-style *pottery and cultic objects and architectural remains with close parallels in the Aegean. A newly discovered inscription from *Ekron lists five local *kings, two of whose names are non-*Semitic; these names, along with other linguistic evidence from the *Bible, also point to the Philistines' Aegean origin. The original homeland and fate of most Sea Peoples are unknown, but the Philistines illustrate the process of acculturation that followed this mass movement of peoples.                      GLM

T. DOTHAN, 'Sea Peoples and the Philistines of Ancient Palestine', *Civilizations of the Ancient Near East*, ed. J.M. Sasson (New York 1995) 1267–79.
T. DOTHAN and M. DOTHAN, *People of the Sea: The Search for the Philistines* (New York 1992).
S. GITIN, A. MAZAR and E. STERN (eds), *Mediterranean Peoples in Transition* (Jerusalem 1998).

The Horus Falcon of Ramesses III smiting a kneeling figure wearing the so-called Philistine headdress, from the temple at Medinet Habu, Egypt, c.1185 BC (courtesy of K.A. Kitchen).

N.K. SANDARS, *The Sea Peoples: Warriors of the Ancient Mediterranean 1250–1150*, rev. ed. (London 1985).

I. SINGER, 'The Origin of the Sea Peoples and Their Settlement on the Coast of Canaan', *Society and Economy in the Eastern Mediterranean (c. 1500–1000 B.C.)*, eds M. Heltzer and E. Lipinski (Louvain 1988) 239–50.

L.E. STAGER, 'The Impact of the Sea Peoples in Canaan (1185–1050 BCE)', *The Archaeology of Society in the Holy Land*, ed. T.E. Levy (London 1995) 333–48, 583–5.

**Seals**  There were two types of seals used in the ancient Near East: *cylinder and *stamp. Their use was either decorative and/or functional where the impression in clay acted as a mark of authority or of ownership. Generally the design was carved in intaglio so that when it was impressed the design in reverse appeared in relief. Some seals were made of *wood, *bone or *ivory but few of these have survived. The majority were made from *stones of various kinds (fashion and availability of exotic stones dictated their use). *Dynastic and royal seals have been found, as have the seals of individuals and institutions, for example government departments. Seals are associated with ownership and recording but can have other uses as amulets or votive objects. Changes in the design of seals can be traced through excavation of the seals themselves or more generally through the sealings (impressions) made on datable styles of *pottery or clay tablets and envelopes. Sealings far outnumber actual seals in the archaeological record and many designs are known only from impressions. At certain periods the seals themselves were inscribed in reverse so that the inscription can be read on the impressions, and this early form of 'printing' also enables seals to be dated.      PTC

D. COLLON, *First Impressions: Cylinder Seals in the Ancient Near East* (London 1987).

——, *Near Eastern Seals* (London 1990).

McG. GIBSON and R.D. BIGGS (eds), *Seals and Sealing in the Ancient Near East* (Malibu, CA 1977).

**Semiramis**  Two statues set up by a governor of *Nimrud about 800 BC bear *prayers for *King *Adad-nirari III and his mother Sammu-ramat. On a stela defining the border between Kummuh and Gurgum in southern *Anatolia she is named with her son, and a stela was erected to honour her at *Ashur among stelae of kings, *eponyms and a few royal ladies. Nothing else is known of her from contemporary records. Greek writers tell of Semiramis, a *Babylonian *queen, and this figure is agreed to be an echo of Sammu-ramat.

Diodorus Siculus in the first century BC related the tales of Ctesias who was a physician at the *Persian court about 400 BC. Semiramis married Ninus, and ruled for fifty-two years, building and beautifying *Babylon. Some writers report that she killed her husband and replaced him by Ninyas. A *Hellenistic romantic wrote a drama, known from papyrus fragments, about Ninus' love for the maiden Semiramis, and Armenian tradition told of her great campaign into Armenia (Diodorus says it was Ninus') and construction of *Van. The queen's name continues to be popular throughout the Near East.      ARM

W. EILERS, *Semiramis Entstehung und Nachhall einer altorientalischen Sage* (Vienna 1971).

D.D. LUCKENBILL, *Ancient Records of Assyria* 1 (Chicago 1926) 260, 264.

Stamp seal, Phoenician or Aramaic, engraved with an Egyptian-style figure and the name of the owner Mitsri. 13 mm high (courtesy of the Bibliothèque Nationale, Paris, De Luynes Collection 223).

Achaemenid seal from Borsippa, BM 89337 (Rich).

**Semites** *Israelite tradition gives twenty-six names as sons or descendants of Shem, son of Noah (Genesis 10: 21–31). Many are names known as places and, observing that people in some of them spoke related *languages (e.g. Asshur (=*Assyria), Hazarmaweth (=Hadramawt in South *Arabia), *Aram), in 1781 A.C. Schlözer categorized all these as 'Semitic' (=Shemitic, latinized). The languages taken today as Semitic have long been divided on the basis of shared and distinctive features into three branches, East, South and North-West, and the whole forms part of the wider Hamito-Semitic or Afrasian family, which includes Egyptian, Berber, and languages of sub-Saharan Africa.

The East Semitic branch is *Akkadian, attested from the middle of the third millennium BC onwards, South Semitic embraces the languages of the ancient Arabian kingdoms of the first millennia BC and AD, written in the South Arabian *alphabet, and the Semitic languages of Ethiopia carried across the Red Sea to the Horn of Africa (principally Amharic, Ge'ez, Tigre, Tigrinya). Arabic is commonly placed in this group. North-West Semitic covers *Amorite, *Ugaritic and *Canaanite (all in the second millennium BC), *Phoenician, *Hebrew and *Aramaic in the first millennium BC, the last two continuing thereafter.

Research on the Semitic languages has uncovered a range of words and forms spread through or shared between them, which seem to belong to the hypothetical 'Proto-Semitic', and sufficient is common between them and the 'Hamitic' languages to surmise an earlier ancestor for the whole Afrasian family. The resultant vocabulary indicates that it belonged to a *Neolithic pastoral society becoming acquainted with *agriculture but not yet with *metalworking, probably at home in north-east Africa or the *Levant.

Attempts to identify Semitic characteristics, whether through physical features, thought patterns, religious beliefs, desert lifestyle or other particularities do not withstand critical scrutiny. It is their language which distinguishes them. Semites have been conquerors, like *Sargon of *Akkad or *Sennacherib, ancient Semitic poets produced masterpieces like the *Epic of *Gilgamesh and the poems of the *Hebrew *Bible which also contains masterly narratives. The greatest Semitic *legacies to modern times are the practical one of the alphabet, the moral one of the Ten Commandments and their underlying monotheism which lives on in Judaism, Christianity and Islam.                        ARM

I.M. DIAKONOFF, *Afrasian Languages* (Moscow 1988).

R. HETZRON (ed.), *The Semiitc Languages* (London 1997).

S. MOSCATI, *An Introduction to the Comparative Grammar of the Semitic Languages* (Wiesbaden 1964).

V. OREL and O.V. STOLBOVA, *Hamito-Semitic Etymological Dictionary: Materials for a Reconstruction* (Leiden 1995).

**Sennacherib** '*Sîn has replaced his brothers' became *king of *Assyria in 704 BC, following the death of his father *Sargon in battle. Experienced in strategy and *administration, he took steps to secure his empire, quelling rebellions in the *Zagros and *Iran and in the *Levant (Hezekiah of *Judah). *Babylonia was an intractable problem. Merodach-Baladan, the *Chaldaean leader, was driven out and an Assyrian nominee, Bel-ibni,

Sennacherib in a chariot, overseeing transport of a colossal bull. Or. Dr. I,57.

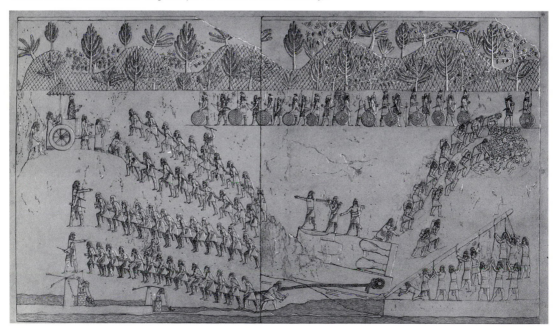

made king of *Babylon (703 BC). He rebelled, so Sennacherib set his son, Ashur-nadin-shumi, in his place. Babylonian rebels handed him to *Elamite forces and made Nergal-ushezib king (694 BC). He was followed by Mushezib-Marduk – both called Shuzubu in Sennacherib's texts. The Assyrian warded off Elamite forces supporting the Babylonians and captured Babylon and its king after a hard siege in 689 BC. Sennacherib avenged his son by diverting canals to level the *city and by carrying away the statue of *Marduk to *Ashur. Shorter campaigns took Sennacherib's forces into Cilicia, to *Tarsus and Tabal in 696 and 695 and into *Arabia, to *Duma about 690 BC. For the later years of his reign there are no narrative reports.

At the start of his reign, Sennacherib embarked upon the rebuilding of *Nineveh to replace his father's new city at *Khorsabad. The town was enclosed by a wall 12 km long, pierced by fifteen *gates. The king's 'Palace without a Rival' was erected at the south-west end of the ancient *tell and decorated lavishly with carved *stone slabs and pillars at the doorways resting on cast *bronze figures of bulls and lions. His scholars tried to assimilate the 'defeated' god *Marduk of Babylon to *Ashur, who replaced him as conqueror of *Tiamat in copies of Enuma eliš (see *Creation legends) and in bronze reliefs on doors of the *New Year shrine at Ashur.

Inscriptions on rock faces, stelae, relief *sculptures and *foundation prisms are the chief sources for Sennacherib's reign, all reporting in the first person in the '*annals' style. The Babylonian Chronicle gives another point of view, and the *biblical accounts (notably 2 Kings 18, 19) exult in his failure to capture *Jerusalem. *Family and *court intrigues led to Sennacherib's assassination in 681 BC by two of his sons, which was followed by a short period of uncertainty until his nominated successor, *Esarhaddon, who was not the eldest son, gained the throne.                                                                    ARM

A.K. GRAYSON, 'Sennacherib', Cambridge Ancient History 3.2, 2nd ed. (Cambridge 1991) 103–22.
D.D. LUCKENBILL, The Annals of Sennacherib (Chicago 1924).
——, Ancient Records of Assyria and Babylonia 2 (Chicago 1927) paras 231–496.
J.M. RUSSELL, Sennacherib's Palace without a Rival at Nineveh (Chicago 1991).

## Sexual behaviour

**Sexual behaviour** The *Hellenistic distaste for sexuality which informed *biblical and later Christian writing represented the Near East (and famously *Babylon) as the area given over to harlotry and fornication. This negative view of physical sexuality which contrasted civilized restraint with primitive licence also pervaded Near Eastern scholarship, resulting in an enduring fascination with such topics as the *Sacred Marriage and cult *prostitution.

Information about sexual behaviour and attitudes in the ancient Near East is based on literary texts, especially erotic *poetry, references in the *omen literature, *medico-*magical spells against impotence, and legal statutes regulating matters of concubinage, *adultery,

incest and, occasionally, *ritual defilement (see Law). In addition, there are archaeological objects, statuettes of naked females (and, rarer, males), genital parts, reliefs and *seals depicting copulating couples. From these indirect sources it is clear that sexuality was understood as the major life-force, the generative principle that ensures the perpetuation of the species and that binds human beings, vegetation and animal life in a shared concern with regeneration as the opposite to *death. The importance and sacredness of the erotic is part of the divine order and ritually affirmed.

While heterosexual and reproductive sexuality was seen as the natural manifestation of the erotic principle, alternative forms (either homosexuality or non-reproductive acts) were condoned as suitable for particular circumstances. Generally we know little about the social norms regulating sexual life, and there must have been considerable variations throughout the millennia, with differences between *social groups, classes and perhaps ethnic affiliation. Matters such as premarital sexuality, the relative importance of virginity, knowledge of female orgasm, incidence of homosexuality, promiscuity etc. remain difficult to determine.

In *Sumerian *literature, *Inana, *goddess of sexual desire and erotic drive, is the main protagonist in texts that celebrate female sexuality, rejoicing in the '*marriage-bed'. Her partner in many of these '*songs', which although showing all the stylistic refinements of courtly poetry may have had counterparts in vernacular songs, is the shepherd *Dumuzi. In royal *hymns the *king is likened to Dumuzi, like him 'he sweetens the lap of Inana'. In some myths of origin, the god Enki (*Ea) represents male and phallic sexuality, whose semen fills the *rivers with water; there is a marked correlation between *irrigation and ejaculation. *Babylonian literature develops the theme of erotic suffering (*Ereshkigal's loneliness in the *underworld, sexual jealousy) and the more problematic and ambiguous aspects of physical

Terracotta figures of couples engaging in sexual activity were probably used in rituals to overcome impotence. Nineteenth to seventeenth centuries BC. WA 115719.

attraction (*Gilgamesh, *Ishtar's descent).

*Hittite and *Hurrian texts also acknowledge the power of female sexuality and its limitations, as when the naked goddess confronts the dragon monster Illuyanka.

In *Canaanite mythology the vigour of the *weather-god, often conceived in the guise of a bull, correlates with the fertilizing powers of rain. The potency problems ascribed to some other, older weather gods (*El) reflect the instability of precipitation in the *Fertile Crescent. There are as yet no direct references to any orgiastic rituals of spring such as those described by *Greek writers for the *Phoenicians.

The accounts of the patriarchal period in the *Bible (Abraham, Jacob and their wives) reflect the social setting and norms of pastoralists, eager to enlarge their flocks and *families. The Song of Songs is a much debated collection of poetry, exulting erotic love, the beauty of the beloved and the emotional intensity of infatuation with such mastery of poetic artifice that it has remained canonical within the sacred traditions of two major religions.                                                        GL

B. ALSTER, 'Sumerian Love-songs', *Revue d'Assyriologie* 79 (1985) 127–59.

H. BALZ-COCHOIS, *Inanna: Wesensbild und Kult einer unmütterlichen Göttin* (Gütersloh 1992).

R.D. BIGGS, *ŠA.ZI.GA: Ancient Mesopotamian Potency Incantations* (Locust Valley, NY 1967).

J.S. COOPER, 'Enki's Member: Eros and Irrigation in Sumerian Literature', *Dumu-é-dub-ba-a* in Honor of A. Sjöberg, eds H. Behrens, D. Loding and M. Roth (Philadelphia, PA 1989) 87–9.

J.J. FINKELSTEIN, 'Sex Offenses in Sumerian Laws', *Journal of the American Oriental Society* 86 (1966) 355–72.

G. LEICK, *Sex and Eroticism in Mesopotamian Literature* (London 1994).

J.H. MARKS and R.M. GOOD (eds), *Love and Death in the Ancient Near East* (Guildford, CN 1987).

**Shahr-i Sokhta** Located in south-east *Iran, close to the border with Afghanistan, at 150 ha Shahr-i Sokhta is the largest known proto-historic settlement in the area. Excavations by an Italian team (1967–78) uncovered eleven phases grouped into four periods dating between c.3000 and 1800 BC.

The settlement of Period 1 (c.3000–2800 BC) was relatively small and little excavated, with *cylinder seals and impressions having parallels to Proto-*Elamite types and to Early Dynastic I *Mesopotamia. In Period II (c.2800–2500 BC) the site became a proto-urban centre, with well preserved groups of *houses, evidence for *copper *metallurgy, and long-distance trade attested by lapis lazuli, turquoise, alabaster and carnelian from the north and east. The site reached its maximum size in Period III (c.2500–2300 BC) when it became a regional centre, consisting of a large walled complex including a building with a drainage system, and distinct *craft quarters in the outer portions of the *city, each specializing in a specific material such as copper or lapis lazuli. Occupation contracted in Period IV (c.2300–1800 BC): the 'Burnt Building' extended over 500 sq m, with massive walls, a

corridor and staircases, followed later in the period by small-scale and lightly built structures.

The *cemetery to the south yielded *graves dated to Periods I–III, including graves of craftsmen, for example stone-bead makers buried with their *tools and raw material.                                                         PB

R.C. HENRICKSON, 'Shahr-i Sokhta', *The Dictionary of Art* 28, ed. J. Turner (New York/London 1996) 538.

M. TOSI (ed.), *Prehistoric Sistan* 1 (Rome 1985).

**Shalmaneser** 'The *god Shulman is pre-eminent' was the name of five *Assyrian *kings.

Shalmaneser I, son of *Adad-nirari I, c.1274–1244 BC. At his accession, *Urartian tribes in the *Zagros rebelled and were reduced and other tribes in the north-east were brought to heel. Shalmaneser's major success was the defeat of Shattuara of Hanigalbat, last of the *Hurrian rulers of former *Mitanni. His territory was put under *provincial governors, and Hurrians entered Assyrian service. Assyria's expansion worried the *Hittite King *Hattusilis, who made a *treaty with *Babylon and urged its king to attack Assyria, but any action was of little effect. Building inscriptions from *Ashur and *Nineveh detail the king's achievements.

Shalmaneser II, who ruled c.1031 to 1020 BC in the 'dark age', is known only from *King Lists, the *Eponym List, a stela from Ashur and a later copy of a list of gifts to the *temple of Ashur.

Shalmaneser III ruled from 858–824 BC. His policy was to consolidate the gains of his father, *Ashurnasirpal II, extending the frontiers where hostilities occurred. His inscriptions, on stelae, statues and tablets of clay and *stone, record thirty-four campaigns. He began with a sweep to the Mediterranean, attacking the *Aramaean state of Bit-Adini, a centre of resistance, reduced to a province on a second campaign. In 853 BC he marched west again, collecting tribute as he moved towards Aleppo, then fighting a league of twelve kings led by Adad-idri of *Damascus at Qarqar on the Orontes. Shalmaneser returned in 849, 848 and 845 BC to subdue western *Syria, an indication that his vaunted victory at Qarqar was indecisive, and in 841 BC ravaged the kingdom of Damascus under its new king Hazael, without taking the *city. In 856 and 844 BC he rampaged through parts of *Urartu, attacking again in 832 and 830–827 BC. In 835 BC his troops fought the *Medes in the Zagros. To the south, Babylon had a treaty with Assyria, but a local quarrel involved Assyria, so Shalmaneser entered Babylon in 851 and 850 BC, attacking the restless *Chaldaean tribes further south. From 832 BC onwards generals led the *army, and the king did not campaign personally, but was still credited with the victories his agents won. A son began a revolt in 827 BC which spread through the towns of Assyria, except *Nimrud, continuing beyond the king's *death. Shalmaneser built a great military headquarters and arsenal at Nimrud, now called Fort Shalmaneser. There a stone slab forming a throne base was carved with miniature reliefs depicting the kings of Assyria and Babylonia making a pact. Similar small reliefs on the Black

The 'Black Obelisk' of Shalmaneser III is one of the most famous Assyrian monuments. The pictures and inscriptions on all sides relate the submission and tribute of regions from Iran to Israel. Height 1.98 m. WA 118885.

Obelisk show tribute from Jehu of *Israel and others, and reliefs in the same style decorate *bronze bands once fastened to temple doors at *Balawat. From Ashur and Nimrud come stone statues of this king.

Shalmaneser IV, son of Adad-nirari III, 782–773 BC, is known only through the monuments powerful officials set up in his name, the *Eponym List and the *King List. The commander-in-chief led campaigns against *Urartu and there were others to the west, notably against Damascus in 773 BC.

Shalmaneser V, son of *Tiglath-pileser III, 726–722 BC. His reign is very poorly documented: the entries in

the *Eponym Chronicle are broken and there are no royal inscriptions. His name and titles appear on bronze *weights cast as lions found at *Nimrud. The Babylonian *Chronicle and the *Hebrew *Bible (2 Kings 17: 1–6) report his capture of *Samaria in 722 BC and a letter in the next century refers to action against Bit-Adini. Babylonian King List A, an *Aramaic letter on an *ostracon from *Ashur and the Canon of Ptolemy call him Ululayu, 'born in the month Elul'.                                    ARM

Shalmaneser I:
A.K. GRAYSON, *Assyrian Royal Inscriptions* 1 (Wiesbaden 1972) 79–100.
——, *Assyrian Rulers of the Third and Second Millennia BC (to 1115 BC)* (Toronto 1987) 180–230.
M. MUNN-RANKIN, 'Assyrian Military Power 1300–1200 B.C.', *Cambridge Ancient History* 2.2, 2nd ed. (Cambridge 1975) 279–84.

Shalmaneser II:
A.K. GRAYSON, *Assyrian Royal Inscriptions* 2 (Wiesbaden 1976) 68–70.
——, *Assyrian Rulers of the Early First Millennium BC I (1114–859 BC)* (Toronto 1991) 124.

Shalmaneser III:
A.K. GRAYSON, *Assyrian Rulers of the Early First Millennium BC II (858–745 BC)* (Toronto 1996) 5–179.
——, 'Assyria: Ashur-dan II to Ashur-nirari V (934–745 B.C.)', *Cambridge Ancient History* 3.1, 2nd ed. (Cambridge 1982) 259–69.
M.E.L. MALLOWAN, *Nimrud and its Remains* 2 (London 1966).

Shalmaneser IV:
A.K. GRAYSON, *Assyrian Rulers of the Early First Millennium BC II (858–745 BC)* (Toronto 1996) 239–44.
——, 'Assyria: Ashur-dan II to Ashur-nirari V (934–745 B.C.)', *Cambridge Ancient History* 3.1, 2nd ed. (Cambridge 1982) 276–79.

Shalmaneser V:
F.M. FALES, 'Assyro-Aramaica: The Assyrian Lion-weights', *Immigration and Emigration within the Ancient Near East*, eds K. van Lerberghe and A. Schoors (Leuven 1995) 33–55.
A.K. GRAYSON, 'Assyria: Tiglath-pileser III to Sargon II (744–705 B.C.)', *Cambridge Ancient History* 3.2, 2nd ed. (Cambridge 1991) 85–86.
——, *Assyrian and Babylonian Chronicles* (New York 1970) 73.

**Shamash** The *Akkadian word for the sun and therefore the name of the *Assyrian and *Babylonian sun-*god (*Sumerian Utu), who also served as god of justice. From the first appearance of the name as an element in some pre-*Sargonic Akkadian personal names (e.g. 'My mother is Shamash') and by analogy with the sun-goddess Shapash at *Ugarit, it seems possible that this deity was originally female, perhaps transformed into a male god by association with Sumerian Utu. Utu's principal shrines were at *Sippar in Akkad and *Larsa in southern Sumer. In the *city of Ashur the Assyrians built a *temple dedicated jointly to Shamash and the *moon-god.

As the sun, Shamash emerges in the morning from the eastern gate of heaven and traverses the earth, seeing

The sun-god Shamash is imagined on this cylinder seal design cutting his way through the eastern mountains at dawn. To the left are a warrior-goddess, perhaps Ishtar as the morning star, and a warrior-god, to the right the water-god Ea. The two-faced god behind him is his attendant. The inscription names the owner as 'Adda the scribe'. Height 3.9 cm. Akkadian period, c.2250 BC. WA 89115.

all things and accompanying travellers. *Cylinder seals depict him standing between two large open doors, held by a pair of gatekeepers, and emerging from between two mountains, the twin-peaked Mount Mashu, said to be located near the eastern gate of heaven in the Babylonian *Gilgamesh *epic. In *art he often brandishes his distinctive pruning-saw, which has an arc-shaped blade with jagged teeth; this he uses to cut his way through the mountains and, metaphorically, to cut decisions in his court of *law. At night the god re-enters the 'interior of heaven' through its western gate. There he dines and sleeps in his chamber (and does not, as is often stated, spend the night travelling through the *underworld).

As the god of justice he destroys wrongdoers, rewards the just and supports the downtrodden. He was also credited with giving *omens, granting happiness and long life and controlling the seasons. Sometimes, especially in Neo-Assyrian inscriptions, he is also cast as a warrior. Shamash does not play any great part, however, in *mythical narratives, although he figures with some importance in the legend of *Etana and in the Epic of *Gilgamesh.

Though it has often been ascribed to the god *Ashur, the *divine symbol of Shamash was probably the winged disk. It might be thought strange that Shamash, and not the supreme deity Ashur, should be seen hovering within the disk over Assyrian scenes of battle, but this should perhaps be related to the belief that victory on the battlefield was due to a favourable verdict in the court of the sun-god.

The sun-gods corresponding to Shamash in *Anatolia were the *Hattic deity Eshtan and the *Hurrian god Shimige; Wurusemu, identified with Hebat, was the sun-goddess of the town of Arinna, important in the Hittite cult.
AG/JAB

G.R. CASTELLINO, 'The Šamaš Hymn: A Note on its Structure', *Kramer Anniversary Volume,* ed. B.L. Eichler (Neukirchen/Vluyn 1976) 71–4.

F.M.T. DE LIAGRE BÖHL, 'Das Problem ewigen Lebens im Zyklus und Epos des Gilgamesch', *Das Gilgamesch-Epos,* ed. K. Oberhuber (Darmstadt 1977) 237–75.

W. HEIMPEL, 'The Sun at Night and the Doors of Heaven in Babylonian Texts', *Journal of Cuneiform Studies* 38 (1986) 127–51.

W.G. LAMBERT, *Babylonian Wisdom Literature* (Oxford 1960) 121–38.

M.J. SEUX, *Hymnes et prières aux dieux de Babylone et d'Assyrie* (Paris 1976).

K. TALLQVIST, *Akkadische Götterepitheta* (Helsinki 1938) 457–8.

**Shamshi-Adad** Shamshi-Adad, 'Adad is my sun', was the name of five *Assyrian *kings, only the first and the last being significant.

Shamshi-Adad I (c.1813–1781 BC) was an *Amorite chief who, according to the Assyrian *King List, sought refuge in *Babylonia from the current ruler of Assyria, then moved back and seized the throne. His father, Ilakabkabu, had not been king, but perhaps belonged to a branch of the royal family. Shamshi-Adad proceeded to enlarge his realm, fighting tribes in the *Zagros to the east

Shamshi-Adad V dedicated this stela to the god Ninurta at Nimrud, having his figure carved on it with an account of his achievements. It is the major source of information for his reign. Height c.2 m. WA 118892.

and reaching westwards to conquer *Mari and much of Upper *Mesopotamia, then reached the *Lebanon and erected stelae on the coast, securing good relations with the kings of *Aleppo and *Qatna. Shamshi-Adad made his capital in the *Khabur region, at Shubat Enlil (Tell *Leilan), whence he could better control his kingdom. *Letters found at Mari illustrate his energy and skills and his relations with his sons, Ishme-Dagan, ably governing in Assyria and immature Yasmah-Adad posted at Mari. After his death they could not resist neighbouring powers or the claimant to Mari and only Ishme-Dagan was left, holding Assyria. Shamshi-Adad's rule aided the *trade already established with *Anatolia (see Kanesh) and set a pattern for later rulers to imitate. There are building inscriptions of his from *Ashur, *Nineveh and Terqa and letters and dedicatory notices from Mari, and the number of *seals and seal impressions of his officials indicates the extensive administrative machine he set up.

Shamshi-Adad V (823–811 BC) had to spend the early years of his reign crushing the rebellion led by his brother which had clouded the end of the rule of *Shalmaneser III, his father. Thereafter he mounted three campaigns against Nairi (*Urartu) and also the *Medes, the second being led by an official, securing territory in the north and east and receiving *horses as tribute. His last years (814–811 BC) were occupied with Babylonia. King Marduk-zakir-shumi had apparently helped him against his brother and made a *treaty in which Assyria took the junior place (a fragment survives). The next king of *Babylon behaved differently, so Assyria invaded and captured that king, finally reaching Babylon and capturing the next king, leaving the land in chaos. Shamshi-Adad set up stelae at *Nimrud, Nineveh and Ashur, some written in archaic script, and did building work at Nineveh and at Ashur, where his empty *stone *coffin was found. Fragmentary information about his campaigns comes from what appears to be a divine response to a request for an oracle.                    ARM

Shamshi-Adad I:

A.K. GRAYSON, Assyrian Royal Inscriptions 1 (Wiesbaden 1972) 18–28.

——, Assyrian Rulers of the Third and Second Millennia BC (to 1115 BC) (Toronto 1987) 47–76.

J.-R. KUPPER, 'Northern Mesopotamia and Syria', Cambridge Ancient History 2.1, 2nd ed. (Cambridge 1973) 1–8.

P. VILLARD, 'Shamshi-Adad and Sons', Civilizations of the Ancient Near East, ed. J.M. Sasson (New York 1995) 873–83.

Shamshi-Adad V:

J.A. BRINKMAN, 'Babylonia, c.1000–748 B.C.', Cambridge Ancient History 3.1, 2nd ed. (Cambridge 1982) 308–9.

A.K. GRAYSON, Assyrian Rulers of the Early First Millennium BC II (858–745 BC) (Toronto 1996) 180–99.

——, 'Assyria: Ashur-dan II to Ashur-nirari V (934–745 B.C.)', Cambridge Ancient History 3.1, 2nd ed. (Cambridge 1982) 269–71.

**Shanidar** Shanidar cave is located in the north-east corner of Iraq at an elevation of 822 m above sea level. It is on the south face of the Baradost mountain overlooking the Shanidar Valley. It is a large cave with deep sediments (c.13 m) first occupied 100,000 years ago. Apart from providing a key early sequence in the *Zagros from Middle through Upper *Palaeolithic and *Epipalaeolithic, it has particularly important Middle Palaeolithic and possibly late Epipalaeolithic/early *Neolithic *burials and evidence for Late Epipalaeolithic settlement.

In the Middle Palaeolithic Phase D are a number of remains of Neanderthals, one of the most easterly finds of this species of hominid. There are the remains of nine individuals representing the largest sample of Neanderthals in the Near East. Whilst some of these remains were disturbed, at least one seems to be an undisturbed burial. Flower pollen suggests that this corpse was deliberately buried with flowers, though this claim has been contested. Detailed analysis of these bones suggests interesting features of the life and *death of these Neanderthals. Shanidar 1, a male, suffered head injuries and crushing of the right side of his body followed by infections and partial paralysis. Though disabled he lived with his injuries for several years, indicating that he was cared for in Neanderthal society. The Shanidar 3 male had a partly healed rib wound suggesting violence within Neanderthal society, resulting in his case in eventual death although the man lingered for some weeks.

In Shanidar level B is a *flint assemblage that seems to belong to the tenth millennium BC, spanning the development from late Epipalaeolithic to earliest Neolithic. Storage pits and fragmentary arcs of *stone suggest structures and storage facilities, paralleling developments found in the contemporary *Natufian. The flint industry of Shanidar B is similar to the nearby open-air site of Zawi Chemi.

In the upper part of the Shanidar B deposits were twenty-six burials believed by the excavators to belong to the late Epipalaeolithic. More recently it has been suggested they might have been cut into these deposits during the Neolithic. This is significant as the pathology of the remains suggests indications of conflict (disputed) and (less controversial) dental wear associated with the consumption of processed plant *foods.                    DB

R. SOLECKI, Shanidar: The First Flower People (New York 1971).
E. TRINKHAUS, The Shanidar Neanderthals (New York 1983).

**Shasu** The *shasu* are mentioned only in *Egyptian texts, mostly lists of conquered *towns and enemies, between c.1500 and 1100 BC. They are variously described as tribes of semi-*nomadic pastoralists who live in tents, rebels, highwaymen, mercenaries, and possibly occasionally as town-dwellers. The references place them particularly in *Transjordan, specifically *Edom and *Moab, but also elsewhere in *Palestine, the *Negev, southern *Syria and even in Nubia. The *shasu* are represented pictorially on Egyptian reliefs, but it is difficult to distinguish them from other Asiatics.

The meaning of the word *shasu* is uncertain: it is related either to the Egyptian 'to wander' or to the *Semitic 'to plunder'. They were not an ethnic group but, rather like the *habiru*, a *social class of quarrelsome trouble-makers.                    PB

R. GIVEON, *Les bédouins Shosou des documents égyptiens* (Leiden 1971).

D.B. REDFORD, *Egypt, Canaan, and Israel in Ancient Times* (Princeton, NJ 1992) 269–80.

W.A. WARD, 'The Shasu "Bedouin": Notes on a Recent Publication', *Journal of the Economic and Social History of the Orient* 15 (1972) 35–60.

M. WEIPPERT, 'Semitische Nomaden des zweiten Jahrtausends: über die *S3sw* der ägyptischen Quellen', *Biblica* 55 (1974) 265–80, 427–33.

**Sheba**  Saba' appeared earlier and lasted longer than any of the other South *Arabian kingdoms. Sheba is the form in which the name appears in the *Old Testament, but the native form is Saba'. There are still grave difficulties in establishing the *chronology of ancient Yemen but the most recent evidence, based on radiocarbon dates from a number of sites in the north of the country, points to the following. In the eighth century BC a number of 'states' were clustered around the edges of the Sayhad desert (the modern Ramlat-al-Sab'atayn) in the centre of Yemen. Although they were heavily involved in the *trade in aromatics, particularly frankincense (see Incense and spices), their *economies were based on *agriculture. Near the Sabaean capital, Marib, on the edge of the Sayhad desert, a huge dam was constructed, possibly in the second, or even the third millennium BC, on a wadi which received the run-off from a vast network of valleys during the twice-yearly monsoons. This dam, which lasted until the sixth century AD and was considered one of the wonders of the ancient world, was designed not to stop and store the *water but to break its force and deflect it into a system of *irrigation channels and smaller storage tanks covering an immense area.

At the beginning of the seventh century BC Karib'il Watar, son of Dhamar'ali, the Mukarrib (federator) of Saba', extended his rule over most of South Arabia and initiated a period of Sabaean hegemony which lasted until the fourth century BC. It seems very likely that this is the 'Karibilu, king of Saba'' who sent gifts to the *Assyrian King *Sennacherib between 689 and 681 BC.

The earliest references to Saba' date from the eighth century BC and are found in both the Sabaic inscriptions in Yemen and in the Assyrian *annals. It used to be thought that, at this period, the Sabaeans were a *nomadic North Arabian tribe which moved to the south only several centuries later. However, recent archaeological and epigraphic research has shown that this view is untenable. In the Old Testament, Saba' (Sheba) is very often associated with *Dedan, the oasis settlement through which South Arabian goods reached *Palestine and the Mediterranean, whereas in the Assyrian and *Babylonian records Saba' is usually linked with *Tayma, the oasis through which merchandise travelled to *Mesopotamia. A *cuneiform report by Ninurta-kudurri-usur, the governor of Suhu on the Euphrates in the eighth century BC, describes how he ambushed a caravan of the people of Tayma and Saba' which had tried to evade paying customs dues. He lists the goods it was carrying (unfortunately in a fragmentary passage) which included mauve-dyed (*takiltu*) wool and *iron, but no aromatics. This suggests that the caravan was on its way home with goods bought in exchange for South Arabia's most sought after export, frankincense.

Remains of the dam at Marib, the capital of Saba' (Sheba) (courtesy of M.C.A. Macdonald).

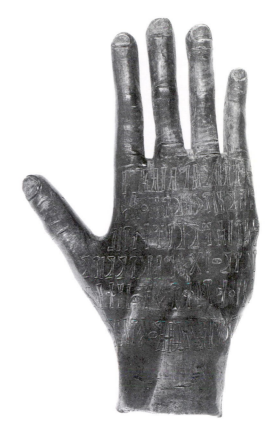

In Hellenistic and Roman times the prosperity of southern Arabia was displayed in the casting of bronze plaques to commemorate pious acts. This Sabaic inscription in the Old South Arabic alphabet, dedicated to the moon-god, comes from Amran, Yemen. Height 44.5 cm. WA 1862-10-28, 4/48456.

Bronze hand, with a Sabaic dedicatory inscription referring to the god Ta'lab. WA 1983-6-26, 2/139443.

The biblical story of the Queen of Sheba (set in the tenth century BC but composed in the sixth) has all the hallmarks of being a literary creation. There is no evidence of *queens-regnant in Saba' or any other South Arabian state at any period.

The Sabaeans were always settled farmers and *merchants. Their *religion centred on a hierarchy of local, regional and communal deities. Social organization was both tribal and regional. The Sabaic *language belonged to a sub-group of *Semitic whose only living relatives are the non-Arabic spoken languages of Yemen and Oman and some of the languages of Ethiopia. The script in which they wrote was one of the South Semitic group of *alphabets which shared a common ancestor with the *Phoenicio-*Aramaic script, but which had followed its own course of development (including its own letter order) in both North and South Arabia since the late second millennium BC. This script, with only minor

differences, was used for monumental inscriptions by all the kingdoms of South Arabia, and at a later period a cursive was developed for private documents which were incised with a stylus on soft-*wood sticks. Such was the prestige of Saba' that the Sabaic language and script continued to be used long after the demise of the kingdom, and it was also employed in monumental inscriptions in eastern and central Arabia by those who spoke quite different languages. MCAM

W. DAUM (ed.), *Yemen: 3000 Years of Art and Civilisation in Arabia Felix* (Innsbruck, no date).

M.C.A. MACDONALD, 'Trade Routes and Trade Goods at the Northern End of the "Incense Road" in the First Millennium B.C.', *Profumi d'Arabia*, ed. A. Avanzini (Rome 1997) 333–49.

C.J. ROBIN, 'Sheba: 2. Dans les inscriptions d'Arabie du Sud', *Supplément au Dictionnaire de la Bible* 12, eds J. Brend *et al.* (Paris 1996) cols 1047–254.

——, *L'Arabie antique de Karib'il à Mahomet: Nouvelles données sur l'histoire des Arabes grâce aux inscriptions* (*Revue du monde Musulman et de la Méditerranée* 61) (Aix en Provence 1991).

**Sheikh Hamad, (Tell)** Situated on the left bank of the *Khabur *river in eastern *Syria to the north of Der ez-Zor, Tell Sheikh Hamad was in *Assyrian times known as Dur-Katlimmu, an important *city with a citadel and lower town. After initial investigations by *Rassam in

Excavations in progress at Tell Sheikh Hamad, showing part of a late seventh-century BC mudbrick building (courtesy of Hartmut Kühne).

1879, in recent years the site has been extensively excavated by Hartmut Kühne (1978–).

Fluctuations in the size of the settlement reflect the fortunes of Sheikh Hamad through the long history of its occupation. Late *Chalcolithic and Early Bronze Age settlements were succeeded by an expansion of the city during the Old *Babylonian period, c.2000–1500 BC, when the citadel was first occupied. Following a spell of *Mitannian domination, the city became the seat of a regional governor during the Middle Assyrian empire, c.1300 BC. Excavation of the governor's *palace recovered an *archive of some five hundred *cuneiform tablets, giving the ancient name of the city as Dur-Katlimmu.

During the late eighth century BC a newly constructed town wall enclosed a total of some 55 ha and settlement expanded beyond the city wall throughout the Neo-Assyrian period, c.800–612 BC. Dur-Katlimmu became the regional centre for a large area of the Khabur during this time, its urban amenities including a palace, well-appointed residences for high officials, wide streets and communal open spaces.

After the collapse of the Assyrian empire in 612 BC, Sheikh Hamad, probably now under the name of Magdalu, came under the control of the Neo-Babylonian empire, which administered the city and its territory through a palace and *administrative buildings. A small group of clay tablets, written in both Assyrian and *Aramaic, indicate the survival of Assyrian and Aramaic traditions after the fall of the Assyrian empire. A reduced scale of occupation continued at the site through the *Persian, *Hellenistic, *Roman, Byzantine and Islamic periods.                                                       RM

H. KÜHNE (ed.), *Die Rezente Umwelt von Tall Šeh Hamad und Daten zur Umweltrekonstruktion der Assyrischen Stadt Dur-Katlimmu* (Berlin 1991).

——, 'Sheikh Hamad, Tell', *The Oxford Encyclopedia of Archaeology in the Near East* 5, ed. E.M. Meyers (New York 1997) 25–6.

H. KÜHNE and A. LUTHER, 'Tall Šeh Hamad/Dur-Katlimmu/ Magdalu?', *Nouvelles Assyriologiques Brèves et Utilitaires* (1998/4, December) 106–9.

W. RÖLLIG, 'Dur-katlimmu', *Orientalia* 47 (1978) 419–30.

**Ships:** see Boats and ships

**Shipwrecks**  Along with the famous story of Jonah and his shipmates in a raging storm at sea, the *Bible contains two famous accounts of shipwrecks. One of these passages, in Ezekiel 27, is a lament for the *Phoenician city of *Tyre, and the shipwreck is a figurative expression of God's displeasure at Tyre's pride. Verses 34–6 prophesied that the great seagoing *ship ('merchantman') of Tyre would be shattered by the sea, and its cargo and crew would go down to the depths. Acts 27: 13–44 contains a detailed account of an actual shipwreck, the sinking of a *Roman grain ship whose passengers included the Apostle Paul. Before this vessel's crew could escape a Mediterranean storm by beaching their ship, they struck a sandbar and the stern was broken apart by pounding surf. These two famous texts draw attention to – or symbolize – a phenomenon that was repeated throughout ancient Near Eastern and Mediterranean history thousands of times. In a recent study, Parker provides

Many of these ships broke up on headlands, sandbars, or reefs while many ancient sailors – like the crew described in Acts 27 – tried to save themselves and their cargoes by running ships ashore in storms. Other ships sank after fires or were abandoned because of *war or piracy. Shipwrecks are documented for every country in the Mediterranean basin, and a smaller number of ancient sites are known in other bodies of water.

The first complete excavation of a seagoing vessel was that of G. Bass at Cape *Gelidonya, in 1960. This small ship went down off the southern coast of Turkey c.1200 BC. The other important shipwreck at *Ulu Burun, also off southern Turkey, dates to c.1300 BC. Bass and other specialists in this field have learned much about ancient ship construction and the nature, origins, ports of call and destinations of ships and cargoes. While much can be known about ancient trade from literary records and artistic evidence, the recovery of actual ships and their contents has contributed immeasurably to the study of international trade in antiquity. Organic materials are far better preserved under water than on land and provide much useful information on trade in perishable substances.

Possibly the world's oldest known deep-water shipwrecks were recently discovered c.50 km off the Mediterranean coast of Israel. Preliminary reports identify the well preserved ships as Phoenician on the basis of their cargoes, and date them to c.750 BC.          GLM

G.F. BASS, *Archaeology under Water*, 2nd ed. (Harmondsworth 1970).
——, *Shipwrecks in the Bodrum Museum of Underwater Archaeology* (Ankara 1996).
L. CASSON, *Ships and Seamanship in the Ancient World* (Princeton, NJ 1971).
J.P. DELGADO (ed.), *British Museum Encyclopedia of Underwater and Maritime Archaeology* (London 1997).
M.-C. DE GRAEVE, *The Ships of the Ancient Near East, c. 2000–500 B.C.* (Louvain 1981).
A.J. PARKER, *Ancient Shipwrecks of the Mediterranean and the Roman Provinces* (Oxford 1992).
P. THROCKMORTON (ed.), *The Sea Remembers: Shipwrecks and Archaeology* (New York 1987).

Lifting balloons raising some of the stone anchors from the Ulu Burun shipwreck (courtesy of the Institute of Nautical Archaeology).

information on 1189 shipwrecks documented in the Mediterranean region. Many times this number must have sunk in antiquity, and future research will undoubtedly expand this inventory. In Parker's list, only thirty-seven ships predate 500 BC, but this small number has already provided a wealth of information concerning ancient *trade and *transport.

Nautical – or 'underwater' – *archaeology is a recent development, which was greatly enhanced by the invention of the aqualung (SCUBA) in the 1940s. Though many shipwrecks had already been located by sponge divers and fishermen, the use of modern diving equipment and other technology has helped scholars gain access to the valuable data on the sea floor. Nowadays nautical archaeologists employ many of the same methods that were developed to excavate sites on dry land. Of course, underwater excavation has its own problems, especially those related to the amount of time divers can stay down and the complications of decompression. Techniques of digging in – or removing – sand and recording finds are different. In terms of the preservation and removal of submerged materials, each shipwreck must be treated as a unique site.

Most of the known shipwrecks are from the Roman period. This indicates that the experience gained from many centuries of navigation was not sufficient to cope with the various factors that sank ships through the ages.

**Shiqmim**  Shiqmim was excavated by T.E. Levy in the 1980s. It is located in the Wadi Beer Sheba in the northern *Negev where a large number of other contemporary *Chalcolithic sites are known. It is close to the limits of reliable rain-fed *agriculture. Indeed claims are made that crops on the site were grown in a regime of 'floodwater' farming. The site dates to the Chalcolithic between c.4500 and 3800 BC.

The site covers approximately 10 ha, one of the largest Chalcolithic sites in the region, and may have been a regional centre. It is interesting to contrast the nature of the evidence from Shiqmim with a proximate site of the same size of a slightly later period such as *Arad in the Early *Bronze Age II period. Arad shows many features of a *town which Shiqmim notably lacks. Nevertheless Shiqmim may indicate some of the features of a central place.

In the earlier phases of settlement dwellings were subterranean, a series of chambers and tunnels cut back into a terrace in the local loess subsoil. These are typical for the earlier phases of a number of local Chalcolithic settlements. It is suggested that such a method of construction would have aided defence or provided insulation for people, *animals and stored goods alike in the hot summers and cold winters.

Later phases are characterized by a series of rectangular structures. Little differentiates these structures from one another. Indeed it is intriguing that *metalworking debris seems to be associated with a number of these building complexes. This debris includes ore and slag as well as evidence of moulds and *tools. It would appear that all stages of metalworking are represented and that *copper was brought as ore from the Faynan area c.90 km to the south-east. Manufacturing seems to have involved the production of simple pure copper tools in open moulds rather than the complex lost-wax alloys of the Nahal Mishmar hoard. Given this acquisition of metals, the Shiqmim community may have played a significant part in the regional distribution of copper and copper tools. However, there is little evidence of specialists on site, and much of the community may have had a role in copperworking. Further, a number of other Chalcolithic sites in the Wadi Beer Sheba and immediate environs have evidence for copperworking. Perhaps it was a major regionally based industry allowing Wadi Beer Sheba inhabitants to engage in wider-ranging exchanges.

There may have been a hierarchy in the community at Shiqmim based on the evidence from a series of circular stone cairns wherein a number of the community were buried. Some cairns are larger than others. These *burials and particularly the larger might indicate the high status of those buried. In addition a few individuals were buried with grave goods including, rarely, a copper macehead, which may have been a symbol of status as much as a weapon.                                                      DB

T.E. LEVY, *Shiqmim* 1 (Oxford 1987).
T.E. LEVY and S. SHALEV, 'Prehistoric Metalworking in the Southern Levant: Archaeometallurgical and Social Perspectives', *World Archaeology* 20 (1989) 353–72.

**Shops and markets** Although supply and demand created a market among the *merchants of *Babylonia and *Assyria, the same forces may not have applied throughout society and there is little evidence for the existence of shops and market places in the ancient Near East. Excavations have tended to concentrate on monumental buildings in settlements, and exploration of areas likely to reveal shops is limited to just a few sites like *Ugarit and *Ur. *Sumerian texts mention pedlars selling roasted barley, salt and alkali (for soap) as well as *beer-makers, but there is little to suggest that this ever took place in shops. From the Old Babylonian period there are references to what might be a small shop possibly selling luxury items.

*Archaeology has revealed what arguably may be a *suq* (oriental market) at the *trading *city of Ugarit as well as

warehouses which might have served a similar purpose. In second-millennium BC *Anatolia, one- or two-room units opening on to the streets at *Alaca Hüyük have been taken to be shops or workshops, while at *Beycesultan there appears to be an example of a grain shop or *food store where large storage jars (some 1.5 m high) were discovered half full of wheat, barley or lentils. Storage jars in the next room were associated with a pile of drinking cups. *Palace courtyards are mentioned in some *Mari letters as the place where goods are unloaded to be taxed. It is possible that large open squares within cities served as places for the exchange of goods or as caravanserais. *Gateways often served as market areas of towns. The control of prices by central authorities is found in the *laws of *Hammurabi, *Eshnunna and the *Hittite laws but how these relate to markets is unknown.          PTC

A.L. OPPENHEIM, *Ancient Mesopotamia: Portrait of a Dead Civilization* (Chicago 1977).
J.N. POSTGATE, *Early Mesopotamia: Society and Economy at the Dawn of History* (London 1992).

**Shulgi**  Shulgi ruled *Ur for forty-eight years (c.2094–2047 BC), reinforcing the kingdom his father *Ur-Nammu had established. His year names report military expeditions, including several to the north-east (Arbela in *Assyria and the *Zagros foothills) and to *Iran, where he gained control of major routes and married one of his

Terracotta drain-pipe from Ur, inscribed with the name and title of Shulgi, king of Ur. WA 118729.

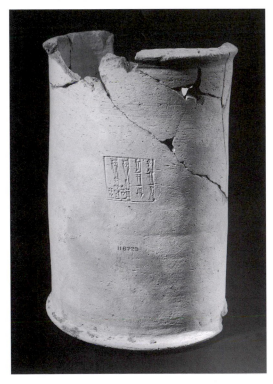

daughters to a local ruler. In the west *diplomacy maintained good relations with *Mari and other places. From Mari, *Ebla and *Byblos sheep were sent as offerings to Ur, joining numerous other *animals and all kinds of produce collected at revenue centres throughout the land. Thousands of tablets from one *city in particular, Puzrish-Dagan (now Drehem) near *Nippur, demonstrate the elaborate *administrative system Shulgi put into effect from his seventeenth year for receiving and using *taxes. The central provinces paid *bala* tax in their main products, the peripheral ones paid *gún ma-da* tax, a sort of rent as they were treated as crown property. This required a hierarchy of officials, from governors down to clerks and workmen to manage income and expenditure most effectively. The meticulous bureaucracy is evident in small tablets recording receipts of single sheep beside large ones summarizing a year's transactions, balancing credits and debits. Standardization of *weights and of the *calendar helped to facilitate the system. Shulgi kept control by placing members of his *family in most of the important positions, even his *queen and daughters playing a role. He followed the lead of *Naram-Sin of *Akkad in deifying himself, and several *hymns express this by describing him in exaggerated terms, lauding, among other things, his ability to run huge distances (from Nippur to Ur and back in one day) and to read and write.

The empire so carefully organized began to weaken after Shulgi's *death and collapsed under external and internal pressures, with his grandson Ibbi-Sin being carried prisoner to *Elam (c.2004 BC).          ARM

C.J. GADD, 'Babylonia c.2120–1800 B.C.', *Cambridge Ancient History* 1.2, 2nd ed. (Cambridge 1971) 595–623.

J. KLEIN, *The Royal Hymns of Shulgi, King of Ur* (Philadelphia, PA 1981).

——, *Three Shulgi Hymns* (Ramat-Gan 1981).

——, 'Shulgi of Ur: King of a Neo-Sumerian Empire', *Civilizations of the Ancient Near East*, ed. J.M. Sasson (New York 1995) 842–57.

S.N. KRAMER, 'The King of the Road: A Self-laudatory Shulgi Hymn', *Ancient Near Eastern Texts*, ed. J.B. Pritchard (Princeton, NJ 1969) 584–6.

P. MICHALOWSKI, 'Charisma and Control: On Continuity and Change in Early Mesopotamian Bureaucratic Systems', *The Organization of Power: Aspects of Bureaucracy in the Ancient Near East*, eds McG. Gibson and R.D. Biggs (Chicago 1987) 55–68.

P. STEINKELLER, 'The Administration and Economic Organization of the Ur III State: Core and Periphery', *The Organization of Power: Aspects of Bureaucracy in the Ancient Near East*, eds McG. Gibson and R.D. Biggs (Chicago 1987) 19–41.

**Shuruppak** Shuruppak, modern Fara, was a large *Sumerian *city in southern Iraq. In Sumerian *literature the city was famous as the home of Utnapishtim, who survived the *Babylonian *Flood and went to *Dilmun where he was visited by *Gilgamesh. Excavations at Shuruppak were conducted by Ernst Heinrich (1902) and Erich Schmidt (1931).

Drawing of a seal impression of late Early Dynastic I date from Shuruppak, showing a bird above two deer, two men and filling motifs including a dagger. Height c.5.25 cm (after H.P. Martin, *Fara: A Reconstruction of the Ancient Mesopotamian City of Shuruppak* (Birmingham 1988) 244 no. 196).

The earliest settlement of the city was in the *Jemdet Nasr period, c.3000 BC. Shuruppak was then extensively occupied through the Early Dynastic period, c.3000–2350 BC, and finally abandoned at the end of the *Ur III period, c.2000 BC. At its largest, the city covered at least 200 ha.

Deposits of Jemdet Nasr date were not extensively excavated, but are substantial. The building in area IIIa–c may have been a *temple of Jemdet Nasr to Early Dynastic I date. A large rubbish dump in area Id/Ie is contemporary with the IIIa–c building and contained large quantities of clay sealings indicating *administrative activity.

Various mudbrick structures of Early Dynastic III date were excavated. Many of these buildings contained large numbers of *cuneiform tablets with Sumerian *writing. Of special interest are: the Tablet House, perhaps a specialized institution dealing in up to 9660 donkeys and 1200 men; the *house in area XVa–d with texts showing ownership of 100 ha of land; the house in area IXa–c where exclusively lexical and literary texts were found; the large building in area XVIIc–d with texts listing up to 6580 workers, some from other Sumerian cities such as *Uruk, Adab, *Nippur, *Lagash, Umma and *Kish; and the house in area XIIIf–i where texts and clay sealings show the execution of administrative practices within an apparently domestic house. Large silos, probably for grain storage, were also excavated.

The Early Dynastic III evidence from Shuruppak has an important bearing on the debate over the nature of Sumerian society. Texts and other archaeological evidence suggest that the Sumerian citizens of Shuruppak fulfilled a dual *economic role, firstly within a household context, and secondly within the wider communal context of the city and its partners on the *Mesopotamian plain.          RM

E. HEINRICH, *Fara: Ergebnisse der Ausgrabungen der Deutschen Orient Gesellschaft in Fara und Abu Hatab 1902/03* (Berlin 1931).

H.P. MARTIN, *Fara: A Reconstruction of the Ancient Mesopotamian City of Shuruppak* (Birmingham 1988).

R.J. MATTHEWS, 'Fragments of Officialdom from Fara', *Iraq* 53 (1991) 1–15.

E.F. SCHMIDT, 'Excavations at Fara, 1931', *University of Pennsylvania Museum Journal* 22 (1931) 193–245.

**Sialk, (Tepe)** On the western edge of the central plateau of *Iran, Tepe Sialk was a key site in the early study of the *archaeology of Iran. Excavations by *Ghirshman (1933–7) revealed a settlement sequence from late *Neolithic (Sialk I–II) to *Chalcolithic (Sialk III–IV), early sixth to late fourth millennia BC. Clay tablets from Sialk IV paralleled those at Proto-*Elamite *Susa. Nearby are *Iron Age *cemeteries of periods V (c.1350–1100 BC, Necropolis A) and VI (c.1100–800 BC, Necropolis B), the individual *graves roofed with gables of terracotta or *stone slabs. These cemeteries are not associated with any known settlements.                                          PB

R. GHIRSHMAN, *Fouilles de Sialk, près de Kashan, 1933, 1934, 1937* (Paris 1938).

R.C. HENRICKSON, 'Sialk, Tepe', *The Dictionary of Art* 28, ed. J. Turner (New York/London 1996) 647.

A. TOUROVETZ, 'Observations concernant le matériel archéologique des nécropoles A et B de Sialk', *Iranica Antiqua* 24 (1989) 209–44.

**Sidon:** see Phoenicia

Silver and copper vase dedicated by Entemena (possibly to be read as Enmetena) of Lagash to the god Ningirsu. Early Dynastic period, c.2400 BC (© Photo RMN – H. Lewandowski. Louvre AO 2674).

**Silver** Ancient *Mesopotamian texts refer to the Silver Mountain, often identified with the Taurus range of southern Turkey, a major source of silver in antiquity. Silver (*Akkadian *kaspu*) appears around the late fourth millennium BC throughout western Asia from *Beycesultan and *Arslantepe to *Byblos, sites in the southern *Levant, and Predynastic Egypt. In Mesopotamia, *Uruk has produced a *copper-silver arrowhead from the Riemchen Building, and a silver vase from the *Jemdet Nasr period. The finely decorated vase of Entemena (or Enmetena) of *Lagash dates to the mid third millennium BC, as does an impressive variety of objects from the Royal *Cemetery at *Ur including belts, vessels, ornaments and decorated *weapons.

In Mesopotamia, silver was used from the late third millennium BC onwards as a standard of value and a medium of exchange. Prices for commodities such as land, livestock and various manufactures, as well as legal fines and compensation, could all be reckoned as amounts of silver bullion. Various hoards dating to the Akkadian period have produced silver rings and coils which might be currency, and from which specific amounts of silver were removed to make payments (see Money). During the first millennium BC, silver was used for the production of *coinage, first in *Anatolia, then in Mesopotamia and other regions.

Silver is generally obtained from smelted lead ores by the process of cupellation. Evidence for this process has been reported from a late fourth-millennium BC context at *Habuba Kabira in *Syria. Silver was less easy to work than *gold, and its hardness was often improved by the addition of a small amount of copper. In both *Egypt and the southern Levant a significant proportion of early silver objects appear to contain several per cent gold. Such aurian silver may be the product of a long worked-out ore body in the eastern desert of Egypt, but recent work has suggested that this alloy is the result of the mixing of silver and gold through the recycling process. It is quite possible that ancient smiths had little idea of the ultimate origin of the materials with which they worked.          GP

P.T. CRADDOCK, *Early Metal Mining and Production* (Edinburgh 1995).

K.R. MAXWELL-HYSLOP, *Western Asiatic Jewellery c. 3000–612 B.C.* (London 1971).

P.R.S. MOOREY, *Ancient Mesopotamian Materials and Industries: The Archaeological Evidence* (Oxford 1994).

J. OGDEN, *Ancient Jewellery* (London 1992).

T. REHREN, K. HESS and G. PHILIP, 'Auriferous Silver in Western Asia: Ore or Alloy?', *Historical Metallurgy* 30/1 (1996) 1–10.

**Sîn (Suen)** In *Sumerian, the *moon-*god was called Suen or Nanna (Nannar), and sometimes he was called by both names together, Nanna-Suen. In *Akkadian, Suen was later pronounced Sîn. Other names included Ashimbabbar, Namrasit ('Who shines forth') and Inbu ('the Fruit', perhaps referring to the natural waxing and waning of the moon). His name is also written simply with the number 30, the number of days in a lunar month.

Nanna was the son of *Enlil and Ninlil. The story of

Enlil's rape of the young goddess is told in a Sumerian poem: Enlil was banished by the other gods, but Ninlil followed him, already pregnant with Nanna. Nanna's wife was the goddess Ningal, and their *children were *Utu, the sun-god, and the goddess *Inana.

The most important shrine of Nanna was the E-kish-nu-gal at *Ur, but another cult centre which became of great importance in the Neo-*Babylonian period was the *temple at *Harran in northern *Syria, where under the name Sîn the god was worshipped together with Nuska as his son. The temple at Harran was especially popular with the Babylonian *King *Nabonidus, whose mother was a *priestess there. Nabonidus made his daughter high priestess of Sîn at Ur.

Although a very popular deity in Old Babylonian times, Nanna always remained subordinate to the chief gods of the pantheon, and in 'Nanna-Suen's journey to *Nippur', he *travels by barge to Nippur to obtain the blessing of the god Enlil.

A symbol of Nanna was a recumbent crescent moon. His beast was a bull, a lion-dragon or a gazelle.    AG/JAB

H. BEHRENS, *Enlil und Ninlil: ein sumerischer Mythos aus Nippur* (Rome 1978).

E.A. BRAUN-HOLZINGER, 'Die Ikonographie des Mondgottes in der Glyptik des III. Jahrtausends v. Chr.', *Zeitschrift für Assyriologie* 83 (1993) 119–34.

G. COLBOW, 'More Insights into Representations of the Moon God: The Third and Second Millennium B.C.', *Sumerian Gods and their Representations*, eds I.L. Finkel and M.J. Geller (Groningen 1997) 19–31.

A.J. FERRARA, *Nanna-Suen's Journey to Nippur* (Rome 1973).

M. KREBERNIK *et al.*, 'Mondgott', *Reallexikon der Assyriologie* 8 (Berlin/New York 1995) 360–76.

Å. SJÖBERG, *Der Mondgott Nanna-Suen in der sumerischen Überlieferung. I. Teil: Texte* (Stockholm 1960).

**Sinai** Few regions in the world have served as a more important land bridge than the Sinai peninsula. This inverted triangle is c.385 km long at its maximum north–south extent and c.200 km wide at its broadest limits, along the Mediterranean coast between Rapha and the Suez Canal. The peninsula, which covers c.38,500 sq km, is surrounded, for the most part, by water – the Mediterranean on the north, Suez Canal and Gulf of Suez on the west, and the Gulf of Aqaba on the east. Only in the north-eastern Sinai is this great wilderness connected with land, the Israeli *Negev. It was primarily the northern part of Sinai, a low, sandy plateau, that served as a corridor between Egypt and Asia. Dozens of armies have crossed this coastal zone through the ages, including the *Egyptians, *Canaanites, *Assyrians, *Babylonians and *Persians. The coastal zone was also used by *travellers and *traders from remote antiquity to the present, while the Sinai bedouin – still numbering in the tens of thousands – have found all of the plateau more hospitable than most.

Research completed under Israeli jurisdiction of the Sinai between 1967 and 1982 has demonstrated that this region was home to *prehistoric peoples from the Upper *Palaeolithic to the *Chalcolithic periods. Some 1300 sites, which date from Palaeolithic to Ottoman times, were documented by the Northern Sinai Survey (1972–82), but other projects have supplemented this work by locating hundreds of additional sites throughout the peninsula. In other words, ancient populations adapted their economy to this 'great and terrible wilderness' (Deuteronomy 1: 19), even though its annual rainfall is normally less than 65 mm, except along the northern coast.

During Early Bronze I, settlements in northern Sinai reflect Egyptian interests in southern Canaan.

Mine 'L' at Serabit el-Khadem in Sinai, one of the turquoise mines in which the Proto-Sinaitic inscriptions were found (courtesy of I. Beit-Arieh).

The Egyptians did not maintain the same interest in southern Sinai in Early Bronze II, even though this region was a source of *copper ore. The material culture of this period shows affinities with Canaanite *Arad (strata III–I). Early Bronze IV *pastoralists and a Middle Bronze Age population that mixed pastoral and *agricultural activities maintained close ties with both southern *Palestine and the eastern Delta.

Although the *Bible gives considerable attention to a forty-year *Israelite sojourn in Sinai, archaeological evidence displays no new ethnic component or sign of a significant population influx in the Late Bronze Age. It is, of course, difficult to fix the geographical location of most episodes in the Bible that relate to the Sinai experience of Moses and the people of Israel. The location of Mount Sinai, famous for its association with *Yahweh's deliverance of the 'Ten Commandments', is disputed, though most traditions point to southern Sinai, to a 2286-m peak named Jebel Musa. From Kadesh-Barnea, in northern Sinai, the Hebrews later attempted to enter Canaan but were unsuccessful.

The important site of Serabit el-Khadem, in west-central Sinai, was a source of Egyptian turquoise from the middle of the third millennium BC. Over four hundred Egyptian hieroglyphic inscriptions are known from a *temple of Hathor that was built at this site, but Serabit el-Khadem is best known because *slaves who worked in its turquoise mines used the so-called 'Proto-Sinaitic' *alphabet.

Some interesting inscriptions and drawings were found on potsherds at Kuntillet Ajrud, south of Kadesh-Barnea. These texts, which date to the eighth century BC, seem to make reference to Yahweh and his *Asherah. Meanwhile, the northern Sinai corridor had become very important in *Iron Age II, when the Neo-*Assyrian monarchs extended their empire to the frontier of Egypt. The site of Tell Ruqeish, near Khan Yunis, served as an Assyrian commercial centre, and the Sinai was crossed regularly by the armies of *Esarhaddon and *Ashurbanipal in their campaigns against Egypt in the 670s and 660s. Sinai continued to serve as a land bridge for later armies right up to the present.          GLM

O. BAR-YOSEF et al., 'Sinai', New Encyclopedia of Archaeological Excavations in the Holy Land 4, ed. E. Stern (New York 1993) 1384–403.

I. BEIT-ARIEH, 'Fifteen Years in Sinai', Biblical Archaeology Review 10 (1984) 26–54.

J.J. HOBBS, Mount Sinai (Austin, TX 1995).

E.D. OREN, 'Sinai', The Oxford Encyclopedia of Archaeology in the Near East 5, ed. E.M. Meyers (New York 1997) 41–7.

B. ROTHENBERG, God's Wilderness: Discoveries in Sinai (London 1961).

——, Sinai: Pharaohs, Miners, Pilgrims and Soldiers (Bern 1979).

**Sippar** Modern Abu Habbah, on the banks of the Euphrates *river in southern Iraq where it runs closest to the Tigris, was identified as ancient Sippar by T.G. Pinches in 1885. The name 'Sippar' in ancient texts sometimes refers to Abu Habbah together with its neigh-bouring twin *city, modern Tell ed-Der. Sippar appears in the *Sumerian *king list as one of the cities divinely chosen to rule over Sumer before the *Flood. Its *temple to the sun-god, *Shamash, was a traditional and prestigious *religious centre. The Euphrates was called 'the Sippar river'. The site was first described by W.B. Selby and J.B. Bewsher (1860), and excavated by *Rassam (c.1880), Vincent Scheil (1894), a Belgian team (1972–3) and Walid al-Jadir from the University of Baghdad (1978–).

Sippar was occupied from the *Uruk period (fourth millennium BC) until the *Parthian period (first to second centuries AD). It is c.100 ha in area, consisting of two *tells surrounded by the ruins of an ancient mud-brick wall covered by a dike which protected the city against flooding. The south-western mound was the religious quarter, with *ziggurat and temples, with the city proper on the north-east mound. Sippar was famous in the Old Babylonian period for its cloister where special *women dedicated to Shamash (nadītu women) were housed. This prestigious cloister included daughters of kings. The recent Iraqi excavations have uncovered streets of two-roomed *houses which may be the nadītu cloister. Also in the religious quarter, the Iraqis discovered a Neo-Babylonian *library, mostly of literary texts, with the *cuneiform tablets still arranged in their pigeonholes. Thousands of tablets from Rassam's excavations are in the British Museum.          PB

H. GASCHE and C. JANSSEN, 'Sippar', The Oxford Encyclopedia of Archaeology in the Near East 5, ed. E.M. Meyers (New York 1997) 47–9.

R. HARRIS, Ancient Sippar: A Demographic Study of an Old Babylonian City, 1894–1595 B.C. (Leiden 1975).

F. JOANNÈS, 'Les temples de Sippar et leurs trésors à l'époque néo-babylonienne', Revue d'Assyriologie et d'Archéologie Orientale 86 (1992) 159–84.

L. de MAYER (ed.), Tell ed-Der 3: Soundings at Abu Habbah (Sippar) (Louvain 1980).

**Slavery** Slavery existed in all parts of the ancient Near East, although it is only from *Mesopotamian and *Hittite texts that we get a clear idea of how it functioned. The Babylonian *cuneiform signs denoting slaves suggest that they were foreigners, probably prisoners-of-war. Foreign slaves could also be supplied by *merchants who specialized in the slave *trade; for example, in the Old *Babylonian period slaves from the mountain fringes of Mesopotamia were popular. Free citizens could also be forced into temporary slavery by economic misfortune, especially debts that could not be repaid, and this practice is also referred to in the *Bible. Slaves were marked either by tonsure or by tattoos or brands; exceptionally they might be chained.

Wealthy *families normally used slaves in domestic service. One slave or more per household was normal, occasionally up to twenty, divided between male and female. They were the property of their masters and could be bought and sold. In third-millennium BC texts, a symbolic act called 'crossing of the pestle' signified the transfer of ownership of a slave; perhaps the slave had to step over a pestle as a symbol of servile labour. Some owners donated their slaves to the *temple; sometimes the slave served his master until the latter's death, and then was 'inherited' by the temple. Slaves could be given away as presents; in one of the *Mari *letters a *woman asks *King *Zimri-Lim not to give away her aged mother as a gift. Most slaves undertook basic domestic or *agricultural duties (although there is little evidence of large-scale slave labour in *palace or temple fields), but skilled slaves worked as *craftsmen for their owners or were hired out for profit where the corvée system prevailed. Others were given responsible administrative tasks, echoing the *biblical story of Joseph in Egypt. Slaves could even accumulate their own wealth to spend as they wished.

Slave girls might be treated as concubines, and any offspring were also slaves, but slave girls could also be supplied by an infertile wife as a surrogate for her, to bear *children who were then treated as the wife's own. According to the Hittite *laws, slaves could marry free persons who for the period of the *marriage also became slaves. Although regarded as *property, slaves were protected by laws and could claim damages for personal injuries. In the Hittite laws, the owner paid any reparations for a *crime committed by his slave; if he refused, the slave was given to the injured party. In some instances a slave suffered the death penalty where a free man for the same crime paid a fine. A slave who attacked his master was put to death.

Occasionally slaves escaped, and in Babylonia a public herald announced their loss and citizens had a duty to turn a runaway in. In the Mari texts, a slave who made a habit of trying to escape might be guaranteed by his fellow workers who would be jointly liable for a large sum if he escaped again (although it is unclear if this applied specifically to slaves).

Slaves could be manumitted (freed), and some might be adopted into their master's family. In some circumstances of debt slavery, freedom could be purchased. Mesopotamian kings periodically issued edicts revoking personal enslavement for debt. Manumission was accompanied by the removal of the slave mark by a barber, which is why manumission was formally known as 'clearing the forehead'. The Bible refers to the freeing of slaves during a jubilee year (i.e. every fifty years).    PB

M.A. DANDAMAEV, *Slavery in Babylonia from Nabopolassar to Alexander the Great (626–331 BC)* (DeKalb, IL 1984).

I.M. DIAKONOFF, 'Slaves, Helots and Serfs in Early Antiquity', *Wirtschaft und Gesellschaft im alten Vorderasien*, eds J. Harmatta and G. Komoróczy (Budapest 1976) 45–78.

I.J. GELB, 'Prisoners of War in Early Mesopotamia', *Journal of Near Eastern Studies* 32 (1973) 70–98.

——, 'Definition and Discussion of Slavery and Serfdom', *Ugarit-Forschungen* 11 (1979) 283–97.

H.G. GÜTERBOCK, 'Bemerkungen zu den Ausdrücken *ellum, wardum* und *asirum* in hethitischen Texten', *Gesellschaftsklassen im alten Zweistromland und in den angrenzenden Gebieten*, ed. D.O. Edzard (Munich 1972) 93–7.

I. MENDELSOHN, *Slavery in the Ancient Near East* (New York 1949).

## Social classes

Ancient Near Eastern *scribes and administrators were more concerned with people's skills, output and wages than with their social status, and there is a danger when discussing social classes that any division will be influenced by our modern preconceptions, especially the Graeco-Roman contrast between '*slave' and 'free' or 'citizen'. The Code of *Hammurabi divided male society into three categories. First came *awēlū* ('men', sing. *awēlum*), citizens who held land or *property in their own right, without an obligation in return to serve someone else, the *palace or *temple. In Neo-*Babylonian times the term *awēlū* was applied more broadly, and a new term, *mār banî* ('free citizens'), described the free class. Second came the *muškēnū* (sing. *muškēnum*), who also held property or land allotments, but with it came an obligation to serve the real owner. *Muškēnū* lived on lands belonging to the *king or temple, and paid part of their yield to the owner, and might also contribute service as auxiliary troops. In the Babylonian *laws, *muškēnū* were consistently treated as less important than *awēlū*. The term *muškēnum* came to mean 'poor' in the *Semitic *languages and survives via Arabic in the French 'mesquin' which has a similar meaning. Third were the *wardū* ('slaves'), who were the property of another person or institution and could be bought or sold. *Hupšū* were manumitted slaves, described as a free but low class.

A thirteenth-century BC letter from a *Hittite king to the king of *Ugarit refers to similar categories: 'sons of the *town', 'king's slaves', 'king's slaves' slaves', chattel slaves and *habirū*. The *Hittite laws, however, divided society only into 'men' and 'slaves', the latter including what the Babylonians called *muškēnū*. In the Hittite empire these were people without land who worked for the palace, temple and the estates of high officials and normally received rations, though occasionally land allotments.

Many scholars of ancient Near Eastern society stress the 'lord versus slave' mentality, everyone having a lord automatically being the 'slave' of that lord. A 'son of the town', that is someone owning property in his own right, who hired himself out for work was actually treated as a temporary slave. The distinction between social classes was relative, not absolute, and based on an individual's relationship to property, means of production and share of produce.    PB

I.M. DIAKONOFF, *Structure of Society and State in Early Dynastic Sumer* (Malibu, CA 1974).

——, 'The Structure of Near Eastern Society before the Middle of the Second Millennium BC', *Oikumene* 3 (1982) 7–100.

——, 'Slave-Labour vs. Non-Slave Labour: The Problem of Definition', *Labor in the Ancient Near East*, ed. M.A. Powell (New Haven, CN 1987) 1–3.

D.O. EDZARD (ed.), *Gesellschaftsklassen im alten Zweistromland und in den angrenzenden Gebieten* (Munich 1972).

H. KLENGEL (ed.), *Beiträge zur socialen Struktur des alten Vorderasien* (Berlin 1971).

J.N. POSTGATE, 'Employer, Employee and Employment in the Neo-Assyrian Empire', *Labor in the Ancient Near East*, ed. M.A. Powell (New Haven, CN 1987) 257–70.

**Songs** Songs were an important part of *religious ceremonies and *rituals in the ancient Near East. One Middle *Assyrian text dating to c.1100 BC lists over 360 *Sumerian and *Akkadian songs belonging to thirty-one song types. There were songs for *work, battle, love, *childbirth, *funerals, rituals, *magic and *hymns. Complete texts exist for some songs, while for others there is only the opening line or title, often determined by the name of the *god or the ritual action concerned, e.g. 'the song of the washing of the feet of the divinity'. Normally we do not know the names of the composers of songs; an exception is Enheduanna, daughter of *Sargon of *Akkad and *priestess of the *moon-god *Nanna, who wrote several *temple hymn cycles, some of which have survived.

Singing in the official sphere was always accompanied by *music, and sometimes by *dancing. *Epics and myths were sung and accompanied by instruments. One *Hittite song was accompanied by the beating of swords. Songs were integrated into ceremonies, for example in processions, rituals, recreations of *wars and battle scenes.

Like musicians and dancers, singers are listed as professionals employed by temples and *palaces, and the title 'master of singers' is known. In the Hittite *archives, singers are distinguished by the *language in which they sing. Texts mention solo singers and choirs. A Sumerian text concerns a famed singer, Geshtinanna, without whom men's choruses could not sing properly. Singers accompanied the army on campaign, and captives, specially *women, were trained to become singers. In *art, singers are sometimes depicted with one hand at the throat or cupped at the ear.                                      PB

A.D. KILMER, 'Music and Dance in Ancient Western Asia', *Civilizations of the Ancient Near East*, ed. J.M. Sasson (New York 1995) 2601–13.

A.D. KILMER et al., 'Musik', *Reallexikon der Assyriologie* 8 (Berlin/New York 1995–7) 463–91.

H.M. KÜMMEL, 'Gesang und Gesanglosigkeit in der hethitischen Kultmusik', *Festschrift Heinrich Otten*, eds E. Neu and C. Rüster (Wiesbaden 1973) 169–78.

S. DE MARTINO, 'Music, Dance, and Processions in Hittite Anatolia', *Civilizations of the Ancient Near East*, ed. J.M. Sasson (New York 1995) 2661–9.

**Sport** In contrast to the huge amount of information about *Greek and *Roman sport, there is sparse evidence from the ancient Near East, unless royal *hunting is included. The range of sports surviving in the evidence is very meagre, and often their context is *ritual. Clay and faience balls are often found on excavations, and their leather or *textile equivalents would not have survived, but there is no indication in the texts of organized ball games. No *horse or *chariot races are mentioned prior to the *Hellenistic and Roman periods.

Wrestling and boxing were practised and are depicted in *sculpture and on *seals. *Cylinder seals often show real and mythical creatures holding each other by the wrist, or a human fighting off such creatures, scenes sometimes explained as representing a game of bull wrestling, and there are also scenes of bull leaping on

Terracotta plaque with man boxing and others playing a drum and cymbals. Width 11.5 cm. Old Babylonian period. WA 91906.

*Syrian seals of the eighteenth to seventeenth centuries BC. Wrestlers, acrobats and jugglers are mentioned in a ritual text from *Mari, performing in the *temple of *Ishtar, and are depicted on reliefs from *Alaca Hüyük. It is possible that wrestlers also performed in the *palace at Mari, since one section of the royal workshops perhaps produced wrestlers' belts. In the *Epic of *Gilgamesh there is a wrestling match between the hero and Enkidu, in which the winner is the one who lifts the other off the ground. *Baal is portrayed in the *Ugaritic texts as an accomplished sportsman, excelling at wrestling, running, throwing the javelin and hunting with a bow. An *Akkadian and Ugaritic phrase, 'to bend the knee', has been interpreted as denoting admission of defeat in a sport contest.

In *Hittite *Anatolia, wrestling, boxing, running, jousting and weight throwing were events attached to religious rituals. A relief at Tell *Halaf shows two swordsmen having a duel. It has been suggested that *bronze arrowheads found in *Canaan, inscribed with a name, perhaps the owner's, were connected with the judging of sporting events, to measure which archer had shot his arrow the farthest.                                      PB

M. DIETRICH and O. LORETZ, 'Ringen und Laufen als Sport in Ugarit', *Ugarit-Forschungen* 19 (1987) 19–21.

G. DOSSIN, 'Un rituel du culte d'Ištar provenant de Mari', *Revue d'Assyriologie* 35 (1938) 1–13.

R.M. GOOD, 'The Sportsman Baal', *Ugarit-Forschungen* 26 (1994) 147–63.

J. PUHUEL, 'Hittite Athletics as Prefigurations of Ancient Greek Games', *The Archaeology of the Olympics*, ed. W. Raschke (Madison 1988) 26–31.

J.M. SASSON, 'The Worship of the Golden Calf', *Orient and Occident*, ed. H.A. Hoffner, Jr (Neukirchen 1973) 151–9.

**Stamp seal** Stamp *seals are generally quite small (1–2 cm across) and were made in many shapes: square, round, oval, conical, elipsoid, biconical, irregular or even representational. Designs, either abstract or figural, were carved on the flat or slightly convex surface of one side. Usually on the other side was carved a loop or a hole through which a line for suspending the seal could pass.

This lapis lazuli stamp seal has a handle on the back, and was originally square. The scene showed two figures facing each other; the surviving one's hair hangs in locks down the sides and back. To the right are a goat and a zebu. Height 3.2 cm. c.2400–2000 BC. WA 1992-10-7.

Prototypes of stamp seals have been found at *Çatal-höyük and a number of sites in the *Levant and north *Mesopotamia dating to the *Hassuna period (7000–6000 BC) but the earliest stamp seals used administratively in the Near East come from excavations at Tell Sabi Abyad and *Arpachiyah dating to the *Halaf period (c.6000–5000/4500 BC). Clay tags and round clay disks were stamped with seals engraved with incised lines and more elaborate designs. The shape of seals was perhaps more important than the engraving since impressions of different shape at Arpachiya are combined on single clay disks. Seals start to be impressed in clay covering the fastening of doors and containers such as jars. Stamp seals continued to be used in the ancient Near East, although in Mesopotamia and in surrounding areas at various periods the *cylinder seal came to dominate until the mid first millennium BC. Among the *Hittites, stamp seals were carved for private, but particularly for royal use. In the third and early second millennium BC, stamp seals were used down the Gulf to the *Indus Valley civilization, which developed its own stamp seal tradition.　　PTC

B. BUCHANAN and P.R.S. MOOREY, *Corpus of Ancient Near Eastern Seals in the Ashmolean Museum, II: The Prehistoric Stamp Seals, III: The Iron Age Stamp Seals* (Oxford 1984, 1988).

D. COLLON, *Near Eastern Seals* (London 1990).
McG. GIBSON and R.D. BIGGS (eds), *Seals and Sealing in the Ancient Near East* (Malibu, CA 1977).
E. PORADA (ed.), *Ancient Art in Seals* (Princeton, NJ 1980).
A. VON WICKEDE, *Prähistorische Stempelglyptik in Vorderasien* (Munich 1990).

**Stein, Aurel (1862–1943)** The first systematic explorer of north-west *India and its relations with *Mesopotamia, (Marc) Aurel Stein was born in Budapest and studied oriental and classical languages and *archaeology in Vienna, Tübingen and England. He went to India in 1888 as an educational administrator, but during his vacations carried out archaeological and geographical research in Kashmir and the north-west frontier. In 1900 he began the first of his four Central Asian expeditions which continued until 1930 (1920–9 while working for the Archaeological Survey of India). He is widely credited with rediscovering the ancient Silk Route between China and the West, but has been accused of robbery for removing the ancient Chinese library at Tun-huang, the Cave of the Thousand Buddhas, which he had discovered. In addition he carried out reconnaissances in Baluchistan and *Persia, attempting to connect the earliest cultures of the Indus and Mesopotamia; researched the routes and battlefields of Alexander the Great's eastern campaigns; and surveyed the *Roman frontier in Iraq, *Syria and *Transjordan, both by air reconnaissance and by ground examination. He also carried out smaller projects on Graeco-Buddhist remains in north-west India.

Stein had always wanted to explore Afghanistan, and was finally granted permission at the age of eighty. He travelled to Kabul, but died a few days later, and was buried in the same city. Described as 'the most prodigious combination of scholar, explorer, archaeologist and geographer of his generation', he was a brilliant and determined hard worker who overcame all obstacles, including the loss of his toes from frostbite in 1908. He became a naturalized British citizen in 1904, and was knighted in 1908. He published the results of his investigations meticulously, often in multi-volume works, and received many awards from academic institutions in different countries.　　PB

J. MIRSKY, *Sir Aurel Stein: Archaeological Explorer* (Chicago 1977).

**Stone** Like *pottery, stone is one of the most common finds on archaeological excavations, because it is virtually indestructible. In the ancient Near East it was used for a wide range of purposes including building, *sculpture, *tools, vessels, *seals, amulets and beads. In most areas of the Near East, the most commonly available surface stones are limestone and sandstone. Dark igneous rocks such as diorite and granite are found only in *Sinai, western *Arabia and parts of *Iran and *Anatolia, with basalt also in *Jordan, *Syria and *Anatolia. This different availability of stone naturally affected what could be used in different areas in antiquity, and sometimes different types of stone were imported from elsewhere. *Babylonia was largely devoid of stone, while in *Assyria limestone, sandstone and alabaster were readily available. Babylonian sculpture was sometimes made from boulders eroded from their banks by the Euphrates and Tigris *rivers and carried south in the annual flooding. The import of dark and decorative stones, particularly favoured by *kings because of their rarity, is documented textually and archaeologically. It is not always clear precisely where imported stone came from, but large quantities or sizes could be moved only using river *transport.

*Mesopotamian *scribes produced lists of stones, described according to their appearance, but often it is difficult to identify these precisely with our modern names for stones. Particular stones were regarded as suitable for *magical amulets, and forty-nine stones listed in the *Sumerian *myth *Lugale* were the children of Asag, helping him in his fight against *Ninurta, who had turned him into stone.                                          PB

P.R.S. MOOREY, *Ancient Mesopotamian Materials and Industries: The Archaeological Evidence* (Oxford 1994) 21–110.

## Stories, myths and epics

The narratives, myths and legends of ancient *Mesopotamia form an exceptionally diverse collection of material. Some are preserved in *Sumerian and some in *Akkadian, the earliest from 2500 BC and the latest from the first century BC. Historically, a rich stream of survivals flowed from *Babylonian *literature, mediated by translations into other *languages and by oral transmission, into ancient Indian, *Greek and Arabic civilization, and from there into the European tradition. From *Anatolia, *Hittite as well as more ancient Hattic and *Hurrian myths of quite different character are preserved in the Hittite language. Myths of ancient coastal *Syria (some North-West *Semitic, some of Hurrian origin) are preserved in the *Ugaritic language.

As might be expected from such a broad field, they display very considerable variety, and in many cases there are several different versions of a narrative, originating from different localities or in different periods, some of which directly contradict other versions. Some myths were created within the historical period; others are of indeterminate antiquity. No doubt they were transmitted orally in many forms and on many occasions: however, the only form in which they survive substantially is the written form. It has proved extremely difficult to identify with certainty artistic depictions of individual myths or mythic episodes. Every myth or legend preserved in written form is preserved as part of a (perhaps fragmentary) work of literature which was created in a specific historical environment and which was intended to serve a specific literary aim. There is no homogeneous system, and the very distinction between myth, legend and history is of course a largely modern one.

Most of the literary works incorporating myths and legends which have been studied and edited so far are now available in English translation, but numbers of the Sumerian compositions are available only in foreign-language editions or in doctoral dissertations (which may not be readily available), or have not yet been published. Apart from these, there are many that have not yet even been read or studied in modern times. The term 'epic' is conventionally used of the Babylonian Epic of *Gilgamesh and the Epic of *Creation, and has also been used of other much shorter mythical narratives because of their style of diction.                                          AG/JAB

J. BOTTÉRO and S.N. KRAMER, *Lorsque les dieux faisaient l'homme* (Paris 1989).
S.M. DALLEY, *Myths from Mesopotamia* (Oxford 1989).
*Electronic Text Corpus of Sumerian Literature* (http://www-etcsl.orient.ox.ac.uk/) (1997–).
J.C.L. GIBSON, *Canaanite Myths and Legends*, 2nd ed. (Edinburgh 1978).
H.A. HOFFNER, JR, *Hittite Myths* (Atlanta, GA 1990).
T. JACOBSEN, *The Harps that Once … Sumerian Poetry in Translation* (New Haven, CN 1987).

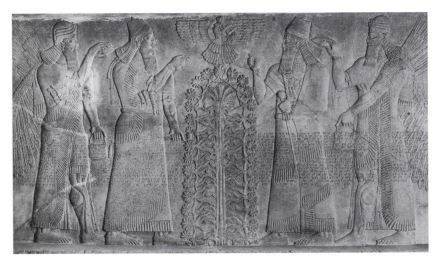

Relief panel which stood behind the throne of Ashurnasirpal II (883–859 BC) in his palace at Nimrud. The king is shown twice, either side of a stylized tree, flanked by winged genie holding buckets and cones. The meaning is debated but may be connected with fertility and prosperity or with a rite of purification. Height 1.93 m. WA 124531.

**Stylized tree** Stylized *trees of differing kinds are widely portrayed in the *art of the ancient Near East from early times. Their forms vary from the very formalized to more naturalistic, but in all cases the tree is generally portrayed as standing on an elevation or placed in a prominent position in the scene. It is often flanked by *animals or anthropomorphic supernatural beings.

Interest in the tree motif has been heightened, and interpretations of the device often influenced, by the *biblical 'tree of life' (Genesis 2–3). At least for *Mesopotamia, however, there is no reason to make any direct connection between the two traditions, and one particular post-*Akkad *cylinder seal which has often been thought to illustrate 'the temptation' can be interpreted as showing an untypical variant of a *banquet scene. In scenes of the second and first millennia BC, and especially popular in *Assyria, a tree, often surmounted by the symbol of the winged disk, is flanked by a pair of genies, one or more holding a bucket and cone. Although the interpretation of this motif, for which there is no known direct textual reference, has been a matter of much speculation, it seems likely that it is *mythico-*religious and represents a rite of purification. AG/JAB

P. ALBENDA, 'Assyrian Sacred Trees in the Brooklyn Museum', *Iraq* 56 (1994) 123–33.

A. GREEN, 'Mythologie. B. I. In der mesopotamischen Kunst', *Reallexikon der Assyriologie* 8 (Berlin/New York 1993–7) 579–80.

C. KEPINSKI, *L'arbre stylisé en Asie Occidentale au 2e millénaire avant J.-C.* (Paris 1982).

B.N. PORTER, 'Sacred Trees, Date Palms, and the Royal Persona of Ashurnasirpal II', *Journal of Near Eastern Studies* 52 (1993) 129–39.

H. YORK, 'Heiliger Baum', *Reallexikon der Assyriologie* 4 (Berlin/New York 1972–5) 269–82.

**Sumer, Sumerians** Sumer and Sumerian are invented modern terms derived from *Akkadian *Šumerum*, the name of the southern part of *Babylonia (from *Nippur south). In the Sumerian *language, this area was called *Kiengir*, or else simply *kalam*, 'the Land' – contrasted with *kurkur* 'the (foreign) countries', principally the less civilized mountain peoples to the east. There is evidence that Sumer was a conceptual unity at least as early as the *Uruk III/*Jemdet Nasr period (c.3000 BC), when the names of *cities throughout the region are linked together on *cylinder seal inscriptions in a way that implies some sort of political interrelationship, even though the individual cities functioned as independent states. After the rise to power of *Sargon of Akkad (c.2340 BC), Sumer was never again an independent political entity, merely a region of Babylonia.

Although there is a distinct Sumerian language, it is more difficult to identify a unique Sumerian culture. It is interesting that Sumerian speakers almost never identified themselves as 'Sumerians' (although apprentice scribes of the Old Babylonian period liked to call themselves 'Sumerians', that is, students of Sumerian, rather like the term 'Latinist'). Southern *Mesopotamia was a bilingual culture from virtually the earliest period from

(*left*) The Sumerians are typified by votive statuettes, such as this woman, although no physical features can be distinguished as 'Sumerian'. The eyes appear large because they were originally inlaid. Height 22.1 cm. Early Dynastic III period, c.2500 BC. WA 116666.

(*right*) Sumerian votive figure found in the shrine at Ubaid. The staring eyes and large nose have often, wrongly, been considered 'Sumerian' characteristics. Height 40 cm. Early Dynastic III period, c.2500 BC. WA 114207;

which written records can be read, with *Semites living among and alongside Sumerians. How much earlier a distinct 'Sumerian' people existed is a matter for speculation; there is a danger in projecting a discrete ethnolinguistic group called 'the Sumerians' indefinitely far back into history. Parents with Akkadian names gave their *children Sumerian names and vice versa. At least one inscription of a royal lady probably buried in the 'Royal Cemetery' of *Ur was written in Akkadian, although these are people whom we tend to think of as Sumerians *par excellence*. 'Sumerian' culture was an evolving process within southern Mesopotamia during the third millennium BC, and it is defined by use of the Sumerian language. The 'Sumerians' were those who participated in that culture.

However, this has not prevented violent scholarly debates in modern times about the possible origins outside southern Mesopotamia of a 'Sumerian race', who allegedly entered the area as immigrants; about the (almost certain) existence of non-Sumerian-speaking substrate populations, and about rivalry between the 'Sumerians' and the other inhabitants of what became Babylonia who spoke Semitic languages such as Old Akkadian or *Amorite. Most of these disagreements are now merely part of the history of ancient Near Eastern studies, as a reflection of twentieth-century theories about race and ethnicity, since much of their factual basis has been overtaken by more recent discoveries and improved understanding of Mesopotamian *archaeology and the languages involved.                    JAB

J.S. COOPER, 'Sumerian and Aryan: Racial Theory, Academic Politics and Parisian Assyriology', *Revue de l'Histoire des Religions* 210/2 (1993) 169–205.
T.B. JONES, *The Sumerian Question* (New York 1969).
R.J. MATTHEWS, *Cities, Seals and Writing: Archaic Seal Impressions from Jemdet Nasr and Ur* (Berlin 1993) 33–50.

## Sumerian (language)

**Sumerian (language)** The Sumerian *language was the vernacular tongue of southern *Babylonia until approximately the end of the third millennium BC. Thereafter its use was much restricted to formal public contexts, as it was gradually overtaken by *Akkadian (to which it is completely unrelated, although many words were loaned into Akkadian). By about 1650 BC it had probably died out entirely as an everyday spoken language, but it continued to remain an important vehicle of literary and, especially, religious culture until the very end of the *cuneiform tradition. Poems in Sumerian were still being copied by *scribes in *Babylon in the first century BC.

The earlier history of Sumerian extends back as far as the beginning of the third millennium, and it is very likely that the earliest written clay tablets of all (dating from c.3400 BC) were already written in Sumerian. No information survives about the other languages of the family of which Sumerian was a member, since none of them was ever written down, and they may even have died out before *writing was invented. However, Sumerian

influenced and was influenced by Akkadian in many ways, especially vocabulary.

The main variety of Sumerian is called Emegir. In addition, a dialect called Emesal, the so-called '*women's language', is known; this was also the dialect of certain *religious *literature. Structurally, Sumerian is an agglutinative and ergative language, which certainly posed problems for Babylonian apprentice scribes who had to learn it as part of their professional training. Their difficulties are apparent both from the surviving Sumerian–Babylonian grammars, vocabularies and bilingual texts, and from humorous dialogues describing life at *school in the 1800s BC.

There is an extensive literature in Sumerian, with narrative poems (including poems about *Gilgamesh), praise *poetry addressed to *kings, *hymns to *gods and *temples, dialogues, debate poems, diatribes, fables, folk songs and proverbs. It has been estimated that the preserved literature in Emegir extends to over sixty thousand lines of verse; that in Emesal may be almost as extensive, but has not yet been quantified.                    JAB

D.O. EDZARD, 'The Sumerian Language', *Civilizations of the Ancient Near East*, ed. J.M. Sasson (New York 1995) 2107–16.
*The Electronic Text Corpus of Sumerian Literature* (http://www-etcsl.orient.ox.ac.uk) (1997–).
P. MICHALOWSKI, 'Sumerian Literature: An Overview', *Civilizations of the Ancient Near East*, ed. J.M. Sasson (New York 1995) 2279–91.
M.L. THOMSEN, *The Sumerian Language* (Copenhagen 1984).

## Suppiluliumas

**Suppiluliumas** Two *Hittite *kings called Suppiluliumas appear in the Hittite records. Almost nothing is known of the second.

Suppiluliumas I (c.1370–1330 BC) was one of the most powerful monarchs of the period, who established lasting Hittite control from western Turkey to north *Syria. An outline of his conquests can be reconstructed mainly from a later text called 'the Deeds of Suppiluliumas'. He sacked Washshukanni, capital of *Mitanni which had dominated Syria. One of his sons was left to govern the region from Aleppo and another was installed at *Carchemish. Friendly relations were established with *Egypt (under either Akhenaten or Tutankhamun). There is a reference in a later Hittite text to a *letter from Egypt requesting a son for *marriage, perhaps for the widow of Tutankhamun. Suppiluliumas was wary and the son he eventually despatched was murdered. To the east of Hatti, the 'Upper Land' and Azzi-Hayasa were retaken and the capital, *Hattusas, which had been lost was recovered, *fortified and rebuilt. The king probably died from plague which was brought back by Hittite soldiers from the *wars in the *Levant.

Suppiluliumas II (c.1210 BC–?): Son of *Tudhaliyas IV and brother of Arnuwandas III, he is the last recorded Hittite king. He is known to have conducted a sea battle off *Cyprus and constructed a rock sanctuary for his father's cult. It is not known how long he reigned, as the Hittite records fall silent and the capital Hattusas was massively destroyed by fire.                    PTC

T. BRYCE, *The Kingdom of the Hittites* (Oxford 1998).

O. GURNEY, *The Hittites*, rev. ed. (Harmondsworth 1990).

H.G. GÜTERBOCK, 'The Deeds of Suppiluliuma as Told by his Son Mursili II', *Journal of Cuneiform Studies* 10 (1956) 41–68, 75–98, 107–30.

J.G. MACQUEEN, *The Hittites* (London 1986).

G. WILHELM and J. BOESE, 'Absolute Chronologie und die hethitische Geschichte des 15. und 14. Jahrhunderts v. Chr.', *High, Middle or Low* 1, ed. P. Åström (Gothenberg 1987) 74–117.

**Susa**  Susa, modern Shush, dominates the great plain of *Elam in the south-west *Iran that is an extension of the alluvial plain of *Mesopotamia The site comprises three mounds, called the Acropolis, Apadana and Royal City after *Achaemenid-period constructions, covering some 120 ha and rising 15–20 m above the plain.

First excavations were by the British archaeologist W.K. Loftus in 1843–5. Thereafter Susa fell to the French, first under Dieulafoy (1884–6), followed by de Morgan (1897–1908), who constructed a great French château that served as the headquarters of the Delegation until the Iranian Revolution of 1979. Ride Mecquenem worked there from 1912 to 1939 and was succeeded by *Ghirshman in 1946 and, finally, in 1968, by Jean Perrot. Mining engineers by training, Morgan and Mecquenem attacked the mound as though it were an open-cast pit, a tradition followed by Ghirshman.

Susa I, the earliest period, became the capital of Elam from the late fifth millennium BC. A mass of *burials and a ceremonial centre on a mudbrick platform yielded exceptionally fine painted *pottery and *stamp seals, both distinctively Iranian. Susa II, from the mid fourth millennium BC, developed extensive cultural links with *Uruk-period *Mesopotamia and, like southern Mesopotamia, made the transition from record-keeping by means of tokens to the development of *writing called proto-Elamite. The extent to which Susa II fell under direct control from Uruk is disputed, but by Susa III, c.3000 BC, it had regained full independence and dominated the plain.

During the Old Elamite and following periods, c.2700–1500 BC, Susa was conquered by both *Akkad and the Third Dynasty of *Ur before regaining independence from Mesopotamia under the rulers from *Anshan. In the late second millennium BC Susa reached its apogee in what is termed the Middle Elamite period, c.1600–1100 BC, under the kings of Anshan and Susa. At the peak of its imperial power Susa defeated the *Kassite regime and brought back amongst the trophies two of the most important early Mesopotamian monuments, the Victory Stela of *Naram-Sin and the *Law Code of *Hammurabi. Susa's own distinctive culture flourished, indicated by a wide variety of *arts and crafts. In the Neo-Elamite period, c.1100–539 BC, Susa declined, with a resurgence of power in the late eighth century BC. On the Acropolis a small *temple to Inshushinak was decorated with glazed bricks. Rich burials from this period have also been excavated.

The Elamite city was destroyed by the *Assyrian King *Ashurbanipal in 647/6 BC, an act from which it never

Glazed brick reliefs decorated palace walls in Elam and Babylonia in the Neo-Babylonian and Persian periods. A royal guard from the palace of Darius I at Susa, c.500 BC. Height 1.99 m. WA 132525.

fully recovered. It was chosen by Darius I for the construction of a summer *palace and associated structures on the main mound. The later *Persian king Artaxerxes II built a second palace on the other side of the Shaur river. Susa was the centre of Achaemenid *administration and communications, including the Persian Royal Road that ran to *Sardis in western Turkey.                    GDS

J.E. CURTIS, 'William Kennet Loftus and his Excavations at Susa', *Iranica Antiqua* 28 (1993) 1–55.

P.O. HARPER, J. ARUZ and F. TALLON (eds), *The Royal City of Susa: Ancient Near Eastern Treasures in the Louvre* (New York 1992).

J. PERROT and D. LADIRAY, 'Susa – City of Splendour', *Royal Cities of the Biblical World*, ed. J.G. Westenholz (Jerusalem 1996) 197–254.

**Swastika**  The swastika, fylfot or gammadion is a rare motif in the ancient Near East, but often provokes interest because of its wide international and multicultural use elsewhere, and especially because of the notoriety of the symbol in our own time owing to its adoption by National Socialist parties and regimes in the 1930s, including the German Third Reich. In *Mesopotamia the device is clearly shown on *prehistoric painted *pottery, especially *Samarra Ware, and on Early Dynastic *seal impressions. It then disappears from use, although there have been some rather dubious attempts – especially by scholars writing just before and during the Second World War, when interest in the history of the swastika was especially high – to recognize the form of the symbol in various arrangements of men, *animals and other geometric motifs throughout the long history of ancient Mesopotamian *art. The motif does recur, painted in bitumen, on a limestone slab on the façade of a Neo-*Assyrian *temple at *Ashur.

A swastika is surrounded by birds and fish on this prehistoric painted pottery bowl from Samarra.

A pre-War theory, promoted by some Nazi propagandists, saw the swastika as an essentially *Indo-European ('Aryan') symbol, in contradiction to the winged disk, ubiquitous in *Semitic cultures. The rarity of the swastika motif in Mesopotamia is certainly striking, but it was equally rare in *Iran, which from *Achaemenid times took over the winged disk from Mesopotamia and used it extensively. The meaning of the swastika has been explained in differing ways, for example as a solar symbol, as the sign for a fortress, and as symbolizing a whirlwind or the four winds. In Mesopotamia, another cruciform device, the Maltese (or '*Kassite') cross, was apparently interchangeable with the solar disk or winged disk as a symbol of the sun-*god, but there is no evidence for the swastika in such a role. The form of the cross might well be intended to indicate a circular movement of some kind.                    JAB/AG

R. DAVIS, *La croix gammée* (Paris 1967).

K. JÄGER, *Zur Geschichte und Symbolik des Hakenkreuz* (Leipzig 1921).

J. LECHLER, *Vom Hakenkreuz* (Leipzig 1921).

E.D. VAN BUREN, *Symbols of the Gods in Mesopotamian Art* (Rome 1945) 120–3.

T. WILSON, *The Swastica, the Earliest Known Symbol and its Migrations* (Annual Reportof the Smithsonian Institution, Washington, D.C. 1896).

**Syria**  The modern state of Syria lies between *Israel, *Jordan, *Lebanon, Iraq and Turkey, although the older geographical term designated an area known in Arabic as *Bilad ash-Sham* between *Sinai in the south, the Mediterranean to the west, *Anatolia to the north and the Syrian desert to the east. The climate changes from temperate Mediterranean, through steppe to true desert as one moves east. A range of mountains, the Jebel Ansariye, separates the narrow coastal plain from the interior plateau, across which flows the Euphrates *river.

The name 'Syria' is a *Greek derivative from '*Assyria', and was not used in ancient times as a geographical or political term. It is first recorded by *Herodotus in the fifth century BC, later becoming a name of the provinces of the Seleucid, Ptolemaic (see Hellenistic period) and *Roman empires.

Syria was an important area of *agricultural development and includes some of the major *Neolithic sites such as Abu Hureyra and Mureybet. Later, Syria was part of the *Halaf and *Ubaid cultures which stretched across much of *Mesopotamia. An urban culture emerged in the Early Bronze Age, and much of northern Syria was under the control of *Ebla until its defeat by the *kings of *Akkad.

New urban centres became the nuclei of small Middle Bronze Age states, in particular *Yamhad, *Carchemish and *Qatna. *Shamshi-Adad I of Assyria moved his capital into Syria, to Shubat Enlil (Tell *Leilan). A major source for the history of this period are the *archives from *Mari, which show complex relations between the states and with *pastoralist populations. During this period the *Hurrians infiltrated and became a significant part of

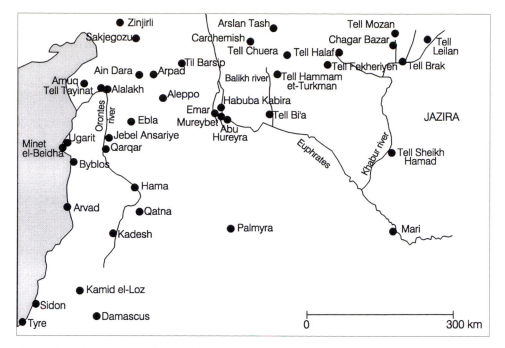

Map of Syria showing main archaeological sites.

the population, the Hurrian state of *Mitanni eventually developing into a major power. The Middle Bronze Age ended with a *Hittite raid on Syria which continued into Mesopotamia and destroyed *Babylon c.1595 BC. During the Late Bronze Age, Syria was mostly controlled by the competing foreign powers of Mitanni, *Egypt and the Hittites. The ever-growing Hurrian influence is documented by tablets from *Nuzi, *Alalakh and *Ugarit. The period ended with destructions and incursions of new groups such as the *Sea Peoples and the *Aramaeans.

During the *Iron Age, Syria was divided between the *Phoenician *city-states, the Aramaean states, and the states in the north-west often called Neo-Hittite because of the continuity of Hittite culture: these included Carchemish, *Ain Dara, *Zinjirli and Sakçagözü. Neo-

Hittite *cities included *administrative buildings and *temples in a distinctive *bīt hilāni style. Later, Syria came under *Assyrian, *Babylonian and *Persian domination, which is sometimes reflected in the local architecture, especially the Assyrian provincial *palace at *Til Barsip.

PB

M.W. CHAVALAS, 'Ancient Syria: A Historical Sketch', *New Horizons in the Study of Ancient Syria*, eds M.W. Chavalas and J.L. Hayes (Malibu, CA 1992) 1–21.
P. HITTI, *A History of Syria* (London 1957).
H. KLENGEL, *Syria 3000 to 300 B.C.: A Handbook of Political History* (Berlin 1992).
H. WEISS (ed.), *Ebla to Damascus: Art and Archaeology of Ancient Syria* (Washington, D.C. 1985).

# T

**Tammuz:** see Dumuzi

**Tarsus** The prehistoric mound at Tarsus, capital of the east Cilician plain on the southern coast of Turkey, is known as Gözlü Kule in Turkish. Excavations by Hetty Goldman (1934–9) provided one of the most important sequences for the *archaeology of Turkey because of

the links with the *Anatolian plateau, north *Syria and *Cyprus that are evident in the assemblages. Although no longer adequate, the results have not yet been superseded.

Occupation began in the *Neolithic. Early Bronze Age levels were 18 m deep, spanning the entire period. By Early Bronze III extensive contacts with north Syria are seen in *ceramics, *glyptic and *metallurgy. Settlement continued though the Middle Bronze Age, when successive levels were burnt, and the Late Bronze Age. Late Bronze II culture has strong *Hittite elements, some Mycenaean pottery and a few imports from Cyprus and Syria. At that time Tarsus lay in the region of Kizzuwatna. There is clearly a hiatus following the end of the Late Bronze Age, with reoccupation in the Middle and Late Iron Ages. Tarsus was under Assyrian rule in the seventh century BC, and thereafter under local rulers entitled 'Syennesis'.                                                    GDS

E. FRENCH, 'A Reassessment of the Mycenaean Pottery at Tarsus', *Anatolian Studies* 25 (1975) 53–75.

H. GOLDMAN, *Excavations at Gözlü Kule, Tarsus* 2 (Princeton, NJ 1956).

## Taxation

Once communities grew, rulers required the populace to contribute to communal purposes. The simplest way was by corvée duty or military service, and those continued throughout *Mesopotamian history. As society developed, payments in kind became common and taxes were imposed on crops and trade. Under *Naram-Sin the provinces of *Akkad were required to contribute to the centre, and *Shulgi organized them to pay the *bala* tax in their particular produce, the peripheral provinces sending *gún-mada* tax, in effect rent for the land occupied by soldiers. The goods received at central collection points were redistributed to pay government expenses, all meticulously recorded.

Old *Assyrian *merchants paid tax on the goods they took from *Ashur and paid tax on them when they arrived at *Kanesh (10 per cent on garments). A *king of *Isin about 1860 BC boasts of halving tax on barley from 20 per cent to 10 per cent. Service for land (*ilku*) is attested in *Hammurabi's *Laws and many other texts throughout the second millennium BC across to *Ugarit. Documents from *Nineveh reveal a wide variety of taxes imposed on corn (10 per cent), straw (25 per cent) and on fruit, livestock and its produce, ferry-crossings and *trade, all assessed by tax-collectors travelling the country to estimate yields, sometimes accompanied by armed guards.

Taxes were also paid to *temples in the form of tithes, 'a tenth'. Tithes were also imposed on crops and livestock in *Israel to support the religious personnel (Leviticus 27).

The 'Royal Standard' of *Ur and many later monuments depict captives loaded with booty and the Assyrian '*annals' delight in listing the spoils. Defeated kings who became vassals paid tribute to their suzerains as a rent for their thrones, taxing their subjects accordingly. Lists of taxes paid by *villages in the kingdom of Ugarit for the *Hittite overlord and the tax imposed by Menahem on Israel's landowners to meet *Tiglath-pileser III's imposition (2 Kings 15) illustrate the impact of such demands across society.                                           ARM

J. BÄR, *Der assyrische Tribut und seine Darstellung: eine Untersuchung zur imperialen Ideologie im neuassyrischen Reich* (Kevelaer 1996).

J.N. POSTGATE, *Taxation and Conscription in the Assyrian Empire* (Rome 1974).

E. SALONEN, *Über den Zehnten im alten Mesopotamien* (Helsinki 1972).

P. STEINKELLER, 'The Administration and Economic Organization of the Ur III State: Core and Periphery', *The Organization of Power: Aspects of Bureaucracy in the Ancient Near East*, eds McG. Gibson and R.D. Biggs (Chicago 1987) 19–41.

## Tayma

Tayma is a major oasis in north-west *Arabia, lying between Yathrib (modern al-Madina) and *Duma (modern Al Jauf). It has a pivotal position on the *trade route between southern Arabia and the north since from here caravans could turn either north-eastwards to *Mesopotamia or north-westwards (via Duma) to the *Levant. Taking the latter route would have cut out the rival oasis of *Dedan and this probably accounts for the 'wars against Dedan' mentioned in some of the inscriptions found near Tayma.

As at Dedan, the basis of Tayma's *economy was *agriculture, as shown by the remains of extensive field systems fed by an elaborate underground *irrigation network. Although the presence at Tayma of some *pottery of the Qurayya type and apparent references to the name in *cuneiform documents of the third and second millennia BC hint at earlier occupation, the first secure evidence for the oasis dates to the eighth century BC. Tayma is mentioned along with *Saba' in a list of tribes, oases and peoples which attempted to placate the *Assyrian *King *Tiglath-pileser III (744–727 BC) after

Fragment of an Assyrian stela showing booty being weighed on scales. From Nimrud, ninth century BC. WA 118800.

the revolt of Samsi, *queen of the *Arabs. Tayma and Saba' are again linked in a report by the governor of Suhu on the Euphrates about a punitive raid he made against 'a caravan of the people of Tayma and Saba" passing through his territory.

Like the inhabitants of Dedan and Duma, the population of Tayma spoke an Ancient North Arabian *language and wrote it in a distinct form of the Ancient North Arabian script. It appears that this was already in use and well known to Tayma's trading partners in the eighth century BC. At this date, the regent of *Carchemish, Yariris, erected an inscription in which he boasted that he knew twelve languages and four scripts: his own (*hieroglyphic Luwian), *Phoenicio-*Aramaic, cuneiform and Taymanite.

For reasons that are still obscure, the last king of *Babylon, *Nabonidus, left his capital and spent the major part of his reign at Tayma, at the same time establishing his authority over the other major oases on the so-called '*incense road'. He killed the king of Tayma, slaughtered much livestock and forced the inhabitants to build him a *palace and other public buildings. The remains of several large buildings and huge *city walls can still be seen in and around the oasis but it has not yet been possible to date these with certainty.

It is clear that the cultural life of Tayma was cosmopolitan and eclectic. Its *art, *religious beliefs and personal names all show a mixture of native North Arabian, *Egyptian, Mesopotamian and South Arabian elements. The Aramaic language and script were in use at the oasis in the second half of the first millennium BC, perhaps introduced by Nabonidus or his *Persian successors.                                                           MCAM

H.I. ABU-DURUK, *Introduction to the Archaeology of Tayma'* (Riyadh 1986).

G. BAWDEN, C. EDENS and R. MILLER, 'Preliminary Archaeological Investigations at Tayma', *Atlal* 4 (1980) 69–106.

P.A. BEAULIEU, *The Reign of Nabonidus King of Babylon 553–534 B.C.* (New Haven, CN 1989) 149–203.

M.C.A. MACDONALD, 'Trade Routes and Trade Goods at the Northern End of the "Incense Road" in the First Millennium B.C.', *Profumi d'Arabia*, ed. A. Avanzini (Rome 1997) 333–49.

P.J. PARR, 'Aspects of the Archaeology of North-West Arabia in the First Millennium B.C.', *L'Arabie préislamique et son environnement historique et culturel*, ed. T. Fahd (Leiden 1989) 39–66.

**Technology:** see Science and technology

**Teleilat Ghassul:** see Ghassul, (Teleilat)

**Telepinu**  A *Hittite ruler whose name is the same as an important vegetation-*god of this period, Telepinu reigned c.1525–1500 BC. The *king claims in the 'Edict of Telepinu' (preserved in a Hittite and an *Akkadian version) to have put an end to years of murder and usurpation by the bloodless deposition of his brother-in-law Huzziya, whom he exiled, and to have restored the land of Hatti to a golden age. He also established the rules of succession which the assembly of nobles was expected to uphold. During the earlier period of anarchy, Hittite territory probably shrank but while Telepinu claims total collapse this is probably exaggeration. It is probable that the Hittite domination of central *Anatolia was not seriously undermined.                                              PTC

O. GURNEY, *The Hittites*, rev. ed. (Harmondsworth 1990).

A. KUHRT, *The Ancient Near East c. 3000–330 BC* (London/New York 1995).

J.G. MACQUEEN, *The Hittites* (London 1986).

**Tell, tepe**  *Tell* and *tepe* are the Arabic and Turkish words respectively for an artificial mound or low hill formed from the successive remains of ancient settlements (in Turkish *höyük* or *hüyük* are also used). Such mounds are characteristic of the Near East. They were formed over long periods of time as settlements, normally of mudbrick, were built over the ruins of previous settlements. Over time the mass of decayed mudbrick walls grew progressively higher, and after abandonment erosion smoothed the mounds into dune-like shapes. Such mounds are stratigraphically complex since contemporary features

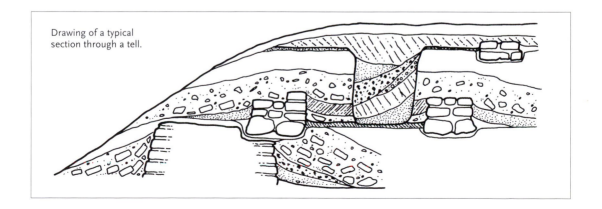

Drawing of a typical section through a tell.

Deep section through the tell at Jericho, cut by Kenyon's excavations in the 1950s (courtesy of Piotr Bienkowski).

like walls and pits can be located at different absolute heights and often cut through remains of older features. Earlier generations of archaeologists either did not excavate stratigraphically at all, or sliced off strips of equal depth across a mound, making it impossible to correlate features of similar date. Modern controlled stratigraphic excavations carefully follow individual layers and keep a record of what has been removed by means of vertical sections which relate layers to each other (see *Petrie). New scientific techniques now enable the huge amounts of sediment from mounds to be analysed to provide environmental evidence.                                    PB

S. LLOYD, *Mounds of the Near East* (Edinburgh 1963).
A.M. ROSEN, *Cities of Clay: The Geoarchaeology of Tells* (Chicago 1986).

**Temples** The ancient Near Eastern temple was not a place of popular worship, but was regarded as the *house on earth of the *city *god. The words used for 'temple' in *Sumerian and *Akkadian, *e* and *bītu*, literally mean 'house'. The god lived in the main shrine of the temple in the form of a cult statue or a *divine symbol. The role of the temple *priests was to undertake a daily regimented rota of feeding and *clothing the cult statue, and occasionally, during *festivals, taking it outside the temple to visit gods in other towns.

The oldest structures identified as temples or shrines date to the *Mesolithic period, e.g. at *Jericho. In *Mesopotamia, a sequence of mudbrick temples at *Eridu dates to the fifth and fourth millennia BC. The earliest, only 9 sq m, already shows the essential characteristic of all later Mesopotamian temples, an *altar for the cult statue or divine symbol in a niche opposite the doorway. In later periods the plan became more complex, with rooms added on either side, and the mounds created by sequential rebuilding of the temples may have led to the notion of the *ziggurat.

The constituent parts of Mesopotamian temples were the inner sanctuary, with the altar; an outer sanctuary, where the daily *rituals, especially *food offerings, were carried out; a vestibule, the transition between the temple and the outside world; occasionally a court, e.g. for *sacrifices; and subsidiary rooms for storage and living quarters for the priests. Inner sanctuaries were either long rooms, with the altar in the middle of a short side, or broad rooms, with the altar in the middle of a long side; and either bent-axis, where the main entrance was at right angles to the altar, or direct-axis, where the main entrance was opposite the altar. A characteristic of Mesopotamian temple architecture was the use of alternating buttresses and recesses on the exterior, perhaps in imitation of vertical reed bundles that supported the walls of reed houses.

Mesopotamian temples eventually expanded into huge complexes which included temples, chapels, ziggurats and other structures arranged around several courtyards, e.g. at *Uruk, *Nippur and *Babylon. Other areas of the Near East had a great variety of temple plans, some single rooms, some bipartite or tripartite structures, but always with the essential component of the main shrine with an altar.

Mesopotamian temples owned large amounts of land and had thousands of employees and dependants, with a complex hierarchy of priests (see Administration). The temples played an important social role by storing food surpluses for times of shortage or famine, and also protected the disadvantaged such as widows, orphans and prisoners-of-war. PB

A. BIRAN (ed.), *Temples and High Places in Biblical Times* (Jerusalem 1981).

W.G. DEVER, 'Palaces and Temples in Canaan and Ancient Israel', *Civilizations of the Ancient Near East*, ed. J.M. Sasson (New York 1995) 605–14.

E. HEINRICH, *Die Tempel und Heiligtümer im alten Mesopotamien: Typologie, Morphologie und Geschichte* (Berlin 1982).

J.-C. MARGUERON, 'Sanctuaires sémitiques', *Supplément au Dictionnaire de la Bible* 64B–65 (Paris 1991) cols 1104–1258.

M. ROAF, 'Palaces and Temples in Ancient Mesopotamia', *Civilizations of the Ancient Near East*, ed. J.M. Sasson (New York 1995) 423–41.

**Terqa** Modern Ashara, ancient Terqa, stands on the Euphrates c.70 km north of *Mari and was often under Mari's control in antiquity. The site has been excavated by French (1923), American and French archaeologists (from 1974). The Early Dynastic *town had three strong walls, later re-used, and a long-lived *administrative building. Major areas of Middle Bronze Age occupation were exposed. A large building dated to the Old Babylonian kingdom of Mari by numerous texts may have served, in part, as a *scribal *school. The slightly later *temple of Ninkarrak, a simple shrine on a bent-axis plan, yielded, among other finds, some *Hyksos-style scarabs. One room of a *house contained a variety of domestic articles and *cuneiform tablets dated about 1720 BC. Detailed observation showed that the texts were probably old documents stored in a lumber-room. An adjacent room yielded a jar containing cloves, the earliest sign of *trade links between *Mesopotamia and the Far East. Other tablets reveal occupation continuing into the seventeenth and perhaps sixteenth centuries BC under local *kings, some with *Kassite names. The following period saw *Mitannian control, a large building violently destroyed perhaps being an administrative centre. A fine *bronze harpe-sword (like a scimitar) found in it preserves some of its mounts. There was also evidence for working in *glass paste. Slight traces exist of later use of the site, including a provincial stela of *Tukulti-Ninurta II. ARM

G. BUCCELLATI and M. KELLY-BUCCELLATI, 'Terqa', *The Oxford Encyclopedia of Archaeology in the Near East* 5, ed. E.M. Meyers (New York 1997) 188–90.

A.H. PODANY, 'A Middle-Babylonian Date for the Hana Kingdom', *Journal of Cuneiform Studies* 43–5 (1991–3) 53–62.

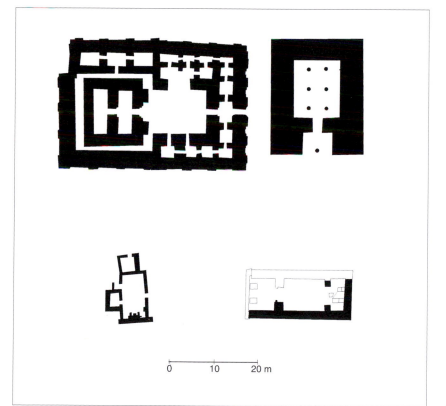

Sketch plans of temples: (*top left*) Temple of Enki at Ur, c.2000 BC, with direct access through a courtyard surrounded by service room and storerooms.
(*top right*) Tower temple (migdol) at Shechem, c.1650 BC. One tower flanking the entrance may have contained a staircase.
(*lower left*) Late Bronze Age 'Fosse Temple' at Lachish, with indirect entry ('bent axis').
(*lower right*) Iron Age temple adjacent to the palace at Tell Tayinat, the plan comparable with the biblical description of Solomon's Temple in Jerusalem.

O. ROUALT, *Terqa Final Reports I: L'Archive de Puzurum* (Malibu 1984).

——, 'Terqa: rapport préliminaire (1987–1989)', *Mari: Annales de Recherches Interdisciplinaires* 8 (1997).

——, 'Recherches récentes à Tell Ashara-Terqa (1991–1995)', *Subartu* 4 (1998) 313–30.

**Teshup**  A storm-*god who became the head of the *Hittite pantheon during the New Kingdom or Empire period, Teshup has a *Hurrian name and was worshipped in *Mesopotamia (where he was also known as Tishpak), *Syria and *Anatolia and often identified with or assimilated to local *weather-gods. In one Hittite *myth, *Kumarbi attempts to regain the *kingship of the gods from Teshup and creates a stone monster that threatens the world and the gods with destruction. Teshup's defeat of the monster confirms his authority. He was the symbol of royalty and his epithet was 'king of heaven'. In the rock carvings of the Hittite pantheon at Yazýlýkaya, Teshup leads the procession of the gods. He was depicted carrying a mace, axe or trident, sometimes a bolt of lightning, and wearing a sword. His *sacred animal was the bull. He often appears on *cylinder seals, especially from *Nuzi, where there was a cult and a *temple of Teshup. Teshup also appears in the *Urartian pantheon, lending support to the supposed link between the Hurrian and Urartian *languages.                                             PB

E. LAROCHE, 'Tešub, Hebat et leur cour', *Journal of Cuneiform Studies* 2 (1948) 113–36.

——, 'Tešub', *Dictionnaire des mythologies et des religions des sociétés traditionelles et du monde antique* 2, ed. Y. Bonnefoy (Paris 1981) 486–7.

**Textiles**  Many products are subsumed under the study of textiles – *clothing, soft furnishings (carpets, rugs, cushions, curtains, tapestries), tent and sail cloth, containers (pouches, bags), rope, netting, basketry, mats. These were manufactured out of a variety of raw materials, including linen (flax), wool, mohair, cotton, silk, reeds, palm fibre and hemp. The fabrication of textiles was time-consuming and labour-intensive and often called for specialized skills. This means that some textiles were expensive, depending on the type and quality of raw materials and the quality of production. High-quality materials were part of a long-distance *trade network, and textiles were used for tribute, special gifts, and dowries.

Even when the textiles themselves have actually deteriorated, their presence – or details about the kind of weave used – can be detected by impressions left on other substances. For example, at *Jarmo impressions made on clay objects betray the presence of fabrics, reed matting and baskets that have long since disappeared.

Artistic representations of textiles are abundant. For example, reliefs from *Persepolis provide much information about clothing and other textiles, even though actual garments from *Iran are extremely rare. It is important to remember that *art and *sculpture often portray the royal or elite class, while *tomb *paintings might present clothing in an idealized manner because of their *religious setting. Artistic portrayal of clothing worn by *gods and goddesses may have reflected conservative values.

Most textual references to textiles relate to *economic activities (e.g. shipping, cost, inventory). Tablets from *Ebla, *Ur III, *Mari and *Kanesh shed much light on the international exchange of textile products for the centuries around 2000 BC. *Merchants of Ebla traded textiles with their counterparts in Ur, *Kish, and *Megiddo, and the Old *Assyrian tablets from Kanesh documented the exchange of textiles between *Anatolia and Assyria. The wool industry was very important to *Sumerian merchants, who traded their products on the *Arabian peninsula and in *Akkad and *Syria.

The strands of *plant or *animal fibre were turned into yarn or thread by spinning, normally with a hand spindle and a whorl. Spindle whorls dating back to the

The rich carpets that covered the floors of Assyrian palaces were imitated on stone slabs at doorways where the heavy doors would rip textiles. From Sennacherib's palace at Nineveh. c.700 BC. WA 124962.

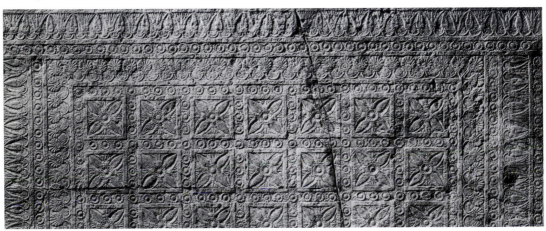

sixth millennium BC are common on archaeological sites, together with *bone and *bronze needles. Ancient weavers used various kinds of looms (horizontal ground loom, warp-weighted vertical loom, two-beam vertical loom). This work was divided between men and *women, but women were probably more active in the production of textiles. Woven fabrics ranged from the very simple to more elaborate decorative patterns (e.g. twill, brocade, embroidery).

Dyes of various colours were made from animal, vegetable and mineral substances, and some colours were 'fixed' to the cloth with mordants. Tomb paintings depicting 'Asiatics' from Beni Hasan in *Egypt show them wearing brightly striped garments. Perhaps the best-known dyeworks were associated with the *Phoenicians, who made rich purple dye from murex shells.

The earliest fragments of manufactured 'textile' are charred twisted plant fibres from Ohalo II in *Palestine, dating to 19,000 BP ('before present'; see Epipalaeolithic), tentatively identified as cord used for nets or bags. Rectangles of cloth made from flax from Nahal Hemar in the Judaean desert dating to Pre-Pottery *Neolithic B (c.8000 BC) have been interpreted as net-like headgear and parts of what may be string skirts. Rope, netting, matting, thread and linen cloth have been found there and at later Neolithic sites (e.g. *Çatalhöyük, Jarmo, *Jericho). Thereafter, linen and wool textiles of various styles appear at sites throughout the Near East. Cotton, native to *India, gradually spread to the West but is first documented in *Sennacherib's *annals c.700 BC. Silk was used in China by the third millennium BC, and was exported to Europe as early as the sixth century BC. Neither cotton nor silk became important in the Near East until much later. GLM

E.J.W. BARBER, *Prehistoric Textiles: The Development of Cloth in the Neolithic and Bronze Ages* (Princeton, NJ 1990).

——, 'Textiles: Textiles of the Neolithic through Iron Ages', *The Oxford Encyclopedia of Archaeology in the Near East* 5, ed. E.M. Meyers (New York 1997) 190–5.

C. BIER, 'Textile Arts in Ancient Western Asia', *Civilizations of the Ancient Near East*, ed. J.M. Sasson (New York 1995) 1567–88.

J. HARRIS (ed.), *Textiles 5000 Years: An International History and Illustrated Survey* (London 1993).

D. NADEL et al., '19000-year-old Twisted Fibers from Ohalo II', *Current Anthropology* 35/4 (1994) 451–8.

F.E. PETZEL, *Textiles of Ancient Mesopotamia, Persia, and Egypt* (Corvallis, OR 1987).

T. SCHICK, 'Cordage, Basketry and Fabrics', *Nahal Hemar Cave*, eds O. Bar-Yosef and D. Alon, *Atiqot* English Series 18 (1988) 31–43.

J.P. WILD, *Textiles in Archaeology* (Aylesbury 1988).

**Tiamat** Tiamat is an *Akkadian name meaning 'sea'. This female creature is the personification of the primeval salt waters in the *Babylonian *Epic of *Creation known by its opening words as *Enūma eliš* ('When on high'): 'When on high the heavens were not yet named, and below, the earth was not called by a name …' According to this unique Babylonian account (which differs from other *Mesopotamian narratives of the earliest periods in the development of the world), the only creatures in existence were Tiamat and Apsû. The latter represented the subterranean fresh waters. In the epic, Tiamat and Apsû are female and male respectively, and apparently they were able to give birth by their waters mingling together. Between them they produced a line of *gods including *Anu, Anu's son *Ea and various other deities. The noisy doings of these younger gods were irksome to Apsû, so much so that, despite the protests of their mother Tiamat, he plotted to kill them all. But Ea anticipated Apsû and killed him; and Tiamat, desiring revenge, created eleven monsters who fought *Marduk, champion of the younger gods, under the leadership of Tiamat's champion, her lover the god Qingu. Marduk heroically defeated the monsters, as well as Qingu and Tiamat, splitting open her skull with his mace. Breaking her in two 'like a dried fish', he used one half to roof the heavens and the other to surface the earth; her breasts formed mountains, Tigris and Euphrates flowed from her eyes, and her spittle formed clouds. However, it is difficult to form a precise image from the poem of how Tiamat was envisaged. JAB

S. DALLEY, *Myths from Mesopotamia* (Oxford 1990) 228–77.

**Tiglath-pileser** 'My help is the son of Esharra' (a *temple in *Ashur), name of three *Assyrian *kings.

Tiglath-pileser I (1115–1077 BC) briefly increased Assyrian power which had been in decline until the reign of his father, Ashur-resh-ishi. Tribes moving in southern *Anatolia had smashed the remnants of the *Hittite empire, and one, the Mushki (perhaps *Phrygians), crossed the Taurus and advanced along the Tigris towards Assyria. The Assyrians repelled 20,000 men, pacified the mountainous region and penetrated to the north of Lake Van, leaving inscriptions on the rocks. From Jebel Bishri in the west, Akhlamu-*Aramaean tribes were raiding as far as the Tigris, and Tiglath-pileser reports that he crossed the Euphrates twenty-eight times to fight them, passing through Tadmor (Palmyra) to reach the Mediterranean, where he took a sea voyage from *Arvad, caught strange marine creatures and received tribute from *Byblos and Sidon. Carvings of the *animals were made to decorate his new *palace at Ashur. The *Babylonian king had attacked Assyria, so Tiglath-pileser invaded, sacking *Sippar and *Babylon, taking plunder but not attempting to stay in control. Booty, new *trade routes and access to mineral resources added to Ashur's wealth. The later years of his reign are not recorded; a fragment of a *chronicle-like text may speak of Aramaean attacks and famine close to Ashur. Tiglath-pileser was the first king to leave lengthy *annals inscribed on octagonal clay prisms, as well as shorter versions on tablets, to commemorate his extensive building works at Ashur and similar tablets at *Nineveh. His texts are the first to tell of royal prowess in *hunting, in his case including four wild bulls, ten elephants and 920 lions! From his reign survive large tablets bearing the Middle Assyrian *Laws and fragments of the edicts regulating behaviour in the palace

Tiglath-pileser III is led in procession in his chariot with the driver and parasol-bearer. Relief carving from Nimrud. WA 118908.

enacted by several kings from Ashur-uballit I (1365–1330 BC) onwards. There is also a *hymn praising the king and part of an *epic about his exploits and a number of literary texts found at Ashur and Nineveh were copied in his reign.

Tiglath-pileser II (967–935 BC) ruled near the end of the obscure period of Aramaean incursions and is known only from the *King List, *Eponym List and a stela at Ashur.

Tiglath-pileser III (744–727 BC): Revolt in *Nimrud led to Tiglath-pileser taking the throne in 746 BC, although he was not in line to succeed. An able ruler, he increased Assyria's control of its territories, improving the organization and equipment of the *army and breaking the enormous provinces governed by the highest state officials into smaller areas, so reducing the officials' power (see Provincial administration). Almost every year saw a military campaign, starting with Babylonia. Its forces had taken Assyrian land in the east, so Tiglath-pileser regained it and marched south to the Gulf, supporting the new Babylonian king Nabu-nasir against *Chaldaean threats. That problem took him to Babylon again in 731 and 729 BC when he crushed rebel Aramaeans and Chaldaeans and made himself king of Babylon. Immediately north of Assyria, *Urartu incited rebellion, requiring repeated attention (739, 738, 736 BC), then Tiglath-pileser's troops entered Urartu, defeated its king at his capital, now Van, and turned Urartian lands into provinces. In the north-west Urartu had headed a league against Assyria, which was defeated in 743 BC and one centre, Arpad in north *Syria, was besieged and captured (742–740 BC). Further south a rebel Azriyau was

obliterated in the *Hamath area and neighbours paid tribute, including *Damascus and *Samaria (738 BC). In 734 BC Tiglath-pileser progressed through the *Levant to the Egyptian frontier at Gaza, but Rezin (Rahyan) of Damascus headed another uprising which was suppressed in 733 BC, with Damascus taken and turned into a province in 732 BC. *Tyre paid a heavy tribute and *Arab tribes brought more, including *spices. Regions and tribes in western *Iran were subjected to Assyrian rule in 744 and 737 BC.

Tiglath-pileser began a new palace at Nimrud but *Esarhaddon's workmen dismantled the slabs carved in relief and they have been only partially recovered. Their style reflects *Ashurnasirpal's, with both life-size figures and double registers of action scenes, but, where the earlier *sculptures had a repeated standard inscription between them, here narrative 'annals' filled the space.

Babylonian *King List A, the *Bible (2 Kings 15: 19; 1 Chronicles 5: 26) and *Hellenistic sources give him a nickname, Pulu.                                          ARM

Tiglath-pileser I:
B.R. FOSTER, *Before the Muses* (Bethesda, MD 1996) 237–39 (hymn).
A.K. GRAYSON, *Assyrian Royal Inscriptions* 2 (Wiesbaden 1976) 1–45.
——, *Assyrian Rulers of the Early First Millennium BC 1 (1114–859 BC)* (Toronto 1991) 7–84.
D.J. WISEMAN, 'Assyria and Babylonia c. 1200–1000 B.C.', *Cambridge Ancient History* 2.2, 2nd ed. (Cambridge 1975) 457–64.

Tiglath-pileser II:
A.K. GRAYSON, *Assyrian Royal Inscriptions* 2 (Wiesbaden 1976) 73–4.

——, *Assyrian Rulers of the Early First Millennium* BC *1(1114–859* BC*)* (Toronto 1991) 129–30.

Tiglath-pileser III:

R.D. BARNETT and M. FALKNER, *The Sculptures of Ashur-nasir-apli II (883–859 B.C.), Tiglath-pileser III (745–727 B.C.), Esarhaddon (681–669 B.C.) from the Central and South-West Palaces at Nimrud* (London 1962).

A.K. GRAYSON, 'Assyria: Tiglath-pileser III to Sargon II (744–705 B.C.', *Cambridge Ancient History* 3.2, 2nd ed. (Cambridge 1991) 71–85.

H. TADMOR, *The Inscriptions of Tiglath-Pileser III, King of Assyria* (Jerusalem 1994).

**Til Barsip** Til Barsip (also Til Barsib and Tarbusiba) has been identified by *Assyrian inscriptions with modern Tell Ahmar. It lies on the Euphrates downstream from its confluence with the *River Sajur, south of *Carchemish, in fertile country where a land route comes down from Amedi (modern Diarbekir) via Edessa (modern Urfa) or *Harran, through Suruj (Serug in Genesis 11, Neo-*Assyrian Sarugi, Christian Serugh). Across the river

Black-and-white pebble mosaic courtyard in the Assyrian residential building in the lower town at Til Barsip (courtesy Guy Bunnens and Melbourne University Expedition to Tell Ahmar).

from Tell Ahmar lies Pitru, biblical Pethor; and Membidj-Hierapolis (Assyrian Nappigi) is 15 km down the road towards Aleppo.

Its Luwian name was Masuwari. The *city or part of it was named Kar-Shalmaneser from 856 BC when *Shalmaneser III conquered it. At that time it was a royal residence of Ahuni, ruler of the *Aramaean tribe Bit-Adini. Its *Hellenistic name was Bersiba.

French excavations (1929–31) on the high citadel mound found a Neo-Assyrian *palace with *wall paintings, above *tombs of the third millennium BC. Large basalt lions and various basalt stelae and *sculptures, set up at city *gates and elsewhere, some inscribed in *Akkadian, *Aramaic and Luwian, help to reconstruct the history of the site in the early first millennium BC, including a *dynasty founded by Hapatilas and prosperous under Hamiyatas and an independent governor Shamshi-ilu c.796–752 BC. Assyrian royal inscriptions indicate *boat-building there under *Sennacherib, and continuing importance under *Esarhaddon. The patron *god of the city was probably the *weather-god.

Australian excavations from 1988 onwards found a large Assyrian residential building in the lower town, with an audience suite and a black-and-white pebble courtyard like the *Bâtiment aux ivoires* at *Arslan Tash. It contained some *Syrian-style *ivories, legal and administrative Akkadian texts from the mid seventh century BC indicating relations with *Nimrud, *Samaria and Cilicia, and two Aramaic tablets. There is another seventh-century BC residential area in the northern part of the settlement, with more pebble mosaics. On the citadel, an Early Bronze Age *temple or palace has been found. The city name for that period is still unrecognized. There is also Middle Bronze Age architecture and burials on the *tell. A Hellenistic temple was built into the Assyrian palace on the citadel. Seleucid *coins were also found there.                                                                          SMD

G. BUNNENS, 'Til Barsib under Assyrian Domination: A Brief Account of the Melbourne University Excavations at Tell Ahmar', *Assyria 1995*, eds S. Parpola and R.M. Whiting (Helsinki 1997) 17–28.

——, 'Carved Ivories from Til Barsib', *American Journal of Archaeology* 101 (1997) 435–50.

G. BUNNENS *et al.*, 'New Texts from Til Barsib', *Abr-Nahrain* 34 (1996–7) 59–117.

J.D. HAWKINS, 'The Political Geography of North Syria and South-East Anatolia in the Neo-Assyrian Period', *Neo-Assyrian Geography*, ed. M. Liverani (Rome 1995) 87–101 and pls I–X.

A. ROOBAERT, 'A Neo-Assyrian Statue from Til Barsib', *Iraq* 58 (1996) 79–87.

F. THUREAU-DANGIN and M. DUNAND, *Til-Barsib* (Paris 1936).

**Timber:** see Wood

**Timna** Timna is the name of a valley on the western side of the Wadi Arabah; it is located c.29 km north of Eilat. This valley, famous for its *copper ores, contains a large number of *mines, mining camps and smelting sites which were used sporadically from the *Chalcolithic to Late Islamic periods. *Glueck linked exploitation of copper ores at Timna with his excavations at Tell el-Kheleifeh and claimed that both dated to the days of Solomon (tenth century BC), but it is now clear that this was not the case. Timna was excavated by B. Rothenberg (1959–90).

A variety of copper ores, especially malachite and chalcocite, were extracted from the sandstone cliffs by means of vertical shafts and horizontal galleries. The Timna mines represent the earliest extensive use of this system, and associated artefacts (e.g. tuyères (nozzles of bellows), grinding *tools, *pottery) and slagheaps reflect intensive activity. Some of the vertical shafts are over 30 m deep and include footholds for climbing in and out of the mine.

Apart from the important *prehistoric copper mines and smelting furnaces at Timna, this valley was used extensively by *Egyptian miners between the fourteenth and twelfth centuries BC. A sanctuary dedicated to the Egyptian goddess Hathor, patron deity of mining, was constructed in the reign of Seti I (c.1306–1290 BC) and rebuilt under Ramesses II (c.1290–1224 BC). Egyptian artefacts, including scarabs which name pharaohs from Seti I until Ramesses V (c.1156–1151 BC), reflect the long-term use of this *temple. Pottery that is typically associated with the *Midianites points to a later, post-Egyptian (mid twelfth century BC) use of this site.                    GLM

W.G. DEVER, 'Timna', *The Oxford Encyclopedia of Archaeology in the Near East* 5, ed. E.M. Meyers (New York 1997) 217–18.

B. ROTHENBERG, *God's Wilderness: Discoveries in Sinai* (London 1961)

——, *Timna': Valley of the Biblical Copper Mines* (London 1972).

——, *The Egyptian Mining Temple of Timna'* (London 1988).

—— (ed.), *The Ancient Metallurgy of Copper: Archaeology, Experiment, Theory* (London 1990).

——, 'Timna', *New Encyclopedia of Archaeological Excavations in the Holy Land* 4, ed. E. Stern (Jerusalem 1993) 1475–86.

## Tin

**Tin** The main function of tin was for alloying with *copper to produce *bronze, although tin solders were also used. It occurs in nature as the ore cassiterite, deposits of which are scarce in the Near East. Third-millennium BC sources from *Ebla mention tin as passing through Dilmun (modern *Bahrain), but this was clearly a transhipment point, not a source. Old *Babylonian documentary sources also provide information on the distribution of tin rather than its origins, and indicate its dispatch from *Susa in south-west *Iran to *Sippar south of modern Baghdad, from where it was sent westwards by a variety of routes. It may have originated in Afghanistan. Some tin passed through *Mari, from where texts mention onward shipment to *Hazor in northern *Palestine and *Ugarit on the *Syrian coast.

More recently it has been suggested that there was Early Bronze Age tin *mining in the vicinity of Göltepe in the Taurus mountains of southern Turkey. This may have been related to the extraction of lead or *silver, although *Hittite and Neo-*Assyrian documents refer to tin from

Tin ingot in the shape of an oxhide (maximum length 62.5 cm) from the Ulu Burun shipwreck (courtesy of the Institute of Nautical Archaeology).

places which lie within modern Turkey. *Phoenician settlement in the western Mediterranean may have been stimulated by the search for *metals, although evidence for the export of tin from west to east is scarce.

Tin (*annaku* in *Akkadian) was expensive, appearing at one-tenth the value of silver at Mari during the nineteenth to eighteenth centuries BC. Its importance is clear from early second-millennium BC texts from the Old Assyrian colony at *Kanesh in central *Anatolia, which refer to *merchants from *Ashur transporting tin to Anatolia, where it was *traded for locally produced silver. Actual tin ingots are rare, although their existence is confirmed by the discovery of several examples in the Late Bronze Age *shipwrecks at *Gelidonya and *Ulu Burun. Tin artefacts are also rare, although a number are known from *graves of the nineteenth century BC at Tell ed-Der in Babylonia.                    GP

P.T. CRADDOCK, *Early Metal Mining and Production* (Edinburgh 1995).

J.E. CURTIS (ed.), *Bronzeworking Centres of Western Asia, c.1000–539 BC* (London 1988).

P.R.S. MOOREY, *Ancient Mesopotamian Materials and Industries: The Archaeological Evidence* (Oxford 1994).

J.D. MUHLY, 'Mining and Metalworking in Ancient Western Asia', *Civilizations of the Ancient Near East*, ed. J.M. Sasson (New York 1995) 1501–21.

## Tombs

**Tombs** The way a society treats its dead reveals much about its cultural values, and the details of *burial customs vary according to time and place. Just as ceramics and other artefacts vary from region to region, no typology of tomb styles can be applied across the entire Near East. In most regions, the simple graves of earliest times were later replaced with elaborate designed tombs, with above-ground or subterranean architecture.

*Palaeolithic burials in Mount Carmel's Skhul cave are among the earliest reflections of the human response to death. During the early *prehistoric periods, graves consisted of little more than a pit in the floor of cave dwellings or *houses. At *Natufian *Jericho the dead were placed underneath floors, or their skulls were buried in

Interior of a Middle Bronze Age tomb at Jericho, showing the skeleton in the middle lying on the remains of a wooden bed. To the left are the remains of a wooden table and a wooden platter, with various pottery vessels and a lamp. A basket in the left-hand corner contained the remains of a wooden box with bone inlay (courtesy of Piotr Bienkowski).

pits. In the *Neolithic period, skulls were plastered, decorated with shells and placed beneath floors of houses. After *pottery was invented, infants were sometimes buried in jars and adults were placed in cairns or mounds. In the *Chalcolithic period, ossuaries were used for secondary interments, as at the recently discovered Peqi'in cave in northern Israel. Stone-lined cists, rock-cut tombs and caves were used in some regions. Pit graves continued, alongside jar burials under floors, at Teleilat *Ghassul, while stone circles called *nawamis* were used in the *Sinai. This variety was accompanied by a trend to bury the dead outside settlements, rather than in and around houses. Intramural burials were still preferred in some places, especially for the interment of infants. In parts of *Palestine and *Transjordan, megalithic tombs called dolmens were used in the Chalcolithic period and continued into the Early Bronze Age.

The Early Bronze Age witnessed a shift towards rock-cut, cave or shaft tombs. The chambers that radiated off the shaft could hold multiple interments, as in the huge cemeteries of Bab edh-Dhra in *Jordan. At this same site, the Early Bronze Age occupants also built above-ground round tombs and large rectangular charnel houses. Grave furnishings in the large pit burials of *Ur's Royal Cemetery illustrate the wealth of *Sumer. The royal *family of *Ebla was also buried in elaborate tombs. The Early and Middle Bronze tombs at Jericho do not reflect such a wide disparity in social status, however. *Kenyon detected differences in the shape and content of Jericho's Early Bronze IV tombs and suggested that they revealed ethnic diversity in the *town's population. Middle and Late Bronze Age tombs continued the Early Bronze types but added other regional variations. For example, some of *Ugarit's Late Bronze Age houses had corbelled funerary chambers under them. The appearance of anthropoid clay *coffins at numerous sites in Palestine and Trans-

jordan in the Late Bronze to Iron I transition probably illustrates the influence of *Egyptian burial customs. Late Bronze *Hittite tombs contained jars filled with ashes from *cremation and very few grave goods.

Iron Age I saw a continuation of Late Bronze Age practices, but the typical grave in much of Palestine during Iron II was the rock-cut chambered tomb. This type included a forecourt, low entrance and raised stone benches. When the bench was needed for another interment, the skeletal remains were often placed in repository pits within that same chamber. The *Judaean kings were probably buried in tombs like the eighth-century BC rock-cut chambers of Silwan. In contrast, *Ashurnasirpal II and *Shamshi-Adad V were entombed at *Ashur in underground chambers which contained huge *stone sarcophagi. They, like so many other tombs, were plundered in antiquity. Graves of high-ranking *Assyrian *women, perhaps *queens, were found in four subterranean chambers with barrel-vaulted roofs in Ashurnasirpal's *palace at *Nimrud. The bodies were originally interred in *pottery or stone sarcophagi, three of them with rich collections of *jewellery. In *Phrygia, the massive burial tumuli of *Gordion date to the eighth and early seventh century BC and enclosed elaborately furnished tombs built of *wood.                    GLM

S. CAMPBELL and A. GREEN (eds), *The Archaeology of Death in the Ancient Near East* (Oxford 1995).

M.S.B. DAMERJI, 'Gräber assyrischer Königinnen aus Nimrud', *Jahrbuch des Römisch-Germanischen Zentralmuseums* (Mainz) 45 (1998).

R. GONEN, *Burial Patterns and Cultural Diversity in Late Bronze Age Canaan* (Winona Lake, IN 1992).

S. LOFFREDA, 'Typological Sequence of Iron Age Rock-Cut Tombs in Palestine', *Liber Annuus* 18 (1968) 244–87.

J.B. PRITCHARD, *The Bronze Age Cemetery at Gibeon* (Philadelphia, PA 1963).

R.T. SCHAUB and W.E. RAST, *Bab edh-Dhra': Excavations in the Cemetery Directed by Paul W. Lapp (1965–67)* (Winona Lake, IN 1989).

D. USSISHKIN, *The Village of Silwan: The Necropolis from the Period of the Judean Kingdom* (Jerusalem 1993).

**Tools and weapons** When objects are found on archaeological excavations, it is sometimes difficult to decide whether they were used as tools or weapons, or perhaps both. *Bone was frequently used for harpoons, arrowheads, awls, needles and pins. *Metal tools replaced those in *stone gradually, and first become common during the fourth millennium BC. The first stone tools to be replaced by metal were large, heavy-duty implements such as axes, adzes and chisels. However, there is a lack of evidence for metal tools because metal was extensively recycled, because tools were rarely placed in *graves, and because much research has focused on public buildings, rather than workshops or domestic areas. Occasional groups of tools do occur, such as a hoard from Tell Sifr in southern Iraq. Of Old *Babylonian date, the hoard is dominated by woodworking and *agricultural equipment, with most of the items made from unalloyed *copper, rather than *bronze. A group of tenth-century BC *iron tools from Tell Taanach in *Palestine shows a similar range of implements.

Early depictions of weaponry appear on the so-called Standard from the Royal Cemetery at *Ur, dating to c.2600 BC. This shows soldiers wearing helmets, and carrying spearheads and shaft-hole axes. The most extensive records come from reliefs of the Neo-*Assyrian date, while *Egyptian representations of campaigns in western Asia provide valuable evidence for the *Levant during the Late Bronze Age. Although these contain valuable information, some scenes are stereotyped, and the evidence cannot always be taken at face value.

Actual weapons mostly come from graves, and may not be representative of the tools of *war. For example, the *Mari texts, which date to the early second millennium BC, refer to sieges, mention various forms of military engineering and indicate the large-scale use of metal projectiles, but the contemporary grave goods are dominated by weapons designed for close-quarter fighting between individual warriors. The archaeological evidence for pre-*Bronze Age weapons includes stone and copper maceheads and a range of projectiles with stone, bone or wooden points. Although fourth-millennium BC graves at *Byblos produced a number of daggers, there appears to have been a big increase in the deposition of weapons in graves around the mid third millennium BC when large quantities of daggers, axes and spearheads appear at sites throughout western Asia, for example at Ur. There is mid-third-millennium BC documentary evidence from *Ebla in western *Syria for the production of weapons in bronze, and their decoration with precious metals. These feature alongside other precious objects as high-status gifts.

The increasing use of casting in two-piece moulds led, around the beginning of the second millennium, to the appearance of a range of elaborately styled objects including fenestrated and narrow-bladed axes and daggers with decorated blades. Spearheads hafted by means of a socket now replaced earlier tanged forms. Considerations of style and fashion may sometimes have been more important than mechanical efficiency, especially for weapons intended as gifts or status markers. The discovery of many weapons, including examples in *gold and silver alongside other 'valuable' materials, in a group of *temple offerings at Byblos confirms that these objects had multiple levels of meaning.

Longer daggers with the hilt and blade cast as one appeared in the Late Bronze Age. Metal arrowheads appeared at the same time, probably coinciding with changes in the technology of the bow. Self-bows, made from a single piece of wood, were an old tradition, but had serious limitations. In contrast, a composite bow constructed from layers of wood, horn and sinew was more powerful than a self-bow of equivalent size, and could be kept strung for long periods. While these may have originated in mid-third-millennium BC *Mesopotamia, and are mentioned in early second-millennium BC texts from *Mari under the term *tilpānum*, bows are perishable and rarely survive, so arrowheads often remain as the only evidence of their presence. An exception is a bow dating to the fourth millennium BC, found in the 'Cave of the Warrior' in the Judaean desert.

*Chariot and scale armour developed in the later second millennium BC. Chariot drivers and archers were equipped with coats of scale armour which were relatively light, and did not overly restrict the wearer's movement. A lot of armour was probably made from leather rather than metal, but surviving evidence for bronze armour appears in the form of groups of perforated metal scales, designed to be laced together in overlapping rows to form a coat long enough to cover the body and upper legs. The organization of warfare was revolutionized with the appearance of specialist chariot-troops, the *maryannu*, as well as the growth of an extensive support network: farriers, wrights, harness-makers and armourers.

In many ways *Iron Age weapons were simply developments of earlier equipment, but in iron. *Assyrian reliefs show archers protected by coats of mail, and infantrymen with swords or spears and shields, many wearing pointed or plumed helmets.                    GP

R. GONEN, *Weapons of the Ancient World* (London 1975).

O.W. MUSCARELLA, *Bronze and Iron: Ancient Near Eastern Artifacts in the Metropolitan Museum of Art* (New York 1988).

G. PHILIP, *Metal Weapons of the Early and Middle Bronze Ages in Syria–Palestine* (Oxford 1989).

Y. YADIN, *The Art of Warfare in Biblical Lands in the Light of Archaeological Discovery* (London 1963).

**Toprakkale** Toprakkale, a great fortress atop a low, steep-sided hill on the north side of the modern city of Van in eastern Turkey, was the second and last capital of *Urartu. It was founded by Rusa II (c.685–665 BC?), a most prolific builder of Urartian fortresses, and thus called Rusahinili. The reason for moving the centre of

A bronze sickle-sword (harpe), 54 cm long, inscribed for Adad-nirari I of Assyria (c.1305–1274 BC), now in the Metropolitan Museum of Art, New York.

Fenestrated axe, Byblos. Bronze, Middle Bronze Age WA 116633.

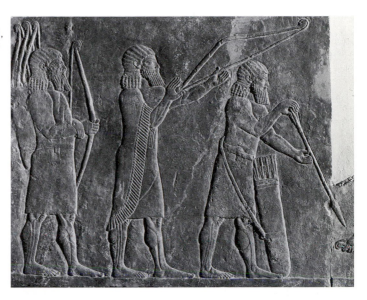

(top) Bows and arrows being prepared for King Ashurbanipal's hunt. Relief from the North Palace at Nineveh. WA 124884.

(left) A relief showing construction work on Sennacherib's palace at Nineveh includes workmen carrying saws, picks and spades. WA 124823.

(below) Bronze blades for small wooden spades of the Old Babylonian period, from Tell Sifr, near Larsa. Each is c.10 cm long. WA 91202, 91204.

Lead overlay for a wooden statue with ivory face and hands, inlaid with ivory and glass. From Toprakkale. Height 24.3 cm. Eighth to seventh centuries BC. WA 123870 + 123881 + 123883 + 4.

Human-headed winged figure of Assyrian style, cast in bronze, part of a support for a piece of furniture. From the shrine of Haldi at Toprakkale. Height 20.3 cm. Urartian, c.700 BC. WA 91247.

and a statuette. Also found were carved *ivories, *stone inlays and other objects that form the core of the Urartian collection in the British Museum. Lehmann and Belck dug at the site in 1898 and their discoveries are in Berlin. Later work has been undertaken by Professors A. Erzen and E. Bilgiç.

Major architectural elements that have been recognized, besides the *fortifications which might be reconstructed with reference to the bronze model fragment, are the *temple to Haldi (*god of *war and head of the Urartian pantheon), great magazines or storerooms and a rock-cut staircase, with fifty-six steps, leading down to a large cistern.                                                                    GDS

R.D. BARNETT, 'The Excavations of the British Museum at Toprak Kale near Van', *Iraq* 12 (1950) 1–43.
——, 'More Addenda from Toprak Kale', *Anatolian Studies* 22 (1972) 163–78.
A. ERZEN, 'Untersuchungen in der urartäischen Stadt Toprakkale bei Van in den Jahren 1959–1965', *Archäologischer Anzeiger* (1962/2) 383–414.
H. RASSAM, *Assur and the Land of Nimrod* (New York 1897).
J. READE, 'Hormuzd Rassam and his Discoveries', *Iraq* 45 (1993) 39–62.
R.-B. WARTKE, *Toprakkale* (Berlin 1990).

**Tower of Babel** In the *Bible (Genesis 11) there is a description of the building of a *city and tower of Babel. Humankind had only one *language and wished to build a prestigious city to prevent their dispersal and a tower to reach heaven. God punished them for their pride by confusing their language and scattering them across the earth. There is a play on words between *Babel* ('gate of god', i.e. *Babylon) and the *Hebrew word *bālal* ('confusion').

The term 'Tower of Babel' does not appear in the Old Testament, but is generally used to describe the prominent tower associated with the city. It has normally been assumed that it was a *ziggurat, or *temple tower, of the type built in *Babylonia from the third millennium BC on. Travellers throughout the centuries have attempted to locate the ruins of the tower of Babel. Some identified it with the ziggurat of Babylon, of which nothing now re-

A small Babylonian tablet of c.500 BC bears a diagram of a miniature ziggurat with six or seven stages, each six cubits (c.3 m) high. WA 38217.

*administration from Van Kale to Toprakkale is not known.

Like most fortresses, Rusahinili met a violent end and was put to the torch around the middle of the seventh century BC. The crumbling mudbrick walls reddened in the blaze and collapsed into a great mound of earth, hence the modern name which means 'earth castle'.

Early digging at the site was carried out by *Rassam, who was able to recover a number of important objects, including the decorated ceremonial *bronze shields inscribed with dedications to Haldi by Rusa III. Other bronze objects included quivers, cauldrons and other vessels, parts of a bronze model city, *furniture elements

mains, others with the remains of ziggurats at *Borsippa or *Aqar Quf. One Dutch traveller, Leonhardt Rauwolff, visited Babylon in 1574 and claimed that he found the tower of Babel 'full of Vermin' which he described as 'three-headed poisonous lizard-type insects with multi-coloured spots on their backs'. The tower of Babel became a central theme in European art from the twelfth century AD on, and especially during the Renaissance.

Modern scholars are divided as to whether the Old Testament account reflects any genuine allusion to real architecture, or whether the role of the story is purely theological. A *Mesopotamian tradition possibly related to the tower of Babel story in Genesis is found in the *Sumerian *story '*Enmerkar and the Lord of Aratta', in which all people worshipped *Ellil with one voice until *Enki introduced diversity into their *language.　　PB

H. MINKOWSKI, *Aus dem Nebel der Vergangenheit steigt der Turm zu Babel: Bilder aus 1000 Jahren* (Berlin 1960).

A. PARROT, *The Tower of Babel* (London 1955).

F.A. SPINA, 'Babel', *Anchor Bible Dictionary* 1, ed. D.N. Freedman (New York 1992) 561–3.

**Towns:** see Cities, towns and villages

**Toys and games**　Toys are not always easily identifiable in archaeological contexts, since it is not usually clear whether an object was primarily for play, or perhaps had an unknown symbolic meaning, for instance if found in a *grave. Representations in Near Eastern *art sometimes help with identification, supplemented by copious evidence from *Egypt, especially tomb paintings.

From the *Neolithic period on, and especially in the *Bronze and *Iron Ages, objects identified as toys include rattles, terracotta model wagons and *chariots, clay *animals, balls, tops (also represented on an eighth-century BC relief from *Carchemish), and the 'buzz' (a small clay disk with a string run through two holes, which is stretched and whirled). Probably the earliest game involved astragali, or animal knucklebones, which could be used as four-sided dice. The earliest dice come from

the *Indus Valley, dating to the third millennium BC, and by c.2300 BC are found at *Shahr-i Sokhta in north-east *Iran, made of *wood, with four numbered sides, the numbers indicated by *ivory and mother-of-pearl inlay or by incisions. Six-sided dice in various materials are known from the late third millennium BC onwards all over the Near East. Some 'toys' have not survived archaeologically, but we know of their existence from texts, for example skipping ropes.

The Egyptian board game *senet* was known in Egypt and *Palestine at least from the third millennium BC, if not earlier, and occasionally found elsewhere in the Near East later: it consisted of moving pieces, made of different materials, around a chequerboard of thirty squares, though the rules are uncertain. Other games played on boards with different numbers of squares or holes are also known from all areas of the Near East; one was called 'pack of dogs', and its rules have survived in a *cuneiform text. Similar games have survived to the present day; a game similar to backgammon was introduced in the *Roman–Byzantine period.　　PB

W.W. HALLO, 'Games in the Biblical World', *Eretz-Israel* 24 (1993) 83*–8*.

U. HÜBNER, *Spiel und Spielzeug im antiken Palästina* (Göttingen 1992).

——, 'Games', *The Oxford Encyclopedia of Archaeology in the Near East* 2, ed. E.M. Meyers (New York 1997) 379–82.

A.D. KILMER, 'Games and Toys in Ancient Mesopotamia', *Actes du XIIe Congrès International des Sciences Préhistoriques et Protohistoriques* (Bratislava 1993) 359–64.

**Trade**　Peoples of the ancient Near East were accustomed to obtaining products through trade since *prehistoric times. Local materials and products were exchanged between one settlement and another by land or *water, and it was only a matter of time before more elaborate trade networks extended the range from which items could be acquired. Once the exchange system began, *merchants and middlemen developed more sophisticated means to *transport, protect, document and market their materials and products. Ancient trading activities

Hollow wooden gaming board and counters. The board was inlaid with engraved shell, red limestone and lapis lazuli. Found in the Royal Cemetery at Ur. Length 27 cm. c.2500 BC. WA 120834.

Pull-along lion and hedgehog from Susa, limestone and bitumen, c.1150 BC (© Photo RMN – H. Lewandowski. Louvre Sb 2905, 2908).

included the exchange of genuinely essential items, not just exotic luxury products. Ancient Near Eastern trade was also an important channel for the exchange of information, technology and world views.

*Coinage was not invented until the seventh century BC; before this, materials and products were bartered – for other goods and services – or exchanged for certain amounts of metals. One of the earliest known Near Eastern trade materials was *obsidian, which was already exchanged in *Neolithic times. On later Neolithic and *Chalcolithic sites, the number of items that reflect trade increase significantly (e.g. lapis lazuli from Afghanistan, *wood, *copper, *foods), but there was an explosion of trading activities in the Early Bronze Age. The *Bronze Age network of trade facilitated the exchange of copper and *tin, *bronze weapons and *tools, precious *metals, *jewellery, *pottery, *textiles (including purple cloth, which became significant in the first millennium BC), *building stone, timber, *furniture, *ivory, bitumen, livestock, olive oil, *wine (from the early second millennium BC onwards) and foods. The Late Bronze Age cargo of the *Ulu Burun *shipwreck reflects the range of items that could be exchanged over great distances by *ship. Sea and overland routes opened the market for goods from Europe and the *Aegean, Africa and ports in the Gulf and Indian Ocean.

Much of the Bronze Age trade was documented in thousands of *cuneiform tablets in a variety of *languages, mostly administrative and economic accounts. One of the most important windows on Near Eastern trade is the collection of over twenty thousand tablets from *Kanesh, the *archive of an Old *Assyrian trading colony that flourished from c.1920 BC for almost two centuries. *Ugarit was another significant trading entrepôt. During the Late Bronze Age, ships from *Greece, Crete, *Cyprus and *Egypt made regular stops at Ugarit, while other products went in and out of Ugarit via overland routes through *Syria.

The *Phoenicians filled the vacuum left by the collapse of the Late Bronze Age. Mediterranean seaports like *Tyre and *Sidon flourished with long-distance trade that reached far into the interior of Asia and all the way to Spain and Morocco. Some of the trade products reached the *Lebanese coast by ship and others came overland by *camel caravan. *Arabs specialized in camel caravans enabling products to be shipped across the region's deserts; their particular specialities were *incense and spices.                                                        GLM

M. ASTOUR, 'Overland Trade Routes in Ancient Western Asia', *Civilizations of the Ancient Near East*, ed. J.M. Sasson (New York 1995) 1401–20.

N.H. GALE (ed.), *Bronze Age Trade in the Mediterranean* (Jonsered 1991).

J.D. HAWKINS (ed.), *Trade in the Ancient Near East* (London 1977).

A.L. OPPENHEIM, 'Trade in the Ancient Near East', *5th International Congress of Economic History* (Leningrad 1970) 1–37.

J.A. SABLOFF and C.C. LAMBERG-KARLOVSKY (eds), *Ancient Civilization and Trade* (Albuquerque 1975).

N. YOFFEE, 'The Economy of Ancient Western Asia', *Civilizations of the Ancient Near East*, ed. J.M. Sasson (New York 1995) 1387–99.

**Transjordan**  Although the term 'Transjordan' is not ancient, the *biblical writers referred to this region as 'beyond the Jordan'. Obviously, this reflects a *Palestinian perspective, a view of Near Eastern geography held by people who lived west of the Jordan river, in 'Cisjordan'. Transjordan usually refers to the territory east of the Jordan rift valley, between Mount Hermon in the north and the Gulf of Aqaba in the south. A modern political distinction was made between Palestine (west of the Jordan) and Transjordan (east of the *river and stretching towards the *Syrian desert). Between 1872 and 1881, the Palestine Exploration Fund completed an archaeological survey of 'Western Palestine' and 'Eastern Palestine'. *Glueck conducted a monumental surface study of *Ammon, *Moab and *Edom between 1932 and 1947. He used the earlier terminology and published his results in four volumes as *Explorations in Eastern Palestine*; Glueck's popular account of his research and discoveries was published as *The Other Side of the Jordan*. The Crusaders called this region Oultrejourdain; nowadays most of the land formerly known as Transjordan falls within

Map of Transjordan showing main archaeological sites.

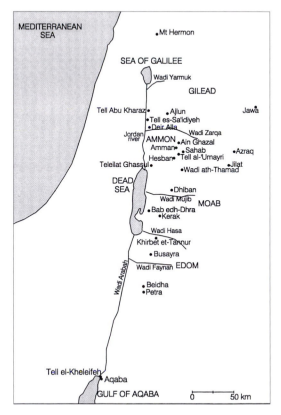

the boundaries of the Hashemite Kingdom of Jordan, although part is in southern Syria.

Transjordan includes a wide variety of topographic features and environmental zones, and the region's history reflects its strategic position. Much of this territory is a high plateau that rises above the Great Rift Valley to the west and slopes down to the *Arabian desert on the east. The higher parts of the plateau have a Mediterranean climate and are agriculturally productive; in the lower elevations and in southern Edom, desert conditions prevail. The plateau is cut by four great canyons, whose tributaries drain winter rainfall into the Rift Valley – Yarmuk, Jabbok (Wadi Zarqa), Arnon (Wadi al-Mujib) and Zered (Wadi al-Hasa). These canyons were central to the formation of ancient Transjordan's distinct political and cultural identities, which were known as Bashan, Gilead, Ammon, Moab and Edom. Archaeological research in these regions has increased dramatically in recent years, and the history of Transjordan from its *prehistoric foundations to the arrival of the *Assyrians, *Babylonians and *Persians can be written in some detail. Since antiquity, the peoples of Transjordan have interacted with *nomadic tribes from the eastern desert, and the region's position along the caravan routes between Arabia and Syria is reflected in its cultural developments. Important ancient cities in Transjordan include Rabbath-ammon (modern Amman), Madaba, Dibon (modern Dhiban), Kir-hareseth (modern Karak) and Bozrah (modern *Busayra).                                              GLM

Y. AHARONI, *The Land of the Bible: A Historical Geography*, rev. ed. (Philadelphia, PA 1979).

P. BIENKOWSKI (ed.), *The Art of Jordan* (Stroud 1991).

N. GLUECK, *The Other Side of the Jordan*, rev. ed. (Cambridge, MA 1970).

J.A. SAUER and L.G. HERR, 'Transjordan in the Bronze and Iron Ages', *The Oxford Encyclopedia of Archaeology in the Near East* 5, ed. E.M. Meyers (New York 1997) 231–5.

G.A. SMITH, *The Historical Geography of the Holy Land*, 25th ed. (London 1931).

(*right*) When armies had to cross rivers, chariots were ferried in boats or, as here, wicker coracles. Relief from the palace of Ashurnasirpal II (883–859 BC) at Nimrud. WA 124543.

(*below*) Where practicable, the Assyrian army built bridges of boats or coracles, as shown in this section of the Balawat gates, c.845 BC. WA 124660.

H.O. THOMPSON, *Archaeology in Jordan* (New York 1989).

——, 'Transjordan', *Anchor Bible Dictionary* 6, ed. D.N. Freedman (New York 1992) 642–3.

**Transport and travel** For certain segments of the ancient Near Eastern population, travel was a regular part of life (e.g. *merchants, caravaneers, *diplomats, soldiers, sailors, messengers). In its ancient Near Eastern context, the term '*road' should normally be thought of as an unpaved route, i.e. a dirt track by which travellers went from one place to another. Pack *animals and mounts for riding were available, but wheeled vehicles were primitive. Passengers and cargoes could be transported by *boat or ship, but travel by land, *river, or sea was complicated by poor roads, unpredictable weather, lack of security, technological limitations and lack of lodging, *food and *water. A number of ancient texts mention problems that caravans had with brigands. Since antiquity, one of the most important components in standing armies was its corps of engineers, men who prepared the way for *military forces by identifying routes, clearing (and, in the classical period, actually building) roads and constructing bridges. When a commercial or other civilian traveller moved beyond the boundaries of ancient Near Eastern *cities, conditions were not necessarily equal to the standard established for military or official travel. Merchants and transportation professionals accepted the hardships and risks of travel because of the profit involved, but the number of tourists and pilgrims was quite limited until a much later period.

Ports grew up along safe and convenient stretches of seashore or river bank, and techniques for *navigation – on land and sea – improved through time. Many roads (especially in *Mesopotamia) stayed close to the courses of rivers, where settlements were frequently located. Caravan routes took advantage of the unique qualities of the *camel but still followed traditional routes from one water source to the next; oases and 'caravan cities' became famous because of this logistical mandate. The Middle Bronze Age donkey handlers who made the 1200-km journey between *Ashur and *Kanesh referred to the latter destination as a *kārum*, a 'quay', and the camel became known as the 'ship of the desert'.

When merchants in the trading colony of Kanesh imported *tin and *textiles from Assyria by ass or donkey caravans, they employed a means of transportation that had been available for over a thousand years. Before oxen pulled two- or four-wheeled wagons in Mesopotamia, where the wheel was invented late in the fourth millennium BC, they pulled *Sumerian sledges. Donkeys pulled wheeled vehicles in the third millennium BC; well designed horse-drawn *chariots were developed early in the second millennium BC. Better-quality horses were bred for cavalry units in the first millennium BC and employed by couriers who carried messages for royal administrators. Even though animals had been domesticated as 'beasts of burden' or draught animals, the principal means of land travel for human beings was walking.

Boat travel and transport began as early as the *Neolithic period, when the Tigris and Euphrates were recognized as important thoroughfares. These great rivers were excellent highways and provided a rapid, inexpensive means to transport food and other commodities. The value of canals as roads was quickly recognized, and many ditches were widened so that they became navigable. Long-distance seafaring opened international *trade routes for a vast array of raw materials and manufactured products. Although long-distance trade by sea became more common with the passage of time, the story of Wenamon, who sailed from Karnak to *Byblos c.1100 BC, reflects the perils of such travel.

Ashur, *Nimrud and *Nineveh were all located on the Tigris, and these Assyrian capitals prospered because of easy and inexpensive riverine transportation. Long quays were built at Nimrud and Nineveh, and *Sennacherib used these facilities to bring colossal statues to Nineveh by boat. Sennacherib employed *Phoenician ships and sailors in his long-distance trade.                    GLM

G.F. BASS, 'Sea and River Craft in the Ancient Near East', *Civilizations of the Ancient Near East*, ed. J. M. Sasson (New York 1995) 1421–31.

B.J. BEITZEL, 'Travel and Communication (OT World)', *Anchor Bible Dictionary* 6, ed. D.N. Freedman (New York 1992) 644–8.

R.W. BULLIET, *The Camel and the Wheel* (Cambridge, MA 1975).

L. CASSON, *Travel in the Ancient World* (Baltimore, MD 1994).

M.-C. DE GRAEVE, *The Ships of the Ancient Near East (c. 2000–500 B.C.)* (Louvain 1981).

M.A. LITTAUER and J.H. CROUWEL, *Wheeled Vehicles and Ridden Animals in the Ancient Near East* (Leiden 1979).

Marduk-zakir-shumi of Babylon and Assyrian Shalmaneser III make a treaty. Carved throne base from Nimrud (courtesy of British School of Archaeology in Iraq).

Stela from Ugarit, carved with a scene which probably shows two people making an agreement, their elbows perhaps resting on clay tablets on a table. Fourteenth century BC (after C. Schaeffer, *Syria* 17 (1936) 114–9, pl. 14).

**Treaties and covenants** When one ruler conquered another he might replace him with one of his own retinue or leave him or another local on the throne as a subject or tenant, his position defined by a vassal-treaty. *Kings who thought themselves to be, or proved to be, of equal stature, 'brothers', might regulate their relationships by a parity treaty. Where treaties were made orally the parties would call on human and divine beings as witnesses who could be called to testify if a treaty was broken, the divine witnesses perhaps also punishing the guilty party. When it becomes possible to write the agreements, the texts themselves become witnesses.

The wars between *Lagash and *Umma in the Early Dynastic III period involved broken pacts, and the oldest treaty texts come from *Ebla at the end of that period, although they are only partially understood. An *Elamite version of the treaty *Naram-Sin made with a king of Awan in *Iran c.2250 BC, found at *Susa, contains the basic terms of all treaties: 'My friends will be your friends, my enemies will be your enemies'. From the Middle Bronze Age there are several treaties, draft treaties or quotations from treaties from *Mari, Tell *Leilan, *Alalakh (level VII) and other sites, but the largest number come from the *Hittite *archives of the Late Bronze Age. They are written in *Akkadian and Hittite and include *cuneiform versions of the parity treaty between Ramesses II and Hattusilis III, which is also

Felling trees was a common act in war. Assyrian artists took care to represent the variety of trees they saw in foreign countries. From Sennacherib's palace at Nineveh, c.700 BC. Or. Dr. II, 57.

preserved in Egyptian. These Hittite treaties, of which over three dozen are known, share a clear common structure. The principal elements are: (1) title, (2) historical prologue (a sometimes lengthy rehearsal of events leading to the conclusion of the treaty), (3) stipulations, (4) instructions for depositing the document in a shrine or other safe place, (5) instructions for periodic reading of the text, (6) lists of witnesses, (7) blessings on those who keep the terms and curses on those who break them, (8) oath-taking ceremony and affirmation of the sanctions. Variations occur and not every element is present in every treaty. This formula was widely accepted and is evident in the covenants involving Moses and Joshua in the *Bible.

With the *Iron Age a change of pattern appears, although the number of treaty texts is smaller. The basic formula becomes: (1) title, (2) stipulations, (3) curses, (4) witnesses, although the order varies. *Aramaean treaties between an unknown king and Mati-el of *Arpad, Akkadian ones between Mati-el and *Ashur-nirari V of *Assyria, between *Esarhaddon and Baal of *Tyre, between Esarhaddon and *Median rulers illustrate this well. The well preserved last set concludes with some seventy curses on treaty-breakers using vivid similes drawn from widespread traditions reaching back to the third millennium BC.

Treaties became integral to ancient *diplomacy, and their breach was often cited as the reason for attack by the 'righteous' party (e.g. *Tukulti-Ninurta I against the *Kassite king of *Babylon, *Sennacherib against Hezekiah of Judah). The Israelite concept of God making a covenant with his people has no direct parallel, but its operation was explained in the same way as a political vassal treaty, its breach resulting in similar punishments, as the prophets repeatedly warned. ARM

G. BECKMAN, *Hittite Diplomatic Texts* (Atlanta, GA 1996, 2nd ed. 1999).

J.S. COOPER, *Reconstructing History from Ancient Inscriptions: The Lagash-Umma Border Conflict* (Malibu, CA 1983).

E. EDEL, *Der Vertrag zwischen Rameses II. von Ägypten und Hattusili III. von Hatti* (Berlin 1997).

A. GOETZE, 'Hittite Treaties', *Ancient Near Eastern Texts*, ed. J.B. Pritchard (Princeton, NJ 1969) 201–6, 529–30.

K.A. KITCHEN, *The Bible in its World* (Exeter 1977) 79–85.

D.J. McCARTHY, *Treaty and Covenant* (Rome 1978).

S. PARPOLA and K. WATANABE, *Neo-Assyrian Treaties and Loyalty Oaths* (Helsinki 1988).

E. REINER, 'Akkadian Treaties from Syria and Assyria', *Ancient Near Eastern Texts*, ed. J.B. Pritchard (Princeton, NJ 1969) 531–41.

J.A. WILSON, 'Treaty between the Hittites and Egypt', *Ancient Near Eastern Texts*, ed. J.B. Pritchard (Princeton, NJ 1969) 199–201.

**Trees** Much of the Mediterranean basin today is covered by so-called *maquis*, evergreen thickets that often include oaks. In antiquity the Near Eastern forests were more abundant, and different trees were better represented. While deforestation was well under way in the *Bronze Age, the rapid destruction of trees in the eastern Mediterranean was largely post-*Roman; some regions were deforested in relatively modern times. The Near East's limited *timber resources were in great demand for construction projects, shipbuilding (see Boats and ships) and fuel; trees were cut in large quantities when there was a need for more agricultural land and when armies besieged *cities. Ancient texts reflect the speed with which forests were reduced, and by *Hammurabi's day *laws were needed to curb abusive cutting.

Poor-quality timber was available in the lowlands of the ancient Near East. Trees like tamarisk, acacia, terebinth, sycamore, poplar and willow were used for fuel, the manufacture of *tools, *furniture and household implements, and the construction of small buildings. A variety of trees also supplied resins and *medicinal ointments. Of course, nut (e.g. almond, pistachio) and fruit trees (e.g. fig, pomegranate, date) were important sources of *food, and the olive tree provided oil that filled a multiplicity of uses.

The local supplies of timber rarely fulfilled the demands of more urban civilizations. The need for longer logs and more fragrant, durable wood led the *kings and wealthier citizens of *Mesopotamia, *Syria–*Palestine and *Egypt to import high quality timber from the mountainous regions of *Lebanon, Syria, *Anatolia and Upper Mesopotamia. In the third millennium BC, the Egyptians shipped logs from the well watered slopes of Lebanon; eventually they were joined by competing work crews from *Babylonia, *Assyria and *Israel. *Sargon of *Akkad was one of the first monarchs to use *war to secure raw materials, including timber, when he expanded his empire to the 'Cedar Forest', presumably Mount Lebanon and the Amanus range.

The cedar (*Cedrus libani*) was the most prized wood, but other kinds of trees were cut in the high mountains, especially fir, juniper, cypress and pine. Nowadays only a few stands of cedars are found in the Lebanon. Once crews cut the trees, they were removed from the mountains with teams of oxen and sometimes dragged great distances overland. More frequently the logs were loaded on ships, floated singly, or lashed together as rafts and hauled down the Mediterranean coast or down the Euphrates and Tigris *rivers. The *Phoenicians played an important role as middlemen in the international timber *trade. Timber was an important part of the Phoenician tribute sent to the Assyrians.                GLM

H.A. FORBES and L. FOXHALL, 'The Queen of All Trees', *Expedition* 21 (1978) 37–47.

N.F. HEPPER, *Baker Encyclopedia of Bible Plants* (Grand Rapids, MI 1992).

——, 'Timber Trees of Western Asia', *The Furniture of Western Asia: Ancient and Traditional*, ed. G. Herrmann (Mainz 1996) 1–12.

R. MEIGGS, *Trees and Timber in the Ancient Mediterranean World* (Oxford 1982).

J.N. POSTGATE and M.A. POWELL (eds), *Trees and Timber in Mesopotamia*, Bulletin on Sumerian Agriculture 6 (Cambridge 1992).

M. ZOHARY, *Plants of the Bible* (London 1982).

**Troy**  The story of the Trojan war recounted in Homer's *Iliad* concerns an Achaean expedition against Troy (or Ilios) to regain Helen, the abducted wife of Menelaus, king of Sparta. A ten-year siege ends with the destruction of the *city after an enormous *wooden horse, thought by the besieged to be a gift but actually full of Achaean soldiers, is brought into Troy by its defenders. It is generally accepted that these legends evolved into their final form in the eighth or seventh centuries BC after a process of oral transmission by court bards, but that their roots are in Mycenaean times in the late second millennium BC.

Since Byzantine times, the mound of Hissarlýk on the north-west tip of *Anatolia has been identified as the *Hellenistic/*Roman city of Ilion; it was first identified as Troy by Charles Maclaren in 1820, an identification still not proved beyond doubt. The site was a harbour, until that silted up, where ships waited for favourable winds before sailing through the Dardanelles, which now lie 5 km away. The mound is c.25 m high, with a lower town 1 km square. Troy/Hissarlýk has been excavated by Frank Calvert (1863, 1865), *Schliemann (1871–90), Wilhelm Dörpfeld (1893–4), Carl Blegen (1932–8), and Manfred Korfmann (1988–). The debate concerning the identification of Hissarlýk with Troy continues, as do the arguments about which levels might reflect 'Homer's Troy', but the site itself, with nine major strata numbered Troy I–Troy IX, constitutes one of the best *Bronze Age sequences in the region. The settlements dating from Early Bronze II (c.3000 BC) to the Byzantine period were all *fortified and provided with *gates, and consisted of citadels with major public buildings.

Troy II (Early Bronze III, 2500–2000 BC) was chosen by Schliemann as Homer's Troy because of its sixteen treasure troves of *jewellery, *gold and *silver vessels and six palatial buildings. Dörpfeld preferred Troy VIh, destroyed c.1250 BC, though Blegen later claimed that the VIh destruction was caused by an earthquake. Troy VIIa and b were both destroyed by fire. Blegen identified the VIIa destruction with the Trojan war, dating it to c.1250 BC, but it was probably later. VIIb was destroyed between 1100 and 1000 BC. One can speculate endlessly about which destruction (if any) should be associated with Homer, but there is no archaeological proof at all for a long siege and deliberate destruction. Troy VI, VIIa or VIIb could plausibly have been destroyed by Mycenaean Greeks.

It is not clear whether Troy was abandoned until a *Greek colonial settlement of the eighth century BC (Troy

Reconstruction of Troy VI looking north, showing the citadel and part of the lower town (courtesy of Christoph Haussner).

VIII); there may have been some continuous occupation. Alexander the Great certainly believed the site to be Troy: the Hellenistic city of Ilion, with two temples, was destroyed and rebuilt in Roman/Byzantine times before final abandonment. PB

C.W. BLEGEN, J.L. CASKEY and M. RAWSON, *Troy: Excavations Conducted by the University of Cincinnati, 1932–1938* 1–4 (Princeton, NJ 1950–8).

W. DÖRPFELD, *Troja und Ilion: Ergebnisse der Ausgrabungen in der vorhistorischen und historischen Schichten von Ilion 1870–1894* (Athens 1902).

L. FOXHALL and J.K. DAVIES (eds), *The Trojan War: Its Historicity and Context* (Liverpool 1985).

H.G. JANSEN, 'Troy: Legend and Reality', *Civilizations of the Ancient Near East*, ed. J.M. Sasson (New York 1995) 1121–34.

M. KORFMANN *et al.*, 'Excavation Reports and Studies on Troy and the Troad', *Studia Troica* 1 (Mainz am Rhein 1991) and subsequent volumes.

**Tudhaliyas** The name of four *Hittite *kings of the Hittite New Kingdom (c.1430–1210 BC). There is some confusion about the attribution of texts to the first two rulers.

Tudhaliyas I (c.1430–1410 BC) may have been the founder of a new royal line. Texts once dated to the end of Hittite history are now redated to this king. He attempted to control Cilicia and north *Syria, especially *Aleppo, and expanded eastward into territory directly north of *Mitanni.

Tudhaliyas II (c.1400–1390 BC) is known from a few contemporary inscriptions and *seal impressions at *Hattusas.

Tudhaliyas III (c.1380–1370 BC) is best known as the father of *Suppiluliumas I, who conducted a series of campaigns to the east of Hittite territory before coming to the throne himself.

Tudhaliyas IV (c.1245–1215 BC) was the son of *Hattusilis III. He is known for his massive rebuilding in and around Hattusas. *Treaties suggest that territory was lost in the west although part of *Cyprus was conquered. More land was lost in the east and in north Syria to the expanding power of *Assyria. PTC

O. GURNEY, *The Hittites*, rev. ed. (Harmondsworth 1990).

P. HOUWINK TEN CATE, *The Records of the Early Hittite Empire (c. 1430–1370 BC)* (Leiden 1970).

J.G. MACQUEEN, *The Hittites* (London 1986).

**Tukulti-Ninurta** Tukulti-Ninurta, 'the *god *Ninurta is my help', was the name of two *Assyrian *kings.

Tukulti-Ninurta I (c.1244–1208 BC) was an active warrior and builder. Following his father *Shalmaneser I to subdue unruly tribes in the *Zagros and *Anatolian foothills, whose men had been raiding Assyrian territory, he penetrated into the realm of Nairi, later *Urartu. In that way, he opened sources of *copper to Assyria. Westwards, his forces reached and crossed the upper Euphrates, clashing with the *Hittite king *Tudhaliyas, causing repercussions that reached *Ugarit. Before that,

Tukulti-Ninurta enjoyed his major triumph. The *Kassite King Kashtiliash IV took over some frontier *towns, breaking a *treaty, so the Assyrian fought and captured him, slighted the *fortifications of *Babylon and set his man in charge there. His forces moved on as far as the Gulf. Beside many inscriptions made for his building works which report his campaigns, a lengthy epic poem describes his confrontation with Kashtiliash, explaining the faults of the Babylonian king and lauding Tukulti-Ninurta. It tells of booty brought from Babylon, including *cuneiform tablets of both literary and administrative content. Assyrians always felt culturally inferior to their southern neighbours (see Akkadian), so this was an unusual opportunity to take advantage of their knowledge and skills. Tukulti-Ninurta constructed city walls and *temples in *Ashur, worked at *Nineveh and built a new capital, 3 km upstream from Ashur called Kar-Tukulti-Ninurta. A prayer for the king implies unpopularity and opposition at home and he was eventually murdered by his son and courtiers.

Tukulti-Ninurta II (890–884 BC) maintained control of regions west of the Tigris gained by his father, *Adad-nirari II, quelling rebels and marching from *Babylonia up the Khabur *river to 'show the flag', a journey reported in the style of an itinerary in his '*annals' and marked by a stela found at *Terqa on the mid Euphrates. In 885 BC he campaigned against an *Aramaean king, reaching one source of the Tigris, where his son says he left his monument. He decorated his *palace at Ashur with colourful glazed tiles and also built at Nineveh and sites in the Jazira (Kahat and others). ARM

Tukulti-Ninurta I:

B.R. FOSTER, *Before the Muses*, 2nd ed. (Bethesda, MD 1996) 209–36 (epic and prayer).

A.K. GRAYSON, *Assyrian Royal Inscriptions* 1 (Wiesbaden 1972) 101–34.

——, *Assyrian Rulers of the Third and Second Millennia BC (to 1115 BC)* (Toronto 1987) 231–99.

M. MUNN-RANKIN, 'Assyrian Military Power 1300–1200 B.C.', *Cambridge Ancient History* 2.2, 2nd ed. (Cambridge 1975) 284–94.

Tukulti-Ninurta II:

A.K. GRAYSON, *Assyrian Royal Inscriptions* 2 (Wiesbaden 1976) 97–113.

——, 'Assyria: Ashur-dan II to Ashur-nirari V (934–745 B.C.)', *Cambridge Ancient History* 3.1, 2nd ed. (Cambridge 1982) 251–3.

——, *Assyrian Rulers of the Early First Millennium BC* 1 *(1114–859 BC)* (Toronto 1991) 163–88.

**Tyre** Prior to Alexander the Great, Tyre was a small island off the coast of southern *Lebanon. It is located c.39 km south of *Sidon, just south of where the Litani *river empties into the Mediterranean. In 332 BC, Alexander took this fortified island out of *Persian hands by building a causeway that linked it with the mainland. Before Hiram I (c.969–936 BC), who linked them together, Tyre in fact comprised two small islands. It served primarily *administrative and *religious functions and was tied to the coastal *town of Ushu, which was dismantled for fill when Alexander created a small peninsula. Ancient writers noted Tyre's original status as an island. It had port facilities on its north and south, and Tyre's importance and fame reached enormous proportions because of its role in *Phoenician shipping and *trade.

Early excavations made little progress in locating Tyre's pre-classical remains, but P.M. Bikai's 1973–4 excavations successfully probed into the city's most ancient past. Her work established the phases of settlement between c.2700 and 700 BC. Tyre, which according to *Herodotus was established c.2750 BC, has yielded substantial ruins from the Early Bronze Age, followed by a gap in occupation from c.2000 to 1600 BC. The earliest undisputed references to Tyre are the *Ugaritic tablets and the *Amarna Letters. During the fourteenth century BC, Abdi-Milki, the *king of Tyre, appealed to Amenophis IV (Akhenaten) for help against Tyre's enemies. The city is named in *Egyptian texts from the Nineteenth and Twentieth Dynasties, and it does not appear to have been destroyed at the end of the Late Bronze Age.

In the *Iron Age, Tyrian development turned westward and thrived through maritime activities and colonization; eventually *Cyprus, North Africa and Spain fell within the Phoenician commercial sphere and Tyre, along with Sidon, led the way. Carthage was the most famous colony of Tyre, but King Hiram is known from the *Bible for his trade relations with the *Israelite monarchs David and Solomon. Tyre and other coastal cities of Phoenicia and *Philistia prospered during Neo-*Assyrian expansion; when Tyre failed to pay tribute, the city was threatened with force – and into compliance. Josephus reports that Tyre withstood a thirteen-year siege by the *Babylonians, and the weakened city fell under Persian rule in 538 BC. GLM

P.M. BIKAI, *The Pottery of Tyre* (Warminster 1978).

D. HARDEN, *The Phoenicians*, 3rd ed. (Harmondsworth 1980).

N. JIDEJIAN, *Tyre through the Ages* (Beirut 1969).

H.J. KATZENSTEIN, *The History of Tyre*, rev. ed. (Beersheba 1997).

H.J. VAN DIJK, *Ezekiel's Prophecy on Tyre* (Rome 1968).

W.A. WARD, 'Tyre', *The Oxford Encyclopedia of Archaeology in the Near East* 5, ed. E.M. Meyers (New York 1997) 247–50.

# U

**Ubaid** The late *prehistoric and *Sumerian site of Ubaid lies in south Iraq, 6 km west of *Ur and 16 km north of *Eridu. A main significance of the site is that it gives its name to a long phase of *Mesopotamian *prehistory, the Ubaid period. Excavations were conducted by Harry Hall in 1919, by *Woolley in 1923–4 and by Pinhas Delougaz and *Lloyd in 1937. *Pottery from Ubaid and related sites, such as Eridu, Ur and Tell el-'Oueili, forms the basis for the definition of a multi-phase Ubaid period lasting from c.5500 to 4000 BC, and, in northern Mesopotamia, from c.4500 to 4000 BC. This period witnessed the earliest human settlement on the alluvium of the south Mesopotamian plain, lying between and around the *rivers Euphrates and Tigris.

Material of prehistoric date excavated at Ubaid includes modest *houses built of pisé (pressed mud), of

(*left*) Spouted bowl from Ubaid with dark painted patterns which characterize the Ubaid-period style. WA 117119.

(*below*) Proposed reconstruction of a tableau, copper plating over bitumen, from the temple at Ubaid. Early Dynastic IIIa period, c.2500 BC. Height 1.07 m. WA 114308.

(*left*) Terracotta figurine of a woman, perhaps originally nursing a baby, typical of the Ubaid culture. Height 16 cm. From an Ubaid-period burial at Ur. WA 122872.

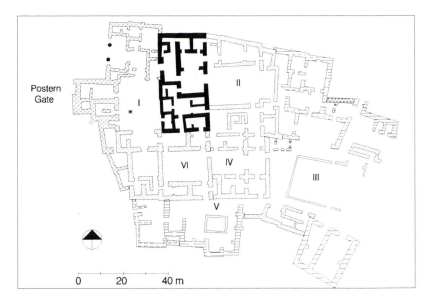

Plan of the royal palace at Ugarit in the thirteenth century BC, showing different construction stages. Most of the rooms open from courtyards, and courtyard V had a sunken pool in the centre.

Postern Gate

0    20    40 m

Late Ubaid date around 4000 BC. Typical painted pottery was recovered, as well as implements of baked clay. To the south-west of these buildings an extensive *cemetery of almost one hundred *graves was investigated. A few of the graves were approximately contemporary with the Late Ubaid structures but most belonged to the Sumerian Early Dynastic period, from c.3000 to 2350 BC. Considerable quantities of Sumerian pottery were deposited inside the graves, some of which may originally have been cut through floors of mudbrick houses.

The main excavated structure at Ubaid is a large *temple complex dating from Early Dynastic III, c.2500, to Ur III, c.2000 BC. The temple is set in an oval enclosure, similar to examples at *Khafaje and *Lagash (Al-Hiba), and inscriptions record its dedication to *Ninhursanga by A-ane-pada, *king of Ur. The temple itself does not survive but originally stood on a large mudbrick platform within the enclosure. Decorative elements from the temple were found at the base of the platform. These items, many now on display in the British Museum, include a massive *copper plaque showing a lion-headed eagle between two stags, heads of bulls, *birds, lions and leopards, and figurative panels of shell and bitumen. This collection of artefacts gives us a unique insight into temple decoration of the third millennium BC.      RM

H.R. HALL and C.L. WOOLLEY, *Ur Excavations I: Al-'Ubaid* (Oxford 1927).

J.L. HUOT, 'Ubaid', *The Oxford Encyclopedia of Archaeology in the Near East* 5, ed. E.M. Meyers (New York 1997) 251–2.

H.P. MARTIN, 'The Early Dynastic Cemetery at Al-'Ubaid: A Re-evaluation', *Iraq* 44 (1982) 145–85.

**Ugarit**   Following a farmer's discovery of a rich *tomb on the *Syrian coast 10 km north of Lattaqia, *Schaeffer began excavations in 1929 and a French expedition continues the work. After exploring Minet el-Beidha, a port of the Late Bronze Age (ancient Mahadu), with a

magazine full of *Canaanite jars and other *trade goods, Schaeffer turned to the *tell of Ras Shamra, 800 m inland. *Cuneiform texts found in the first seasons proved that the site was ancient Ugarit.

Situated in a fertile well watered plain, at the end of a route from the Euphrates, Ugarit was a prime site, settled from the Pre-Pottery *Neolithic to the end of the Late *Bronze Age, with short *Persian and *Roman use. A deep sounding revealed evidence of *Halaf and *Ubaid-period imports, extensive Early Bronze Age settlement followed by a period of abandonment. A major Middle Bronze Age *town arose, which a *letter found at *Mari says the *king of Mari visited, while pharaonic sculptures point to strong links with *Egypt. After a decline, Ugarit prospered in the fourteenth century BC, when its kings corresponded with the pharaohs (*Amarna Letters 45–9), until its hasty abandonment about 1185 BC in the face of the marauding *Sea People. The excavations have uncovered large areas of that last city.

On the west side stood the Royal *Palace, covering about 10,000 sq m, its external wall shutting it off from the rest of the town. It had a *fortified *gateway on the city rampart and, in an earlier period, a postern through it, but only one or two other entrances. Dozens of rooms were arranged around courtyards, with staircases to upper storeys and, at one point, a large *burial vault under the floor. The main entry led up steps through a two-pillared porch, through a reception room into a large courtyard with an ablution slab, from which another porch gave access to the throne room. Elsewhere there was a courtyard with a shallow central pool and another enclosing a *garden. A vaulted drain ran from the palace past other structures to the edge of the mound. Generations of *kings had enlarged and altered the buildings, all in the same fashion of rubble cores and squared *stone facings, especially at doorways, with horizontal timber baulks laced through the stonework for strength. The stone walls were originally plastered and painted. Outside the palace were *houses of all sizes, palatial and poor, built in the same way, many with their own wells, arranged along narrow, winding streets. At the summit of the tell stood two *temple-towers, both badly ruined, thought to be dedicated to *Baal and *Dagan. The *road into the south of the city crossed a stream-bed by a bridge.

The rich finds include *golden bowls and *jewellery, *bronze *weapons, tools and *figurines, stone stelae and *sculptures and large amounts of locally made, usually plain *pottery. Egypt was the source of scarabs, *faience and alabaster vases, the *Aegean of Mycenaean pottery, *Cyprus of Cypriot wares, *Babylonia of *cylinder seals, but all were imitated locally. The written documents demonstrate the city's wide connections. Egyptian and *Hittite *hieroglyphs, the Cypro-Minoan syllabary and the local cuneiform *alphabet were read beside the cuneiform script used for the *Sumerian, *Akkadian, *Hurrian, *Hittite and, rarely, Ugaritic *languages. Tablets from royal *archives were recovered at six sites in the palace, many fallen from the upper floor(s). They are legal deeds, often validated with the *dynastic seal, letters between the king and his fellow rulers and his Hittite suzerain, many administrative documents and *magic, *medical and literary compositions. The majority are in Akkadian, with a notable proportion in the local *Semitic language, Ugaritic, and cuneiform alphabet. *Archives and groups of tablets found in several houses, personal and official documents mixed together, reveal their owners' activities. Between the temples, in the 'High *Priest's House', were found the major manuscripts of the Ugaritic *myths and legends (see Aqhat; Keret).

Ugarit is the most important site in the *Levant for knowledge of Late Bronze Age culture, a small kingdom lying outside *Canaan, but sharing much with the towns there in language, *religion and lifestyle. The Ugaritic texts contribute to the understanding of *biblical *Hebrew and the history of the Semitic languages.   ARM

A. CURTIS, *Ugarit: Ras Shamra* (Cambridge 1985).

G. SAADÉ, *Ougarit: Métropole Cananéene* (Beirut 1979).

C.F.A. SCHAEFFER (ed.), *Ugaritica* 1–7 (Paris 1939–78).

C. VIROLLEAUD and J. NOUGAYROL, *Le palais royal d'Ugarit* 2–6 (Paris 1957–70).

M. YON, *The City of Ugarit at Tell Ras Shamra* (Winona Lake, IN 1998).

M. YON, D. PARDEE, and P. BORDREUIL, 'Ugarit', *Anchor Bible Dictionary* 6, ed. D.N. Freedman (New York 1992) 695–721.

**Ulu Burun** Located c.8 km south-east of Kas, along Turkey's southern shore, the *shipwreck at Ulu Burun yielded a unique treasure in both the literal and figurative sense. This late fourteenth-century BC merchant vessel is the oldest seagoing *ship to have been excavated. Its hold was filled with cargo from all over the eastern Mediterranean, and the ship provides many valuable insights into ancient *trade and *technology. Examined in light of ancient texts and compared with finds from sites on dry land, the Ulu Burun shipwreck offers an unparalleled glimpse into the international route that was plied by *merchants and sailors from a number of ancient lands.

The wreck was discovered in 1982 just 60 m from the cliff face at Ulu Burun. This vessel was built out of cedar with mortise-and-tenon joints and was originally c.15 m long. When it went down, the hull came to rest on the sloping floor of the sea at a depth of 44–52 m, and some artefacts were strewn downslope to a depth of 61 m. Word of the wreck's discovery came to the Bodrum Museum of Underwater Archaeology, and the site was excavated by the Institute of Nautical Archaeology (Texas A & M University) in eleven campaigns (1984–94). Under the leadership of G.F. Bass and C. Pulak, this exceptionally rewarding venture required a total of 22,413 dives (6613 hours) to complete. During this time the site was fully mapped, the area beneath and around the hull was excavated, and much of the cargo was recovered. The INA's study of the hull and contents of the ship – the process by which these unique data were recovered and analysed – is exemplary.

Unlike the smaller, excavated *Bronze Age shipwreck from nearby Cape *Gelidonya, which dates to c.1200 BC, the Kas ship is a microcosm of the shipping network that connected the Near East, the *Aegean and *Egypt. This Late Bronze Age vessel carried cargo from *Syria–*Palestine, *Cyprus, the Aegean, Italy, Egypt and *Mesopotamia. The artefacts reflect at least seven cultural backgrounds – Mycenaean Greek, *Canaanite, Cypriot, Egyptian, *Kassite, *Assyrian and Nubian. The nature of the voyage represented by the Kas shipwreck is unclear,

An archaeologist examining the Ulu Burun ship's keel and planking; two stone anchors are on the left, and a row of copper ingots on the right (courtesy of the Institute of Nautical Archaeology).

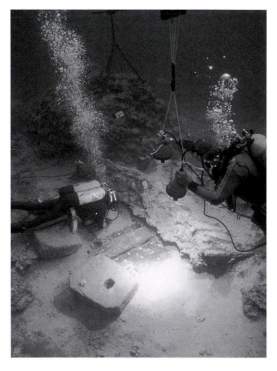

reflecting features of both private enterprise and official exchanges of 'royal gifts'. The cargo was mostly raw materials and included 10 tonnes of Cypriot *copper ingots, nearly a tonne of *tin ingots from an unknown source, over 150 *glass ingots in various colours, pigments, terebinth resin, precious *wood, *ivory (elephant and hippopotamus), large jars filled with Cypriot *pottery, and *silver and *gold *jewellery. Along with numerous other artefacts, the excavators recovered a vast quantity of seeds and *food remains (e.g. almonds, pine nuts, pomegranate, fig, grape, olive, coriander).

Excavators date the ship to c.1306 BC on the basis of tree-ring analysis of a log, firmly dated Mycenaean pottery, the presence of a gold scarab of Nefertiti, and a reworked *cylinder seal. The national origin of this ship is difficult to determine, since its style of construction is not distinctive and its cargo comes from so many places. The use of a particular type of *stone anchor (a total of twenty-four on board) points to a Syro-Palestinian origin, but the crew could have come from many places and it is thought that there were high-ranking Mycenaeans aboard. GLM

G.F. BASS, 'Oldest Known Shipwreck Reveals Splendors of the Bronze Age', *National Geographic* 172 (1987) 692–733.

——, *Shipwrecks in the Bodrum Museum of Underwater Archaeology* (Ankara 1996).

E.H. CLINE, *Sailing the Wine-dark Sea: International Trade and the Late Bronze Age Aegean* (Oxford 1994).

A.J. PARKER, *Ancient Shipwrecks of the Mediterranean and the Roman Provinces* (Oxford 1992).

C. PULAK, '1994 Excavation at Uluburun: The Final Campaign', *Institute of Nautical Archaeology Quarterly* 21 (1994) 8–16.

——, 'Shipwreck! Recovering 3,000-year-old Cargo', *Archaeology Odyssey* 2/4 (September/October 1999) 18–29, 59.

C. PULAK and G.F. BASS, 'Uluburun', *The Oxford Encyclopedia of Archaeology in the Near East* 5, ed. E.M. Meyers (New York 1997) 266–8.

## 'Umayri, (Tell el-)

Tell el-'Umayri represents the remains of what must have been a very important *Ammonite settlement. This site is located c.15 km south of Amman and sits just west of the main highway that connects Jordan's capital city with its international airport. The main *tell, which covers 6.5 ha, is one of three archaeological sites that cluster around a perennial spring. The ancient name of 'Umayri West (the main site under consideration here) is unknown, but some have identified it as *Amorite Heshbon or *biblical Abel-keramim. In fact, a spring with the name *krmn* appears in an itinerary of the Egyptian King Tuthmosis III and probably refers to this location. The modern Arabic name probably derives from a root referring to the site's copious source of *water. 'Umayri's strategic position is reflected in the nature and extent of ruins which occupy this tall, steep hill.

The excavation of Tell el-'Umayri is the focal point of a large multidisciplinary project known as the Madaba Plains Project, focusing on the history of *food systems within a 5-km radius of 'Umayri. Excavations at this site

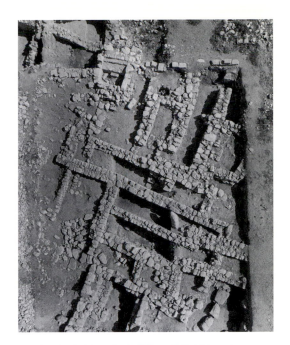

Iron Age II administrative building at Tell el-'Umayri (courtesy of L.G. Herr, balloon photography by Elli and Willi Myers).

(1984–96) have uncovered stratified remains from the middle of the third millennium BC (Early Bronze III) to the first century AD; surface sherds reflect evidence of site use in the *Chalcolithic and Byzantine periods as well. In the Early Bronze Age, 'Umayri's inhabitants had already turned this hilltop into a prosperous, albeit unfortified, *village. Evidence of occupation in the Middle and Late Bronze Ages is not as substantial, but remains from these periods demonstrate that 'Umayri's fortified Iron I town was the continuation of a relatively steady history of settlement. A *seal impression of Tuthmosis III appears on an Iron I jar handle, an indication of international commerce. Excavation on the site's western slope has recovered an elaborate Iron I defence system which includes a casemate wall, rampart and dry moat. Typical collared-rim jars were found in the deep destruction layer which marked the end of this period.

Impressive building remains from the latter part of Iron II and the *Persian period point to 'Umayri's continuing importance. Though many seals and seal impressions were found, one impression is very important; it dates to c.600 BC and mentions the name of a Milkom-'ur, servant of Ba'al-yasha'. This is the first time that the name of Milkom, the principal Ammonite deity, has turned up in a personal name. The second name is almost certainly that of the Ammonite King Baalis, who is mentioned in the Bible (Jeremiah 40: 14). GLM

L.T. GERATY, ''Umayri, Tell el-', *The Oxford Encyclopedia of Archaeology in the Near East* 5, ed. E.M. Meyers (New York 1997) 273–4.

L.T. GERATY and L.G. HERR, ''Umayri, Tell el-', *Anchor Bible*

*Dictionary* 6, ed. D.N. Freedman (New York 1992) 722–4.
L.T. GERATY *et al.* (eds), *Madaba Plains Project* 1, 2, 3 (Berrien Springs, MI 1989, 1991, 1997).
L.G. HERR, 'The Servant of Baalis', *Biblical Archaeologist* 48 (1985) 169–72.

**Underwater archaeology:** see Shipwrecks

**Underworld** Many different cultures believe in the existence of an 'underworld', a parallel world located physically beneath the surface of the world on which we live, where the dead go when they die and where they have some sort of continuing existence. For the polytheistic peoples of the ancient Near East, this appears to have been the exclusive vision of life after *death, although there are traces of a belief that the other world was located in a remote and inaccessible area of the earth's surface rather than beneath it. Generally the underworld was thought to be located at the bottom of a stairway which led down from earth, or even from heaven. The exact location of this stairway is not specified. Apparently it was even lower down than the *apsû* or subterranean freshwater ocean. It was dark, dusty and unpleasant, and the dead wandered there thirsty and naked (or sometimes described as having feathered wings like *birds), together with various 'dead' *gods and multitudes of *demons, who emerged from the underworld to pester humankind. Unlike those beliefs which make allowance for a special location for the favoured dead, in ancient Near Eastern beliefs all the dead without exception end up in the underworld. There are only rare suggestions of moral discrimination amongst them: in *Hittite belief, evildoers had to eat excrement rather than dust after death.

The *Mesopotamian underworld was organized like an earthly kingdom, with a *palace (called Ganzir) with seven (or fourteen) *gates leading to a great courtyard, ruled over by the *queen of the underworld *Ereshkigal, with her husband *Nergal. Other deities functioned as her *scribe (Geshtin-ana), major-domo (Ningishzida), administrator (Pabilsang), messenger (Namtar) and gate-keeper (Neti).

Literary compositions and *rituals indicate a belief that the afterlife could be made more tolerable if living relatives provided regular *food and drink offerings. Of course return from the underworld is impossible for mortals, and the only gods who return from visits there do so by providing substitutes to take their place (notably Inana/*Ishtar in the *Mesopotamian *myths of 'Inana's/Ishtar's Descent to the Underworld'). It seems that, as time progressed, accounts of the underworld gradually became more detailed, specifying the numbers of deities who lived there and describing the horrible demons in grotesque specifics.

In Hittite belief, certain waterways and springs were directly connected to the underworld, and these entrances were important in certain rituals for 'disappearing deities'. Similarly to Mesopotamian ideas, it was thought that the dead needed regular food and drink offerings to prevent them returning to haunt the living. JAB

V. HAAS, 'Die Unterwelts- und Jenseitsvorstellungen im hethitischen Kleinasien', *Orientalia* 45 (1976) 197–212.
——, 'Death and the Afterlife in Hittite Thought', *Civilizations of the Ancient Near East*, ed. J.M. Sasson (New York 1995) 2021–30.
M. HUTTER, *Altorientalische Vorstellungen von der Unterwelt* (Göttingen 1985).
A. LIVINGSTONE, *Court Poetry and Literary Miscellanea*. State Archives of Assyria 3 (Helsinki 1989) 68–76.
J. SCURLOCK, 'Death and the Afterlife in Ancient Mesopotamian Thought', *Civilizations of the Ancient Near East*, ed. J.M. Sasson (New York 1995) 1883–93.

**Uqair, (Tell)** The multi-period mounds of Uqair, south of Baghdad in Iraq, were excavated in the 1940s by *Lloyd and Fuad Safar and briefly in the 1970s by Michael Müller-Karpe.

Uqair has extensive settlement of the *Ubaid period,

Reconstruction of frescos in the Painted Temple at Tell Uqair, c.3300–3000 BC (from S. Lloyd and F. Safar, *Journal of Near Eastern Studies* 2 (1943), pl. X, courtesy of University of Chicago Press).

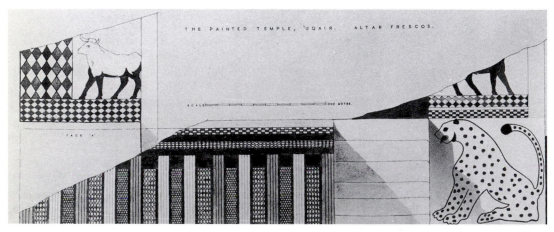

the earliest level resting on virgin soil several metres below the present level of the plain. At the north of mound A, a substantial building of long rooms with thick walls suggests at least an architectural sophistication in central *Mesopotamia by the Late Ubaid period, matching contemporary developments in the north at sites such as Tepe *Gawra. A street and small private *house were excavated adjacent to the large public structure, recovering great quantities of painted Ubaid *pottery and baked clay *tools.

On the western side of mound A, a remarkable platform and *temple, the Painted Temple, of Late *Uruk date, c.3300–3000 BC, were excavated. The platform was built of solid mudbrick, its buttressed façades decorated with mosaic of bitumen-tipped clay wall cones. Staircases gave access to the top of the platform where a mudbrick temple was located on an upper terrace. The heavily buttressed temple had a long central hall with ranges of rooms to north and south, its exterior façades painted white. Extremely fragile *wall paintings were discovered on the interior wall faces of the temple, with skirted humans, large felines, other *animals and geometric designs depicted in brilliant shades of red, orange, white and black. After abandonment the Painted Temple was carefully packed with mudbrick prior to the construction of a later temple which did not survive.

Immediately to the east of the Late Uruk platform, excavations revealed a small temple with *altar and rich deposits of painted vessels of the *Jemdet Nasr period. In addition, four clay tablets inscribed with proto-*cuneiform writing were found. These tablets, along with others from the nearby site of Jemdet Nasr, have suggested that the ancient name of Uqair may have been Urum.

Little work has been conducted on mound B apart from the excavation of Early Dynastic III and *Akkadian *graves and fragmentary walls.                    RM

R.K. ENGLUND, *Proto-cuneiform Texts from Diverse Collections* (Berlin 1996).

M. GREEN, 'Urum and Uqair', *Acta Sumerologica* 8 (1986) 77–83.

S. LLOYD and F. SAFAR, 'Tell Uqair: Excavations by the Iraq Government Directorate of Antiquities in 1940 and 1941', *Journal of Near Eastern Studies* 2 (1943) 131–58.

J.N. POSTGATE and P.J. WATSON, 'Excavations in Iraq, 1977–78', *Iraq* 41 (1979) 141–81.

**Ur** The ruins of the *Sumerian *city of Ur, one of the most important archaeological sites in ancient *Mesopotamia, lie in south Iraq, near a dried-up bed of the Euphrates *river. Occupation at Ur, modern Tell al-Muqayyar, spanned the *Ubaid period, from c.4500 BC, until the end of the fourth century BC. *Rawlinson identified the site on the basis of inscriptions recording *Nabonidus' work on the *ziggurat at Ur found by J.E. Taylor in 1854. From that time it has been generally regarded as Ur 'of the Chaldees', the birthplace of Abraham (Genesis 11), although some doubt this identification. H.R. Hall excavated in 1918–19 for the British Museum, followed by the major Joint Expedition of the British Museum and the University Museum of Pennsylvania, directed by *Woolley (1922–34).

The earliest occupation at Ur belongs to the Ubaid period, although remains of this period were not extensively explored. Artefacts include typical painted Ubaid *pottery, and *tools of baked clay and *stone. A few Ubaid *graves were also encountered. During the *Uruk and *Jemdet Nasr periods, c.4000–3000 BC, there is evidence for the construction of substantial public buildings in the form of a *temple platform with wall cone decoration. A large *cemetery, spanning the Uruk to Early Dynastic periods, was partly excavated.

Although never attaining the immense size of other Sumerian cities such as *Lagash or *Shuruppak, Ur was a city of major importance during the Early Dynastic period, c.3000–2350 BC. The architectural evidence for public buildings during this time was obscured or destroyed by the later building programmes of the Ur III rulers of Ur at the end of the third millennium BC. Much of the Early Dynastic evidence from Ur comes in the form of rubbish deposits near the main temple platform, the so-called Seal Impression Strata. From these deposits came great quantities of clay lumps with distinctive *seal impressions, tablets with proto-*cuneiform writing and pottery, all probably the debris from the everyday func-

One of a pair of figures of he-goats standing with its forefeet in the branches of a tree. Wood overlaid with gold, silver, shell and lapis lazuli. From the Royal Cemetery at Ur. Height 45.7 cm. c.2500 BC. WA 122200.

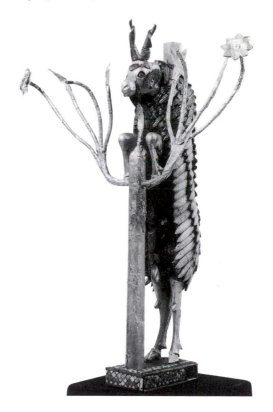

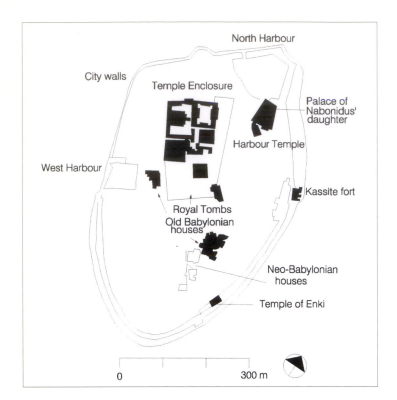

tioning of a large institution such as a temple. Some of the seal impressions bear symbols representing the names of about ten cities, suggesting the existence of a league or loose confederation engaging in as yet unknown forms of interaction. Similar evidence comes from the sites of Uruk and Jemdet Nasr.

Into the rubbish deposits had been dug deep pits for sixteen 'Royal Tombs' of Early Dynastic III, Woolley's most famous discovery. Important persons had been buried in *stone-built chambers with a wealth of equipment, much in *gold and *silver, accompanied by numerous attendants in outer chambers, all furnished with instruments for their courtly roles. Woolley recovered the material, including mosaic panels, such as the 'Royal Standard', and the forms of long-perished *wooden objects, harps, lyres, a sledge, with admirable skill. They exemplify the splendour of the Early Dynastic III elite, the ability of the *craftsmen and the amount of *trade in precious materials. Debate continues over the role of the people buried – were they *kings and *queens, *priests and priestesses, partners in a *sacred marriage, *fertility *sacrifices? The names on *seals and other objects, accompanied by royal titles, are not found in the *Sumerian *King List or *epic traditions. However, in layers above the *tombs were impressions of the seal of Mesannepada, a king of the First Dynasty of Ur, similar in style to some seals from the tombs, suggesting that they are close in date. The 'Royal Tombs' lay within a much larger cemetery where citizens were buried, rich and poor, until at least the end of the *Akkad period.

*Sargon of Akkad dedicated his daughter, Enhedu-

anna, to Nanna, the *moon-god at Ur, and a *sculpture of her making a libation was discovered, but it was during the Ur III period, c.2100–2000 BC, that the city of Ur was the capital of a wide-reaching and important empire, with harbours on the Euphrates carrying *trade to and from the Gulf and the *Indus. Immense quantities of cuneiform documents attest Ur's centrality in the bureaucratic management of its extensive conquests across much of the Near East. Many of the excavated public buildings at Ur, including the *ziggurat of *Ur-Nammu, the temenos (sacred enclosure) of Nanna (patron *god of Ur), the Ehursag *palace and the Giparu *priestess residence, date to this period. The Ur III city was destroyed by invading *Elamites from *Iran, c.2000 BC, but was soon rebuilt by rulers based at the *Mesopotamian cities of *Isin and *Larsa.

During the Old Babylonian period, c.2000–1600 BC, Ur remained of major importance. Excavation of two areas of private *housing with associated graves has provided much information relating to daily life at Ur during this period. The following centuries saw impoverishment until the *Kassite Kurigalzu I reconstructed the ziggurat with its enclosure and rebuilt other shrines, one decorated with moulded brick reliefs. A few dozen tablets document commercial and social life. Subsequent kings undertook various repairs. In the seventh century BC an *Assyrian governor, Sin-balassu-iqbi, restored many old buildings and in the sixth century BC *Nebuchadnezzar II built a new enclosure wall for the precinct and *Nabonidus reconstructed the ziggurat with seven stages, topped by a shrine of blue-glazed bricks. He also built a palace for his daughter the high priestess. *Cyrus II undertook some other repair work, but thereafter the city gradually declined, tablets showing some activity down to the end of the fourth century BC.                    RM

C.J. GADD et al., Ur Excavations, Texts 1–9 (London/Philadelphia, PA 1928–76).

O.R. GURNEY, The Middle Babylonian Legal and Economic Texts from Ur (London 1983).

R.J. MATTHEWS, Cities, Seals and Writing: Archaic Seal Impressions from Jemdet Nasr and Ur (Berlin 1993).

P.R.S. MOOREY, Ur 'of the Chaldees': A Revised and Updated Edition of Sir Leonard Woolley's Excavations at Ur (London 1982).

S. POLLOCK, 'Ur', The Oxford Encyclopedia of Archaeology in the Near East 5, ed. E.M. Meyers (New York 1997) 288–91.

C.L. WOOLLEY et al., Ur Excavations 1–10 (London/Philadelphia, PA 1927–76).

**Urartu** The *Iron Age state of Urartu expanded from a core area in the region of Lake Van to include much of north-western *Iran and Armenia, as far as Lake Sevan, and the highlands of eastern Turkey to Altintepe (Erzincan) on the headwaters of the Euphrates. At its most powerful Urartu was able to rival the Neo-*Assyrian empire. Urartu was the Assyrian name for the lands around Mount Ararat, the Urartians themselves using the name Biane. Assyrian texts from the thirteenth century BC mention the Nairi lands.

The state seems to have been formed through the confederation of *Hurrian tribes in the ninth century BC under Sarduri I (c.840–830 BC). The greatest period of expansion was under Menua either side of 800 BC and a late resurgence of power under the last *king Rusa II (c.685–665 BC?), who moved the capital from *Van Kale to *Toprakkale.

The earliest inscriptions, on the Sardurisburg at Van Kale (ancient capital of Tushpa) are in Assyrian, but all later inscriptions are in Urartian, a late form of Hurrian. *Cuneiform texts on *stone include *annals, religious texts and building inscriptions. Few cuneiform tablets have been found in Urartu but a wealth of information can be gleaned from Assyrian texts, notably the account of *Sargon II's eighth campaign in 714 BC.

The Urartian state exercised control by constructing mighty fortresses, containing *palaces, *temples to the state *gods and storehouses. These fortresses were located on prominent steep-sided rock outcrops and were sited so as to control the inter-mountain plains and few communicating valleys in the mountainous highland massif. Architecture, with structures partly cut out of living rock and partly of built stone (ashlar masonry), all surmounted by mudbrick, represents the highest and most original achievement of Urartu. The restricted size of the plains did not produce sufficient wealth for the growth of *cities, and only modest towns surround some fortresses. Most archaeological research has focused on the fortresses; thus little is known of the surrounding settlements and countryside. Huge *irrigation works, long canals and impressive dams watered vineyards and orchards.

Urartian *art, notably *metalwork, was distinctive and innovative but became repetitive and stereotyped. Metalsmiths were skilled in the production of military equipment (see Tools and weapons), of which the most impressive pieces are votive.

Urartu spans the modern national borders of Turkey, Iraq, Iran and the *Caucasus, a circumstance that has

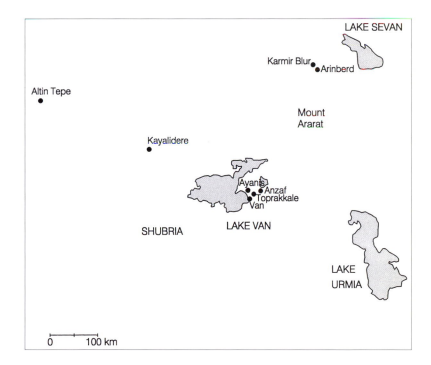

Map of Urartu showing main archaeological sites.

Copper figure of Ur-Nammu carrying a basket of earth for building. The inscribed lower half represents a peg to hold a brick symbolically to the earth. From Uruk. Height 27.3 cm. WA 113896.

Libation scene of Ur-Nammu on limestone stela from Ur (University of Pennsylvania Museum, neg. S4-140070).

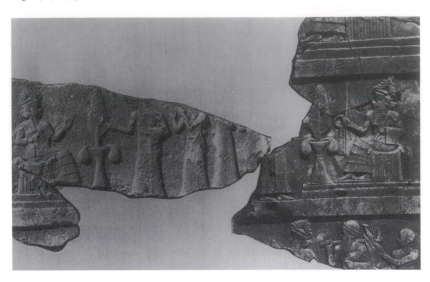

tended to impede research. New work in eastern Turkey, particularly at Anzaf, just north of Van, and Ayanis, on the east side of Lake Van, is greatly expanding our knowledge.

GDS

T.B. FORBES, *Urartian Architecture* (Oxford 1983).

W. KLEISS and H. HAUPTMANN, *Topographische Karte von Urartu: Verzeichnis der Fundorte und Bibliographie* (Berlin 1976).

B.B. PIOTROVSKII, *Urartu* (Geneva 1969).

M. SALVINI, *Geschichte und Kultur der Urartäer* (Darmstadt 1995).

L. VAN DEN BERGHE and L. DE MAYER, *Urartu: een vergeten cultuur uit het bergland Armenië* (Ghent 1983).

M.N. VAN LOON, *Urartian Art* (Istanbul 1966).

P.E. ZIMANSKY, *Ecology and Empire: The Structure of the Urartian State* (Chicago 1985).

**Urkesh:** see Mozan, (Tell)

**Ur-Nammu**  About 2112 BC a governor of *Ur under Utuhegal of *Uruk, who drove the *Guti out of *Babylonia, took the *kingship when his master was drowned and founded the Third Dynasty of Ur. Ur-Nammu left few, rather uninformative, building inscriptions, and the names of his years add little. *Diplomacy may have enabled him to extend his influence, so that one year was named after his 'making straight the road from below to above', that is, throughout the land, possibly even from the Gulf to the Mediterranean. On that route one of his sons was married to the daughter of an independent governor of *Mari. Military action ended the independence of the *Gudea *dynasty of *Lagash and ousted *Elamite forces occupying the north-east of Akkad. This firm rule, coupled with extensive canal digging and clearing, brought prosperity, with *trade from the Gulf, from the north and the west. Ur-Nammu's lasting achievement was to build the *ziggurat at Ur and associated shrines in honour of the *moon-god Nanna (*Akkadian *Sîn) and his wife Ningal. He also did construction work at Uruk, *Nippur and *Larsa. *Sumerian was the *language of royal inscriptions and *administration and the earliest Sumerian code of *laws is apparently a product of this reign. Ur-Nammu was celebrated in several *hymns, and a eulogy on his *death tells of his honoured place in the *underworld. It is possible that he died fighting the Guti (c.2095 BC). He was succeeded by his son *Shulgi.

ARM

C.J. GADD, 'Babylonia c.2120–1800 B.C.', *Cambridge Ancient History* 1.2, 2nd ed. (Cambridge 1971) 595–631.

Laws:

J.J. FINKELSTEIN, in *Ancient Near Eastern Texts*, 3rd ed., ed. J.B. Pritchard (Princeton, NJ 1969) 523–5.

M. ROTH, *Law Collections from Mesopotamia and Asia Minor* (Atlanta, GA 1995).

**Uruk**  Uruk is one of the most important archaeological sites in *Mesopotamia. Situated along an old course of the Euphrates *river in southern Iraq, the ruins of the ancient *city stretch across a vast area of the flat alluvial plain. Known today as Warka and in the *Bible as Erech, Uruk was occupied from the late fifth millennium BC until around the time of the Arab invasion in the seventh century AD. The first excavations at Uruk were conducted by William Loftus in the mid nineteenth century. A long series of German excavations at the site commenced in

Part of a mudbrick wall covered with black-and-white clay cones, arranged in a pattern probably intended to imitate palm-tree trunks. Uruk, late fourth millennium BC (courtesy of Alan Millard).

1912 and has continued up to the present, most recently directed by Rainer M. Boehmer.

The earliest levels at Uruk have not been extensively explored, largely because of difficulty of access through the accumulation of later deposits and buildings but also because of modern groundwater levels. The site seems to have been first settled in the Late *Ubaid period, towards the end of the fifth millennium BC, and remains of mud-brick structures, some perhaps *temples, have been excavated in the later central cult area of the city, the Eanna precinct. Typical Ubaid painted *pottery and baked clay implements were recovered.

The site may originally have consisted of two settlements surrounding shrines to a male and female deity, *Anu and *Inana. Uruk's real predominance started with the Uruk period, named after the site. During this thousand-year timespan, the fourth millennium BC, Uruk developed into the most important city-state, colonial power and sophisticated centre of cultic and administrative capability in the whole of Mesopotamia.

Architecturally the Uruk period is best known at Uruk from a series of immense *religious buildings excavated in two cultic areas of the city, the Eanna precinct and the *Anu *ziggurat, also known as Kullab. Some of these buildings, including those known as the Limestone

Temple, the Stone Building and the Stone Cone Temple, probably date to c.3600 BC. Many new monumental buildings were constructed during the Late Uruk period, the late fourth millennium BC, including the Riemchen Building, Buildings A–E and the Great Court. Architectural decoration included the use of coloured wall cones in mosaic patterns and engaged pillars. During this time Uruk was the central power in an economic and political empire which reached up the Euphrates into northern *Syria and *Anatolia as well as into *Iran to the east. It is within this context that the world's earliest *writing system, known as proto-*cuneiform, was first devised and put to use at Uruk itself in the latter part of the fourth millennium BC, later spreading across much of Mesopotamia and evolving into true cuneiform writing in subsequent centuries and millennia.

Through the Early Dynastic period, c.3000–2350 BC, Uruk maintained its importance, with the construction of a new city wall, some 10 km in length, attributed to *Gilgamesh. By the mid third millennium BC the ruler of Uruk, Lugal-zaggesi, had conquered all of south Mesopotamia before being defeated by *Sargon, who founded the *Akkadian empire. Further building activity continued during the Akkadian and *Ur III periods, up to c.2000 BC when Uruk went into a decline for several centuries.

In the later second millennium and through the first millennium BC, Uruk regained to some extent its role as a major city, with the renewal of massive building programmes in the cultic precincts. In the centuries after the death of Alexander the Great, Uruk was ruled by three important rulers who may be buried in three large tumuli north of the ruins of the city. *Greek influences on the *art of Uruk can be seen in the many baked clay figures of this period. Uruk later came under the control of the *Parthian empire and then the *Sasanians. The city gradually declined until a final abandonment at some time before or at the Arab invasion of AD 634. RM

*Ausgrabungen in Uruk-Warka: Endberichte* (Mainz am Rhein 1987–).

G. ALGAZE, *The Uruk World System* (Chicago 1993).

R.M. BOEHMER, 'Uruk 1980–1990: A Progress Report', *Antiquity* 65 (1991) 465–78.

——, 'Uruk-Warka', *The Oxford Encyclopedia of Archaeology in the Near East* 5, ed. E.M. Meyers (New York 1997) 294–8.

R.K. ENGLUND, *Archaic Administrative Texts from Uruk: The Early Campaigns* (Berlin 1994).

**Utu:** see Shamash

Gypsum trough, carved in relief with processions of ewes and rams approaching a reed building, from which two lambs emerge. Uruk period. Length 1.03 m. WA 120000.

# V

**Van** The modern provincial capital of Van, in eastern Turkey, lies on the east side of Lake Van, a natural soda lake (altitude 1650 m) that never freezes. Van perhaps stems from Biane, the name that the *Urartians gave to themselves. The plain of Van is the largest and most productive in the region, able to provide for the capital of Urartu.

Earlier settlement in the region was more modest. *Chalcolithic levels, including *Halaf *pottery, have been excavated at nearby Tilkitepe and there are many small sites belonging to the Early Transcaucasian culture (see Caucasus). The second millennium BC remains largely blank.

Van Kale (Castle) is justly famous: the huge natural rock close to the lake shore, said to resemble a kneeling *camel, rises above copious springs. A UNESCO World Heritage Site, Van Kale was the Urartian capital Tushpa, a fortress too strong for the *Assyrians to besiege. Under Rusa II (c.685–665 BC?) the capital moved to *Toprakkale, north of Van city, but Van Kale retained its symbolic importance, not least as the royal mausoleum. It remained of considerable importance until the early twentieth century AD when the modern town was established.

Much remains of the Urartian fortress despite subsequent occupation. The rock is 1.5 km long and 80 m wide and rises 100 m from the plain. The earliest structure is the Sardurisburg, so named from the building inscription of Sarduri I (c.840–830 BC). This massive *stone platform was associated with the springs gushing from its base and would have supported a substantial mudbrick building. Stone curtain walls with buttresses and towers ringed the fortress. Some impressive parts are extant, the line of other stretches being indicated by the step-like bedding cut into the rock. Much of the defensive wall of the crowning inner citadel is Urartian, and here parts of the oldest *palace were revealed. A new palace, perhaps of Argishti I (c.785–756 BC), has been recognized at the western end of the rock, the remnants comprising

The medieval castle (*kale*) at Van is built over the remains of the first Urartian capital. On the nearest rock outcrop on the left can be seen the fortress of Rusahinili (modern Toprakkale), the second and last capital of Urartu (courtesy of Dominique Collon).

a series of rock-cut platforms characteristic of Urartian architecture. Several rock-cut sacred complexes survive, the Anali-Kiz at the western end being the most impressive with inscribed andesite stelae set in niches.

Rock-cut royal *tomb complexes survive at various locations around the fortress, each comprising connected chambers with rows of niches that apparently contained *cremated remains. Platforms in front of the tombs were for ceremonial purposes. The tomb of Argishti I, close to the new palace, has the *annals of the king inscribed into the rock-cut access passage.                                    GDS

C.A. BURNEY, 'Eastern Anatolia in the Chalcolithic and Early Bronze Age', *Anatolian Studies* 8 (1958) 157–209.

M. KORFMANN, *Tilkitepe: Die ersten Ansätze prähistorischer Forschung in der östlichen Türkie* (Tübingen 1982).

M.T. TARHAN, 'Recent Research at the Urartian Capital Tushpa', *Tel Aviv* 21/1 (1994) 22–57.

**Villages:** see Cities, towns and villages

# W

**Wall painting** From *Neolithic times, paint was applied not only as decoration on *pottery but on walls of *houses, *temples and *palaces. Colour was used on mudbrick walls surfaced with mud, lime or plaster. The most common technique was distemper, painting on a dry surface; painting on a damp surface (fresco) does not appear to have been used before the second half of the

second millennium BC. The basic colours were red (iron oxide), white (gypsum), black (bitumen), and later blue (copper oxide, lapis lazuli) and, rarely, green (malachite), but these could be mixed, for example to produce yellow or grey. The colours were mixed with *water, probably with a binding medium such as egg white or casein from milk.

Wall painting from the palace at Til Barsip (Room XXIV) showing Assyrian soldiers with prisoners, one being held by the hair. Watercolour copy by Lucien Cavro (© Département des Antiquités Orientales, Musée du Louvre AO 25068 B).

The earliest wall painting discovered so far is at Mureybet in *Syria, dating to the eighth millennium BC, consisting of black and red chevrons on a white background. Wall paintings are thereafter found in most areas of the ancient Near East, for example at *Alalakh, *Anshan, *Aqar Quf, *Beidha, *Çatalhöyük, Tepe *Gawra, *Nippur, *Nuzi, *Qatna, Tell *Sheikh Hamad, Teleilat *Ghassul, Tell *Uqair and *Uruk. The most common decoration was geometric motifs such as chevrons, triangles and lozenges in friezes, sometimes with human and *animal figures, often in procession.

The widest Neolithic repertoire is found at Çatalhöyük, where there are geometric motifs possibly imitating *textile hangings, reliefs of confronted felids which were repeatedly repainted in varying patterns, vultures with human corpses, scenes of festivity in which bulls and stags are teased and baited, *hunting scenes, and a landscape with a settlement and erupting volcano. The paintings were sometimes renewed on a fresh layer of plaster, suggesting to the excavator that they were made in connection with certain events.

No site has produced more wall paintings than the eighteenth-century BC palace at *Mari, where twenty-six rooms or courtyards are decorated. Internal walls and door frames were plastered and painted, sometimes with plain red dados with black bitumen for the skirting, or with scenes of ceremonial and mythological action, each scene framed with a decorative border. The largest composition shows the *king before *Ishtar, taking an *oath with his hand upon the *divine symbol in the presence of other deities; below are two figures of the 'goddess with flowing vase', *sacred trees and other symbolic figures.

This scene has been compared with the entrance to an *Assyrian temple at *Khorsabad which is also flanked by 'flowing-vase' figures and trees. The Assyrians regularly painted their palace walls, from the thirteenth century BC at Kar-Tukulti-Ninurta north of *Ashur, and later at

*Nimrud and Khorsabad. The best-preserved Assyrian wall paintings are in the provincial palace at *Til Barsip, dating to the eighth century BC. The scenes are similar to those found on Assyrian reliefs, which were also originally painted (see Sculpture). The throne room was decorated with *horses led by soldiers, including galloping horses never painted in. In another room, the largest scene is 22 m wide, showing the enthroned king with his soldiers, *chariot and horses, and in front of him officials, soldiers and prisoners. Other scenes show fantastic beasts and the execution of prisoners. The drawings were outlined in black or red. Scenes were framed with friezes of geometric and floral decoration.

Assyrian themes influenced the wall paintings of *Urartu, at Arinberd and Altintepe, where animals, genies, sacred trees and rosettes are all found. The Assyrians also decorated their walls with coloured enamelled bricks, known from Ashur and Nimrud. This type of decoration was used by *Nebuchadnezzar II for the lions, bulls and dragons adorning the Ishtar Gate and Processional Way at *Babylon, and was later imitated by the *Persians at *Susa (the *Elamites had used coloured glazed brick earlier).                                          PB

D. CASTRIOTA, 'Wall Paintings', The Oxford Encyclopedia of Archaeology in the Near East 5, ed. E.M. Meyers (New York 1997) 325–30.

A. MOORTGAT, Alt-Vorderasiatische Malerei (Berlin 1959).

A. NUNN, Die Wandmalerei und der glasierte Wandschmuk im alten Orient (Leiden/New York 1988).

A. SPYCKET, 'Malerei', Reallexikon der Assyriologie 7 (Berlin/New York 1988) 287–300.

**Warfare** Already in the *Neolithic period, *fortifications around *towns in the ancient Near East indicate that warfare was a threat. Later written and pictorial evidence, primarily from *Mesopotamia and *Hatti,

(*right*) Reliefs from the palace of Tiglath-pileser III (744–727 BC) at Nimrud showing a city under attack by scaling with a ladder, a battering ram and archers, with captives being slaughtered and impaled. WA 115634+ 118903.

(*below*) Urartian bronze shield, embossed with rows of animals and inscribed with the name of Rusa II, king of Urartu, c.685 BC. Such a decorated shield was probably for parade or decoration. Diameter 85 cm. WA 22481.

(*right*) Six rows of bronze scales originally sewn to leather or cloth to make a coat of mail. Found at Nimrud. Seventh century BC (courtesy of the British School of Archaeology in Iraq).

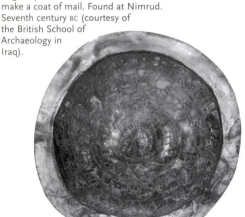

provides detailed insight into the practice of war.

Wars were given *religious justification. The enemy had sinned against the opponent's *gods, and victory was described as the triumph of one god over another or as a triumph of justice. The will of the gods was made known through oracles or *divination. *Assyrian royal inscriptions especially refer to *Ishtar as the goddess who went into battle at the *king's side. The practical and acknowledged causes of war were disputes over *boundaries and *irrigation, plunder of wealthy cities, protection of *trade routes, imperial expansion and punishment of disloyal tributary rulers.

Actual war seems to have been a last resort, even for the Assyrians, who attempted to persuade enemies to submit willingly. Large *armies were normally levied from cities, districts or provinces, who had to provide troops, *weapons and supplies. *Treaties make it clear that, if an ally sent troops to help a treaty partner, the host country had to supply and support those troops. Foraging and living off captured booty was normal, although Hittite documents indicate that, while in territory considered Hittite, the troops were under strict orders against raping and plundering.

Diviners marched with the army and took omens to discover the favourability of every military plan. The

original strategy approved by the gods did not always work, and there is a Hittite account of alternative tactics being adopted under pressure in the field by Mursilis II. Tactics prior to full-scale battle included gathering intelligence and spreading misinformation using spies and infiltrators, night marches, surprise attacks and deceptive manoeuvres. Warfare consisted of raids and ambushes, especially against trading caravans, or besieging cities, and sometimes pitched battles on open ground outside a city under threat of siege. Armies were divided into divisions and wings, each with its own patron deity and standard. The king often led the army into war, accompanied by a bodyguard, or was at least credited with the actual leadership. The Hittites normally sent a challenge to battle to the enemy king; there is some Hittite evidence, though uncertain, that very rarely a battle of champions might settle an issue.

Already in c.2500 BC, the Stela of the Vultures from *Lagash shows the *Sumerian infantry advancing in a phalanx, protected by shields and armed with spears, accompanied by spearmen in *chariots. Chariots were later used both as an assault weapon to break up infantry formations and as a mobile firing platform for archers. In the first millennium BC, cavalry emerged as an independent force, with archery still the supreme weaponry. The Hittites and especially the Assyrians used siege towers and mobile battering rams to attack fortified cities, supported by spearmen, archers and slingers. Sieges could be long and might attempt to starve a city into submission, but were problematic for the besieger. A number of Hittite *rituals are *magical attempts to rid army camps of *diseases and to pass them to the enemy. Sometimes a siege was called off because of the onset of winter.

When a city was captured, it was usually looted and often burned, and the booty carried back to the victor's capital. In the third millennium BC, prisoners-of-war are depicted naked and tied, while the enemy dead were *buried together in large mounds. The Hittites divided prisoners and booty between the king and the troops. The Assyrians took prisoners in huge numbers, slaughtering and blinding many, and cutting off heads, hands or lower lips to help in counting. Some were hung on stakes or walls as a deterrent to rebels. From the eighth century BC, the Assyrians carried out a policy of mass *deportation of conquered peoples, later continued by the Neo-*Babylonian empire.                                                     PB

R.H. BEAL, 'Hittite Military Organization', *Civilizations of the Ancient Near East*, ed. J.M. Sasson (New York 1995) 545–54.

S. DALLEY, 'Ancient Mesopotamian Military Organization', *Civilizations of the Ancient Near East*, ed. J.M. Sasson (New York 1995) 413–22.

H. KLENGEL, 'Krieg, Kriegsgefangene', *Reallexikon der Assyriologie* 6 (Berlin/New York 1980–3) 241–6.

Y. YADIN, *The Art of Warfare in Biblical Lands* (London 1963).

**Water** A reliable source of fresh water was a major concern for all inhabitants of the ancient Near East. Water was needed for drinking and cooking, but it was used also in washing, dyeing cloth and producing *pottery. Livestock and crops needed water, and it was used in *religious *rituals. In days before pumps and pipes and access to deep groundwater, the availability of water was the chief factor that allowed human settlements to expand and develop. Drought and famine resulted from too little rain or depletion of river water for *irrigation. *Agriculture and pastoral activities depended on a certain minimum supply of water; this was obtained from rainfall, perennial sources of water (i.e. *rivers and springs), and/or a variety of water installations.

The amount of water available to a particular ancient people varied widely. For example, the *Hittites and *Assyrians lived in well watered regions, and the kingdom of *Urartu centred on Lake Van had access to abundant water. Generally speaking, the amount of rainfall in the Near East is less in the interior zones (places further away from the Mediterranean) and at lower elevations in the more southerly regions. For agricultural purposes the distribution of rainfall is as important as the amount, and many regions did not receive enough annual rainfall to allow for significant cultural development.

Ancient Near Eastern peoples had many ways to retrieve, store and *transport water. The easiest way to solve the water problem was to live near a permanent source, and the perennial springs and rivers of the Near East are intimately linked with the rise of civilization. The great oasis at Azraq, in *Jordan, is surrounded with remains of *Palaeolithic camps, and residents of the *Syrian city of Tadmor (ancient Palmyra) – half-way

between the Euphrates and *Damascus – still irrigate their orchards and fields from the spring that made this caravan city possible. *Jericho developed alongside a copious spring, as did *Qatna. *Mesopotamia would not have existed without the Tigris and Euphrates.

Cisterns were cut out of soft bedrock and were often plastered and fitted with channels and drains to capture surface runoff. Wells were dug to gain access to the water table, which was recharged with winter rainfall. Larger amounts of water were retrieved and conserved in pools and reservoirs, and more elaborate water systems, including shafts and tunnels, were constructed to supply the water needs of whole *cities. Such waterworks were built in *Phrygia and *Palestine in the Late Bronze and *Iron Ages, e.g. at *Hazor, *Megiddo, *Gezer and *Jerusalem. *Sennacherib constructed an aqueduct over 48 km long to supply *Nineveh with adequate water. Elaborate irrigation networks watered the alluvial plain between the Tigris and the Euphrates. These projects were possible because of a centralized political system that built and maintained dams, canals, dikes and water-lifting devices for many centuries.

Although the threat of drought and famine was constant, the problem of too much water was not unknown. The *Bible and the *Gilgamesh *epic include accounts of great *floods, but the annual flooding of the Tigris and Euphrates routinely threatened the young crops that were planted in the spring before the early summer flood.

                                                     GLM

P. BEAUMONT, 'Water Resources and Their Management in the Middle East', *Change and Development in the Middle East: Essays in Honour of W.B. Fisher*, eds J.I. Clarke and H. Bowen-Jones (London 1981) 40–72.

T. BOIY et al., *Changing Watercourses in Babylonia: Towards a Reconstruction of the Ancient Environment in Lower Mesopotamia* (Chicago 1999).

C.J. EYRE, 'Agricultural Cycle, Farming, and Water Management in the Ancient Near East', *Civilizations of the Ancient Near East*, ed. J.M. Sasson (New York 1995) 175–89.

R.J. FORBES, 'Water Supply', *Studies in Ancient Technology* 1, 2nd ed. (Leiden 1964) 149–94.

D. HILLEL, *Rivers of Eden: The Struggle for Water and the Quest for Peace in the Middle East* (New York 1994).

R. MILLER, 'Water Use in Syria and Palestine from the Neolithic to the Bronze Age', *World Archaeology* 11 (1980) 331–41.

J.P. OLESON, 'Water Works', *Anchor Bible Dictionary* 6, ed. D.N. Freedman (New York 1992) 883–93.

**Weapons:** see Tools and weapons

**Weather-gods** Throughout the Near East, a number of deities were venerated who were considered primarily to be responsible for, and whose characters were little more than personifications of, natural meteorological phenomena such as storms, rain, winds and frost. Generically these are termed 'weather-gods'. Especially for the *Hurrians and *Hittites, who dwelt in upland *Anatolia, the cloudy and stormy mountains of eastern Turkey and north *Syria, some of their principal deities were weather-*gods, who acquired special prominence when the *Mitannian and Hittite states achieved political dominance.

In *Mesopotamia proper, the best-known weather-god was *Adad (*Sumerian Ishkur). Several North-west *Semitic weather deities were worshipped locally in *Syria and *Palestine under the name *Baal (meaning 'Lord'). In Syria and on the middle Euphrates, a storm-god under the name Mer or Wer was known.

However, the many local names of these deities are not always recoverable, and in *cuneiform writing are often written simply as 'weather-god', especially in Hittite, where an unnamed storm-god plays an important role in several Hattic *myths. Typically the weather-god or storm-god is shown standing alone, wielding an axe and a symbolic flash of lightning.

*Teshup was the Hurrian name of an important weather-god widely worshipped in Anatolia, Syria and northern Mesopotamia. In Mesopotamia he was also known as Tishpak. As with other storm-gods, the bull is his *sacred animal, reminding us of the 'bull-calves' (storm clouds) of the Mesopotamia storm-god Adad. The consort of Teshup was the goddess Hebat, who was worshipped together with him at *Aleppo and various *cities in Anatolia. Their son is Sharruma.

Taru, the consort of Wurusemu, the Hattic sun-goddess of Arinna, was a weather-god who, in the Hittite state *religion, was exalted to a major position as 'King of Heaven and Lord of the Land of Hatti'. In an early Hattic myth the storm-god slays the serpent *Illuyanka, celebrated every spring at the *purulli* festival. In another Hattic myth in the Hittite tradition, a different sort of weather-god is represented by 'Jack Frost' (*Hahhimas*), a personification of winter cold which paralyses the land when the sun-god disappears. The weather-god of the Luwians and the Neo-Hittite kingdoms was Tarhunt (meaning 'the Conqueror'), a name which was the origin of the Etruscan Tarchon (and Roman Tarquinius).    JAB

H.J. DEIGHTON, *The Weathergod in Hittite Anatolia* (Oxford 1982).
O.R. GURNEY, *The Hittites*, rev. ed. (Harmondsworth 1990) chapter 7.
H.A. HOFFNER, JR, *Hittite Myths* (Atlanta, GA 1990).
J.G. MACQUEEN, 'Nerik and its "Weather-god"', *Anatolian Studies* 30 (1980) 179–87.

**Weaving:** see Textiles

**Weights and measures** Systems of measuring weight, capacity, length and area are known in detail only from *Mesopotamia, although related but different systems existed at *Ebla, *Alalakh, *Ugarit and in *Hatti. In the third millennium BC, local Mesopotamian systems were sexagesimal (based on multiples of sixty). Around 2200 BC an integrated system linking all measures was created and incorporated into mathematical training for *scribes. It became the standard system of calculation and accounting until about 1600 BC but continued to be taught for more than a thousand years.

(*top*) Dome-shaped weight of pink limestone found at Lachish. The incised Hebrew letters *bq'* give its value as 'half (a shekel)'. Weight 6.095 g. Seventh century BC. WA 132828.

(*above right*) Babylonian stone weight inscribed '1 shekel'. Present weight 7.98 g. WA 95823.

(*above*) Basalt 'duck' weight inscribed for Eriba-Marduk, king of Babylon, c.770 BC, 30 'true' minas. Weight c.15 kg. WA 91433.

Measures of length were based on cubits (forearms) or portions of cubits, divided into palms of four or five fingers, and sometimes into fingers and smaller subdivisions. A cubit measured about 50 cm. Measures of area were derived from multiples of cubits, called 'garden plots'. Weight was measured using a mina of about 500 g, consisting of sixty shekels or 10,800 barleycorns. The capacity measure was the *Sumerian SILA or *Akkadian *qû*, approximately one litre. Fractions or sub-units of surface, volume and capacity were expressed using shekels and barleycorns.

In practical terms, weight was measured using *stone or *metal weights which are occasionally inscribed with their values. Stone or *pottery jars or bowls are sometimes inscribed with a measure of capacity; *wood and metal may have been used for standard measuring vessels, but no inscribed examples are known. Cubit rods of *wood, stone and metal measured length. The oldest examples, dating to c.2200 BC, are engraved on a *bronze bar from *Nippur and on statues of *Gudea, and show graduated rules divided into a palm of five fingers with smaller subdivisions.

The basic measures were unchanged after 1600 BC, although areas of land were expressed in units of capacity. All systems remained essentially sexagesimal, but a system of unit fractions was incorporated into the weight system, creating ¼, ⅓ and other fractions including ¹⁄₂₄, identified with the seed of the carob *tree (*Ceratonia siliqua*), part of whose Latin name has survived to modern times as the carat. The *Babylonian system was used and adapted elsewhere, for example at *Nuzi, which also used decimal patterns (based on multiples of ten) which were eventually incorporated into *Assyrian measures.

Hundreds of small stone weights found in *Judah attest a standard system based on a shekel of 11.33 g in the seventh century BC, partly correlated with Egyptian weights. The problems arising from varied systems of weight are revealed by specific qualifications, such as 'weight of *Carchemish', 'royal cubit', and condemnations of sub-standard weights in *laws and *wisdom literature reveal the easy opportunities for fraud.     PB

R. KLETTER, *Economic Keystones: The Weight System of the Kingdom of Judah* (Sheffield 1998).
M. POWELL, 'Masse und Gewichte', *Reallexikon der Assyriologie* 7 (Berlin/New York 1990) 457–517.
——, 'Weights and Measures', *Anchor Bible Dictionary* 6, ed. D.N. Freedman (New York 1992) 897–908.
——, 'Weights and Measures', *The Oxford Encyclopedia of Archaeology in the Near East* 5, ed. E.M. Meyers (New York 1997) 339–42.
T.P.J. VAN DEN HOUT, 'Masse und Gewichte: Bei den Hethitern', *Reallexikon der Assyriologie* 7 (Berlin/New York 1990) 517–27.

**Wheel:** see Transport and travel

**Wine**   The earliest traces of wine are found in sediments in a *pottery jar from the *Neolithic village of Hajji Firuz in *Iran, dating to c.6000 BC. Analysis of the wine showed that it contained an additive of terebinth resin, which inhibits the growth of bacteria that convert wine to vinegar and masks offensive taste or odour.

Most wine was made from grapes, but in *Assyria also from the fermented juice of dates. Grape wine was produced in areas of higher rainfall, such as the *Levant, *Anatolia and Assyria, but not usually in *Babylonia. Wine was imported into Babylonia, normally by *boat, in Old Babylonian times via Mari and *Sippar. Its expense restricted it in that area to *food offerings for the *gods and to the rich, who drank it chilled by ice brought from the highlands. The profession of wine-mixer is known at Mari. Wine could be 'red', 'clear' (white), 'sweet', 'strong', 'of good quality', 'second-rate', 'early' or 'old'. In Neo-Babylonian times it was described as 'mountain beer' or 'bright wine like the uncountable waters of the river'. A wine connoisseur of the period wrote a letter of complaint that wine had been sent in a boat normally used for bitumen, the smell of which had spoiled the wine.

Wines were generally named after their place of origin. Wine from the Near East was exported to *Egypt, where it was used at religious festivals. A *Syrian vintner is named on wine-jar sealings found in the tomb of Tutankhamun. In Assyria, the best vineyards were east of *Nineveh, but wine was also delivered from the *Aramaean states as booty and tribute. *Israelite vines

are depicted on the reliefs of *Sennacherib's siege of *Lachish, and many wine presses, especially of the *Iron Age, have been found in excavations of Levantine sites.

At the inauguration of *Nimrud, *Ashurnasirpal II served 10,000 skins of wine to his 69,574 guests. His *palace could store 2000 litres of wine in jars arranged in rows, and many large jars were found together with dipper jugs in the storeroom of Karmir Blur in *Urartu. Some of the earliest wine jars, from *Godin Tepe, dating to c.3500 BC, were stoppered and stored on their sides, perhaps to prevent the wine from changing to vinegar. *Cuneiform tablets record the *administration of the wine ration for the 6000 people of the royal household at Nimrud, the standard amount per person being about two decilitres.

Four paragraphs in the code of *Hammurabi concern *women wine sellers, who were threatened with being thrown into *water if they poured short measures. The amount of grain the wine seller should receive at harvest-time in return for supplying drinks on credit is stipulated. Undesirables clearly congregated in wine *shops, and it was the wine seller's duty, on pain of death, to arrest outlaws and deliver them to the palace. Certain *priestesses were forbidden from entering wine shops. If they even opened the door, the penalty was death by burning.     PB

H. FINET, 'Le vin à Mari', *Archiv für Orientforschung* 25 (1974–7) 122–31.
J.V. KINNIER-WILSON, *The Nimrud Wine Lists: A Study of Men and Administration at the Assyrian Capital in the Eighth Century B.C.* (London 1972).
H.F. LUTZ, *Viticulture and Brewing in the Ancient Orient* (Leipzig 1922).
P.E. McGOVERN, S.J. FLEMING and S.H. KATZ (eds), *The Origins and Ancient History of Wine* (Luxembourg 1996).
P.E. McGOVERN et al., 'Neolithic Resinated Wine', *Nature* 381 (6 June 1996) 480–1.
L. MILANO (ed.), *Drinking in Ancient Societies: History and Culture of Drinking in the Ancient Near East* (Padua 1994).

**Wisdom literature**   This term, originally coined to refer to certain *biblical books, has been used to group together various works of *Sumerian and *Akkadian *literature which are considered to resemble them thematically, and indeed any related Near Eastern compositions (such as ancient *Egyptian, *Aramaic and Syriac).

The major works of wisdom literature in Akkadian are the '*Babylonian Theodicy', a long acrostic poem exploring the justice of the *gods; *Ludlul bēl nēmeqi* ('I will praise the lord of wisdom'), an extended poem of the cult of *Marduk which bears some resemblance to the biblical Book of Job; and the 'Dialogue of Pessimism', a gloomy exchange between master and *slave. Sumerian proverbs were grouped into thematic collections, and later given Akkadian translations. Sometimes proverbs and wise sayings were presented in a dramatic setting, as in 'The Instructions of Shuruppak', when a father instructs his son in the ways of the world. In *Mesopotamian debate poems, personified *animals, *plants, objects or seasons (such as 'Sheep and Grain', 'Tree and Reed', '*Copper and *Silver', 'Winter and Summer', 'Palm and Tamarisk') formally debate their respective benefits to humankind. Dialogues of *scribal life incorporate ethical recommendations, while riddles and fables often point up moral themes.

Babylonian wisdom literature was copied in the west during the Late Bronze Age (at *Emar, *Ugarit). No local, western compositions are known, although some proverbs are quoted in certain *Amarna Letters (e.g. no. 259). In the first millennium BC West Semitic wisdom literature is available. The Bible preserves a collection of Proverbs, similar to Babylonian and Egyptian collections, Job (see above) and a philosophical treatise on the meaning of life, Ecclesiastes. 'Wisdom' concepts appear in some Psalms and Judges 9: 8–15 contains a short debate reminiscent of Mesopotamian ones. A fifth-century BC papyrus from Egypt preserves the Wisdom of Ahiqar, described as a courtier of *Sennacherib and *Esarhaddon, a series of proverbs with introductory story circulated later in many languages and versions.                        JAB/ARM

B. ALSTER, *The Instructions of Šuruppak* (Copenhagen 1974).

——, *The Proverbs of Ancient Sumer: The World's Earliest Proverb Collection* (Bethesda, MD 1997).

M. CIVIL, *The Farmer's Instructions* (Barcelona 1994).

W.G. LAMBERT, *Babylonian Wisdom Literature* (Oxford 1960).

J.M. LINDENBERGER, 'Ahiqar (Seventh to Sixth Century B.C.)', *The Old Testament Pseudepigrapha* 2, ed. J.H. Charlesworth (New York 1985) 479-507.

R.E. MURPHY, 'Wisdom in the Old Testament', *Anchor Bible Dictionary* 6, ed. D.N. Freedman (New York 1992) 920-31.

G.J. REININK and H.L.J. VANSTIPHOUT (eds), *Dispute Poems and Dialogues in the Ancient and Medieval Near East* (Leuven 1991).

J.J.A. VAN DIJK, *La sagesse suméro-akkadienne* (Leiden 1953).

**Women/gender** In the societies of the ancient Near East, as is generally the case in pre-modern, traditional societies, the gender-specific distribution of social functions was more rigidly governed by tradition than in most modern societies. But it is as much due to the origins of the majority of the written sources available to us that there is more mention of the activities of men than there is of women. The *scribal class was almost exclusively male, although a few cases of women scribes are documented. The functions of scribes and their spheres of operation – at *court, and in the civil and religious *administration – mainly involved the recording of men's activities in politics, in the *military, in *law and in *religion. Certain areas can be identified where the activities of women were more visible, either in interaction with those of men or on their own. In the law, there was explicit provision in most collections of laws for women, and specifically for widows and orphan girls, as also for *children, generally because these were all perceived as being vulnerable and exploitable groups. Women are sometimes prominent in legal documents, especially those concerned with *marriage arrangements, dowries, *adoptions and so on, and it is clear that at certain periods independent ownership of *property by women was regarded as normal.

In religion, certain categories of religious personnel were the exclusive preserve of women, e.g. the *en* *priestesses of male deities, or the secluded *nadītu* women of the Old *Babylonian period. It has been suggested that certain cults were practised mainly by women, e.g. the cult of *Dumuzi. In *Mesopotamian society at various periods, some social functions were fulfilled exclusively by women. Examples are the brewing and selling of *beer; and *weaving. An interesting treatment of the themes of women's social functions is found in the last section of the *Sumerian *myth '*Enki and the World Order'. Female *prostitution was organized in some way under the patronage of the goddess Inana/*Ishtar.

For the rest, it is mainly a question of chronicling notable occurrences of female prominence. In literature, one may cite the priestess and poetess Enheduanna (c.2400 BC), to whom several literary compositions were attributed. She happens also to be the earliest identifiable author in Sumerian – indeed, any – *literature. Sumerian has a 'women's *language', Emesal, which was used as the literary dialect for a large body of cultic and love *poetry. It has been noted that Sumerian love poetry is composed almost without exception from the female perspective.

In political history, the name of the woman Ku-Bau is mentioned as an early (but probably legendary) ruler of the *city of *Kish. Bara-namtara, the perfectly historical wife of Lugalanda, the ruler of *Lagash (twenty-fifth century BC), administered an extensive *temple organization of which many records survive. An extensive correspondence between the lady (or *queen) Iltani and her associates is preserved among the documents excavated at the *palaces of *Mari and Tell al-*Rimah (eighteenth century BC). Sammu-ramat, the mother of *Adad-nirari III, was a power to be reckoned with in the *Assyrian empire during the reign of her son; she survived in legend as *Semiramis. Adda-guppi, the mother of *Nabonidus, was a powerful influence on her son, and was buried with royal honours when she died at the age of 104 in 547 BC.

Bitumen relief from Susa, showing a woman spinning, c.700–600 BC (© Photo RMN – H. Lewandowski. Louvre Sb 2834).

In religion and *mythology, female deities were enormously important. Inana/Ishtar was responsible both for *war and for (unmarried) love; most other female deities represent aspects of *fertility or activities specifically assigned to women in Mesopotamian society (such as Uttu for weaving, and Ninkasi for beer-making).

Non-textual sources can also sometimes provide information on gender roles and status, and on the *family. But the evidence of *burials has often been misapplied, with the presupposition that graves containing *jewellery, for example, are the burials of women. Where the sex (and age) of skeletal remains has been reliably determined through osteometrical means, however, correlation with other data, such as the grave location, construction and funerary goods, can be illuminating. On this basis it does seem possible to say, for instance, that *weapons are absent from the *graves of women, while long eye-hole pins – so-called toggle pins – appear to be found only in female burials. However, jewellery, *cylinder seals (sometimes inscribed with the name of the female owner) and, in the first millennium BC, fibulae are found in both male and female graves (see Clothing). By and large there seems to be no great differentiation of burial practices or the location of burials of men and women, who usually share the same *cemeteries.

Representations of men, women and children in *art provide information about their respective dress, *work, activities and sometimes status. Only men are shown in combat or *hunting. Household activities, such as spinning or weaving, are shown as exclusively performed by women. Both women and men are seen in *ritual performance and involved in *agricultural tasks, including heavy labour. The common scene of a woman's face gazing out of a window almost certainly represents a prostitute: the goddess Inana is said to appear at the window like a harlot. A figure common in Old Babylonian art of a nude woman with a distinctive hairstyle – long hair parted at the crown and falling either side of the face, curled or bunched at the ends and apparently tied with ribbons – may represent a *kezertu(m)*, a type of *temple prostitute in the cult of Ishtar whose name implies a particular way of dressing the hair. Depictions not only of mortals but also of gods and goddesses are pertinent here, though often difficult to interpret. For example, the common scene, especially on Old Babylonian and *Ur III *seals, of a goddess entreating an important god may reflect a genuine female social role of intercession with the husband or other male relatives; it was considered a duty of a wife to pray for her family.

Architecture can also be used to infer social conditions and, with caution, something of the status of women. The ground plans of domestic housing give insights into the conditions of family life but, except where documentary sources provide details of the ownership of particular properties (see Property ownership and inheritance), do not normally allow any assessment of relative gender roles. At the top end of the social spectrum, separated wings of large *houses and palaces have often been interpreted as women's quarters (although the application of the term *harem is disputed) and some-times related finds and inscriptional evidence make the suggestion plausible.

Direct physical evidence of women at work has not yet been extensively studied but may provide some information on gender. For example, the numerous finger impressions on *pottery seem to belong primarily, perhaps exclusively, to women (and perhaps children). A parallel study of the fingerprints on clay door seals and other marks of property ownership would also be valuable. Ethnographic parallels provide a potentially illuminating source, but only when applied in close relation to archaeological and documentary evidence.     JAB/AG

P.-A. BEAULIEU, 'Women in Neo-Babylonian Society', *Bulletin of the Canadian Society for Mesopotamian Studies* (Toronto) 26 (1993) 7–14.

G. BECKMAN, 'From Cradle to Grave: Women's Role in Hittite Medicine and Magic', *Journal of Ancient Civilizations* (Changchun) 8 (1993) 25–39.

M. BROSIUS, *Women in Ancient Persia, 559–331 BC* (Oxford 1996).

J.-M. DURAND (ed.), *La femme dans le Proche-Orient antique* (Paris 1987).

B.S. LESKO (ed.), *Women's Earliest Records from Ancient Egypt and Western Asia* (Atlanta, GA 1989).

S. ROLLIN, 'Women and Witchcraft in Ancient Assyria (c. 900–600 B.C.)', *Images of Women in Antiquity*, eds A. Cameron and A. Kuhrt (London/Canberra 1983) 34–45.

M. STOL, 'Women in Mesopotamia', *Journal of the Economic and Social History of the Orient* 38 (1995) 123–44.

**Wood** Although wood was relatively scarce in some parts of the ancient Near East, it was employed in a surprisingly large number of ways, especially in the construction of buildings and *ships and in the production of *furniture. Throughout antiquity, *Levantine builders made more use of *stone and wood than did their counterparts in *Mesopotamia, where mudbricks were more common. In Mesopotamia, especially, the cost of a building was related to the amount of wood used in its construction, and roof timbers were recycled because of their value. Nevertheless, objects made of wood appear in a large number of ancient texts, and much effort was made to acquire the *trees necessary to fill these needs.

The procurement of wood was an important feature in an early and far-reaching *trade network. Since the *Egyptian, *Babylonian and *Assyrian demand for larger logs was great, these peoples developed elaborate systems to cut and *transport trees from the mountains of *Lebanon and the mountainous region where *Syria, *Anatolia and Mesopotamia meet. They were especially interested in the tall cedar trees (*Cedrus libani*), but fir, juniper, cypress and pine were also valuable. Such trees were prized for their use as roof beams and in the production of *gates (which would smell of cedar when opened), wood panelling and fine furniture. At *Gordion, wooden *tomb chambers and the furniture in them were primarily of juniper inlaid with boxwood. Other exotic woods from as far away as *India and sub-Saharan Africa were also obtained for aristocratic use (ebony was found on the *Ulu Burun shipwreck). The *Phoenicians, and especially *Byblos, became famous in the international transport of timber.

Local sources of wood were sufficient for many uses. Over fifty samples of oak were recovered from *Jarmo. Willow, terebinth, olive, palm, acacia and tamarisk trees were accessible in many parts of the Near East; these woods were used to manufacture numerous small-scale objects (e.g. *tool and weapon handles or shafts, bows, bowls, spoons, *coffins, small boats, wagons, boxes, furniture, doors, windows). Some of the Middle Bronze Age furniture from *Jericho's tombs was made from tamarisk, willow and a wood resembling cherry. Both local and imported woods were used for furniture (e.g. tables, stools, beds, thrones).

Knowledge of ancient logging and woodworking comes from artistic representations, texts and archaeological evidence. Many carpentry tools have been recovered from Egyptian tombs; the range of tools and the techniques (e.g. mortise-and-tenon joints, inlay) used by ancient woodworkers were remarkably uniform. Several important occupations resulted from the ancient demands for wood and wood products: lumberjacks, transporters, *merchants, and carpenters. Although some wooden implements were made in the home, skilled *craftsmen manufactured other products.            GLM

G. KILLEN, *Egyptian Woodworking and Furniture* (Aylesbury 1994).

P.I. KUNIHOLM, 'Wood', *The Oxford Encyclopedia of Archaeology in the Near East* 5, ed. E.M. Meyers (New York 1997) 347–9.

A. LUCAS, *Ancient Egyptian Materials and Industries*, 4th ed. revised by J.R. Harris (London 1989).

P.R.S. MOOREY, *Ancient Mesopotamian Materials and Industries: The Archaeological Evidence* (Oxford 1994).

J. PERLIN, *A Forest Journey: The Role of Wood in the Development of Civilization* (New York 1989).

J.N. POSTGATE and M.A. POWELL (eds), *Trees and Timber in Mesopotamia*, Bulletin on Sumerian Agriculture 6 (Cambridge 1992).

**Woolley, C. Leonard (1880–1960)** The influential British archaeologist Charles Leonard Woolley's first taste of archaeological fieldwork was in Nubia and Italy before he directed excavations at some of the most important sites in the Near East: *Carchemish (1911–14, 1919), *Amarna in Egypt (1921–2), *Ubaid (1922), *Ur (1922–34), Al Mina (1936–7) and *Alalakh (1937–9, 1946–9). His survey of the 'Wilderness of Zin' in *Sinai (1914) with T.E. Lawrence ('of Arabia'), on the eve of the outbreak of the First World War, was less concerned with *archaeology than with military intelligence. Indeed, Woolley served as an intelligence officer in Egypt during the war, before being blown up at sea and becoming a prisoner-of-war in Turkey (1916–18).

Woolley was an intuitive and observant field archaeologist, with particular insight into methods used by ancient *craftsmen and builders, and he saved many important decayed artefacts by careful excavation. He had a flair for breathing life into the past by imaginatively recreating the individuals who lived in the houses and walked in the streets he excavated, although he tended to

(Sir) Leonard Woolley, right, and T.E. Lawrence ('Lawrence of Arabia') with sculptured slabs they excavated at Carchemish. E3070.

stretch evidence to its limits by reconstructing buildings known only from foundations. A clergyman's son, he had studied theology at Oxford and used the *Bible instinctively as a historical source. He uncritically associated Ur, and even particular levels, with Ur 'of the Chaldees', home of Abraham in the *Old Testament, without questioning whether the biblical traditions had a historical basis. On discovering a layer of water-laid silt in a fifth-millennium BC deposit, he claimed this was evidence of the great *Flood known from *Sumerian and biblical sources. Criticized for this biblical approach, Woolley was quite inflexible and loath to modify his overall interpretations in the face of new evidence, despite being prepared to reconsider matters of detail.

Woolley was conscientious about publishing both scientific and popular accounts of his excavations, although much of his final report on Ur remained in typescript for years because of war and lack of funds, some volumes appearing only after his death. He was knighted for services to archaeology in 1935. He was an archaeological adviser to India in 1938, and to the Allies during the Second World War; on his advice the supreme commander, General Eisenhower, issued an order prohibiting looting and damaging of buildings which included art treasures such as those of the Uffizi in Florence.            PB

M.E.L. MALLOWAN, 'Woolley, Sir (Charles) Leonard', *Dictionary of National Biography 1951–1960* (Oxford 1971) 1082–4.

P.R.S. MOOREY, *A Century of Biblical Archaeology* (Cambridge 1991) 78–80.

H.V.F. WINESTONE, *Woolley of Ur: The Life of Sir Leonard Woolley* (London 1990).

C.L. WOOLLEY, *As I Seem to Remember* (London 1962).

**Wordplay** Oral compositions use similarities of sound in various ways for effect and to aid memorization, and *writing expanded those possibilities. *Mesopotamian *scribes wrote riddles and developed devices like acrostics, so that taking the first sign of each line of a text produced a sentence, even giving an author's name.

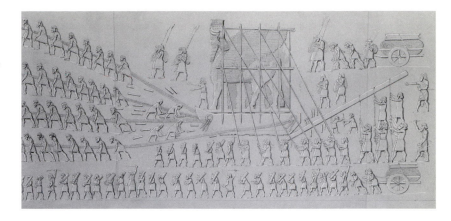

Drawing of a relief from Sennacherib's palace at Nineveh showing a colossal stone sculpture being moved with ropes, log rollers, levers and manpower. c.700 BC. Or. Dr. II, 65.

The *cuneiform script lent itself to ambiguity, so scribes might indulge in paronomasia and interpret syllabic signs as if they were word signs and give meanings quite different from the original intention. In the first millennium BC this is a feature of commentaries 'explaining' older texts. Some words and divine names had associated numerical values and so could be written entirely as numbers. The physical shapes of the signs also allowed re-interpretation, as when *Esarhaddon claimed that he could restore *Babylon because the god *Marduk had reduced the number of years decreed for its desolation under *Sennacherib by reversing the cuneiform number 70 to make it 11, as reversing roman XI makes it IX. *Babylonian scribes also used abbreviations of words and numbers In the *Bible paronomasia is found and *alphabetic acrostics occur in several Psalms (e.g. 37, 119) and the Book of Lamentations. The prophecy of Jeremiah 25: 26; 51: 41) includes a simple code whereby *Babylon (*bbl*) becomes Sheshach (*ššk*) on the system A=Z, B=Y etc.
ARM

w.m. soll, 'Babylonian and Biblical Acrostics', *Biblica* 69 (1988) 305–23.

e.f. weidner, 'Geheimschrift', *Reallexikon der Assyriologie* 3 (Berlin/New York 1957–71) 185–8.

**Work** The work carried out in the ancient Near East can be divided into *agricultural and domestic labour, public works, crafts and trades. Ancient sources do not give a balanced view of the world of work. Most texts come from *palaces and *temples, so the evidence is biased towards the large-scale organized labour which generated those texts.

Little is known about the private sector. Agricultural work could be carried out by the owner of the land and his *family, *slaves, hired workers, or by free men working off a debt. Temples and palaces employed their own labourers and *craftsmen, but might also employ independent workers for a particular piece of work. Self-employed craftsmen worked in their own workshops and concluded *contracts with customers for the manufacture of various objects. Apprenticeship agreements are known, and by the Neo-*Babylonian period contracts of employment were regularly drawn up.

In the large institutions, craftsmen were hired, raw materials supplied and finished products distributed under separate departments headed by an administrator. The *bureaucracy of state-employed labour is best known from the *Ur III period. Daily rosters were kept: craftsmen had to turn up regularly for work each day, and are occasionally registered as sick or absent. An Ur III *textile factory known from the *archives of *Lagash employed over six thousand workers, mostly *women and *children. State employees received rations of grain, wool or cloth and oil, and occasionally other commodities, the amount of rations varying with the responsibility of the position. A normal Ur III male worker received rations of 60 l of barley a month and 2 kg of wool a year, with extra at *festivals. The normal daily hire rate for an Ur III worker was 10 l of barley, although many work contracts were for less. By the Neo-Babylonian period, the wage was normally paid in *silver, but sometimes partially or entirely in barley, wool or dates. The normal monthly wage for a labourer was between one and three shekels of silver (one shekel could buy one *kur* or c.180 l of barley or dates). The receipt of rations did not necessarily mean that the worker was a slave or dependent; private work contracts make clear that free persons working for hire also received rations, although it is not always possible to distinguish between rations and wages in administrative and legal documents. In any case, the wage for the labour of a hired slave was the same as that for a free hired worker.

Some of those who received rations worked for the state at other times of the year doing state service which could include civilian duties such as dike repairing and canal cleaning, as well as military service (see Military organization). From the Old Babylonian period this state service was called *ilkum*. It was separate from the obligations of the *muškēnū* (see Social classes) and was essentially a mechanism for conscription, an obligation to serve in the army in return for the right to hold state land. Some individuals were able to get exemption from military service, or hired substitutes. In the Neo-*Assyrian period, the large numbers of *deportees were put to work on the massive state building projects.

Employees and hired workers were entitled to holidays, and free days are sometimes mentioned in contracts. Holidays were given particularly at religious festivals, which could last several days in each month. The *New Year festival was the main public holiday of the year, lasting between eleven and fifteen days.          PB

J.N. POSTGATE, *Early Mesopotamia: Society and Economy at the Dawn of History* (London 1992) 229–43.

M.A. POWELL (ed.), *Labor in the Ancient Near East* (New Haven, CN 1987).

**Writing and the alphabet**  Writing is one of humankind's supreme inventions, enabling people to transmit their thoughts across the limits of time and space. Writing arose, so far as available evidence shows, in *Sumer. The rulers of the first urban cultures needed means to organize and control the growing populace. From *Neolithic times small clay tokens of various simple shapes were used for basic accounting. In the fourth millennium BC we find some tokens completely enclosed in hollow clay spheres which were covered with *cylinder seal impressions. The spheres might accompany deliveries, being broken upon receipt to ensure the consignments agreed with the number of tokens. On some spheres marks indicating numbers were impressed, heralding the next step when the tokens were abandoned for small clay tablets imprinted with numerical marks and, eventually, signs denoting the objects counted. This was a simple system of notation, not writing proper, which, however, followed quickly. The first script, known from the *Uruk IV level, was pictorial, each sign representing a word (logogram), and so could be read in any *language (like modern traffic signs). The signs might be pictures of complete objects, parts of them (e.g. the head of an ox), or symbols. Very

soon, *scribes recognized how they could expand the range of the system and its precision, without enlarging the number of signs, by applying the 'rebus' principle. A sign could be read for its sound value rather than its meaning, thus pictures of a thin man and a *king could mean 'the thin man is king' or 'the king is a thin man' or, by sound, 'thinking', and grammatical elements could be marked. The language written on tablets from the Uruk III period is *Sumerian. Over five thousand tablets and fragments have been recovered from Uruk IV–III, the majority at Uruk itself, with small collections from other sites, such as *Jemdet Nasr and Tell *Uqair. This distribution reveals the adoption of a uniform writing system throughout Babylonia by about 3000 BC. For the subsequent development, see Cuneiform script.

At the end of the fourth millennium BC *trade links carried the script to nearby *Elam, where a local form was created, and it may have moved from there to the *Indus Valley, stimulating the still unread script of that culture. Most importantly, the idea travelled, with other Babylonian creations, to Egypt, where the Egyptians turned it into their distinctive form, the hieroglyphs, incorporating the rebus principle.

However flexible such scripts (see Cuneiform script) proved to be, with their hundreds of signs they remained the monopoly of the scribes. The invention of the *alphabet changed the picture in due course, superseding all other writing systems in the Near East.          ARM

G.R. DRIVER, *Semitic Writing, from Pictograph to Alphabet* (London 1976).

H.J. NISSEN, P. DAMEROW and R.K. ENGLUND, *Archaic Bookkeeping: Writing and Techniques of Economic Administration in the Ancient Near East* (Chicago/London 1993).

D. SCHMANDT-BESSERAT, *Before Writing* (Austin, TX 1992).

# Y

**Yahweh**  The name of the national *god of *Israel is written with the consonants *yhwh* in the *Hebrew *Bible, in ancient Hebrew inscriptions and in the *Moabite Stone (c.830 BC). It is shortened to *yhw*, *yw* or *yh* in personal names (e.g. *yhwntn*=Jonathan, *mkyh(w)*= Micaiah). *Assyrian *scribes wrote it as they heard it in personal names, *yahu*. The origin of the name is unknown. The Bible assumes that it was current in the earliest human society and familiar to Abraham and his family (Genesis 4; 12ff; see Patriarchs), but its meaning was revealed only in the time of Moses (see Exodus), when God appeared to him at the Burning Bush saying, 'I am that I am' (Exodus 3). This explanation points to the root of the name in the Hebrew verb *hāyāh*, 'to be', but the form is archaic and the commonly accepted meaning 'he who causes to be' and the reconstructed form

Yahweh itself are not wholly certain.

After *Cyrus II allowed the Jews to return from exile in *Babylonia, such sanctity became attached to the name that it was no longer spoken, the word 'my lord' being substituted for it, even in reading the Bible aloud. When it grew necessary to preserve the pronunciation of the Hebrew text in the Middle Ages, the vowels for 'my lord' (*'adōnāy*) were combined with the consonants *yhwh*, giving the hybrid which came into Reformation Europe as Iehouah or Jehovah.

While Yahweh was to be Israel's sole deity according to the Bible, it also condemns Israel for its apostasy with other deities. Discoveries of Hebrew inscriptions from the ninth and eighth centuries BC referring to Yahweh and his consort (*Asherah) illustrate that failure, but it is noteworthy that Israelite personal names in the Bible and in ancient inscriptions, especially *seals, rarely embody any other gods.

Attempts to trace this divine name outside ancient Israel have been unsuccessful. A place named Yahwa in Egyptian lists of the New Kingdom, thought to lie in *Edom, was associated with it, but is now believed to belong in *Syria, and seems too remote to be related. The same is true for a supposed divine name Ya at *Ugarit. When the *Ebla tablets were first read, the occurrence of *ya* at the end of personal names was compared with the Hebrew *-ya*, but it is now clear that it is not the same.

ARM

T.N.D. METTINGER, *In Search of God* (Philadelphia, PA 1988).
M.S. SMITH, *The Early History of God* (San Francisco 1990).

**Yahya, (Tepe)** Significant for its long sequence of occupation from the *Neolithic to *Parthian–*Sasanian periods, with gaps, Tepe Yahya lies in south-east *Iran, 130 km north of the Straits of Hormuz which lead into the Persian Gulf. It was discovered in 1967 and excavated until 1975 by C.C. Lamberg-Karlovsky. The site is c.3 ha in area and 19.8 m high. Of particular importance was a series of Late Neolithic villages (c.7000–5500 BC), and a late fourth-millennium BC Proto-*Elamite colony consisting of a single building complex containing inscribed tablets. In the late third millennium BC Tepe Yahya was probably part of the kingdom of Marhashi, known from *Ur III texts from *Mesopotamia. Regional survey complementing the excavation has provided the fullest understanding so far of settlement patterns in south-east Iran.

The most distinctive objects from Tepe Yahya, from all periods but particularly from the third-millennium BC levels, were vessels, beads, figurines and other types made of chlorite which was mined and manufactured locally. Over one thousand fragments of chlorite bowls were found, of the type known from third-millennium BC sites in Mesopotamia and the Indus Valley, and it is likely that

Tepe Yahya was a primary centre for long-distance trade in this material. Many of the bowls were carved with complex designs, including snakes, felines, scorpions, geometric motifs and architectural façades.

PB

P. DAMEROW and R.K. ENGLUND, *The Proto-Elamite Texts from Tepe Yahya* (Cambridge, MA 1989).
C.C. LAMBERG-KARLOVSKY, *Excavations at Tepe Yahya, Iran, 1967–1969* (Cambridge, MA 1970).
——, 'Urban Interaction on the Iranian Plateau: Excavations at Tepe Yahya, 1967–1973', *Proceedings of the British Academy* 59 (1973) 282–319.
C.C. LAMBERG-KARLOVSKY and T.W. BEALE, *Excavations at Tepe Yahya, Iran, 1967–1975: The Early Periods* (Cambridge, MA 1986).

**Yam** The word means 'sea' in the *Semitic *languages and refers to a divine figure who features in the *Ugaritic *myths as the *god of the unruly waters of the sea. Ugarit as a port was dependent on *shipping, and since the god of the waves had an important role to play he had a cult and received regular offerings. In the *Baal cycle he is, like *Mot, one of the antagonists of the storm-god. He challenges Baal to a fight but is overcome with the help of *magical weapons devised by the craftsman of the gods, Kothar-wa-Hasis. The theme of a struggle between sea and a young god, usually a storm-god, has parallels in *Mesopotamia and may represent a conflict between an older cosmogonic system with a new divine order. The *Babylonian god *Marduk's battle against *Tiamat, the representative of the primeval waters, is an example; the Theogony of Dunnu has a similar conflict between generations of gods, whereby the older ones are linked to the watery element.

GL

J.M. DURAND, 'Le mythologème du combat entre le dieu de l'orage et la mer en Mésopotamie', *Mari: Annales de Recherches Interdisciplinaires* 7 (1993) 41–61.
P. MATTHIAE, 'Some Notes on the Old Syrian Iconography of the God Yam', *Natural Phenomena: Their Meaning, Description and Depiction in the Ancient Near East*, ed. D.J.W. Meijer (Amsterdam 1992) 169–92.
N. WYATT, 'The Source of the Ugaritic Myth of the Conflict of Baal and Yam', *Ugarit-Forschungen* 20 (1988) 375–85.

Fragment of a typical chlorite vase from Tepe Yahya, carved in relief with architectural motifs. Mid third millennium BC (after C.C. Lamberg-Karlovsky, *Proceedings of the British Academy* 59 (1973)).

**Yamhad** Yamhad was a major state during the second millennium BC in north *Syria; its capital was at modern Aleppo. Aleppo was settled from at least the Early Bronze Age. By the eighteenth century BC Yamhad was the most powerful state in Syria, in conflict with *Shamshi-Adad I of *Assyria. Its core territory is unclear and changed over time, but Yamhad probably stretched from the Euphrates in the east to the Orontes *river in the west, and from *Qatna in the south to *Carchemish in the north. Most of the evidence comes from the *Mari, *Alalakh and *Hittite archives. Nine *kings of Yamhad are known covering a period of about two hundred years, and they were regarded as 'great kings' by the *Hittites. The Hittite king Mursilis I attacked and destroyed Aleppo c.1600 BC as part of his raid into Syria and *Mesopotamia which also destroyed *Babylon. Yamhad ceased to exist as a state.

King Niqmepa of Alalakh (fourteenth century BC) sometimes used a cylinder seal that had been made about four centuries earlier for Sharran (or Sharra-el), king of Yamhad, whose name and titles it bore (from D. Collon, *The Seal Impressions from Tell Atchana/Alalakh* (Neukirchen/Vluyn 1975) 170).

Aleppo remained relatively unimportant from then on, although Neo-*Hittite remains have recently been excavated on the citadel, and was important again in Islamic times.                                                                              PB

H. KLENGEL, *Syria: 3000 to 300 B.C.: A Handbook of Political History* (Berlin 1992) 44–64.

**Yarim Tepe** Yarim Tepe (Turkish for 'half mound') comprises six mounds near the town of Tel'afar in north-western Iraq. Excavation of three of these mounds by a team from the Soviet Union has shed much light on the early *prehistory of northern *Mesopotamia in the millennia after the full-scale adoption of *agriculture and *animal husbandry.

Occupation at Yarim Tepe I is principally of the *Hassuna period, c.7000–6000 BC. Twelve levels of pisé (pressed mud) architecture were excavated, including multi-roomed *houses, store-blocks and kilns, with many *burials. Following the use of incised and painted Hassuna-type *pottery, in the upper levels painted pottery of *Samarra type indicates increasing contact with central *Mesopotamia towards the end of the seventh millennium BC. Domesticated crops and *animals occur in all levels, as do *flint and *obsidian tools.

Yarim Tepe II was occupied during the *Halaf period, c.6000–4500 BC. Nine architectural levels were excavated, predominant features including circular structures,

known as *tholoi*, which appear to be largely domestic but with some *ritual function, as well as rectilinear buildings. Burials of the Halaf period were found in both Yarim Tepe I and II, the most spectacular being the 'hunter's burial' where an individual was buried with a buffalo skull, pots and maceheads. Beautifully painted pottery, including a vessel in the shape of a *woman, indicate the full participation of Yarim Tepe within the cultural sphere of the Halaf world, which flourished across northern Mesopotamia from south central Turkey to eastern Iraq and south into *Lebanon.

Occupation at Yarim Tepe III includes further levels of Halaf date and also settlement during the transition from the Halaf to the *Ubaid periods, c.4500 BC, as well as during the Ubaid period itself. Again *tholoi*, rectilinear buildings and burials of Halaf date occur. The Ubaid levels comprise rectilinear buildings only. Painted pottery has motifs painted in styles common to both Halaf and Ubaid periods.                                                        RM

R.J. MATTHEWS, *The Early Prehistory of Mesopotamia, 500,000 to 4,500 BC* (Turnhout 1999).

N.I. MERPERT and R.M. MUNCHAEV, 'The Earliest Levels at Yarim Tepe I and Yarim Tepe I', *Iraq* 49 (1987) 1–36.

N. YOFFEE and J.J. CLARK (eds), *Early Stages in the Evolution of Mesopotamian Civilization* (Tucson, AZ 1993).

**Yazýlýkaya:** see Boghazköy

Halaf-period vase in the shape of a woman, from Yarim Tepe.

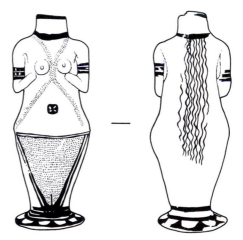

# Z

**Zagros** The Zagros mountains separate the plateau of *Iran from the plains of *Mesopotamia. They contain many sheltered basins linked by deep, narrow gorges cut by perennial *rivers, and the routes through them were the main avenue for contacts between Iran and Mesopotamia in antiquity. A number of sites, such as *Jarmo and *Ganj Dareh, are of importance for the origins of *food production and the earliest *pottery in the Near East. The area is covered by forests degraded through cultivation, *pastoralism, and cutting for fuel. The wild ancestors of wheat and barley, goats and sheep all flourished here. Goats were probably domesticated in this region c.7500–7000 BC, sheep a little later, and pigs by the end of the seventh millennium BC (see Animal husbandry). Later, the Zagros formed part of the territory of *Elam, and also incorporated *Luristan. PB

F. HOLE (ed.), *The Archaeology of Western Iran: Settlement and Society from Prehistory to the Islamic Conquest* (Washington, D.C. 1987).

**Ziggurat** Anglicized form of *Akkadian *ziqqurratu*, the name in *Assyria and *Babylonia for a stepped pyramid with a *temple or temples on the summit. Such structures are first found in southern *Mesopotamia dating from c.2200 BC, and continued to be constructed until 550 BC, also being imitated in the north by the Assyrians. Throughout most of their history these structures were free-standing, but the Assyrian examples were part of larger temple complexes. Three principal theories have emerged as to the origins of the ziggurat. According to one idea, ziggurats were first developed as a mechanism for the elevation of grain to keep it dry during spring flooding. Another view sees them as artificial mountains, with the presumption that the original home of the *Sumerians was a mountainous land. Most widely accepted, however, is the theory that the ziggurat was seen as a ladder to heaven, the shrine on the summit elevating the *priests closer to the *gods themselves. The ziggurat should probably be seen as deriving from the raising of temples, at first by the mounds created through sequential rebuilding, as with the temples at *Eridu of the late fifth to early fourth millennia BC; and subsequently by the deliberate construction of a raised platform on which the temple was built.

Ziggurats were constructed of solid brickwork, without internal rooms or spaces, except for draining shafts. Where physical evidence survives, access to the summit was by an outside triple staircase or by a spiral ramp; in other cases, if there was access, it may have been from the tops of surrounding buildings. Usually the pyramid was square or rectangular, on average some 40 by 50 m at base.

The largest surviving ziggurat is at *Chogha Zanbil in *Iran, built in the thirteenth century BC, 100 m square and standing 24 m tall, thought to be just under half its original height. Uniquely, access to the summit was by means of internal stairways. The best preserved ziggurat

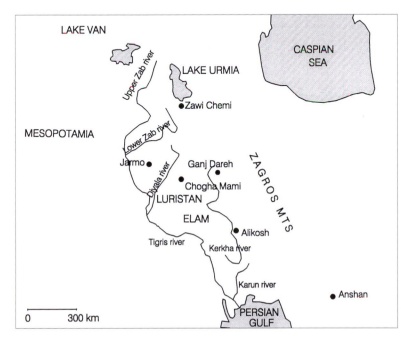

Map of the Zagros region showing main archaeological sites.

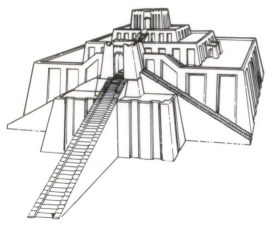

Reconstruction of the ziggurat at Ur.

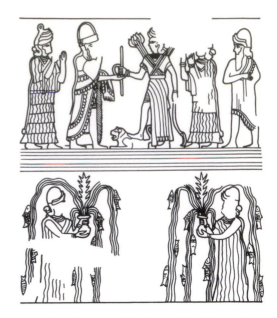

A mural from the palace at Mari shows Zimri-Lim receiving the insignia of kingship from the goddess Ishtar. Below, two goddesses hold vases flowing with water, symbols of fertility.

is that at *Ur in southern Mesopotamia, built by *Ur-Nammu c.2110 BC. It is 64 by 46 m at base and originally some 12 m in height, with three storeys (increased to seven by *Nabonidus in the sixth century BC).

The *city ziggurat or ziggurats (some places had more than one) served as the urban focal point, visible on the skyline from afar, and from the summit providing an aerial view of the metropolis. Although it was not their real purpose, it is possible that at certain times the ziggurats were used as vantage points, above the grime of the city, for *astronomical observation.          JAB/AG

T. BUSINK, 'L'origine et évolution de la ziggurat babylonienne', Jaarbericht van het Voorazijatisch-Egyptisch Genootschap Ex Oriente Lux 21 (1970) 91–141.

R. CHADWICK, 'Calendars, Ziggurats, and the Stars', The Canadian Society for Mesopotamian Studies Bulletin (Toronto) 24 (November 1992) 7–24.

R.G. KILLICK, 'Ziggurat', The Dictionary of Art 33, ed. J. Turner (New York/London 1996) 675–6.

H.J. LENZEN, Die Entwicklung der Zikurrat von ihren Anfängen bis zur Zeit der III. Dynastie von Ur (Leipzig 1942).

M. ROAF, Cultural Atlas of Mesopotamia and the Ancient Near East (New York 1990) 104–7.

E.C. STONE, 'Ziggurat', The Oxford Encyclopedia of Archaeology in the Ancient Near East 5, ed. E.M. Meyers (New York 1997) 390–1.

**Zimri-Lim**   Zimri-Lim (c.1775–1761 BC) was the son of Yahdun-Lim, *king of *Mari. When Yahdun-Lim was conquered by *Shamshi-Adad I, Zimri-Lim found refuge at Aleppo, where his father-in-law ruled as king of *Yamhad. The weakening of *Assyrian rule after the *death of Shamshi-Adad enabled Zimri-Lim to regain his ancestral throne where he became a powerful ally of *Hammurabi of *Babylon, who eventually dispossessed him. He was the last occupant and builder of the great *palace at Mari, but the only inscription he has left records the construction of a house for ice brought from the mountains to cool the royal drinks. The enormous *archives of Mari shed brilliant light on his reign, in-

cluding over two thousand documents concerning provisions for the king's table and the correspondence of his *queen, Shibtu. International relations were regulated by *treaties, often cemented by royal *marriages. Zimri-Lim had at least eleven daughters and several left home in that way, accompanied by rich dowries.          ARM

S. DALLEY, Mari and Karana: Two Old Babylonian Cities (London 1984).

**Zinjirli (Zencerli, Zincerli)**   The Neo-*Hittite or Syro-Hittite city of Sam'al, a circular *city with a central citadel atop an earlier mound, Zinjirli represents the centralized urban planning of a new ninth-century BC foundation. It lies in the plain of Islahiye in south-eastern Turkey, close to the border with *Syria. Nearby open-air *sculpture quarries are known at Yesemek where, in all likelihood, many of the city's *stone sculptures originated.

The city was excavated by C. Humann, F. von Luschan and *Koldewey (1888–92), digging being concentrated on the citadel and the outer double wall with its three *gates. Unravelling the precise sequence of construction and the long sequence of use and re-use of many of the buildings is fraught with difficulties.

A *Phoenician inscription of King Kilamuwa I dates to the third quarter of the ninth century BC and attests the spread of Phoenician *language that is witnessed also at *Karatepe and Ivriz. Different styles of sculpture show the admixture of Luwian and *Aramaean traditions, superseded by a style with strong *Assyrian influence under the auspices of the eighth-century Aramaean king, Barrekub. A colossal statue of a *king may represent Kilamuwa,

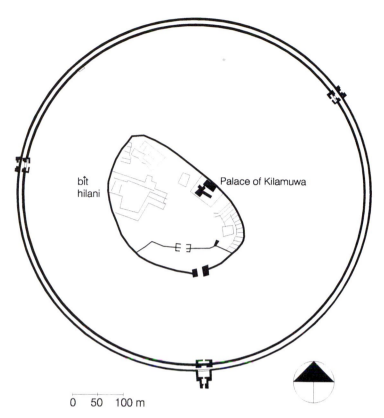

The defensive wall and citadel of Zinjirli, c.830 BC.

bīt hilani

Palace of Kilamuwa

0  50  100 m

but it is not inscribed. The Assyrian King *Esarhaddon erected a stela in the citadel gate. Further carved ortho-stats (standing stone slabs) were recovered from the southern gate of the city wall.

The citadel has a surrounding wall with a single gate adorned with sculpted orthostats, depicting protective lions and gate bulls and individual panels rather than an integrated scene. A second, inner, wall and gate afforded extra defence. The interior is further divided by walls. Buildings within include two palaces of the *bīt hilāni type, each approached by a short flight of wide steps and entered by way of columned porticoes.          GDS

E. AKURGAL, *The Birth of Greek Art* (London 1966).

H. FRANKFORT, *The Art and Architecture of the Ancient Orient*, 5th ed. updated by M. Roaf and D. Matthews (New Haven, CN 1996).

B. LANDSBERGER, *Sam'al* (Ankara 1948).

F. VON LUSCHAN, *Ausgrabungen in Sendschirli* (Berlin, I 1893, III 1902, IV 1911, V 1943).

**Ziwiye**   The site of Ziwiye is in Kurdistan in north-west *Iran. In about 1946, antiquities dealers reported the discovery there of a rich *burial containing a *bronze *coffin and objects of *gold, *silver, bronze and *ivory. Since then, hundreds of objects allegedly from Ziwiye have appeared on the antiquities market and it is imposs-ible to establish what really did come from the *tomb. Some of the objects are decorated in the 'animal art' style

of the *Scythians, with stylized lions, stags, ibexes and *birds, leading to suggestions that it was the tomb of a Scythian or *Median prince. In fact none of the objects has a certain context, and some may even be forgeries. Survey and excavation at Ziwiye in 1964, 1976 and from 1994 revealed a fortified structure dating to the seventh century BC, approached by a monumental rock-cut stair-case, but no objects resembling the 'treasure'.          PB

O.W. MUSCARELLA, '"Ziwiye" and Ziwiye: The Forgery of a Provenience', *Journal of Field Archaeology* 4 (1977) 197–219

Detail from a decorative gold strip with two 'Scythian'-style animals and a border of eagles' heads, said to be from Ziwiye. Eighth to seventh century BC. WA 134383.

## Babylonia

| | | | |
|---|---|---|---|
| Kish: | Enmebaragesi c.2650 | | |
| | Agga | Uruk: Gilgamesh | |
| | Mesalim | | |
| | | Ur: Royal Tombs | |
| Kish: | Ur-Nanshe c.2500 | | |
| | Akurgal | | |
| | Eannatum c.2454 | | |
| | Enanatum c.2424 | | |
| | Enmetena c.2402 | | |
| | Enanatum II c.2374 | | |
| | Enentarzi c.2364 | | |
| | Lugalanda c.2358 | | |
| | Uruinimgina/Urukagina c.2351 | | |
| Uruk: | Lugalzagesi c.2340 | | |
| Akkad: | Sargon c.2340/2296 | | |
| | Rimush c.2284/39 | | |
| | Manishtusu c.2275/2229 | | |
| | Naram-Sin c.2260/2213 | | |
| | Shar-kali-sharri c.2223–2198/2175–2150 | | |
| Gutian rule | | | |
| Uruk: | Utuhegal c.2119 | | |
| Ur: | Third Dynasty: | Lagash: Gudea | |
| | Ur-Nammu c.2112 | | |
| | Shulgi c.2094 | | |
| | Amar-Sin c.2046 | | |
| | Shu-Sin c.2037 | | |
| | Ibbi-Sin c.2026 | Larsa: | |
| Isin: | Ishbi-Erra c.2017 | Naplanum c.2025 | Babylon: |
| | Shu-ilishu c.1984 | Emisum c.2004 | |
| | Iddin-Dagan c.1974 | Samium c.1976 | |
| | Ishme-Dagan c.1953 | Zabaya c.1941 | |
| | Lipit-Ishtar c.1934 | Gungunum c.1932 | |
| | Ur-Ninurta c.1923 | Abisare c.1905 | |
| | Bur-Sin c.1895 | Sumuel c.1894 | Sumu-abum c.1894 |
| | Lipit-Ishtar c.1934 | Nur-Adad c.1865 | Sumulael c.1880 |
| | Ur-Ninurta c.1923 | | |
| | Enlil-bani c.1860 | Sin-iddinam c.1849 | |
| | | Sin-eribam c.1842 | Sabium c.1844 |
| | Zambiya c.1836 | Sin-iqisham c.1840 | |
| | Iter-pisha c.1833 | Silli-Adad c.1835 | Apil-Sin c.1830 |
| | Urdukuga c.1830 | Warad-Sin c.1834 | Erishum II |
| | Sin-magir c.1827 | Rim-Sin I c.1822–1763 | Sin-muballit c.1812 |
| | Damiq-ilishu c.1816–1794 | | Hammurabi c.1792 |
| | | | Samsuiluna c.1749 |
| | | Rim-Sin II 1741 | Abi-eshuh c.1711 |
| | | | Ammiditana c.1683 |
| | | | Ammisaduqa c.1646 |
| | | | Samsu-ditana c.1625–1⟨ |

**Assyria**

Puzur-Ashur I

Shalim-Ahum
Ilushuma
Erishum I c.1939–1900

Ikunum

Sargon I

Puzur-Ashur II

| | Mari: |
|---|---|
| Naram-Sin | Yaggid-Lim c.1820 |
| | Yahdun-Lim c.1810 |
| Shamshi-Adad I c.1813–1781 | Sumu-Yamam c.1794 |
| | (Shamshi-Adad) |
| Ishme-Dagan I c.1780–1741 | (Yasmah-Adad) |
| | Zimri-Lim c.1775–1761 |

| Babylonia | Assyria | Elam |
|---|---|---|
| **Kassite Dynasty:** | | |
| Gandash c.1729 | | |
| Agum I | | |
| Kashtiliash I c.1660 | | |
| | | |
| | | |
| Burnaburiash I c.1530 | | |
| | | |
| | Ashur-rabi I | |
| | Ashur-nadin-ahhe I | |
| | Enlil-nasir II c.1432 | Inshushinak-shar-ilani c.1450 |
| | Ashur-nirari II c.1426 | Tan-Ruhuratire |
| Karaindash c.1413 | Ashur-bel-nisheshu c.1419 | |
| Kadashman-Harbe | Ashur-rem-nisheshu c.1410 | |
| Kurigalzu I | Ashur-nadin-ahhe II c.1402 | |
| Kadashman-Enlil I c.1374 | Eriba-Adad I c.1392 | |
| | | |
| Burnaburiash II c.1359 | Ashur-uballit I c.1365 | Tepti-ahar c.1365 |
| Karahardash c.1333 | Enlil-nirari c.1329 | Hurbatila c.1330 |
| Nazi-bugash c.1333 | Arik-den-ili c.1319 | Ige-halki c.1320 |
| Kurigalzu II c.1332 | Adad-nirari I c.1307 | Pahir-ishshan |
| Nazi-Maruttash c.1307 | | Attar-kitah c.1310 |
| Kadashman-Turgu c.1281 | | Humban-numena c.1300 |
| Kadashman-Enlil II c.1263 | Shalmaneser I c.1274 | Untash-napirisha c.1275 |
| Kudur-Enlil c.1254 | | Unpahash-napirisha c.1240 |
| Shagarakti-Shuriash c.1245 | Tukulti-Ninurta I c.1244 | Kidin-Hutran c.1235 |
| Kashtiliash IV c.1232 | | |
| (Tukulti-Ninurta c.1225) | | |
| Enlil-nadin-shumi c.1224 | | |
| Kadashman-Harbe II c.1223 | | |
| Adad-shum-iddina c.1222 | Ashur-nadin-apli c.1207 | Hallutash-Inshushinak c.1205 |
| Adad-shum-usur c.1216 | Ashur-nirari III c.1203 | |
| Meli-Shipak c.1186 | Enlil-kudurri-usur c.1197 | Shutruk-Nahhunte c.1185 |
| Marduk-apla-iddina I c.1171 | Ninurta-apil-Ekur c.1192 | |
| Enlil-nadin-ahi c.1157–55 | Ashur-dan I c.1179 | |
| **Second Dynasty of Isin:** | Ninurta-tukulti-Ashur | |
| Marduk-kabit-ahheshu c.1154 | Mutakkil-Nusku | Kudur-Nahhunte c.1155 |
| Itti-Marduk-balatu c.1140 | | Shilhak-Inshushinak c.1150 |
| Ninurta-nadin-shumi c.1132 | Ashur-resh-ishi I c.1133 | |
| Nebuchadnezzar I c.1126 | | Hutelutush-Inshushinak c.1120 |
| Enlil-nadin-apli c.1104 | Tiglath-pileser I c.1115 | Silhina-hamru-Lakamar |
| Marduk-nadin-ahhe c.1100 | Ashared-apil-Ekur c.1076 | |
| Marduk-shapik-zeri c.1082 | Ashur-bel-kala c.1074 | |
| Adad-apla-iddina c.1069 | Eriba-Adad II c.1056 | |
| Marduk-ahhe-eriba c.1047 | Shamshi-Adad IV c.1054 | |
| Marduk-zer-x c.1046 | Ashurnasirpal I c.1050 | |
| Nabu-shum-libur c.1034 | Shalmaneser II c.1031 | |
| **Second Sealand Dynasty:** | Ashur-nirari IV c.1019 | |
| Simbar-Shipak c.1026 | Ashur-rabi II c.1013 | |
| Ea-mukin-zeri c.1009 | | |
| Kashshu-nadin-ahi c.1008 | | |

| Hittites | Mitanni | Ugarit |
|---|---|---|
| Hattusilis I c.1650 | | |
| Mursilis I c.1620 | | |
| Hantilis I c.1590 | | |
| Zidanta I c.1560 | | |
| Ammuna c.1550 | | |
| Huzziya c.1530 | | |
| Telepinu c.1525 | Parratarna c.1480 | |
| 6 kings | Kirta ? | |
| Tudhaliyas I c.1430 | Parsatatar | |
| | Saushtatar c.1430 | |
| Hattusilis II c.1410 | Parratarna II ? | |
| Tudhaliyas II c.1400 | Artatama I c.1400 | |
| Arnuwandas I c.1390 | Shuttarna II c.1390 | |
| Tudhaliyas III c.1380 | Artashumura | Ammishtamru I |
| Suppililiumas I c.1370 | Tushratta c.1370 | Niqmaddu II |
| Arnuwandas II c.1330 | Shuttarna III | Arhalbu |
| Mursilis II c.1330 | Shattiwaza | Niqmepa |
| Shattuara I | | |
| Muwatallis II c.1295 | Wasashatta | |
| Mursilis III c.1282 | Shattuara II | |
| Hattusilis III c.1275 | | Ammishtamru II |
| | | |
| Tudhaliyas IV c.1245 | | Ibiranu |
| | | Niqmaddu III |
| | | |
| | | |
| Arnuwandas III c.1215 | | |
| Suppiluliumas II c.1210 | | Ammurapi |

| Babylonia | Assyria | Elam |
|---|---|---|
| **Bazi Dynasty:** | | |
| Eulmash-shakin-shumi c.1005 | | |
| Ninurta-kudurri-usur I c.988 | | |
| Shirikti-Shuqamuna c.986 | | |
| Elamite ruler    Mar-biti-apla-usur c.985 | | |
| | | |
| **Dynasty of E:** | | |
| Nabu-mukin-apli c.979 | Ashur-resh-ishi II c.972 | |
| Ninurta-kudurri-usur II c.944 | Tiglath-pileser II c.967 | |
| Mar-biti-ahhe-iddina c.943 | Ashur-dan II c.934 | |
| Shamash-mudammiq c.905 | Adad-nirari II 911 | |
| Nabu-shuma-ukin c.895 | Tukulti-Ninurta II 890 | |
| Nabu-apla-iddina c.870 | Ashurnasirpal II 883 | |
| Marduk-zakir-shumi I c.854 | Shalmaneser III 858 | |
| Marduk-balassu-iqbi c.818 | Shamshi-Adad V 823 | |
| Baba-aha-iddina c.812 | Adad-nirari III 810 | |
| 6 kings | Shalmaneser IV 782 | |
| Marduk-bel-zeri | Ashur-dan III 772 | |
| Marduk-apla-usur | | Humban-tahrah c.760 |
| Eriba-Marduk c.770 | | |
| Nabu-shuma-ishkun c.760 | Ashur-nirari V 754 | |
| Nabu-nasir 747 | Tiglath-pileser III 744 | Humban-nikash c.742 |
| Nabu-nadin-zeri 733 | | |
| Nabu-shuma-ukin II 732 | | |
| Nabu-mukin-zeri 731 | | |
| (Tiglath-pileser 728) | | |
| (Shalmaneser 726) | Shalmaneser V 726 | |
| Marduk-apla-iddina II 721 | Sargon II 721 | Shutruk-Nahhunte c.717 |
| (Sargon 709) | | Hallushu-Inshushinak 699 |
| Various kings | Sennacherib 704 | Kudur-Nahhunte 693 |
| (Esarhaddon) | Esarhaddon 680 | Humban-nimena 692 |
| Shamash-shum-ukin 667 | Ashurbanipal 668 | Humban-haltash I 687 |
| Kandalanu 647 | | Shilhak-Inshushinak II 680 |
| | | Tempt-Humban-Inshushinak c.668 |
| | | Humban-nikash III 653 |
| | | Atta-hamiti-Inshushinak 653 |
| | | Tammaritu II 651 |
| | | Humban-haltash III 648–644? |
| | | |
| **Chaldaean Dynasty:** | | |
| Nabopolassar 626 | Ashur-etel-ilani 630?/626? | |
| | Sin-shar-ishkun 622? | |
| | Ashur-uballit II 609 | |
| Nebuchadnezzar II 604 | | |
| | | |
| Amel-Marduk 561 | | |
| Neriglissar 559 | | |
| Labashi-Marduk 556 | | |
| Nabonidus 555–539 | | |

| Urartu | Damascus | Israel | Judah |
|---|---|---|---|
| | | Saul | Saul |
| | | David c.1011 | David |
| | Rezon c.955 | Solomon c.971 | Solomon |
| | Hezion | Jeroboam c.931 | Rehoboam c.931 |
| | | | |
| | Tabrimmon | Nadab c.910 | Abijam c.913 |
| | | Baasha c.909 | Asa c.911 |
| | | Elah c.886 | |
| | | Zimri & Tibni c.885 | |
| | Ben-Hadad I | Omri c.885 | |
| | | Ahab c.874 | Jehoshaphat c.870 |
| Sarduri I c.840 | Ben-Hadad II | Ahaziah c.853 | Jehoram c.848 |
| Ishpuini I c.830 | Hazael c.843 | Joram c.852 | Ahaziah c.841 |
| Minua c.810 | | Jehu c.841 | Athaliah c.841 |
| Argishti c.785 | | Jehoahaz c.814 | Joash c.835 |
| | Ben-Hadad III c.796 | Jehoash c.798 | Amaziah c.796 |
| | Hadian | Jeroboam II c.782 | Uzziah c.767 |
| | | Zechariah c.753 | |
| Sarduri II c.756 | Rezin c.750?-732 | Shallum c.752 | |
| | | Menahem c.752 | |
| | | Pekahiah c.742 | |
| | | Pekah c.740 | Jotham c.740 |
| Rusa I c.730 | | Hoshea c.732-22 | Ahaz c.732 |
| | | | Hezekiah c.716 |
| | | | |
| Argishti II c.713 | | | |
| | | | |
| | | | Manasseh c.687 |
| Rusa II c.685 | | | |
| Erimena ? | | | |
| Rusa III c.655 | | | Amon c.642 |
| | | | |
| Sarduri III c.645 | | | Josiah c.640 |
| Sarduri IV | | | |
| | | | |
| | | | |
| | | | Jehoahaz c.609 |
| | | | Jehoiakim c.609 |
| | | | Jehoiachin 597 |
| | | | Zedekiah 597-586 |

Page numbers in **bold** refer to main entries on the topics, while numbers in *italic* refer to illustration captions. Commonly occurring topics have been indexed only to the main entry.